A FAMILY MEMOIR

I SLEPT WITH
JOEY RAMONE

MICKEY LEIGH

WITH LEGS McNEIL

A TOUCHSTONE BOOK
Published by Simon & Schuster
New York London Toronto Sydney

Touchstone
A Division of Simon & Schuster, Inc.
1230 Avenue of the Americas
New York, NY 10020

First Touchstone hardcover edition December 2009

TOUCHSTONE and colophon are registered trademarks of Simon & Schuster, Inc.

For information about special discounts for bulk purchases, please contact Simon & Schuster Special Sales at 1-866-506-1949 or business@simonandschuster.com.

The Simon & Schuster Speakers Bureau can bring authors to your live event. For more information or to book an event contact the Simon & Schuster Speakers Bureau at 1-866-248-3049 or visit our website at www.simonspeakers.com.

Designed by Joy O'Meara
Artwork from iStockphoto.com

The names and details about some individuals have been changed.

Manufactured in the United States of America

1   3   5   7   9   10   8   6   4   2

Library of Congress Cataloging-in-Publication Data
Leigh, Mickey.
I slept with Joey Ramone : a family memoir / Mickey Leigh
with Legs McNeil.— 1st Touchstone hardcover ed.
p.   cm.
Includes bibliographical references and index.
1. Ramone, Joey, 1951–2001. 2. Rock musicians—United States—Biography.
3. Ramones (Musical group) I. McNeil, Legs. II. Title.
ML420.R2832L45   2009
782.42166092—dc22
[B]
2009022791

ISBN 978-0-7432-5216-4

DEDICATED TO MY MOM, CHARLOTTE LESHER.

If her everlasting love weren't greater than my heartbreak, I'd be a goner.

CONTENTS

AUTHOR'S NOTE

It took me, with the help of Legs, many years to finally tell the story of Joey Ramone—from his origins in the suburbs of Queens as Jeff Hyman to the glitter rock scene; the Ramones; CBGB; and his incredible music, energy, and innovation. To tell the story, we interviewed dozens of our family, friends, colleagues, and industry professionals both to aid our narrative and to give the perspective of those who were there as Joey's life unfolded. We've included some of these first-person accounts throughout *I Slept with Joey Ramone*, and while they offer a twist to something billed as a "memoir," I also feel they help give the fullest picture of his life that I can offer. I hope that in these pages you'll share in the spirit of my brother, a true punk rocker, Joey Ramone.

PROLOGUE

It was one of those crystal-clear evenings in the late winter of 1969. My mother, my brother, and I had recently moved into a new high-rise apartment building in Forest Hills, Queens, with a spectacular view of Manhattan.

I was sitting in our new bedroom with Arlene, a friend who'd stopped by after our last class at Forest Hills High School. We could see the entire skyline from my bed by the window and watched the sun set over Manhattan. Arlene gazed at the city lights as I passed her the joint.

All of a sudden, on the other side of the bedroom there was a stirring beneath a huge, homegrown pile of rubble. It was as if this unidentifiable mass of a mess had taken on an animated life of its own.

"What's that!?" Arlene asked in a hushed but urgent tone; she was ready to bolt should the inexplicable commotion continue.

"Oh, that's my brother," I answered, deadpan.

On one side of the bedroom by the window was your average teenage mess, plus a few oddities: a skinny ten-inch-long mirrored hash pipe made by Mexican Indians; an eight-track tape deck; an issue of the *East Village Other*; a copy of *How to Talk Dirty and Influence People* by Lenny Bruce; and some guitar picks.

On the other side, my brother's side, was the pile.

It had levels, or more like tiers: clean and dirty shirts; pants, socks, and assorted underwear; a pair of brown suede, calf-high fringed boots (like the ones Ian Anderson wore on the cover of the Jethro Tull album *Stand Up*); all covered by a huge Afghan shepherd's coat. Below, in another layer, were records, newspapers, rock magazines, and wrappers and boxes from various food groups, all surrounded by dishes, cups, and glasses that doubled as ashtrays, containing liquids that had created multicolored foam—beer-mug-type heads that had risen up to and above the rims of the glasses.

Sheets and blankets snaked their way in and out of the living sculpture. An unseen mattress lay on the floor supporting the escalating geological wonder that was my brother's side of the room.

"Uh, are you sure that's him?" Arlene asked, somewhat confused, in that I hadn't even glanced over in the direction of the mysterious mass. "I don't see anybody."

"Yeah, that's him," I replied, "unless there's a new tenant in there that I don't know about."

Arlene giggled, half genuinely, half nervously.

Hearing our voices, my brother cleared through enough of the debris to pop his head up and see what was going on.

His sunglasses were already on.

They were rarely off.

"Hey, how ya doin'?" he said to Arlene. They'd seen each other around the neighborhood.

"I'm okay," Arlene said to my brother. "Did we wake you up?"

Looking out the window and seeing that it was almost dark, my brother replied, "No, no, that's okay, I was up."

As he started to clear his way out of the heap, we realized *he didn't have any pants on.*

Arlene said, "You know, I kinda gotta get goin'. I told Alan I'd stop upstairs."

"Yeah," I said. "My mom will be home soon, anyway."

I moved to the middle of the room to shield Arlene's view.

I didn't have many girls come over after that.

My brother—the guy without the pants—lived on to become Joey Ramone, with quite an amazing story.

I lived on to tell it.

1.

I SLEPT WITH JOEY RAMONE— AND HIS MOTHER TOO!

Our parents, Charlotte Mandell and Noel Hyman, grew up within a few miles of each other in Brooklyn, New York.

Oddly enough, they met for the first time over a hundred miles away at the Nevele Resort in the Catskills. The upstate resort area, also known as the "Borscht Belt," had become a post–World War II hot spot for young Jewish singles looking to hook up.

Fortunately for my brother and me, not to mention millions of Ramones fans, our mom and dad *did* hook up, on New Year's Eve in 1946.

They met when my mother, Charlotte, was nineteen. By the time she was twenty, she'd married Noel: "I wanted to get out of the house," she said.

Our father's parents were born in Brooklyn of European Jewish descent and humble means. Mom's parents were also born in Brooklyn and Jewish, but were more affluent. Charlotte's family wasn't sure about the match.

"I wasn't living up to my father's expectations," Charlotte explained. "In the beginning, Noel was fun. He was an older guy with a convertible. I wanted excitement in life, and so did he. We had a good time together."

After their wedding, the couple moved into a modest flat on Ninety-fifth Street on the Upper West Side of Manhattan.

Noel was the hardworking owner of a fledgling trucking company called Noel's Transfer. Charlotte took a leave from her job as a commercial artist at an ad agency when she became pregnant with my older brother.

Jeffry Ross Hyman was born on May 19, 1951, at Beth Israel Hospital in downtown Manhattan. The young couple and their mutually ecstatic families celebrated the joy of Jeff's arrival, but the blessed day did not pass without extreme distress. The major encumbrance in my brother's life had actually formed before he'd ever taken his first breath. As nature would have it, a mass of what might have been another fetus that never developed had become attached to his spine. The medical term for the condition is "sacrococygeal teratoma"; it describes a type of tumor with cells vastly different from the surrounding tissue. It occurs once in every thirty-five to forty thousand births, with 75 percent affecting females. If the tumor is promptly removed, the prognosis is good. If elements of the teratoma are left behind—or diagnosis is delayed—the risk of malignancy increases. When he was born at six pounds, four ounces, the teratoma was the size of a baseball.

Surgery to remove the teratoma was extremely risky due to the location of the mass, but it was unavoidable, as far worse complications would occur if it were left intact. A few weeks later, when doctors deemed Jeff's tiny body strong enough to withstand the trauma of surgery, the procedure was successfully completed. Some scarring of the spinal tissue was inevitable, which could cause neurological problems down the road. The extent of these problems was indeterminable at the time, but doctors were hopeful it wouldn't have a devastating effect, if any, on Jeff's development.

A relieved Mom and Dad nurtured Jeff back to health, and it appeared that my big brother was on his way to growing up a normal, happy boy.

About a year later, Dad, Mom, and Jeff headed to Queens, settling in a middle-class Jewish area called Forest Hills. They moved into a garden apartment snuggled in a corner of the neighborhood where the Long Island Expressway and the Grand Central Parkway intersect. Their apartment was conveniently located smack between the city's two major airports, La Guardia and Idlewild Airport.

In front of the house, there was a footbridge that spanned Grand Central Parkway and took you into the huge Flushing Meadow Park, the site of the 1939 World's Fair. The park featured Meadow Lake, where people could rent rowboats during the day and at night watch great displays of fireworks staged throughout the summer. Forest Hills was a friendly little community, a fun place for kids to grow up safe and sound.

THEN ONE NIGHT in October 1953, via Dad's instinctive impulses and with Mom's unyielding assistance, I began gathering myself together. Nine months later, I met up with them and Jeff for the first time.

They named me Mitchel Lee Hyman.

Born on July 15, 1954, in Forest Hills General Hospital, I passed inspection with only a couple of webbed toes noted on my permanent record. Dad drove us to the new house he'd recently purchased for the expanding family. It was right across the street from the garden apartment complex they'd lived in previously. Our house had a great little backyard with a small cherry tree, and as Jeff and I grew, so did the tree.

As far as my brother and I knew, we were a happy family then; but only a few years later, we began to hear harsh tones coming from our parents' room. Jeff and I shared a bedroom down the hall from Mom and Dad's, on the top floor of the house.

Jeff was a good big brother. When I would get scared at night, either from the boom of the fireworks across the lake or after seeing a scary movie like *Invaders from Mars*, *The Crawling Eye*, or *The Thing*, I'd run to his bed for protection.

"Jeff! Help!" I'd scream. "The monsters are under my bed and they're trying to get in!"

"Come on in," Jeff offered, pulling back the covers. "You can sleep with me. You'll be safe here."

Jeff was only five years old, but he seemed oblivious to the dangers that lurked under his bed. Maybe for Jeff, real life was scary enough; the crescent-shaped scar across his lower back reminded him what real danger was.

Our friends David and Reba lived down the street, and our mom became well acquainted with their parents, Hank and Frances Lesher.

"I remember," said David Lesher, "we used to run around in the parking lot by my house and make up crazy games, like Doody Boy."

The game was basically tag with a glorified name. Instead of "it," you were the "Doody Boy." The main strategy was to not get stuck with the name at the end of the day, or you'd have to walk home with everybody laughing at you, yelling, "*Hey, Doody Boy!*" Somehow, Jeff often wound up the Boy.

One day, a bunch of us were playing in the dimly lit basement labyrinths of a nearby apartment complex.

All of a sudden, some kid yelled, "Run! There's a ghost!"

We all screamed and bolted for the exit.

Even above the din of kids shrieking, everyone could hear the clang as my skull became intimate with an iron pipe in my path. I crumpled to the floor and started to cry. The next thing I knew, Jeff was picking me up and saying, "We better go home."

Though everyone was running away, Jeff stayed to get me out of there.

Blood covered my eyes and face. Jeff put his arm around me, held my hand, and got me home to our horrified mom and dad, who rushed me to the doctor. I got my first taste of hard drugs and first feel of stitches—five of them, right in the middle of my head.

When the anesthesia began to wear off, I opened my eyes to see Jeff smiling down at me as he held a mobile of little colored airplanes above my head. He'd made it for me while I was sleeping.

"Do ya like it?" Jeff asked.

"Say thanks to your big brother," Mom said to me. "He got you home."

"Thanks, Jehhh . . . ," I mumbled, still half-asleep, as Dad hung the mobile over my bed.

Actually Jeff and I didn't call our father "Dad." We called him "Bub," a nickname we gave him when he'd come home shouting, "Hey Bub!" as he'd hoist us in the air.

"Hey Bub," we'd shout back to him repeatedly, hoping for a second or third ride. The name stuck.

Our mom was loving and vibrant. She was always teaching us things, reading us stories, or showing us how to draw. She made sure we listened to all kinds of music, everything from kiddie songs to classics like Prokofiev's *Peter and the Wolf*. We did everything together as a family. Mom, Dad, Jeff, and I would walk down the street, laughing, all holding hands.

We often had friends and family over for parties in the basement, where Jeff and I would provide the entertainment. We were comfortable playing that room. We would stand on top of the piano and sing songs like "When the Saints Come Marching In" and "She'll Be Comin' Round the Mountain."

Grandma Fanny, Dad's mom, bought Jeff an accordion, which he loved. He picked it up pretty quickly, playing everything in "oompah" time—probably from listening to too much Lawrence Welk. They got me a little ukulele, which I loved too. Unfortunately, I smashed it to pieces one night, after our "set," by jumping off the piano and cracking the little uke on the basement floor. That made quite a memorable sound.

One day, after we'd come home from seeing our first circus at Madison Square Garden, Jeff exclaimed, "Hey! Let's try the knife-throwing act!"

"Yeah!" I said. "Just like the Fantastic Fontaine Family!"

Jeff grabbed half a dozen steak knives from the kitchen. We went out on the grass by the side of the house, and I lay down with my arms and legs stretched out. Jeff made a drumroll sound.

As he let fly the first knife, Mom shrieked from the kitchen window, *"Jeffry! Don't you throw that knife!"*—just as it sailed past my head.

"Aw, c'mon, Mom," I explained. "We're just playing circus!"

She came running out of the house with some paper and a box of crayons.

"Don't you two ever play with knives again, you hear me? Here, play with these," she said as she handed us the crayons.

As soon as Mom was out of sight, I stretched back out on the grass, Jeff made the drumroll sound—and he threw the *crayons* at me.

In the winter Mom and Dad would often take us upstate to Bear Mountain to go ice-skating or sleigh riding. At the end of the day, we'd go into the lodge and have dinner in front of the huge fireplace.

One time up at Bear Mountain a big motorcade pulled up just as we were about to enter the lodge. We were made to wait outside, along the path to the entrance, while a parade of police officers and men in suits escorted someone inside.

"*It's the president!*" Dad yelled. "*Wave to him, maybe he'll say hello to you!*"

Jeff and I looked at each other and then started jumping up and down, shouting, "*Hey, President! Say hello!*"

We were a little nervous. A few months earlier we'd been on the overpass above the Grand Central Parkway when a similar-looking motorcade had been passing underneath. That day, a bunch of us kids knocked some pebbles off the railing of the bridge that trickled down onto the cars below. Jeff Storch, the neighborhood bully, who frequently picked on my brother, threw a rock that made contact with one of the cars in the motorcade. Worse, some cops stationed on the overpass saw us all running away. Jeff and I were now afraid that the president was being escorted by those *same* cops—who might recognize us. But given that we didn't want to tell our parents about that incident, we kept waving and shouting to the president.

As he came closer, we caught his attention. The president of the United States stopped for a second and summoned us past security. We thought we were in big trouble, but before we knew it, we were shaking hands with President Dwight D. Eisenhower. Ike told us we'd better be good boys and listen to our parents.

We figured the president had pardoned us.

In the summer, we would walk over to Meadow Lake to go fishing, have picnics, and take out the rowboats. Dad taught us a game called Sink the *Bismarck*. We'd float a can or bottle in the water and throw rocks at it until it submerged. It was our favorite game, though neither of us knew what the hell the *Bismarck* was.

Jeff had a penchant for catching butterflies; he even had a mounting set. He would mount his bounty on a special board with little pushpins and write the name of the species in a designated space underneath. The Mammoth Viceroy was his prized catch. The only problem was that Jeff never followed the instructions for preservation correctly, and invariably they would dry up and turn into bug dust about a week later.

Jeff was as happy a kid as you could find in Forest Hills in the 1950s: rolling down the grassy hills laughing; standing up, spinning round and round in circles with his long gangly arms outstretched; then falling over like a drunken monkey.

Jeff would coax me to join him but warned, "Don't throw up on me!"

I did both of the above.

We found ways to share just about everything, boosting each other up trees on sunny days and switching off verses of "Oh! Susanna" in the basement on rainy ones.

My big brother was outgoing and adventurous, cheerful and talented, and, as I said before, brave. He wasn't weird. He wasn't angry or removed or troubled or sickly or lonely or concerned. Jeff was the smiling, happy kid with the long legs, running through the thick grass, chasing butterflies, calling to me.

When I close my eyes and think of my brother, those are the first things I see.

2.

THE DAY THE MUSIC LIVED

When Jeff started first grade, it became apparent that he was having some difficulty learning to read, which prompted his teacher to suggest that my mother take him to the eye doctor. In addition to getting him glasses, Mom gave him a little tutoring in the mornings.

As a result, I got some residual "preschooling" at home. At breakfast Mom would teach Jeff the alphabet on big index cards. Though *he* was struggling, I could almost read before I started kindergarten.

One morning after Jeff left for school, while Mom was cleaning off the kitchen table, a song came on the radio I can still hear in my head as clearly as when I heard it the first time forty-five years ago. This song changed our lives completely and forever. It was part nursery rhyme and parts unknown. It took me to a place I'd never been to, though I'd heard the nursery rhyme part already, in songs about "tiskets, taskets, green and yellow baskets" and little brown jugs. But I couldn't even begin to identify the subject of this tune. More important, the beat made me giggle, clap my hands, and jump up and down.

Rock & roll! Perfect for kids of all ages: No music ever made us jump before, unless we were so instructed by the lyrics ("Put your left foot in . . . put your left foot out"). Neither Jeff nor I was too hot on "The Hokey Pokey," but this new movement didn't require a narrator. It just happily . . . *happened.*

"You like that, huh?" Mom noticed.

Later that afternoon when Jeff came home, I told him about the song I'd heard that made me jump up and down and feel wild. I couldn't wait for him to try out this new game—it was even better than spinning in circles!

"It's called 'Ah Ya Ba Ba,' " I said excitedly. "I think."

"What's that?" Jeff asked, sensing I was onto something big.

"I don't know," I told him. "Didja ever hear it?"

" 'Ah Ya Ba Ba'?" he answered. "The one about the barber?"

"Well," I told him, "ya can't tell what it's about 'cause it's too fast! But it doesn't matter!"

"It's called 'La Bamba,' " Mom laughed. "It's in Spanish."

"Where's Spanish?" we asked.

The next morning, Jeff asked Mom to turn on the radio in the kitchen before he went to school. He was really hoping to hear the "Ah Ya Ba Ba" song, and that morning he finally did. Once he heard it, Jeff never played oompah music on his accordion again. In fact, he didn't take the thing out of its big black case much after that. Ritchie Valens killed Joey Ramone's accordion career but planted the seed for a new one.

We were very excited about this phenomenon we'd discovered but were quickly distracted from our newfound utopia. Jeff came down with a bad case of scarlet fever, which was serious for a seven-year-old kid. It wasn't a normal childhood disease, like the chicken pox or mumps; Mom and Dad were very concerned.

Mom moved him into the guest bedroom to prevent me from catching the contagious disease. Jeff must have been in there for a good two weeks, maybe more. I had nowhere to go when I got scared.

Around this time, Mom and Dad's relationship took a turn for the worse.

Jeff and I heard a lot of yelling and saw things like Dad pushing Mom around, an obvious sign of trouble to anyone but five- and eight-year-olds. We knew something was wrong, but kids that age are never prepared for something like their parents splitting up.

Dad started coming home later at night and sleeping downstairs on the living room couch. We didn't do things together anymore.

We still didn't understand why they couldn't be together, why we couldn't be like the families in the TV shows like *Father Knows Best.* Dad told us he didn't want to split up with Mom, but they continued to fight with each other.

Mom felt that Dad resented her: "He had become very domineering," Charlotte recalled. "I wanted to go back to my job as an artist, and he wouldn't hear of it. He'd tell me, 'You have to stay home and take care of the children.' Noel didn't want me to be independent. I started realizing I couldn't spend my whole life with this man. But he didn't want a divorce. He not only fought me tooth and nail, he also put private detectives on me. He suspected I was running around with Hank Lesher, the guy who lived down the street."

Dad might have been onto something.

It started out innocently, when Hank walked Mom home after Scrabble games she played with his wife, Frances. They'd walk and talk, and occasionally take the long way home. Then the Leshers moved out of their garden apartment.

One day about six months later, Jeff and I were taking a walk in the neighborhood with Dad when we spotted Hank Lesher with his kids, David and Reba. We hadn't seen them since they moved away from our block. David was about six years old now, and Reba just three.

We walked over to them as they were about to get into their car, but instead of saying hello, Dad started yelling at Hank and cursing.

Jeff and I were getting really scared.

Hank was saying, "Come on, Noel, this isn't necessary. Let's talk about this some other time. We have kids here!"

When Hank tried to walk away, Dad pinned him against the side of the car with his body—and slapped him in the face.

Hank had a still-sleeping Reba in his arms. "What are you doing?" he reasoned. "I have a baby here!"

"Well, put her down then!" yelled Dad. Dad yelled, then cursed—and slapped Hank again.

David, Jeff, and I all started crying and begging him to stop. Just then, Dad turned his head and looked down the block to see a police car turning the corner. Dad grabbed Jeff and me by our hands and started running with us full speed down the street. We were still crying when we got to our house and ran to Mom, who was in shock. Dad didn't come into the house, but the reality of the situation did. We knew we weren't going to be like the happy families on television.

"What's gonna happen to us?" I asked Jeff before we went to sleep.

"Dad's gonna come back," Jeff tried to assure me, and himself. "You'll see!"

"I hope so," I said. "But what if he doesn't? Will Mom stay with us?"

"I don't know," Jeff said, shuddering.

The next day Mom assured us that she and our father still loved us more than anything in the world, but for the time being it would be just the three of us living in the house.

For the next year, the atmosphere at home was calmer. I'd started school, and Jeff and I were adjusting to life without Dad in the house. We still went on day trips with him, though. That summer, he took us to a few games at Yankee Stadium, then down to Chinatown for dinner. We'd take Broadway the entire way, driving from the northernmost tip of Manhattan straight through Times Square, all the way down to Chinatown. Dad's brother Sy gave us our first lesson in physics there, mixing the hot Chinese mustard with the duck sauce, among other things. But we were still confused about our family's chemistry.

About a year later, after Jeff finished fourth grade and I finished first grade, Mom sat us down and informed us that she and Hank Lesher had gotten married.

"I divorced Noel in Juárez, Mexico," Charlotte explained, "and married Hank the very next day." She told us that we were going to move in with Hank, David, and Reba. We were shocked and confused. Apparently, Frances, Hank's wife, had passed away.

Even worse, the Leshers had moved to a more remote part of Queens called Howard Beach. We would have to leave our house, our friends, the stray cats that lived in the backyard, and life as we knew it in Forest Hills.

The move to Howard Beach was a major turning point for Jeff and me. We were lost in this new world. The serious confusion began with what we were supposed to call Hank: Dad? Stepdad? Hank?

And what about David and Reba—brother and sister?

Jeff and I were given David's room, and he was exiled to Reba's.

What did they think of us? What did they think of Jeff, whose legs now encompassed more than two-thirds of his body?

"It was hard for me," David Lesher confessed. "Sometimes I went along with the crowd and ignored Jeff because he was so tall, skinny, and awkward, and other times I felt sorry for him. I wanted to keep my friends, and yet Jeff was my stepbrother. I was torn."

Getting used to Hank as a person with absolute control over us was surely the most difficult transition. This new arrangement seemed to take authority away from our real father, which instinctively is where a kid wants authority to be. It was a painful process and gave rise to rebellion.

"I don't wanna listen to Hank," Jeff said as we lay in our new beds. Our voices sounded different at night here. There were new echoes and new shadows. At least there were no more monsters under my bed. But for the first time in our lives, we had real live enemies. One had stolen our mom.

"Do we have to listen to Hank?" Jeff asked.

"No," I said. "He's not our dad."

"Mom said he's our stepdad," Jeff mused. "But David and Reba have to listen to our mom, right?"

"I think so," I answered.

"It's not fair," Jeff went on. "They don't have to listen to our dad like we have to listen to theirs. We have to listen to two dads now, and they don't have to listen to their mom; that's two more people we gotta listen to than they do!"

"Huh?" I said, attempting to grasp the two-father concept.

"Well, do you like him?" Jeff asked me.

"He's okay, I guess."

"What about David and Reba?"

"They're okay too," I answered, feeling very sad. "But I wish we could go back to our old house."

"Me too," Jeff answered. "The kids around here are real stink-heads."

Luckily, we had one another to commiserate with, but we were still very lonely.

Of course, the kids on our new block put us through the wringer. Neither of us got picked to play in games when they were choosing sides for stickball or baseball. Jeff took the bulk of the bullying. They told him that if he wanted to play stickball, he could be the bat. "Daddy Long-Legs" was his new moniker—as if "Four Eyes" wasn't bad enough.

When there weren't enough kids around to play a game and they needed us to complete a squad, they would flip a coin to determine who had to take Jeff on their team.

"I'm not playing with him. He stinks!" was the typical reaction.

"It sucked to watch Jeff try and run," David Lesher recalled, "because he wasn't really capable. When he ran, he was kind of slow, and the kids would spit on his back. After that, I don't remember him being around for a lot of sports."

When Jeff ran, his feet kind of kicked out to the sides instead of straight back, like the rest of us. Since it was the way I had always seen him run, it was normal to me. But now that it was being pointed out, I noticed it, too. Jeff was definitely different.

We looked forward to weekends, when Dad picked us up and took us out. Sometimes he took us back to the house in the old neighborhood, which he still owned. He had rented it out to strangers; it was really weird seeing other people in *our* house.

We were anxious to reconnect with our old pals, the ones we'd performed "blood brother" rituals with; but even they acted different. They had new best friends now.

We got the sense that since we were part of a "broken family," we were now considered damaged goods and possibly even troublemakers. We weren't sure if, or where, we belonged. Alienation brought us closer to one another. That's when Jeff and I became each other's best friend.

3.

"DO YOU REMEMBER ROCK 'N' ROLL RADIO?"

Hank Lesher was a caring man and a loving father—he just wasn't ours. He had gone to college and gotten his degree, so he certainly had an educational edge over our dad. Hank put more emphasis on academics and liked to keep us thinking, periodically quizzing us with mathematical problems and brainteasers. Along with his brother-in-law Lou, he owned a dry cleaning business in Manhattan that catered to an upscale clientele, but Hank was far more intellectual than his career in that industry indicated.

He also was a huge enthusiast of hi-fi equipment and had a console in the living room the likes of which we'd never seen, even in the appliance stores. He attempted to explain how the system worked to Jeff and me, though we didn't quite understand. He also informed us that if we ever touched it when he wasn't there, we'd be in a lot of trouble. *That* we understood.

Nonetheless one day we tried to get it going while Hank was out with Dave and Reba. Of course he could tell from our grimy little fingerprints alone. But instead of getting really mad, Hank chose to give us another, more in-depth demonstration. He was a smart man and must have known that a gesture such as this would go a long way toward making Jeff and me more comfortable with him.

It worked.

"This is the Marantz crossover," Hank explained, "with a Fischer tuner, McIntosh amplifiers, and a Rek-O-Kut turntable. They're the best there is. This sends the frequencies to the speakers or channels you want them to go to . . ."

We were fascinated. Hank put on a record, Tchaikovsky's "1812 Overture," and cranked the machine. The sound impressed the shit out of Jeff and me for years to come. We went outside and bragged to the other kids. We figured no one else had anything like it—not in this neighborhood.

We were living in a part of Howard Beach called Lindenwood Village, smack on the border of Brooklyn. It was a white, working-class, family-oriented development comprised mainly of garden apartments. There were several six-story apartment buildings in the center of the sprawling "village," with many more to be built.

The makeup of the community was more mixed—in other words, not everyone was Jewish. The kids there were hipper, more streetwise, tougher, and in a sense, more worldly than the kids in Forest Hills. They wore blue jeans with big cuffs and rolled up the sleeves on their white T-shirts.

There were more bullies per block, too. The Garillo brothers, Billy and Bobby, were far worse than our former tormentor Jeff Storch back in Forest Hills. David warned us about them, and sure enough, the "Bully Brothers" gleefully chased Jeff and me around the block.

A lot of the kids there had colorful nicknames. There were guys like Victor "Moody" Mootel, who we had seen smack Roy "Pimple Tuchas" Brown over the head with a stickball bat (Roy had ranked on Moody's mom).

There were other cultural differences, too: Kids huddled in little groups singing strange songs with foreign-sounding words, snapping their fingers in time. The unidentifiable words sounded like "yip" and "sha la la la" and "wop doo wop."

It reminded us of "La Bamba," but it was weirder. It had a similar spirit, though, and it was exciting to know that the spirit hadn't disappeared—we'd just lost track of it. It was our stepbrother, David, who put us back in touch. One day he pulled something out of his shirt pocket, a little rectangular box with a wire attached to it. The other end of the wire was stuck in his ear.

We asked him what he was doing and what the heck that thing was.

"It's an eight-transistor," David said to enlighten us.

"Whaddaya mean?" Jeff asked. "It does eight things?"

David pulled the wire out of the little box, and suddenly we heard the whooshing noise of the crowd at Yankee Stadium cheering a home run by Roger Maris, followed by a voice: *"And that's the first homer for number nine of this 1961 World Series!"*

"Wow! That's neat!" we exclaimed in unison. "What about the other things?"

David rubbed his thumb on a little dial on the side of the box—and *there it was!* *"Who put the bomp in the bomp sha bomp sha bomp? Who put the ram in the rama lama ding dong?"*

He rubbed it again, and we heard "Sha da da da, sha da da da da, Yip yip yip yip yip yip yip yip, Mum mum mum mum mum mum. Get a job, sha da da da, sha da da da," and then, "Hey, kids, this is Murray the K, keep it tuned to eighty-eight on your dial for more rock & roll!"

Jeff and I nagged our dad until he finally got each of us our own little transistor radios, with our own earphones! We weren't so lonely anymore. Now we had Murray the K, Cousin Brucie, Dandy Dan Daniels, Harry Harrison, and all the other DJs as our new friends and constant companions. They provided us with as much rock & roll as we could ever want—and we wanted as much as we could get.

Soon we were reconnected with our old friend Ritchie Valens, who had a new hit song, "Come On, Let's Go." This time he wasn't singing in Spanish, but in our language, rock & roll. Though this revelation was an emotional lifesaver, it didn't completely fill the emptiness we were experiencing. We still wanted to be accepted and included, as we had been by our former friends. Rock & roll was a common denominator, and we hoped it would help us connect with our new classmates.

Since there were no schools yet in Lindenwood Village, we were bused over to the public school in Ozone Park, Jeff for fifth grade and me for second.

It was a horrible experience.

The school was a gray lead-painted, asbestos-tainted, vermin-infested place we detested. The teachers were mean, the classrooms pea green. We saw our first fights. The days trudged into nights and we couldn't wait to move on. In a year we were gone.

Never happier to hear that last school bell ring, we knew we were never coming back. After the summer, we would be going to a brand-new school in our own neighborhood, just six blocks down the street, right past the swamps.

The area or "block" before the new school was a vast marshland—wide enough that it would someday accommodate a dozen six-story apartment buildings. Jeff, David, and I would spend much of our free time there playing in the ten-foot-high reeds. We'd come home filthy, with ticks embedded in our heads. Mom would pull the buggers out with tweezers.

When we disappeared into those reeds, everything real, except the sky above our heads, disappeared as well. We became soldiers, cowboys, big game hunters, monsters, and creatures from the black lagoon—anything we wanted to be, as long as there was something dangerous about it. If we didn't want to be found, or caught, this was where we went. There were even rumors of mobsters floating around beneath the reeds and weeds. We were swamp rats and knew all the good spots to become invisible.

One day, a mud ball thrown by Jeff landed on the back of a kid cutting through the mire on his way home. Just our luck, he was a friend of the Garillo brothers. They heard about our "first strike" soon enough. The Garillo clan came upon us in the swamp armed with buckets of mud balls and dirt bombs.

Victor "Moody" Mootel became our new squadron leader. He suggested we pack some pebbles into the mud balls. The pebbles escalated into small stones, and by the third day, an all-out rock fight ensued across a putrid stream. It finally ended when Jeff and I whipped a spray of pebbles across at the enemy and Dave hoisted a large, football-shaped slab of stone up above his head and then reared back, *smack into my face*.

He heaved the missile across the battle line as I watched my front tooth fall into the creek, the victim of friendly fire.

"Shit!" Jeff swore. "You're bleeding! We better go!"

We dropped our ammo and retreated back to the street. When we got out of the swamp, Jeff and Dave looked at me and started laughing at my tooth. Then we heard some shouts and spotted the Garillos, who were *pissed*. One of the rocks we'd thrown had connected: We could see the red stuff on the kid's crew cut.

We took off again. They wanted Jeff, the slowest, but we *couldn't* leave him behind!

"C'mon! Run, you faggot!" Moody urged Jeff on the only way he knew how. The enemy was closing in.

All of a sudden Hank came driving down the street on his way home from work. He stopped the van and yelled, *"What the hell is going on here?! What did you kids do?"*

The pack that was chasing us also stopped short when they saw Hank.

"We were just playing around," said David, covering for all of us.

Hank told us to get home, "*On the double!*" He waited to make sure the Garillos didn't chase us down again and launch a counterattack.

When we got to our door, Mom dropped her jaw and gasped in horror as we filed in.

"All right, hold it!" she said as she checked out my bloody mouth. "*Does one of you want to tell me what's going on here?!*"

"Somebody threw a rock," Jeff said in a temporary lapse of sanity.

"*A rock fight?!*" Mom yelled, "*Are you kids CRAZY or something?*"

As the sun set over the battlefield, it was a big victory for the stray dogs. As Jeff and I lay in bed that night in the late summer heat, he hit me with some philosophical queries: "Do you think it's worse to kill someone or get killed by someone?"

"Well, if you kill someone," I deduced, "you go to the death chamber, right? So you die anyway."

"What if they don't catch you?" Jeff asked.

I would have answered but my tongue was too busy exploring the new gap between my front teeth.

"Why does that guy Mootel have to call me a faggot?" Jeff continued.

"Because *he's* a faggot," I tried to explain. "That guy's just a stinkpot. Remember what we saw him do to Roy, when we first moved here?"

"You mean Roy 'Pimple Tuchas'? Yeah. He hit him with the stickball bat," Jeff remembered.

"But maybe that was because Roy said that his *dog* had almost as much hair on its legs as Victor's mother!" I suggested, attempting to smooth the path of friendship toward our newfound allies.

"Yeah, maybe," Jeff said. "But I hear him calling me names all the time. When I see those other guys at school, they start with me, too.

"I made *one* friend last year," Jeff rambled on, "Mitchell Becker, but he lives all the way past the swamps. He's got a record player and a lot of good records, too. You should come over there with me. He's got that new one by the Dovells, 'You Can't Sit Down,' and one by that guy, 'The Duke of Earl.' I love that song."

"I think he's gonna be on *The Clay Cole Show* this Saturday night. We gotta watch it! I hope they let us. And I think the Four Seasons are on *American Bandstand!*"

"You know," Jeff continued, "I was thinking about 'Walk Like a Man' today when Victor was ranking on me. He kept saying I run like a girl. I don't know why I can't run as fast as him. Mom said that shouldn't matter, anyway—and that just 'cause *they* don't need glasses doesn't make them any better than me. They're just big idiots. Someday, someone's gonna show those guys . . ."

The sound of girls' voices surfed in on a breeze that played with the window shade for a few seconds. It was that sound young girls make—half laughing, half shrieking. We'd usually hear it when a guy was chasing them and they were about to get caught. Or more often, it appeared they were letting themselves get caught—but still shrieking.

"Do you like girls?" I asked my big brother.

"Well, I liked Karen Klein, from our old block," Jeff admitted. "She was my friend . . ."

"Your *girlfriend*?" I asked.

"Nah," Jeff responded quickly. "I don't really talk to girls now."

"Only sissies like girls, right?" I reminded him. "Holding hands and picking flowers—and being all clean and everything. And dancing with them in school, ya know? Those stupid dances they make you do?"

"I *hate* that dancing," Jeff said, and then warned, "Girls always want you to dance with them. And they always want you to tell them you like them and then they kiss you. Yecchhh!"

"I think it's different when you get older," Jeff added.

"I guess so," I answered before I closed my eyes and waited for sleep to swallow me.

Under our window, in the driveway between the two buildings, some teenagers were attempting an a cappella version of the Tokens' "The Lion Sleeps Tonight." They got a good echo from the sound bouncing off the brick walls.

"That's cool when they do that," Jeff whispered.

Yeah.

It was things like that that made us think and made us dream. There's not a doubt in my mind that Jeff was digesting a child's dosage of the ultimate fantasy right then and there. I know I was. Could *we* do that someday?

It was stirring. The song was infectious. The spirit these guys had was contagious. We'd caught the fever, and it burned slowly somewhere deep inside us.

Jeff could be within earshot of a Yankees World Series game seven broadcast and walk away uninterested, but this music excited and aroused his imagination. He could get lost in a world of songs that streamed out from the little radios, from the TV set, in the movies, in the nighttime breezes. There he could fit in. He could be invisible. He could be in love. He could be the Wanderer. He could be the Duke of Earl—and nothing could stop him.

4.

"WIPEOUT!"

In addition to Hank's sophisticated hi-fi console, there was a little phonograph for us kids to use, but we didn't have any rock & roll records yet. I saved my trick-or-treat money from Halloween and didn't buy baseball cards for a week. As soon as I had enough saved up, around $0.58, Jeff and I rode our bikes over to the store to pick out the first record of our collection.

There was a chart on the counter that listed the current top ten songs, and we loved them all. Since it was my money, for our *first* record, I said, "Let's get the number one song!" It was Lesley Gore's "It's My Party."

The collection grew at a rapid pace: the Crystals' "He's a Rebel," Dion's "The Wanderer," and Boris Pickett's "Monster Mash."

When we weren't listening to our records, we were listening to our radios, even taking them to bed with us armed with our earplugs. Jeff lost interest in just about everything but rock & roll. When he outgrew his first baseball mitt, he didn't exactly go running to the store for a new one.

Soon enough my interest started drifting away from sports, too, and focusing almost completely on music. On weekends, if Jeff and I weren't out with our dad, we would rock around the clock—well, *almost* around the clock.

First came the cartoons on Saturday morning TV, then roller derby, followed by *Rin Tin Tin, Sky King,* and *American Bandstand.* Rainy Saturdays were the best. There'd be a whole day for us to play games and pick singles out of our 45 RPM carrying case, which was rapidly filling up.

Occasionally around five p.m. the scent of perfume and the smell of freshly cleaned clothes would float out of Mom and Hank's bedroom, creating that special Saturday night aura. We could always tell when our parents were going out—alone. Any minute, Mom would come out in a snazzy dress, shortly followed by Hank, emanating the aroma of aftershave and leather shoe polish.

While Mom put dinner on the table, they'd tell us we'd better behave ourselves and listen to the babysitter. If we were lucky, it was a young girl who liked rock & roll. Jeff, David, Reba, and I would soon be blasting the music and throwing each other around the living room in preparation for Killer Kowalski, Haystacks Calhoun, Bobo Brazil, and the other wild men of *Saturday Night Wrestling* on WOR TV, channel 9.

We would put each other in headlocks, armlocks, half nelsons, and full nelsons. No one could pin Jeff, though: His legs were too long and strong.

If he got anyone in a scissor hold with those stanchions, it was all over.

"I give! I give!" was all we could say, if he hadn't squeezed the air out of our lungs yet.

Jeff and I were beginning to feel more at home. David and Reba were starting to feel like family, not just friends.

Of course, we still loved our dad, but we were all still adjusting. Dad hadn't taken Mom's rejection very easily, and we could sense his anger. One day he got really pissed when he heard Jeff refer to Hank as "Dad."

On the other hand, when he wasn't pissed off, our real father was actually a much looser personality than Hank, and Jeff and I still had many good times with him when he took us away on weekends. Dad would often bring "friends" along with him—"broads," as he liked to call them. He fancied himself an honorary member of Frank Sinatra's legendary Rat Pack and often had the radio in the car tuned to a station playing Tony Bennett, Dino, or Sammy.

Dad drove a big Cadillac convertible and always wanted the top down, which Jeff and I hated. We'd get nothing but a constant faceful of air—and the gale forces destroyed the pompadours we worked so hard on. Plus, you couldn't hear the radio!

Whenever Dad got out of the car, we'd immediately switch the station to WABC or WMCA. He'd let us listen for a while, but then try to make us feel like "our" music was silly. He'd clap and clown around, mimicking the words. We would get embarrassed and beg him to stop.

Dad would often take us horseback riding at places called "dude ranches." We *loved* it. The best thing about the ranches, aside from the mud, horses, and dogs, was that they had bands playing at night—*rock bands*!

"Can you play 'Wipeout'?" was always our first question, directed at the drummer.

"That's all you little runts ask for," griped the drummer. " 'Wipeout.' 'Wipeout'!"

"Yeah, but could ya play it?" we'd beg. *"Please?"*

"Yeah, yeah, kid, later."

We were amazed that these guys would even take the time out from setting up their stuff, or making out with their girlfriends, to talk to us. They were in their late teens or early twenties, and like the guys singing under our window that one night, they impressed us. They had flashy outfits and looked cool as they played all our favorite songs.

Even after Dad took us to our room and put us to bed, we'd still be listening—through the walls.

But more than anything in the world, we wanted to see the *real* bands we'd been hearing on the radio. We bugged our old man relentlessly to take us to the *real* rock & roll shows. Soon enough, he gave in. He took us to Murray the K's Rock & Roll Extravaganza at the Brooklyn Fox Theatre for an incredible bill featuring Marvin Gaye, the Supremes, the Temptations, Jay and the Americans, the Shangri-Las, and the Ronettes.

A thousand more *"PLEASE DAD"*'s got us to the WMCA Good Guys show at Brooklyn's Paramount Theatre, where the Animals headlined *another* amazing bill. We always wanted Dad to drop us off in front of the theater and let us go in by ourselves—especially then-twelve-year-old Jeff— fearing the old man would embarrass us in front of the other kids.

Dad didn't always want to stay for the whole show and sometimes he'd mimic the stage moves, trying to be funny. The hipper Dad tried to be, the more we shriveled up. Typical kid stuff, except we knew that Dad really didn't want us to get too involved in this scene.

He would have been thrilled if Jeff wanted to play football or do some boxing, like he had as a kid. Dad had a macho, tough-love approach. He knew how to humiliate us about things, like running away from the neighborhood bullies. If we got upset, he'd mock us for crying.

He wanted Jeff to get tougher and wasn't thrilled with what he was seeing. Dad told us Jackie Wilson was a fruitcake. He thought these rock & roll kids, with their funny-looking hairdos and crazy language, were disrespectful. I think my father found the whole rock & roll phenomenon threatening to his entire way of life.

"Look at these guys," Dad would say. "With their sequins and sparkles, they look like sissies!

SINATRA WORE A SUIT AND TIE, GODDAMN IT!"

Dad sensed the rebellion in the performers, in the audience, and in us as well.

He wanted us to respect authority and to be obedient. Jeff was learning that being obedient didn't always score him popularity points in life.

"*Stand up straight!*" Dad would yell at Jeff, occasionally amplifying it with a smack on the ass.

Jeff had begun to slouch already, to fit in better—or to not stand out so badly.

"*And stop playing with your hair!*"

Jeff had begun a nervous habit of twirling his hair round his index finger at the back of his head.

Dad didn't like sissy boys. Daddy liked *men*. So he kept trying to make men out of us, and he worked hardest on Jeff. "It's for his own good," he would say.

There was an inherent problem: When it came to machismo, Jeff was simply unsuited physically and at a disadvantage.

Our father certainly *did* love Jeff and me, in his own way.

When we would spend the night at Dad's apartment on Fifteenth Street and Seventh Avenue in Manhattan's Chelsea area, he would pull out the convertible bed in the living room couch for us. Sometimes he'd get in too, and hug us real hard and tell us how much he loved us.

We'd squirm around, telling him, "Stop it, Dad, we're tired—you're takin' up the whole bed."

Some of the times we stayed with him in the city were great. He'd take us to movies on Forty-second Street and to Chinatown. We'd go bowling or ice-skating, the one sport Jeff was really good at. Jeff and the old man bonded at the skating rinks, which made it more fun for all of us—although the smell of overused cooking oil, the stench of stink-foot rental skates, and the cheesy organ music made me queasy.

On car rides Dad would turn off the radio and encourage us to talk. Given that we were on the shy side, it took a little prodding.

"Okay, talk to me now," he'd insist.

Then we'd clam up even tighter—which he didn't take well. Dad would still ask us questions about Mom and Hank. When we could satisfy him with a few words about school and friends, we could all relax. Then he'd suggest that we all sing songs. Dad taught us "Show Me the Way to Go Home," which Jeff and I loved, because we would all pretend to be sloshed when we sang it.

That was the strange thing about our father—one minute he'd be clowning around like he was in a Jerry Lewis movie, and the next he would be like the prison warden in *Midnight Express*. When Dad was the prison warden, we couldn't wait for him to drop us off in Howard Beach, where we were beginning to feel more and more comfortable. Jeff and I were almost . . . home.

Though we were becoming more accustomed to life there, we were still considered "outsiders" in the new neighborhood.

One day we spotted a stray black and white cat with a very pink nose. Jeff and I courted her with a piece of tuna sandwich from our lunchboxes and consummated the relationship with a little container of milk from the school cafeteria. She came around the next day, and the next. We named her Pinky. Since we weren't allowed to bring her into the apartment, we'd take her into the staircase of the building and feed her scraps from dinner that we'd stashed in napkins.

We'd sit her on our laps and tell her our problems, like how sad we were about our parents and how much we hated moving. If we cried, she would start to purr. We had to put her outside at night, but she always came back. She got us through that horrible period better than any therapist could have. Pinky became our best friend and most loyal companion: She was our Lassie.

Things were definitely settling into a more positive state of affairs when all of a sudden we were informed that Mom and "Dad," as we now called Hank, were looking for a house; they were seriously considering moving back to Forest Hills. Jeff and I were psyched, envisioning a hearty welcome back to our old neighborhood. Mom and Hank settled on a nice, big house on Sixty-seventh Drive, a tree-lined street one block from Forest Hills High School. We were scheduled to make the move as soon as the school year ended.

In the summer of 1963, we began packing up all our records and magazines. On our last evening in Howard Beach, David, Jeff, and I, keeping a safe distance, taunted the Garillo brothers as much as possible, while not letting on that we were moving. *"Tomorrow, you're goners,"* the ignorant bullies warned us.

The next morning Jeff and I tracked down Pinky, and we all piled into Hank's Jaguar and headed to Forest Hills.

Our new house was only about twelve blocks from our old one. We rode our bikes to our old block but found that it wasn't remotely the same. The only constant was our old nemesis Jeff Storch. He was right in form, slapping Jeff on the back so hard that he practically fell off his bike.

"Well, Four Eyes," Storch assured him, "I'll be seeing you around in school. Betcha can't wait! Ha ha!"

But the start of school was a long way off. We spent the remainder of that summer exploring our new block and our new house. We had a backyard again and a basement where Hank put the big hi-fi system.

David, Jeff, and I shared the big master bedroom upstairs. Reba had her own room next to ours. There was a bedroom for our grandmother Nanu, upstairs, too. Mom and Hank took a room downstairs near the den and made it their bedroom.

There were a lot of kids on the block and we made friends with them right away. Their parents were another story. There was a large contingent of relatively wealthy European Jewish immigrants with snobby attitudes. It didn't help that our parents had been divorced and remarried—which carried a stigma in 1963. The neighbors would look at us and mutter to each other. We looked back and gave them big smiles. Then they would turn away, shaking their heads to each other. Lord knows what would've happened if we hadn't been Jewish. It helped that there was one Italian and one Latino family on the block.

On our street there were two kids my age, Kenny Slevin and Michael Goodrich, who'd be in my class going into fourth grade. PS 3 is one of the oldest schools in the city, an authentic "little red schoolhouse" built in the 1920s, with only one classroom for each grade.

Michael's neighbor, Bernard Tinter, was Jeff's age. We all became fast friends. Jeff and I fit in better back in Forest Hills. The kids were more characteristic of middle-class Queens Jews, more interested in being funny and entertaining than tough and athletic.

But Jeff wasn't getting along so well in seventh grade at Stephen A. Halsey Junior High School in Rego Park. A few times he came home with the mark of someone's sneaker-bottom imprinted on the back of his white shirt. Being so tall and skinny, Jeff was easy prey. Even David and I were in awe of how fast our brother was shooting into the upper atmosphere.

As if things weren't bad enough for Jeff, a new toy store opened up called Toys "R" Us. On their commercials a creature called "Geoffrey Giraffe" was the featured mascot. Every time the commercial came on, David and I howled, because it reminded us of Jeff. It was good-natured ribbing, if there is such a thing at that age.

As we laughed, Jeff would shoot back at me, *"Well, you're Daffy Duck!"* alluding to my two webbed toes. *"Quack quack!"*

With the new phonograph in our bedroom, the four of us would "rock out" with our 45s and go crazy jumping from bed to bed. We'd go ape to the Trashmen's "Surfin' Bird," hang ten to Jan and Dean's "Surf City," and bop 'til we dropped to the Ran-Dells' "Martian Hop." We'd pull every sound imaginable out of our musical box of tricks.

When we caught our breath, we looked up to see the 1964 World's Fair being assembled right down the street in Flushing Meadow Park. People from all over the globe would be coming to *our* neighborhood to witness the most remarkable display of modern technology ever assembled.

The world really needed a fair, too. The past few years had seen some foreboding events.

After the 1962 Cuban Missile Crisis brought the world to the brink of nuclear annihilation, President Kennedy initiated a $17 billion nuclear missile program and advised Americans to build fallout shelters. The United States had begun underground nuclear testing. Racial tensions were also coming to a head, and violent confrontations between oppressed black Americans and white bigots were intensifying. Governor George Wallace had given his "segregation forever" speech in Alabama, prompting President Kennedy to propose the Civil Rights Bill on June 11, 1963. The next day, the NAACP's Medgar Evers was assassinated outside his home. On November 22, President Kennedy was assassinated in Dallas. On November 24, President Johnson escalated America's military involvement in the Vietnam War.

There were nuclear bomb tests and various treaties to ban the bomb. But from our perspective, the biggest bomb to drop on our shores fell right there in Queens, at JFK airport: "Beatlemania" exploded in the USA.

We'd heard they were coming for weeks. Murray the K, Cousin Brucie . . . *everyone* on the radio was talking about them. *The Beatles!*

Glued to the radio that February, we couldn't go to sleep without conferring with each other on how many days were left until the Beatles would be arriving in America for their appearance on *The Ed Sullivan Show.* We knew this was the biggest thing to ever happen in our lives. We pooled our money and bought every Beatles record we could find. Our first score was the hit single "I Want to Hold Your Hand." Later, we got the *Meet the Beatles!* album.

Instantly, everything else seemed old. These guys were obviously the future. They didn't dress in preppy frat-boy outfits, like Pat Boone, or in schmaltzy shiny jackets.

They weren't a continuation of the greasy-haired doo wop–era bands or Elvis Presley. They wore their hair straight down in the front, like we used to before we combed it neat with grease. They were funny, loose, fresh, and they were *ours.* The Beatles became the center of our lives and provided us a new source of style, sound, and philosophy.

The Beatles finally arrived just a few miles from our doorstep at Idlewild International Airport, which had been renamed John F. Kennedy International Airport in honor of the late president. Jeff and I rode our bikes down to the overpass across the Grand Central Parkway. We knew they'd be passing by—probably in big black shiny limos, just like the great leaders we'd seen before them.

It would be only two days until *Ed Sullivan,* on Sunday night.

For the first time in our lives we made absolutely *1,000 percent* sure we had all our weekend homework done by Sunday afternoon. There was nothing in the world that would prevent us from being in front of that television set at eight p.m. We sat and watched in reverence, savoring every second of their way-too-short appearance.

Waves from the British Invasion continued to douse American shores with bands like the Rolling Stones, Dave Clark Five, and Herman's Hermits—while homegrown acts just tried to keep their heads above water.

We hadn't consciously abandoned the Beach Boys or Chubby Checker. We still loved it all, from the Four Seasons to the Four Tops. AM radio was unbelievably abundant with great songs and great artists, like James Brown, the Supremes, Aretha Franklin, and Little Stevie Wonder. Hell, even our father suddenly had trouble finding something for himself on the dial in the Caddy. The stations that played Tony Bennett, Sinatra, and the rest of the Bow Tie Brigade were being reformatted.

Rock & soul had taken control. While the California Sound was reluctantly being nudged into the Pacific, the Motown Sound was spreading from Detroit toward both coasts. But we didn't have any money left over for records made by anyone who didn't have a funny accent and bowl haircut.

5.

ALL FALL DOWN

During this period of music and fashion transition, Jeff's exceptionally long legs actually came in very handy for me. We would have "chicken fights" on the lawn, with kids sitting atop the shoulders of their partners, battling to push or tug the others down. When I was on Jeff's shoulders, we had a huge advantage, as our opponents had to reach up high to try to grab my arms.

One day my friend Kenny Slevin stuck his foot out and tripped Jeff as we were celebrating our victory. I had my fists raised high in triumph as we suddenly toppled over—to everyone's glee. I cracked my head on an in-ground oil pipe, and once again, Jeff picked me up and took me home. Immediately, Mom took me to the hospital, where I was sewn up with fifteen stitches in the middle of my head. The upside was that for at least a month I had a get-out-of-haircut-free card. We all wanted to grow our hair over our ears and wear bangs like our heroes, but no one had been allowed to—yet. I was the first kid in school to have a Beatle haircut!

I garnered all kinds of attention from the girls in my fourth-grade class, who told me that I looked like Ringo Starr because of my big nose. Girls in Jeff's school weren't as kind to him; neither were the boys.

Reed-thin, Jeff would come home from Halsey regularly with stories about being mugged, tugged, pushed, and shoved in the hallways and staircases of the school. He was becoming more introverted socially. He didn't hang out after school with classmates; he hadn't made many friends.

Jeff had to attend gym classes for the first time in his life. Imagine this skinny kid trying to pull that long body up a twenty-five-foot rope, with the gym teacher goading him and the other kids razzing him. The whole class watched to see how my brother would handle the balance beams, waiting to explode into laughter. Jeff's grades paralleled his self-esteem: Both were poor.

Mom and Hank gave him some special attention and help with his schoolwork. Hank was very encouraging. He'd graduated from Brooklyn College and wanted us to earn *our* degrees. Jeff got help, but he also became even more frustrated.

Jeff had begun taking lessons to prepare for his bar mitzvah on his thirteenth birthday in May. It became a big point of contention between our mom and dad. Though our father was adamant about Jeff being bar mitzvahed, he didn't want to help our mom foot the bill, either out of hurt or just pure spite.

We were not a very religious household and always celebrated both Hanukkah *and* Christmas, with a tree as well as a menorah. We thought of Christmas as an American holiday and Hanukkah as a Jewish holiday. There was some sincere thought given to Judaism and tradition, but Jeff wanted the bar mitzvah mainly for the same reasons every kid in the neighborhood did—the gelt!

Normally, kids in Forest Hills had swanky affairs in fancy hotels or catering halls and made out like bandits. Mom and Hank threw Jeff a modest party in the house, but he still fared pretty well with the loot.

A month later, I received a few presents as well. I'd wrapped up the fourth grade having the highest reading level in the entire school. The school presented me with several prizes, including an award certificate, a globe, and a world atlas. And there were big pats on the back from my parents.

I also tried out and got accepted to the school glee club, which would be performing at the New York State Pavilion at the World's Fair. But a slightly bigger performance was coming up later that summer of '64. In August, the Beatles would be appearing *right in our neighborhood*! They'd be doing two shows at the Forest Hills Tennis Stadium, just blocks from our house. Mom and Hank warned us we were too little for this kind of thing and insisted that we stay away from the pandemonium. I was ten years old and knew it was out of my control. Jeff was pissed: He was thirteen. We settled for our father taking us to see *A Hard Day's Night*.

Dad had taken us to the country the weekend the movie opened in theaters, and we wouldn't give in until he agreed to drive to the theater where it was playing, which was at least thirty miles away.

"Drive faster, Bub, faster!"

Jeff started taking a big interest in sports cars, no doubt because of the songs we were listening to about little deuce coupes, Mustangs, and Corvettes. He loved it when our old man took us to the National Car Show every year at the New York Coliseum and always wanted to stay all day.

He got into slot car racing with miniature replicas of race cars propelled electronically on a model racetrack, controlled by handheld gizmos. We had a little track in the basement. There were also stores that rented time on their big tracks in elaborate settings. Jeff did well at this sport, where muscles weren't a factor.

Toward the end of fifth grade, my teacher, Mrs. Lacy, assigned the class a homework project to write a composition called "If I Had One Wish . . ." I handed in a positive but apparently alarming piece, "The School Would Blow Up!" Most likely inspired by the "duck and cover" drills that were supposed to save us from nuclear bombs, it was a harmless little fantasy about how some good might come out of destruction. The school blows up—and kids could all stay home, help their moms with chores, and play games. No one gets hurt or arrested, and everybody's happy.

But once Mrs. Lacy read my fantasy composition, she called my mom into school for a discussion. Mrs. Lacy knew I was a good student but thought I needed some focus. She suggested a hobby—perhaps a musical instrument.

I eagerly agreed. Playing music and being in a band was something I'd been dreaming about since the days back in Howard Beach when we'd listened to those guys singing in the alley. My first choice was to play the drums, like Ringo. Mom and Hank nixed that idea because they thought it would be too noisy.

My second choice was guitar. Mom took me to a little bargain shop in the neighborhood, where I picked out a $15 Harmony acoustic steel-string guitar. I rushed home, and within minutes I was plucking out riffs from the Stones' "Satisfaction" and the McCoys' "Hang on Sloopy." I played until my fingers couldn't take the pain. I couldn't really play any chords yet but was having a ball picking out melodies of new songs and revisiting old favorites such as "Wipeout."

Jeff was impressed—and extremely encouraging. Sometimes when I was practicing he'd tap out the beat with pencils. We were having fun, but a huge dilemma was looming: The Beatles would be performing at Shea Stadium in August, while us four kids would be spending our first summer at sleepaway camp upstate. We'd be missing them—*again*.

Jeff was so upset that he mentioned it years later, in a rough draft of a magazine article he began but never completed.

"It was 1965," he wrote. "I was thirteen, fourteen. My mother remarried. I was a loner, me and my brother, and proud, and rock & roll was my salvation. Now every summer, spread across Queens Boulevard, there would be a huge banner of the coming concert events at Forest Hills Tennis Stadium. This year it said, 'Aug. 15th—The Beatles at Shea Stadium.' It was exciting, I wanted to go, but NO, I had to go to sleepaway camp. It killed me."

At least I got to bring my guitar to camp and continued to progress.

At camp, Jeff initially took the usual ribbing from kids who hadn't yet seen anyone quite like him. But after they'd had their fun with him, the jocks and elitist boneheads—the "popular" kids—stopped taunting him, allowing some actual camaraderie among Jeff and his fellow campers. Like any kid, Jeff got into the spirit of summer camp, as he expressed in a letter to our dad.

Dear Dad,

How are you? I'm fine. Since my last letter we had tribals and a carnival, which was a lot of fun. Last week we went to Tanglewood, a very beautiful place. Another camper and I wandered off, and down in a field we saw a big barn. In this barn is where they keep all their drums, bells, gongs, bongos, etc. We found some drumsticks and we played around with the drums and all the other things there. Then we went back to hear the concert of the Boston Pops Orchestra which hadn't started until 8:00.

I met a lot of kids that went to my school there also. I had a very nice time. This week Aug. 9th we went to "How to Succeed in Business Without Really Trying." That was good too. On our last Day Off we went to the State Capitol and then we went to the movies and saw "Batman" and also "Disk-O-Teen Holiday." Batman was good but I liked the other picture better. It had all the singing groups in it. I saw a group in it called the VAGRANTS who live in Forest Hills, and I know. They're very good and just saw recently they made their first record. This week we went on an overnight Hike. We slept out at Thomson's Lake in sleeping bags, made our own food and campfire. It was real rugged living. In all we hiked 10 miles. Today is Aug. 12th and Color War should be breaking out very soon now. Well that's all the news that's happened up till now.

See You Soon!!!
Love, Jeff

WHILE WE WERE at camp, Mom and Hank had gone to Stuttgart, Germany, to buy a new chocolate-brown Porsche 911. They planned to drive around Europe until the middle of August and return to the United States on the SS *France*, their beautiful new car in its hold.

When they didn't show up on visiting day in August, we were concerned. Our aunt, Elaine Gindy, who worked at the camp, informed us there had been a complication but said we certainly should not worry. With our dad visiting, Jeff and I were preoccupied and didn't give it too much thought.

But when camp ended and the bus dropped us off in Queens, only Mom was there to meet us. She hugged us all like never before. I thought she must have really missed us. Mom told us that Hank wasn't able to come with her to pick us up and that she'd explain as soon as we got home.

When we got back to the house, she asked us to come into the den. We could tell that something was wrong. The four of us sat on the couch. Instinctively we began to panic.

"Dad won't be coming home today," Mom started. All of a sudden her face looked noticeably different than when we left for camp. "We had an accident in the car," she said quietly, "and your dad passed away."

David doubled over and fell to his knees in front of my mother, weeping uncontrollably. Reba looked shocked for a few seconds and then did the same, as my mom reached out to hug them. They were stricken beyond description.

Though dismayed, Jeff and I were certainly not as affected. When we looked at each other, we saw more fear than grief.

By this point, Mom had broken down; Jeff and I began bawling uncontrollably as well. Finally Dave composed himself enough to ask what had happened.

Mom told us they'd been having a wonderful time and were driving down a road in France when they had a head-on collision.

Because she'd been sleeping, Mom didn't even realize she'd been propelled right through the windshield. She said she was very lucky to be alive—but Hank was not as fortunate. We all began to cry again and hug each other.

Now Jeff and I were freaking out as well—over the notion that we had come so close to losing our mother. We also knew why her face looked so different: She'd had stitches in her mouth and bruises on her face.

Within a month or so things eased up a bit, and the enduring household—now us four kids and Mom—managed to find some relief and laughter together. We felt like we were in one of those Doris Day movies where tragedy bleeds into comedy. Then Jeff and I came home one day and found Mom crying again.

There was a little Spanish bench in the hallway between the kitchen and the den. Mom sat us down on the bench and told us that David and Reba had gone to live with their uncle and aunt. They wouldn't be coming back. Mom told us that it wasn't what she wanted, but it could not be changed.

"It's just the three of us again," she said, "and we'll be all right. Don't you worry, we'll be all right . . ."

Mom hugged Jeff and me. The three of us quietly sobbed as we squeezed each other. Before Mom let us go, she gave us another big squeeze and kissed the tops of our heads.

Well, the top of one of our heads—Jeff's was beyond her reach.

6.

THE HILLS ARE ALIVE!

I n Forest Hills in the mid-1960s, rock bands were forming at a phenomenal rate. It was as if you'd win a prize just for starting one—which, in a way, you did. Several neighborhood boys had been at it for a while already, and some had attained substantial success: Tom and Jerry, a.k.a. Simon and Garfunkel; Spirit; and the Vagrants, to name a few.

Herds of local bands were striving to break ahead of the pack, hoping to be noticed. Every band was trying to outdo their competition, whether it was through their style, or musicianship, or whatever else they could come up with. Maybe it was finding a singer who could throw a tambourine twenty feet into the air and catch it behind his back, or a drummer who could twirl his sticks while he smashed his skins, or a guitar player with really long hair who could pace menacingly around the stage, like a lion in a cage.

The kids of Forest Hills took the term "battle of the bands" literally, and sabotaging the competition was not just an option—it was customary. Traditionally, drum skins were found slit and amps were suddenly unplugged during a band's set in a school gym.

A band called the Tangerine Puppets had thoroughly established themselves as the most popular of the local bands. My friend Michael Goodrich's older brother, George, was a drummer, and guys from the Puppets were always coming over to his house to jam with him. One day in the fall of 1965, Mike and I were up in his attic reading *Archie* comics when we heard the sound of music spreading upstairs from down in the basement.

"Let's go down and see 'em rehearse," Mike said. "Maybe we can pick up some tricks for our stage show." Michael was the designated lead singer of the band we were forming in our minds.

We thought the guys in the Tangerine Puppets were the coolest in the world. They had Beatle haircuts and wore mod-style clothes. They had cool moves when they played. And they had *girlfriends*!

One of the Puppets' guitarists who'd come over was a kid named Tommy Erdelyi. Another was John Cummings, who played bass in the group.

"Watch out for that guy," Mike Goodrich warned me about John. "Sometimes he's in a bad mood."

"I met John Cummings at the Forest Hills High School cafeteria," Tommy Erdelyi remembered. "Bob Roland, who became the lead singer of the Tangerine Puppets, took me over to John's table and introduced me. He had personality; he was funny and had a lot of people sitting with him.

"Sometimes I'd go sit at John's table," Tommy continued, "and I would arm-wrestle him. John was a bodybuilder and I weighed like ninety-five pounds at the time. He would just slam my hand into the table. John Cummings liked to dominate, verbally or physically. He had a need to take charge and feel superior. He seemed to not feel whole unless he could do that."

When Michael and I slipped down to his basement to watch the Puppets in awed silence, we made sure to stay out of John's way, especially after seeing him go ape on Bob Roland at one of his shows.

"John tried to kick our singer Bob Roland in the head when we were playing one of those battle of the bands in Forest Hills in 1966," Tommy Erdelyi remembered.

"John's amplifier started making a noise," said guitarist Richard Adler. "It was cutting in and out, so John started kicking the side of the amp. Bob Roland went over and started to kick it, too, except he was kicking it from the front and stuck his foot right through the speaker.

"John got so mad," Richard recalled, "that he put down his bass right in the middle of the song and, as the rest of the band was playing, started punching and kicking our singer right onstage in front of the audience.

John was beating him up until we put down our instruments and stopped him."

John, Tommy, George, and the other guys were six years older than Michael and I, more or less. But they'd *been* "us" just a few years prior, so they let Michael and me hang out and observe. They knew it was never too early to start learning or to get performing experience.

One day when the Tangerine Puppets were taking a break, Tommy laid his Fender guitar down on a chair. I went over and just looked at it. Tommy spotted me and walked over. "Do you play?" he asked.

"Uhhh," I said.

"Let's see," Tommy said as he handed me his guitar.

"I only started a few months ago," I warned him, and strapped on an *electric* guitar for the first time in my life. Since I didn't know anything very complicated, I opted for my old favorite, "Wipeout."

"Wow, that's pretty good!" Tommy said with surprise. "Who taught you to play?"

"Nobody," I answered him. "I've been learning it myself. Think you could teach me? I got a guitar about six months ago, a Harmony, but I think there's something wrong with it. Think you could come over and take a look at it?"

After rehearsal, he came over to my house and saw my guitar: "How do you play this thing?" he laughed. "The neck is bowed to crap! It's warped. You can stick your whole hand between the strings and the neck!"

Tommy took out his guitar to show me for comparison and then started playing "The House of the Rising Sun."

"Can you show me that?" I begged him. "Please!"

After he started teaching me the chords, I was getting it, but my fingers were killing me, and I couldn't switch from one chord to another quickly enough.

Jeff came down to see what was going on. "This is my brother, Jeff," I informed Tommy, making the introduction between the two future bandmates.

"Do you play too?" Tommy asked Jeff.

"Nah," Jeff replied, not mentioning his stint on the accordion.

"Well, you're really good. Keep practicing," Tommy advised me, "and get a new guitar. You could shoot arrows off that thing!"

"Wow, thanks, Tommy," I gushed.

A week or so later, after I had the chord changes down and Michael had practiced singing, he suggested we perform "The House of the Rising Sun" during our sixth-grade class show-and-tell day. Our teacher Mrs. Wolfson loved it so much she insisted we go around and perform it for every class in the school. We had our first tour booked and took our act on the road, making our bones in the daunting classrooms of PS 3.

We loved the way the kids watched us. We loved the applause—and getting out of class! It even got me a date for the sixth-grade prom with the most desired girl in the school, Dee Dee Friedman. We considered ourselves pros already and started writing our own songs. When Jeff saw me and Michael having all this fun, he wanted to get in on the action, too.

Jeff started saving not money, but King Korn trading stamps. King Korn was a supermarket chain that used the stamps as a marketing gimmick. Jeff pasted the stamps into booklets, which were redeemable for prizes. There were "redemption centers" in most neighborhoods, where people would go to trade in their stamps for the items of their choice. Jeff had his eye on a red-sparkle Maestro snare drum.

Mom had said she and Hank didn't want the noise of drums in the house. But with all the noise coming out of the basement now—with me and Michael singing and playing our guitars, and Jeff banging out beats on the table with whatever makeshift "drumsticks" he could find—she knew it was a losing battle. David and Reba were gone, and sadly so was Hank and our grandma Nanu, who'd recently passed away. So Mom gave Jeff the thumbs-up for just *one* drum.

We went to the trading center and got his Maestro snare drum. But when we got it home, we realized that a snare drum needs a snare drum *stand*. Jeff would just put the drum on his lap and tap along with us until he got a stand. He really wasn't sure of what he was doing, and neither was I, but we were having fun.

My guitar neck had gotten so warped I could hardly get the strings to touch the neck. Mom could tell that I was dead serious about playing, and after I'd whined enough, she took me to Austin Street and got me a brand-new Hagstrom electric guitar, a little Univox amp, and a Shure microphone and mike stand. I wanted to sing now too, like John, Paul, George, and Ringo. I started to take my equipment around to kids' birthday parties and sang songs by the Beatles, the Stones, the Dave Clark Five, and Herman's Hermits, among others.

After a while, just banging on the drum all day wasn't challenging enough for Jeff. I had a band in the making already, and he wanted to get into one, too. A few weeks before we were to depart for sleepaway camp, Mom gave Jeff the OK to get a full set of drums, with cymbals, stands, stool, and everything. It cost about $350 in those days, which was quite a bit. She gave Jeff $100 toward the set, the same sum my guitar had cost, and he used his bar mitzvah gelt for the balance. Amen.

We piled into the station wagon, and Mom took us to Manny's Music on Forty-eighth Street in Manhattan to get Jeff his set of "white pearl" Gretsch drums. The house was noisier than ever, and some nights Mom even pulled the power on us. Kids on the block started coming around to hang out by the basement windows and listen to us play.

Sometimes they'd tell us how good we were, other times how *bad*. But they came; our house was becoming the center of a scene on the block. It was great!

One thing that wasn't great was Jeff's ninth-grade report card. But Mom and our real dad—the only Dad now—were certainly happy to see Jeff graduate from Stephen A. Halsey Junior High.

Meanwhile, I once again overachieved academically and was informed in a letter that next semester, at Halsey, I'd be placed into an accelerated-progress program called the SP. It combined three years of junior high school into two, skipping from seventh right into ninth grade. Mom was very proud and she even got me my own telephone line and Trimline telephone as a reward.

When we got back from summer camp, we all got serious about starting a band.

Michael Goodrich met a kid named Andy Ritter, who auditioned on my brother's drums. Andy had been playing for a year or so and was damn good for a twelve-year-old. Now we had a real band—almost. We didn't have a bass player, but we forged ahead and named the band the Overdose of Sound.

Andy brought his drum set over, and now we had *two* sets of drums in the basement, along with amplifiers and microphones. Eventually we'd add a small PA system for the vocals.

In a few months, Jeff was also looking to form a band. He was in his first term in Forest Hills High School in the tenth grade and had met a classmate named Demetrious who played guitar pretty well and could sing, too.

Demetrious was an odd duck. He had a beautiful Fender Stratocaster. He'd kiss his guitar and cover it with a blanket before closing the case. He and Jeff struck up a nice friendship and began forming what would be the first band for both of them, the Intruders. Mom designed a logo for them and Magic Markered it onto the skin of Jeff's bass drum.

They were having a difficult time filling out the rest of the lineup, as Demetrious was quite temperamental and Jeff was still trying to get up to speed on the more difficult beats. Jeff still couldn't play "Wipeout" very well, but he was intent on having a band, and he was certainly showing that despite his extreme shyness, he had the will, the drive, and the guts to do whatever it took to get it together.

A year and several months after Hank died, Mom was beginning to have financial worries. It cost a lot of money to maintain a house that size. She hadn't really been working since the accident.

It was now the fall of 1967. The boiler had broken down; the price of heating oil had gone up; the storm windows gave in; and the TV blew out. Winter was headed our way, but there was no money coming in to help prepare for it.

Our mom had to be creative. She came up with the idea of renting Nanu's old room to airline stewardesses, since we were smack in the middle of both airports.

Jeff and I were now fifteen and twelve years old—and maturing, if you know what I mean. We thought, *"Airline stewardesses! Great idea, Ma!"*

A stewardess from Pan Am responded to her ad, and Jeff and I eagerly awaited her arrival. Late at night we would share our fantasies.

"I hear these stewardesses are pretty wild!" Jeff told me the night before the first one arrived.

"This could be great, man!" I added. "Like in that Tony Curtis movie *Boeing Boeing*. But," I wondered, "do you think they'd really do anything with us? I mean, you and me ain't exactly Tony Curtis."

"No," he agreed, "but at least, we're . . . *younger*."

The first to move in was a cute Pan Am stewardess named Joanie. She was sincerely warm and friendly, but she was pretty straight, and she had a boyfriend, a pilot named Skip, or was it Chip? So much for "coffee, tea, or me."

Then Mom made friends with a recently divorced woman named Geraldine Einhorn. Gerri was also a bit wacky. She had two kids, Richard and Amy, and nowhere to go temporarily. They became transitory boarders in Reba's room.

The house was brightening up again, and Jeff and I thought it was great. It was all kids and women—there was no one to get tough with us.

It was like a big commiseration party in a way, because we were all in the same boat. We could all relate to each other—and laugh about our woes. Plus it was the sixties, and the idea of abandoning old-world conventions for new ones helped us not get *too* upset about being abnormal.

Sometimes we even reveled in it. "We are the modern world, we are the future," we told ourselves. Then we'd all watch some family-oriented Hallmark Hall of Fame show on TV and get really sad.

MY BANDMATES ANDY Ritter and Mike Goodrich brought over a kid named Doug Scott, who was a bit of a stray cat himself. He'd lost his dad, and his mom made a modest salary as a nurse. He became my best friend and a constant fixture in our house.

Doug had been playing guitar about two years longer than me, from the age of nine. He was the best in our age bracket. Doug became a band member, replacing me on guitar. I would switch over to bass guitar. We went to a pawnshop, where I picked up a used Höfner bass just like Paul McCartney's. Now my band was complete!

Jeff seemed to be spending more time with himself upstairs in the bathroom. I thought I knew what he had been doing in there; I figured it was the same thing I was doing as I began to . . . discover myself. But now I really wasn't so sure.

When Jeff finished up there, the bathmat would be all wet, towels left unhung. He would let the hot water run for an hour—and he wasn't shaving yet. The room was so steamy that the walls would be sweating and the mirror so frosted I couldn't see myself without wiping it ten times. Jeff had no answer when I'd ask him what he was doing in there for so long. There was nothing glaringly indicative of a specific problem, but something more than just *unusual* was happening.

I knew my brother was different. But now with everyone else gone, and no other brothers, or sisters, or stepfathers to distract me, my attentions were more focused on Jeff. I began noticing things about him—like when he'd move his toothbrush in and out of the holder several times, for no reason, and when he'd turn the light off as he left the bathroom, then go back in and turn it on again.

Jeff would get into bed and out again—put his feet back on the floor, pause, and get back into bed. Other mysterious happenings began to occur: Dirty glasses and plates were left *next* to the kitchen sink, not *in* it. Ice cream was left out all night on top of the refrigerator. Empty food containers were not thrown away. Half the time, I'd get blamed for these things. Sometimes I actually was the culprit, but I had a solvable problem—I was *a kid.*

Our mother was really becoming annoyed with Jeff's increasing sloppiness and seemingly intentional lack of consideration. The last thing she needed was to lose the stewardesses, who found themselves waiting for Jeff to get out of the bathroom when they needed to get ready for their flights. Confrontations between Mom and Jeff became more frequent as his weird behavior became more of a burden.

Mom was already running the house, shopping, cooking, and cleaning. She had no one to help pay the bills, replace fuses, fix a broken chair, or make sure the gutters on the roof were clear—all the things a father normally does.

Initially she tried to reason with Jeff, but he responded to her complaints with complete denial and a perplexing mockery. We hoped it was nothing more than a phase he would pass through.

There was another possible explanation for this strange behavior.

Things were changing fast in 1967. The Beatles were not just funny, innocent mop tops; they had evolved.

Elvis, Dion, and the whole slicked-back doo-wop crowd were just big grease marks that could be wiped away with a new space-age spray. They were all just campy now, as campy as the cover of our new Beatles album, *Sgt. Pepper's Lonely Hearts Club Band.* These songs weren't about schoolgirls wearing lace, a pretty face, and a ponytail hangin' down.

Now they were girls with "kaleidoscope eyes" who worked as lovely "meter maids." They could be seen floating in the sky with diamonds, after meeting you at the turnstile—then, with the sun in their eyes, they'd be gone.

Penny Lane? Very strange.

Everything and everyone now looked and acted different, and there was a good reason—drugs. There was nothing stopping Jeff and me from happily succumbing to the ways of the "counterculture." Head shops popped up, even in Forest Hills. Jeff and me would go to the "In" Market on Austin Street to smell the incense and look at the Day-Glo posters. Jeff even traveled into the city by subway on his own. His favorite place to hang out was

Greenwich Village. West Fourth Street in the Village was just one subway stop past where we'd get off for my dad's house in Chelsea. Jeff talked about the clubs he saw, like Cafe Wha?, the Bitter End, and Folk City—clubs we'd read about on the liner notes of our Lovin' Spoonful albums.

Except for our futile attempt to smoke some banana peels, inspired by Donovan's song "Mellow Yellow," I hadn't done any drugs yet. And though Jeff was behaving strangely lately, I was *pretty* sure Jeff hadn't either—he would have told me. We were certainly more than curious. We'd listen to the sitar drone dripping from the tracks of the recent Beatles albums, especially Harrison's "Within You Without You" on *Sgt. Pepper's*, and pretend to be on LSD trips. We'd get giddy and convince ourselves we'd reached some mystical zenith from a "contact high."

"Are you floating yet?" we'd ask each other.

THAT JUNE JOANIE moved out, and a new Pan Am stewardess named Rickie arrived. She had a little red Volkswagen Beetle and told us she'd teach us how to drive it when we came back from summer camp. Sleep-away camp that summer was the best, because we knew it would be our last. We'd enjoyed the color wars, water-skiing, rifles, bows and arrows, building fires, and bra-stealing raids on the girls' bunks. But we'd had enough of that good, clean fun and vowed to go out in style.

One night Jeff and I broke into the head counselor's shack just before dawn and sacrificed one of our favorite old 45s, "The Martian Hop." We blasted the song over the PA system and bolted back to our bunks as the song blared throughout the entire camp! We were laughing so hard, hearing the crazy song echoing off the mountains, that we got caught by the karate instructor, of all people. But it was well worth it as our way of saying farewell to our fellow campers.

Jeff was really happy not to be coming back. He wanted to get back home, where his drums were, and back to the Village, where his future was.

7.

IT AIN'T US, DAD

Safe to say, my brother and I were now headed down a clear path, but it certainly wasn't the straight and narrow. As soon as we got back from camp, which was healthy for the body, we got right to work on our heads.

We'd heard the "youth rules" rebellious rumblings in the Who's "My Generation," but Jeff and I realized that what they'd melted down in that song was just the tip of the sociological iceberg. One night in an upstate motel room with our dad, we turned the TV on to watch *Where the Action Is*, the nightly Paul Revere and the Raiders show. Dad staunchly switched the channel to news coverage of the Vietnam War and told us that this was what we *should* have been watching.

"Aww, come on, man!" Jeff challenged him. "The Turtles are gonna be on tonight!"

Even in a Turtles song there could be some vital message, one we might choose to use to shape our frame of mind: *"You say you're lookin' for someone / Never weak but always strong, / To protect you an' defend you / Whether you are right or wrong . . . But it ain't me, babe."*

Those lines neatly summed up the ideology we'd been hearing, thinking, talking, and singing about. We related it not only to girls, but also to society, our country, and even our parents. Though these were actually Bob Dylan's words that the Turtles were singing, it didn't matter; we were all on the same page now.

"Our parents just may have fucked up; we can't defend what they've done to this world, two wrongs don't make a right," was the proverb of our fable.

After all, adults were lynching people in the South; there was talk of air and water pollution that would kill us after our parents were gone; and our teachers were telling us to duck under our desks to protect ourselves from atomic bombs. We really *did* believe that we were on the eve of destruction. We also believed that the youth of America had the numbers now, and we were taking over—with music!

We had it all figured out.

Of course, we really didn't; but these were the things Jeff and I talked about to each other, sometimes all day and all night.

Dad supports the war, Mom doesn't. Who's right, who's wrong?

We knew about the war, we just didn't want to hear about it from our father's sources. We didn't trust them.

"This is important, and you're gonna watch it," Dad said, continuing his motel room lecture. "These soldiers are fighting over there and dying for America, like we did when *I* was in the service."

"We heard that this war is stupid," Jeff persisted, reaching over to switch the channel. "And Mom told us you never went to France. And this is different anyway, man. Nobody even knows why they're going there!"

"*Hey,*" Dad yelled, smacking Jeff's arm down and thrusting a finger in his face, "*you do what I tell you to do. I joined the service and was ready to fight, and you're gonna go too, when it's time. You better learn some respect. The way you two are starting to look, I'm not surprised what I'm hearing. What's that mother of yours teaching you? How to be your beatniks! And your hipniks! Whatever you call 'em. And you don't call me 'man.' I'm not your 'man,' I'm your father. I'm not one of your beatniks!*"

That was for sure.

As we left the motel room to go out for dinner, Jeff turned the thermostat all the way up so that it would be warm when we got back, as it was freezing up there in the mountains. When we returned, the room was like an oven. The old man got so pissed at Jeff that he flung him across the room—clear over the bed—splattering him against the wall. It was the most violent punishment I'd ever seen him dole out. Jeff wasn't hurt, at least not physically, but he was pretty shaken up. He stayed quiet for the rest of the weekend. I felt really bad for him and pretty much gave the old man the silent treatment too.

This didn't exactly bring us closer together, which was what these trips were supposed to accomplish.

Dad had one of his steady broads with him, a divorcée named Nancy, along with her six-year-old boy, Jonathan. She was totally submissive and would never interfere or intercede when our father was going off on Jeff or me, which he now did more frequently. She wouldn't even defend herself when he would taunt, tease, and insult her mercilessly, calling her stupid or fat.

"Jelly Legs" was one of his favorite nicknames for Nancy, referring to her less-than-perfect thighs. This was meant to be funny, and we were all supposed to laugh with him at this humiliation.

Nancy would just giggle and say, "Oh, stop it, Noel!"

We liked Nancy, so we felt bad and were embarrassed at the way Dad was treating her. We now understood why our mother didn't want to stay and endure Dad's behavior for the rest of her life.

JEFF WAS SIXTEEN, a year and change away from the draft. I'd turned thirteen over the summer and was having my big bar mitzvah party in September. I'd actually studied and learned how to read Hebrew. All our friends were having their parties in fancy hotels in Manhattan or Long Island, but ours were in the basement, which was okay with us. We didn't really care about the schmaltzy bar mitzvah thing.

But even on this scale, again our father didn't think he should contribute. He resented being asked to pay for things. "Let *her* pay for it. That's the way she wanted it," was his reasoning. He paid the minimum amount of child support required by law. We'd heard Mom trying to squeeze a drop more out of him on several fruitless occasions.

Hence we had our "affairs" in the house; better that than not having one at all, which would have stigmatized us in this solidly Jewish neighborhood. At the time, it was a status thing and as much about appearances as a religious rite of passage. Call it "prayer pressure." We were not ashamed, just not very religious Jews. We were probably the worst Jews on the block. Kids talk and have a tendency to repeat things their parents say. Many of our neighbors would express their disappointment with a caustic glance or a disdainful shake of the head when they walked by our house.

It's not like we went out in the front yard and barbecued ham on the high holy days, but we did play loud rock music in the basement on several of them. Maybe that wasn't exactly kosher, and maybe they had a legitimate beef, but we were surprised at how intolerant such a recently persecuted people could be.

As a result, Jeff and I developed a weird resentment toward our "own people." Then we realized their problem with us was more about money. "The *meshugana* neighbors," as they referred to us, were fucking up the property values on the block. If that's what it was all about, then we Jews were just the same as everyone else—no better and no worse.

Regardless, we had a nice party with all of us kids chasing each other in and out of the house. One of my friends had raided his big brother's pot stash and lit up behind the garage during the party; the smell crept into the backyard. I got a little mad; after all, it was *my* party, and they didn't even offer me any. Maybe it wasn't the right occasion to smoke my first joint, given that I was already kind of dizzy after stealing one of Mom's cigarettes and puffing on it. We'd all be getting high soon enough.

Mom had read us newspaper articles about people overdosing on heroin and the dangers of drugs in general. Glue sniffing had become popular, and she warned us about losing brain cells and being stupid for the rest of our lives.

But Jeff and I weren't interested in glue or heroin. We wanted to become "experienced," as Jimi Hendrix put it. We wanted our souls to become "psychedelicized," as the Chambers Brothers sang in "Time Has Come Today." No earthly limits; we wanted visions beyond those our normal abilities could provide. These were not normal times.

We started to dress like our rock star idols, in bell-bottoms, satin shirts with big collars, scarves, and vests, anything that looked like something the Who or Jimi Hendrix might wear. Even Forest Hills had two stores that catered to the counterculture. Jeff and I began collecting Day-Glo posters from the "In" Market, and he also brought a few back from Greenwich Village. We bought an ultraviolet black light and another light that sent colors dancing around the room. We bought some fluorescent paint and dabbed little stars on the ceiling that you could only see under black light. We turned our bedroom into a psychedelic experience, replete with light show and music.

One night we brought Mom in for the cosmic experience. She was actually very impressed and realized how artistic it all was, and, in her opinion, harmless. She was even encouraged by our creativity.

"Just be careful with that incense," she said. "Don't burn the house down!"

We were on our way to hippie freakdom.

The room right next to ours was the total converse of our rebellion. Rickie, the Pan Am stewardess, could not have been more straitlaced. With all that was going on next door, she showed the tolerance of a saint—or a stewardess, depending on your religious beliefs. She was also leaving us to get married and would be replaced with another stewardess, a Russian beauty named Titanya.

She insisted we call her Tanya, because we were not able to say the "Tit" part with straight faces.

Another family moved into Reba's old room, a woman named Bea and her daughter Sandra. Bea was hot, even to us kids. Then again, even Mrs. Howell on *Gilligan's Island* was fair game in a pinch when fantasies of Ginger and Mary Ann were overused and in need of some time off.

Bea had been married to a wealthy man and acted like she was above us. Her daughter was extremely cute, but she was also a snob. I'm sure Bea instructed her to set her sights higher than screwups like us. Soon enough, they were gone, too.

It was strange, being frowned upon in our own home. With all these people coming and going in and out of our lives, we became increasingly aware of how far we were from being the "typical family." We had already become outsiders on our own block. Jeff and I designated the Doors'"People Are Strange" as our theme song for the year.

We were the black sheep of the block, and we kind of liked it. Jeff was becoming the darkest of us. As he got older, he traveled to Manhattan more frequently.

"When I was around sixteen, I went to see the Who at a Murray the K show on 59th Street," Jeff wrote in his journal. "It was the first time they came to America, and it was a really big bill; the Who, Cream, Mitch Ryder and the Detroit Wheels, the Vagrants, a whole bunch of bands. I got there really early in the morning; if you got there early enough you might get a free album or something. I even brought my Instamatic camera.

"The Who only played three songs: 'I Can't Explain,' 'Happy Jack,' and

'My Generation,' and they just blew me away," he wrote. "They were so exciting, visual, and fun. Then they destroyed their equipment! The Who was my favorite band."

Though his schoolwork was hurting, Jeff started hanging out in Greenwich Village, even on weeknights. He was coming home later, too. This caused Mom some grief, but she was having trouble controlling him at this point. Jeff was almost seventeen years old. His band, the Intruders, had fallen apart, and he was searching for new prospects in the clubs and cafés around MacDougal Street. An unexpected little find in a Village boutique turned out to be historic.

One night he came back with a new pair of sunglasses and asked me how they looked on him.

"Way cooler than those Mr. Peabody glasses you got," I told him. They were similar to John Lennon's and really fit his face. But the lenses weren't prescription.

He asked Mom to take to him to the eye doctor to get a pair he could use. She agreed. Jeff walked out of the eye doctor's office wearing his new gold-framed, oval-shaped, rose-colored glasses. The rest is history: They became an extension of his head. But since Jeff had no medical reason to wear them in school, his teachers objected. As a result, he spent a lot of time in the principal's office, where he "hung out and ate Popsicles."

Jeff was becoming very defensive about removing his glasses. Our father refused to let him wear the "freako" glasses when we went out with him.

The cracks in their relationship were beginning to show—and they weren't pretty. Between our old man yelling at him on the weekends and the tension at home between Jeff and my mother, due to his increasingly strange behavior, it was beginning to get to us all.

For a year, my mother had been taking Jeff to doctors and psychiatrists, trying to get to the root of his problem. I'd spent some of those evenings doing my homework in the car while waiting for them, which I didn't mind. But I did mind all the yelling. Jeff was getting pretty nasty with Mom, and sometimes I'd become protective and lash out at him. On the other hand, tolerance, peace, and loving your brother were the messages blowing in the wind, and he and I were probably the tightest we'd ever been.

My band the Overdose of Sound had been renamed Purple Majesty and Jeff really liked it. We were hanging out in the Village, too. We'd leave in the afternoon and be greeted at the West Fourth Street subway stop by change-begging street hippies. The most radical of the revolutionaries would taunt us if we didn't give them money.

"*Hey, yo-yos,*" they'd yell, "*you don't live here, man! Why don't you go back to your rich mommy and daddy in Queens, or wherever you came from!*"

"Yo-yo" was what they called people who came to hang out in the Village but didn't live there—kind of the precursor to the "bridge and tunnel" label but more obnoxious, because these hippies thought they were ethically above us. It was the beginning of the "hipper than thou" era.

Once we got past them, we'd check out the head shops and the clothing and record stores. We'd go down to Cafe Wha?, where Hendrix had played, and the Night Owl, where Bob Dylan and the Lovin' Spoonful had performed. They wouldn't serve us alcohol, of course, but we could come in and order a soda and watch the bands. Not many bars would let a bunch of thirteen-year-olds do that today.

Jeff joined a band called the Hudson Tube, named after the train line that delivered his new bandmates from their native New Jersey to their new crash pad in the West Village. He was playing in the Bitter End, Cafe Bizarre, and Cafe Wha? The Hudson Tube broke up shortly after it began, and Jeff joined another band called 1812. My brother was having a good run and making strides toward gaining the confidence and acceptance he wasn't getting from his peers in Forest Hills.

Mom was a bit concerned by the hours Jeff was keeping and the strange people calling on the phone—people with cosmic names who talked in psychedelic mumbo jumbo. Sometimes if Jeff wasn't home, they'd talk to me for hours about war and politics. I wondered why these cool older guys would talk to a thirteen-year-old kid for so long. I learned soon enough: These people were speeding, or tripping their balls off.

Jeff was in the thick of it now. One night he told me he had experimented with some pills. I begged him to describe it.

"It's just like you think," he said, stating what I later found is ultimately the only right answer.

"Wow!" I said.

Through his shyness, my brother had found a way of saying a whole lot with just a few words.

8.

WILD IN THE STREETS!

One winter day Jeff's band was rehearsing in the basement, so my band went to Michael Goodrich's house. The Tangerine Puppets didn't jam down there anymore because it stank horribly from dog shit. Their crazed German shepherd, Beylon, was kept confined either in the basement or the backyard. Their once-cute little puppy had become a ferocious beast.

Walking up to Michael's back door, I looked up and saw Beylon spring five feet in the air, headed right toward me, baring his teeth and growling like I'd never heard before. He was always trying to jump that backyard fence. Finally he made it.

He pounced and knocked me down flat. I yelled, hoping he'd recognize my voice—but Beylon was *possessed*. I hunched my shoulders and pressed my chin into my chest as he gnawed away at my back and shoulders. He bit into the collar of my coat and pulled, thrashing his head and dragging me down the driveway. He was going for my throat, and he was bigger, heavier, and stronger than me.

My bandmate Doug froze. Michael came running outside but was not strong enough to pry Beylon off. If I tried to get up, the dog pulled me right back down. Luckily my hands were still in my pockets, so he couldn't bite my fingers and screw up my guitar playing. Finally Michael's eldest brother, Bob, who had been in the shower upstairs, came running out with just a towel wrapped around him and was able to restrain the dog.

I racked up a career-high twenty-six sutures on my face, back, shoulder, and right arm. But my fingers were preserved, and though my right arm was in a sling, I still wanted to play the show we had booked at the Halsey JHS Battle of the Bands in two weeks. During the show, while Doug took his guitar solo in "Purple Haze," I ripped the sling off my arm, grabbed up my old acoustic guitar by the neck, raised it as high as possible without reopening any wounds, and *kaboom*! Just like Pete Townshend! We didn't win, but we came in second. Later I'd find out that John Cummings of the town-famous Tangerine Puppets was in the audience that night and was impressed!

Jeff really liked what we were doing, too. We'd started writing some original songs and even had a bite from a record company A&R guy. Jeff especially liked a new one Doug had written called "In This Day and Age," a combination of Hendrix's "If 6 Was 9" (replete with a jazz-inspired jam in the middle) and "Shape of Things to Come" by Max Frost and the Troopers from the *Wild in the Streets* soundtrack.

Possibly inspired by his longtime idol Phil Spector, Jeff came down to our rehearsal and said he wanted to take us into the studio and produce a single. At Saunders Studios on Forty-eighth Street in Manhattan, you could record your songs and walk out with an acetate, a ten-inch vinyl record that deteriorates after a few dozen plays. Quite remarkably for a sixteen-year-old in the 1960s, Jeff took his first plunge into the music business.

He listened to us rehearsing the song and then went to Manhattan, put down a deposit, and set the studio date for the next Saturday afternoon. Jeff took me into the studio to record my first record and produce his.

"Jeff really wanted our record to be done *right*," Andy Ritter explained. "He didn't like the tone of Mitch's Höfner bass guitar *at all*. So he ran out to Forty-eighth Street and rented Mitch a different bass, a Fender Jazz."

"Jeff had this vision and couldn't see *any* roadblocks," Doug laughed. "He got us in this studio, this little teeny room. He was *sure* we'd have a big hit!"

Maybe it was because Jeff wasn't having luck with his own bands that he was becoming interested in the entrepreneurial aspects of music. Or maybe he just thought we were, as he would classify certain things, "really fuckin' great!"

Jeff not only produced and paid for our record; he also started booking us. He got us into the clubs where he'd been playing in the Village, booking a two-weekend stint at Cafe Bizarre. Of course, we had to be finished playing by midnight and had to be accompanied by an adult. With Mom acting as chaperone, Jeff, Doug, Andy, and I piled our stuff into the Chevy station wagon and went to do our first real "gig." We even got paid, $12.50 each a night, and gave Jeff 10 percent for being our "agent."

They were great times for us all. We played well. The crowd really liked us, and not just because we were little kids. Jeff beamed. Mom was proud too and took us all out for a late-night snack after the last set. When we got back and unloaded the equipment, Jeff promised to get us more shows.

One night a few weeks later I was lying in bed with my little transistor radio tuned to *The Alex Bennett Show*. Doing the first "alternative" talk show on WMCA-AM, Bennett came on at midnight and went 'til six a.m. *The Alex Bennett Show* was the predecessor and prototype of call-in radio shows like Howard Stern's. It was hysterically funny but far more intellectual and political than Stern's.

We listened to Bennett religiously; he was a tremendous influence on us. Sometimes we were up so late we'd hear the clunking of bottles as the milkman made his predawn deliveries. One particular night Jeff hadn't come home, and several hours before the milk bottles clanged, a ringing telephone broke the night's silence.

It was the police. Jeff had been arrested in the Village with pills in his pocket. Belladonna, they told my mother, a form of hallucinogenic. The sergeant told her that Jeff had called my father as well, and Noel was on his way over to the precinct to get him out of the tank.

Fortunately for Jeff, this precinct was in the same district as our old man's Hyman Trucking terminal on Charles and Hudson streets. As he loved to tell us, Dad had a "relationship" with the cops. Sometimes a box of goods would "accidentally" fall out of one of the shipper's trucks—and *maybe* a cop would wind up with one of the items. Then the guys who got the rest of the box would somehow make sure that certain trucks would receive "fair treatment" by the longshoremen at the loading docks on the river. In 1968, this was a typical business day on the docks of the Hudson River.

Dad got Jeff released relatively quickly and with a clean record. Apparently, some of Jeff's new Village pals were either cops or were using him to transport pills from one nightclub to another. Either way, he'd been set up and busted right on MacDougal Street. That's what cops did in Greenwich Village back then. They'd approached him knowing he was carrying the pills. Luckily for him, he hadn't taken any of them yet, or it would have been an even more horrifying experience.

The next morning, Dad dragged Jeff into the house. He was furious — and was giving it to our mother pretty good, too. Now he could say he'd been right all along. This proved his point: Mom was too lenient. He knew better; his tough approach with us was what was called for. Though it was hard to argue with him, she gave it her best try.

Dad ranted about sending us to military school.

"Neither of them is going anywhere!" Mom guaranteed us. "You've got to calm down, Noel!"

He didn't take her advice. Dad had already taken Jeff to his barber in the city for a shearing. It was bad. I don't think I ever saw Jeff that sad.

Then Dad took Jeff's rose-colored glasses, threw them on the kitchen floor, and ground them into pieces. When Jeff protested, he got a smack across the face. He started to pick up the glasses and got another one on the ass.

It was a horrible day.

Later that night, Jeff told me that the worst thing was that he felt betrayed by his new friends, who he'd thought were "right on."

Mom knew her kid had been through hell, and she assured Jeff he'd get another pair of sunglasses. She knew that to blame anything on his shades, haircut, music, and clothes was misdirected, if not stupid. All over the country, kids were getting their asses kicked, unknowingly paving the way for the youth of today who show up at the office sporting torn jeans, tattoos, and nose studs. Fortunately for us, our mother knew the importance of being flexible, or she might have wound up with kids as broken as those glasses. Being an artist herself, Mom also knew the importance of individuality and allowed us to nurture ours. She even encouraged it; this was the most critical stage of our development.

This is essentially when, and where, Joey Ramone was born: different, disadvantaged, but undaunted.

Those days saw the borehole of the generation gap. Our mother tried to position herself in the middle of the breach in an attempt to pull the two sides together. After Jeff's big bust nothing really changed at home, except that his relationship with our father was severely strained. We stood united on that front.

He didn't go into the Village as much anymore, either. I think he was biding his time until his hair grew back.

We started to have wild parties in the house when Mom was out, especially when she was spending the night somewhere. By this time, Doug had started to play in a band with a guy Jeff's age named Steve Marks. Steve's friends always had good pot and lots of hippie-type girlfriends. Steve was Jeff's age and a very mellow guy—except when his little brother Larry would steal his LSD.

Steve and Jeff got along well, and so did Larry and me. When Steve brought the crowd over to party, it was total mayhem. There were naked girls in the bathtubs, and people freaked out on bad acid trips. I smoked pot with my brother, and Jeff discussed politics with the hippies. Music blasted all night long, while Andy Ritter and I climbed out the upstairs windows and walked all over the roof of the house to watch the sunrise from the apex. Somehow, with everybody's help, we got it together before Mom got home.

Even then there was still a good feeling in the house. Mom had a friend, Pearl, who wanted to become a comedienne, and the two would sit in the kitchen, laughing, drinking coffee, and writing material for her act. Eventually they would try it out on us. Mom and Pearl also started a little business designing handbags created from lunch pails and lunch boxes, which they sold to several boutiques in the Village. This was definitely a creative atmosphere.

Doug and I started a little creative business venture, too. On the weekends, we'd get ten dollars' worth of pot from one of Steve Marks's friends, divide it into three piles, and sell them for five bucks each. We weren't smoking all the time—yet. And it didn't *seem* to be screwing us up.

I'd already purposely fucked up as much as I could in my last year at Halsey Junior High. I didn't want to go into Forest Hills High School without my friends, so I purposely tried to get left back. I cut classes constantly and managed to tie for the lowest mark in my grade on the math Regents. I tied with Manny Pedillo, a member of the Forest Hills/Rego Park/Corona gang called the 108th Street Men.

The Men were not your typical Forest Hills Jewish kids. They were tough teenagers. They hit people with bats and carried knives. Our old nemesis Jeff Storch had become a member of the Men. There were other tough guys in the gang, like Phil "the Butcher" Russo and Melvin "the Pimp" Jones (one of the few black kids in the neighborhood). These were the guys who left their footprints on my brother's back and "borrowed" his lunch money. A few years later, Manny Pedillo got arrested and convicted for the murder of Jeff Storch in Flushing Meadow Park in the wake of a heroin deal gone bad.

We weren't doing any hard drugs yet, except for the occasional black beauties, Seconals, and Tuinals friends would steal from their parents.

Pearl and my mom had seen the marijuana movie *I Love You, Alice B. Toklas* and seemed curious. Though Mom had an inkling that we smoked and didn't particularly condone it, her main concern was that we didn't do it all the time or anyplace where we could get caught. She said if we ever did smoke, we should do it in the house.

One day we convinced Mom and Pearl to try it. Jeff, Doug Scott, Andy Ritter, and I were sitting around the kitchen table passing a joint, teaching my mom and her friend how to hold it and how to hold it in. Finally we were appreciating Pearl's comedy routine.

Throughout all this, Jeff's odd behavior hadn't changed; even *he* was becoming more concerned about himself. He couldn't figure out why he felt so compelled to do these strange things. He'd started to tap spoons and forks over and over. He would come to the table and pick up a knife and then drop it. He'd pick it up, put it down, pick it up, and put it down again; it seemed like he was counting. As it got worse, Jeff wanted help in solving this mystery.

He saw one doctor who recommended an endocrinologist, who referred him to a psychiatrist, who told my mother that Jeff was not well at all and that he would never be productive in society. "He'll most likely be a vegetable."

So much for doctors. We didn't accept this as anything other than the opinion of a confounded quack from Queens, although it had to be extremely disconcerting for Jeff. As his frustration level increased, my brother started smoking cigarettes.

The back-and-forth between Jeff and Mom was becoming more and more uncompromising as my brother went into denial mode.

"You were supposed to go the dentist today," Mom told him.

"You didn't tell me," Jeff said, trying to blame her.

"I certainly did! I told you five times!"

"No, you didn't."

"I asked you to throw out that garbage you left in the basement."

"Yeah, yeah, I'm gonna."

"You said that yesterday!"

"You said that yesterday!" he'd mimic.

It would go on like this until they wore each other out, which usually took about half an hour. Then everything would be okay. It got very ugly sometimes. I felt bad for both of them.

Though the youngest in the household, somehow I became the family buffer. On Mother's Day in 1968 I wrote in my card, "P.S. Mom, next time don't get so uptight about Jeff. It's not worth it." She kept the card for years.

Whatever the problem was, it had become overwhelming for both of them. Jeff was losing his grasp. Our mom was losing her battle to keep our house clean—to keep the house at all. The expense had become too much. It was time to move again.

In the fall of 1968 Mom sold the house, and the three of us settled into a two-bedroom apartment about four blocks away. We were living on the twenty-second floor of a new, semiluxury high-rise building called Birchwood Towers, on Yellowstone Boulevard. We had awesome views of the boroughs and Long Island. The Empire State Building looked almost touchable. We could see into Shea Stadium with our binoculars.

It was expensive, but Mom had some money from the sale of the house. Still, most people living there were much wealthier than we were.

Jeff and I were still as shy as schoolboys could be, especially around the pretty and popular girls, the Jewish American Princesses. JAPs characteristically zeroed in on either the popular guys with rich parents or the tough guys from nearby Corona who made them feel protected and important. Going out with a guy from Corona would almost ensure a JAP of getting a new car from Daddy, as a perquisite for breaking up with him.

Of course, we were neither tough nor rich. As tall as Jeff and I were, these girls rarely lowered their noses enough to make eye contact with either of us. Jeff, however, was having more luck than me—that is, he had a girlfriend or two and was actually having sex with someone other than himself. I don't know how he found these girls, but he did.

One of them, Lois, was from Brooklyn. "At that time I didn't really get many chicks," Jeff remembered. "Nobody really had any girlfriends and there was just like one Brooklyn chick named Lois, who'd give me a blow job down in the basement.

"Everyone would go there on a Friday night and the guys would line up," Jeff elaborated. "Lois was hideous-looking. She was about twenty-seven, and it was very hard to get her to fuck. So I'd turn her on to LSD and take her to my house on Sundays. At that time I was living with my mom. It was very rough trying to get Lois to my house without anyone seeing."

Though Lois obviously suffered from some type of cerebral malfunction, it was hard to peg. She'd call up just about every day. After starting off slowly, rapidly she'd blurt out the sentence she was trying to finish.

"Hello?"

"Uh"—then a very long pause, then another "Uh," followed by another long pause, and *finally*, "Hi, it's Lois."

"Hi, Lois," I sighed, knowing it would take her just as long to ask for Jeff.

"Is, uh, uh, uh, is Jeff there?"

"No, Lois; no, he's not home. I'll tell him to call you back."

"Uh, uh, uh, uh, thanks, bye-bye."

She always giggled at the end. At least Lois was properly medicated, a virtue lacking in some of Jeff's other girlfriends.

Not all the women in Jeff's life were always giggling, though.

Mom took a job at a women's clothing store and would get home around six p.m. She'd walk into these huge messes in the kitchen—and get pissed. *Very pissed.*

Jeff would enter the kitchen, tilt his head with a coy little smile, and say, "What? I didn't do that," unable to keep from breaking into a small, embarrassed laugh. For the next hour or so, he'd engage my mother in a test of endurance. They'd bash it out in what had become a daily struggle, with my mother fighting to keep her sanity and my brother fighting to defend his insanity. In fact, Jeff was almost incapable of cleaning up his messes. Even if he tried, it would take him many frustrating hours.

We all knew he had a problem. Eventually we'd find out there was a medical term for his condition, but that would be years later.

"I can't stand this!" Mom would say. Then she'd start crying and go into her room.

I felt sorry for my brother, but I was starting to get pissed at him. He'd been getting too rough with our mother lately and was becoming very hard to live with, especially in these new, smaller quarters.

9.

THE SEEKERS

Our new high-rise apartment building was just two blocks from Forest Hills High School, where Jeff was in the twelfth grade and I had started tenth. One drawback was that hundreds of less fortunate black kids walked right past our building on their way to Forest Hills High. They were being bused over from Jamaica High as part of the new integration plan. Here were these "rich" white Jews coming out of this fancy building, walking along with kids who were understandably resentful. And out came Jeff, tall, skinny, fragile, more than a bit freaky-looking—easy prey.

Jeff and I were both hippies, so we understood why these kids resented us, because we represented "the man," or at least the children of the man. But a guy named Jarod continually bullied Jeff beyond reason. One night we formulated a plan to get him to stop.

The next day at school, wearing our tie-dyed rock & roll rags, we were greeted with the usual taunting from bused-in kids and local idiots alike. When we got near the high school, Jarod walked into our path and approached Jeff.

"Hey, skinny! Whatchu got for me, rich boy? Gimme something!"

Jarod was a small guy but wiry, with an intense energy and a crazy look in his eyes.

As Jeff fished through his pockets, piles of junk poured out: half-wrapped chewing gum, dirty tissues, handfuls of tobacco and broken cigarettes, class schedules, assorted crumpled papers, cough drops, and broken pencils.

Jarod started to get restless. I did too. It *was* remarkable how much stuff was in my brother's pockets. He just couldn't throw anything away.

"Yo! You two fuckin' with me?"

Just in time, Jeff pulled out a big, fat joint and held it out to Jarod. "Here, man," he said. "We don't want any trouble. We just wanna be friends."

But our plan backfired.

"I know you got something else for me, rich boy! I'll cut your pockets open, motherfucker," Jarod threatened.

When Jarod got right up in Jeff's face and grabbed his shoulders, my brother tried to get around him. I didn't know what to do. As my older brother, he was supposed to be protecting *me*. "Hey, man!" was all I could get out.

"You better bring me that tomorrow, you skinny-ass motherfucker!" said Jarod as he shoved Jeff into the hedges, where I soon joined him.

A friend of mine who'd seen the incident helped us out of the bushes. Fortunately he had a tougher older brother with a lot of friends. After they talked to Jarod on our behalf later that day, he didn't bother us anymore. But finding my brother in the bushes did become the source of a running joke among some of my friends.

In fact, to *most* of the kids in that school Jeff was a running joke, and they liked to keep him running. Wherever we went—a restaurant, the lobby of a movie theater, even the lobby of our own building—kids would invariably point and say, "Look!" Adults would nudge each other and gesture in Jeff's direction. When we walked into a room, you could hear the buzz, then the snickering. This upset our father when we were out with him, and he would blame it on Jeff's clothes, hair, or glasses.

But high school was the worst. The kids there really let Jeff have it, physically as well as verbally. Though it was the height of the hippie era, macho high school kids still tried to impress each other by picking on the oddball. Some things never change.

Having a compatibly freaky family saved Jeff from going totally over the edge. Home was a safe haven. Rock & roll was heaven, and we were a rock

& roll household. After graduating high school, except for a few outings he spent most of his time in the house, listening to records, smoking cigarettes, twirling his hair, making horrible messes, and returning to regularly scheduled screaming matches with our mother.

One of Jeff's big outings was to San Francisco. He wanted to hitchhike across the country, a popular mode of travel for seekers of "Real Life Experience." I tried to talk him out of it. We'd just seen *Easy Rider*. Instead, Jeff opted to experience a jet plane. He flew to "Frisco," where he met other hippies and walked around Haight-Ashbury barefoot. Three days into his journey, he called to say that someone had ripped him off in the "crash pad" where he'd slept.

He had no money left, but he did have a big cut on his foot, which he thought might be getting infected. He was coming home. As a souvenir, he brought home a nasty case of crabs. They were easy enough to get rid of, but the infection in his foot took much longer to heal than it should have.

Another outing resulted from his sudden interest in George Harrison's new book of Eastern philosophy which Jeff began to carry around like the Bible. Soon enough bald-headed minstrels lured Jeff into a Hare Krishna temple in Brooklyn. He called and told us he was going to stay there for a while. He even considered moving in.

Just hours after we got the phone call telling us about the temple, me, my mom, and her new boyfriend Phil were sitting at the table when all of a sudden Jeff walked in.

"What happened?" we chorused.

They had told him, "Cleanliness is next to godliness. To please God, you should clean the Lord's house, and *then* take the Lord's food."

"Well, I'm not sure," Jeff told us, "but I think they wanted me to clean the bathrooms . . ."

We all busted up laughing, including Jeff.

"But I *did* want to please the Lord, so I took his food." He held two huge shopping bags filled with Hare Krishna vegetarian delights. Jeff had cleaned out the whole temple.

Though we all laughed about it, we were very relieved he had come home; Jeff seemed so lost. He was very lonely, almost desperate, and fair game for some cult or another. We were thrilled that he didn't come back in robes, with his head shaved, a white dot on his forehead, and a little ponytail in back. He could still call upon his sense of humor, but his soul-searching far exceeded the normal teenage daily requirement.

All the while, Jeff was sinking into a mysterious world he could not live in much longer. His bizarre, compulsive behavior was worsening, and none of us could really help him. Not Mom's former boyfriend, Dr. John Stevens, a stylish black man who seemed to much prefer it when we weren't around, nor her new flame, Phil Sapienza.

Phil worked in the school system with kids Jeff's age. He was a tolerant, easygoing man and seemed concerned and helpful, but we were just getting to know each other. Phil was Mom's fourth or fifth boyfriend since Hank had died.

Phil remembers well the first time he saw us: "When I went up to Charlotte's place, Mitch was there, and he looked like a standard, typical sixteen- or seventeen-year-old. Then Jeff walked in—he's six foot five with hair down to his chest, wearing big, fringed boots. I just said, 'Wow.'"

Phil became a surrogate father to us, and he soon noticed that Jeff had serious problems. How could he not?

My brother and I had a bathroom in our bedroom. One night, Jeff was in there washing his purple eyeglasses for about two hours. He would put them under the water for a few seconds and then pull them out. After a while, the sound was torture.

Sshhhhhup . . . Sshhhhhup . . . Sshhhhhup.

It was driving me crazy: I had a big test the next morning, and it was already two a.m. After about three hours of this, I finally lost it and threw a sneaker at the door—*boom!*

"Awright, awright!" I heard Jeff say, the water still running. The bang on the door had to have scared the shit out of him; I feel bad about it to this day.

I knew I'd fuck up my test the next day and that academia was probably not in the cards for me. And I knew that it wasn't my fault or anyone else's. I remember thinking that music was the only hope for my brother and me, that one of us *had to* make it somehow. But since we'd moved out of the house and lost our basement and rehearsal space, neither of us had been as active.

I knew Jeff was itching to do something musically, but he couldn't even practice now that we were in an apartment building. His drums were packed up in the hallway closet. I wanted to play again badly, but my Hagstrom guitar had caved in at the input jack, and my Höfner Beatle bass had separated into two pieces. Only the strings connected the body and the neck. The reality that "you can't always get what you want" was one I was battling with and sadly had to face. I was dreading the thought I might never play in a band again. But as another saying goes, "Timing is *everything*."

One day in the winter of 1968–69, Doug Scott reintroduced me to John Cummings in the street. I told John I'd met him years ago in the Goodriches' basement. Though John said he remembered me, I didn't really think he did.

About a month later, there was a knock on my door: It was John Cummings and another guy. Unbeknownst to me, Doug had told John that he and I had a little side business going on out of my apartment in Birchwood Towers.

Oddly enough, John had lived in the same building but moved up the block just before we moved in. The doorman normally called up when there was a guest, but John knew his way around.

"Who's there?" I asked.

"Hi, Mitchel, it's John."

"And Michael," chimed in John's friend Michael Newmark.

"Yeah, what's up?" I said through the door.

"Well, you know, dontcha?" John said cagily. "Ya know, uh, can we come in?"

I opened the door a little. "What are you talking about?"

Johnny pressed, "Doug told me ya had stuff . . ."

"C'mon, John, I hardly know you," I said, "and I don't know that guy at all."

"Aw, come on, man, don't be that way." John kept pushing it. "You know who I am, I'm not a narc. Come on, just this one time."

He half charmed, half guilted me into letting him and Newmark come into the apartment. We went into my room. Jeff wasn't home that day.

They wanted to buy ten dollars' worth of pot, so I started measuring it out. Then, like everyone else who'd just acquired some pot, they wanted to roll a joint and smoke. My nerves calmed down as we started to talk.

"I saw you smash your guitar at the battle of the bands at Halsey," John said as he passed me the bone. "I was impressed."

"Yeah, I heard you were there," I said coolly. "I used to go see your band, too. Me and Goodrich snuck in the night you kicked the guy in the nuts. Why'd ya do that, anyway?" I asked, quickly adding, "I mean, it was pretty funny, but it looked like you hurt that guy."

Johnny laughed.

It was a bit confrontational for our initial conversation, but I didn't want John to think he intimidated me. It surprised him that I would question his actions, but at the same time he seemed to respect it. "Well . . . you know how it is when you're playing, right?" said John.

I nodded in agreement.

"Ya don't want anybody getting too close to you, like when you were swinging your guitar around. They might get hurt, or . . . kicked," Johnny added.

We all laughed, and the tension was broken.

They hung out for about an hour and smoked pot and listened to eight-track tapes on the Panasonic tape deck my father had given me as a reward for graduating Halsey early. It had fallen out of one of his trucks. Jeff and I shared it, of course.

John liked our selection: Led Zeppelin, Steppenwolf, and our newest treasure, the Who's *Tommy.* Looking at the Who album, John said I reminded him of Pete Townshend, especially when I was playing guitar. He asked who I'd been playing with and what band I was in. I told him of my equipment woes.

John told me I was too good not to be playing. He suggested we get together again and talk about starting a band. He said he would lend me his Gibson SG, which was the exact guitar Pete played when he wasn't smashing them to pieces.

I couldn't believe it!

I knew John was twenty, six years older than me, but thought absolutely nothing of it. The only thing that bothered me was the intense gleam Johnny would get in his eyes occasionally—like the look he had when we were talking about kicking the guy in the nuts onstage.

John and I became fast friends and started to hang out together often. We'd get some pot, roll about ten joints, and smoke them all. Often we'd go over to his house because no one was there in the daytime. We'd smoke a few joints, listen to records, and practice songs for our band. John would heat up the spaghetti his mother had left for him. Then we'd finish the joints and wind up watching an afternoon horror movie on TV.

John decided he would play bass. He thought I'd make a better guitar player because I picked things up quickly and was able to figure out songs easily.

One day I started playing Led Zeppelin's "Communication Breakdown," and John was really impressed.

"Wow, you know about downstrokes, huh?" John said.

"Whaddaya mean, downstrokes?" I answered.

"Ya know, how you're picking everything downward," John said, motioning.

"I'm just trying to play it how it sounds," I explained.

"Yeah, well that's really important," John told me. "Most people don't realize that. That's how rock & roll should be played. All of it! Everything should be a downstroke, unless you're playing folk music or the banjo or something like 'Mrs. Brown You've Got a Lovely Daughter.' That may be okay, but it's not *rock & roll!*"

In retrospect, I believe Johnny had begun formulating the concept for the Ramones' sound even back then.

John knew a drummer named Peter McAlister, and before long we were playing songs by Led Zeppelin and the Who, "My Little Red Book" by Love, and "Pushin' Too Hard" by the Seeds.

We didn't have a lead singer. John thought I had a really good voice but had to convince me to take on the double role.

We read about a freak named Humphrey Lynch who committed bizarre robberies in the Midwest and we used his name for the band. After we'd polished enough songs for a set, we started playing around the neighborhood. In those days, they still had bands at the Rego Park and Forest Hills Jewish centers on Saturday nights.

My father was starting to relax a little, almost approving of me playing in a band. I had done well in school that year and hadn't gotten busted for drugs. Dad was a member of an organization called the SWORDs, which stood for "Single, Widowed, or Divorced Men." He had us play at one of their weekly parties.

He also booked us to provide the entertainment at a benefit to improve conditions in the Alimony Jail in Manhattan, where dads who didn't pay up were locked up. We actually got press in the *Daily News* for performing songs like "Communication Breakdown," "Good Times, Bad Times," and "I Can't Explain" for the occasion.

By the summer of 1969, John and I had become best friends and were hanging out just about every day. Most of his friends accepted me, but a few would say things like, "Who's the baby?"

"Mitch is the guitar player in my band," John would tell them.

One day John took me over to his friend Richard Freed's house in the Lefrak City apartment complex. Everyone was shooting dope, including John. John had been taking Thorazine for many years. He was going to a psychiatrist for the prescription. Working construction, he'd made a lot of money, so he and Richard scored a lot of good heroin.

Fortunately, shooting *anything* didn't appeal to me, but I soon wound up taking my first hallucinogenic with John: big, purple mescaline pills. John showed me how to sneak into the former New York State Pavilion in Flushing Meadow Park, where they were now having rock concerts. After we climbed over several fences and skirted security, we heard the MC say, "Ladies and gentlemen, *here's Joe Cocker!*"

So we left.

Since it was July 4, things were popping all over the park—or at least they appeared to be. When we got back to the neighborhood, we hit the supermarket after they delivered the bread and milk, which they left unguarded in those days. We grabbed what we could run with and pigged out on Swiss rolls and chocolate milk.

During the day we'd go down to the laundry room and tie-dye T-shirts or bleach our jeans. Sometimes we'd play handball or stickball. John had wanted to be a pro baseball pitcher at some point earlier in his life. We'd always wind up at Thorneycroft, the apartment complex across the street from John's building. The flat roof of the huge garage in the center of the complex doubled as a recreational area. One side had an inclined walkway leading up to it that we called "the Ramp." Invariably everyone would meet up at the Ramp to shoot the shit, pull pranks, hide from the cops, and of course get high. We would regroup there after hitching to Rockaway Beach to hear everyone's crazy stories and see who didn't make it back.

One day a neighborhood kid brought up some mysterious green pills and handed them out. John gave a handful of them to his friend Jay and mischievously told him he could take them all. Jay took way more than he should have and went crazy in front of half the neighborhood. He took off his clothes, ran down the street, and did a swan dive onto the hood of an approaching police car.

This was nothing compared to some of the stories John told me.

"I was sniffing glue on occasions," John remembered, "doing pills, robbing kids in the street, things like that. Did I have a knife? No, I'd just go up to them and punch 'em, and say, 'Give me your fuckin' money!'

"I'd steal old ladies' pocketbooks, grab a pocketbook and run, or throw TV sets out the window. Once I dropped a TV set two feet in front of some old ladies. I painted swastikas all over the place in a predominantly Jewish neighborhood. At the time, these things were amusing to me. It was fun."

There was a girl who lived in Thorneycroft named Arlene Kohn who I'd seen around in school. Arlene was going out with my friend Alan Wolf, who lived in my building in the penthouse.

Although John was much older than Arlene, she had gone out with him for a while. Apparently, she had broken up with him, and he wasn't happy about it. In fact, the first week I started hanging out with John, we ran into Arlene and Alan Wolf walking past the Ramp.

John approached them and started smacking Arlene in the face. He kept yelling, "Why'd ya do that, huh?" and slapping her.

"Stop it!" she yelled. "What are you talking about?!"

John smacked her again and said the same thing. "You know what I'm talking about! Why'd you do that to me, huh?"

John wasn't hitting her hard, but it was definitely violent—and humiliating. This was a twenty-one-year-old man yelling at a fifteen-year-old girl.

I didn't like it at all, but I didn't feel it was my place to do anything. My best effort was to say, "Come on, John. Let's go," and walk away, hoping that he'd walk away, too.

In order to get along with him, I viewed John's actions as if they were scenes from a James Dean movie or something. Somehow it seemed exciting. John became the cool older brother Jeff just wasn't turning out to be.

John didn't want to have anything to do with Jeff. To him, Jeff was just a spaced-out hippie. And John didn't like hippies, though, oddly enough, he looked just like one.

"I met John Cummings through my brother," Jeff later recalled. "Sometimes I'd hang out with him and John. We went to shows at the Fillmore together. I remember going to see Mountain and the Who."

One day that summer, Jeff suggested that we all go to Woodstock for the big festival coming up in August.

John said, "No fuckin' way, man. Sit there in the dirt with those dirty hippies? You *would* want to go there. Not *me*." John turned to me and asked, "You wanna go there and sit with the smelly hippies in their dirty underwear for three days?"

"Uh, no, I guess not," I lied.

Jeff made the big trip but never made it to the concert. He caught a ride upstate with Bob Roland's band, which was playing at one of the hotels in the Catskills in the Borscht Belt. Because of the overload of cars trying to get to the concert area, the roads were blocked up, and Jeff couldn't get anywhere near it.

John just laughed when he heard about that; he didn't have the patience to deal with Jeff.

I didn't exactly convey much empathy for my brother at that particular time. I guess I felt let down and probably took it out on him.

From Jeff's perspective, he resented the fact that in a lot of ways our roles were reversed. The younger brother was more athletic, had more friends, and played in a band with older guys.

Having to ask me if it was okay to tag along—and not always being told yes—had to have been brewing a big resentment inside Jeff.

If John and I were going out for pizza, to get high, or whatever, Jeff would ask, "Can I come?"

"No, we want to talk about the band," John would reply, leaving Jeff sitting by the record player in the living room listening to Quicksilver Messenger Service.

"I saw what he was doing," John remembers, "but I had no idea what his problem was called. The guy was nuts. He wasn't eccentric; he was *nuts*. You're only eccentric if you're rich. Otherwise, you're just nuts."

At the least, the relationships established here undeniably paved the way for the ones to come.

I really just wanted to brag about my big brother like other guys did. But I never considered whether he might be disappointed in himself for not measuring up to typical big brother standards. I didn't understand why he would lash out so horribly at our mother. At fifteen, I wasn't wise enough to pick up on the emotional beating Jeff was taking. I had all the reasons in the world to be more in tune with my own problems.

But I was also sharing Jeff's problems. My life was immersed in his mess. I never embarrassed him and always tried to stick up for him.

Still, it was Jeff's mess, and when I got out of that room and out of the house, I just wanted to forget about it. The exclusion had to hurt Jeff and would take its toll in the months ahead.

10.

"THEY'RE COMING TO TAKE ME AWAY!"

Over the next year, Johnny and I started to take what we were doing a bit more seriously. Though Johnny was really encouraging me to be the lead singer, I wasn't feeling very extroverted in those days, so we got our old friend Tommy Erdelyi into the band to take over as front man and do most of the lead singing. It was a dream come true to be in a band with two members of the legendary Tangerine Puppets. We added a few new songs to the repertoire and started playing in local bars. Tommy started writing original songs and tried to convince Johnny and me to concentrate on this, but Johnny was lukewarm on the idea of songwriting.

"I don't wanna do some inferior songs just 'cause we wrote them. I just wanna play *great* songs, the best songs we can play," Johnny would say.

But Tommy was determined; he wanted us to go and record one of his songs. He had a connection with a guy who owned a recording studio in Manhattan. Tommy told us that the guy lived in the building right next to his and had been in the music business a long time—he'd even had a hit record himself.

"So who is it?" we asked, wondering who the hell lived in that building that had a hit record.

"His name is Jerry Samuels," Tommy said, "but you know him as Napoleon the Fourteenth. He's the guy who did 'They're Coming to Take Me Away, Ha-Haaa!'"

"You're kidding!" we said.

Jerry met us at the door of his house wearing a ponytail in the front of his head and holding a cereal bowl full of M&M's—except they weren't M&M's but tabs of acid. After we sat down, he started playing us his new experimental project, "Birth," which was the sound of a baby crying while being slapped by, I hope, a doctor. And a similar stroke of genius called "Rape."

Both songs got a lot better after a few M&M's—unforgettable, actually.

The next day we went to Samuels's studio above the Metropole Cafe and recorded Tommy's song "Lady Lane."

"'Lady Lane' was inspired by Jimi Hendrix. It was a rip-off of 'Little Miss Lover,'" Tommy explained. "I'd been playing in this band with John and Mitch for a few months and finally convinced John to do a recording of one of my songs."

It was a fun song, but Johnny wasn't crazy about it.

The recording went well and we took to hanging out at Napoleon XIV's place. One night we brought Jeff over to his house, but it didn't turn out to be the greatest experience.

Jerry Samuels was a generous host and perfectly weird gentleman, and he told Jeff to help himself to the M&M's. Jeff confessed to me later that night that he was having a really bad trip and getting really nervous that he might go off the deep end. Sometimes on LSD just being worried about going over the edge is what will actually take you there. I'd talked people down from bad trips before, so I kinda knew what to do.

"Just relax, ya know?" I whispered calmly. "Don't fight it, and try to feel like you could even enjoy it. Don't take anything too seriously that you're thinking right now, 'cause you're probably gonna forget it tomorrow anyway. You know that! It only lasts for a little while. I'm right here."

We talked for a while; then he said he was doing better. "You wanna listen to some music?" I asked him. I gave him my headphones and put on "Bourée" from Jethro Tull's *Stand Up* album, a semisoothing flute song of hybrid jazz and classical. Jeff said it was great and made him feel much better. Eight-track tapes play to the end of the album and start over. Jeff let the tape play about four times around. The next day, he kept thanking me for helping him through it.

It was real nice but not exactly an encouraging indication of stability.

Johnny, Tommy, Peter, and I continued playing together but then ran into some personnel problems. Nothing had materialized with the recording we'd made, but Tommy had attracted some interest as a singer/songwriter on his own.

"When we were recording 'Lady Lane,' I'd already had one falling-out with John," Tommy remembers. "When Richie Demedia joined the Tangerine Puppets, I said, 'We're going to have two lead guitar players?' John chose Richie Demedia over me, and I said, 'Good-bye, John.' The second rift took place in Jerry Samuels's recording studio when we were recording 'Lady Lane,' and this guy wanted just me, and not the whole band, to record for him. I said, 'Okay,' and left. That was me paying John back. It was just over."

Johnny and I continued playing and hanging out, doing things like scaling records off my terrace and sneaking into concerts. Over the course of the next year or so, Jeff was visibly plummeting deeper into despair. This mental flux caused him to neglect his hygiene. Of course this was driving our mother to the brink, as we still did not know the cause of this behavior, or even if there was one.

Jeff couldn't seem to throw anything away. He would wear the same item of clothing every day. His sneakers had become so horribly smelly and disgusting that one day when he was taking a shower, Mom threw them down the incinerator. He was furious when he found out. It was becoming worse and worse. Jeff was hitting bottom.

At night after John and everyone else had left, Jeff would open up a little more and tell me what he was experiencing. He was hearing voices in his head and didn't know where they were coming from or how to deal with them. He said that sometimes it got so bad and he felt so hopelessly crazy that he thought about jumping out our twenty-second-floor window. Jeff talked about committing suicide on several occasions.

The more frustrated he got, the more violent he became with our mother. This caused big problems between Jeff and me. He would sometimes back Mom against a wall with his large frame and blame her for his physical and emotional misfortunes. I couldn't stand by and watch him, or anyone, cursing and cornering my mother.

One day during a particularly vicious shouting match, Jeff pulled a big knife out of the kitchen drawer and held it threateningly to Mom's chest.

I lost it this time. I ordered him, "Put that fuckin' knife down, you sick motherfucker," or I was going to kick his ass.

Finally Mom decided to take him to a psychiatrist.

The next day, as Jeff and I scrapped verbally, he pulled the knife out again and stuck the point in my belly.

"Go ahead," I dared him. "Are you gonna stab me?"

I slapped him across the face, sending his glasses flying. In all the fights we had, throughout our whole lives, neither of us had ever hit the other in the face.

Jeff dropped the knife and started swinging; we grabbed each other's shirts by the shoulders and started pulling each other all over the house. I threw him up against the living room window and broke it. Broken glass dropped twenty-two floors. I was now sixteen and stronger than Jeff. It was the worst fight we ever had.

Later we drank some of his favorite wine, Boone's Farm Strawberry Hill, and talked. Jeff said he wasn't really going to do anything. I told him I knew he was just posturing, but I couldn't let someone treat my mother that way.

Jeff said he understood.

He hardly left the house anymore. He just stayed in and kept going through his repetitive rituals: putting on the same clothes every day; not throwing anything away; tapping; turning switches and faucets on and off; and repeatedly picking things up and putting them down. It could take him ten minutes to put a container of milk in the refrigerator and leave it there.

My brother was in agony, trying desperately to hang on to his sanity. He began listening less to the heavier rock & roll and more to soft, introspective music. We had heard that James Taylor's song "Sweet Baby James" was about the time he'd committed himself to a mental institution in Massachusetts for nine months. Jeff got heavily into the song and that album.

I'll never forget walking out one night when Jeff was sitting in the living room in his usual position, on the floor with his knees up and his arms wrapped around them while he twirled his hair with one hand and his smoke-stained fingertips clutched a cigarette with the other. Jeff was listening to that James Taylor song as I said good-bye to him. He looked so sad, tormented, and confused.

He didn't even bother asking me where I was going anymore or if he could come. I went over and listened to "Sweet Baby James" with him for a minute. We gave each other a long look. I knew what Jeff was thinking. I knew he was going to be leaving one way or another—whether it would be out the door or off the terrace was the question.

All I could do was tell him I was going out for a little while and would definitely see him later. That night I couldn't think about anything else. I realized my brother needed my help and support. I knew I had to accept things and start treating him differently or he was not going to make it. I grew up a year, or ten, that evening.

As bad as things had become, I didn't want to lose my brother. But I didn't want to hear James Taylor and Cat Stevens for ten hours every day, either.

Thank God for psychotherapy—and Alice Cooper.

11.

A LITTLE GENIUS IN EVERY MADMAN

It would be several years before Mom and Phil Sapienza got married, but Phil had already come to be like family to us. We couldn't have been happier to have him in our lives. Phil was an extremely intelligent and open-minded guy in whom we felt totally comfortable confiding, something we dared not do with our own father.

Phil worked as a guidance counselor at Benjamin Franklin High School in East Harlem, one of the city's more dangerous neighborhoods at the time, especially for a white man. In 1970, he had participated in a march protesting the substandard conditions endured by schoolkids in the heart of the ghetto and the disparity of inner-city schools in general. Tempers flared and the protest almost became a riot. The incident succeeded in catching the attention of the press, and the next day there was an article in the paper about it with a picture of Phil standing alongside the children and parents of the Harlem community.

In our eyes, Phil was already a hero. Jeff and I had been going to all kinds of marches, in New York and Washington, protesting the war in Vietnam. We related to Phil on just about every level. Phil was also working toward his degree in psychology and was invaluable in helping Jeff feel comfortable about his decision to seek help. We all did as much as we could to ease Jeff's mind as he decided to voluntarily admit himself to St. Vincent's Hospital for psychiatric evaluation.

Dad thought Jeff was being coddled and argued with my mother that Jeff should go into the army, like he did. They would make a man out of him.

Jeff had made his decision but naturally was apprehensive. He was afraid of what might happen to him there, but more afraid of what was happening here and now. Jeff would be going for a two-week evaluation period, hopefully no longer. I thought he was showing tremendous courage and told him so.

The days leading up to his departure, I spent all the time I could with him, talking to him about it at night and well into the morning. I told him not to worry; lots of people had problems like this.

"Yeah, Bellevue is full of 'em," Jeff joked, alluding to the infamous New York City mental hospital.

Jeff was handling the situation well but was concerned about the stigma of being in a mental hospital and the haranguing he would most certainly come back to. The kids in the neighborhood would have new ammunition to hit him with.

They would have an A-bomb to drop on him.

In the minutes before Mom and Phil took him into the city, I could sense Jeff's increasing sadness and see the fear in his eyes. It was time to go. I gave my brother a quick hug.

"Don't worry, it's gonna be all right," I reassured him. "Remember, there's a little genius in every madman."

"Isn't it the other way around?" Jeff laughed.

"Well, it must work both ways, right?" I said.

Jeff thought for a moment, "Yeah, I guess you're right. Thanks."

He was in St. Vincent's for around a month. When we visited him, he couldn't talk because his tongue was so thick from the Thorazine. Excerpts from Jeffry Hyman's psychological report from St. Vincent's Hospital made it clear he was having real problems:

EMOTIONAL FACTORS: The patient essentially sees himself with low self-esteem, as a combination of being both dangerous and in danger, approaching the unfamiliar with considerable caution and suspicion, frequently employing poor judgment in the process.

Experiencing great pain in the form of anxiety, Jeff feels at the mercy of external and internal forces beyond his control, culminating in explosive behavior, accompanied by confused depression.

His sense of self is of a passive, dependent person with ambivalent sexual identification, against which he is inclined to defend himself by means of distancing maneuvers to the point of estrangement when ritualism can no longer bind up his anxiety.

His view of authority is markedly fearful, feeling his life to be in danger in the presence of such figures. He becomes unable to reconcile this danger because of the complications introduced by his own poorly contained rage reactions. He resorts to unconscious fantasy which doesn't find acceptable conscious outlets, creating further spiraling tensions and culminating in explosive acting-out behavior.

SUMMARY AND CONCLUSIONS: The patient's personality structure is consistent with diagnosis of Schizophrenia, Paranoid type with minimal brain damage (the latter probably of long-standing duration). It is strongly recommended that he be in intensive psychotherapy whose aim would be toward strengthening his obsessive-compulsive defenses while helping to interpret, first external reality and finally his own reality, particularly his rage reactions.

IT WAS HARD to tell how much St. Vincent's helped Jeff.

Even though Dad was still heavily pushing the army, Jeff decided to stay with him in Manhattan rather than come back to Forest Hills. Dad was certainly showing concern for Jeff, but as usual he seemed even more concerned about the reflection he saw of himself in his son. Dad seemed oblivious to what was extremely obvious to me. This kid was not going to get into a boxing ring, like his father did. This kid was not going to survive in the army. This kid was not going to stand up to bullies the way his father had—Jeff would find a different way.

Dad couldn't accept it, so he kept on Jeff's case about his hair, his glasses, his clothes, and his bad habits. Dad kept trying to prove that real toughness was going to make the difference, that he'd been right all along and the woman who'd ditched him had been wrong.

After two weeks of Dad's attempted reconditioning, Jeff came home, but it was not long before he attempted another escape from Forest Hills. He found an apartment in the West Village, almost across the street from St. Vincent's Hospital.

"I went to live in the Village, on Jane Street," Jeff recalled. "I remember walking into this apartment expecting it to go somewhere. But it was like a jail cell. In bed, it was like your feet were in the oven. It was crazy."

The apartment was tiny, more like a bedroom, except that the room was actually smaller than the bed. When we helped Jeff move with the family station wagon, we couldn't fit both the mattress and the suitcase in the room. The rent was paid for two months, but I don't think Jeff ever stayed there. It was back to the family, back to the Hills.

Jeff was different after his St. Vincent's experience. We were all different, because it helped to know what was really going on. We had a much clearer understanding of his behavior and could be more compassionate about his situation. Jeff was also more relieved but nonetheless frustrated. At the time, there was no real treatment for his condition. In fact, they recommended Jeff extend his stay in the hospital, but none of us wanted that. Instead, my brother went to St. Vincent's as an outpatient several times a month.

Jeff would also return to his standard routines, but instead of listening to "Sweet Baby James" ten times a day, the soundtrack to his life became a song by Alice Cooper titled "Ballad of Dwight Fry." Jeff played it over and over. Occasionally he'd play the rest of the album as well, which was fine with me.

We actually discovered Alice via Frank Zappa. My friend Larry Marks had loaned me his copy of *Weasels Ripped My Flesh*, and on the inner sleeve was an ad for an album called *Zapped*, a compilation of songs by bands, or acts, that Frank Zappa had "discovered." The only way to get it was to mail two dollars in to Zappa's label, Bizarre Records. The album contained material that was light-years ahead of its time, by truly weird acts like Captain Beefheart and His Magic Band; Wild Man Fischer; Lord Buckley; the GTOs; Zappa's own band, The Mothers of Invention; and a guy called Alice Cooper.

We liked Alice's tracks, so we went and bought his album *Love It to Death*. It became Jeff's favorite record, to say the least. It became his inspiration. Jeff was still in hippie mode and still listening to bands like the Grateful Dead and Jefferson Airplane, but the relevance of Alice Cooper's words really got through to him during his adjustment period. How could they not? They were almost telepathic:

> I was gone for fourteen days
> I coulda been gone for more

Held up in the intensive care ward
lyin on the floor
I was gone for all those days
but I was not all alone
I made friends with a lot of people
in the danger zone
See my lonely life unfold
I see it every day
See my only mind explode
Since I've gone away
I think I lost some weight there
and I—I'm sure I need some rest
Sleepin don't come very easy
in a straight white vest . . .
See my lonely life unfold
I see it every day
See my lonely mind explode
when I've gone insane
I wanna get out of here
I wanna, I wanna get out of here!

Jeff would turn it up at the end of the track where Alice breaks down, screaming, "*I wanna get outta here*," repeatedly, faster and faster.

We both derived much amusement from this controlled display of insanity. It desensitized the issue for us and brought it straight up to the surface: Alice is mentally disturbed. It was okay to be sick. It was like an extension of the glee we would feel singing along with Jerry Samuels (a.k.a. Napoleon XIV)'s "They're Coming to Take Me Away, Ha-Haaa!" Our whole perception of the word "sick" changed. We also liked *The Sick Humor of Lenny Bruce*. Suddenly we all wanted to be "sick."

John Cummings didn't like Lenny Bruce or Frank Zappa, but he *did* like the release of acting out like we were "sick," odd, or different, which, comparatively, we were. Maybe John wasn't acting.

Johnny was starting to enjoy the exploits of Charles Manson, whose murder trial was in full swing. Johnny viewed Manson as a rock star. It didn't seem to matter that Manson was responsible for murdering people, at least not in John's view. Manson's followers did it for him because they both worshipped and feared him. To John, that seemed really cool. Though John was my best friend, he and I were not on the same wavelength. He was outspokenly bigoted, but I didn't take him seriously because 98 percent of his friends were Jews.

Johnny was also prone to violence and didn't seem capable of much compassion. I chalked this up to the fact that he was the son of a blue-collar construction worker. At the time, they were infamous for being racist and beating up hippies.

John also didn't believe Manson was racist, even after reading in the newspaper, "Manson grew obsessed with death and 'Helter Skelter,' his interpretation of a Beatles song predicting race war in America. In Manson's view, once 'Blackie' had been driven to the point of violence, helpless whites would be annihilated, leaving Manson and his family to rule the roost."

"Well, he's not saying to *kill* the blackies," John explained. "He's saying that *they* will kill the helpless whites, meaning the poor, dumb hippies. How is that racist against the blackies?"

"John," I would tell him, "he's calling them *blackies!*"

But Johnny remained fascinated with Manson.

"Isn't he sick?" he'd say, laughing. "He's like Hitler, only cooler."

It scared me.

12.

IN WITH THE OUTPATIENTS

By 1971 Jeff and I had begun to actively rebel against our father. Dad's conservative values made us recoil in disgust and rebel further. He'd pick us up in front of our building in his gold Cadillac with an American flag on the window. It was the height of the Nixon era, and at this point we were more inclined to burn flags—*and* Cadillacs.

Given that Jeff could no longer deal with our father and rarely visited him anymore, Dad's attention turned to me. One night he took me out for dinner, along with one of his broads named Barbara, and started getting on me about my hair and clothes and music, becoming increasingly loud and nasty. People started looking over.

Dad kept pushing until I finally blew my stack.

"My mother's fine with the way I look, and I'm not going to change it for the days I see you. Neither is Jeff. He can't take your crap anymore. Don't you get it? And you don't pay for our clothes or books. You hardly give my mother anything. You're just a weekend father!"

Understandably, this didn't go over very well; it *was* pretty harsh.

When Dad dropped me off, he and his broad came up to the apartment. I was hoping my brother and mother would be home, but neither of them was.

"So, I'm just a weekend father?" Dad yelled. "Well, then I guess you don't appreciate these things I gave you, and you don't deserve them." Then he walked into my bedroom closet and removed the pair of skis he'd just bought me.

In silence he took the boots and poles and anything else he had ever given me. Then Dad went for the kill, ripping a plug out of the wall and picking up my eight-track tape deck and speakers.

"You can't do that; those are my things," I yelled.

"You shouldn't have talked to your father that way," Barbara said.

"I didn't really mean it. I'm just a kid. Come on!"

By that time Dad had taken the stuff to the elevator and begun to pile it in. I couldn't believe it. Practically in tears, out in the hallway I yelled, "Fine, take it. I'll never talk to you again," just as the elevator doors closed.

A second later the other elevator door opened, and John Cummings walked out.

"Whatsa matter with you?" Johnny asked.

"My fuckin' father took my tape player," I told him, with a tear escaping down my face. This was one of those situations when you don't know whether to wipe it and risk drawing attention to it or leave it in the hope that the tear will drop before anyone notices.

Don't worry, Ramones fans; Johnny didn't come over, put his arm around me, and tell me everything would be all right.

"Fuck 'em. Don't worry about it," he said with a shrug. "Let's smoke some pot and play some songs. You'll feel better."

If you were a good friend of Johnny's, he was loyal and protective — sometimes too much so. My friend Doug Scott had owed me a little money for a long time, maybe $5. When we ran into him on our way to rehearsal one day, Johnny got on him about it. He came up behind Doug and put his knee in his back, and then pulled his arms.

I got my $5, but my friend got hurt.

"John was definitely someone who felt he was always right," says Richard Freed. "You could be having a normal conversation and disagree with him, and he would fly into a violent rage."

There seemed to be one incident after another that soured me on my friendship with John. One day when we were passing Thorneycroft, we came across one of my classmates, Teddy Gordon, a kid from Hungary, who was showing off his newly acquired karate techniques.

John made a remark about how these moves weren't going to do some-one like him any good in a real fight.

Teddy responded with, "Of course it will! What are you, crazy?"

To John, "crazy" was all he needed to hear. "What was that? You calling me crazy? You want to start something and find out?"

Teddy mistakenly didn't back down. "Yeah, I said crazy; so? It's just a word, John, why don't you relax?"

Slap! Right across Teddy's face.

"Don't tell me to relax!" Johnny exclaimed. "And you don't *ever* call me crazy! You wanna see crazy?"

Smack!

"All right, John," Teddy said, backing off a bit. "Calm down! What are you, out of your mind?"

Whoops.

"What did I just tell you?" Johnny said, delivering another whack across Teddy's face. "Where's your karate now, huh?"

"John, he didn't mean it like that," I said, trying to cool him down.

"No, he started this," replied Johnny, still in Teddy's face.

"I didn't start anything," Teddy said.

"*Oh no?*"

Smack!

All of a sudden, Teddy's father showed up. A little Jewish immigrant in his fifties, almost a foot shorter than John, he shouted at him in his thick European accent.

"Vaht are you dooink to my son?" he yelled as he walked up the ramp toward us.

Johnny laughed at him.

"Leave heem alone! Vaht are you, crazy or sumpting?"

Oh boy.

Johnny went into a boxing dance, like Muhammad Ali, faking a few jabs and then hauling off with a smack across Teddy's dad's face.

"You want more?" Johnny hit him with a closed fist on the jaw. At that point, another kid and I urged Teddy to get his father out of there.

"Come on, Poppa; let's go now." Teddy started pulling his father by the arm and led him away, still shouting at Johnny, who was laughing.

Not only was I becoming increasingly uncomfortable around John, I didn't fit in with my classmates anymore. They were caught up in the typical Forest Hills syndrome of impressing girls with fancy clothes—pressed bell-bottoms and expensive leather boots—and talk of how their fathers were going to buy them new sports cars when they graduated high school. Some of my former friends would comment on my ripped jeans and ragged "Aqualung" raincoat.

"What's with you? You look like you're about to fall apart," they'd tell me.

This was one of the reasons I started hanging out with Johnny to begin with, but now it seemed he had crossed a line.

Doug Scott was now playing with guys like Bob Roland, Steve Marks, and a bass player named Ira Nagel, who were actually getting jobs at dude ranches and hotels upstate and at strip joints like the Metropole in Manhattan. Doug said that they were interested in having me play some jobs with them.

The Metropole! Naked dancing girls! I was a sixteen-year-old boy— sorry, Johnny.

Finally I got up the nerve to tell John I wanted to quit our band and start playing with other people.

"Why do you want to do that?" Johnny said, insulted. "Those guys aren't cool. They're not your friends."

"Well, yeah, I just want to do something else," I told him.

"If that's really what you want," Johnny said with disappointment.

But I think Johnny knew it was more than just that, and it hurt his feelings. He told me to forget about the money I still owed him for the guitar. Of course, this put a dent in our friendship, but I wanted to get some experience and distance from John's violence and craziness.

JEFF WAS FEELING a bit more secure after surviving the nightmare of being in a psychiatric ward for two weeks. One undeniable upside to the experience was that it had made him stronger. It didn't kill him or his spirit. Though Jeff was still at odds with himself and reserved around certain people, he did seem anxious to have more of a social life again.

Richard Freed had been in the hospital a few months previously, deathly ill from abusing himself in a variety of unsavory ways.

"I was really messed up," Richard Freed admitted. "I was doing drugs at the time—barbiturates a lot, some heroin."

Now that he was feeling better, he had become closer friends with Jeff and was hanging out at our house regularly. Richard would come over to our apartment, smoke some hash, do something in the bathroom for a while (most likely dope), go into the kitchen, fill himself a big bowl of ice cream, and then plant himself in our bedroom in front of the TV.

Like clockwork, after ten spoonfuls Richard's head would begin to drop a little and then pop back up and drop down again until he was in full nod, with his face in the bowl. We'd wake him up after we stopped laughing.

Watching Richard nod out was our prime-time family entertainment. Richard had been leading a life that made even John Cummings's existence look mellow. He was the craziest Jew we'd met to this point. As crazy as he was, Richard was a good friend to Jeff.

"Jeff always walked over that bridge to see me in Lefrak City with no shoes on," Richard Freed recalled. "His foot would be all cut up. I tried to help Jeff emotionally, telling him, 'You gotta wear shoes!' Jeff almost had to have his foot amputated because it was so puffed up."

Jeff had also established relationships with some of the kids he'd met in St. Vincent's psych ward, who were in similar situations. It was a good thing for him. He would joke that they were all "cracked in the head, but had a lot of good pills holding 'em together."

Jeff was "in" with the outpatients—especially the female ones.

When Jeff turned twenty, he said he was going to do something different for his birthday. A few days later he walked in with a full-blown teased-out Afro perm—high and round and as frizzed out as a white boy's follicular density would allow. We realized what the motivation behind Jeff's Afro was when he informed us that he had a new girlfriend, a black girl from Brooklyn. Wilna was still in the psych ward at St. Vincent's, but Jeff wanted us to meet her as soon as she got out.

Wilna was a nice-looking girl with a friendly smile, but she had a frightened look in her big brown eyes, as if something terrible might happen any second. We tried our best to make Wilna feel welcome and relaxed. We knew she was fragile emotionally. Jeff brought her home frequently and Wilna would stay overnight when our mom was away or spending the night at Phil's apartment on Ninth Street and Third Avenue in the East Village.

Jeff seemed very serious about this relationship and we were happy for him. Wilna was a handful, though, and you had to keep a close eye on her—and on any sharp objects in her vicinity. Mostly she and Jeff hung around the apartment listening to music and watching TV.

Sometimes Wilna was very lucid, and we all talked about music, politics, and various social issues, including the stupidity of racism. Wilna said her parents would not approve of her going with a white boy or the mixing of races in general. Jeff would joke that they "must be members of the KKK or something."

The fact was that in 1971 a white hippie "Jew-boy" and a black hippie girl traveling together outside of the city were still in danger. They talked about taking a Greyhound bus to Florida and visiting our relatives down there. The prospect of what might become of a couple like that on a bus going through the Deep South was frightening. If they got off the bus at some truck stop in Jacksonville, the real KKK could have been a big problem.

Wilna alone was a very real problem. She took medications for her psychological needs, and then she and Jeff would drink and sometimes smoke some pot, or hash, or angel dust. Sometimes she would start hallucinating and have extreme paranoia attacks. She would suddenly get hysterical and talk about things that weren't happening.

We'd try to calm her down, telling her, "Nothing is going to hurt you, you're safe here, and everything is okay." Something would click, and Wilna would seem to regain her focus and recognize us again. Then just as suddenly she'd start laughing. It was hard to tell if it was real or if she was acting out to get attention.

One morning when Jeff was out, I woke up to hear Wilna screaming. I rushed into the living room, where she was sleeping on the couch. I tried to wake her, but she was deep in a nightmare. When I shook her shoulder, Wilna jumped up screaming, pulled off her wig, and threw it at me.

Not knowing what had just hit me in the chest, I jumped up and screamed in horror. Wilna put her hand to her head, realized what she'd done, and screamed back.

Then Jeff walked in, and Wilna screamed some more and then ran into the bathroom. A minute later, she ran back out, grabbed her wig out of my hands, and ran back in the bathroom, screaming all the way.

In the summer of 1971, Mom and Phil prepared to take off on a four-week trip to Europe. Our cousin Renee, who was a year older than Jeff, came up from Florida to stay at our house. She had aspirations to become an actress and wanted to spend the summer in New York City.

Renee promised Mom she'd keep an eye on things in her absence. As soon as Mom and Phil took off, Jeff had Wilna move in. She brought her cat, which didn't get along well with my cat, Stymie, a stray kitten I'd picked up at Thorneycroft.

The fun started right away. Wilna's initial fascination with my mother's liquor cabinet quickly became her summer hobby. Mom's liquor cabinet was certainly ample and had a nice variety of top- and midshelf hard stuff, several cognacs, and a few liqueurs. Wilna seemed very enthusiastic about "experiencing" all the new things she'd never tasted before. Jeff was drinking pretty heavily too, but his taste still leaned toward his old favorites, Boone's Farm Strawberry Hill or apple wine.

Regardless of Renee's reminder of our promise not to destroy the place, soon there were teenage bodies spread out on the living room floor almost nightly.

Jeff and Wilna didn't leave the apartment very often that summer. It was getting a little stuffy in there, so my friend Allen Brooks and I decided to take advantage of the Youth Fare discount airline tickets to Europe. We each bought $60 in American Express Travelers Cheques. He stole mine, and I stole his. Then they replaced all of our "stolen checks" immediately. We repeated the scam as we traveled around Europe for about two weeks.

When I got back home, Wilna was gone. So was every bottle of booze in Mom's liquor cabinet. Things seemed a little tense.

"They took her away," Jeff said.

"Who?" I asked him.

"The KKK," Jeff said with a laugh.

I found out later that my mother had called Wilna's parents to tell them that their daughter had cleaned out her liquor stock, that her cat was shitting all over the house, and that they should come and get her.

By this time Jeff's Afro perm was growing out, and he was starting to look like his old self, but was also alone again and not doing much besides playing records. Thankfully, Jeff started getting into David Bowie, Lou Reed, and T. Rex, and getting creative again. He wanted to steal something out of Andy Warhol's bag of pop-art tricks, so instead of just painting a picture of a Campbell's Tomato Soup can, he came up with the idea of painting a tomato with the tomato soup itself. Then he tried split pea.

Mom was still painting at the time and gave Jeff a few canvases to "experiment" on. After Jeff ran out of soup colors, he smeared on some blueberries and stroked on some strawberry ice cream and chocolate syrup. Jeff thought this concept was going to be the next big thing, and that he could sell the pieces in the art gallery Mom would be opening with her best friend Jeanie.

It seemed like a good idea until the downside became apparent. Though the syrup never really dried, the ice cream did; but when it crusted off, the soups began to crack and flake. Jeff hadn't thought it out completely. He tried brushing honey on the canvas to coat everything, then putting it under a fan to dry. You can imagine what the kitchen looked like afterward and what ensued when he didn't clean it up.

Next Jeff moved on to a new enterprise, making flowers. The flowers came in a kit and were made of wire. The wire was shaped like flower petals at one end. He dipped the petal end into liquid plastic solutions of different colors and let it dry. Jeff made bouquets of these plastic flowers and sold them out on the street. He did well with them at Le Drug Store on the Upper East Side, a trendy nightclub for spoiled rich kids owned by our friend Ira Nagel's cousin.

"Jeff was walking around barefoot, wearing a belt with little bells hanging from it; he was really a hippie," Ira Nagel remembered. "He was selling these plastic flowers on the sidewalks down in the Village and in Forest Hills, and he kept getting summonses from the cops. So I got my cousin to let him sell them in front of Le Drug Store.

"These flashy guys up there were all wired up on coke," Ira continued, "and they would laugh at Jeff. Then their stoned-out girlfriends would feel sorry for him, so they'd make their boyfriends buy some flowers."

While Ira had found Jeff a safe spot to sell his wares, he had also found me a spot playing guitar in his band, Sneaky Pete. It was comprised of former Tangerine Puppets lead singer Bob Roland on vocals, Wayne "Lippy" Lippman on drums, and Ira on bass. We were working steadily, and the experience was invaluable. We played every weekend and sometimes during the week. If the job paid well enough, we had Tommy Erdelyi join us.

They had a booking agent who got them tons of work in dingy, mob-owned joints in the Bronx, Brooklyn, and Jersey, and at army and navy bases in the tristate area. Jeff would often come along and hang out when we played. Best of all were the topless bars. We had a regular gig at the Wagon Wheel on Forty-fifth Street, near the famous Peppermint Lounge, where beautiful girls surrounded us, dancing to the hits. It was a seventeen-year-old boy's dream come true.

We had to do a few slow songs, and since we hated corny ballads, we chose to do BB King's "The Thrill Is Gone," a slow, steamy blues classic. One night after escaping into a guitar solo, I sucked the drool off my lower lip and realized that the sleazoid drunks and derelicts at the bar were giving me a standing ovation. These horny guys who came for nothing but tits and ass had apparently been *moved*. It remains among the most memorable achievements of my career.

In the spring of 1972, the band got an offer to play at the combined army, navy, and air force base in Keflavik, Iceland. It was a two-week stint in one of the most extraordinary geological locations on the planet. Only the abundance of beautiful and willing girls was more astounding than the landscape. But we were thrown out of Iceland a week into the gig for causing an "international incident" as an onslaught of troops, rotating from their tours in Vietnam, began making nightly jaunts to our room to "party with the band." How could we turn them away?

The soldiers had great weed and other things, and we had two go-go dancers traveling with us. Ultimately, things got out of hand, and the Icelandic police were called to the base to break up the party and search our room. The next morning, we were *advised* to sign a document and sent back to the States on a cargo plane—the kind with straps for seats. The band was in free fall.

When I got back, Jeff was hanging out with a new girlfriend named Lori. She was also an outpatient but was actually decent looking and from the neighborhood. Unlike us, Lori had wealthy parents.

While Lori tried to come off as a free-spirited hippie gypsy, she seemed very spoiled. She was loud, outspoken, and obnoxious if she didn't get her way. She was also the proud owner of several drug prescriptions, which she was more than willing to share. However, if we turned down her offer, Lori would get suspicious—if *she* had to take them, then *everyone* should.

Lori was also a poet and introduced herself to everyone as an "artist."

There were also noticeable scratches on my Yamaha acoustic guitar. Apparently Lori and Jeff had been trying to write some songs together. She wrote horrible lyrics, things along the lines of: *"I'm Mother Nature, unleashed and unformed. All the cold, cold people are in need of my cosmic warmth. You, too, are beautiful, sad and shy. Touch me, and we will sparkle like stars in the sky."*

Her singing was even worse.

13.

"I'M EIGHTEEN AND I DON'T CARE"

Jeff was hesitant to tell me that he and Lori had been fucking around with my guitar without asking me. We'd had some spats over him using my stereo. I'd just bought my first one, with a brand-new tuner, amp, and turntable. I got it with the money I'd made working as a messenger after school, a sucky job Jeff and I both did for a while.

Jeff could listen to my radio anytime, that was fine with me; but he was playing records that had scratches and puncture marks on them. I had just spent $75 on a new Pickering needle and cartridge—and my brother was putting out cigarettes on his records. I told Jeff he had to play those records on the old turntable in the living room. But I'd walk in once in a while and he'd be picking the needle up and putting it down—fifty times, bludgeoning the record until it was pockmarked and the needle was blunt, and I'd have to buy another. Jeff's spirits had certainly improved, but his OCD hadn't. In fact, it was getting worse.

I told Jeff I knew he had been playing my guitar and that it was okay. It was a relatively cheap one, and I was thinking about smashing it soon anyway and getting a classical guitar. I wanted to learn how to read music and had started studying a little music theory.

In May 1972, what we were left with in music culture was either the flamboyant rock star or the outdated idealistic hippie rock star. Or a combination, like working-class hero John Lennon, singing lyrics like "imagine no possessions" while being filmed in a multimillion-dollar mansion playing a piano that cost more than many Americans earned in their entire lifetime. Much as we loved Lennon and our old ideals, something was beginning to smell rotten. Bands like Yes ultimately left us nothing but confused. What else was out there? Elton John, "American Pie," Black Oak Arkansas? Hendrix was dead, and so were the Beatles and the Doors. Everything seemed so pretentious; everybody seemed to be pushing themselves, their philosophy, or their lifestyle—everyone but Frank Zappa and a very few others.

I started listening to jazz and classical music. The soundtrack from A Clockwork Orange had sparked a big interest in Ludwig van Beethoven. Jeff, and even John Cummings, liked Beethoven after that movie—as long as John could imagine someone being kicked in the "bollocks" to the accents of the music.

Jeff had discovered the world of "glam rock." Lou Reed's Transformer and David Bowie's Ziggy Stardust albums now dominated his playlist. He was making the transition from the California bands like Jefferson Airplane, later renamed the Jefferson Starship, and the Youngbloods, who sang lyrics such as "Come on people now / Smile on your brother / Everybody get together / Try to love one another right now."

Gender-bending glam rock and the new sexual decadence in rock & roll was a trickle down from the free-love current of the 1960s. It was like a love-in run amok. Though the sixties credo was that everybody should do their own thing, homosexuality had still been concealed—even in rock & roll. Bowie, Reed, and Andy Warhol did just about everything to change all that. The difference now was that the boundaries of gender didn't separate male from female but included them both. You were what you were, at whatever time you chose to be.

Nobody ever said this wasn't confusing.

For whatever reason, this greatly appealed to Jeff. Physically, due either to nerve damage from the teratoma or his genetic composition in general, Jeff was neither athletically inclined nor macho. Finally it didn't matter.

David Bowie had become his new inspiration. Jeff very much related to the introspective identity-crises angle of Bowie's message. Bowie had him, and millions of other kids, convinced that the ugly ducklings of the world would transform themselves into beautiful swans, if only they'd believe they could. No one had to be left out of the parade. The thinking now was, "We could be pretty! We should be stars!" Jeff seemed particularly affected by the words to Bowie's song "Rock 'N Roll Suicide":

> No matter what or who you've been
> No matter when or where you've seen
> All the knives seem to lacerate your brain
> I've had my share, I'll help you with the pain
> You're not alone

We listened to a lot of Bowie, but this particular song he played over and over, every day. Lyrically, to me it just seemed like a lot of overemotional whimpering—more intellectual than, say, Melanie's "Beautiful People," but just about as melodramatic. Almost like the kind of crap Liza Minnelli would be singing. Don't get me wrong: I loved Lou Reed's Velvet Underground songs and most of Bowie's stuff, too, but now Lou's material was all about celebrating "coming out of the closet," and I just couldn't relate. Though I was very happy for him, I wasn't interested in "transforming" myself into a "Diamond Dog" or a she-male in "Venus and Furs." I was more concerned with just growing hair on my nuts. I didn't feel an urge to put on lipstick or space suits and platform boots. Some people did, and that was fine with me. Jeff did.

Yeah, it's a little weird watching your older brother in the bathroom, experimenting with Mom's cosmetics.

This is where we finally began to part ways in our musical tastes, except for a few things we still loved in common. Jeff brought home a new Stevie Wonder album, the first one where he wasn't called "Little" Stevie Wonder. It was called *Music of My Mind* and had a song on it called "Happier than the Morning Sun" that we both loved and listened to every day. We loved the whole album.

At this point I just wanted to learn to play more challenging things than jerk-me-off rock solos. The phony grimaces on the faces of the current "rock gods" playing these dreadfully extravagant guitar solos made me recoil and retreat. They were the same riffs we'd heard a jillion times already. I was getting too old for "Crocodile Rock," or it was too old for me. I bailed on it and went searching for new saints. Bring on more Mingus, Django Reinhardt, Miles Davis, and Igor Stravinsky.

John and Richard Freed thought I was nuts.

I told Jeff he could have my Yamaha when I got my new guitar. He asked me if I would teach him how to play and offered to pay me for lessons with the Supplemental Security Income (SSI) payments he'd started receiving. He had turned twenty-one and was eligible for financial aid from the government based on his disability. I told my brother he didn't have to pay me but that it would be really hard to teach him, as he was left-handed and my guitar was strung for righties. I would have to make it as simple as possible.

I'd noticed how folksinger Richie Havens tuned his guitar to a chord and just barred the frets with one finger. I adapted that technique for Jeff, using just the bottom two strings for starters.

Normally, a chord is formed with three or more notes from the musical scale—think of the Three Stooges singing, "Hello," "Hello," "Hello!"

Playing the two bottom strings formed an inverted chord with just the fifth and the tonic (the first "hello" and last "hello"). It was just enough to imply the chord, especially if you sang over it—and enough to mimic a song.

I showed Jeff how to hold the pick and play downstrokes. I got him accustomed to the fret board on the guitar and tried to show him where the chords found in standard rock progressions lay on the neck. Of course it was rough, but for a lefty, he seemed to be doing well with this simplified two-string method. Jeff was catching on quickly, which made it enjoyable for both of us. He had only played drums and didn't sing, so it had been hard to tell previously if he had good pitch or not. We were finding out that Jeff had a pretty good ear.

Jeff asked me to teach him a song. He'd been listening to Alice Cooper's "I'm Eighteen" about twenty times a day, so I figured that was a good one to start with. It wasn't terribly difficult chord-wise—there were only three. I showed him the frets to put his finger on and sang the song as he changed the chords. After two times around, he was doing it by himself.

A few days later I came home and Jeff was sitting there with the guitar again. He had become totally attached to it.

"Hey, Mitch, tell me what you think of this!" Jeff said, very excited. He began to play the chords to "I'm Eighteen."

"Yeah, that's it, that's 'I'm Eighteen,'" I said to him.

"Yeah, wait, wait," he said, starting over.

Jeff started playing the chords to "I'm Eighteen" again, but then started singing different words over them.

"*I don't care, I don't care, I don't care about this world. I don't care about that girl. I don't care.*"

"Whaddaya think?" Jeff said after he went around it twice.

"Well, it's a start," I said, "but dontcha think you need a little something more in there?"

"Okay," Jeff said. "How about this?"

He used the same chords in a different sequence but continued singing, "I don't care," over and over.

"Yeah, right, something like that," I laughed. I had meant the words but tried to encourage him, saying, "But that's pretty good for a beginning!"

"Well, I think it's *really* good!" Jeff said.

Surprisingly enough, he called it "I Don't Care."

It turned out to be the first Ramones song ever written.

A few days later he wrote another great song called "Here Today, Gone Tomorrow"—with the same three chords!

Richard Freed, John, and a kid named Doug Colvin who lived across the street from us had been going to see a band called the Stooges whenever they came to New York City and had a new hero in the singer, Iggy Pop. Richard would occasionally bring Jeff along with them. Jeff had become a big Stooges fan as well. Jeff had also become friendly with Doug Colvin.

Doug's father was in the army, and though Doug was born in Virginia, he'd been raised in Berlin and Munich in Germany. His German mother was a war bride. "We lived with other U.S. military people. I lived outside American society, but within it," he explained years later.

"We moved to the base in Pirmasens," said Doug, "where there was some old bombed-out houses. I used to wander around looking for war relics, like old helmets and gas masks and bayonets. I had a bad childhood and what I did to compensate for it was to live in a total fantasy world, to just get outta myself before I knew about drugs. I first started getting high on morphine.

"When we moved to America," Doug continued, "we went right to Forest Hills." Jeff and I lived on Sixty-sixth Road; Doug lived right across the street, as did Tommy. John lived right up the block. We all lived on the same street, within one block of each other.

Doug and I had first acknowledged each other one day when we both walked out of our buildings at the same time carrying guitar cases. We talked a bit about bands; he'd said his favorites were the Byrds and the Beatles. Now all Doug would talk about was Iggy Pop and the Stooges.

Jeff and I first saw the Stooges one day in June 1970 when John was over at the house. John had rushed in and turned on the TV to watch a great concert he said we had to see. It was the Cincinnati Pop Festival, where the lineup included Mountain, Grand Funk Railroad, Alice Cooper, Traffic, Bob Seger, Mott the Hoople, Ten Years After, Bloodrock, Brownsville Station, and the Stooges.

Aside from the headliners, there were a lot of horrible bands. Then one finally came out playing with an intense ferocity. Unfortunately, it sounded like a buzz of fuzz coming out of the little TV speaker. The graphic displayed the name the Stooges. We liked them from their name alone. Iggy came out, dressed in blue jeans and no shirt, rolled around the stage, taunted the crowd, and then smeared himself in brown shit we thought was diarrhea.

"Did you see that?" Johnny asked, laughing hysterically. "He smeared shit all over himself!"

"No!" said Richard Freed. "That's like . . . pumpkin pudding or something!"

"No," Johnny said, "I've read about this guy. He does things like that."

We were still arguing whether it was or wasn't when, minutes later, Iggy boldly stepped into, or more like onto, the crowd.

"Look, he's trying to walk into the audience but they won't let him 'cause he's got shit all over him," Johnny continued, laughing, while we watched in awe with our mouths open. "They're holding his feet so he can walk over them!"

In 1970, Jeff and I weren't quite sure what to make of it. It was cool and reminded us of *Saturday Night Wrestling*.

By 1972, Jeff was heavily influenced by Iggy and the Stooges. He'd bought all of Iggy's albums that had come out since we'd seen that concert two years before. Things had changed, though; now Iggy was decked out in glam from head to toe—silver lamé pants and cheetah-skin tops.

Jeff was also beginning to dress for success. He was discarding his old hippie clothes (well, not really discarding them—his OCD prevented him from discarding anything) and overhauling his image completely. My brother felt more comfortable hanging out with the cross-gender Warholians. He fit in better with this crowd—and wanted to be a part of it. He thought he could make it. And the more accessories he borrowed from my mother, the more I sincerely hoped he would, too.

In New York City the glitter movement was in full force. Jeff, John, Richard, and Doug were all over it, and it would soon be all over them.

Mom had a friend in our building named Edna Gladys Geer. We called her "the EGG Lady of Forest Hills." She was a small, sweet woman who'd recently moved up from the Deep South and spoke with a heavy drawl. A seamstress by trade, Edna made her living doing custom alterations out of her apartment, where an impressive collection of egg-shaped items crammed every room in her home. Aside from that, she was relatively normal and probably attended church every Sunday.

Edna soon found herself being approached by Jeff, a six-foot-five-inch twenty-one-year-old man, with a request to make him a one-piece, form-fitting jumpsuit out of either sequins or another shiny material—preferably in red or gold. It had to be long enough to cover his three-inch platform boots.

"Um, well, of course, Jeff," Edna said. "If that's what you really want."

Jeff had already ordered the knee-high platform boots at a store called Granny Takes a Trip, an English boutique that specialized in rock & roll garb. They had just opened a shop in Manhattan but were having trouble locating a pair in a men's size ten, so they shipped them over from London for him.

Edna told Jeff that she only had enough material on hand to make his suit in a soft, black cotton fabric—which wasn't shiny. Jeff was disappointed, but as Edna measured him, she advised him that it would be more comfortable and durable than sequins or glitter material. Also, she would have to spend much more time looking for the right color and density if he wanted the sparkly stuff.

Jeff settled for the black.

The boots finally arrived, but Jeff didn't like their light tan color, so he soaked them in lavender shoe dye for a few hours. The lavender platform boots created a striking complement to the black jumpsuit.

Jeff Hyman's metamorphosis was almost complete.

But there were just a few wrinkles to iron out before he would be ready to burst onto the glitter scene. Jeff was finding his footing in the platform boots and started feeling comfortable at that elevated altitude (in the shoes he now towered slightly over six foot eight).

Jeff began to peruse the "Public Notice/Music" section of the classifieds in *The Village Voice*, where bands post notices looking for musicians. The way the *Voice* ads read was indicative of the current trend. The "We're all beautiful, let's strut," movement was basically sparked by Andy Warhol's declaration, "In the future everyone will be famous for fifteen minutes," combined with Bowie's beckoning of his fans' inner Starman to "come out!"

The ads would read something like "The Smoking Manholes looking for pretty singer with rough voice. Let's dress up and be stars tomorrow. Call Dean Deanie."

Jeff placed his own ad saying he was looking to join or form a band. To better fit his new image and further boost his confidence, he considered a name change.

In the fall of 1972 there were no answering machines and no screening of calls. You actually had to pick up the phone to get it to stop ringing. The day the ad came out, Jeff was in his new outfit—he hadn't taken it off since Edna finished it—and was sitting on the kitchen counter near the wall phone. But I was closer when it rang.

"Hi, is this Jeff Starship?" the caller asked.

"Huh? Jeff Starship?" I said as Jeff grabbed the phone from me.

Jeff Starship was the name my brother had chosen for his ticket to stardom in the world of glam rock.

The mecca for glam wasn't really in Manhattan. It wasn't Max's Kansas City, where the New York Dolls hung out with people like Warhol, Iggy, and David Bowie. Max's was still more of a cabaret than a rock club and wasn't booking many original, unsigned rock bands yet. Oddly enough, the emerging scene was thriving in Queens.

It was all happening at a club called the Coventry in Sunnyside, about a mile down Queens Boulevard from the Fifty-ninth Street Bridge. There really was no other place for local bands playing original music to perform in the city, except for the old-guard West Village clubs, which were now viewed as passé tourist traps. Jeff was becoming a regular at Coventry. John Cummings, Doug Colvin, and Richard Freed would go occasionally to check out the bands. Jeff would dress up in the black jumpsuit, purple boots, and whatever accessories he could "borrow" from Mom.

Jeff had Edna make the jumpsuit skintight, with just a little give by the knees. It had a zipper down the front that Jeff would lower to his midriff, exposing a hairless, ghost-white chest. He tied Mom's chiffon scarves to his belt, which he wore at hip level, and adorned the suit with pins from my mother's jewelry chest. It was a look that said—well, actually, I'm really not sure what the hell that look was saying, but it spoke volumes.

Initially, Mom didn't mind sharing her scarves, belts, jewelry, necklaces, and bracelets with her son—or even some of her vests and shirts, if he could make them fit. But as dictated by his disorder, when Jeff put something on, it rarely came off without a struggle. The jumpsuit became his regular outfit, and Jeff wore it during daylight hours, as well. It was quite a sight.

"Dressing meant so much to Jeff," Phil Sapienza recalled. "He'd break his mother's chops about the jumpsuit looking just right. He became obsessed by how he looked. 'How do I look? Am I coming across?' "

Jeff Starship would walk out of Birchwood Towers from the third-floor exit, where you had to pass through a children's playground to get to the street. The kids would climb off the seesaws and monkey bars to view Jeff in his jumpsuit and platform boots, the likes of which they'd never witnessed before (good thing Edna didn't have the gold lamé). The kids peppered Jeff with the kind of remarks you'd expect little kids to make. Their mothers, who were as spoiled as the kids, did nothing to curb them and made no attempt to teach them that it wasn't polite to point at and jeer at someone who was a little different.

Jeff suppressed his anger at the little brats but later used it as inspiration for a song.

After enough of Mom's wardrobe came back to her smelling of beer, smoke, sweat, and piss—or, worse, didn't get returned at all—a new and unusual sort of problem arose. Mom forbade Jeff from further use of her apparel, but that didn't stop him. He still tried to sneak a scarf or string of pearls out with him and would still *borrow* her compacts and mess around with her makeup, which led to many bizarre exchanges between mother and son.

Just as I was asking myself, "What next?" Jeff's wacky girlfriend Lori started coming on to me. His crazy girlfriends all seemed to come on to me at some point; maybe it was because I appeared to be more stable, or maybe they were just crazy. If it bothered him, Jeff never let it show. It never came close to being an issue because: 1) horny as I was, I wasn't interested; 2) horny as I was, I wouldn't do that to him.

Lori also was upset that Jeff's outfits were getting more attention than her.

It became such an issue for her that Lori broke up with him over it. That was about the only time I really appreciated Jeff's jumpsuit and lilac boots.

14.

GALL THAT GLITTERS

few other kids in the neighborhood were now getting into the glitter thing. Doug Colvin was hanging around with John Cummings's old pal Michael Newmark. Doug and Michael liked to dress up and walk around the neighborhood. They would come up to Thorneycroft, act out like drag queens, and try to shock us. But nobody was terribly shocked. We thought it was funnier that they would think they scared us. Everyone up there had pretty much seen and heard it all already. We'd all developed a very droll, jaded sense of humor.

"Yo, here comes Doug Colvin," we'd say. "He's wearing the frilly shirt and makeup again!"

"Nice," would be the stoned response. "Looks like my grandma's blouse. He looked better in the red."

When Milton Berle came out in drag on our black-and-white TV screens in the 1950s, maybe we were shocked. In the midsixties when the Mothers of Invention all sported women's dresses on an album cover, it made an impact. Later when a male singer came out wearing makeup and calling himself "Alice," it was fun.

By now, it was just a joke.

We really didn't think Doug and Michael were gay, and if they were, we really didn't give a fuck. To us Forest Hills outcasts, dressing like that and running down to Max's was tantamount to being politically correct. After all, that's what all hip people did and how all the "beautiful people" were dressing.

Johnny was conscious of that and confided to me that hanging out with those people basically annoyed him. But he wanted to compete and thought that was what he had to do at the time. More often, he preferred that we all just take a few hits of pot, go to Jack in the Box for tacos, and then go back to his place to watch some horror movies.

Suddenly, Doug was mocking me now because like most kids in the neighborhood, I'd toned down my mod, hippie look several years ago and opted for the old standby: tight blue jeans, T-shirts, and Keds tennis sneakers. It was a look that I considered timeless and unpretentious. Plus it was comfortable, practical, and durable. But since I didn't get into the glitter thing with them, Doug would tell me that I wasn't cool anymore, dismissing me as a faggot and a hippie.

At least one worthwhile lesson I came away with from our nonconformist hippie days was not to give a fuck about doing things just because "everybody's doing it!"

Johnny had been working construction and making decent money. When I met up with him to check out the used Jaguar he had just bought, he was wearing silvery spandex pants, a velvet shirt, and a chinchilla fur coat. He seemed a lot cooler emotionally. Johnny had just gotten married to Rosanna, who lived in his apartment building. She was closer to my age, and I had noticed her in Forest Hills High School; so had every other guy.

Rosanna was an extremely sexy, brown-eyed, bronze-skinned Jewish girl from Morocco. She'd been living in America for several years but still had an accent. Rosanna was short and petite, wore high heels and microminiskirts, and boasted bosoms that caused schoolboys to drool on their desks.

"John had a crush on me from the first time he saw me," Rosanna remembers. "I would get out of the car with some guy driving me home from high school, and John used to hang out in front of our building just so he could see me. The first line outta my mouth was, 'Can you teach me how to play the guitar?' I wanted to learn 'The Twilight Zone.'

"In my eyes John was a rock star from day one. He had the aura about him. It's like I fell in love with the image more than I fell in love with the person, 'cause the person was a pain in the ass."

When Rosanna went to John's apartment, they listened to records and talked about rock & roll. Eventually she married John, partially to escape her ultra-strict parents and partially because she saw John as a rock star.

"It was fun while it lasted, which wasn't long," she said. "John had a rule that I had to be less than a hundred pounds or so. And so the fight would be, how did I dare to put more than eight zitis on my plate? I never had an eating disorder 'til I met him."

The scene at the Coventry was blossoming. Local glam bands like the New York Dolls and Harlots of 42nd Street had gotten record deals and were spawning new bands. Kiss had begun their career playing the Coventry sans makeup and then suddenly conceived the Kabuki-monster-from-space look.

Richard Freed had a drummer friend named George Quintanos who was forming a glam band called Sniper. Since they already had a drummer in George, and since Jeff Starship was becoming so noticed at the Coventry, they decided to try him out as the lead singer. Jeff already had the suit, the name, and the right attitude; apparently he convinced them that he had a voice, as well.

"It was the first time I sang lead in a band, 'cause I was a drummer up until then, ya know?" Jeff said. "I made some good friends at the time and it was fun—like when it's naïve and sort of innocent, but good. It was the 'glitter days' and the Dolls and Kiss would come play the Coventry; all those bands would come in from Manhattan."

Jeff would have the guys in Sniper over to talk about their stage show and image and to work out some songs. At that point the guitarist was still singing with them. A few weeks later, Jeff told me they had a show booked, and that I "gotta come!"

Though I thought it was going to be lame, I was stunned when Sniper came out. Jeff had now taken over as their lead singer, and I couldn't believe how great he was. He'd gone from sitting in my house with my acoustic guitar to being this guy you couldn't take your eyes off onstage.

I was blown away. I was shocked. I didn't think much of Sniper as a band, but I was really impressed with my brother. He moved like he would in the early Ramones days, mimicking Bowie's flirty drag-queen shtick. That was the one aspect of his performance I could have lived without—although a six-foot-eight-inch rail of a man dressed up like a rock & roll diva brazenly confronting you with the stance and attitude of a drunken Forty-second Street hooker certainly *will* grab your attention. It was a real freak show, but for my brother, this was an epiphany.

After their set, I told him, "I can't believe it. It's amazing how strong you're coming off, how great you're performing!"

"I sort of became like a star in my own right, hanging out at the Coventry," Jeff said.

"I saw Sniper play one night," Doug Colvin said. "Jeff was the lead singer, and he was great. I thought Jeff was the perfect lead singer because he was so weird looking. And the way he leaned on the mike was really weird. I kept asking myself, 'How's he balancing himself?' All the other singers were copying David Johansen, who was copying Mick Jagger, and I couldn't stand that anymore. But Jeff was totally unique."

Though Jeff's singing was improving rapidly, he hadn't yet gotten his footing onstage. He tried to do things up there that he'd seen other singers do, but he was floundering for stability, like a newborn calf taking his first steps. I was always afraid he was going to trip. Sometimes he did. But as awkward as he looked, posturing with that fey, come-hither sexiness that he was attempting to make his "act," his powerful voice easily negated the clumsiness.

Apparently, his bandmates didn't see it that way. They told my brother he just wasn't "pretty enough" and threw him out. Jeff was now at a bit of a crossroads, but he certainly had my vote of approval to keep going for it. Easy for me to say: It wasn't my apparel he was borrowing, and it wasn't my roof he was living under. At twenty-two he was spending the little money he had on cigarettes, costume jewelry, makeup, and drinks. Mom was getting fed up.

Now, picture, if you will, a strange-looking figure towering over a curious crowd of onlookers—origin unknown, gender uncertain, clothed in a uniform unidentifiable to the bewildered citizens of this fair metropolis—as he is hitchhiking down Queens Boulevard. Determined to rejoin his people at a place called the Coventry, he would miss the signpost up ahead saying that he was now entering the Danger Zone.

"I was always hitching," Jeff said. "Usually I'd be completely decked out; I used to wear this custom-made black jumpsuit, and I had on these like purple knee-high boots, platforms, all kinds of rhinestone pins, lots of belts dangling, and gloves. It was crazy."

I told Jeff repeatedly that he was taking his life in his hands hitching dressed like this. It was a catastrophe waiting to happen. Sure enough, one spring evening we got the call from the emergency room at Elmhurst Hospital.

"Inevitably, somebody beat the shit out of him on Queens Boulevard," Phil Sapienza said. "But at that time, people beat the shit out of him with some regularity."

"I guess that was my first time experiencing queers, ha ha," Jeff laughed. "All of a sudden, you'd be halfway there and they'd say, 'Hey, do ya know somewhere we can go and take a piss?' Usually if I was close enough to the Coventry, I'd just jump outta the car. But sometimes I had to fight my way out of it."

Mom was becoming frustrated with Jeff once again but didn't really have time to deal with him. After months of hard work, she and her partner Jeannie were ready to debut their art gallery on Queens Boulevard. They'd named it the Art Garden and planned a big party for the opening. Basically they were selling the works of the lesser-known artists they'd discovered and had been representing to galleries in Manhattan for several years. It was a bold undertaking in a neighborhood where there was little demand for paintings of anything except rabbis at the Wailing Wall.

The opening was a big success, and the venture appeared to be promising. Many of the artists came to show support for the new gallery, and *all* of our friends turned out to show support for the free wine and cheese.

We had already adapted the basement of the gallery into a rehearsal room with drums, amps, and a PA. It was ideal for after-hours playing. The only problem was that it was brimming with water bugs.

When things settled down a little at the gallery, Jeff's problems became the more pressing issue again. He seemed more belligerent about doing anything about his future. Mom and Jeannie offered Jeff a job as a salesman if he cleaned himself up a little. Jeff wouldn't have to dress up conservatively or anything, but the jumpsuit certainly wouldn't fly—though it might crawl away when he finally took it off.

"Jeff was working in the art gallery," Charlotte remembered. "Little old Jewish ladies would come in wanting frames for their Wailing Wall paintings. They were all afraid of Jeff, but that was *their* problem."

Jeff and I found out that Mom was planning to move again after the summer. There were several reasons for this, she explained. She'd sunk a lot of money into the Art Garden and was a bit extended financially. Our lease was up in October, meaning there would be a rent increase for our apartment. We were surprised when Mom told us that she'd found another apartment right in our building, but the real bombshell was that it was much smaller. She told Jeff he was going to have to find his own place. It was time for him to sink or swim on his own.

"I got kicked out of the house," Jeff laughed. "My mother told me it was for my own good, ha ha! So I moved into my mom's art gallery. I had to barricade myself in real fast so the cops wouldn't catch me. The cops would come by, I'd see a flashlight and hear the police radio going, and they'd be banging on the door, like they thought I was a burglar. It was kind of a tense situation. I was always worried they'd get me. So I'd barricade myself in with the paintings and sleep on the floor. I had a sleeping bag, a pillow, and a blanket, and then I'd work there during the day."

I felt bad that Jeff had been thrown out but figured it was what Mom had to do if he was ever going to survive—and if *she* was going to survive. She just couldn't deal with him anymore.

The prospect of Jeff never finding his way was very real. I'd pondered what the doctors had said about my brother never being able to function or be productive, as I'm sure my mother had. I worried that he might be a burden on her someday, and on me later on. I'd call him and let him sleep on the couch when Mom was away. I knew she was trying to teach him a lesson, but *I* didn't have to.

Jeff was working part-time at the art gallery, and at the age of twenty-three, he was on his own for the first time. I was starting classes at Queensborough Community College and had my own room for the first time in my life.

My old friend Michael Goodrich was working as a bartender at a disco called Butterfingers on Queens Boulevard a few blocks from the Coventry. Mike's brother Bob was part-owner of the place, so they hooked me up with a job as a bar back, eventually leading to a bartending slot. I'd be at school all day studying music—music history, music theory, composition, keyboard harmony, sight singing, and performance. I'd work at night to the wretched repetition of the pounding bass drum and high hat beats that comprised the foundation of "The Hustle" and other disco delights.

Occasionally I'd run into John and Doug, who were still dressing up when they weren't working construction jobs John's father had gotten them. John talked about starting a band, but Doug didn't think I would be interested, because I was still sporting the old blue jeans, T-shirts, and sneakers and wasn't into the glam thing. He said I didn't want to be in "the scene" and that I probably thought I was above them now because I was going to school studying classical music and classical guitar.

"You're *special*, Mitchel," Doug mocked me. "*We* can't play that Andrew Segovia stuff. You're very *learned* now."

"Ya know what I learned, Doug?" I asked him. "That the greatest composers in history got inspiration from the simple music of the peasants — which today is what you call rock & roll." I probably sounded like an ass when I said, "Everything has its value, ya know?"

"Okay, Mitchel," Doug said. "You're real smart, and you can go to school, but that doesn't mean you'll make it, and it doesn't mean you're better. You can play bolerios and concertios, but you're not a star. You're twenty years old and still just a punk, like the rest of us."

It was always hard to tell when Doug was giving you a compliment.

Jeff told me that Doug and Johnny talked to him about starting a band, but he wouldn't be singing; he'd be playing drums. A few weeks later, I walked into the Art Garden and heard something rumbling in the basement.

The door to the basement of the Art Garden was on the floor in the back of the gallery. When I pulled it up, the sound came rushing up out of the hole — the sound that would soon make history. At this point it was thoroughly crude and hard to define. It was familiar but different and new.

There were some other new developments as well, like new names for my brother and friends. Jeff Hyman was now calling himself Joey Ramone, Doug Colvin was now Dee Dee Ramone, John Cummings was now Johnny Ramone, and Tommy Erdelyi was now Tommy Ramone.

"Dee Dee got the name 'the Ramones' from Paul McCartney," Tommy said. "McCartney would call himself Paul Ramone when he checked into hotels and didn't want to be noticed. I liked it because I thought it was ridiculous. The *Ramones*? That's absurd! We all started calling ourselves Ramones because it was just a fun thing to do. There *were* times we were pretty lighthearted when we were putting this together."

"Jeff didn't like the name 'Jeff,'" Tommy remembered. "He chose 'Joey.' I wanted to call him Sandy Ramone, because it sounds Beach Boyish, but he hated that. I thought it was a cool, funny name . . . *Sandy Ramone*. Jeff said, 'Hell no!'"

Dee Dee and Johnny also had new guitars.

"I picked up a guitar when I got laid off from my job as a construction worker, which would have been in January 1974," Johnny remembered. "Affirmative action had come in; they had to get their quotas made right away. And who got shafted? The white people with the least seniority—I lost my job. Dee Dee was workin' downstairs in the mailroom. Before I got fired we'd sit and have lunch."

"I was a mail clerk in office buildings," Dee Dee explained. "I'd pack up the mail in the morning and sort it out. Johnny was a construction worker at 1633 Broadway, and I got transferred there. We'd meet every day for lunch. Usually we'd go to the Metropole and have a few beers. The Metropole was like a go-go place, and after we got a little tipsy we'd go over to Manny's on Forty-eighth Street, which was next door, and look at the guitars."

"We were still friends with Tommy Erdelyi," Johnny continued. "He was always telling me that me and Dee Dee should start a band."

"I felt John was charismatic and had good stage presence," said Tommy. "When the Tangerine Puppets would play, John would hold his bass real high like a machine gun and move it around. He was a great performer. So I said to him, 'You should get a band together.'"

Johnny told Tommy that he didn't really even know how to play guitar, but Tommy reassured him that he shouldn't worry about that. There was a bit of a conflict of ideas between them. But when Johnny went to see the New York Dolls again, it helped him make his decision.

"I go see the Dolls," Johnny remembers, "and I say, 'Wow, I can do this, too. They're great; they're terrible, but just great. I can do this.'

"Then I saw a rock & roll movie, *That'll Be the Day*, that really helped prompt me to start the band," he continued. "In the end, the boy looks in a music shop. He sees a guitar in the window. The movie ends like that. And I thought, 'I'm bored, I'm restless, this is how I feel. I *should* be in a band!'"

Tommy may have replanted a notion in his head, but basically John initiated the forming of the Ramones because he wanted to be in a band again.

"One payday," Dee Dee said, "we both bought guitars and decided to start a band. Johnny bought a Mosrite and I bought a Danelectro, but then we didn't know what to do with them. We started tryin' to play either some Wombles or Bay City Rollers songs. We absolutely couldn't do that; we didn't know how. So we just started trying to write our own stuff and put it together the best way we could."

Johnny and Dee Dee started trying out drummers, but the drummers would come down and basically reject their offer even before an offer was made, saying, "Nah, I don't think I wanna do this."

They knew my brother had played drums, and though Johnny wasn't thrilled about it, he gave in.

"I always thought that a band with me and John and Dee Dee would be cool," Joey Ramone remembered. "'Cause we would be a good-lookin' band, image-wise. So one day I got a phone call and they asked me if I wanted to join the band as a drummer. I said, 'Yeah.'"

"I might've seen Sniper," Johnny said, "when Jeff was calling himself Jeff Starship. I wasn't impressed. I didn't think he was an asshole, I just thought he was a hippie and he was just a little out of it. Then he played a couple of songs he wrote, and I said, 'These are okay.' They were a little Alice Cooperish, but good. I was surprised he was able to do that. Me and Dee Dee hadn't been able to write a whole song yet. So he became our drummer."

"When they auditioned me to be their drummer," Joey related, "I played them two songs I'd written already: 'I Don't Care' and 'Here Today, Gone Tomorrow.' That's how I got in."

Joey was still living in the Art Garden, and Dee Dee was living with a girl in Brooklyn. They were meeting at Johnny's house.

"We were forming a band, somehow, listening to singles like 'Yummy Yummy' and '1-2-3 Red Light,'" Dee Dee said. "Why a bunch of Stooges fans were listening to bubblegum music, I don't know."

It could have been brilliant planning, pure instinct, or just dumb luck that led them to emulate the simplest style of rock & roll—though realistically, considering their abilities, they didn't have much choice.

Characteristic of most things Johnny got involved in, the band had to be suited to his personality and abilities. If it wasn't it wouldn't have lasted very long. It had to be in an arena where he could excel and at a level where he could be the authority; logically, he started at the most minimal. Fortunately, Joey and Dee Dee were on the same level, technically, as Johnny. So they took baby steps—and it turned out to be the right move, allowing them to reach an achievable goal and take it from there. Or not.

"But Johnny and me couldn't write any songs yet," said Dee Dee.

Essentially it was Joey who provided the formula for future Ramones songs with his initial contributions: the stark minimalism, the two-minute length, the maximum of three chords, the existential lyrics comprised of two lines in their entirety. The other members of the band saw how he made it work, and the group's dynamic snowballed from there. Initially the Ramones had no material and no concept. Had Joey not contributed "I Don't Care," the Ramones sound and concept more than likely would have been something different.

"I started strumming down to keep time," Johnny explained. "I thought 'Communication Breakdown' was down-strums. I'd go, 'One, two, three, four, five, six, seven, eight! One, two, three, four, five, six, seven, eight!' to keep time, because I didn't know how to play any other way. I'd just be countin' 'em out."

"It was just the three of us," Joey recalled. "I was drumming, and Dee Dee was playing rhythm guitar and singing lead. But when Dee Dee would start singin', he would stop playing guitar, 'cause he couldn't sing and play at the same time. Then our friend Richard Freed was playing bass, but he didn't last long. He never played before, and he wasn't getting it fast enough for John. I think he was gonna snap!"

Johnny's track record as a leader was, for better or worse, well established. Joey and Dee Dee happily followed.

John's forte as a Ramone was as organizer, and as such he was invaluable. No doubt he picked up some tips in military school and while working construction. He was ultimately perceived as "the General," who made sure everybody was doing what he was supposed to do. Actually, he was functioning more like the foreman on a work site. Johnny had finally gotten Archie Bunker's dream job.

"I wanted to get rid of Joey as a drummer," Johnny recalled, "'cause he wasn't keepin' up as we practiced. I would get better each day, and he'd stay the same."

"It took Joey two hours to get the drum set ready," Dee Dee said. "We waited and waited for him. I couldn't take it anymore, so we started playing. We stopped after the first song and I looked over at Joey and he didn't have the seat on the stool. He was just sitting on the point!"

After that, they asked him to sing. "Actually, it was Dee Dee, 'cause he thought I was unique in the band Sniper," Joey recalled. "I wasn't like anybody else. Everybody else was doing an Iggy or a Mick Jagger."

"Joey was a perfect singer," Dee Dee explained. "I wanted to get somebody real freaky, and Joey was really weird lookin', man, which was *great* for the Ramones. I think it looks better to have a singer that looks all fucked up than to have one that's tryin' to be Mr. Sex Symbol or something."

"Joey was not my idea of a singer," Johnny said, "and I kept telling Tommy that. I said, 'I want a good-lookin' guy in front.'"

Tommy convinced Johnny that Joey looked good between him and Dee Dee. It all worked visually.

"Was Joey a star?" Johnny mused. "I don't know. With him in the center and me and Dee Dee on each side, that played into it. You have to be in the right surroundings. Just about everyone has to be in the right surroundings, but some people have more star appeal than others."

And some people have less star appeal than others, but sometimes they shine far brighter than those with more.

15.

OUT-ZAPPING ZAPPA

Johnny always took pride in being "different." Now it seemed as if he knew that it was okay to let his ego rise to the occasion. He started to believe he was different for a reason and that all that had preceded this was preparation for what was about to come. He always believed he had the power, the charm, the charisma—and he did, given the right circumstances. Now he seemed determined to claim his destiny, corny as it sounds. He believed he was the star—of *his* band.

He also knew he was flawed, in that he couldn't dance the dance required in the music industry—sucking up to people he'd more enjoy peeing on. Tommy would handle that. Johnny knew that he was limited creatively but was savvy enough to utilize the resources surrounding him.

"Tommy was friends with John and sort of acting as our adviser," Joey said. "We'd audition drummers and everybody was real fancy; nobody would play the way we wanted. So Tommy would show them how to play. Tommy'd never played drums in his life. But when he sat down on the drums, that style of the band emerged."

"When we finally got Tommy to be the drummer things started to gel," Johnny agreed. "I did the down-strumming and speed. I'd say, 'It doesn't seem fast enough, *play faster.*' Dee Dee wasn't gettin' no better on guitar, so I made him the bass player."

"The sound was just the chemistry of the four of us—a chemical imbalance," Joey laughed.

"At the beginning, we were thinkin' about doin' some covers, some bubblegum songs," Joey recalled. "But then we wrote songs for ourselves, 'cause we weren't hearing anything on the radio that we liked. All of the great music was gone, and at that point every radio station was playing 'soft rock'!"

Our friend Ira Nagel had also done a short stint as bass player in the band after Richard Freed imploded and was thrown out of the band. Ira and a few other guys had moved into a big house in neighboring Kew Gardens and were looking to rent out the spare rooms. After Joey and Dee Dee moved in, the band moved rehearsals from the basement of the Art Garden to the basement of the house.

"We'd keep rehearsing here and there, and we would invite all our friends down, but we were awful," Johnny said. "I didn't think our friends would want to talk to us ever again after hearing us—and that was probably after about two months of rehearsing."

They still had trouble getting through a whole song at that point. They didn't have many yet, aside from the ones Joey had written back in Birchwood Towers. They were all out of tune and kept starting and stopping. We would watch and root for them to actually finish a song. We were entertained but weren't sure yet if these guys were really serious or not. Regardless, they were unwavering and kept at it. Before long they had written enough songs for a set.

Whether they could play them all the way through, in front of an audience, would soon be determined. They booked their first live shows in Manhattan. The first was at a rehearsal/showcase facility called the Performance Studio, and the second was at a new bar on the Bowery called CBGB.

It was actually Dee Dee who had first told the others about the dingy little club on the Bowery.

"I knew about CBGB's because Television played there first, before anyone," Dee Dee remembered. "I knew Richard Lloyd. He got the job in Television that I went to audition for before I was in the Ramones."

"CBGB's was a slum bar," Joey recalled. "There weren't any customers. I remember walking in with the sawdust on the floor, with the dog shit all over the place, playing a couple of songs. There was just a bartender and his dog."

"The Ramones contacted me shortly after the New York Dolls disinte-grated and asked me if I would manage them," Marty Thau, former manager of the New York Dolls, remembered. "I said, 'Actually I'm not interested in managing anybody, but I'd like to meet you.'

"I went down and saw them play CBGB's," Marty continued. "I said, 'I would be interested in producing a couple of singles with you.' And they said, 'Okay.' We went up to a studio in Rockland County, we did a couple tracks, and I always felt that that resulted in them getting their record deal."

Johnny wanted to get the songs copyrighted, but at that time you couldn't just send in the printed lyrics and a cassette tape. In fact, cassettes weren't around yet. Johnny gave me the reel-to-reel tape and hired me to transcribe the songs into music notation form, which they could then send to the Library of Congress. He paid me $15 a song.

The first song I heard was called "Judy Is a Punk."

> Jackie is a punk, Judy is a runt.
> They both went down to Frisco, joined the SLA
> And oh, I don't know why
> Oh, I don't know why
> Perhaps they'll die

After I cracked up laughing, I thought, "Holy shit! This is almost like Zappa's song 'Flower Punk,'" which went, "*Hey, Punk, where you goin' with that flower in your hand? Well, I'm goin' down to Frisco to join a psychedelic band.*" "This is amazing!"

"Once I heard 'Judy Is a Punk,' I saw it all," Tommy Ramone remem-bered. "I saw that this was totally different and unique and that these guys were so out of their minds. They were so original—we had something in-credible. These guys didn't know what they we were doing. They weren't just doing a song but inventing a whole new genre together. Before that, I knew they were good. But once I saw they could write songs, it was a new dimension."

As I listened on, almost *all* the words kind of reminded me of Frank Zappa lyrics. And the music was just so raw and unusual it fit perfectly with the bizarre lyrics. In fact, it seemed to me this stuff could have been on that *Zapped* album I loved so much. It would've fit right in there with Captain Beefheart, Lord Buckley, Wild Man Fischer, and of course Alice Cooper.

David Walley had written a book about Frank Zappa called *No Commercial Potential*, which dealt with the concept of having financial success while going totally against the corporate grain. It was about using that contrast to your advantage in defining your audience and using the negative publicity to garner attention—and ultimately record sales.

With songs like "Now I Wanna Sniff Some Glue," "Beat on the Brat," and "Loudmouth," and lyrics like *"You're a loudmouth baby / You better shut up / I'm gonna beat you up / 'Cause you're a loudmouth babe,"* that's where I saw a marketing possibility for this stuff.

I didn't see these guys becoming the next Beatles, much as I liked what they were doing. That they were doing something worthy of being on the *Zapped* album was cool enough for me—*cooler*, even, than being "the next Beatles." They even outsmarted Frank, I thought. At gut level, I became a Ramones fan instantly. And they would evolve.

When I called Johnny to tell him I was finished transcribing, the first thing he asked was, "So? What do ya think?"

"It's the best thing I've heard in years! I love it!" I told him.

"Oh, yeah?" he said. "I'm surprised."

"John, there's not one guitar solo on there. Not one!"

"Yeah," Johnny said. "I decided that's too much work, and I don't want to do that, anyway."

"That's great, ya know? I'm so sick of that riff-god, face-making crap," I told him.

"Oh, but I thought you didn't listen to this kind of music anymore," he said condescendingly.

"Yeah, but that's why—because everyone else is doing everything that *you're not*," I explained.

"Yeah, I know what you mean," Johnny said. "Well, come down and see us."

The first time I saw the Ramones do an actual show was at the Performance Studio, where Tommy's old friend and former bandmate Monte Melnick was working. Fortunately, I'd heard the tape before I went to see them. The show was sloppy but funny and fascinating, and sometimes even frightening.

"Chris Stein and I ran into Tommy Ramone on the street," Blondie's Debbie Harry remembered. "He said, 'Oh, I've got this band. We're doing a showcase this weekend, you should come by.' So we went, and it was *great*!

"It was hilarious, because Joey kept falling over. He's just so tall and ungainly. Joey couldn't see very well, plus he had shades on, and he was just standing there singing, then all of a sudden, *WHHHOMP*, he was face-down on this flight of stairs that led up to the stage. Then the rest of the Ramones pushed him back up and kept going."

People did not know what to make of this. They laughed when Joey fell because you really couldn't tell if he was doing it on purpose or not. He'd get up off the floor with a hole in the knee of his jeans and blood dripping. People around me were laughing hysterically, but I was thinking, "Oh man! What the fuck is he doing? He's gonna kill himself."

Dee Dee seemed to keep losing his place in the songs and missing his fingering on the bass guitar frets. He would stop playing and then look over toward John questioningly. These were the simplest songs we'd heard in years, yet the band convincingly looked as if they were struggling for dear life. And they looked mad about it.

Johnny sported a wicked snarl, accompanied by a glare reminiscent of his hero Charles Manson. The snarl would morph into a menacing scowl at Dee Dee when he fucked up. Dee Dee responded with a helpless, child-like shrug until he found his place and resumed playing the song—if it wasn't over already. Throughout all this Tommy sat on the drums, totally deadpan. I knew this wasn't part of the show, but no one else there did. All this combined with Joey's fey gestures, feigned British accent, remarkably odd vocal styling, and near-fatal attempts at rock acrobatics made for a true spectacle. It could almost have passed for a parody, like some downtown, way-off-Broadway production.

"They had maybe five or six songs at the time," Richard Hell remembered. "'I Don't Wanna Go Down to the Basement,' 'I Don't Wanna Walk Around with You,' 'I Don't Wanna Be Learned,' 'I Don't Wanna Be Tamed,' and 'I Don't Want' something else. I wondered, 'Are these guys serious? Is this an act? If it is, this is great! It's like being at the circus!'"

"John was thinking our songs might be too depressing," Joey said, "'cause they were all 'I Don't Wanna' do this and 'I Don't Wanna' do that."

"We didn't have a positive song until we wrote 'Now I Wanna Sniff Some Glue'!" Dee Dee explained.

By this time, Joey was burning through his monthly Supplemental Security Income checks like he was smoking 'em—which was partially true. The yellow tobacco stains on his fingertips practically glowed against his pale skin. He'd also burned a few holes in his mattress at Ira's house. The albums I'd lent him were melted all over the radiator and windowsills, and piles concealed where the floor ended and walls began in his bedroom, which was like a Salvador Dalí painting come to life. After getting about three months behind in his rent, he'd worn out his welcome.

Fortunately, he met some girls at the Coventry who lived a few blocks from Ira's house. They'd seen the Ramones and took a liking to Joey, in a maternal sort of way. They offered him shelter and more. He was finding out he could take advantage of new opportunities that wouldn't have been there had he not been in a band.

Meanwhile, back at home, Mom was experiencing severe pain in her abdomen. In the fall of 1974 it became so unbearable she asked me to take her to the doctor. On his orders, I immediately drove her out to Long Island Jewish Hospital. The next day they removed a huge piece of her intestine, which had become perforated. She was in the hospital for a good three weeks.

Joey got in touch with Mom but never came there to see her. She never complained about it or appeared disappointed that he hadn't come, but it's hard to imagine that she wasn't.

There were certain things we'd come to expect from Joey and certain things we didn't. I didn't expect my big brother to do things normal big brothers do, like protect me. Our mother had similar resolves respective to their relationship. It was an unspoken thing between the three of us. By now, we'd accepted that he had his own problems to deal with, which kept him plenty busy. So we cut him slack on certain things. In return, he came to expect that of us. And he actually *was* getting pretty busy.

The Ramones were beginning to play more frequently. A small contingent from "the Ramp" in Forest Hills, Billy Banks, Merc "the Jerk" Railin, Ira, Richard Freed, Arlene, Rosanna, a few others, and I, continued to support and encourage them. We helped them carry their amps, got people to come to the shows, and did whatever we could.

We distributed and pasted up new posters the band had made to advertise the next show they were doing at CBGB, where they were becoming the house band by default. No one really knew about the place yet.

Alan Vega, lead singer of Suicide, picks up the story: "About a year or two after Jeff Starship got thrown out of Sniper, I caught a band called the Ramones at CBGB's, and who's up there singing but *Jeff Starship*, who's now Joey Ramone. I said, '*Good* for him, man!'" Alan laughed. "I caught their first gig and I laughed my ass off. I thought it was great.

"I loved the name, I loved the way they started every song with Dee Dee shouting '*ONE, TWO, THREE, FOUR!*' into the mike. I thought they were the fucking greatest—so cool.

"I talked to Joey after the gig, and you could tell he was different. You could tell this kid was special."

"Around August 1974," Johnny Ramone said, "we played CBGB's for the first time. We didn't have it down quite yet, but you know, the music was getting closer.

"I think there were two people there. Alan Vega from Suicide was there, and he goes, 'Wow, this is what I been waitin' for! You guys are great!' I told Dee Dee that this guy's sick, and that if we can fool him, maybe we can fool more people. Sure enough, a few more started showing up each time."

The new posters for the Ramones shows had the image of the American eagle on them. They'd been made up by a new friend of Dee Dee's named Arturo Vega, who lived right around the corner from CBGB. The eagle was actually Arturo's belt buckle.

"Dee Dee used to come to my building at Six East Second Street to see his girlfriend, Sweet Pam," Arturo Vega recalled. "She used to live upstairs with Gorilla Rose and Tomata du Plenty, who were original Cockettes from San Francisco."

The Cockettes were a flamboyant drag-oriented theatrical group. Arturo was kind of flamboyant himself at the time.

"Dee Dee started telling me that he and his friends were putting this band together and how he thought that I was a really cool person and that I should design things for them. In those days when you first saw the Ramones, you didn't know what to think. Your senses told you there was something happening there, but what?"

Arturo was totally enamored with the Ramones, and he invested much of his time doing whatever he could to help them, artistically or otherwise. Though they didn't pay him, he continued to develop new designs for flyers, posters, banners, backdrops, and later, T-shirts. Arturo stuck with the eagle theme. Eventually, with the help of two old-time artists named William Barton and Charles Thomson, and some input from the band, he came up with a logo that would become one of the most recognizable in the genre.

After a few months, the girls who had taken Joey in as a boarder requested some contributions from him, financially and domestically. When he didn't comply, they tossed him out. Joey soon followed Dee Dee to Arturo's loft, which was fast becoming the sanctuary for wayward Ramones.

"I thought Joey was really nice," Arturo recalled, "but I didn't know what was wrong with him. Occasionally, I would try to make him act normal. I gave him a hard time. I would make him clean up, or rather, I would try to get him to clean up. But Joey never could."

Everyone was moving. Mom was about to marry Phil Sapienza and move into his place in the East Village, so I found a studio apartment in Forest Hills Gardens for $150 a month. I had to have Mom cosign the lease, as I wasn't twenty-one yet.

Fortunately, bartending at the disco, I was making just enough to cover my rent, car insurance, and food. Money, and time for school, were a bit of a problem. I still wasn't talking to my father; Joey wasn't really, either. Now we were both officially out of the nest and flying on our own wings.

In early 1975 the Ramones' shows were still raw and unrefined; their presentation was still amateurish. But they were creating a buzz heard in circles that listened. John and Tommy were convinced they had something unique but knew they couldn't get to the next level just by putting up posters. The four of them kept writing songs. Johnny, Joey, and Dee Dee made sure that the songs didn't waver from their persona, while Tommy pursued help in the form of a manager.

"We wanted Danny Fields as our manager," Johnny said. "We thought it would be the best route to go with somebody who could understand what we're doin', since Danny had managed the Stooges and the MC5 and worked with the Doors."

"Tommy Ramone was harassing me," Danny Fields recalled. "I was at *Sixteen* magazine when Tommy Ramone started calling me and sending flyers. I thought they were Spanish or Puerto Rican, with a name like Ramone, probably a salsa band or something. So I ignored them.

"I guess Tommy was jealous," Danny Fields continued, "because I wrote about Television in my column in the *SoHo Weekly News*. I loved Television's music, but I had no interest in them financially or professionally. Of course the Ramones were jealous," Danny explained, "because they're jealous of everything that's ever been that wasn't them. So they wanted to know why Television was getting written about and they weren't."

Finally Lisa Robinson, the editor of *Hit Parader* and *Rock Scene* and a rock & roll columnist for the *New York Post*, came down for one of the Ramones' sets, and then called Danny Fields and said, "You gotta get down here and see these guys."

"The Ramones had been harassing Lisa Robinson the same way they were bothering me," Danny explained. "But Lisa said I'd love the Ramones. They did songs one minute long, very fast; it was all over in less than a quarter of an hour. It was the funniest thing she'd ever seen."

"Finally one day Danny comes down to CBGB's," Johnny remembered. "Before I met Danny, I never knew anyone gay—I'd see gay people out, but I didn't know anyone gay, and I didn't want to know anyone gay. Even though I wasn't a kid anymore, and even though I was a delinquent punk, still, somehow I'd led a fairly sheltered life."

"I went to see the Ramones at CBGB's on a Monday or Tuesday night," Danny recalled. "I got a seat up front with no problems. And I fell in love with them. I just thought they were doing everything right. They were the perfect band. They were fast, and I liked fast. Beethoven quartets are supposed to be slow. Rock & roll is supposed to be fast. I loved it."

"I introduced myself to them afterward and told them, 'I love you so much I'll be your manager.' And they said, 'Oh good, we need a new drum set.'

"When I went to Miami to see my mother, I asked her for three thousand dollars. She gave it to me and I bought them a new drum set. I bought myself into their management."

"Danny has a different story of how he became our manager," Johnny said, contradicting Danny Fields. "What I remember was that we told Danny that Lee Childers wanted to manage us and Danny said, 'If that fag is going to manage you, it might as well be me.' Danny says that's not true, but that's what I remember. But we always wanted him as our manager anyway, so Danny buying us the drums was never a condition."

Either way, Danny Fields was now the official manager of the Ramones.

Tommy may have had the hardest job in pulling the three of these guys together and getting the most out of them musically. He was also very clever about communicating their message to the public, intelligently putting the band's philosophy into words even though they weren't totally solid on it themselves. So far he was doing an extremely smooth job.

"I would have Tommy as the spokesman," Johnny recalled. "This way I could keep Dee Dee and Joey away from talking. I thought that Dee Dee and Joey weren't the brightest guys in the lot. We were already getting the image of being dumb, so I let Tommy do the talking. At least he sounded intelligent. I wouldn't be talking either. If you're cool, you don't really talk. I let Tommy be a spokesman for me."

Each of the band members had their functions and understood their roles. For the time being at least, the four acknowledged and accepted each other's strong points and weaknesses—a rare and magical thing—thus allowing their precarious chemistry to develop.

The end result was that their creativity began to flow like a natural spring, or more accurately, a toxic creek. Songs like "Beat on the Brat," "You're Gonna Kill That Girl," and "Chain Saw" proved the waters to be dangerous but certainly exciting.

16.

"1-2-3-4!"

Johnny and I were becoming friendly again. I went with him to the first couple of Ramones shows at the Performance Studio. I'd pick him up in my car, or he'd pick me up in his.

But our friendship was different now: Everything revolved around the band. We still had common interests, though, things like the Yankees, the Mets, and especially movies. Johnny and I were both real film buffs who particularly loved old black-and-white movies and horror films. The 1940s classic *Nightmare Alley* was a mutual top-five favorite we often talked about. It was also an inspiration to the whole band.

It starred Tyrone Power as a drifter who gets a job as a scam artist in a carny. He is fascinated by an illegal sideshow attraction called "the Geek," a near-lunatic who bites the heads off live chickens and is then "paid off" with a cheap bottle of rotgut and a warm place to sleep it off.

Tyrone Power upgrades his mind-reader scam to one where he conjures up spirits of departed loved ones. He leaves the carny to soak the pockets of unsuspecting millionaires. When he's exposed as a fraud, he is shamed into the life of a derelict, alcoholic bum on the run from the cops and the people he scammed. Desperately seeking work, he approaches another carny, where he's told the only job available is as the Geek. The last scene shows Tyrone in a torch-lit tent, glaring ghoulishly at the crowd and the chicken.

Movies like this intrigued and delighted us. They were odd and creepy but certainly intelligent. This was the stuff Ramones songs were made of, in the beginning. The members of the band wanted to convey the essence of those movies in their songs, and when they hit their mark, the songs were as classic as the films. I know this is what Johnny wanted—and that was basically what counted, since he was the self-proclaimed leader of the band.

Johnny wanted a psycho/horror/carny-sideshow songfest. And the story/song should be embodied in a two-minute wrap, maximum, so that you don't even have time to decide if you like it or not: "One-two-three-four," *bam*! Too late, that song is already over . . . now listen to this one . . . "One-two-three-four," *bam*!

Fortunately the others were on the same page.

"In the beginning," Joey remembered, "the Ramones shared a dark sense of humor. We had a persona onstage, but I'm talking about the subject matter of our songs. Not all our songs," Joey laughed, "but a lot of the early ones. We were having fun. There were too many serious people out there at that time. Rock & roll is about fun. Fun hadn't existed in rock for a long time until the Ramones came along."

Johnny had his own idea of fun, a fascination with depraved people like Hitler and Charles Manson. Dee Dee shared it, especially the Nazi thing—possibly resulting from his boyhood fantasies while growing up in post–World War II Germany, or possibly because he was just mentally unbalanced. For whatever reason, some of this found its way into the fabric of the band's compositions.

Tommy brought a few songs to the table, as well. He'd written "I Wanna Be Your Boyfriend" himself and had come in with a new one called "Animal Hop." "Animal Hop" is a prime example of how the personalities, styles, and visions of the band's members clashed and how the collaborative process really paid off.

"I wrote 'Blitzkrieg Bop,'" Tommy Ramone declared. "I wanted to contribute, too, but the guys weren't real receptive to my input. Whenever I wrote a song for the band, it'd have to be incredibly good. This wasn't John, but mostly Dee Dee, because Dee Dee was very competitive. I don't know how Joey felt, because Joey was very quiet. Joey would just sit there not saying anything. But I wrote this song originally called 'Animal Hop,' and it was too good to be rejected. It wasn't about Nazis. It's about kids going to a show and having a good time.

"It went, 'They're forming in a straight line, they're going through a tight wind, the kids are losing their mind, the Animal Hop.'

"There's a line that goes, 'Hey, ho, let's go, they're shouting in the back now.'

"Dee Dee said, 'Animal Hop'? Let's call it 'Blitzkrieg Bop'! Dee Dee was sabotaging the song," Tommy recalled, exasperated. "He said, 'I don't like that line "They're shouting in the back now"—say, "They shoot 'em in the back now."'" He wanted to do the Nazi thing, so that it would never get played on the radio!"

As Johnny summed up the confusion: "Basically we decided to write some crazy bubblegum music."

The first time I went to CBGB was with Johnny. I picked him up in the Plymouth Duster I'd bought for $600. We loaded his guitar, a bag of cables, and the two Mike Matthews Freedom amps that Johnny and Dee Dee were using at the time. They were small amps, about the size of a seventeen-inch TV, and very economical, but they could get loud and created a unique harmonic distortion when you turned them up all the way.

On the ride in, Johnny and I talked about the band's performances—what could be better, what worked and what didn't. Keeping the songs coming in rapid succession seemed to be something that suited them the few times they were able to string two or three together. Johnny didn't want any cute stage patter between the songs—he thought that was corny.

I told him I could easily live without that crap. Say the name of the song, and play it. Sometimes you didn't even have to say the names of the songs—just keep 'em coming.

But getting to the point where you are able to do that isn't so simple. We realized you had to be prepared for anything. We'd say, "Let's look at the other bands we've seen. Study them, see how they do it."

That's when John broached the subject of me working for the band as their roadie. I was still in school, and still bartending, but I told him I would help out whenever I could. I was willing to start that night if we could just work our way past the stumbling, piss-soaked drunks who occupied the entrance to CBGB, relentlessly begging change and cigarettes. There was a typical Bowery bum flophouse directly above CBGB called the Palace Hotel; at one time, apparently CBGB was the hotel's bar.

I walked into CBGB carrying one of the amps and was immediately taken by the fragrance. The combined aroma of dog shit and wood paneling reminded me of my friend Michael Goodrich's basement and made me feel right at home. It wasn't like a "rock club" per se but seemed warm and friendly compared to some of the mob-sponsored joints I'd played in.

There was nobody in there but the owner, Hilly Kristal, the bartenders Merv and Ritchie, Hilly's dogs, and a Hell's Angel playing pool on the table behind the stage.

We set up the equipment and did a little sound check. Johnny kept the volume knobs on the guitar and the amp turned up full, which is where they had to be to get the sound he wanted. When he stopped playing, his guitar would squeal horribly from feedback. It took too much time between songs to turn the volume knob on the guitar down and up. We determined he needed some kind of floor pedal connected between the guitar and the amp so that he could simply step on it and stop the shrieking feedback. Then Johnny's hand would be in position to strike while Dee Dee counted off the next song, which took as long as "1-2-3-4!"

We went over things like that until it was time for the set.

Later a carload of friends from Forest Hills showed up, and Arturo Vega and his friends Gorilla and Tomata du Plenty came too. There might have been fifteen of us in the place, including the dogs.

Though the show was a mess, it was still awesome. There were false starts, mistimed endings, various technical delays, and set order screwups.

The antics that went on during these mishaps could be as funny as the show, with Johnny snarling and barking out orders, Tommy disagreeing, Dee Dee struggling to get his opinion in, and Joey either posturing and falling off the stage during the songs, or standing silently between them in performance-ready stance, waiting for them to decide what the hell they were doing.

When they were able to keep going for a good six-to-seven-minute stretch, which allowed time for at least three of their songs, you could see the potential.

Who the hell knew what might ever happen with them at this point? I didn't even think about it. They could so easily have fallen flat on their faces. But whether anything was going to happen for them or not, I gave them a ton of respect for getting up there and trying. That's more than I was willing to do. I had pretty much given up rock & roll for dead. These guys

forced me to reconsider. There was absolutely nothing going on for us anywhere. At least now there was something to do—something to get me out of
Forest Hills. I was certainly grateful for that.

They started to play regularly at CBGB on Monday nights.

"When we first went to CBGB's, it was rough for a while," Joey said,
"because of the neighborhood, with all the drunks. We tried to encourage
other bands to come down and play, and nobody would, because the neighborhood was so bad. But we liked the atmosphere, and the place had great
acoustics."

When they were playing those first shows at the Performance Studio and
CBGB, the Ramones didn't have their definitive image down yet.

"At that point John was wearing spandex pants and David Bowie glitter
jackets," Tommy said. "But then he slowly went back to motorcycle jackets
after the glitter phase. I thought that black leather jackets looked the best,
but it wasn't something that was new, really."

Johnny recalled, "We'd still get dressed up to go out, to go see the New
York Dolls, but now we're starting a band—*now* what do we do? An image like that is fine for New York and L.A., but it's gonna be so limited. I
had on silver lamé pants and a leather jacket with leopard-print fur around
the collar. How you gonna get people coming to the shows like that? We
wanted every kid in Middle America to be able to identify. We realized we
gotta get uniformed: jeans, T-shirts, leather jackets, sneakers. Then there'd
be no problem with kids coming to the shows dressed like *us*. We defined
the image, and then we had to work out exactly what we were doing up
there.

"Some bands will come on and they'll start talking, they'll start tuning,
and I'm bored already. This is the most exciting moment of the concert so
you gotta make sure you go right into the song and not lose that excitement
before you even start. We had to have the guitars tuned up before we got up
there, so we held the stage from the minute we came on."

They would film their shows whenever possible and study them to figure out what they needed to do.

"We learned from that big-time," continued Johnny. "Joey's falling down
with this faggy Alice Cooper routine—horrible. Dee Dee's still playing with
his fingers. We watched the tape and made corrections. Dee Dee got a pick.
We told Joey, 'You look better standing, not falling down. Just don't let go
of the mike stand, stay glued to it.' That's how we thought Joey was going to

look his best and how the band would look its best. Everybody had to hold down their positions, keep it really symmetrical."

It took a while to figure out that doing what came naturally was the best way to go. The Ramones shed their spandex and reemerged in the uniform of suburbanites. Now they came off like regular guys from the boroughs instead of another bunch of celestial, untouchable rock stars.

We had our boys back; they were like one of us again. The Forest Hills outcasts could *really* get behind them now in full force. We proudly put up flyers and posters at Queensborough Community College, Queens College, NYU, Hunter, Hofstra—all over the neighborhood, and Manhattan, too. We were the beginning of the Ramones' future core following.

Usually, after the shows Johnny, Rosanna, Arlene, Alan Wolf, and I wound up stopping at the Jack in the Box back in Queens for tacos and milkshakes before splitting up. Exciting, eh? We were bored and had already done our worst—and we weren't teenagers anymore. There was nothing else to do. We were just waiting for something to happen. At the same time, although we didn't know it, something *was* happening.

ONE NIGHT, JOHNNY approached me at CB's to tell me that Danny Fields was getting close to getting the Ramones a record deal. They had an important show coming up out of town, and they really needed someone reliable to work with them full-time.

Johnny was very flattering while listing his criteria for the perfect roadie: someone smart, fast, agile, with a good ear for tuning guitars, who'd been in bands, knew what he was doing, and knew what this band was doing. He said they all wanted me to do it and assured me that when they got their record deal they would put me on a salary.

Somehow it was an offer I couldn't refuse. I'd broken my thumb playing basketball and couldn't play guitar myself at the time, anyway—but I *could* tune theirs.

I agreed. In the summer of 1975, I became the Ramones' sole official— yet untitled and unpaid—crew member. I did tell Johnny that I wanted to play again myself someday.

A week or so later, for the show in Waterbury, Connecticut, we put the guitars in the trunk of my Duster, and Johnny and I went to pick up Danny Fields and the rest of the band in the city. It was the Ramones' first road trip and their first time performing at a theater-size venue, opening up for the legendary Johnny Winter. Since they were a late addition, their name was never added to the billing on the marquee.

"When we were still trying to get a record contract," Tommy Ramone remembered, "Danny Fields was good friends with Steve Paul, who had the Blue Sky label, which had Johnny Winter. To audition us, Steve Paul had us open for Johnny Winter in Waterbury, Connecticut."

A band called Storm, a classical/rock/fusion hybrid comprised of former members of Yes, were the openers. We needed to set up quickly after they performed an hour of elitist, virtuosic sludge to the delight of the slightly out-of-touch audience—an audience the Ramones thought they could convert.

For some reason, the house crew and crew from the other bands seemed to have real contempt for us. I suppose they were just not happy about this extra band on the stage. They were really slow in giving me the space and power needed. By the time I had the stage set up for the Ramones, the crowd was restless and chanting for Johnny Winter. When the curtains opened and the Ramones were standing there, the crowd was, well, let's say surprised—in more ways than one.

"WE'RE THE RAMONES AND YOU'RE A LOUDMOUTH BABY!" my brother shouted. "TAKE IT, DEE DEE!"

"ONE-TWO-THREE-FOUR . . ."

The crowd gave it a minute, which was about one whole song. They thought there was a technical problem or something. But when the Ramones began their second song, and it was just like the first one, the kids in the audience realized this was indeed the show—and then they turned. The look on their faces is a priceless memory for me today, but that night it was pretty scary. Damn, it was only some guys playing music, but the crowd acted like they were stoning a bunch of murderous child molesters.

"When we came out and did Ramones songs," Tommy recalled, "they started throwing everything they could at us."

"Waterbury was a very nasty town," Dee Dee added. "Before we went on, this cop was in the dressing room. When he heard us warming up, he said, 'I really feel sorry for you guys.'

"We said, 'What do you mean?' He went on about us not making it off the stage alive.

"I started worrying a little," Dee Dee continued. "But I didn't know what to expect, 'cause I never seen a band get it worse than we did that night. We weren't even on the bill, so when all these lights went on, the audience didn't know who the hell we were. Everyone was standing up, cheering, just going crazy. As soon as we started playin', that crowd turned ugly. I never got so many bottles and firecrackers and so many people givin' me the finger."

There were even D-cell batteries going by that must have come out of the ushers' flashlights. In between attempts to clear the debris piling up on the stage, I took cover behind Johnny Winter's Marshall stacks until the band decided to call it a night.

"We got booed off the stage," Tommy explained.

The ride home was a mix of encouragement and depression. Danny Fields was encouraging; the band was depressed.

At the end of September, Johnny told me that I "had to be" at shows coming up in October at a place called Mother's on Twenty-third Street in Manhattan. At Danny Fields's instigation, the president of Sire Records, Seymour Stein, was coming to see the Ramones. Everything had to go smoothly.

"It was a snowy, snowy night," recalled Seymour's ex-wife, Linda Stein. "Seymour was supposed to see this band that Lisa Robinson and Danny Fields had raved about. But he had the worst flu. He stayed home and I went with Craig Leon from the office.

"Mother's was an old gay bar," said Linda, "full of elderly queens. In the back was this little room. I heard the Ramones playing '53rd and 3rd' and thought, 'Oh, God, this is amazing!'"

Thankfully, the show that the Sire people attended went very smoothly, except for Johnny breaking a guitar string and Dee Dee losing his place once or twice. Aside from that, the band maintained a blistering pace. The Sire people were certainly impressed.

Linda Stein raved to her husband about the show.

"On the way home, I could sing all the songs," Linda Stein laughed. "And each song was *a hook*, you know? I came back and said, 'Seymour, you have to see this band! *You have to see this band!*'"

"Linda Stein discovered the band," Danny Fields confirmed. "She and I set up an audition in a rehearsal studio so Seymour could see them."

Two or three days later, the Ramones auditioned for Seymour, with producer Craig Leon, Sire publicist Janice Schacht, Danny Fields, and Linda Stein also in the audience at the Performance Studio.

"Seymour was like a little kid," Joey Ramone remembered. "He was all excited. He was just knocked out, ya know? And that's when things started getting rolling. At the time, nobody had been signed in New York since the New York Dolls, and their failure was leavin' a black cloud on New York 'cause Mercury Records didn't push them enough."

"The bottom line," Danny Fields said, "is that Seymour Stein simply had great taste in rock & roll."

The word was starting to get out about CBGB. Now at a Ramones show, when you turned around after the band finished, there might actually be someone standing behind you. A whole crop of new bands was emerging. Kids were beginning to come in from Queens, Long Island, Brooklyn, and New Jersey, even as far away as Connecticut. It was a renaissance in a way, a revolution of sorts, but one without a slogan or a battle cry.

It might have faltered if it remained undefined. A couple of energetic, ambitious kids from Connecticut had the remedy for that. John Holmstrom, Legs McNeil, and Ged Dunn, three buddies from Cheshire, had come south to start a new magazine that would represent and reflect the activities and spirit of what was happening on the Bowery.

"I wanted *Punk* to be a rock & roll humor magazine," John Holmstrom explained. "Patti Smith and Television were the two most important bands in New York City in 1975 until we came on the scene and ruined everything for them. *Punk* magazine turned the whole scene upside down. We changed the agenda from poetry readings, quoting Rimbaud, long guitar solos, and beatnik outfits to punks, burgers, beer, leather jackets, and sneakers."

"When we went to CBGB's for that first time to see the Ramones, it was quite impressive," Legs remembered. "There were only around thirty-five people there that night. They counted off a song—and all started playing *different* songs. So they threw down their guitars in disgust and marched off. I'd never seen anything so authentic onstage. Then they came back a few minutes later and played the best set I'd ever seen."

John Holmstrom was bright and funny, a great cartoon illustrator with a style all his own. Legs, the writer, was a beer-guzzling, trash-talking, good-natured wiseguy. Friendly as your favorite class clown, he felt like a friend from the first time you met him. We all became instant pals. Legs and Joey struck up a fast friendship.

With all this positive activity, Joey finally seemed to be attaining genuine self-confidence, which was great to see. This was no fleeting occurrence that could be erased the next time some kids pointed at him and laughed.

Though Joey was still very shy, especially around Johnny and Tommy when we all hung out drinking beer and checking out the bands at CB's, my brother seemed like a new man. We could laugh and fuck around with each other like we hadn't in years. I didn't have to worry about him getting into fights with my mother over making messes; that was Arturo's problem now. The pressure was off of us as brothers—and we were having the best times we'd had together since we were little kids.

Joey and I didn't talk much about the Ramones; I was around all the time and knew pretty much everything that was going on. I actually talked to Johnny and Tommy about band stuff more than I did with Joey. Except for playing me some new songs to get an opinion, my brother talked to me more about other bands and other things—like what our old man would think of this whole scene.

Toward the end of October, Johnny Ramone called with the news about the Sire Records deal. He didn't sound very excited, but Johnny was never one to be overemotional—except when displaying anger. Johnny simply said, "We got the deal with Sire, you gotta quit that job."

I gave notice at the disco, quit school, and dedicated my life to the Ramones. They paid me $50 a week.

The band had a bunch of local shows booked for the rest of the year and would go into the studio in the beginning of February to record their first album. We got very serious then about what needed to be done to make the shows flawless. Everything had to be right for the record's release—and the tour to support it.

The first thing the Ramones needed was equipment. The $20,000 advance they got from Sire took care of that. Then we had to figure out a way to avoid any disruption of the momentum of the show. We needed two of everything to make that happen. We got two Fender Precision basses for Dee Dee. Johnny got a Fender Stratocaster for the ballad they would do in the middle of the set or if a string broke on the Mosrite.

I suggested we work out a spot in the set for the band to take their leather jackets off all at the same time, instead of stopping two or three separate times. We figured this should all be done within ten seconds, tops. I'd hold Johnny's guitar while he took off his jacket, which left me with maybe five seconds to dart across the stage to Dee Dee and grab Joey's and Tommy's leather on the way back. This also needed to happen earlier in the set rather than later, because as the crowds began to grow in size, the temperature increased onstage.

Hilly Kristal had sprung for some new stage lights and had even hired a lighting guy, Cosmo; but Johnny only wanted him to turn the lights on and off. He didn't want any "psychedelic" lighting effects. Johnny also wanted the lighting to be equally bright on all of them, meaning he didn't want the spotlight on the singer, as is usually the case. Plus they wanted to stand out from the other bands. They had Cosmo remove the colored gels from all the spotlights to have only bright white light on the stage. That heated things up, too.

The middle of the set was the designated spot for the "ballad," where we would do the guitar switch. I'd have to be 1,000 percent sure the guitar was in tune before I handed it back to Johnny or receive the evil eye. In 1975, there were no convenient little digital guitar tuners.

Previously, I'd run back to the dressing room—the bathroom or basement at CB's—to tune the guitars by ear. Then Johnny and Tommy came in one day with a gadget called a Strobotuner that looked like they'd stolen it from a submarine. It worked on an oscilloscope. Though it was a pain in the ass to operate, using it was much easier than running around the clubs trying to find a quiet spot. Now I could give the guitar back to Johnny completely tuned by the time the next song came up. We choreographed the switch so it would take just seconds. This was also the band's designated time to take a drink. Unlike most bands, their water bottles actually contained just water.

I taped extra guitar picks onto the bottom of their guitars. I taped up their guitar straps so they wouldn't fall off during songs. When the new Marshall guitar amps and Ampeg SVT bass amps came, we rigged them up so that I could instantly switch to the spare head if the main one went out. We had a spare snare drum and spare bass drum pedal for Tommy. He was getting a lot stronger and breaking the skins more frequently. We had plenty of spare guitar cables now, as those were usually the first things to break.

I taped my brother's microphone cable to the mike so he wouldn't break the connection when he handled it. Joey also had a habit of breaking the metal bases off the bottom of the mike stands. He'd bang it on the floor until the threads would give, and I'd crawl in front of him and attempt to screw it back on.

Some nights, if things started breaking down all at the same time, it was dizzying. When things went smoothly I could bop my head to the beat and at the same time be giving Johnny a reaffirming signal that everything was good. It was hard to tell if everything was good with Johnny, as his face was in a constant grimace. When I saw the scowl and he would motion with his head, I knew something was up and would spring into action.

We devised a routine for the beginning of the show. The stage would go dark after I finished setting it up, with the guitars tuned and plugged in, everything checked for power and ready to go. The guys would come on the dark stage while the music was still playing—I'd lead them onstage with a flashlight. My brother had his shades on, so I had to hold Joey's arm and guide him to his spot so he wouldn't trip.

Once they got up there, they didn't make a sound. When they were ready, I'd give the soundman a signal, and the music would stop. After my brother yelled his quick opening line, Dee Dee would almost cut him off with the count, "One-two-three-four," and *boom*—the white-hot lights would flash the instant they hit that first chord. The Ramones were on their way and didn't let up until it was all over.

It was so exhilarating when the show went so smoothly that there were no interruptions at all—just nonstop action. It was awesome, and I could see the excitement reflected on the faces in the audience.

The wheels were greased. Going into the studio, we were confident that the live show was now as tight as could be. We were ready to hit the road, to spread the sound, and to support the first Ramones album.

1 7.

LIKE COFFEE FOR JESUS

The Ramones took some time off from live shows in January to prepare for the recording of their first album at Plaza Sound, the recording studio above the legendary Radio City Music Hall. I went in a few days in advance to bring all the guitars and to set things up so that the band could get started as quickly as possible. They were paying the studio by the hour. The clock would be ticking and the meter running.

It was easy to get lost inside the cavernous music hall, but fun. Just getting up to the studio was an adventure—only certain elevators went all the way up. Getting off the wrong elevator on the wrong floor and seeing all the props and the Rockettes' costumes was awesome. This was right after the big Christmas show, and all the huge wooden soldiers, angels, and elves were still lying around all over the enormous backstage area. I wound up walking around on the catwalks, high above the stage. There was no one in the whole theater; it was so quiet up there that it was eerie.

On the first day of the recording session, Joey and I went down to get some coffee while the engineer, Rob Freeman, was getting the tape ready. We got lost coming back up to the studio and walked into a huge room where they kept Santa's sleigh and the Jolly Old Soul's red suit, boots, and beard. Joey and I turned a corner and saw the reindeer props, then walked down a hallway and into a dimly lit room where we found ourselves face-to-face with the son of God himself, leaning against the wall, looming larger than life. He was stiff as Styrofoam, but we swore he was looking right at us—forgivingly.

We left him a cup of coffee.

Craig Leon, the house producer at Sire Records, was coproducing the album with Tommy Ramone. Before they started rolling tape, they spent time getting sounds to their liking. Back then, most bands would spend a week doing that; the Ramones did it in a few hours. Tommy had me play the drums while he and Craig listened and adjusted levels and changed the placement of the microphones. Fortunately, I had a little knowledge of the drums from practicing on my brother's set in the house.

To speed things up, Johnny had me play his guitar so he could listen to it in the control room. Given that the hallway from the studio to the control room was a quarter mile long, this was faster than having him run back and forth.

Before they started doing takes, Johnny and Tommy had a dispute about how the songs should be tracked. Tommy wanted to double-track the guitars to thicken the sound, the method commonly used in the studio at the time. In fact, Tommy, who had worked at Electric Lady Studios, where Jimi Hendrix would layer dozens of guitar tracks together, thought it would be crazy to have no overdubs on the recording. Tommy believed it wouldn't hold up to the fidelity standards of the albums they would be competing with at the time.

Johnny wanted no overdubs at all. For one thing, it would admittedly take him who knows how long to play two tracks exactly the same. Besides, he wanted to transport the bare-bones, minimal sound of the live band onto the record.

Tommy argued that it would sound too thin. He said you couldn't record just one track each of guitar, bass, and drums on a studio album.

"I just wanted to fatten up 'Now I Wanna Sniff Some Glue' and some other songs, and double up the guitars," he said. "I did some overdubs on it, but Johnny didn't want to do it. He thought it slowed the song down, sludged it up. I thought it sludged it up but also fattened it up."

When Johnny called me into the fray, I brought up the fact that we all loved the Who's *Live at Leeds* album and that it sounded big and full even though there are no overdubs. Tommy pointed out that the Who's album was live—and hence had to have that live sound. Johnny said that was exactly what he wanted, and he didn't see any reason why they couldn't do it that way, too. The argument was over.

Thirty years after the album came out, I still believe Johnny made the right call. It set the standard for what became known as punk rock. If that album had been any more "produced," the trademark simplicity, the concept of punk—the idea that any kid could imagine picking up a guitar and doing it, too—would have gone out the window. That approach is what gave the album its charm and character—and *balls*.

By dinnertime on the second day of recording, Tommy, Dee Dee, and Johnny were already finished laying down all fourteen songs. We took a break to get some food. When we came back, Joey had already started on the vocals. But after he tried several different microphones and different techniques, Joey's voice was getting tired. He laid down some scratch vocals and they canned it for the night.

The next day Joey's voice was fresher and stronger; he hadn't been sitting around smoking all day. He had a little work to do under the scrutiny of the high-tech microphones: Sometimes he'd pop on the "P" and "T" sounds, and he had to learn to adjust his sibilance. The intensity of the recording situation seemed to magnify any bad notes. Joey had to adjust for that, too, which took more concentration. He also had to sing some new words.

Seymour Stein came up to the studio in the afternoon and complained, "You can't say, 'I'm a Nazi baby, I'm a Nazi, yes I am,'" referring to the opening lines of the song "Today Your Love, Tomorrow the World," which had become the Ramones' signature closer at live shows. It was kind of ridiculous, but not to Seymour. The words are:

I'm a Nazi baby; I'm a Nazi yes I am
I'm a Nazi shatzi, y'know I fight for the Fatherland.
Little German boy, being pushed around
Little German boy, in a German town

It didn't offend me, and *I'm* a Jew.
It didn't offend my brother.
Tommy, whose parents had narrowly escaped the death camps during

the Holocaust, was more sensitive to this issue but acquiesced so as not to impede the band's artistic freedom and black humor. To me, the song conjured up the image of a weak, skinny German kid, who, after being bullied in his own little burg, found a way to become one of the bullies. It was like a glimpse into the mind-set of a typical Hitler Youth member, brilliantly summed up in two lines.

Seymour was insistent that the band change the lyrics. The Ramones were sticking to their guns. A heated and emotional argument ensued; it looked as if this could be a deal-breaker.

Then they started talking about alternatives and came up with the line, *"I'm a shock trooper in a stupor, yes I am."*

Even that was too much for Seymour; to him, it was equally offensive.

But after a big struggle he finally gave in and allowed them to go with "shock trooper."

"I don't know if I should admit it," Seymour later confessed, "because I got over it pretty quickly, but I wasn't pleased with the Nazi references in the songs. You can't throw away twenty years of Jewish upbringing in Brooklyn."

"We got away with a lotta stuff then that we wouldn't have if we'd been big," said Johnny. "Dee Dee came up with '53rd and 3rd' on the first album. I thought it was funny: I didn't know it was anything from real experience. I thought we were just singing about warped subjects that no one else sang about. It doesn't mean that we had to be *doing* it."

Fifty-third Street and Third Avenue in Manhattan was the notorious spot where young male hustlers made themselves available.

"To Johnny's dying day," Danny Fields laughed, "Johnny would never admit to knowing that '53rd and 3rd' was about Dee Dee turning tricks!"

On the third day, Joey finished all his lead vocals. When they got to the background vocals, they ran into some problems that could have potentially slowed things up drastically. For those long "ooohs," Joey had to hold the notes steady for quite a while. He had done an amazing job on the lead vocals, especially for someone who'd started singing only a few years prior. His instincts, talent, style, and uniqueness carried him to a place in history that day. But he wasn't cutting it on the backgrounds, and his voice was getting burned out.

"We tried Joey and Dee Dee," producer Craig Leon remembered. "At that point, neither one could hold the long notes too well. We needed to find somebody to sing."

Tommy, Johnny, and Craig knew they had a problem on their hands and started looking around the room. Tommy tried first, but his voice didn't quite sound full enough behind my brother's. Then Craig Leon, Arturo Vega, and the engineers gave it a shot.

"All right, Mitchel," Johnny said to me, looking at his watch. "Why don't you go and try it?"

"Mitch was on a lot of the background vocals," Craig Leon remembered. "There weren't a lot of other options. I know that's him on 'Judy Is a Punk' and on 'Blitzkrieg Bop,' as well. As far as the rest of the songs, Mitch sang some stuff, and me and some of the engineers sang others."

I went out and sang one take of the "ooh"s in the bridge of 'Blitzkrieg Bop,' and it worked. It felt great. "Wow," I thought, "I'm actually going to be on this album!"

I was really excited, but the feeling was short-lived.

When I bounced back into the control room, Johnny seemed annoyed—like he was protecting his turf. Or maybe he was still holding a grudge about my quitting his band five years ago.

"When Johnny held a grudge," Tommy recounts, "he *really* held a grudge. It didn't matter if it took a lifetime—he'd get back at you."

Begrudgingly, in order to keep things moving, he told me to go back out there. I sang a harmony to the first part I'd done to finish the backgrounds on "Blitzkrieg Bop." Then Tommy had me sing the "ooh" following Joey's "you" on "I Don't Wanna Walk Around with You" and the long "ooh" in the middle of "Judy Is a Punk."

It sounded good, because it was close enough to my brother but just a little different—it blended right in.

Tommy came out with me to double up the "ooh la la" harmonies for the bridge of "Chain Saw." Then I did the "oooh" in the middle of "I Wanna Be Your Boyfriend." The engineer, Rob Freeman, sang the refrain at the end of "Boyfriend." And that was it. I did all my parts on the first take, so the whole thing took about an hour.

Back in the control room, my brother said, "Wow, that was really good. You saved the day."

I said, "Thanks a lot, just remember me when the album comes out."

Dee Dee said I should change my name for the credits on the album cover. I liked the name Mickey, like former Yankee great Mickey Mantle, and Lee is my middle name. Dee Dee said, "Yeah, Mickey Lee, that's a really good name."

I later changed the spelling so as to not get lumped in with already well-known Lees such as Ten Years After's Alvin, blues great Albert, Peggy, Sara, or Bruce Lee.

Craig Leon went out and played the studio's huge pipe organ on "Let's Dance." Me, Tommy, Arturo, and even Danny Fields went out to do hand claps on a few songs. After that, Craig Leon and I worked out the "bomb" sound effect for "Havana Affair."

I stroked the side of a guiro (a grated Latin percussion instrument) for the sound of the fuse, and Craig whacked a huge bass drum with a tympani mallet for the bomb — *tsssss BOOM!*

And then it was done. I was glad I could help and thrilled that my name would be mentioned on a major album.

Tommy, Craig, and Rob immediately began setting up for the mixing. To Johnny, more time in the studio meant less money for other expenses, so he wanted to get the album done as quickly as possible. I had sky-high hopes for the album and the band. Within sixty hours of beginning the recording session, I began putting the guitars away, wrapping the cables, and getting ready to load everything.

"We did the album in a week and only spent $6,400 making it," Joey said. "Everybody was amazed. At that time, people didn't have that much regard for money. There was a lotta money circulating. Some albums were costing $500,000 to make and taking two or three years to record, like Fleetwood Mac and Boston. Doing an album in a week and bringing it in for $6,400 was unheard of, especially since it was an album that really changed the world."

The day after they finished mixing the album, we hit the road for the first advertised dates out of town.

Johnny, Joey, Dee Dee, Tommy, Danny Fields, and I piled into a van I rented on Queens Boulevard and headed up to a high school in Nashua, New Hampshire, where the Ramones would open up for a popular local cover band. These guys wore makeup, dressed in tight rock star clothes, and played Aerosmith and Boston covers. The big gymnasium was packed with little girls.

The next night the Ramones headlined their own show in Boston. It went relatively well. It wasn't very crowded, but there was a lot of interest from Boston's independent press. The press and audience alike displayed a definite curiosity as they watched the band — in other words, they were baffled.

The next night, the Ramones opened for the cover band again in Brockton, Massachusetts. The cover band's fans couldn't have been less interested in the Ramones. After that, Johnny swore they wouldn't open up for *anyone* anymore.

Danny booked as many shows as he could around the tristate area. There weren't a hell of a lot of places for bands like the Ramones to play. My Father's Place in Roslyn was the only club that welcomed original music in Long Island; the Ramones and the Heartbreakers broke ground there in March. Max's Kansas City, of course, was their home away from CBGB in Manhattan. There were a few adventurous clubs in New Jersey that booked the Ramones and Blondie for a few shows. Then we went back up to Boston for a three-night stint and made a few trips up to Connecticut.

Traveling was difficult. Most of the time, it was just Danny Fields, me, and the members of the band. We'd get two rooms in the hotel, three of us in each. They couldn't afford any more help at that point, so the band had to pitch in unloading the equipment. I'd play the drums during sound checks, while Tommy went out to the board and mixed the sound—and instructed the soundman not to fuck with the settings. We would enlist the aid of any fans willing to help us load out at the end of the night.

I was roadie, road manager, stage manager, driver, security, and whatever else the situation called for. Arturo Vega would come when possible but still had to keep his job as a busboy, as the band couldn't pay him. Tommy's old friend Monte Melnick came on one or two trips to do the sound. Otherwise, I had to do it all; I got a 20 percent raise to $60 a week.

At the time, none of us realized the importance of what we were doing. If we had, it never would have happened. The friendships between many of us continued to thrive and solidify. In Legs McNeil, Joey had a friend *and* a fan.

"I loved the Ramones. Joey loved *Punk* magazine. It was that simple," Legs remembered. "Joey's normal pose was like a question mark, with his tall body wrapped around itself, his back slightly hunched over, his arms crossed, his fingers constantly playing with his hair. But onstage, Joey was an exclamation point—which made him absolutely commanding. When he stood at the microphone, you couldn't help but look *right* at him. And when he opened his mouth and you heard that voice, he became the leader of the Ramones.

"There weren't too many girls that wanted either Joey or me in the early days," Legs confessed. "When we'd try to pick up girls, we usually wound up at Arturo's loft watching *Mary Tyler Moore* until the station signed off for the night.

"We both felt like we were helping create something new and different. In 1976, there wasn't much that was cool, except for Fonzie on *Happy Days* and old black-and-white monster movies. Our whole lives were about redefining what *cool* was. It was pretty serious business, because we were all defining the future."

The first Ramones album was a huge factor in that defining.

"The Ramones' original idea was to make their record cover look like *Meet the Beatles*," John Holmstrom recalled. "But it came out horribly, so they were desperate for any alternative they could find. They asked for photographer Roberta Bayley's pictures from the *Punk* magazine photo shoot.

"The Ramones were uneasy about using Roberta initially," said Holmstrom. "I reassured them that Legs and I would be there to direct the shoot, so what could go wrong? Well, a lot did. Getting the Ramones to pose was like pulling teeth. They complained about everything. We managed to get a few group shots against a brick wall."

"The hard part was getting the Ramones in a symmetrical line," Legs remembers. "Though they looked like they were the same height, if you look on the album cover you can see Tommy standing on his tiptoes and Joey hunched over a bit, to give that impression."

"The photo that ultimately became the album cover image was just one of those perfect moments when everything came together," Roberta Bayley said. "The frame before it and the frame after it aren't that great, but for that one moment everyone looked right—exactly like the Ramones. Then when I was changing film, Dee Dee stepped in dog shit."

"If you look at the contact sheet," Legs said, "you see Dee Dee trying to wipe the dog shit off his sneaker with a stick. Then he chases everyone with the dog-shit stick, and the photo session is over."

Roberta's photo became the classic Ramones album cover. And the image of a band in ripped blue jeans and motorcycle jackets lined up in front of a brick wall became one of the most copied of all time: Even Alvin and the Chipmunks used it on their *Chipmunk Punk* album.

We were at Johnny's apartment in Forest Hills when the Ramones' first album came out. We were all excited. Johnny cracked open the box of albums he'd just received and handed one to each of us. It looked great: black-and-white, pure and simple, and totally cool. Johnny even broke out some beers for the occasion. Then he put the album on the turntable, and we listened almost in disbelief and reveled in the moment, quite amazed at this remarkable event. We listened to the album several times and looked at the cover. I heard the vocal parts I did on the record, and it made me feel great. It also made me remember that my name was on there somewhere, but I couldn't find it.

I said to Johnny, "What happened? You know, I thought I was getting a mention."

Johnny said, "Well, we didn't want people to get confused with who's in the band or who's not."

"It was just supposed to say 'Background' or 'Additional vocals,' right?" I said to Johnny. "Not that I'm in the band or anything."

He said, "It's our first album, you know, and we didn't want people to get confused."

Of course I was upset and disappointed, but it sort of made sense. What could I do? It was a done deal. I just had to accept it and move on. We all had our disappointments. We were all swallowing our pride.

"I wrote a song called 'Swallow My Pride,'" Joey recalled. "It was about signing with Sire. Tommy always used the expression 'You gotta swallow your pride,' and we did when we signed to Sire."

"Sire Records was a small independent label," Joey claimed, "that had other companies distribute them, like ABC. And they sucked. We'd fly into some city where we were gonna play, and there'd be nobody there to meet us at the airport or nothin'. And we thought we had a lot of songs that shoulda been hits, but that didn't happen, so you swallowed your pride."

Johnny Ramone had to start swallowing a bit of *his* pride, as well. He wasn't too thrilled that John Holmstrom ultimately opted to put only Joey on the cover of *Punk* magazine. Johnny thought it was going to be the whole band. At that point a little tension, or competition, might have started to brew between Johnny and Joey.

"As soon as the third issue of *Punk* came out," John Holmstrom said, "we started getting distributed in England. The one with Joey on the cover was our first issue sold over there. I really think this helped the Ramones with the rabid following they had in England. The third issue sold so well that they wanted more and more of every issue."

There was a slight difference of opinion between the Ramones and the guys at *Punk* magazine as to *who* was driving sales of *what*. Johnny scoffed at the idea that this fledgling magazine was contributing to the popularity of his band. He was well aware of the importance of press but was more of the opinion that *Punk* magazine, among others, was enjoying the residual effects of the band's groundbreaking success, not the other way around.

After having studied music history in school, I tend to think that Johnny Ramone was more on target—that music precedes not only magazines but even the written word itself by several centuries, if not millennia. Art comes before articles. One thing was for sure: All of a sudden, Joey was getting a lot more of the attention. He was even starting to speak up for himself. I was really proud of him. I didn't mind being his roadie at all. I didn't mind the job, either.

Traditionally, as the roadie I was supposed to be the guy you order around and abuse, but they couldn't do that to me. Johnny was still very capable of getting nasty, but it was sort of understandable with the enormous pressures involved.

I liked the pressure. As the only stage worker, I was solely responsible for whatever happened during their shows. And when a band known for starting and stopping repeatedly during performances started to get a reputation for doing slam-bang, nonstop barrages of songs, I knew I had done my part—and more.

One day before a sound check at CBGB, Johnny and Tommy got into another ugly dispute. Tommy thought they were beginning to play the songs too fast and were running the risk of losing the groove. Johnny totally disagreed and wanted to keep playing them faster and faster. They were arguing fiercely as I passed between them, bringing equipment into CB's. Johnny stopped me and asked what I thought about the matter.

"Mitchel! Are we playing the songs too fast?" Johnny asked me.

"*I* don't think so. Not yet, anyway," I told him, and started toward the stage.

Johnny stopped me. "So? Is it better faster?" he continued.

"Well, there's this thing I learned in music theory called accelerando," I offered.

"Yeah, great, Mitchel. Big word," Johnny responded. "So what does that mean?"

"It's a device used in music composition," I explained, "when if you want something to be more exciting, you speed it up."

"Right! Exactly. Well, I want to be as exciting as we can be," Johnny said, ending that argument.

Aside from being a consultant when Johnny and Tommy were having disputes, and singing on the first album, I also got to pitch in with a few lines and ideas here and there.

One day I was in Tommy's loft packing the amplifiers into the new road cases while the band was writing songs for their second album. The four of them were huddled, adding words and melody to chords Johnny had come up with. The song was called "Suzy Is a Headbanger." It went: *"Ooh-whee! Do it one more time for me . . . Can't stop that girl / There she goes again / I really really love to watch her / Watch her headbangin'."*

Then they got to the bridge: *"Suzy is a headbanger . . ."* And they got stuck. I figured something associated with the movie *Nightmare Alley* would appeal to everyone, so I threw out the line "Her brother is a geek."

Johnny laughed, my brother shot me a little look, and they changed the "brother" to "mother" for some reason. But the line stuck.

When we went to Cleveland for the first time, the show got canceled and we had the night off. We looked in the newspaper and saw that the movie *Freaks* was playing downtown. Band and crew—which now included Monte Melnick—piled into the van and went to see it. We were just fascinated by dementia of all varieties. It helped us deal with our own, I suppose.

When the wedding scene came on where the midget groom does a dance on the banquet table and sings, "Gooble gobble, we accept you, one of us," to his bride, we all started cracking up. I suggested to Johnny that they should make a song out of it—an audience participation song. He liked the idea. Ultimately it developed into the punk rock classic "Pinhead."

The song ended with the repeated chant "Gabba gabba hey." I'd run out with a big sign bearing those words and pass it off to my brother, who'd hold it up to the people in the crowd, urging them to join in. They did. It became one of the highlights of Ramones shows.

The night after we saw *Freaks* in Cleveland, we drove to Youngstown to play at the Agora Theatre, a large venue that was about two-thirds empty. We were welcomed by a greasy-looking bunch of guys in a band called the Dead Boys. They were obviously big fans already. They were certainly friendly and made us feel very welcome there, which was more than the promoters of the show did. They were pissed that the show was a bust and gave Danny a hard time about getting paid.

Danny offered me the official title of "road manager" if I would go and collect the money for the band. I had already been doing the job anyway, he reasoned. I turned it down. I didn't want to make a career out of working for the Ramones. For now, I had enough responsibility for $60 a week. The thought of having to snap to even more of Johnny's brusquely barked orders and field Dee Dee's drug-fueled requests was scary. I preferred we remain friends.

He then offered Monte the opportunity. Monte accepted and successfully collected the money. Monte was better suited for the job; he had a better temperament to deal with all the complaints that lay ahead as the band got to be more famous and more demanding.

Not that my brother was complaining; things with him were better than ever. Joey was totally appreciative of what I was doing.

As we headed back to the highway after the show Joey nudged me with his elbow and pointed out the window of the van. "Look at that," he said.

The guys in the Dead Boys were in their car, leading us back to the highway. Going about fifty miles an hour, their singer Stiv Bators had climbed onto the roof of the car, pulled down his pants, and was mooning us all the way to the toll booth.

Joey and I cracked up laughing.

He and I had a great relationship now. It was the kind of friendship I'd always wanted us to have.

18.

WILL THE KIDS BE ALRIGHT?

As Joey's status and confidence grew, so did his appeal to women. Joey now had a girlfriend even Johnny couldn't call a retard. Pam Brown was Joey's first girlfriend who wasn't from the "nuthouse" and wasn't on medication. She was intelligent, pretty, lean and sexy, and very tall. Standing more than six feet high with a thick mane of wavy black hair, Pam bore an eerie resemblance to Joey, especially from behind.

Pam saw the Ramones perform at CBGB and decided he was for her. "I fell madly in love with Joey," Pam said. "I packed my bags and moved right in with him in Arturo's loft. I don't think Arturo was too happy about it at first, but soon he really liked me. I cleaned up Joey's old cereal and everything."

Pam and Joey looked so much alike that their relationship struck me as nearly incestuous.

But as much as I liked her, something didn't seem quite right. She was such a contrast to Joey in many ways. She seemed so together and very sure of herself, while Joey still hadn't found himself. He would slip into speaking in a feigned English accent, evoking his idols in *Help!* and *A Hard Day's Night*—like we did when we were kids pretending to be rock & roll stars.

He was happy as a kid on Christmas but living in a bit of a dreamworld. He hadn't fully realized that his dream was actually becoming reality—that it was really *him* people were interested in now.

At this point, Dee Dee and Joey were still coasting on a craft skippered by Johnny and Tommy, with the social, political, and musical atmosphere adding wind to their sails. Everything seemed to be falling into place. Joey was just enjoying all the positive attention, and I was thrilled to see it. Pam's affection seemed to be part of the natural flow. It did seem a little odd that she moved in so quickly, but everything was happening quickly. And it was all good—it was all fun.

Except for several occasions in Arturo's loft, where Dee Dee's new girl-friend, Connie, had moved in with him. They fought violently.

"Joey and I would be in bed every night, with the covers over our head, hoping nothing would hit us," recalled Pam. "Connie and I would go into CBGB's to get a beer, and she'd rip off the pocketbooks of punk girls. Connie was really nuts. She was hooking. I did it once, too, when I was really broke.

"I thought the Ramones were going to rule the world. Instead we were sitting around eating cream cheese and tomato sandwiches. Every now and then Joey would get some money, from steamrolling his mother or something.

"One night I was walking back to Arturo's loft by myself, from Club 82, at four in the morning, and I was drunk. This guy in a Cadillac pulls up next to me and he says, 'I'll give you fifty dollars for a blow job.'

"I said, 'Okay.' I was just drunk enough to do it," Pam admitted. "The guy called me afterward, and then every few weeks or so. But I didn't tell Joey. I kept it to myself."

Pam kept several other things to herself, as well.

"Rock journalist Lester Bangs was my idol. I had an affair with Lester when I was living with Joey," Pam confessed. "Lester was still living in Detroit when he was editor of *Creem*, and he started giving me work. I wrote the first Ramones article for the magazine. I was sleeping with the enemy!"

Despite these goings-on, everything *seemed* fine between Pam and Joey—until the *Creem* magazine article came out in December 1976. The title was "Baby-Sitting with the Ramones: Will the Kids Be Alright?"

When Joey read the article, he was less than pleased, especially with the line "Walking down the street with Joey Ramone is like having a pet giraffe and taking it to the newsstand with you to buy the latest copy of *Zoo World*."

Of course, Pam had no way of knowing that Joey was called "Geoffrey Giraffe" as a kid. Still, the article was too personal for Joey, exposing his private life and his secrets.

Pam wrote, "He's taller than anybody and weighs less than anyone at the same time. He always smiles and never lies, but makes up great stories about people getting hit by buses, girls turning into vegetables, and giant cockroaches breaking through walls. Joey sleeps in his leather jacket. He has a plastic bug zoo. Once he made me and Dee Dee catch a huge water-bug for him and he fed it bread until it died a few days later, then he kept it anyway."

Joey felt Pam made him sound like a freak, that she'd used him.

Pam went on to write, "Joey is nowhere around. He's up in a dingy at-tic somewhere with a shitty old record player, hundreds of scratched LPs strewn in a mess at his feet. He's playing song after song like some demented reclusive disc jockey, just listening and thinking.

"He hasn't showered or changed his clothes for days. Half-eaten bowls of cornflakes and old cups of coffee turn sour on the windowsill. Joey notices nothing."

The things she was talking about were part of his sickness. Pam hit a raw nerve.

I'd been concerned about how some of his peculiarities might get por-trayed. Even as an adult, I was protective of my big brother. But this was different than when I tried to help him fight off Jarod and the kids picking on him in high school. It was even part of my job now, as a roadie *and* as a brother.

Pam's article came out of left field for Joey. He wasn't ready for his per-sonal life to be scrutinized in that fashion. It was a first, out of a shitload more to come.

"I got the idea from the way Pam talked about Joey that their relation-ship was not a romantic one," recalled Scott Kempner, guitarist for the Dic-tators. "Pam cared about Joey, but his problems made it impossible for her to have a full-on romantic relationship with him. I never saw any signs of them actually interacting as boyfriend and girlfriend."

I came up to Arturo's loft one day and all signs of Pam were gone. When I asked my brother where she was, Joey simply said, "She's gone."

Pam had moved in with Scott Kempner in the Bronx.

Joey seemed neither disturbed nor undisturbed about it; he just never mentioned her name again. For Joey, it might have been about denial. On some level, I think my brother knew she was fucking everybody. But it was the *Creem* article that really disturbed him. He never forgave Pam for revealing so much about him. In some ways I think Joey also realized that Pam was more than he'd bargained for. I was happy she moved on to Scott Kempner before my brother got really hurt.

But there was no time to dwell on Pam's departure. Things were happening so fast. The Ramones were booked for the Fourth of July weekend in London, England, and we'd be leaving very soon.

"Linda Stein, Seymour Stein's wife, my partner in managing the Ramones, was very internationally minded," Danny Fields explained. "She was hypnotized, and rightly so, by the lucrative possibilities open to the Ramones in the European market. From the very beginning, she sensed that we were likely to find an easier niche in the United Kingdom. We tried to get to England, especially as it seemed less and less likely that we could move beyond New Jersey.

"Our first show in England was July 4, 1976, the weekend of the Bicentennial, which I thought was metaphorically appropriate," Danny laughed. "On the two hundredth anniversary of our freedom, we were bringing Great Britain a gift that was forever going to disrupt their sensibilities."

Since Monte Melnick had not yet assumed the tasks of road manager, they were still my responsibility. The band had opted to not take Monte or Arturo Vega to England with us on this trip. I prepared a rider, identifying all the equipment we would be bringing through customs and arranged transportation to the airport for the band. We only took four guitars and some accessories with us, so it wasn't too much of a struggle. Danny Fields helped me lug everything through customs and keep tabs on Dee Dee's whereabouts so he wouldn't get lost in the terminal and miss the plane.

We arrived in London early the morning of July 3 and went directly to the hotel to try to rest, but no one could sleep. Joey, Tommy, Johnny, Dee Dee, Danny, and I met up in the lobby and decided to walk around the streets of London. Seymour and Linda Stein had an apartment there, and somehow we wound up near it.

Danny Fields thought it would be fun to pay them a visit. We entered the building through an unlocked door and barged in on the couple, still in bed, asleep.

It was definitely awkward talking to Linda and Seymour while they were lying there naked. We kept the visit short. As we wandered the streets, we marveled that people still had milk delivered to their doors and helped ourselves to a few bottles.

We didn't go out that night, as the show was the next day. In the hotel lobby, we met up with some of the guys from the Flamin' Groovies, the band that would be headlining the shows the next two nights. In the hotel bar I wound up talking to their manager, Greg Shaw, who was with his beautiful blond girlfriend, Sable Starr. Greg was also the founder of the well-respected garage-pop "indie" record label Bomp, which would soon become legendary in its genre.

So would Sable Starr.

We liked the Flamin' Groovies. It was no insult opening up for them. Their song "Shake Some Action," a Beatles-esque pop tune that played routinely on CBGB's jukebox, was a favorite of everyone in the band.

The first show would be at a place called the Roundhouse, an actual obsolete railroad car "roundabout." Everybody was a little nervous in the car as we drove through London on our way to the sound check, because we were off our turf for the first time and didn't know what to expect.

When Danny took the band to the dressing room to meet the press, things warmed up after a somewhat surreal arrival. No one seemed to want to acknowledge that they knew the band. I brought the guitars to the dressing room and listened in as the British press attempted to intimidate the "Yankee punks," trying to ruffle their feathers, albeit good-naturedly. Then it became apparent that they liked the Ramones' album but wanted answers.

I waited for the Flamin' Groovies to finish their sound check, then went to look over the stage and get things ready.

As I stepped on the stage I was welcomed to the Roundhouse by the house DJ, Andy Dunkley, "the Human Jukebox." He was very friendly and reassuring.

"Don't worry about anything," he said. "You're going to have a great show, mate. Everybody is *so* anxious to see the Ramones. They just don't act all star stricken, and they put up a bit of a front. Don't let those stiff-upper-lip bastards throw ya. That's just our style."

It was still a little scary; I had no help at all on the stage. We didn't have our own equipment or soundman. There was confusion as Tommy took off to the soundboard and I stepped up to play the drums. Photographers started snapping pictures, and Johnny started getting weird. We were playing "Beat on the Brat," and for some unfathomable reason, Johnny started yelling at me.

Then he decided to do "Judy Is a Punk," which he knew was too fast for me. Halfway through the song I started floundering on the fast high hat beats as my right arm grew leaden. Now it was clear that I was not the drummer, which I suppose was the whole point. As I stumbled and crumbled in front of the entire British music press and a curious crowd of onlookers, Johnny laughed.

"Ha, ha, can't handle it, huh, Mitchel?" he said loudly enough.

Johnny still got his kicks that way.

"Well, I'm not a drummer, John," I said, offering him the drumsticks, "I'm a guitar player. Let's see *you* do what I just did. Wanna switch?"

The crowd laughed at the roadie barking back at the rock star. They seemed to like it. This was what they were expecting—punk rock!

"Tommy, get back up here," Johnny yelled toward the sound booth.

After the sound check the band went back to the hotel, and I went to Seymour Stein's house to pick up the box of promotional baseball bats Sire had made up to give away for promotional purposes, miniature Louisville Sluggers that said, "It's a Hit, on Sire Records!"

When we went back to the Roundhouse to do the show there was a huge crowd outside. Inside, the place was packed. London was in the midst of one the nastiest heat waves in memory, and everyone was already drenched in sweat. A lot of guys were shirtless—and so were the girls.

It was incredibly exciting. There was a tremendous buzz and energy in the room. It appeared that everyone had heard the first Ramones album, or were at least certainly aware of it. There was a sense of rivalry with a new band called the Sex Pistols, the British equivalent of the Ramones. Some kids over there seemed protective of the Pistols, who in their opinion were the originators and provocateurs of this new "movement," not the Americans.

There was also a bit of friendly taunting, as this was July 4, 1976, the two hundredth anniversary of America's bloody battle to free itself from English rule. It was Independence Day for us, not them. Little did we know that together we were founding a new revolution—a musical one. We weren't aware that we were about to launch an entire cultural movement. No one was.

"Our album was an import in England for three months before we arrived there on July 4, 1976," Joey remembered. "Maybe we were drawing five hundred people at CBGB. But at the Roundhouse, we played a sold-out show for three thousand—and we drew all kinds. That was like the height of it. They called it the 'Summer of Hate' as opposed to the 'Summer of Love.' It was really weird, with all these punks hanging around with different hair colors."

For the most part, the fans didn't look anything like us. The fashion statement they were making was far more purposeful, outrageous, and rebellious than in New York City and seemed to hold as much importance for them as the music did. They wore torn-up sport jackets, S&M-styled trousers replete with buckles and straps, and a lot of plaid—very colorful and British-looking. They had black makeup under their eyes and safety pins sticking out all over the place. The intent was to be shocking.

The motorcycle jacket, T-shirt, and blue jeans is a classic and ever-revered American look that still clings to the connotation of toughness and biker gangs. But while the Hell's Angels were still sporting that look, so was Fonzie on Happy Days. The British punks' getups were more original and menacing than those of the American punks, but also more contrived.

They were all very conscious of what was going on in New York and seemed very competitive. They were taking the whole punk thing much more seriously than us, but I think we were having more fun with it. We thought they might be overcompensating a bit, as the scene there was so much more violent in spirit—more political and radical. It made what was going on in New York seem almost tame. In actuality, they were more appreciative of what "Yankee punk" and the Ramones were all about than the Yanks themselves.

"I remember like bein' treated real well," Joey recalled. "Like royalty, and I remember meeting Paul Getty and all these people. Everyone came out to see us. In the USA, there was nothing. It was a different story over in England."

After the show at the Roundhouse we all went back to the hotel and hung out in the lobby, except for Dee Dee, who went up to his room. Two people came by to meet him up there, and later that night, Dee Dee took off. He just disappeared.

He still hadn't returned to the hotel as we were getting in the car the next day to go to a club called Dingwalls. We were waiting in a big old black taxi as Johnny freaked out. He was really pissed. Johnny was like a military school drill instructor—everybody had to be straight and sober. Johnny wasn't going for what Dee Dee was doing—looking for dope.

Fortunately, they didn't put the responsibility of keeping track of Dee Dee on me. Danny Fields had that job.

Dee Dee's enthusiasm for getting high was becoming a predicament. There had been many occasions where Dee Dee would go blank in the middle of a song, lose his place, and stop playing. Fortunately, I knew the songs and fret board well enough to anticipate the notes and could run over and point out where Dee Dee should place his finger on the guitar neck.

Then something seemed to click, and he'd be okay. I could usually tell when it was going to happen, as Dee Dee's "stage face" would suddenly be replaced by a look of bewilderment. Then he'd lose it. It was a matter of concentration. Johnny and Tommy attributed it to drugs and were getting agitated; the last thing they wanted to do was give the hypercritical British press fodder for mockery.

The Ramones couldn't depend on Dee Dee to be where he was supposed to be. Johnny fumed when he heard that Dee Dee had ordered $700 worth of stuff from room service and was talking about getting rid of him.

I liked Dee Dee; he'd get pot and hash and share it with me. But Dee Dee would also get *really* fucked up. Just as we were about to head to the club to attempt a sound check without Dee Dee, he came running down the street and jumped in the taxi. Johnny threatened Dee Dee with the notion that he'd get Richard Hell to replace him. He was seriously trying to scare Dee Dee.

Of course, Dee Dee was apologetic and kept saying, "I'll be better, don't worry about me, I'll be good. I know I've fucked up. I'm going to make sure I'll be there."

Dingwalls was more like the CBGB of London. When we got to Dingwalls, the scene in front was even more overwhelming than at the Roundhouse. Out in sordid splendor, the mob was coming toward the taxi.

It was still scalding-hot outside. The half-naked horde looked almost tribal. They had war paint on their faces and spiked-up Day-Glo-colored hair, and they wore rags all safety-pinned together. They adorned themselves with oddly placed piercings and had rings and chains hanging from them. The tribe circled the cab and stood there, arms crossed.

It was like a scene out of *Lord of the Flies*. I expected to hear them start chanting, *"KILL THE BEAST! SPILL HIS BLOOD! BASH HIM IN!"*

We had to go down a long alley to get to the back entrance. Standing in the alley like a posse were kids trying to look real tough. They were doing their best to intimidate us, and they were succeeding. Because of their accents, we didn't know what the hell they were talking about when they went on about "No bollocks," "No wankers," and "We're winding you up."

We were all a little scared. Johnny, Dee Dee, Tommy, my brother, and I thought that we were going to get beat up.

"I was trying to figure out how to defend myself," Tommy recalled. "I took the spurs from my drums, those big metal things, and put them in my pocket, just for reassurance."

The kids formed a gauntlet down the alley. It was a confrontation of sorts, like the British invasion that had happened a decade earlier—except this time an American band was invading. The crowd came close to blocking our way. They would get up in our faces as we walked by, challenging us to look them in the eye. I stayed close to my brother, just in case, but had at least three guitars in my hands and arms. One guy stepped in Joey's path and asked him if he'd like a mouthful of hair.

I stepped over and asked him, "What flavor?"

The English punk laughed, shook his head, mumbled something, and stepped aside.

I had no idea what I was talking about, but we soon found out that that was exactly what we were supposed to do—act like we were not afraid of them. Then they would either respect you or give you a mouthful of hair (a head butt to your mouth).

We would later come to learn that a lot of it was just a stance. They were acting "punk." They were acting tough, because they figured that being from New York, we were real tough guys.

As we got near the door to the club two guys approached us, all hyped up.

It was Mick Jones and Joe Strummer, who said, "We're the Clash, man. And we're gonna be bigger than the Sex Pistols!"

Well, great. Go ahead. Do it!

Bands in New York weren't as competitive with each other. It was like a real war in the UK. Ultimately, in my opinion, the Clash did go on to become the big winners.

"It wasn't until we played Dingwalls," Joey admitted, "that we found out what was going on with these English punks. At the sound check all these kids came to watch, and talk to us, and tell us that it was 'Blitzkrieg Bop' that inspired a call to arms. That's what got them all starting their bands."

During the show the band wanted me to go to the mixing board at the back of the room periodically, to make sure everything sounded good. I was running back and forth—yelling at the soundman to turn up the guitars and the microphones over the high hats and cymbals—while the crowd kept bumping me playfully with their shoulders.

Then all of a sudden the entire audience began spitting on the band. Called "gobbing," the newly created ritual was meant to be a compliment, an expression of approval: They were showering the band with affection. We'd never seen anything like it. The mucous and saliva came sailing through the room toward the stage like sea-to-land missiles. The gob was hanging off the necks of the guitars before finally falling to the stage floor, which was slippery with the stuff. It flew off the cymbals as Tommy whacked them. It flung itself around Joey's mike stand. By the end of the set we were all covered in it, signifying a successful show.

Everything was different over there.

1 9.

"TODAY YOUR LOVE . . ."

While Joey was absolutely thrilled with the Ramones' reception in London over the Fourth of July weekend, Johnny Ramone remained a die-hard pragmatist.

"Who cares about London?" Johnny stated. "London doesn't matter. I'm not gonna live there, I'm just gonna go for a week once a year. The real world is America, you know? I'm not succeeding unless I make it in America."

We got off the plane from England and hit the ground running. Danny Fields had the Ramones booked practically every night for the rest of the year, and beyond. After a string of dates in Long Island, New Jersey, and Connecticut, the band did two nights, August 6 and 7, at Max's Kansas City, before commencing a mini-tour of the West Coast. It would be the first time the Ramones played Los Angeles.

The band would be flying to L.A., while Monte and I drove to L.A. in a rented U-Haul truck. We had a little more than three days to make a trip that usually takes five. The band hired another Forest Hills guy known as Big Al, for additional help on the tour. After the band's last set at Max's, Monte, Big Al, and I quickly packed up the truck, crammed ourselves into the crowded cabin, and began our nonstop traverse from the East Side of New York City to the other side of America.

By the end of the second day, we were comparing the experience to astronaut training. The heat in the middle of the Texan desert was becoming unbearable when, not surprisingly, the tired old truck broke down.

We'd lost precious time, so Monte had to fly to L.A. to start making preparations. Big Al and I loaded everything into the new truck the next day and headed out. Somewhere at the edge of Arizona, the "new" old truck gave out. They had me fly to L.A., too. I got to the Roxy Theater just as the Flamin' Groovies were finishing up their sound check and just in time to set up the equipment Monte had rented for the Ramones.

I walked into a wildly chaotic scene. There were far more than the usual number of crew and club workers milling about just for a sound check. It was as if these people just couldn't wait to see what they had been hearing, and hearing about. From the buzz in the room, I could tell that once the Ramones took the stage, Los Angeles would never be the same.

After the first show we all wound up hanging out with Ron and Scott Asheton of the Stooges at their apartment on Sunset Boulevard. They were really drunk and rowdy—throwing bottles out of their window onto Sunset, and pushing us to do it too. They thought it might make good press for the Ramones to get arrested while they were beginning their tour. And maybe it would have—but Johnny didn't want to take any chances. We exited the jam-packed apartment when the cops arrived.

We were staying at a fancy hotel near the Sunset Strip called the Sunset Marquis, at that time the preferred hotel of rock stars. Danny Fields thought it was important for the Ramones to be among them. But unlike most of the bands that stayed there, the Ramones were still sharing their rooms with the roadies.

Ariel Bender of Mott the Hoople was hanging out by the pool the next afternoon, spraying everyone with beer. Joey and I were soaking up some sun when all of a sudden, Johnny and Tommy got into another argument. It was a total power struggle this time, with Johnny flat out stating, *"This is my band, and I am the star of this band, not you! What are you gonna do about it?"*

"I wasn't looking to take over the band," Tommy said, remembering the poolside argument. "All I wanted was an acknowledgment of my contributions. I think Dee Dee and Johnny were worried that if I got a *little* power,

I would get too much power. At the time, the hierarchy of the band was Johnny, me, Dee Dee, and Joey—in that order. Dee Dee would pick every opportunity to brainwash Johnny against me, successfully. I was being manipulated by all three of 'em.

"When I was in the studio, I was in total charge," Tommy explained. "When we recorded, we would cut the tracks, do the vocals, and the rest of them would leave. I was there all by myself: the engineer, an assistant, and me. It was great. I was happiest in the studio. When I had to go on the road with them and deal with being a Ramone twenty-four hours a day, it really took its toll. I was so stressed out and so unhappy, without realizing it."

It was the first serious indication of such fragility regarding the band members' relationships with each other. Tommy suggested they drop the subject, and things went back to normal—as normal as the Ramones could be.

After the last show at the Roxy, we all went to a party at Sable Starr's house up in the Hollywood Hills. Sable had been the girlfriend of Iggy Pop and Johnny Thunders and, like many of her friends at the party, had hung out with a wide assortment of rock stars. This was the closest Joey and I had come to actual association with reputed "groupies."

Sable had a sister named Coral, the most beautiful, sexy creature I'd ever been close enough to touch. She asked me to lie down so she could place a Carbona-doused cloth over my face. I had totally refrained from sniffing glue but couldn't resist Coral's offer. A few whiffs of that really helped my confidence—diminish.

Joey and I were a bit intimidated by all the beauty, wealth, and power surrounding us.

"Havin' fun?" Joey asked me.

"Um, yeah, sort of. Whaddaya wanna do?" I asked my brother.

"I dunno," Joey said, a little uncomfortable, "play pinball? I don't know any of these people. I mean it's cool, but it's weird . . ."

Joey had turned down the offer from Coral. We wound up huddling in a corner drinking a few beers before giving ourselves a tour of Sable's house. Joey and I hung out together most of the time when we were out on the road.

The next night provided us another occasion to bond. We'd all gone to a club called the Rainbow, near the Whisky a Go Go on Sunset Boulevard. When we were ready to leave, I went to get the car and pulled up in front of the club to pick up Tommy, Joey, Arturo, and two girls we'd met. Just as I was pulling away, a cop car raced over with its lights and sirens blaring and signaled me to pull over.

Apparently, as the cops later told me, drivers were not allowed to stop their cars on Sunset Boulevard, not even to pick up a passenger. They made us all get out and put our hands up against the wall while they checked everyone's ID—except mine, as I'd left it at the hotel. They let Tommy and the girls go but handcuffed me, Joey, and Arturo. The cops shoved us in the squad car and took us to the Beverly Hills Police Station. The snappy-looking Beverly Hills cops jumped for joy in the station house when they went into the pocket of Joey's motorcycle jacket and pulled out a handful of pills.

"*Yeah! We got 'em!*" the cops proclaimed with glee. "*This wasn't very smart, now, was it?*"

"Ha ha!" Joey merrily informed them, "Those are vitamins!"

"*You idiots!*" we all added foolishly. "*You ain't got nothing!*"

Assuming they would have to release us, we continued to taunt them from our holding cell. They were still trying to figure out what to do with us. Eventually they decided they would charge Joey with drunkenness and make him stay the night. Since I had no ID on me, I was screwed. Supposedly they would release me when Monte brought in my license. Arturo had ID, but they made him stay until they checked him out for warrants. We were put in a big cell with a dozen assorted drunks, johns, junkies, and acid casualties.

"This is like being back on the Bowery," Joey observed.

"If they opened a bar here, this place could do really well," I replied.

After Arturo got out, Joey and I were left with a nut job preaching about penance and worlds colliding. At least we had some entertainment.

There's nothing like sharing a night in the pokey with your brother to bring you together. They let us out after morning grits.

When we got back to New York, Joey and I recovered a bit of confidence in ourselves. Hanging out at CB's with Legs, we met girls who made it easy—well, easier. Legs was adept at kicking off conversations with really good-looking women, something neither my brother nor I was comfortable with after years of rejection. CBGB was now filled with new faces and hordes of curiosity seekers.

Legs would say, "Who are those girls over there? Check them out!

"Hi. I'm Legs McNeil, from *Punk* magazine."

"*Funk* magazine? What's that?"

"No, not funk, *Pu*—never mind. You know who this is, right? This is Joey Ramone!"

"Oh. Hi. What band are you in?"

At least that would get things started.

"Joey and I started getting laid on a regular basis at the same time," Legs McNeil remembered. "What was great about it was that we had different tastes in women, so we never had any problems."

Outside of the city, it was a little different.

A frenzied string of tristate-area shows in September and early October concluded with the Talking Heads opening up for the Ramones at My Father's Place and Max's. At a show in Connecticut, a mini-riot broke out. The biker bar's clientele were so angered by the Ramones' musical response to their requests for "Free Bird" that they smashed the windows on our van and threatened to kill us all, including Big Al. It was a pretty good indication that we still had a ways to go.

In October, the band took some days off here and there to record their second album, *Leave Home*.

"The second album was the first time we worked with Tony Bongiovi," Joey remembered. "That's when we met Ed Stasium, the engineer on *Leave Home* and *Rocket to Russia*."

Later Tommy and Ed Stasium would become a production team.

"I'd never heard of the Ramones," Ed Stasium said. "Tony Bongiovi brought me in to engineer the record. Keep in mind I'd been listening to Pink Floyd, Supertramp, the Eagles, and Fleetwood Mac. So when I walked into Sun Dragon Studios and heard the Ramones, it was jaw-dropping.

"For about a minute," Ed admitted, "I didn't get it. But then I said, '*Holy shit, this is fantastic!*'

"At that time Tommy was calling the shots in the studio," Ed continued. "The band was all rehearsed. The basic tracks only took three days. We did a couple little overdubs, and Johnny doubled his guitar.

"Joey's voice was excellent," Ed elaborated. "He could double-track his voice at the drop of a hat. He sounded fantastic!"

THERE WERE SEVERAL shows booked sporadically in between the recording sessions. On October 16 the band did its first show in Detroit, and after the sound check they had me drive them out to the headquarters of

Creem magazine to do an interview in a creaky old house in the sticks. There we met the magazine's editor and a few of the other writers. When we entered, they were sitting in a dark room, and the place stunk of beer and garbage. One of the two guys sitting in the dark room introduced himself.

"I'm Lester Bangs," spoke the one with the larger silhouette. He had a slight tone of arrogance in his voice but offered a cordial welcome. "Thanks for coming all the way out here," Lester added. "Want a beer?"

"No, thanks," said Johnny. "We got a show soon, we can't stay long."

Lester began asking oddly pointed questions, not the typical ones like "Who were your influences?" and "What is your favorite food?"

It was almost as if Lester was testing the Ramones' intelligence and ethics.

"Do you consider the social implications of your lyrics before or *after* you record them? Do you think your first album was a failure? Do you care about how many records you sell?"

Even Tommy Ramone was stumped during this interview. It ended with Lester saying he very much liked the Ramones' first album and asking how it felt to be labeled "dumb" by the mainstream press. Lester's last question prompted the other *Creem* writers in the room to ask if the harsh reviews of the first album bothered the members of the band.

It's a trick question, because if you say no, you're lying, and if you say yes, you're a pussy for letting bad reviews bother you.

Tommy wasn't sure how to answer.

"One last question," Lester said as we got ready to leave. "What would you like to read in the press about your next album?"

I offered an answer:

" 'Ramones' Second Album Goes Gold,' " I said, paraphrasing an imaginary headline. Everyone laughed, even Johnny.

"Now that's an honest answer," Lester said as we walked out.

BACK IN NEW York City, I ran into Arlene in Forest Hills, who told me she had broken up with Alan Wolf. Arlene gave me some signals that she was interested. Initially, I resisted.

Arlene had sparked a friendship with a girl called Roxy, a.k.a. Cynthia Whitney, of the Chicago Whitneys, who had become Johnny's paramour. Though he was still married to Rosanna, he had become obsessed with this sexy, rebellious, hard-drinking thorn in the side of socialite parents—and vice versa.

"I moved out of my apartment in Queens and left my wife Rosanna for no good reason in August 1976," Johnny remembered. "I think it was after I came back from London. I was bored. Rosanna was fine, no complaints at all, but at that point I got attracted to Roxy, maybe 'cause she was really smart. But I didn't understand alcoholism."

Roxy started appearing at shows out of town. Johnny would pull her off to a corner backstage, scream at her, smack her a few times, and then start making out with her. Then they would leave. Roxy got her own hotel rooms, but John never seemed to stay in them.

On the band's first trip to Washington, DC, Roxy hooked up with Arlene, who had a car, and they drove down to DC to meet us.

Roxy came up to me after the show at the 9:30 Club, half-plastered.

"Arlene is over at the hotel," Roxy informed me, raising her eyebrows. "She's waiting for you . . ."

Though I went to visit Arlene that night, aside from smoking pot, we didn't do a thing. I was confused and a wuss. I wasn't sure if I really wanted anything to happen. Arlene and I had been hanging out a lot, but as friends. Arlene was beautiful and giving me every signal a woman could, short of unzipping my fly. I was as horny as could be but not looking to fall in love— or even have a girlfriend.

Joey was also striking up a new relationship with a friend of Arturo's named Robin Rothman. Something of a holdover from the hippie days, Robin was an aspiring poet, the total opposite of Arturo's typically ostentatious friends. The diminutive, plain-looking, shaggy-haired brunette grew up in Brooklyn but escaped the boroughs for her beloved Greenwich Village.

Robin was down-to-earth, to say the least, and so unglamorous I felt totally comfortable with her. Dressed in jeans, leather boots, a button-down velvet shirt, and a vest, wearing no makeup or jewelry and sporting a Bob Dylan–style haircut, Robin could be mistaken for a cute little fourteen-year-old boy—which is probably why Arturo liked her.

"I had no idea that Arturo was gay," Robin remembered. "He wasn't with a guy. He never told me. We just picked each other up at CBGB's one night. I had coke, and so did he. Then he invited me back to his loft and we had sex. The next morning this guy, Mark, wakes me up.

"Mark says, 'Who are you?'"

"I said, 'I'm Robin. Who are you?'"

"He motions toward Arturo and says, 'I'm his boyfriend.'"

"We all had breakfast together, me, Mark, and Arturo, and everything was fine," Robin laughed. "Then Arturo got sick with the flu, so I made him some homemade chicken soup and brought it over to the loft. I was feeding Arturo chicken soup and Joey walked through the door of the loft. There he was—this guy I'd been eyeing and was kind of curious about."

Joey connected with Robin on many levels. Robin and I also struck up a warm friendship. An unyielding nonconformist, she was much more the intellectual/political activist variety of hippie than the spaced-out Cheech and Chong type, although she did smoke plenty of pot.

Robin's political views were brazen and she was not ashamed to express them, given the opportunity. That bothered some people, like Johnny Ramone, but Joey and I respected her for it. Robin was a staunch feminist, but she never mislaid her appreciation of what humans of both genders have to offer, unlike the most hard-core feminists so desperate to condemn any living thing with testicles.

A devotee of Bob Dylan, Robin was not a huge Ramones fan, but she was trying to adjust to appreciate the humor of a band singing about beating up their girlfriends. Robin found herself adapting to a new breed of bohemian—the punk.

"The girls at CBGB's used to beat me up constantly," Robin said, "because I was Joey's girlfriend. After saving me from three or four fights outside the club, Merv, CB's bartender/bouncer, finally said to me, 'Robin, you've got to get yourself a fucking leather jacket, and stop wearing all that velvet!' I finally got a black leather jacket and became a punk."

Joey was also adapting to a new version of himself. And Robin handily bridged the punk/poet gap.

At the end of October, Sire Records gave the band a used van that one of their other acts had outgrown. To us, it was high luxury. It had couch-type seats on the sides and back, and a little table in the middle. It could accommodate band and crew well enough that we were no longer sitting in each other's laps. We got a trailer for the equipment.

We traveled to Johnson City, Tennessee, to open for Blue Öyster Cult in a big arena. Danny Fields said it would be good for exposure. BÖC were a Long Island band that had been floating around for most of the 1970s and now had a huge hit with "Don't Fear the Reaper."

The Ramones played to a typically mystified Southern crowd of metal-heads who were anxiously awaiting a customary rock show and some slick guitar playing. Blue Öyster Cult rewarded them with laser-light-shooting pistols, high production on long songs with extended solos, and conventional hard-rock choreography. That's what this crowd wanted.

The contrast between the stark minimalism of the Ramones' show and Blue Öyster Cult's mega-show was truly illuminating. You could almost see the future changing hands, the baton being passed. After the Ramones' set, Joey and I walked out into the crowd to look around and observe. "Don't Fear the Reaper" was a great song, but we smirked as we watched this old-school, circus-like rock show. The Ramones and the scene on the Bowery made this all seem surreal.

We had a great feeling about what would happen when the second Ramones album was finished and couldn't wait to hear it. Tony Bongiovi, Tommy, and Ed Stasium would finish mixing it in Montreal.

"One thing that struck me as odd when we were making that second record was that Tommy Ramone was always involved with the mixing, the production, with everything," Ed asserted. "Johnny Ramone never wanted to have anything to do with that. Johnny would just come in at the end and listen to what we had done."

A few weeks before Thanksgiving, I was hanging out with Arlene at CBGB when a girl I'd gone home with once started making her way down the bar in our direction. She was nice but really flaky.

"Uh-oh," I said to Arlene.

"What's up?" she asked.

"See that girl coming up behind me?" I warned her, "I was with her once, and now she won't leave me alone. She just doesn't get the message."

As the girl was about to tap me on the shoulder, Arlene and I spontaneously embraced and locked lips in a steaming kiss—and that was it.

That was all it took. Something clicked on, or off, or both. When I kissed her, every light in the place went out—except the one shining on her. Like it or not, I was in deep. I was a goner. I can still hear the Flamin' Groovies' "Shake Some Action" playing in the background.

At the end of November, the Ramones had a four-night booking at the Electric Ballroom in Atlanta, with Graham Parker and the Rumour. It was the first time any of us weren't home for Thanksgiving. Joey and I talked about going to dinner somewhere; we asked Monte and Tommy what they were going to do.

Johnny decided we should all have a Thanksgiving dinner together: It was an American tradition, and it would be unpatriotic if we didn't. In an unusual display of sentiment, Johnny added that it would also be good for morale, as we were all working toward a mutual goal. It established a slight sense of family among us old friends, like the kind a sports team or a troop of soldiers share. Actually, under Johnny's reign, this outfit was becoming not unlike some kind of military unit, but it was a troupe instead of a troop. Either way, we were all soldiers fighting a war on boredom, and we were making good ground until someone on the front line went down.

Unwittingly, Joey had been testing his health. Several times he had gotten very hoarse, partially because of all the singing and traveling, but mainly from partying and the packs of Winstons he was smoking. The fingertips on his cigarette hand were now a glowing golden brown. Joey was getting sore throats much too often. When it became apparent to him that he was jeopardizing his career and his dream, he quit—just like that. Cold turkey. It was an amazing display of willpower and discipline on the part of someone with an extreme obsessive disorder.

Something Joey couldn't control, though, was his immune system and the neurological blow his body had been withstanding since before he was born. Joey had stepped on something in Arturo's loft and developed another bad infection in his foot, the same one that got infected during his trip to San Francisco in the sixties. This time Joey wound up in the hospital on intravenous antibiotics and was laid up for several weeks.

"I wrote 'Sheena Is a Punk Rocker' the first time I was ever in the hospital," Joey remembered, "when they said I had osteomyelitis. I wrote it there in the hospital, in my head."

Our mom and our stepdad Phil Sapienza were overseeing the doctors, their diagnosis, and the hospital bills. I came to visit every day, usually with my new girlfriend, Arlene. Our father even came once or twice. It was very awkward as we tried to avoid each other. Arlene finally convinced us to talk and try to bury the hatchet.

Well, at least we talked. We forgot about the hatchets, and soon the old man and I were on good terms again.

The hospital room became like a daily party, with Legs and Holmstrom bringing up beer and cheeseburgers.

While things were on temporary hold for the Ramones, new sounds were abounding at CBGB and Max's Kansas City. I saw the B-52's make their CB's debut, and a band called Devo did their first show at Max's, to a crowd of about ten people. Every night offered something new.

Because of my low salary, I had to sell my Plymouth Duster. Taking the train home could sometimes take two hours at four a.m. Fortunately, all the CB's regulars came to know each other sooner or later, and Justin Strauss, from Long Island, would occasionally drop me off in Queens on his way home.

Justin was the singer in a pop band called Milk and Cookies. I'd noticed his girlfriend several times at CBGB and Max's, Linda Danielle. A typical Italian girl from Queens, she was shrewder than her accent let on. She was only seventeen years old but had already been hanging out at the clubs for years. Linda was not a groupie but was certainly not shy, and she relished the attention she got as a result of her close friendship with gossip columnist Janice, a.k.a. "Pressed Lips," who wrote for *Rock Scene* magazine.

Though Justin was at least nineteen, he looked like he was fourteen—a cute little guy. The girls loved him. Linda was a cute little thing, also. They made an adorable couple. They were nice enough to get off the Long Island Expressway at five a.m. to drop me off on Queens Boulevard. Over the years our paths would continue to cross.

2O.

" . . . TOMORROW, THE WORLD"

Joey got out of the hospital a week before Christmas, but the shows scheduled to coincide with the release of the Ramones' second album had to be canceled, as the doctors could not say for certain how long his foot would take to heal. In the meantime, we anxiously awaited copies of the album.

"In January 1977," Legs McNeil recalled, "about a month before the Ramones' second album, *Leave Home*, came out, Danny Fields held a private listening party for me and John Holmstrom at his loft on Twentieth Street. After we listened through it twice, Danny reappeared and asked us what our favorite song was and what should be the single. I blurted out, "Carbona Not Glue," which to me was clear'y the best song on the record. The song was written as a follow-up to 'Now I Wanna Sniff Some Glue.' It was meant to clarify that while glue might not be good for you, the cleaning fluid Carbona was definitely a better high.

"Danny said, 'I was afraid you were going to say that. Carbona is a registered trademark and we might have to take it off the album.'

"I was shocked," Legs recalled. "It was such a great song, so radio-friendly—like a song the Beatles or the Rolling Stones would have written if they were just starting out in 1976, with great harmonies and catchy lyrics."

"Carbona Not Glue" a "radio-friendly" song?

Though Legs's enthusiasm was totally sincere, his logic had betrayed him.

As much as I loved *Leave Home*, I didn't expect to see radio programmers adding a song about getting high by inhaling toxic cleaning products to their playlists anytime soon. Not with lyrics like *"Wondering what I'm doing tonight / I've been in the closet and I feel all right / Ran out of Carbona, Mom threw out the glue / Ran out of paint and roach spray too . . . And I'm not sorry for the things I do / My brain is stuck from shooting glue / Oooh, Carbona not glue."*

Call me silly or naïve, but I didn't see the Ramones' love/murder tune "You're Gonna Kill That Girl" pushing "You Light Up My Life" off the charts, either. It just wasn't realistic—not in those times.

Here is a sample of what was being played on the radio when the Ramones' *Leave Home* came out: "Looks Like We Made It" by Barry Manilow, "You Light Up My Life" by Debby Boone, "How Deep Is Your Love" by the Bee Gees, "I'm Your Boogie Man" by KC and the Sunshine Band, "Dancing Queen" by Abba, "Nobody Does It Better" by Carly Simon, "Don't It Make My Brown Eyes Blue" by Crystal Gayle, and "I'm in You" by Peter Frampton.

It was a sad time for rock & roll.

Of course, *Leave Home*'s "Gimme Gimme Shock Treatment" would've been the perfect radio follow-up to Napoleon XIV's "They're Coming to Take Me Away, Ha-Haaa!" in the 1960s. But things were different now; "Shock Treatment" wouldn't even get played as a novelty song.

But "Disco Duck" would.

"We thought we had a lotta songs that should've been hits," Joey continued. "If you grew up in the sixties, things would just get played and be hits right off the bat. So we thought since our music was doin' something unique that everyone would pick up on that. What really happened was we were so alien that no one wanted to touch us. And so we wouldn't get played. It was fucked up!"

America was tightening up after the looseness of the hippie generation. The sixties rebel yell of "We can change the world!" gave way to the seventies yuppie cry of "Can you change a $100 bill?" If the Ramones were really

looking to become the next Beatles and get accepted by radio programmers, they were going to have go back to the drawing board and rethink the
plan—maybe even change their image, like the Beatles had.

"There were always punks in rock & roll," Joey told an interviewer.
"You know, early Beatles, early Elvis, Gene Vincent—all these people were
punks. The Beatles were wearing black leather jackets when they were playing in Hamburg, Germany. Elvis would be wearing his motorcycle jacket
and riding his motorcycle if you go back to 'Jailhouse Rock.' It was always
like that."

But what Joey forgot to add was that they all changed their appearance
and image to become more marketable. Like the great athletes, boxers, or
military field generals, they knew what they had to do to win.

Johnny Ramone had his plan and a great competitive spirit, but he
didn't know how to win at this game. Selling the Ramones as a radio-friendly
band was a battle they were losing. But if they could hold it together, they
could still win the war.

"Most people didn't get the joke," Joey elaborated. "They thought we
were just real sick and violent. I remember writers being afraid to interview us 'cause they thought we were gonna kick the shit outta them. They
thought we were real nasty and violent and their lives were threatened. A
lot of the radio stations felt that, too. If only they would've given the songs
a chance and played 'em. It didn't make any sense. 'Punk rock' became a
dirty word. All along we were trying to do somethin' positive for music, to
make it exciting and fun again."

The Ramones had no intention of changing anything.

One of the first songs the band wrote was called "I Don't Wanna Be
Learned, I Don't Wanna Be Tamed," and those were also the lyrics, in their
entirety. It was the Ramones' ability to be simple that was the key. It's not
as easy as you think to have the audacity to choose to be more primal and
be proud of it. The Ramones were getting more popular by doing *less* then
everyone else. The main ingredients were there. They believed in what they
had, and so did a rising flock of fans who loved the band just the way they
were. Sooner or later, the rest of the world would catch on—if not today,
tomorrow.

Nassau Coliseum on Long Island is an eighteen-thousand-seat arena
where the New York Islanders hockey team plays. For years, we'd been going to see bands there. Now the Ramones would be one of those bands,
opening up for Blue Öyster Cult again, and for Patti Smith.

The Ramones were received well by the hometown crowd. A few came already knowing and liking the Ramones, but many more left as fans. At the time, it seemed like it was happening slowly. But looking back, it's clear that this bunch of guys who had hardly been playing at all just a few short years ago were making real headway.

After doing the opening set at Nassau Coliseum, we headed straight to CBGB for two sets. Then we went out to the West Coast to pick up where we left off, for a more far-reaching expedition this time.

The highlight of the tour, and possibly Joey Ramone's career, happened at its outset in L.A. with five sold-out nights at the famed Whisky a Go Go. As I brought the guitars into the dressing room after the first show, I noticed a man in a black cape talking to Joey. It was his idol, the legendary Phil Spector. It was obvious that there was a mutual admiration between them.

Phil zoomed in on Joey, who had to be in heaven as Phil showered him with praise. This was the most awesome thing I'd seen happen to my brother. This was *huge*. As I watched Phil bonding with Joey, I could feel waves of wariness floating over from the other side of the dressing room.

"Phil Spector was obsessed with Joey Ramone," Tommy Ramone remembered. "It was all about Joey.

"For some reason, Phil Spector liked tall guys," Tommy continued. "He had a picture of Wilt Chamberlain on his wall. Phil Spector treated Joey like a king. I didn't treat Joey like a king; I treated him like a coworker."

Phil wanted us all to come back to his house and spar with his bodyguards, especially the roadies, who in Phil's mind doubled as the Ramones' bodyguards. That was definitely weird, and creepy, and exactly what I'd expected from the notoriously eccentric prodigy.

When Phil and his guards left, Joey stood in the dressing room glowing. He couldn't get the smile off his face.

"What did you two talk about?" I asked excitedly.

"Well, ya know," Joey said, "I was trying to tell him what a big fan of his I am, but all Phil wanted to do was tell me what a great voice I have, and that I'm like one in a million and stuff like that."

"That's amazing, man!" I told him. "Holy shit, *THAT WAS PHIL SPECTOR!*"

"I know, I know, I can't believe it," Joey said. "He just kept saying how much he wants to work with me, and that he's just been waiting for this kind of talent.

"Funny, though," Joey continued. "He didn't say much about working with the band."

"Uh-oh," I said, and Joey and I cracked up laughing.

For Jeff Hyman, Phil Spector's approval was the kind of medicine no doctor on earth could provide.

We continued up the coast to the other major cities, and to any place Danny Fields could find a club to book the Ramones. With the Sex Pistols emerging in the UK and the U.S., word of this new weirdness called "punk rock" preceded the Ramones to some of these places, to good ends and bad.

"At the time, the Sex Pistols were tryin' to destroy punk rock," Joey recalled. "Punk rock just became negative and derogatory. So a lotta people wouldn't even bother to see that we were doin' something different."

In lumberjack areas such as Aberdeen, Washington, and roughneck towns like San Bernardino, California, the misunderstanding got pretty ugly. But for the most part it was tremendously encouraging to see these curious kids who'd been anxiously waiting for the Ramones to bless their burgs with some real excitement.

In San Francisco, Dee Dee overdosed on PCP and an assortment of pills, and narrowly avoided permanent brain damage.

"Somebody gave Dee Dee angel dust in San Francisco," Joey remembered. "It was real intense. Dee Dee was really freaking out."

Just when we thought it was safe to continue the tour, Dee Dee's girlfriend Connie showed up. Connie freaked out *everyone.* She was either drugged up or desperate, but *always* dangerous. Connie was infamous in New York City for being the girl who chopped off the thumb of the New York Dolls' bass player. Maybe Johnny was right about not bringing girls on the road.

Johnny instructed me to keep Connie out of the clubs before and after the shows—and during them, too. I was working the stage during the show while keeping an eye out for Connie, who might be lunging toward the stage with a meat cleaver.

We got back to New York toward the end of March and worked nonstop for a month, doing shows in places like Countryside, Illinois; Ann Arbor, Michigan; and Salisbury, Massachusetts. Everywhere we went there would be a sprinkling of loners in ragged T-shirts and tight "straight-legged" jeans, with DEATH TO DISCO buttons on their motorcycle jackets. Small contingents of punk rockers would come to shows and tell us how everyone in the town thought they were crazy for liking the Ramones.

There were curiosity seekers, as well, who wanted to see what this new phenomenon was all about. We would soon find out there was that much more curiosity and interest in Europe, too.

We were about to embark on a six-week tour of countries that included just about every major city west of Berlin. Sire Records had signed the Talking Heads and released their single "Love Goes to a Building on Fire." The Heads would be the opening act on the tour.

The Ramones, the Talking Heads, Danny Fields, Monte Melnick, Arturo, Mike the tour manager, and I shared a large tour bus. It wasn't a "rock tour" bus—more like a sightseeing bus. When the Heads' bass player, Tina Weymouth, played James Brown tapes two days in a row, Johnny began to squirm. No one else minded. We knew it was just a matter of time before Johnny erupted. There was a definite culture clash between them.

"The first indication to me that Johnny Ramone was weird was on that first European tour," said Chris Frantz, former drummer for the Talking Heads. "We flew to Switzerland and we went straight to the sound check. After that we went to a little café, and the services promoter ordered us a beautiful *caprese*—a really nice salad, with mozzarella cheese, tomato, and delicious, high-quality lettuce. Johnny said, *'What's this?! They call this lettuce?!'*

"Johnny was actually upset that the lettuce wasn't *iceberg* lettuce," Chris Frantz laughed. "That's when I knew this guy was really messed up."

Sire Records hired a sound and light company for both bands. Called Brit Row, the company sent a two-man crew out in a truck with the gear. Ian Ward and Frank Gallagher were seasoned veterans, with experience in just about every performance situation imaginable. And they were real funny characters with *real* English accents. They made life bearable for me and just about everyone on the tour. Overall, conditions were just bearable, the hotels slightly above hostel level; no phones, no TV, communal bath and toilet down the hall. Some of the venues in France were so ancient that the power would short out, leading to constant electricity and grounding problems. Joey was always getting shocks. David Byrne got a jolt from the microphone in Lyon that knocked him to the floor for a good ten minutes. Fortunately it was during sound check, though it would've made great theater if it happened during the show.

Though the pace was exhausting, everywhere we went the turnout and the shows were tremendous.

In the middle of the tour, the Ramones, Monte, and I flew to Scandinavia for a week of shows in Sweden, Copenhagen, and Finland. In Copenhagen, the energy of the band drove the crowd to insane heights. They worked themselves into a violent frenzy and tore the club into pieces. This was truly frightening, and the first time I thought I might get seriously hurt was while stopping these drunken maniacs from tearing up the stage. In Tampere, Finland, just a skip and a jump from the Soviet Union, the crowd was not allowed to move from their seats and could only applaud between songs. They *were* allowed to clap to the Ramones' beat, though, as they had for the Elvis impersonator who opened the show, if you can picture it.

On our return to London, we found that the English punks had their own scene going full force. They were sporting even more safety pins — from tongues to tits — more Mohawks, bondage pants, makeup, and above all, more anger. They had an agenda, and an edge — called poverty. It seemed that they now felt they'd surpassed what was going on in New York and were way beyond anything happening in America.

In many ways, they were right. The Sex Pistols had huge radio hits in England with "God Save the Queen" and "Anarchy in the UK," and the London-based punk band was getting major coverage on British TV, which wouldn't have happened in America in a million years. And though we were hoping the fad had passed, once again the gobs of phlegm rained down on the stage relentlessly, emanating from as far as the back of halls twice the size of Dingwalls.

Interestingly, the crowd didn't gob on the Talking Heads, nor did they execute some other odd actions we'd never seen before. For the Heads, they were attentive and appreciative but relatively sedate. When the Ramones played, the entire crowd began vigorously bouncing up and down to the beat. Some of them were jumping high in the air and flailing their heads. From the stage, it kind of looked like salmon flying upstream. This amazing "dance" was called pogoing.

The Heads *did* get encores, though. No one expected the Talking Heads to go over as well as they did with the Ramones' audience, especially Johnny, who couldn't wait until they got off the stage.

"The Talking Heads liked to enjoy things and the Ramones loved to hate everything," Chris Frantz mused. "Or it *seemed* like they loved to hate everything. Like when we went to Stonehenge and Johnny stayed in the van. He'd snarl, '*I DON'T WANT TO STOP HERE. IT'S JUST A BUNCH OF OLD ROCKS!*'

"Johnny got upset with us once for not keeping the same seats in the van," Chris remembered. "I would sit by Joey, and another time by Tommy, then Dee Dee—and Johnny didn't like that. He liked everybody to have the same 'assigned' seats and stick with them."

On a night off, we went to London to stay in a hotel. For some reason, Joey and I lingered on the bus and were the last ones to get off. In front of the hotel we noticed a big crowd composed of the drunkest bunch of scalawags we'd yet come across. They were British football fans, and they pounced all over Joey like he was the football. They blocked our way into the lobby and provoked Joey with remarks about his hair, his body, and his frail appearance. It was like he was back in Forest Hills, but much scarier. These morons were aching for a reason to rumble and break a bottle over someone's head—especially someone like Joey. Somehow I talked our way around them.

That night Joey and I shared a room. We lay there while the drunken football fans continued to carry on outside the window, cursing and shouting. They'd start brawling with each other, then sing and play flutes—then do it over again, all night long.

The next day Roxy appeared. I'm sure Johnny was happy to see her—I could tell by the way he immediately started smacking her around. I thought it might relieve some of his aggressiveness, which was getting harder for me to withstand.

"Mickey took a lot of abuse from Johnny on the road," Chris Frantz remembered. "Johnny was just pissed. Tina used to say, 'We move our *own* equipment. We don't have roadies to yell at!'

"Johnny really hated that—and he'd just get more abusive to the guys that worked for the Ramones, Frank Gallagher, Ian Ward, and Mickey."

In Birmingham Johnny tried to humiliate me in front of a whole crowd of people. The night before, John wanted the guitars taken off the truck so he and Dee Dee could practice a new song. Monte would bring the guitars on the bus with the band the next day. I was now leaving early in the mornings, traveling to the venues in the equipment truck with Frank and Ian, to have everything set up when the band arrived.

When they got to the club, Johnny walked in and immediately started yelling at me, "*Mitchell! Why aren't the guitars all set up?*"

I said, "Because they're on your bus."

Johnny shouted, *"You're supposed to have everything ready."*

I said, "John, how could I have them ready if they came with you on the bus?"

Johnny screamed, *"Fuck you, Mitchel!"*

"Well, fuck you too, John!" I said, not backing down.

It's the first time somebody had talked back to Johnny.

I think he dropped it because he knew I was planning on calling it quits soon. He'd tried to convince me to stay, but I wanted out. My brother, Dee Dee, and Tommy had all encouraged me to start playing again, too.

A few nights later, I came backstage after the show to wrap things up in the dressing room, and Johnny was in the hallway with Roxy. Johnny had her up against the wall, and he was doing the same routine I'd seen before.

"What were you doing? Who were you looking at over there?" Johnny grilled her.

As she would blurt out a response, Johnny would give her a quick slap in the face.

"I saw you. You were smiling. Who were you smiling at?" Johnny persisted.

"Nobody!" Roxy whined, expecting a slap at any moment. "You're crazy. Stop it!"

Slap!

"John," I interrupted. "There's some press people on their way back here. Maybe you should chill out."

"Fuck 'em!" Johnny snarled.

"You want them to see this?" I said, my last try.

"Mind your own fuckin' business, Mitchel," Johnny added.

I took that as very good advice. I didn't want this to be my business anymore.

"It probably took a while to sink in that Roxy was an alcoholic," Johnny confessed years later. "I kept thinking she was doing it to me. I didn't know how to deal with her, so I smacked her around."

"Johnny would make life hell for everybody in the Ramones," said Chris Frantz.

The job was becoming less and less appealing to me, spiritually and financially. When Frank and Ian and I were comparing salaries one day, they just looked at me and said, "Why? You're a sap."

I was getting $60 a week. Toward the end of the tour, they gave me a $10 raise. Frank and Ian were getting paid more than three times that! I knew I was being taken advantage of, but I didn't mind in the beginning. It was my brother and our friends. But things, and people, were obviously changing.

"On the road in the beginning, I shared a room with Johnny," Tommy recalled. "I couldn't have shared a room with anybody else. Johnny was fine as long I was alone with him, but as soon as someone else came along, he'd start playing us off each other."

"Tommy says that no one was respecting him," Johnny continued. "I don't remember giving Tommy a hard time; I think Joey and Dee Dee gave him the hard time."

"Dee Dee, Johnny, and Joey made it pretty uncomfortable for me to be in the band," Tommy confessed. "After a while they wore me down. I was startin' to go nuts, which they all thought was amusing. They were on thin ice themselves. Looking back, I think I was suffering from clinical depression, which I didn't know at the time.

"Johnny also felt I was holding back," Tommy continued. "He thought my drumming was too slow. Toward the end of the tour, we were playing in Newcastle in England, and he turned and gave me a really dirty look. I just snapped. I couldn't take it anymore. So I started playing really fast.

"Johnny was always insinuating that the reason I was playing slow was because I couldn't play fast. That wasn't true. I started playing faster and faster and faster and faster. After the set, Johnny said, 'What was that all about?! What the hell were you doing?!'

"I said, 'You wanted it played faster, so I played faster.'

"Johnny yelled, '*You're trying to sabotage the band! You're trying to fuck us up!*'

"Johnny didn't hit me," Tommy confirmed, "but it was close."

"**MAN, THIS IS** amazing," my brother said to me as we sat on a table in the dressing room of the Roundhouse on the last night of the Ramones' first European tour. They'd just finished their pre-show warm-up and would be going onstage in about an hour. Johnny told Danny Fields to open the door and let in the stream of press, photographers, and well-wishers who'd come to greet the band or bid them farewell.

Joey and I looked around at the musicians, writers, and artists. There were poor punks who'd snuck in and beautiful stick-thin girls in patent-leather pants who were said to be some kind of royal bluebloods. Guys from the Pistols, the Clash, the Damned, and other future legends were filching our after-show beer from the coolers, which is exactly what we would have been doing if it were the other way around.

I left to hear the Saints do their hit "(I'm) Stranded" and told Monte to have the band ready to hit the stage in thirty minutes. The Ramones played their set and three encores to a wildly passionate audience full of throbbing, gobbing converts. But there was no mainstream press or BBC camera crew that last night at the Roundhouse, and there weren't throngs of fans screaming for the Ramones at the airport the next day.

"I thought punk rock would become huge and that the Ramones, the Sex Pistols, and the Clash would be like the Beatles and the Rolling Stones," said Johnny. "But it wasn't happening like that."

"Today your love, tomorrow the world," sang the Ramones—but it's a big world, and their fans were only a small part of it. The rest of it still belonged to Billy Joel and Abba. Regardless, the three sold-out shows at the Roundhouse, as well as that entire first tour of Europe, was a big triumph for the four freaks from Forest Hills. Whether all the members of the band appreciated that fact was hard to tell.

As we got off the plane the next day and headed through U.S. customs, an ever-irritated Johnny Ramone decided to take another unnecessary swipe.

When I asked Danny what I should put as my occupation on the immigration form, he said, "Put whatever you want, it doesn't matter."

As a gesture of good luck and an omen for the future, I wrote "musician." When Johnny saw it, he freaked out.

"*Whaddaya puttin' that in there for?*" he screamed at me. "*You're not a musician! You're not a professional!*"

"Why are you getting so upset, John?" I answered calmly. "I have been, and I will be again. I'm a musician when I'm pointing out the notes to Dee Dee on his bass, aren't I? You want me to be a musician then, right? Anyway, why does it bother you so much? Big deal!"

It was John getting his jollies by humiliating someone. What else was new? I'd given the band notice already. I would work the three shows they had booked at CBGB, and that would be it. For this eventuality I had been training Matt Loyla, another Forest Hills kid. It did feel odd when I passed the baton to Matt.

I remember standing on CBGB's stage closing up the last road case and taking a deep breath. A spectacular and phenomenal thing had been happening in the world of music the past two years, and I'd had the best seat in the house. It had been an experience like no other, but moving on felt right. I certainly didn't feel like I was abandoning them. I'd done everything I could to help them get to this point and was certain I'd contributed something.

I'd seen the Ramones' shows go from three people to three thousand, from them stopping ten times during their set to never stopping at all. They had confidence when they went on the stage and were confident I wouldn't let them down. After all, I was family: At twenty-three, I'd known the guys more than half my life.

I leaped off CBGB's stage to start looking for my brother, who wanted to have a little farewell party. Before I could get to the bar, I ran into my old friend John Cummings. Even ol' Johnny must have felt a speck of emotion: He stayed far longer than he normally would have after they'd finished their set.

"I hired Mickey as a roadie," Johnny Ramone explained, "because throughout my career, I wanted to be surrounded by as many friends as I could. I always thought it was better to work with friends."

With the crowd gone, Johnny sat at one of the tables in front of CB's stage. He'd been waiting 'til I'd finished packing up. I sat down across from him.

"Well, I guess you're really gonna quit, huh?" Johnny asked. "You sure you wanna do this?"

He made it sound like I was betraying them somehow.

I almost felt bad.

"Yeah, John, I don't want to be a roadie for the rest of my life, ya know?" I answered honestly, with no malice toward him—or the job. "Anyway, I *can't*. I'm two months behind in my rent and—"

"Well," Johnny cut me off, "how about if we raise your salary?"

"You just did, from sixty dollars to seventy dollars," I replied matter-of-factly.

"How about if we paid you two hundred and fifty dollars a week?" Johnny asked. "And we'll raise your per diem, and you can take Arlene on the road with you if you want."

"Wow, that's a big change. I thought you guys couldn't afford it," I said, before finding out they would be hiring two guys to replace me: Matt Loyla and another, bigger, brawnier kid from Forest Hills named Matt Nadler. Nicknamed Big Matt and Little Matt for easy identification, they would each be getting $250 a week.

"No, thanks, John," I told him quietly. "I really do appreciate the offer and that you want me to stay on, but I really want to start playing again myself."

"Well, it's really hard to make it, Mitchel, ya know?" Johnny advised me. "It ain't easy to get a record deal. You might be better off working with us for a while longer . . ."

"Nah," I said. "I've made up my mind. I know what I'm up against, but I gotta at least try—I'll be miserable if I don't."

"Awright," Johnny said, exasperated, "if that's what you wanna do. I guess I'll be seein' ya."

I watched my former boss get up and leave. Then I yelled good-bye and joined my brother, Robin, Legs, and John Holmstrom at the bar.

Joey couldn't have been more supportive. He encouraged me wholeheartedly to either start my own band or get into one that was already forming. I'd heard from Blondie's guitarist, Chris Stein, that the group was looking to replace their bassist, Gary Valentine. At Plaza Sound Studios, where Blondie was recording their second album, I talked to Chris and Debbie Harry. Chris said we should get together and jam and see what happened, which sounded pretty exciting. I liked Blondie, and they were doing pretty well. But since they'd been together for quite a while already, this felt more like a sideman situation.

In the interim, other options arose.

21.

"I WANNA BE SEDATED"

One night in July, Robin and Joey walked into CBGB with Lester Bangs, who had moved to New York City. By this time he'd become the poster boy for a new breed of subversive rock critic. Joey and I were big admirers of Lester's writing. Though we'd met that night in Michigan, Joey now gave me a proper introduction.

Lester could be described as extremely imperious, and he had no qualms about using erudite language in his articles describing simple pop bands like Abba or rudimentary bands like the Ramones. Though many perceived Lester as arrogant, self-aggrandizing, and overly analytical, I found a lot of humor in his writing. At the least, his style was unique and original, and he made me think. His diatribes raised ideas that had substance—or he tried to convince you that they did.

Although his articles frequently became more about him than the band he was writing about, quite often he was more entertaining. Lester wanted to start a band and be the lead singer, which was the main reason Joey wanted to bring us together that night.

Lester was almost famous, but not quite, and as much as he liked to ridicule "rock stars," apparently he had a desire to be one himself, on his terms of course. That meant unkempt, unshaven, and overweight. Sporting a Wilford Brimley mustache, ample plumber's butt, and the gracefulness of a bull in a china shop, Lester was all revved up—on Romilar cough medicine—and ready to go!

I thought to myself, "Hmmm, we just might have something here."

Like me, Lester's taste in music was diverse. Our long conversation that evening revealed that we both had the same record on our turntables at home, *John Lewis Presents Jazz Abstractions*.

Since Lester and I got along really well from the get-go, we decided to give it a try. Lester was impressed when I started playing a Sonny Stitt sax solo I'd transcribed to guitar, and we developed a mutual respect for each other's abilities.

We started a band, which Lester named Birdland in homage to the jazz club in midtown Manhattan. He had a powerful set of lungs but not a whole lot of experience, having done only two shows at CBGB with a pickup band that included Voidoids guitarist Robert Quine and Patti Smith's drummer Jay Dee Daugherty. Reviews of those shows from CB's regulars were mixed.

Lester had recorded a single called "Let It Blurt," which accurately described his vocal style. I thought that if he could harness that power, he might actually be a great singer. He was an extremely animated character, and he certainly had a lot to say. In fact, if I had to sum up my friend Lester in one sentence, it would be: Lester Bangs was a man with a lot to say.

At the time Lester began to hang out with Joey and me, the Ramones didn't socialize with each other anymore. Johnny rarely left his house if they weren't playing. Dee Dee spent more time with Johnny Thunders, or anyone else with dope and pills. Tommy was more than happy to be busy in the studio, preparing to get the Ramones' third album, *Rocket to Russia*, off the ground. The album would feature a song by Dee Dee that would put Queens on the musical map, called "Rockaway Beach," and one by Joey, "Sheena Is a Punk Rocker," which handily summed up the spirit of the scene and put punk rock on the map. It's about a girl disenchanted with the status quo—"*But she just couldn't stay, she had to break away. Sheena is a punk rocker now.*"

By then Joey had moved in with Robin Rothman, who had a studio apartment on Morton Street in the West Village. He was happy living in his own place—well, actually, Robin's place. But he was happy having some privacy and being away from the dorm-style living at Arturo's loft. Robin had been taking care of him anyway, and Joey still needed a lot of care. He'd been in the hospital once already with the foot infection. Robin tried to keep him clean and healthy, but neither she nor Arlene nor I foresaw the calamity that was about to happen.

On November 19, 1977, the Ramones were headlining a big show, with the Talking Heads and Eddie and the Hot Rods opening up. Arlene and I picked up Robin downtown and headed out to the majestic Capitol Theatre in Passaic, New Jersey.

Joey had a bit of a sore throat, as usual. He was developing a bad habit of screaming instead of singing, and as the band's schedule got tighter, so did his vocal cords. In the dressing room, Johnny was sitting in his "area" (they all had "areas" now), grilling Danny Fields about the turnout and ticket sales and getting on my case for missing a show here and there.

"Loyal fans never miss a show," Johnny lectured.

Dee Dee was mumbling about how he was going crazy. Little Matt set up the practice amps and Tommy shifted his practice set around in preparation for the band's traditional preshow warm-up, wherein they play through the entire set list before playing it again onstage, full throttle.

Joey had begun his recently instituted ritual of drinking about six cups of black coffee to clear his head and breathing steam to clear his throat and loosen up his chest.

"Joey would have his Neo-Synephrine," Big Matt Nadler explained, "and a teapot that was used as a makeshift vaporizer to clear out his bronchi and sinuses before he went onstage."

I hadn't been to a Ramones show for a few months and hadn't seen what Joey was using to breathe steam. I didn't think anything of it when Big Matt plugged in a hot plate and started boiling water in a whistling teakettle. The flip-top on the spout was removed so that the spout stayed open. Matt molded tinfoil around the opening and proceeded to pierce holes in the foil to allow the steam to escape.

I asked them if they'd ever heard of the kind you could buy in stores. They said that this technique worked better—that the other vaporizers were for skin beauty treatments. When the water reached a ferocious boil and the steam started pouring out, Matt put a rubber band tightly around the tin foil covering the spout to keep it from popping off and to prevent the scalding water from possibly being propelled into Joey's face and down his throat.

Joey took off his glasses, draped a towel over his head, and hovered over the teakettle as the steam rose up. He took it in deeply through his mouth, occasionally lifting his head to wipe the moisture from his face. Arlene, Robin, and I sat around the table with Joey, drinking the band's beer and talking about where we would go after the show. Joey came up for a breather and said we could probably make it to Max's in time to check out the last couple of bands.

After Danny Fields came in to inform the band that the Talking Heads were about halfway through their set, Joey bent over to get a few last doses of steam. As I was telling him what bands were playing at Max's that night, suddenly we heard a loud *pop*, followed by a sizzling sound. The rubber band around the spout had snapped. The tinfoil flew into the air, and Joey let out a yell as the scalding hot water shot out of the kettle directly onto his face and neck.

Pandemonium ensued as Joey put his hands to his face, screaming, *"OW, SHIT! SHIT!"*

I grabbed his hands and pulled them away from his face.

"Let me see! Let me see!" I shouted, and within seconds his face and lips began to puff up and blister.

Joey was red from the top of his nose down to the top of his chest.

Fortunately, his eyes escaped injury.

"This looks really bad, man," I said, panicking. "You gotta get to a hospital. Like right away!"

"Wait a minute," Johnny yelled, *"maybe he'll be okay, we gotta do this show!"*

"No fuckin' way," I said. "Look at him, his skin is coming off!"

Danny Fields made the decision to get him to the nearest emergency room. There was still about an hour remaining before the Ramones were supposed to hit the stage. We waited at the theater. Devastated, Big Matt apologized frantically.

After about an hour, word came that Joey was on his way back and that he could do the show. Ten minutes later, they came back to the theater. Joey had cream covering his entire face, but it was melting from the heat of his skin.

"You sure you can do this?" I asked him.

"Yeah, yeah, I think so," Joey said, his words garbled from his swollen mouth and tongue.

"You are a fuckin' warrior, man," I told him as we walked to the stage.

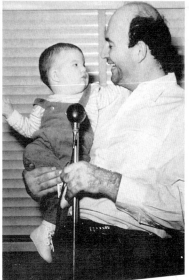

"So, you wanna be a rock & roll star?"
Dad and Jeff (aka Joey), 1952.

"Need a lift?" Big brother
takes me higher, 1955.

Mom always had her hands
full. Forest Hills, 1954.

Showtime!

Beatin' on the brat, in the backyard. Forest Hills, 1957.

LEFT: Our new home for the holidays. With David and Reba Lesher, in Howard Beach, 1962.
RIGHT: Me, Dave, Reba, Jeff, and Jeff's legs. At Lake George, summer 1963.

Hank Lesher, Mom's second husband, with the Porsche bought during their vacation in Europe during the summer of 1965. Only Mom came home.

Check out my drummer! Jeff and me in the basement, Forest Hills, 1965.

BOVE: 1966. Jeff and Mom at his junior high school graduation. Change is gonna come, and none too soon.
RIGHT: Entry level. Jeff's first band, the Intruders, 1967.

Positively Fourth Street. Jeff, Mom, and Phil Sapienza hangin' out in Washington Square Park, 1970.

LEFT: "Hey, ho, let's go!"

BELOW: An era begins for some, an earache begins for others. *Punk rock!*

Can't take my eyes off of you,
or Joey, Tommy, or Dee Dee.
I'm a roadie at work,
Connecticut, 1976.

Joey and Legs share
scary stories.
Joey reads from
The Twilight Zone;
Legs, the *Billboard*
Hot 100.

Free at last. Loud and fast.
The Rattlers, CBGB, 1979.

Arlene and I lock and unload.
Wedding portrait, 1982.

So happy together.
Angela Galetto and Joey, 1983.

Worth a million words.
Joey and me at Richie Ramone's
birthday party, 1983.

Come along with me,
because we're gonna
have a real cool time!
Joey's studio apartment,
1985.

Joey helping Mom do dishes, 1986.

Stop. In the name of love.
Continental, 1996.

One of the greatest rock
singers of all time.

Here's lookin' at you, bro'.
Our last performance together.
His last performance ever. Manitoba's.

When the hot stage lights came on, the remaining cream on his face dripped off.

I don't know where he got the strength, but somehow that night Joey Ramone turned in one of the strongest performances he ever gave. When he came off the stage, he slouched back to the dressing room.

"So you wanna go to Max's?" I kidded him.

Joey managed a laugh and said, "Can ya just take me home?" His voice was totally hoarse. We put him in Arlene's car and headed back to the city. Nobody had said anything about whether or not he should be taken back to the hospital, just to keep an eye on it. He decided to wait until the morning and see how he felt.

Overnight, it got worse. In the morning Robin called me and said that Joey was swelling up. Arlene and I drove in, picked him up at Robin's, and took him to the Cornell burn center. They admitted him immediately.

"It was the next day when Mickey called me and said, 'Don't get crazy, Mom, but Joey got burnt, and I took him to the hospital,'" Charlotte Lesher remembered. "They said they were third-degree burns.

"I don't think he could talk at that point because his whole throat was scalded," Charlotte added. "I couldn't believe he went onstage and sang the night before. He just felt he had to get up there."

Joey looked like Don Knotts's fish-face character in *The Incredible Mr. Limpet*. His lips were so swollen that he looked like a duck-billed platypus.

"I really wasn't aware that he was severely injured," Tommy Ramone confessed. "I knew that they took him to the emergency room that night, but I just thought that was to make sure he was okay. At that point, the Ramones didn't hang out together. After a show, we went our separate ways. What I said might sound insensitive, but the truth is I didn't know that Joey was seriously injured. I didn't know it until the next morning."

In the hospital, Joey started writing "I Wanna Be Sedated," dictating the words to Robin. After he got out, he went back to her place, but things were different between them.

"Don't hold it against me," Robin Rothman laughed, "but I hated living with Joey Ramone. Oh my God, it was like hell! I loved him, there's no doubt about that, but living with him? That was no fun. He was a total mess! It was getting a little too demanding. Living without him? Well, at least then we could still be friends. We had a blast while it lasted, but it was time to send him back to Arturo!"

THE RAMONES WERE on their way to becoming more than local heroes. Despite the lack of radio play in America, the whole Western world was beginning to take notice of punk rock and the Ramones. And aside from the Sex Pistols' Johnny Rotten, no one in the genre was more recognizable than Joey. He was becoming the face and voice of a whole new culture. Joey had more girls hitting on him than he knew what to do with. A girl named Cindy who'd latched on to him had supposedly just come out of a relationship with Denny Laine from Paul McCartney's band Wings.

One night up at Arturo's loft she began to act particularly frisky. We were about to go down to CB's when Cindy stopped to unload a colorful assortment of pills from her bag.

"I want another one of these," she slurred, dropping the whole pile on the floor. She started scrambling for the pills and then just plopped down, rolling around, laughing. Joey rolled his eyes.

The third time Cindy tried to get up, and failed, she stayed down. We called 911 and in a few minutes Cindy, Joey, and I were in the back of an ambulance on our way to the hospital.

"She gonna be all right?" Joey asked.

"She'll live," was the EMS crew's response. "She's going to Bellevue."

Joey and I sat in the dank waiting area of the hospital and watched as water bugs, rats, and mice played happily in a far corner of the room. Finally Cindy came to, and they let us see her.

A week later, Cindy took someone up on an invitation to visit L.A. Joey was disappointed and a bit confused at her sudden departure. I think Joey really liked her, but he knew she was trouble.

"She probably did me a favor," Joey told me after she'd left.

While this was a relatively painless breakup, a far more crucial relationship in Joey's life was also on the brink.

22.

DING DONG!

We had finished making *Rocket to Russia*, a *great* record," Tommy explained. "I was really into the recording process and writing the songs and making the albums, but not the logistics of touring with a bunch of very eccentric, high-strung, crazy people, from one shit-hole club to another. It was pretty depressing. I was making practically nothing. This was okay for a stretch because we thought we were gonna be really good—that we were gonna make it. By now, it had been a while, and there was still no money. This was our third album."

Rocket to Russia didn't sell very well, and Tommy was very unhappy.

"I was thinking, 'What's best for the Ramones?'" Tommy explained, discussing the decision that would change the band forever. "There was all this tension between me and Johnny. I was trying to release the pressure, to keep the band going.

"I told Dee Dee and Joey first that I was leaving the band," Tommy recalled. "They said, 'Oh no, don't go, don't go, blah, blah, blah.' I told them we had to do something, because I was losing my mind."

When Tommy told Johnny he was quitting, Johnny was shocked. He hadn't seen it coming.

Tommy offered to continue working with the band in the studio and with songwriting. He suggested they bring in a new drummer. There was no way he could keep going on the road with the Ramones. Once they'd finally realized he was going for real, they started looking for a replacement.

"I was at the bar at CBGB's when *Rocket to Russia* came out," drummer Marc Bell remembered. "I didn't know the Ramones personally, but obviously I had heard of them. I was the drummer in Richard Hell's band Richard Hell and the Voidoids, and the album *Blank Generation* was also out on Seymour Stein's label. So we were Sire Records mates."

One night at CB's Dee Dee came up to Marc and asked, "Would you ever want to join the Ramones?"

Marc told Dee Dee he'd love to join the band. About a month later, Marc heard from Danny Fields and Monte Melnick; the band was holding auditions. But first Johnny Ramone wanted to talk to him.

"Johnny said, 'You want to be in the band?'

"I said, 'Hell, yeah!'"

Marc ignored Johnny's "dos and don'ts" for being a Ramone, since Dee Dee was not exactly a great example of following the rules.

Instead he said, "Okay, Johnny, all right, yeah, sure."

At the audition, the room was filled with fifteen to twenty guys. Tommy Ramone was there to oversee the choice of his replacement. Marc played "I Don't Care" and "Sheena"—and knew he was in. The newest member became Marky Ramone.

"After I left," Tommy explained, "Joey immediately started leveraging for power, very successfully over time. I think Johnny should've seen that coming. He should've done anything possible to keep me in the band because once I was gone, he had nobody to play off against each other.

"In the beginning," Tommy remembered, "Joey liked Johnny a lot, and I think Johnny liked Joey—as much as Johnny can like anybody. But Joey and Dee Dee weren't treated well. Dee Dee was treated like a little kid, because that's how he acted. And Joey was so quiet, he kinda disappeared."

"Joey was *more* than quiet," said Arturo Vega. "When Joey finally started speaking in public, it came slowly. But eventually he turned into the leader of the band. Joey would be either very funny or very unfunny, but very effective.

"Of course, Joey was never *really* the leader of the band," Arturo added.

"But lead singers are always perceived, ideologically and spiritually, as the leader of the band. Johnny continued giving the orders."

Arturo Vega may have taken his orders from Johnny, but everyone else was becoming more and more interested in Joey. People at the record company, in the media, and in general were beginning to listen to him. And when it came to many of the band's important creative decisions, Joey began to assert himself more and more. After Tommy left, the chain of command in the band was undefined—maybe even up for grabs. Joey soon realized that if he could get up the nerve, and if he wanted it bad enough, he could probably be on equal ground with the domineering Johnny. But he would have to rise to the occasion.

I was surprised that Joey wasn't more upset about Tommy leaving the band. But apparently something had gone down between them, unbeknownst to me.

Years before, they'd argued, and Tommy had told Joey the band should have left him in the basement of his mom's art gallery. Joey never forgave him.

"Tommy couldn't take it," Joey told me at the time Tommy left. "He cracked! He just wasn't tough enough," my brother said, smirking.

Coming from him, the words sounded unusual.

"After Tommy left the band, we went straight into working on the *Road to Ruin* album with Marky," Ed Stasium recalled. "We rehearsed a long time with Marky, just getting it down. Then we went into the studio, recorded, and mixed the record at Media Sound. We spent a lot of money, and the entire summer, on *Road to Ruin*."

At the same time the Ramones were in New York City recording, future filmmaker Allan Arkush was in Hollywood working for Roger Corman, the legendary B-movie mastermind behind such low-budget 1950s classics as *She Gods of Shark Reef*, *Attack of the Crab Monsters*, *Rock All Night*, and *Carnival Rock*.

Unbeknownst to the Ramones, Allan was in Los Angeles cooking up an idea that would put them in a class of their own—as stars of their own movie.

"I started working for Roger Corman, editing trailers and TV spots. I realized the only way I was ever *really* going to get to do anything in Hollywood was to sell Roger on an idea for a film. I wanted to make a movie about blowing up a high school. After I finished working on a film called

Deathsport, which Roger was very pleased with, he said, 'What about that high school movie you wanted to do?'"

Allan still wanted to do it, and with music. Roger suggested something with a disco beat. Allan told him that you couldn't blow up a high school to that music.

When Roger asked why not, Allan got up on the couch and did his imitation of Pete Townshend smashing his guitar, and explained the difference between rock music and disco music. That rang a bell with Roger.

"At a meeting at Warner Bros.," Alan remembers, "a guy named Carl mentioned some bands like Van Halen and Devo, which I passed on.

"Then Carl said, 'Do you know the bands on Sire Records, because we've just acquired Sire Records?'"

"I said, 'Yeah, I like Sire!'

"Carl said, 'What about the Ramones? It's a crazy idea . . . ' Bam! He just threw that out there.

"I said, 'The Ramones! I love *Rocket to Russia!*' To me, the Ramones represented a certain lifestyle, philosophy, and a way of being. I said, 'That could be really funny, if we have a character who worships the Ramones!'"

It so happened that Danny Fields and Linda Stein were in town that afternoon, so Roger and Allan drove down to the Bel Air Hotel to meet them and discuss the idea of the movie. As Allan pitched a scenario of the Ramones showing up at the high school, and in the end blowing it up, Linda and Danny said, "How can we do this?!"

Once Roger got a look at the *Punk* magazine issue "Mutant Monster Beach Party," which was a parody of the B movie *The Horror of Party Beach* featuring Joey as the lead character, he knew this was the band they wanted. Since Allan had never seen the Ramones live, he flew back to New York to see them play at Hurrah's, a rock club on the Upper West Side. He was wiped out after the show, literally.

"The next night I went over to Seymour Stein's apartment on Central Park West for dinner. They'd ordered takeout from a great Italian restaurant," Allan related.

"Dee Dee said, 'I thought we were having Italian food. Where's the pizza?'

"Johnny wouldn't eat soft-shell crab, so they had to order pizza for the band. Joey never said a word. He walked in and out of rooms.

"Johnny seemed really focused. Dee Dee was stoned out of his mind. Marky was kind of new, so he wasn't saying much.

"But the more we talked, the more we found in common. We hit it off that night really well."

After the meal, the whole group went down to CBGB and then over to Arturo's loft, where Lester Bangs was hanging out. When the Talking Heads came by, Lester started screaming at Tina Weymouth about being a sellout. Allan was thrilled to be observing the downtown scene he'd been hearing about. Even more thrilling was that the Ramones agreed to do the movie.

Joey was very excited as well, but they were all a bit apprehensive about how being in this low-budget comedy would ultimately affect their image. It could have raised their profile, but it also might have made them laughingstocks.

"Before we began work on *Rock 'n' Roll High School*," Allan Arkush remembered, "the Sex Pistols came to the States. In the midst of that, the Ramones did a couple of concerts with Black Sabbath and got booed off the stage. Then the Pistols broke up at the end of their tour, and we started making the movie. Dee Dee could barely read his lines. Johnny could read, but he wasn't funny. Joey never said anything.

"We had a lot of people read for the Riff Randell part, including Daryl Hannah, and for the other part, Jamie Lee Curtis. Then PJ Soles read for us; we loved her in *Halloween*. She wanted more than scale, but then she said she'd throw in her own costumes—so she got the part."

At the time, Soles was married to actor Dennis Quaid and had never heard of the Ramones. She was a fan of the Eagles and Jackson Browne.

"When Allan gave me the VHS tape of the Ramones, I put it on, and I went, '*Oh my God!*'" Soles recalled. "It was probably the first time I'd heard punk music. I was amazed. I thought, 'I don't know how *I'm* going to be their number one fan!'"

When she met them on the set, she loved the fact that as people, they were "excruciatingly shy and quiet. They just always had their heads down and always looked like they thought they were in the way."

They were always standing around, just leaning against a wall or something. Soles had to invite them into the trailer: "I remember saying, 'Hey! C'mon in, *you guys are the stars of the movie, you can come in the trailer!*' So they'd come in and sit on the floor.

"When we filmed the bedroom scene for the song 'I Want You Around,'

Joey was spitting as he was singing to me," PJ Soles remembered. "I was lying there with my mouth open—and all this spit is coming into my mouth.
I had to act like I loved it. But Joey and I had a very sweet relationship,
because I respected him, and he respected me."

"When we did the last shot for the movie," Joey laughed, "it was about
thirty degrees—real cold for L.A. All day the technical guys had been working tests for the final scene when the students and the Ramones blow up
Vince Lombardi High School. They put in too much dynamite and the
school really blew up. It was great! That night, everybody got sunburned."

Fortunately they got the explosion on film, as they wouldn't have been
able to reshoot it. I would love to have been there—could have used a
tan—but I couldn't afford to go to L.A. to watch the shoot.

In the fall of 1978, while they were filming *Rock 'n' Roll High School*,
the Ramones stayed at a motel on Santa Monica Boulevard called the Tropicana. It was only a few blocks from the Sunset Marquis Hotel, but several
hundred bucks cheaper. The Tropicana was the undisputed coolest motel
in L.A. It was the place where most New York City rock bands stayed when
they went out there.

Coincidentally, Justin Strauss, the singer of Milk and Cookies, who used
to drop me off on Queens Boulevard on our way back from CBGB, was
also staying at the Tropicana with his girlfriend Linda Danielle. For some
reason, Justin had to go back to New York temporarily and told Linda to stay
in L.A. until he returned.

That's when the romance between Linda Danielle and Joey Ramone
began. It started as a casual friendship. When the manager of the Tropicana
invited people over to her house for Thanksgiving dinner, Joey and Linda
decided to go together. Their relationship started heating up. But things
were interrupted when the band got busy.

When Joey got back to New York a few months later, he and Linda
picked up where they left off. For Joey, it was the beginning of a new and
exciting chapter in his life. Justin, apparently, was now out of the picture,
and Linda was in it.

"I entered Arturo's loft one day and found Joey, Linda, and Arturo happy
and giggling—acting like they'd been naughty," Legs McNeil remembered.
"I knew Linda when she was with Justin, the lead singer of Milk and Cookies, and never suspected her of being a Ramones fan. Now here she was
hanging out with Joey. It was weird.

"I was expecting to hang out with Joey, go drinking and pick up some chicks," Legs explained, "but Joey didn't even wanna go out. I was shocked."

I'd known Linda primarily from those rides home from CBGB at four a.m. with her and Justin. She'd talked mainly about who was at CBGB and which celebrities she'd met at Max's; who was gonna be famous and who wasn't; blah blah blah — mindless gossip. I thought it was insipid and obnoxious but harmless enough.

Linda was the total opposite of the ripped-jeans-and-sneaker-wearing girls who were coming to Ramones shows — not only in fashion, but in attitude as well. She reminded me more of the Forest Hills JAPs who liked expensive clothes and guys with money. But since Linda had been hanging out at CBGB and Max's from the very beginning, I thought she was cooler than the girls in my neighborhood who were still going to discos and raving about Studio 54. The average Forest Hills girl would never have hung out on the smelly, dirty Bowery with bums and punks.

"I remember Joey bringing Linda over to the apartment at 115 East Ninth," Charlotte Lesher recalled of her first meeting with her possible future daughter-in-law. "I didn't really think very much of her. I mean, I had met a lot of the girls that Joey had gone out with or was friendly with, but I hadn't seen him with anybody that flashy-looking before. Linda didn't exactly seem like much of an intellectual."

Any shortcomings Linda may have had, Joey was blind to. And he didn't really care what our mother or anyone else thought. Apparently, Linda had really gotten under his skin.

"*Hangin' out in 100B / Watchin' Get Smart on TV / Thinkin' about you and me, and you and me,*" Joey wrote in his song "Danny Says" about their time together at the Tropicana.

Soon enough, Linda was living up at Arturo's loft with Joey. Even though she seemed materialistic and covetous, I gave her the benefit of the doubt and welcomed her into the clan — and silently wished her luck living with my brother. I had an instant affection, empathy, and appreciation for just about any girl who would venture to live — for even one month — with the guy I'd shared a room with for twenty years.

There were only two ways to survive living with my brother — love him, or kill him — or else you'd go crazy yourself. I hoped it would work out for my brother this time. Given that Linda Danielle did not exactly appear to be a domestic goddess, I hoped for divine intervention. Apparently, someone else in the band was also thinking about an intervention, but not so divine.

"The first time I saw Linda with Joey," Johnny remembered, "I told her to get in the back of the van. I told her that Joey's seats were in the back. Then I asked her, 'Do you smoke? Do you drink? Do you do drugs?'"

Joey and Linda were living happily together, and their relationship seemed solid. He even started taking her on the road with him. When he was in town, Arlene and I hung out with Joey and Linda, almost exclusively. Overall, things were going really well for my brother. Joey was truly happy.

Things certainly could have been going better for me. To pay the bills, I was driving a cab, hoping that things would work out soon with Birdland. I remember being in the garage one day waiting to go on my shift and taking out a copy of the *Village Voice* I'd grabbed on the way over. There was my brother, right on the cover. I wanted to show it around and brag about him to the other cabbies but figured they'd probably never heard of the Ramones or would think I was bullshitting them.

Crowds weren't exactly flocking to see Birdland, but Lester and I had written some great songs we were both truly proud of. The music was eclectic and interesting, lyrically and musically, but not for everyone.

Lester and I were having some difficulties. Though he was constantly stoned on a variety of drugs—mixing speed with cough syrup, with alcohol, with exorbitant amounts of antihistamines and who knows what else—somehow we still managed to remain friends and have a band. Between Lester's crude vocals and his fucked-up lifestyle, it was practically impossible to keep band members from quitting. I had to seek out new players constantly as guys got disenchanted with Lester's antics.

Joey and Lester were still good friends, and though Lester didn't suffer from obsessive-compulsive disorder that we knew of, he did rival my brother in terms of sloppiness. They even wrote a song together called "I'm a Slob."

After going through three drummers, Robin Rothman found us a new one named Matty Quick, who lived all the way on the West Side, downtown on Spring Street and Greenwich. Matty was an old friend of Robin's. He sold pot for a living and helped me get back in the business. He also let us rehearse in his apartment.

"Birdland played at My Father's Place with the Ramones one time," Matty Quick recalled. "But wherever we'd go—maybe because of Mickey—

the kids would come to hear the Ramones. They'd shout at Lester, 'Get the fuck offstage, you fat bastard!'

"Lester scowled back at them and said, 'Name five words that rhyme with purple!'" Matty laughed. "So they shouted back, even harder, 'You suck!'"

My friend Dave U. Hall from Forest Hills, who played bass, left to pursue his master's degree. Through a neighbor of Matty's, we got David Merrill, son of the world-famous opera singer Robert Merrill. I thought it might be helpful to have other well-known names in the band to help diminish the "Joey Ramone's little brother" angle the local press was already pumping. Danny Fields had actually put us on a bill with the Ramones at the Palladium, which I chalked up to him wanting to keep Lester happy. Not that the band didn't have something to offer, but what we did was different. It was basically garage punk, but it incorporated and combined elements of various forms of music—jazz, folk, blues, country, even a bit of classical—and was hard to categorize. Lester's singing style and lyrics were also an acquired taste.

Joey often came over to Matty's house during our rehearsals to lend his advice, offer encouragement, and just hang out. One day Joey brought over an elixir from Kiehl's Pharmacy, the upscale homeopathic drug and beauty-aid store on Thirteenth and Third. Hemotonic was a brown liquid containing a mixture of several forms of vitamin B and other vitamins and minerals. It was supposed to fortify your immune system; he brought it over for Lester to try.

"Lester being Lester, he drank the whole fucking bottle," Matty Quick recalled. "Then he went to sleep and farted out liquid hemotonic all over himself."

There were several other conflicts that arose with Lester.

The Ramones had outgrown CBGB by this time but were going back to do a benefit to help raise money to buy bulletproof vests for "New York's Finest." Birdland could have gotten on the bill since Legs McNeil had organized it, and it was something we would have liked to do. Hell, some of my best pot customers were cops at the 112th Precinct in Forest Hills. A lot of the new bands were going to be playing, but Lester adamantly opposed it, as did Joey, at first.

"Joey wasn't that enthusiastic about it," Legs recalled. "But Johnny Ramone loved it. I got the band I'd just started managing, Shrapnel, to open for the Ramones and all the money was donated to buy the cops bulletproof vests."

The benefit was the last time the Ramones played CBGB. "A few days later," Robin Rothman remembered wistfully, "I was listening to a news story about some cop that was saved by a bulletproof vest, and I thought to myself, 'Wow, the Ramones may actually have saved some lives.'"

After the bulletproof-vest benefit, the discord continued with Lester and our band. Lester continually wanted to stir things up. He liked to annoy, question, or criticize anyone he didn't think was doing enough to turn the world inside out and create the kind of political anarchy he loved to espouse but would never be able to survive in.

I believe Lester really meant well, but he liked getting his paychecks, even from corporate America, just as much as the guy in the suit sitting next to him on the subway. He talked the talk, but he didn't exactly practice what he preached.

Lester went on rants in the press, saying that English punk music, "oi," as he was calling it, was the "real" punk rock because those bands were politically dissident and very vocal about it. He stopped just short of saying that American punk bands were pussies and more akin to innocent "pop" bands. In essence, Lester was giving the British credit for starting the "real punk rock" thing. This started a big debate between Lester and Joey, and Joey and Legs, and Legs and Lester, and on and on.

It was a real "What came first, the chicken or the egg?" argument.

If it didn't start in America with the Ramones, or in England with the Sex Pistols, it started here with the New York Dolls, or Iggy and the Stooges or Lou Reed before him. Or wasn't it the Who, in England, that really kicked it off before them? Or as Joey had said before, "The Beatles were the first punks."

Or was it Elvis, as Johnny Ramone would see it?

Musically, aside from Eddie Cochran, the Beach Boys, and other American bands doing "surf" music, the Ramones' influences were predominantly British. When I first heard them rehearsing in the Art Garden, they were still playing very slowly. It sounded pretty much like Black Sabbath's "Paranoid," same downstroking on the guitar and synchronization with the bass. The basic difference was the way Tommy played high hat on the drums. I could also hear the same guitar riff that Johnny used for "I Don't Wanna Go Down to the Basement" in David Bowie's "Hang Onto Yourself," except that Bowie used an acoustic guitar.

The attitude and twisted humor, though, came from Forest Hills, Queens, New York City, the United States of America—the Ramones.

Punk rock? Who knows where it actually started, and who cares?

Joey did. He was very protective of the Ramones' legacy and didn't react well to anyone attempting to direct credit for it toward the Sex Pistols or the Clash or any English band, for that matter.

"When the Pistols came to the U.S., I was faced with telling the Ramones that I had to cover them for *Punk* magazine," Legs laughed. "Let me tell you, it wasn't fun. Joey had a way of standing there, hunched over, twirling his hair, while he stared at you with piercing eyes from under those rose-colored sunglasses. It was chilling. Joey felt that I betrayed him. He never really understood that I had a job."

While Lester and my brother were fighting over who came first, I was having other problems with Lester. We'd asked him to stop drinking so much and start exercising a little—not so much for cosmetic reasons, but for his health, and for a better performance. Lester said we were just worried about looking like rock stars. When we said we wanted to make a tape and try to get a record deal, Lester said he didn't care what some corporate asshole thought of his band.

I told him I wanted to use the name Mickey Leigh. Lester talked me out of it, saying my real name was fine and again accusing me of acting like a rock star.

Lester was being junketed, feted, and celebrated all over the place, having people kiss his ass up and down, writing articles in big magazines for a living, and getting his name printed in big bold letters. I was driving a cab three nights a week and delivering for a liquor store in Queens—and he was accusing me of acting like a rock star. Right.

To boot, he had already changed his own name, from Leslie to Lester. But that was okay, I suppose, because he played with a typewriter instead of just a guitar. Lester could be quite hypocritical. Thankfully, he did want to record our songs.

Dave Merrill worked as an engineer at Electric Lady Studios and he snuck us in there one night while they were closed for renovations. On April Fools' Day in 1979 we recorded nine songs old-school style—live, straight to tape, no second takes. I put the idea in Lester's head that sometimes a whisper is louder than a scream, offering him options besides his ever-angry "blurt it all out" approach.

He understood and agreed, and it enabled him to feel better about displaying a wider range of emotion in his singing. He was far more effective, and I could tell he was enjoying singing that much more. It appeared that the guy who'd only written about moments like this was finally experiencing one; it felt good to us all. The recording actually turned out really well and was something we would always be proud of.

As much as I admired Lester's writing and valued our friendship, it was becoming more and more difficult to be in a band with him. One day he came to rehearsal really fucked up and our manager, Matty's neighbor Rick Schneider, proposed that Lester just write songs and let someone else sing. Lester did not like that idea at all.

"Mickey wrote a couple of songs and sang them," Matty Quick remembered. "And Lester lost his marbles. He said, 'We're not doing any songs without my lyrics in this band.'

"Lester was really angry," Matty continued. "He started singing right in Mickey's face and got him right in a corner. Lester was all fucked up on a variety of things—he couldn't have been that aggressive without some help, because he was really a peaceful guy when he wasn't fucked up. But I thought Mickey was gonna slug him."

Matty and Dave gave me an ultimatum after the rehearsal. Either Lester had to go, or they would. I'd given it my best shot. I decided to stay with them and part ways with Lester.

It took a while for Lester to get over it, but we did remain friends, which was great, because as a result of his friendships with Joey and me, he'd become part of the family. He'd been coming over to Mom and Phil's house for holiday and birthday celebrations and visiting them at their summer house in Massachusetts. As Phil was now a certified therapist, Lester was also seeing him as a client.

Dave, Matty, and I decided to keep going with me as the singer, but we needed a new name. Joey, who'd just returned from a Ramones tour out west, came over to Matty's house with a little rattlesnake tail he'd gotten for me at a Texas snake farm.

"How about the Rattlers?" he suggested while sitting on Matty's couch, shaking the thing. It stuck.

Now everybody was happy. In fact, I was thrilled. Lester had started another band, and now I was free to write words as well as music and to sing my own songs. Joey thought this was a much better situation for us as well, and not only did he help us name the band, but he also offered to do a cameo on our first record. I thought that was fair enough, since I'd sung on his. Of course, we would put his name on it. We weren't stupid. Or were we?

Ed Stasium, who by now had become a near and dear friend, produced the single for us. We recorded two songs I'd written. The B side—or "In" side, as we labeled it—was called "Living Alone." It was a sequel to the Birdland song "I'm in Love with My Walls" and was a tongue-in-cheek poke at Lester. The "Out" side, "On the Beach," was a sci-fi fantasy inspired by the sixties B movie *The Horror of Party Beach:* A sea monster, created by the famous radiation leak at the Three Mile Island nuclear power plant, swims up onto the beach at Coney Island and absconds with someone's "baby."

Joey loved the song and sang backup vocals on the chorus. It was the first thing any of them had done outside of the Ramones since they started the band. Joey told us that Johnny was totally opposed to Joey being on the single, but Joey didn't care. That was very meaningful to me, and it made our relationship stronger than ever. We put out the single on our own label, called Ratso Records, named for our artist friend James "Ratso" Rizzi, who lent us the money for the pressing.

The record was received very well. It got some radio play and great reviews, including making the "Recommended" list in Billboard magazine, which was quite an achievement for an "indie" record. As came to be common practice, just about every writer began his or her Rattlers review with "Joey Ramone's little brother . . ." and then went on to talk about the band—not mine, his. *Then* they would mention the Rattlers.

It was to be expected and would have happened whether Joey sang on the record or not. That I was Joey's brother was no secret and had already been publicized in pieces about Birdland. But when some of them chose to attribute the entire lead vocal to Joey, who had simply sung a harmony with me on the chorus, it was a little weird. I certainly didn't expect that to happen. But I also thought it was kind of funny. At the time, I took it as a compliment.

BEING A GUY who could never admit he was wrong, our father still maintained some apprehensions about whether his son—his sons, actually—had made smart decisions about their life goals. For me, he had two suggestions. One was that I should work in his truck terminal and learn the business. He also said he would be willing to buy a taxi medallion if I would give up music and drive full-time.

It was a nice gesture, and sincere, and the most generous showing of support he'd ever offered either one of us. But it showed he still didn't get it.

I wasn't looking for a full-time career at anything but playing and recording music. I told him that if he really wanted to help me out, he could contribute to a new guitar and an amp. No deal.

Joey and Linda's relationship was still going strong, but as for the two of them living in Arturo's loft, they had their problems. Arturo placed a lot of long-distance phone calls, which made for an extremely high bill. The agreement with Arturo was that they would split all the bills, but it didn't seem fair to Linda that Joey should have to pay for all of Arturo's calls. A big argument ensued between Linda and Arturo, and culminated in Joey and Linda moving out of the loft.

Uneasily, my brother entertained the notion of asking our father to temporarily host him and Linda in his apartment on Fifteenth Street. Now that Joey's band had achieved substantial notoriety, Dad was beginning to come around. He still had big reservations, as Joey's income was nothing to crow about. But the press, the crowds, and the attention were hard to ignore. Joey's continuing success should have been enough to convince our old man that it was indeed possible to make it; but with him, money was always the main thing. Here he was being asked by his now twenty-nine-year-old son, Joey Ramone, if it would be okay to crash in his house—with his girlfriend, too. No doubt our father was proud of Joey to some degree, but the music still hadn't supplied enough *naches*, as he would say, to satisfy him.

"*Shep naches*" is a Yiddish expression meaning "to bring joy." In the old days it meant that you made your parents proud. These days it meant you made enough money for them to go bragging to their friends about you. To give the old man the benefit of the doubt, this was something normally reserved for kids who either became doctors, lawyers, or rabbis, or married one—not lead singers in punk rock bands.

In the end, Dad let Joey and Linda take over his apartment on Fifteenth Street in Chelsea while he stayed with his girlfriend Nancy at her summer place in East Hampton. This seemed to take the new couple's relationship to another level. Linda hosted a dinner party and we met her mother and her brother. Things were getting more and more serious.

Unfortunately, so was Joey's OCD. When the "old man," as we both now affectionately called our dad, returned to his apartment and was greeted by debris and disarray, he strongly suggested Joey and Linda make their own way—out the door! Joey and Linda began to look for their own apartment.

Mom discovered that there was a studio apartment available at 115 East Ninth Street, the nice, clean building with a twenty-four-hour doorman where she and Phil lived. It was just a small L-shaped apartment, with a tiny kitchen and no view; but it was also huge and monumental. Jeff Hyman, who had been told by psychiatrists and physicians that he would never function in society on his own, now had his own apartment.

23.

ALCOHOLIC SYNONYMOUS

Whenever we were in L.A., we'd run into Phil Spector," Joey Ramone remembered. "He'd follow us around and say, 'Do you guys want to make a good record or a *great* record?' And we'd say, 'Yeah,' and he'd say, 'Well, I'll make you *great!*'

"So we took a chance," Joey laughed. "Which was crazy."

Seymour Stein was looking for a hit record from the Ramones, but they were being totally ignored by American radio. The thinking was that if anybody could get the Ramones a hit, it would be Phil Spector.

"At that point in our careers," Johnny Ramone admitted, "I guess it was just a desperate move to work with Spector. We thought he might get us some airplay."

Seymour Stein told Ed Stasium that Phil Spector was going to be working with the band, and they wanted Ed to be along for the ride. They gave him the credit of "musical director" for *End of the Century*.

When Ed arrived in L.A. he got a call from Phil's secretary Donna, who said that Phil wanted to meet Ed at Gold Star Studio that night at nine p.m.

"I was nervous being in the control room with *Phil Spector!*" said Ed. "Out of the blue Phil says, 'This is the greatest country in the world!' He tried to figure out the chorus to 'God Bless America' on an acoustic guitar that was being passed around. Then he leaned forward in his chair and fell on his face. That was my first meeting with Phil Spector."

Apparently Phil was a little tipsy.

"When we went to talk to Phil about producing our record, he started a fight as a publicity stunt," Johnny Ramone explained. "We were prisoners in his house for about six hours. I said, 'Okay, let's go,' and Phil pulled out a gun and said, 'Do you wanna leave?'

"I said, 'No, that's okay, we'll stay for a while.'"

For hours, the Ramones sat in Phil Spector's living room at gunpoint, listening to him play "Baby, I Love You" over and over again.

"He was drinking from this big gold goblet with jewels on it," Dee Dee related. "Phil looked like Dracula drinking blood. I said, 'Phil, let me have some of that,' and he finally said 'Okay, Dee Dee.' It was Manischewitz wine."

WHILE MY BROTHER was reaching his creative apex, his dream of record-ing with our hero Phil Spector was in some doubt.

"Phil would make us run through the song a thousand times before he'd even do one take," Joey recalled, "and then he'd get drunk. The son of the guy who owned Gold Star Studios would bring Phil these tiny little Dixie cups of Manischewitz and before long Phil would be drunk out of his mind.

"He would be stomping the floor, cursing, yelling, *'Piss, shit, fuck! Piss, shit, fuck! Fuck this shit!'* And that would be the end of the session."

"The third day in the studio," Ed Stasium remembered, "we recorded the song 'Rock 'n' Roll High School,' which starts with Johnny slamming the guitar strings once for a big, loud power chord that rings out for several seconds until the notes fade into feedback."

As legend has it, that's when Phil became obsessed with the first chord of the song, which he had Johnny play over and over and over again. What he was listening for, nobody knew but him—and maybe *he* didn't even know.

After hours and hours of repeating the chord, Johnny couldn't take it anymore. He told Ed, "I'm going home. Tell Seymour I can't work with this guy."

"When I told Seymour Stein that Johnny didn't want to work with Phil anymore," Ed related, "he told me we *had* to save the record."

After Ed got Phil on the phone and told him that Johnny really couldn't work this way, a meeting with the whole band was arranged in Joey's room at the Tropicana Motel. Johnny told Phil he was driving him nuts doing the same song over and over. Phil apologized and said he'd knock it off.

"We told Phil if he didn't stop drinking," Joey said, "we wouldn't be able to work with him."

Johnny agreed to stay and they went back to the studio the next day. Just as Johnny was dealing with all of Phil's eccentricities, in the middle of recording, his father died. He flew to New York to attend the funeral, but the occasion proved to be pivotal in more ways than one, not only for Johnny, but also for my brother and the Ramones.

"When I got back to L.A.," said Johnny, "Joey's girlfriend Linda came to the airport with him and Monte to pick me up. I knew Joey didn't care about comin' to no airport to pick me up—that was Linda's doing."

One day while they were still recording, PJ Soles came to visit Johnny in his room at the Tropicana, and Linda confronted him, asking "What is PJ Soles doing in your room? What's going on!?'

"All of a sudden," Johnny confessed, "I realized I wanted to be around Linda. When Linda stood up to me, she got my attention. We were in the van with everybody and I told Linda, 'Sit in the back where you belong!'

"Linda started sayin' something to me, and Joey told her to be quiet. I just felt Linda was bein' treated badly by Joey. She was something special, and he didn't seem to notice."

Allan Arkush was one of the first people to notice the potential bombshell between Linda, Joey, and Johnny.

"The three of them came over for dinner," Allan remembered, "which already seemed unusual as I'd never known Johnny and Joey to hang out socially. Johnny and Linda were being a little too cozy. Joey wasn't aware of it, though."

Joey was most likely preoccupied with the business at hand and anxiously anticipating the release of the Spector-produced album.

"Before every session," Ed Stasium recalled, "Phil talked about how huge this Ramones record was going to be. He thought it would sell millions and be the biggest record of his career!

"And Phil *loved* Joey. He saw Ronnie Spector in Joey."

The Ramones recorded *End of the Century* in the summer of 1979, and it didn't come out until March 1980—that's a very long time. Usually after they recorded a record, it came out two months later.

Joey was really excited about the record and thought he was finally going to have a hit album, or at least a hit single.

"In the end, I didn't think it sounded good at all," Ed admitted. "The performances were there, but it just sounded soft. It didn't sound like the Ramones."

For someone like me, a fan from the days when Ramones fans totaled single digits, the album was a bit of a conundrum: For those who fell in love with a band blessed with exposed-nerve rawness and no-punches-pulled lyrics, this album was a double-edged sword. One side of the blade cut an interesting new path; the other side just cut the cheese.

The cover of "Baby, I Love You" contained a gooey string section arrangement that sounded right out of Redbone's "Come and Get Your Love." It made me almost embarrassed. At the same time, the combination of Spector's brilliance and Joey's talent turned out a masterpiece in "Danny Says," which remains one of the most captivatingly beautiful songs I've ever heard—and perfectly produced.

It was a risky departure in their career, but they didn't lose me as a fan. It did take some of the edge off of their character, though.

"*End of the Century* was just watered-down Ramones," Johnny Ramone complained. "It's not the real Ramones. 'Baby, I Love You' I didn't play on that at all. What am I gonna do—play along with an *orchestra*? There's no point.

"*End of the Century* was trying to get a hit on each song, instead of trying to get a hit on one or two of the songs on the album and trying to make the rest as raunchy as you can. They ain't gonna play the other ten songs, anyway."

In the end, it was the biggest record the Ramones ever did, going to number 40 on the Billboard charts. "Baby, I Love You" even made it to number 10 in England.

WHILE WAITING FOR *End of the Century* to come out, the Ramones went back to business as usual—touring. It was when they came back to New York City that I first began to hear things about Linda and Johnny, though not from my brother. The Ramones' roadies Big Matt and Little Matt, the band's soundman John Markovich, and of course Monte Melnick all had seen or heard something by then. But nothing they told me really raised warning flags.

The Rattlers were playing with the Ramones that July 1979 at the Diplomat Hotel in Manhattan when Monte made a cryptic comment to me.

"Something's going on," Monte murmured at the show. "Something's weird with John and Linda."

"Whaddaya mean?" I asked him.

"You haven't heard anything?" Monte asked.

"Heard what?" I answered.

"Never mind," Monte said, dropping the subject.

I assumed he was talking about something silly, like Johnny telling Linda not to talk in the van or something. I dropped it, as well.

The band continued to work at a furious pace. They had to in order to survive. They still had no income from record sales, so they played at any club in any town that would pay them. With ever-increasing frustration rising to a peak, the effectiveness of the Ramones' management became an issue for the three original band members, Joey, Johnny, and Dee Dee.

Even after making a feature-length movie and an album with Phil Spector, their career path continued to be disappointing, and the band seemed to be making moves in only one direction—sideways. Apathy and anger had begun to fester with every album that failed to produce a hit for the band. To their credit, the Ramones refused to accept defeat.

At the same time, they needed to lay the blame on someone and concluded that the shortcomings of managers Danny Fields and Linda Stein were the problem. There may have been some truth to that. Another possibility was that they had actually painted themselves into a corner from the very beginning with their own menacing material and image. Or maybe it was just bad luck. Either way, it wasn't happening the way they wanted it to.

Joey and Dee Dee were in agreement that they would be best served having someone else direct this mission for them. Johnny remained loyal to Danny, but he was outvoted and had to accept it. It was a shame because Danny was the guy who had had the foresight and tenacity to get the band their first record deal, against all odds. He moved the band off the Bowery and onto the map. But it appeared that he and Linda Stein had been unable to do what was necessary to deliver the Ramones to the promised land and make them a household name.

While necessity is the mother of invention, desperation is the wicked stepmother of necessity, and the Ramones were desperate. In their relentless quest for success, they canned Danny and Linda and began to search for a savior. It was narrowed down to two prospective managers, Gary Kurfirst and Steven Massarsky.

Gary Kurfirst was from Forest Hills; in fact, his family lived in Dee Dee's building. I had gone to school with his little brother Alan. Gary Kurfirst was someone we were already very familiar with, especially Johnny, as he was closer to Gary's age and grade in school. Gary was renowned in our neighborhood as far back as the late 1960s.

Like Simon and Garfunkel and Leslie West, Gary was a Forest Hills boy who'd made it to the big time. He'd become a rock concert promoter who, even at age twenty, was already presenting big shows in the Singer Bowl and the pavilion in Flushing Meadow Park, as well as other large-scale shows in the tristate area. These were shows we'd always bought tickets for—or snuck into. Gary had become a powerful figure in the music business. He had his own management company, Overland Productions, whose roster boasted several big-name acts, including the Talking Heads, the Pretenders, and Blondie. He also owned a record label called Radioactive.

A family friend, Joe Fontana, had recommended Steve Massarsky. Joe and Steve were friends and business associates. Steve had been successful as manager of the Allman Brothers and Cyndi Lauper. Plus he was a lawyer as well as a manager. Joe spoke of Steve very highly as an extremely intelligent, well-respected guy who didn't play favorites with his clients and showed them all respect.

A meeting was set up for Johnny, Joey, and Dee Dee to meet him. Joey and Dee Dee came away impressed with a good feeling about Steve and seemed to be pushing for him, while Johnny was very much leaning toward Gary.

This was a serious standoff.

After much convincing by Johnny, Joey and Dee Dee agreed to go with Gary Kurfirst. A fresh start with new management seemed to reinvigorate the creative flow, as did another change, a little thing known as acknowledgment. Since *Rocket to Russia*, Joey and Dee Dee had been writing the bulk of the songs. They started a campaign to abandon the scheme of attributing *all* songwriting credits communally to the Ramones, regardless of who actually wrote the song.

Interestingly enough, Johnny, the self-professed Commie-hating enemy of all things socialist, had instituted this rule. In actuality, the whole practice of dividing wealth and prominence equally despite an uneven amount of productivity was totally contradictory to the purportedly pro-capitalist philosophy Johnny was constantly espousing.

Joey and Dee Dee were agreeable to leaving the financial structure as it was, but they were demanding to have their individual names on the album credits, identifying them for their work. As the person who contributed least to the writing, Johnny was totally against this. It would obviously take power, importance, and attention away from him. Johnny certainly would not have let it happen if he hadn't been convinced by Gary Kurfirst that ultimately he himself would suffer for it if this arrangement negatively affected Joey and Dee Dee's input, and output. It turned out to be a good move, as the two were far more productive knowing they would be rewarded with rightful recognition and acknowledgment as prolific songwriters.

With "Beat on the Brat," "Sheena Is a Punk Rocker," "Rock & Roll Radio," "Rock 'n' Roll High School," "I Just Want to Have Something to Do," and "I Wanna Be Sedated," Joey had already written not only Ramones classics, but what would later be recognized as classics in the entire genre of rock & roll. Eventually they would be acknowledged as classics of popular American music, and, even more remarkably, American culture.

For reasons that may or may not have had anything to do with Tommy's departure or the new arrangement regarding writing credits, my brother had suddenly tapped into a stream abundant with ideas for new songs. Over the course of the next year, Joey went on a writing *rampage*. Sometimes he needed help finding a way to make a certain chord transition or to get an effect that he heard in his head but couldn't work out on the guitar. Sometimes, simply for expedience, it was quicker to have someone else play the guitar while he sang the song and decided upon an arrangement.

Normally on these occasions, he would call me to come over and help. I'd play while he'd sing.

Joey would start, stop, say, "No, try this!"

Or, "Yeah, it was better the other way."

Or, "Can ya try another chord?"

Then we would tape it on a little handheld cassette player so that he could listen to it or possibly play it for the band or producer.

We'd already done this on a bunch of songs, including "I'm Affected," "I Can't Make It on Time," "We Want the Airwaves," "This Business Is Killing Me," "I Can't Get You Out of My Mind," and some others. Even Ira Nagel, our old friend and former Ramones bassist, made some contributions.

Ira and I were up at Joey's one day when we helped him write a song called "Chop Suey." I started slapping out a beat on the top of my thighs, Ira came up with a bass line, and then I threw in the guitar riff and chords for the chorus. Joey started singing the words, and it all came together in about an hour. The Ramones only made a demo of the song, but it was recorded by the B-52's and later released on one of their albums.

So far there had been no problems or conflicts between Joey and me. I knew whether I had actually collaborated on the writing or simply helped Joey interpret and record what he had written. But there were definite occasions where the word "collaboration" was more appropriate. Ira, Joey, and I had *definitely* collaborated on "Chop Suey." It was simple and fun for us to write it together.

A few nights after that, Joey asked me to come over to his place and help him with a song he was struggling with. In fact, it was at a stage where aside from having the words and a very vague idea for a melody, he had no idea what to do with it. It was called "It's Not My Place (In the 9 to 5 World)," and the premise and words were great. I knew it was going to be a difficult job putting these words to music, but having just spent two years converting Lester Bangs's overstocked, off-meter lyrics into actual songs, I'd become pretty good at it.

The words for "9 to 5 World" did not make for an even-metered, typical Ramones style song—at least, not the way *I* heard it. In my head I heard a riff somewhere between the Young Rascals' "Good Lovin'" and something Latino-sounding, like the Sharks' "America" in *West Side Story*. Ironically, the riff was more like the one in the song that was our original inspiration, "La Bamba." The seed Ritchie Valens planted some thirty years prior was still growing.

I came up with the music and then a melody for the words that fit into the riff, but it was a very atypical song for Joey. I went over it with him until he got it. He already had a bridge for the song, which he lifted right out of the Who's "Whiskey Man." But the bridge was a half-time "breakdown" deal, which made it even trickier to come up with a good transition into it and then back out. Fortunately, I was able to do that relatively quickly. We wrote the song in a few hours and recorded it on his little cassette recorder. Joey was really happy with the song, and so was I. It was a great collaboration—the first song we'd really written together.

We did consider that this song might not fly with Johnny. It would also be a very atypical riff for him, if he could even play it. It certainly was not all downstrokes. And in the back of my mind—way back—I was hoping they might ask me to play on the track if they decided to record it.

They *had* already used other guitarists on their records, Walter Lure and Ed Stasium to name two. It was not the burning desire of my life to play guitar on a Ramones album, and probably would not have propelled my career tremendously, if at all—but it would have been nice, especially as I had come up with the guitar part.

They did put the song on their album *Pleasant Drams*, but never played it live.

Once again, I was disappointed and disrespected when the record came out and I was not credited or mentioned, which apparently was my brother's decision. It simply read, "Written by Joey Ramone."

I didn't say anything. I played the good soldier, figuring he'd make it up to me some way, someday, and decided not to rock the boat. Joey had been supportive and helpful in trying to get my band recognition, as he had with several other bands he liked. I got the feeling, though, that in *my* case there was some sort of unspoken agreement of give-and-take that existed only in Joey's mind. I continued to help him put some songs together and put them on his little tape recorder: "My, My Kind of Girl," "Real Cool Time," and many others.

I was over at his apartment all the time anyway. I felt a little bad because it was a small studio apartment and Joey and I just took over; Linda had nowhere else to go. But she was tolerant. By this time she was more or less accustomed to Joey's idiosyncrasies.

As my brother got more secure in other areas of his life, his enduring need for acceptance by our father was becoming more noticeable—at least to me and our mother. By now Dad had been completely converted; he had also become a punk rocker himself. Bless his heart, he'd gotten himself a really bad hairpiece, grown his sideburns, and was now wearing Ramones T-shirts on the beach in the Hamptons. He'd even started trying to write songs.

I took it in stride and tried to find the humor in it, but I did cringe when the old man got personalized license plates on his Caddy, dubbing himself the "Rock Pop." It was funny, sort of, but things were getting weird, probably because my brother was taking it *seriously*, as he relished the old man's sudden interest and adulation. When Joey told me that he wanted to compose music around some of our father's lyrics, I really hoped he was joking.

Our father had written words for three or four songs. One was called "No Hope, Can't Cope." Another was called "Cold Turkey for a Hot Poppa." "Hot Poppa" was another one of the nicknames he'd adopted. That was the one Joey wanted to write music for, and unfortunately he asked me to help. Then he had the idea of making it a seven-inch single, with the old man taking on the character of "Hot Poppa"—posing on the cover sitting in a big chair, in a silk robe, smoking his pipe, surrounded by hot "broads."

We went to Daily Planet Studios—Joey and Linda, Hot Poppa, our pianist friend Hilly Balmuth, and myself—and recorded the song. I wound up playing bass, *and* guitar, *and* coproducing the track with Joey.

Apparently, Phil Spector was not interested in "Hot Poppa."

Suddenly the pillar of power in our former young lives was becoming very nervous. I could hear the quivering in Dad's voice as he tried the first few takes. Now he was finding out how difficult it was to be in a studio in front of a microphone and under the microscope—with tape rolling, revealing every flaw, every blunder. Joey and I had trouble containing ourselves. Maybe that was part of Joey's plan.

After his fifth attempt, we all went into the control room to listen to it. Dad wasn't cutting it like he had in the shower stall. We started to feel bad for the guy as the tape revealed the deficiencies in Hot Poppa's ability. Even with both Joey and me coaching him, after several hours of frustration, he was ready to throw in the towel.

It was Joey's enthusiasm that kept the session from sinking: My brother was *determined* to make this happen. Finally we got a montage of performances from "Hot Poppa" that could be assembled into one decent lead vocal track for the song—if there could be such a thing. Dad was, of course, delighted and brought the finished cassette to his girlfriend Nancy's house in the Hamptons. Her son Jonathan made copies, and they played it constantly, in the car—*everywhere*.

It was nice that Joey wanted to do a little family project, but it was still one of the silliest wastes of studio time and money I'd ever encountered. The thought of people actually hearing this thing made me cringe with embarrassment for all of us, but for my father especially. I didn't want people laughing at him. (Or could it be that I was afraid that *he* would get a record deal before I did?)

Fortunately for the time being my brother chilled on the idea of putting the thing out. Thankfully, he put the tape in a box and out of sight—but some things are destined to resurface. Like the disturbing rumblings about this mysterious relationship between Linda and Johnny.

I had forgotten about it since Monte had mentioned it a year earlier. Like the possibility of Joey putting out the "Hot Poppa" record, I didn't want to believe it. I hadn't noticed anything unusual. Could there be more to Linda and Johnny's relationship than met the eye? And now Joey was even talking about him and Linda getting married!

When my brother told me he was going to buy Linda Danielle an engagement ring, I was sincerely happy for him. I didn't think he'd actually get married anytime soon, but it seemed like a positive move. But the buying of the engagement ring turned into scene out of a TV sitcom. Linda wanted a heart-shaped diamond. She said she had never shopped for rings before and had no idea what a ring like that would cost. It was a seemingly innocent request—naïve, but innocent.

The jeweler told them a heart-shaped diamond ring cost $3,000, which was a huge chunk of Joey's savings. In 1980, Joey Ramone's total savings came to not much more than $5,000. The ring would be a serious investment.

A few nights later, Arlene and I, and Joey and Linda, went to Mom and Phil's house for dinner, and the subject came up. It seemed that Mom thought that spending more than half of Joey's savings on this ring was crazy. Joey, Linda, and Mom got into it. Phil and I moved away from the table and tried to watch the basketball game.

Joey, who had apparently told Linda he was okay with the price, suddenly reversed his stance, siding with my mother.

Linda said: "Hey, I didn't even know what it cost!"

At halftime, Phil and I came back to the table for dessert.

Though Mom knew Joey was smitten with Linda, she was worried that she would hurt him. She'd already voiced her concerns when she first met Linda.

"Joey asked me a couple times why I didn't like her, which was pretty obvious. I didn't feel she was right for him, but you can only tell your child this so many times before he resents it. I had good reason not to trust her, because as soon as she could, Linda cheated on him with Johnny."

"The first time we kissed," Johnny explained, "we were in a cab, going to our accountant Ira Herzog's office in the summer of 1980. Me and Linda were the only ones who knew."

By the autumn of 1980, I'd heard from Little Matt, soundman John Markovich, and others that things were getting weird between Johnny and Linda. Little Matt told me that Johnny and Linda were spotted together at a Holiday Inn where the band was staying. Joey had gone to sleep; Johnny and Linda were in a Jacuzzi—holding hands. I just couldn't picture it, nor did I want to.

Even our father had seen Johnny and Linda behaving suspiciously at an out-of-town show. They'd all gone out for dinner, and at the restaurant Dad had noticed Linda attending to Johnny more than Joey—getting him napkins and things. No one had said anything to Joey—not a word. Then Arlene told me things she'd seen.

"Every time Mickey and I were over at Joey's apartment," Arlene Leigh remembered, "Linda would say to me, 'Let's go out for a walk.' So we would go out for a walk, and Johnny would be there, like magic, right in the street. As time went on, Linda would ask Joey if he wanted ice cream, or whatever, so she could go out to see Johnny. And she'd take me. I guess I was a convenient decoy."

Not surprisingly, Johnny had a very different version.

"Arlene would say to Linda, 'Let's call Johnny up and let's have Johnny come downstairs,'" Johnny Ramone claimed. "Arlene would wanna meet me. It would be Linda's way to get outta the house when Arlene would go over to Joey's. I would come downstairs and hang out with them. Arlene hit on me. She'd make little innuendos: 'Why don't you go with a real woman? What do you see in that skinny little girl?' I always found it amusing."

Arlene did say those things, but what Johnny left out was that the "real" woman Arlene was urging Johnny to "go with" was her old friend Roxy, with whom Johnny was sharing an apartment on Tenth Street, around the corner from Joey's building. But Arlene didn't even have Johnny's phone number. No one did except Linda.

"There was no way I could have arranged those rendezvous," Arlene stated. "I could tell something was up with Linda and Johnny—body chemistry. Women are very sensitive to things like that."

Everyone knew what was going on, and it had nothing to do with Arlene. But this is Johnny's side of the story, so I present it as promised to him.

"One day," Arlene recalled, "I flipped out because I saw Johnny put his hand on Linda's thigh under the table in a deli."

"Arlene caught us playing footsie," Johnny Ramone admitted, "underneath the table at the deli on Eighth Street in the summer of 1980. Arlene had been my girlfriend in high school. When she left me, I vowed I'd spend the rest of my life getting back at her."

"It seemed like he was flaunting it," Arlene recalled. "Like he wanted it to come out. If he didn't want people to really know something was up between them, why would he be doing that in front of *me*, when Linda was living with my future brother-in-law?"

Arlene admits she never confronted Linda about her affair with Johnny. She was in a very difficult position and certainly didn't want to be the one to tell Joey. Nobody did.

She did tell *me* that something was going on between Linda and Johnny.

If Joey heard people talking, he wasn't listening. By spring of 1981, I'd heard enough.

24.

GRILL THE MESSENGER

By now I was totally convinced that Linda was having an affair with Johnny. I knew my brother had to be made aware of it and that no one wanted to be the messenger that Joey would slaughter. I didn't, either, but I didn't see any choice. I couldn't continue to let my brother be made a fool out of—especially since Johnny really *was* flaunting it. It was making me feel like a fool as well.

One day when I knew Linda would be out, I got up the nerve to go to Joey's apartment and tell him what I'd heard, let the chips fall where they may—even if it was on my head. I stopped at the deli downstairs so I'd have a few beers in a bag ready, just in case. When I got up to Joey's he was sitting by the table playing his guitar, my old Yamaha. He'd actually made us some coffee and seemed to be in a really good mood—which made it even harder. I sat down on his bed and took a deep breath.

"Joey, I gotta tell you something. Have you noticed anything strange with Linda?"

"Like what?" Joey shot back, in a tone that told me this was going to be ugly.

"I don't want to have to tell you this," I started slowly, "but I keep hearing from people that something is going on between Linda and John."

"Yeah, so?" Joey said, getting more agitated. "So they talk, I know that. What are you tryin' to say?"

I still couldn't tell if he knew about John and Linda and didn't want to deal with it, or if he was in denial, or if he didn't care. I took another deep breath.

"I'm trying to tell you they are fucking around and have been doing it for like a year already," I quickly blurted.

"THAT'S BULLSHIT, MAN!"

"Joey, listen. Everyone's been telling me these things they've seen. Even Dad and Arlene."

I went through the gory details of the things I'd been told.

"I DONT BELIEVE IT! YOU'RE JUST TRYING TO MAKE FUCKIN' TROUBLE, MAN! WHAT, DOES IT BOTHER YOU THAT I HAVE A GIRLFRIEND? WHAT ARE YOU, JEALOUS?"

"Why the hell would it bother me that you have a girlfriend?" I answered. "I'm telling you this because you're my brother and everyone else is afraid to tell you, and because they are making a fucking chump out of you, man! I'm trying to help you here!"

"Well, I don't fuckin' believe you, okay?" Joey snarled.

"Okay, man," I answered. "Don't say I didn't try to warn you."

The way I figured it, I'd probably just confirmed some things Joey had been suspecting but did not want to address.

"STOP TALKING TO John," Joey told Linda shortly after I talked to him.

"Fine, I will," Linda answered.

"Well, it's not really you I'm worried about," Joey told her. "It's John."

"Well," Linda responded, "tell Johnny to stop talking to *me* then."

"I did," Joey said. "But he wouldn't listen. Johnny said you're his best friend!"

Joey had slowed up on his drinking while he was with Linda, but he was now eyeing a bottle of wine on the table.

"So? What can I do about that?" Linda said.

Then Joey just gave up; he was letting Linda go. No yelling, no cursing, no punching. Maybe he was afraid of hitting Linda, who was apparently now Johnny's property.

"Well, ya know what?" Joey said, now freely swigging wine from the bottle. "I think I want to do things on my own; I think I can do that now."

"Well, don't start drinking again or you'll never do anything on your own," Linda said as she headed out of their apartment—toting a nice little chunk of my brother's heart in her handbag. She closed the door and left a guy with a gaping wound behind.

As everyone knew, Joey didn't heal easily.

"There might have been some spite in it," Johnny Ramone remembered. "I don't know. Once I wanted her, I was sticking to it until I got it. I don't accept defeat. It was just a matter of time."

I honestly don't think Linda had a chance. As Johnny said, once he wanted something, he went after it. Johnny really believed he was fighting for Linda and that he actually did *win* her over. But who was his competition? Joey? Johnny knew my brother wouldn't, or couldn't, lift a finger or even confront him verbally. It was cruel: Johnny just took Linda, caveman style.

As a former friend of his, I wish I could say that Johnny Ramone *did* do something to ease Joey's pain. But there was no gesture made of any sort. A big, loud *nothing* was what Johnny offered Joey. We all heard it. And the booming silence would continue to echo.

As if Joey Ramone hadn't been entertaining enough demons in his head, he now had another one to deal with. Born of the humiliation stemming from the John-and-Linda debacle, this new phantasm would heckle him with taunts of "You're shit!" and "YOU'LL NEVER BE ANY GOOD!" It was another voice joining the older, time-honored tenants Joey had been boarding in his brain for many years. The unwanted voices had never gone away, though he'd been doing a good job of living with them. Now he was getting it from inside out, *and* outside in.

"It was a real rocky time," Joey said. "Me and Johnny had almost no communication whatsoever. It probably would have split up most bands. There was a breakdown in the machinery. Things were rolling, but not the way they should have been.

"Things had to change. Maybe we were a little too militaristic. Maybe the egos were running a little too wild."

"At that point, I didn't like Joey," Johnny Ramone confessed. "He didn't like me. I just didn't talk to him and I couldn't have cared less."

The snubbing Johnny was now giving Joey—combined with my brother's inability, or unwillingness, to confront Johnny—had to hurt. For someone like Joey, with more than his fair share of emotional disorders, it was especially damaging. I had never seen his OCD—the tapping, the stepping, the light-switching, the hair-twiddling—worse. Joey even had to ask me to drive him back to the airport terminal when he came home from England, so he could rectify the mistake of not having stepped off the curb properly.

"Johnny crossed the line with me concerning Linda," Joey stated. "He destroyed the relationship and the band right there."

"I knew Joey wouldn't want to talk about it," Legs said, "but since it was such an extreme situation I thought he would eventually open up to me. But he never did. I knew he needed to dump it somewhere, because it was eating him alive."

Joey wasn't changing his clothes. He wasn't cleaning his apartment at all—not that he'd ever cleaned it before. But it was a disaster area, especially for him, as he was always just inches away from stepping on something and winding up in the hospital with another foot infection. He was barely surviving. It probably would have helped if he'd talked about it. The most he would say to me was "Fuck 'em!" or "Screw 'em both," or the deathly sarcastic "Yeah, well, I hope they're real happy!" But mostly he'd just mumble, "I don't wanna talk about John, awright!?!"

I didn't push it.

Thankfully there was someone Joey *did* talk to—Ellen Callahan, a girl he'd first hung out with when the Ramones' second album came out in 1977. Ellen was a very welcome face, especially considering the circumstances. It seemed like she could do Joey some good. She was smart but also kind of wild and fun. And she was going to medical school, studying to become a nurse. Ellen was just what the doctor ordered.

"Joey was very incoherent when he called," Ellen remembered. "I think he was drunk. We talked all night long. He told me how pissed he was at Linda and how he'd like to kill Johnny.

"I never met Linda," Ellen admitted, "though I knew who she was. I thought of her the same way people probably thought of me—as a trashy bridge-and-tunnel kind of person who wore striped tights a lot. When Joey told me that Linda had left him for Johnny, I thought, 'Linda's a fucking little groupie just like I thought she was. She sees that Joey's not going to be the perfect rock & roll husband and Johnny probably fits more into her idea of that.' What she did to him was pretty low. I didn't tell Joey, 'You don't need to kill Johnny.' I just thought these were the kind of ravings that would happen in any band. Joey said he was going to leave the band, and the band was nothing without him—but he said that all the time.

"The way Linda left Joey really kicked in his OCD thing," Ellen continued. "Joey couldn't process or handle it. I think it brought up past events for him, past disappointments, like being passed over by a girl for someone else. Johnny represented that working-class, male machismo type."

After that, Joey and Johnny couldn't agree on anything.

"When things broke down, I felt like . . . 'Fuck this!'" Joey recalled. "I had gotten disgusted with doing the majority of the songwriting. In the early days it said the *Ramones* wrote everything. It wasn't the Ramones, it was me and Dee Dee. I didn't even mind that so much at the time. But some things are off-limits. Some things people just don't do to each other, especially in a band. If you want the band to blossom, then you don't cross that line."

A STROKE OF good timing got Joey and Johnny a short reprieve from being in close proximity to each other. In the late winter of 1981, the Ramones took time off the road to record their sixth album. The record company chose British producer Graham Gouldman, a former member of the 1960s band the Mindbenders, and later 10cc. The Mindbenders were known mostly for their hit "The Game of Love." 10cc was a more sophisticated seventies pop group whose biggest hit was "I'm Not in Love." The combination of the Ramones and Graham Gouldman was an unlikely coupling, but at least he'd written some great songs, such as "I'm a Man" and "Heart Full of Soul" for the Yardbirds; the Hollies' "Bus Stop" and "Look Through Any Window"; and Herman's Hermits' "No Milk Today" and "Listen People."

"We just wanted to produce *Pleasant Dreams* ourselves," Joey Ramone explained, "with Tommy Ramone and Ed Stasium. But Warner Bros. told us if we produced the album ourselves, it would bomb. Warner Bros. got ahold of Graham—and he thought it would be a challenge to produce us."

"Gouldman was a lightweight pop guy," Johnny Ramone offered. "When he told me, 'Your amp is buzzing too much. Can you turn down the volume?' I knew he wasn't right for the Ramones. But we had no choice."

"I went to England with Graham and did some of the vocals," Joey explained. "We went there to mix *Pleasant Dreams* because Graham had these studios, one in Manchester and one in London, where I did the singing and overdubs."

Joey called me from a "haunted" castle in England, where Gouldman had one of his studios. He sounded positive but lonely. Ironically, they had recorded a song called "The KKK Took My Baby Away," which Joey had written well before I'd told him what was going on. I was at his apartment when he was working on the song, and so was Linda. The fluky connection between Johnny and the KKK raised a specter that keeps friends and fans speculating to this day. At the time, though, it had to be an unusual situation for him being that, as often happens with song lyrics, his words now took on a whole new meaning.

When Joey returned from England he was still brooding about Linda, but at least now he was starting to call other girls. He called Ellen to invite her to a Ramones concert on Long Island. She seemed happy to see him again but was going to Stonybrook University Medical School and seriously dating a guy named David.

"Joey told me I was selling out and that I would never be happy," said Ellen. "At that point, Joey was so miserable that he had no capability of being happy for anyone else. When he found out I was engaged, suddenly he wanted me—because I was unavailable.

"People stared at Joey all the time," Ellen continued. "On a ninety-degree day he'd be wearing a black leather jacket with rips in his knees, looking very gangly—and taking two steps forward and one step back. There were seventy different reasons to stare at Joey. I never knew if it was because he was famous, or if it was because he was weird-looking."

But Ellen also noted that fame somehow legitimized the way people looked at my brother: "Part of the wonder of his life was that he was able to turn a negative into a positive. Because of that, girls found him attractive.

"During that summer of 1981," Ellen recalled, "we went to see a Woody Allen movie in Queens. It was Joey, Arlene and Mickey, and my cousin Stacey and her boyfriend, and me. Afterward, we all went back to Arlene and Mickey's apartment. Arlene was telling me that I shouldn't marry David and that I should try to work things out with Joey. I told her, 'I can't work with someone like this!'

"All weekend Joey was obsessing about something he wore on himself somewhere, this thing, his 'little string' he called it. If he didn't have it, then we couldn't walk down the street, we couldn't go out—it was beyond all limits of sanity. Joey would say, 'Just find it, get it for me.' I'd say, 'You must have me confused with some kind of wife.'

"Joey acted very in love with me, but he was also pissed off the whole time. He wanted me to take off my diamond ring, ranting, 'Fucking god-damn woman, fucking bitch Linda, goddamn fucking diamond ring.' Then the last night, he took me up to the top of his building, and we wound up screwing on the roof."

One week after that last fling with Joey, Ellen had a bridal shower. She told my brother they had an internecine relationship, which she defined as mutually destructive. He said that was the only kind he had.

"Joey and Mickey seemed like really close brothers," Ellen recalls, "but when Joey would mumble something, Mickey would do it. Mickey would placate Joey and be his stooge, not in a bad way—but then again, how could you be somebody's stooge in a good way?"

I *had* gotten used to treating my brother a certain way: When we were on the road, my job was to be his roadie/slave/protector/nurse. I think he had gotten used to that as well and was probably taking it for granted. By now, after six years of roadies, he was very comfortable with that kind of treatment, and with barking out orders to people like he did to our mother. Well, like most of us do to our mothers—*when we're little kids.*

At that point we were all kind of handling Joey with kid gloves. Every-body felt bad for him. He was holding his head up and maintaining his sense of humor, but if you knew him well, you knew he was struggling.

"He'd just talk about *'fucking Johnny'* taking her away," Ellen said, "and how he wanted *'fucking Johnny'* dead. He kept repeating himself—I chalked it up to his OCD."

But OCD or no, the law of the jungle is that the male of the species is supposed to kick the other guy's ass in this situation. Joey had a lot to work out in his mind and his heart: love being replaced by anger, trust rewarded with betrayal. Whether he should act on it or not was undoubtedly weigh-ing on him. Joey knew he looked bad, that he was the loser. He was still getting bullied in a passive way—this time by his own bandmate.

If we were back in high school, maybe I could have helped him. But nobody could step in for him on this one. Too many people around the Ramones would become noticeably quiet if Joey suddenly appeared. Were people laughing at him? Some probably were. That would have been con-sistent with Johnny and the Ramones' philosophy: no sympathy, no apologies, and no displays of sentiment or concern. For Johnny, any form of empathy was for hippies and wimps.

It can be tough to keep up the "punk" image, especially if you start to take it seriously and believe it, like Sid Vicious, or even Dee Dee. It's not natural to be *that* insensitive *all* the time. All the Ramones, including Joey, had to maintain the persona of an emotionless being and not break from character often.

"No smiling," Danny Fields would remind them in the early days, "there might be a photographer about to take a picture."

But being miserable came naturally for Johnny.

"I know I'm miserable," he once told me. "I'll probably be miserable 'til the day I die!"

We all feel that way sometimes, and those are the days you need help getting through. In some sick way, that was part of the Ramones' charm.

So was knowing you're a little crazy and then laughing about it.

We were once crossing the street with a bunch of people, and Joey stepped back on the curb. When someone asked him about it, he said, "My head is so far from my feet, I have to make sure I'm making the right decisions." Another time he'd joked, "Uh, I thought my shoe was stuck on something."

But some things about being crazy are just not funny. When we would cross the street, he would pivot from the foot on the curb to the one on the street, and when it felt right to him, he would dart across the street while the gettin' was good. Many times cars would slam on their brakes to avoid hitting him; it was inevitable he would get hit one day. And several times he did get bumped as the cars screeched to a halt. Fortunately, though, they had seen him coming—how could they miss him? My biggest fear was that one day, a driver would *not* see him coming. Or going.

25.

TOMORROW NEVER HAPPENS

When *Pleasant Dreams* was released in August 1981, the disappointment continued. It was another album that didn't produce a hit or sell well. Sire Records had merged into Warner Bros. Records, but they didn't even bother releasing a single from the album in America.

"The record company told us the album would bomb if we didn't use Graham Gouldman," Joey explained, "so we worked with Graham—and the album bombed anyway!"

The results of that collaboration brought mixed reviews from the band and fans alike.

"I didn't write anything on *Pleasant Dreams*," Johnny stated. "The Ramones were losing the respect we'd earned over the years."

"I wasn't crazy about the production on that album," Joey continued. "It lacked aggression. The songs on *Pleasant Dreams* sounded so fantastic live, like 'The KKK Took My Baby Away.' But on the record they didn't have the aggression they were supposed to have. We lost a lot of our fans during that period. They didn't know where we were going."

Insult was added to injury when the Ramones went to tape their inter-

view for *The Tomorrow Show with Tom Snyder* at NBC Studios in Rocke-
feller Plaza.

"We waited all these years to come on *The Tomorrow Show* and meet
Tom Snyder," Joey related, "and we find out he was on vacation. Tom
doesn't even show up!"

The cutesie blond replacement host unwisely disclosed to the TV view-
ers that she'd never even heard of the Ramones and was thereafter hit with a
wave of bitterness and resentment in response to every one of her questions.
When the show aired, the Ramones did not appear to be the carefree, fun-
loving guys everyone imagined them to be.

But then again, after *The Tonight Show Starring Johnny Carson*, most
of the TV sets across rural America would be blaring the national anthem,
anyway.

THE *TOMORROW SHOW* debacle was just one of many public embarrass-
ments the Ramones would suffer during the next decade. Marky was about
to add his contribution.

"By October 1981," admitted Marky Ramone, "I was doing more drinking. Joey was also drinking more, and Dee Dee was doing coke, psycho
drugs, and smoking a lot of pot.

"I always felt I was in the middle of the bickering," Marky continued.
"Every time I'd talk to Joey, Johnny would get upset. If I talked to Johnny,
Joey would get upset. Then there was Dee Dee, with his schizophrenic
personality. Dee Dee would jump out of the tour van and want to fight ev-
erybody. Johnny would tell him to come back in or he'd kick his ass. Since
Dee Dee was afraid of Johnny, he'd do what he said.

"Dee Dee punched Joey once in a restaurant, because Joey said something about his wife. Joey had his glasses on, so I thought that was wrong."

I'd known Marc Bell casually from performing with him at Max's when
he was with Wayne County and the Back Street Boys and I was playing
with Lester Bangs. Later I saw him with Richard Hell and the Voidoids. I
thought he was an excellent drummer and always admired his playing. But
Voidoids guitarist Bob Quine once expressed frustration to me about Marc's
tempo fluctuations, which he attributed to drinking. I hadn't noticed it so
much with the Ramones because everything was basically played at one
speed—maximum.

Marky fit perfectly within the band's New York City street-kid image. He had a Brooklyn accent that could give Bowzer from Sha Na Na a run for his money. His deadpan "acting" in *Rock 'n' Roll High School* was classic and in my opinion took top honors among the Ramones' thespian efforts in the film. When it came to being droll, Marky could outdo any one of 'em. He was always friendly and clowning around.

The first time I came to see Marky in the Ramones, he was mainly concerned with how he looked in his new jeans. I walked into the dressing room as he was contorting nervously with his back to the mirror, straining to check out his butt. The first thing he said to me was, "How do these look, are they awright in the backside?"

I laughed. Then he turned around and I noticed the jeans had some kind of insignia stitching on the back pockets. I gasped. They were designer jeans! Something was not kosher. What was Marky thinking?! Was *more* trouble brewing down the road?

"We were at the Swingo Hotel in Ohio," Marky confessed, "and we had to get to Virginia Beach by the next day. That night, I drank eighteen doubles of 151-proof rum. I couldn't walk. I crawled to my room, ended up sleeping under the desk, literally.

"The next day, I'm still fuckin' out of it, but I have a day off. I tell the band, 'I'll meet you in Virginia Beach,'" Marky laughed. "The groupie I was with—a tall brunette with green eyes—said she'd get me a ride to Virginia Beach the next day. I was all set.

"After a great night with this girl, drinking all night long, it's breakfast time. I'm still suffering a hangover, and I'm ordering beer. As I'm leaving the crowded dining room, who walks into the restaurant but Roger Maris, the famous Yankee baseball player.

"When I was kid, my father bought me a Roger Maris baseball glove. I told him, 'You know, Roger, I had your glove when I was a kid . . . ' We're talking about the Yankees and we're drinking more and more, and it's getting time to leave to get to the show. Of course the ride to Virginia Beach didn't show up. The groupie can't drive, so we're fucked. I was too fucked up to take a bus, and there really wasn't time. So we go to the airport and I try to rent a private plane. I'm drunk out of my mind, and the guy who rents the planes is looking at me, going, 'I don't think so.' He thought I wanted to fly the plane! I tried to call Monte at the club, but no one answered the phone. At least I tried, but nobody could do anything. I missed the show."

The next day Marky got a ride to the next club where the band was scheduled to perform. No one would speak to him.

Then Monte said, "You know, you really screwed up!"

Johnny informed Marky that he had to pay for the whole night. It turned out that Ramones fans had destroyed part of the club because the band couldn't perform. They broke windshields in cars. To cover the damage, Marky had to fork over $6,000 from his own pocket for salaries, per diems, gas, and the club's advertising. He handed it over and admitted he'd been wrong.

"At that time, I was Marc's only friend," Joey remembered. "I tried to keep him in the band. This was at a point when there was a heavy rivalry in the band. It was Johnny and Dee Dee against Marc and me. People were always taking sides. It was them against us.

"I always thought Marc was a great drummer," Joey continued. "I remember watching him during sound checks. I was so impressed."

While the Ramones were having trouble with some of their hired help, I was lucky enough to get some of the greatest help possible, for free. Ed Stasium and Tommy Ramone would each produce a batch of new songs for the Rattlers.

Tommy had recently produced a hit song, "Kiss Me on the Bus" for a new band called the Replacements, and he liked what the Rattlers were doing, "power-pop punk" in its earliest stages. Tommy and Ed saw potential.

On the strength of reviews, our live shows, and the tapes produced by Tommy and Ed, we got signed to a booking agency called Frontier Booking International (FBI), which was run by Ian Copeland, the brother of Police drummer Stewart Copeland. FBI was the premier booking agency for the next wave of bands coming up, like the B-52's, Joan Jett, REM, the Go-Gos, the Buzzcocks, the English Beat, and 999.

Stewart and Ian's brother Miles Copeland had a record company called IRS that put out records by Wall of Voodoo, Oingo Boingo (which featured a young Danny Elfman), the Go-Gos, the Bangles, and the Buzzcocks. Miles Copeland gave us a deal for a single that would come out on his Faulty Products label, and while it wasn't the "real" record deal we were hoping for, we were certainly happy about it.

The Rattlers had already opened for the Plasmatics many times, and thanks to Joey, we even got to open for the Ramones two or three times— but only out of town. My brother told us that Johnny would never let us play with them in Manhattan. From the day I quit working for them, I got the feeling Johnny would go out of his way *not* to help me get anywhere. I didn't know if it was spite or to prove he was right when he told me how hard it was to make it. Maybe it was just Johnny's competitiveness, or even plain fear—his worst one being that I might actually get somewhere. You never know when something might hit. Anything is possible in the music business, and bands had leapfrogged over the Ramones many times already.

In truth I was never thinking, "I wanna be bigger and more famous than my brother!" My aspirations were the same as his—to be like the bands we grew up revering, the Beatles and the Who. They were my gauges of success, not the Ramones. I admired the Ramones and was happy for them, but I really didn't care to be like them—or be *one of* them.

I couldn't imagine being in a band where I couldn't play backstrokes on my guitar. Or not write, or play anything outside a certain formula or style. The Ramones have one song on the *Road to Ruin* album that Dee Dee wrote called "Questioningly," which Ed and Tommy produced more like a country/western song—though in my opinion it turned out to be one of the most beautiful songs the band ever did. Johnny hated it and said, "Never again!" I wouldn't be happy being in the Ramones.

I had my own influences and inspirations. I had my own life, my own dreams. I wanted to make records and play in bands. That's all I was thinking about, not "I gotta have a hit! I gotta have one bigger than the Ramones!"

Sometimes we wound up on the same bill with the Ramones simply because the promoter wanted the Rattlers on it, and Johnny couldn't really make them take us off—though he probably tried.

When our record came out in the spring, the Rattlers began opening for a multitude of big bands, including the Clash, the B-52's, Joan Jett, the Stranglers, the Buzzcocks, and 999. The future looked promising.

Just as things were looking up, something happened that threw me for a loop, to put it mildly.

On May 1, 1982, I got a call from my brother.

"I have some bad news," Joey started, sounding very shaky.

"Uh-oh," I said. "What happened?"

"It's Lester," Joey said. "He died."

I couldn't talk for a minute.

I was walking out the door to do a show in Massachusetts when Joey called. Ironically, we were going to play the Birdland song "I'm in Love with My Walls" for the first time that night. That was the first song Lester and I had written together, and he'd given me the thumbs-up for the Rattlers to do it a few days prior. I had been thinking about him a lot lately. I was in shock. When you spend years in a band with someone they really do become like family. "It happened yesterday," Joey said, breaking the silence.

"Well, how did it happen?" I asked him.

"Nobody's saying," he replied.

Apparently, Lester had been on the wagon, and when he decided to jump off he leaped too high, too fast, with a fatal result—not uncommon in that situation.

It was later determined that the ingestion of the pain-relief drug Darvon, along with several other pharmaceuticals taken while he was fighting off a flu virus, had put too much of a strain on his body and caused his heart to fail. All that abuse to his system had finally taken its toll when he least expected it.

"I really missed Lester around Christmas," Joey Ramone said. "Not that I spent every Christmas with him, but I kept thinking about this time he bugged me for a week to come see his Christmas tree. Finally I did, and it was all roped up like it was on the street and it was decorated with boxes of Romilar. It was total Lester. He liked things spontaneous."

When the curtain closed on that friendship, a window opened to a new one. Angela Galetto was a breath of fresh air, and when Joey started hanging out with her, I had a strong feeling this friendship would last for quite a while. Angela was skinny but built, with long, dark hair and a comfortable attitude.

"My sister, Camille, was living with Monte Melnick when I first met Joey Ramone," Angela Galetto explained. "I was living on Eighty-first Street and Columbus Avenue with this lawyer who worked for Dino De Laurentiis. I lived for a couple of months with him and then found out that he was an alcoholic when he started beating me. One night I called Monte and my sister and said, 'I can't deal with this anymore, you need to come and get me.'

"They were there within a half hour," Angela laughed. "I took all my stuff and moved in with them in Corona, Queens. When we finished moving, Monte asked me if I wanted to go see the Ramones play at My Father's Place in Long Island. That was the night I officially met Joey.

"At My Father's Place we went backstage afterward and of course I got looks from all the girls who were waiting to get into the dressing room. The thing I liked about Joey was that he immediately said something to make me laugh. At that point, with what I'd been through that day, something clicked between Joey and me that would last for years."

Before she got into the van with the band, Monte told her the rules: First, no talking to Johnny. She couldn't sit in Johnny's row, just next to Joey. And she had to make sure she'd gone to the bathroom before boarding, because there'd be no stops.

Whereas Linda was very impressed with people who were famous, Angela couldn't have cared less that Joey was a rock star. She wanted a boyfriend. Joey's friends didn't have to be famous for Angela to want to hang out with them. She was more relaxed, less status-oriented, and far more down-to-earth. That made Joey more relaxed, as well. There were other differences between Angela and Linda that led me to think that this time things would work out better for Joey. Unlike Linda, Angela was very close to her sisters and her family, more like the way we were. Angela liked to do things aside from buying expensive clothing. She liked shopping, but she also seemed content to go to movies, take little trips, or just hang out with the gang and shoot the breeze.

While Joey and Angela's relationship had barely gotten off the ground, my relationship with Arlene had been going strong for five years now. Even though it was really easy for me to come up with reasons why marriage was not a good idea for someone with my lifestyle and career choice, it was time. I did love her.

We set the date for September 12, 1982. I asked Joey to be my best man and he happily accepted. Sadly, about three days before our wedding, Joey wound up in the hospital with another infection in his foot, a really bad one this time. He was put on intravenous antibiotics and couldn't leave the hospital without risking losing a toe—or worse. He talked to the hospital staff about some kind of way to get out for a few hours while remaining on the intravenous feed, but they wouldn't do it. He wasn't well enough anyway—he couldn't even be on his feet. My brother was sincerely upset about not being able to stand by me that day.

Of course, so was I, but I was far more concerned about his health.

When we got back from Arlene's parents' time-share in Puerto Rico two weeks later, Joey was out of the hospital but not completely back on his feet. With Joey laid up, Angela began to come around more frequently. Of course, our mom still took care of him, but she got along much better with Angela than she had with Linda.

"Joey was still going through a hard time about Linda when we met," Angela recalled. "He was devastated about Linda leaving him for Johnny Ramone. When I met him at My Father's Place, he told me that what was so hard was that he didn't know about Linda and Johnny at first—and it was horrible when he found out from Mickey. "Actually, I felt Linda and Johnny were a perfect match. A few nights after the show at My Father's Place," Angela continued, "Joey asked me to meet him at CBGB when Blondie was playing. This was our first real 'date.' We were sitting at one of the tables. When I looked over, I saw he was sliding under the table . . . passed out! I ran looking for Arturo and yelled to him, 'What do I do? Joey's drunk himself under the table!'

"Arturo handed me a little vial and said, 'Get him to do some of this.' That was the first time Joey or I ever did coke."

26.

Joey wasn't the only one in his band who was hitting the sauce too hard. He and Dee Dee were able to keep their inclinations from getting in the way of their careers, but Marky wasn't faring so well.

His drinking got so bad that after a quick stop at the liquor store one day for a liquid lunch, driving his gray 1968 Coupe de Ville Cadillac, Marky passed out at the wheel. With his foot on the gas pedal instead of the brake, he sailed right through the window of a furniture store.

"I wake up," Marky recalled, "with cops on each side of the car—with their guns out! They drag me to jail right then and fingerprint me. Some guy comes into the police station, screaming, 'You ran over my daughter's foot!'

"I spent the night in jail. I had no license, no registration, no insurance, no nothing! Later my lawyer told me the guy who said I ran over his daughter's foot had lied to get insurance. But there were kids who just got out of school waiting at a bus stop. I could have fuckin' killed everybody!"

The next day Marky decided to quit drinking. But after only three or four days of being sober, he was in his parents' kitchen looking into the backyard, when, as he described it, "I saw a shape forming—a fuckin' dinosaur!

"It was the DTs! I turned around, wiped my eyes, then turned back around—but the dinosaur was still there. I ran out of the house, went back to my apartment, and hid under the covers. Later I went to a rehab in Freeport, Long Island, shaking my ass off. They stripped me, took my shoelaces, and then I started seeing things again!

"I was trying to make deals with the matrons, begging them, 'Can you get me some booze?' I stayed in there for three and a half weeks. I got rid of the shakes and the DTs. I was good for a week. Then I started drinking again."

At that point, the Ramones were supposed to record the *Subterranean Jungle* album, with Richie Cordell producing. Marky showed up to rehearse at a studio in Long Island with a bottle of vodka he'd brought along. He was nipping, trying to get loose—and he'd already had a pint of vodka before he got there.

Dee Dee took the bottle out of the trash where Marky had stashed it and ratted him out to everybody: *"Look what I found!"*

"Dee Dee—Mr. Fuckin' Innocent—with his quaaludes, cocaine, pot, and all his psycho drugs. I would never have done that to him," Marky said. "It was like, 'Let Marky be the fall guy.' But I just wanted to drink."

When Marky showed up for the *Subterranean Jungle* album cover photo session at the subway station at Fifty-seventh Street, Monte was the only one talking to him.

The concept was for the Ramones to be photographed in a subway car. Photographer George DuBose suggested going to Fifty-seventh Street and Sixth Avenue, where the B train would come into the empty station and stop for twenty minutes. Johnny asked George to have Marky look out the window, because they were kicking him out of the band, but he didn't know it yet.

"I liked that shot, but I knew something was up," Marky said.

"All our drummers cracked; one every couple of years," Dee Dee laughed.

"I was lying on my bed, watching *Kojak*," Marky remembered, "when Joey calls me and says, 'Mark, I feel bad about this, but, uh, you can't be in the band anymore.' I deserved it. Joey was okay about it, but the others, forget it. No one called me after that. If it was today, Joey would've said, 'Why don't we take off for a month and you get sober?' But I didn't want to tell Joey or the band about my being in rehab, because I would've been admitting my guilt."

The Ramones weren't terribly thrown by the prospect of having to replace their drummer again. By now they'd come to the conclusion that the front line of Johnny, Joey, and Dee Dee was the core of the band. They just needed someone whose drumming style clicked and whose personality blended with theirs—odd as it might be. They got very lucky when they auditioned Richie Reinhardt, because he was everything they needed, and more.

"I used to hang out with this band the Shirts. I went out with their singer, Annie Golden," Richie explained. "The Shirts played at CBGB's all the time and they had this big, three-story house in Brooklyn. One day in 1982, I was hanging out there with the Ramones' roadie Little Matt, and he said, 'I gotta go over to the studio, the Ramones are auditioning drummers.'

"So Little Matt hooked me up, and the next thing I know, I got a message from Monte Melnick saying, 'The Ramones would like you to come down and audition.'

"When I saw them in high school in New Jersey, I didn't like them. No one had heard that kind of music. I didn't own any Ramones records. Before I went to the audition, I had to buy all the records to learn the songs. The first couple of weeks in the band were odd because they never told me I was in the band. I just kept coming to rehearsals and learning the songs."

"We tried out Richie and liked him," Joey remembered. "He was really fuckin' great—and he kept getting better. So we went with him."

Richie performed his first show with the Ramones on February 13 in Utica, New York. Joey called me from the road and gave me the lowdown on how Richie was doing. Joey couldn't have been happier. I hadn't heard him so excited about the band in years. And I got the sense there was something else brewing between Joey and Richie—like the beginning of a great friendship.

"Richie's very talented and he's very diverse," Joey said. "He really strengthened the band a hundred percent because he sings backing tracks, he sings lead, and he sings with Dee Dee's stuff. In the past, it was always just me singing for the most part."

The first time I saw the Ramones with Richie was about a month after he joined, at a club called L'Amour in Brooklyn. To me it looked like the fire was back in a big way, and Richie was providing a lot of the fuel. Though it wasn't the sloppy-but-lovable Ramones I found so entertaining back in 1974, this version was still fun to watch and now had added depth. The band was actually beginning to evolve.

"With Richie singing backing tracks with me," Joey said, "it just adds another dimension to the band. It makes us stronger. I encouraged Richie to write songs. I figured it would make him feel more a part of the group, because we never let anybody else write our songs."

While Richie was finding his way into the band's fiber, the repercussions of Johnny and Linda's affair were still wreaking havoc within it. Though Joey may have gotten over Linda, he definitely hadn't forgiven Johnny. But Johnny couldn't have cared less about how Joey felt. Since Joey and Johnny now refused to speak to one another, they had to incorporate a middleman to facilitate their exchanges.

This new method of communication played out like a comedy routine. Johnny would say to Dee Dee or Monte, "Ask Joey if he wants to play that European tour."

Dee Dee or Monte would turn to Joey and tell him, "Johnny wants to know, do you wanna play the European tour?"

Joey usually answered, in true passive-aggressive manner, "Tell him I'm still thinking about it. Ask me later."

To which Dee Dee would reply, "Okay. Uh, who should ask you later? Me? Or John?"

The funny thing was that these two grown men often had these "conversations" only inches away from each other in the dressing room or rows apart from each other in the van. So Joey's answer would then be repeated to Johnny, who'd fume in the passenger seat next to Monte. While it was funny to watch, a lot of the fallout wasn't so pretty. It had a big effect on other members of the band and their wives and girlfriends.

Vera Davies, Dee Dee's wife at the time, recalled an episode in the hallway of a hotel in London: "Linda told me, 'John won't let me talk to you anymore.' I went back to my room and started crying. Dee Dee saw me crying and asked what happened. I told him, 'Linda's not allowed to talk to me 'cause of Johnny.'

"This did not go over well with Dee Dee," Vera laughed, "because he knew we were friends. So Dee Dee started not speaking to Johnny, and that went on for months. Then out of the blue Linda called to say that she was really sorry.

"But the one she really should have been apologizing to was Joey," Vera added. "Linda simply said, 'It's just the way Johnny is'—like that excused them both."

Dee Dee was glad the two women were speaking again, because he'd never disliked Linda. "When Joey was with Linda," Dee Dee recalled, "he didn't drink too much, because he was totally happy.

"After the crap happened between John and Linda," Dee Dee continued, "Joey started drinking—the ultimate sign of weakness in a man. John and Linda were pushing it in his face—and Joey took it. Johnny was having the time of his life, because he liked being a bully."

Joey and Johnny's conversations through other people were so bizarre, and their behavior so disturbing, that Dee Dee was beginning to look *normal*.

Well, almost.

Because Dee Dee had been diagnosed as bipolar, he was on lithium and a lot of other medications. He'd take a handful of pills every day.

"I was taking Stelazine, Thorazine, BuSpar, and lithium," Dee Dee admitted. "They said I was manic-depressive."

Now, I don't claim to be normal in any way, shape, or form, and I'm certainly not a doctor—but even *I* could've told you that Dee Dee was nuts. I knew it that day he came up to Thorneycroft when I was a teenager, all dressed up in what looked like his grandma's clothes, flaunting an assumed femme personality and provoking us "pussies" for not having the guts to be "fabulous" and different like him.

Dee Dee started getting psychiatric help in 1979. He started seeing a psychiatrist. "Anytime I was home," he said, "I'd see the doctor from Odyssey House, then the guy from Gracie Square, and the guy from Holliswood. I spent a fortune on doctors."

"When he was on the medicine, Dee Dee was at least manageable," Vera said. "You know, some people may have looked at me like I was a little too controlling—but if somebody wasn't making decisions and taking care of things, it would have been complete chaos. Dee Dee couldn't even write out a check."

"I didn't manage money very well," Dee Dee admitted. "For a long time everyone was afraid to give me money, because I'd spend it on drugs. I was spending thousands and thousands a week on jewelry and guns."

The Ramones seemed incapable of sitting down together to write songs. "The Ramones always seemed to find a reason not to do one of Dee Dee's songs," Vera confirmed. "That was really frustrating for him. He didn't feel that comfortable around Joey sometimes, because of petty jealousies within the band."

Dee Dee and Joey didn't collaborate after 1976. "After that, Joey wrote all these love songs, crying about his broken heart, which I thought was embarrassing," Dee Dee said. "I thought a rock star should never have his heart broken. He should be a real lady-killer, not be whining over some woman."

"No matter what Dee Dee wrote, the band said it just wasn't Ramones enough," Vera recalled. "But he always enjoyed writing songs with Mickey."

IN THE SIXTEEN years I'd known Dee Dee, he was always running hot and cold. He knew I respected his creative talents and his amazing ability to write songs, some of which were my absolute favorites. He also respected my songwriting and musical ability. He liked that I could play guitar, bass, keyboards, and harmonica, and program drumbeats as well as figure out the technology of the new gizmos coming out. Dee Dee thought it would be a great idea for us to write together. Since I had a little four-track recorder and all the other necessary accoutrements, he and Vera would come over to my house in Forest Hills.

And since Matty Quick had given me the opportunity to get back in the weed business—which was basically funding my recording career—I usually had enough pot on hand for Dee Dee. But quite often I didn't have enough to satisfy his tireless enthusiasm for the stuff. Sometimes we'd have to stop in the middle of recording and buy something back from a person I'd just sold it to.

Bottom line, I felt better about him smoking pot than doing heroin, which was the alternative. Heroin was something I'd never done, never wanted to do, and didn't want anyone doing in my house. Dee Dee rolled the biggest joints I'd ever seen in my life, and he could smoke me under the table. As much as I liked writing with him, sometimes I couldn't wait for him to leave so I could pass out.

"I smoked over an ounce of pot a day," Dee Dee admitted. "I've never been more addicted to anything in my life. I was just so bored; I had nothing else to do."

"Mickey and Arlene weren't that far from us in Whitestone, Queens," Vera said, "and sometimes I would drop Dee Dee off at their house. Dee Dee was an early bird; he'd be up at eight thirty or nine in the morning. Then he had to wait for six hours for Mickey to wake up."

Arlene and I lived, and still live, in a small one-bedroom apartment on the first floor of our building. The door to our apartment is right next to the elevator. I could just picture the looks on the faces of my neighbors waiting in the hallway as Dee Dee sang/screeched at the top of his lungs in that Popeye-on-crack style he invented and would later use on songs like "Wart Hog" and "Endless Vacation."

Dee Dee knew I'd helped my brother write some songs the band had recorded and was upset that I didn't get acknowledgment for it. He promised that wouldn't happen with the songs we collaborated on, which I really appreciated.

I was used to the Ramones screwing me by never giving me songwriting credit. Joey's excuse was that Johnny wouldn't do a song with my name on it. That may have been true.

During the time Dee Dee and Vera were living in Whitestone, Queens, we reconnected and actually became good friends. Vera and Dee Dee invited Arlene and me over to their house for dinner, or to just hang out and watch TV or listen to music. Dee Dee was unbelievably uninhibited and liked to put on records and dance. We all had a good time with each other. We'd do relatively harmless things, like smoke pot and eat ice cream.

Across the river, Johnny was having his cake and eating it, too.

Though Linda had a place in Chelsea where Johnny would visit her, he was still living in the apartment he shared with Cynthia "Roxy" Whitney on Tenth Street, right next to Joey's building. He seemed to think he was invulnerable and totally in control.

"Roxy was getting beat up all the time by Johnny," Angela explained. "But I think she liked it. I remember going over there when Johnny left her all tied up. Somehow Roxy managed to reach the phone. She called me and said, 'Can you come here and untie me?'"

I was never convinced that Roxy really liked getting beat up. I knew I couldn't continue to stand there and watch it happening when I worked for the band. Even if she did like it, some people just react instinctively to seeing a man hitting a girl. It was a dangerous game they were playing. I knew if Johnny kept this up, sooner or later things were bound to come to a head.

One morning in August, the phone rang much earlier than normal. "Hello?" I answered, half-asleep.

"Hey, Wing," Joey said, using the nickname he'd given me recently when we were passing a Chinese laundry named Wing Lee. "Didja hear the news?" Joey asked. "About John?"

"No," I said. "What about 'im?"

"Somebody kicked John's ass!" Joey said, working hard not to blurt out a hearty laugh.

"What!?" I said, pulling the covers off and sitting up.

"Yeah," Joey said, getting closer and closer to an actual laugh. "John got into a fight with some kid who kicked him in the head—and I think the kid was wearin' combat boots, ha ha!"

"Whooooa," I roared, "you're kiddin' me!"

"Nope." Joey laughed even harder. "Go get the *New York Post*, front page. His head made the headlines. *Ha, ha, ha!*"

"I don't believe it!" I said as a slight smile crossed my face. "I guess it was bound to happen sooner or later, right?"

Joey was still laughing.

When I got back from the corner store with the paper, I called Joey and we read over the story together.

ROCKER FIGHTS FOR LIFE: Superstar Stomped in 10th St. Rage Over Woman He Loves!

Punk Rock superstar Johnny Ramone was fighting for his life today after being savagely beaten by another punk musician. Police said Ramone was injured in a fistfight sparked by jealousy over the rock star's girlfriend, Cynthia Whitney, 27.

Officials said Ramone's attacker repeatedly kicked him in the head as he lay on the ground.

At first, Ramone declined medical treatment after the beating early yesterday outside his girlfriend's luxury Greenwich Village apartment, but later underwent emergency brain surgery in St. Vincent's Hospital.

"Man, they must have shaved his head," I said.

"Yeah," Joey said, "he'll be wearin' a hat for a while. I never saw John in a hat. I think he hates hats."

"Wow, this kid really did a number on him," I said as I scanned the article. "Guess John bullied the wrong guy this time. But it says he's going to live."

"Yeah, I heard he's only gonna be in the hospital a week, maybe two," Joey informed me. "Wonder if he'll have brain damage?"

"Well, you know, he *already* has that!" We both laughed.

The story I got from Seth Macklin, the kid who kicked Johnny and wound up going to jail for his actions, was that Johnny was smacking Roxy and then threatened to hit him as well, which started the brawl. I don't like seeing anyone get hurt, but it was hard for us to feel any sympathy for a guy who had shown absolutely none for anyone else.

"Think he'll be a nicer guy now?" I asked.

"Maybe if they gave him a brain transplant," Joey quipped.

While Johnny was recuperating, I continued to write songs with Dee Dee. But most of my free time was spent with Joey and Angela in the city. Joey, Angela, Arlene, and I hung out together practically every day if we were all in town. We were like a swinging 1980s version of the Kramdens and Nortons, with Joey and me playing Ralph and Ed to Angela and Arlene's Alice and Trixie. But unlike the goofy TV couples, we closed many a club at dawn.

Rounding out the cast of regulars in our crew were Monte and Camille, Richie Ramone, Legs and Holmstrom, Richie Stotts and his girlfriend Jane, and Joey's new friend Kevin Patrick and his wife, Corrine. Kevin was an A&R man for a big record company, but I forgave him for that. He was actually a pretty nice guy for a record company exec.

Since this was the eighties, cocaine had made just about every other indulgence obsolete. Beer and blow went hand in hand; the more you had of one, the more you wanted the other.

Then we discovered another outlet for escape, one that was even legal. It was a new game called Trivial Pursuit, and we got as hooked on the game as we had on the drinks and drugs. They even seemed to complement each other. The more blow we did, the more intensely we played the game. We loved it.

The coke would fuel our obsessive competitiveness. And while the Trivial Pursuit questions weren't at all provoking or inciting, the games often ended in drunken but friendly outbursts. Joey was as competitive as anyone, if not more so. He loved to win. And if he didn't, he would demand a rematch.

"Just one more game," he'd insist. "Aw, come on!"

Sometimes we'd play until the sun came up—that is, if our supplies lasted that long. Pathetically, sometimes we would even gauge how long we would play by how much coke we had. Joey's apartment became the mecca of Pursuit. We usually chose up two teams from the ten or so friends that assembled every Monday night to indulge in the booze-and-snoot-filled contests.

Aside from the aforementioned regulars, bench players were Frank Gallagher, who got hired by the Talking Heads after our Europe '77 tour; Matty Quick; and new additions to the Rattlers: keyboardist Billy Bailey and David U. Hall, who had just replaced David Merrill on bass. There were also occasional visits from various musicians, writers, and artists, such as brothers Billy and Andy Hilfiger, the Smithereens' Mike Mesaros, guitarist Jimmy Ripperton, Randy Dash, *Dirty Duck* cartoonist Bobby London, Billy Altman, and of course Legs.

Sometimes Joey had some very special guest stars attend.

"I was helping Billy Bragg do a gig at the Ritz," soundman Frank Gallagher remembered. "It was one Monday night, which I knew was the designated night for Trivial Pursuit at Joey Ramone's house. So after the sound check, I said to Billy, 'Come with me!' Billy said, 'Where are we going?'

"I didn't tell him where we were going or what we were going to do," Frank laughed. "I just said, 'Come with me!'

"The fool trusted me, so we walked around the corner from the Ritz on Eleventh Street to Joey's apartment on Ninth Street. When we got there, Billy was shocked because Joey was one of his idols. Trivial Pursuit was a new American phenomenon at that time, and Billy was very English. He didn't quite understand.

"Then the Ramones' girls, who had gathered around the table, started arguing with the answers on the Trivial Pursuit cards. They were saying things like, 'The moon is not a planet, it's a star!' There was a level of intelligence and grammatical use," Frank deadpanned, "that I've yet to see matched. Billy was awestruck. He was just astounded with the fact that he was playing Trivial Pursuit with Joey Ramone!"

"Whenever I'd go see Joey," Allan Arkush added, "we would all play Trivial Pursuit, and it was hilarious—because nobody knew any of the answers! I remember a science question that went to Dee Dee: 'What weighs ten trillion tons?'

"And Dee Dee said, 'Your mama!'"

27.

IT'S THE RUM TALKING

For us, life seemed to be a big party. Outside of the Ramones, who were still in turmoil and career limbo, everyone was getting along really well and having a ball. The Rattlers were touring with the Buzzcocks and 999, and Joey was working away as usual. He was happy living with Angela, and although we were partying pretty heartily, he was healthy and staying out of the hospital.

Life was good.

I was still writing a lot with Dee Dee when the Ramones weren't on the road. We'd come up with a song called "Go Home Ann" that we both thought was killer and was too good for the Ramones to pass up. We made a demo in my house, and Dee Dee took it to play for Gary Kurfirst. I didn't get my hopes up, even after Dee Dee told me Gary was considering it.

In April, Arlene and I were planning to go to her parents' time-share in Puerto Rico, as they weren't using it. Since he also had a few weeks off, Joey decided that he and Angela would join us.

This was the third year in a row that Arlene and I had gone to this spot. We rented a car and took Joey and Angela to the rain forest, and drove all around to different beaches and to Old San Juan. The young natives of the island looked at Joey the way people in America had in the 1960s: They pointed and laughed. I wasn't surprised because they did that to me, especially on the beach. We were like ghosts, radiating like fluorescent bulbs in the sand.

At night we went to a rock & roll–type bar in the Condado area, which was about the only place where they recognized Joey. Otherwise we just hung around the hotel and played pool and Ping-Pong and drank.

Nicholas Molina worked the hotel bar and had rightfully earned the reputation for making the best piña coladas on the whole island. Arlene and I had become well acquainted with Nicky over the past three years, as well as with a few couples who had the same designated vacation weeks down there each year. There were Bob and Shirley Boyd from Jamaica, Queens, and Pat and Jimmy Burns from the Bronx. At the time, they had no idea who the Ramones were, but they were happy to meet my brother and Angela and to have more people to drink with.

Jimmy was the kind of guy who wouldn't take no for an answer. If you'd bought him a drink, then he had to buy you two or three. After Joey bought Jimmy a drink or two, before you knew it we were inventing a variation of the standard piña colada called the "302." A normal one is made with a shot of 80-proof rum. We asked Nicky to upgrade it to a shot of Bacardi 151 proof instead. Then we asked him to make one with a double shot of 151, hence the 302. After several of those, we were acting like the natives, pointing and laughing at each other. Then we went out to get some air and something to eat.

As we walked down the street, Joey started acting very strange. I'm not sure if it was the alcohol that made him talk this way or if these issues had been weighing on his mind. All of a sudden, he said to me: "So I hear you're writing songs with Dee Dee?"

I said, "Yeah, so?"

Then Joey said, "Well, ya know, if you ever make it, *I don't know what I'd do.*"

Angela and I looked at each other, wondering, "Where the fuck did that come from?"

I didn't answer Joey. His reaction was something I'd had a gut feeling about for years. I supposed this issue would surface at some point but decided not to worry about what was not happening—yet.

Considering the circumstances and my brother's mental state, not to mention our history growing up, his comment was not something totally out of the ordinary or unexpected. I know he loved me and sincerely wanted good things for me. I know he wanted me to have great success and to stand on the side of the stage and be proud—but he was also afraid of those things.

So how do you respond? "Okay then, Joey, I'll deep-six my chances so that you don't have to worry about anything changing in our relationship or in my life."

It made a knot in my stomach. This was *not* the way I wanted things to be. I don't believe it was the way my brother wanted things to be either, but I wasn't sure he could control that. We all decided not to let it ruin our trip. We woke up the next day ready to forget about it and to continue to have a good time. But neither myself nor Angela nor Arlene was ever able to forget it.

"A few nights later we were back in the bar, and once again Joey was drinking a lot," Angela recalled. "He was drinking those strong piña coladas again that the guys were ordering for him. Joey usually drank beer.

"Arlene had gone up for the night, and when the bar closed, Joey and Mickey got the bartender to make a few more piña coladas and we took them to our room. It was our last night there. I don't remember exactly how the fight started, but I could tell Joey was jealous of Mickey. After what happened between Joey, Johnny, and Linda, Joey was always watching everything that was going on. He was always afraid that something was going on behind his back. In the back of Joey's mind, maybe he thought I was going to leave him for his brother. Joey was always paranoid and very jealous.

"When the thing with Dee Dee came up again, I stuck up for Mickey," said Angela. "Joey was really putting Mickey down. I think it bothered Joey, the idea of Mickey having success, because then Joey would be in the same position he was when they were young. Growing up, Mickey was normal, and Joey wasn't. I don't know if his mother favored Mickey, but Joey was a sick child, so of course he's going to be jealous that he's not normal like his brother.

"I guess Joey was always fighting to be the better brother," Angela elaborated. "That's sibling rivalry. Joey started screaming at me. He was getting really wild. I was sitting on the edge of the bed and there was a dresser with a TV set on it a few feet across from me. Joey went into a rage and grabbed the back of the TV and shoved it at me as hard as he could."

I couldn't believe what my brother was doing. Was he trying to be like

Johnny now? I got a hand under the TV before it hit Angela but it still landed in her lap and hit her in the knees, though at least not as hard. Fortunately she wasn't hurt badly.

"*WHAT THE FUCK ARE YOU DOING!?*" I yelled at my brother. "What the fuck is wrong with you!? Are you out of your fucking mind?"

"*YEAH, HA HA! I'M OUT OF MY MIND, ALL RIGHT!*" he yelled back with an angry, maniacal, drunken laugh. He had really gotten plastered this time. I could tell his head was almost spinning.

"Are you all right, Ange?" I asked her.

"*Are you all right, Ange?*" my brother mimicked me.

"Yeah, I'm okay," she said.

"Aww, isn't that sweet," Joey mocked. "You two care about each other so much. Why don't you take her in another room and screw? I'm sure you'd love to," he slurred. By now he was bouncing off the walls.

"That's it, man," I said. "You got a lot of fuckin' balls saying something like that to me. Fuck you!"

Joey just laughed, and tripped and fell onto the bed as I walked out of their room. I still couldn't believe what I'd just seen and heard. I went down to my room, sat on the terrace, smoked a joint, and looked out at the moon shining over the ocean. I thought about what had happened a few nights before and what my brother had said. I wasn't sure what I should say or do, aside from be very disturbed. I knew if I ever really confronted him, like I did back in Birchwood Towers, it might be over for the two of us. He was Joey Ramone now; I knew that, and so did he. I saw a pattern developing, within myself as well as in our relationship as brothers. It seemed now like it was a game we were playing, without saying it. In Ellen Callahan's observation, I had been playing the stooge.

She may have had a point, but I don't agree, not completely. Yes, I was slightly intimidated by the power my brother wielded now as a result of his notoriety, but I was having trouble seeing the line between his intimidation and my sympathy for him.

I shook my head and went to bed.

Angela called the next morning and told me that Joey had almost drowned in his own puke in bed that night. She said he really wanted to talk to me before they left and was going to put him on the phone.

I told her I wasn't sure I wanted to talk to him right then, but I stayed on the phone.

For the first time since we were kids, my brother apologized to me with a sincere "I'm really sorry." He said he didn't mean any of the things he had said—that he knew he was totally off base and that he trusted me more than anyone.

"I don't know, man," Joey said. "I was really fucked up."

What could I say after that?

An apology is an apology.

I accepted.

"You better try and chill out," I said. "I don't know why you're getting so violent all of a sudden. Call us when you get home, okay? And don't drink too much on the plane or get into a fight with the stewardess!"

"Joey's temper just would get so outta control," Angela explained. "Of course, I used to fight back, which is why it used to get worse. Joey was not a good fighter, but I was only about five-three-and-a-half—and he was six-five!"

MEANWHILE, THE RAMONES kept battling on.

"I tried to pull the band together with *Too Tough to Die*," Dee Dee asserted, "to bring it back to that sound. Before the last album, I wasn't getting along with Johnny. Then I decided to be friends with him again. So I said to him, 'Will you write a song with me?' We sat down and wrote songs and made them real Ramones-like."

As Johnny put it, "I realized the Ramones were losing respect. So I started fighting for things, demanding stuff, and saying, 'I'm not continuing anymore unless we do this, unless we do that . . .'"

"On the last album I wrote 'Psycho Therapy' with Dee Dee," Johnny continued, "and on *Too Tough to Die*, I wrote five songs with him. I felt we'd gotten back on track on that album. At least me and Dee Dee were talking then."

After the previous two albums failed to garner anything close to a hit, the band wanted to get back to the guys who had produced their finest efforts to date, Tommy "Ramone" Erdelyi and Ed Stasium. Even Sire Records president Seymour Stein couldn't argue with that logic and allowed the band to make the call.

"It was Dee Dee who called me," Tommy Ramone laughed. "I was kind of shocked, but pleased, too. Actually, the Ramones had wanted me to produce *Pleasant Dreams* and *Subterranean Jungle*, but the record company kept getting these big producers like Richie Cordell and Graham Gould-man.

"As soon as I started working on *Too Tough to Die*," Tommy claimed, "it was like I'd never left. Even though six years had gone by, to me it felt like a couple of weeks. I was back making another record with the guys. It was great."

They had to start rehearsing without Joey, who was in the hospital for about a month with a bad foot again. So Dee Dee sang and so did Richie Ramone, who was new to Tommy.

"It was interesting to see the Ramones after six years," Tommy continued, "because it looked like they had now formed different camps—four totally separate camps. As far as I could tell, they weren't really dealing with each other or hanging out. There wasn't a band feeling anymore. It was sort of like a corporation that made records. They were very professional, which isn't necessarily bad, it's just not the way people picture the Ramones working together."

The mind games Johnny, Joey, and Dee Dee were playing with each other were not fun, and there were no real winners. The only positive thing to come out of this was that the tension brought their emotions to a boiling point, especially in the highly emotional Dee Dee, which seemed to spur him on creatively.

On *Too Tough to Die*, Dee Dee wrote "Wart Hog" and "Endless Vacation" with Johnny. These songs not only allowed him to blow off steam that had been building inside him for years, but would also prevent the Ramones from falling into the doldrums, as a new form of punk rock, called "hardcore," was emerging. On the heels of punk rock came something called speed metal, popularized most notably by our friends the Plasmatics in the late seventies. Speed metal was an accelerated, more frenetic version of the heavy metal sound originated by bands like Led Zeppelin and Black Sabbath. The hardcore sound was a combination of punk rock and speed metal. Kids at hardcore shows also adapted the straight-up-and-down "pogo" moves from the punk scene and ramped them up several notches into something called "slam dancing," intentionally banging into each other as they jumped in the air. Then they took it even further: A few kids would move in a small circle as they slammed each other, which grew into a larger circle as more kids joined in, forming what is still known today as a "mosh pit."

It was wilder than anything we'd seen. Once Joey and I were at the Ritz watching a band called Suicidal Tendencies from the balcony. Their fans, clad in the extreme garb reminiscent of the seventies British punks—Mohawks, safety pins, piercings, etc.—heaved, weaved, and writhed around and around in a fit of violent motion, relaxing and intensifying as the music directed. From where we stood, it looked like something out of Dante's *Inferno.*

Dee Dee and I had written a fast, crazy song called "My Personal Revolution," which we'd recorded in my house. It was the song on which Dee Dee's "singing" had compelled my neighbors to go complain to the super. Dee Dee and Johnny's new songs, "Wart Hog" and "Endless Vacation," picked right up where "My Personal Revolution" left off. True to the Ramones' form, they were minimal, hilarious, and totally unique.

Faster and more manic than anything the Ramones had offered to date, these songs certainly helped to uphold their reputation as the purveyors of "fast and loud" rock & roll. Unfortunately, though they were the prototype, the Ramones found themselves needing to prove to the blossoming hardcore audience who was boss. The drawback financially was that the nature of this style brought with it a connotation of danger and need for heightened security at the shows, making it harder to get money out of the clubs.

"Hardcore made it more difficult for the Ramones," Monte Melnick elaborated. "The club owners didn't always understand what the hell was going on. They thought a riot was happening! Did you ever see what it's like in the middle of a mosh pit? It's like a whirlpool. Kids got sucked in there and never came out!"

On the upside, "Wart Hog" and "Endless Vacation" provided a desperately needed deviation from what was becoming the Ramones' obvious formula. It also created a two-headed attack with Richie Ramone trading off vocals with Dee Dee, who had found the perfect showcase for his maniacal singing style. The "call and response" singing implemented by Richie and Dee Dee added tremendous impact to their live shows.

"The Ramones needed a shot in the arm," Richie agreed. "Before me, things weren't going too well for the band. With me, it was a whole new thing. Joey knew what I could do. I could produce a song. I was a decent singer; he was happy to have that."

The downside to this battle of wills for Joey was that out of the original band members, he had the least ammunition.

"In the beginning," Richie admitted, "when Joey was having an OCD moment, Johnny would always giggle and say to me, 'Go ask Joey, what is that?'

"I would never have asked Joey anything about his OCD. I kind of put two and two together. Johnny could be very cruel."

Joey felt frustrated and intimidated as the balance of power in the band swung back to Johnny Ramone. Joey's style of songwriting seemed to get shoved to the back of the bus. He was confused about where he fit in. Once again he murmured, albeit louder this time, about his desire to make a solo album. Though Joey had recently experienced one of his most creative and productive periods, now he seemed to be having trouble catching wind in his sails.

Heading into a bit of a writing slump, Joey welcomed as much help as he could get from his friends. I was still there for him if he needed me, as were Richie Stotts, Andy Shernoff, and several others, including our old friend from Shrapnel Daniel Rabinowitz, who later changed his name to Daniel Rey.

"Daniel was a very talented songwriter," Legs McNeil remembered. "Daniel and singer Dave Wyndorf wrote Shrapnel's best songs. After Shrapnel broke up, Daniel started writing songs with Joey Ramone."

Shrapnel were huge fans of the Ramones and had opened up for them dozens of times. Daniel idolized Joey.

"The Ramones were my heroes," Daniel admitted. "Joey was a party guy, so we'd all hang out, drinking. That's when we knew we'd crossed the plateau of not just being fans but actual friends of Joey's."

A while later, Joey invited Daniel to help him with a song he was working on for the *Too Tough to Die* sessions.

"Daniel Rey came in to do some guitar stuff on the song 'Daytime Dilemma,'" Tommy recalled. "I don't think Joey was there. Joey would just be there for the vocals. In fact, nobody was ever there unless they were recording their parts."

The mid-eighties were becoming a blur, with days melding into each other, separated only by the few hours required for recovery. It was a test of endurance. We were constantly cavorting. The night usually began with everyone meeting up at Paul's Lounge on Joey's corner. After the standard first hour of waiting for Joey to come down, we would begin the routine of deciding who was going to go up to his apartment and get him the hell out of there. "Okay, who's gonna get Joey tonight?"

It was determined that no one knew better what to say to my brother that would convince him—at least temporarily—to listen to reason rather than the voices in his head. After thirty-one years of practice, I'd developed a knack for it.

The first thing I'd do was try to get him to relax. Then I would tell him, "Whatever it is you think needs to be done in there [meaning, mainly, the bathroom] you can do when you get back, so you might as well just go now and do it later. And whatever those voices in your head are telling you, just ignore them, at least for right now. They're not even really there, and you know that. I know you expect to hear them, because you have before. But you're letting yourself create them and then you let them talk. So just stop doing that, just for a minute. Get excited about the other voices out there that you'd rather hear, so these will fuck off. Focus, for one minute, on listening to me, on what I'm saying, that we're going out, *right now*, and we're gonna have some fun!"

And he would.

By the time Joey came down, Arlene, Corrine, and Monte would usually be long gone. Those remaining, including newcomer Richie Ramone, would figure out where to go next. Though the band's inner chemistry continued to diminish, Joey and Richie's friendship blossomed. Now they were the only two sharing any sense of camaraderie.

"I hung out with Joey every day," Richie Ramone remembered. "I connected with him right away. It was a long time before someone told me the Johnny and Linda story. Joey never said anything to me."

Mutual respect aside, this bonding could also have been attributed to their joint enthusiasm for getting as fucked up as possible, as often as their schedule would allow.

"Joey and I would take all the beers from the show," Richie laughed, "and go to the room and drink all night—sometimes with Dee Dee. We never saw Johnny. He'd pick a different floor in the hotel and disappear.

"But before we'd get to the hotel," Richie said, laughing even harder, "Johnny would always stop at a 7-Eleven. You gotta picture it: Fans are following our van as we're driving around looking for the nearest 7-Eleven. They think we're these tough punk rock guys, probably going for a case of beer. Then Johnny would jump out and get a pack of cookies and a little container of milk."

Joey and Richie were becoming so tight that it had to be annoying and threatening to Johnny, the control freak—not that anyone cared if it annoyed Johnny.

Our basic contingent of Joey, Angela, Arlene and me, Richie, Monte, Camille, Kevin Patrick, and Corrine was having a great time. Monte had the Ramones' van at his disposal, so we'd pile in, loaded up with beer, bones, and blow for road trips. We'd go out to Action Park water rides in New Jersey, where Angela's sister Camille would delight the patrons with tiny bikini tops that constantly slipped off her mammoth set of melons as she slid down the chutes. Little kids there would elbow each other as they gawked at Joey in his bathing suit. When he'd get out of the pool giggling, we knew he'd gotten his revenge and had deposited some recycled beer in the pool.

"Joey really got into swimming," Richie laughed. "When he got wet, his hair flattened out—and he had a really tiny head. And he still had his glasses on!

"Joey was a really normal guy. Joey loved doing all those things like going to barbecues out by my brother's. I used to take Joey everywhere. I took him bowling in Brooklyn. I took him out to my parents' house in New Jersey. He liked regular-guy activity, away from the band."

Aside from an occasional visit to CBGB, we more often frequented the newer clubs like Danceteria, Irving Plaza, the Peppermint Lounge, Cat Club, and our customary final destination, the Scrap Bar on MacDougal Street. Steve Trimboli, the proprietor, was a generous host, especially to Joey. The Scrap Bar was the epitome of a 1980s rock & roll bar. They actually had a security guy in front of the bathrooms because situations in there got so out of control. The bouncer would bang on the doors to oust the two, three, or sometimes four people who'd exceeded their allotted time in the can, pissing off the long line of fellow deviants waiting to get in to relieve themselves—which they did in just about every way you can imagine.

Val the doorman, a Jimi Hendrix doppelganger who was even taller than Joey, would rarely turn us away, unless we arrived at such a ridiculous hour that it presented too much of a risk with the cops. Sometimes we would stroll up to the door exposed by the ominous rays of the early summer sunrise.

If that were the case, we'd wind up at an after-hours club like Save the Robots on Avenue A, where time did not exist.

Our main hangout was the Ritz: an old ballroom/theater turned into a rock club. It was big enough to attract international acts but still able to enjoy a relationship with the East Village community and support local acts as well. It was run by a guy named Neil Cohen, who became a real friend of Joey's, as did the club's head of security, Jerry Adams, who practically became Joey's personal bodyguard.

Jerry's mentality was far from that of the typical bouncer. He was smart, funny—part of the family. He was dedicated to looking out for Joey as well as the rest of us.

Just about everyone was doing coke, except for John Holmstrom, and Legs, who didn't want to counteract all the alcohol he'd worked so hard to consume all night. People used to hand Joey little packets of the white stuff, either to endear themselves to him or to tell their friends they did.

Some of our friends fell by the wayside and would resurface years later, after the smoke cleared. Some of them simply fell and were not seen again.

Looking back, I feel lucky to have survived those days. We were having too much fun to notice the damage we were doing to ourselves. But the residual effects were becoming noticeable. They seemed to be spiking the intensity in Joey's personality, for one thing. The excessive dosing, combined with events in his recent past, added to the latent biological snags he was dealt at birth, were causing a noticeable imbalance.

"I think the drugs made Joey's OCD worse," Angela remembered. "He'd go into the bathroom and be in there for hours. That's when we would have our fights. They could be over anything. Joey would get all wound up and his OCD would kick in. If I did something that triggered it, he would go crazy. It's not like I would know what I'd done."

He seemed less in control of certain older problems but more in command of others.

My brother had come a long way from the deflated self-image that had held him back. Now he was close to being more like everyone else. In fact, he was more assertive than the average person. These days he was more confident when he spoke, joked, laughed, or acted like a prick. As this new socially improved Joey Ramone emerged, he began to realize that even though he couldn't control what the Ramones said and stood for, he could be responsible for what *Joey Ramone* said and stood for. Joey began thinking for himself again—beyond the claustrophobic, right-leaning world of the Ramones—and went back to what he believed before he joined the band.

He began to allow himself an occasional exodus from the black-leather-clad punk singing about Nazis and Commies, back to his roots as a liberal Jew from New York City who as a youth had concerns about the world and liked to get involved in social issues.

But it was a guy with a "small" name and a big heart who gave Joey the opportunity to open his own heart once again. Little Steven Van Zandt, the legendary producer and guitarist for Bruce Springsteen, called Joey and asked if he would donate his time, name, and talent to a politically motivated project concerning a place in South Africa called Sun City.

Sun City was a resort town in South Africa, like Las Vegas, with big shows and gambling. While several artists were boycotting the racially segregated city, casinos were luring entertainers like Frank Sinatra, Rod Stewart, and Linda Ronstadt with paychecks of $2,000,000 for a two-week run.

"Every time somebody played there, it was kind of in the government's favor," explained Little Steven. "I came back from South Africa and wrote the song 'Sun City,' with the chorus '*I ain't gonna play Sun City.*' The idea was to get celebrities to sing on it and raise awareness about the situation, to end apartheid."

He wanted a representative from each genre of music—like Miles Davis for jazz, and, of course, Joey Ramone for punk.

"I was actually surprised that Joey was so passionate about it," Little Steven admitted. "But apparently he was always quietly aware of what was going on."

When Steven tried to get the song played on the radio, he found that the white rock stations said it was too black and the black stations said it was too rock. So the song got no radio airplay.

"But I still had the 'Sun City' video with all the rock stars in it," Little Steven explained. "So I went to MTV and said, 'Look, you've got a controversy going on that you don't play black people. This is your chance to not only put black people on MTV, but to be edgy—like you're supposed to be!'"

After Steven talked MTV into playing the video, the record raised about a million dollars for the antiapartheid movement.

"We shut down Sun City," Little Steven chuckled. "I swore I'd bring the government down. An entertainment boycott would reinforce the sports boycott. Eventually we'd get the economic boycott, and at that point the government would fall—and that's what happened."

Little Steven surely didn't realize it, but participating in the "Sun City" undertaking was mutually beneficial. It was liberation for Joey as well—and completely contrary to Johnny Ramone's vision of the band as goofy right-wingers.

Unfortunately, even though "Sun City" was a critical success that showcased Joey's talents outside the Ramones, he was still in a songwriting slump.

When Dee Dee called to tell me that the Ramones wanted to record the song he and I had cowritten, "Go Home Ann," he suggested I come to the studio to help lay it down. Ed Stasium would be producing the track, and Lemmy from Motörhead was going to mix it.

It was weird being back in the studio with all the Ramones. I played keyboards, and Johnny actually asked me to play the bass part. I was amazed he allowed me to play at all. Dee Dee even got into a heated argument with his management to make sure I got credited on the record, which I appreciated immensely because I knew he was really going out on a limb. The song was a bit of a rush job, as they needed some tracks for the B side of a single. Coincidentally, Joey and Daniel Rey's "Dangers of Love" was also on the B side.

The A side was a collaborative effort by Dee Dee, musician/producer Jean Beauvoir, and Joey. It was a superbly satirical song inspired by Ronald Reagan's politically motivated visit to an SS cemetery called "Bonzo Goes to Bitburg"—that is, until Reagan advocate Johnny Ramone insisted it be retitled "My Brain Is Hanging Upside Down (Bonzo Goes to Bitburg)."

Because it was unlike a typical Ramones song musically—probably due to Jean Beauvoir's input—and lyrically, due to its sociopolitical content, everyone believed Joey had been the impetus to write the song, though it was actually Dee Dee.

The Beggar's Banquet UK release of "Bonzo" won the New York Music Award for Best Independent Single of 1985. The other Bonzo, Ronald Reagan, was reelected to a second term.

28.

"THEY SAY IT'S YOUR BIRTHDAY"

It seemed as if my brother was still rebuilding his world after the catastrophe of losing Linda to Johnny. As he did, he started adding new self-defense mechanisms. In addition, his old schizoid paranoia had been brought to the surface by the betrayal.

Joey had begun making accusations that weren't always based in reality.

"Joey and I were drinking one night, well, every night," Legs recalled. "Joey turned to me and in a very coaxing voice said, 'So why dontcha just tell me what ya did?'

"'Did what?' I laughed, thinking he was kidding around.

"'What ya did with Cindy?' Joey asked without smiling.

"'Who?' I asked, not placing the name with the face.

"'Ya know,' Joey coaxed, 'Cindy?'

"'That chick you went out with for two weeks in 1977?' I asked, bewildered.

"'Yeah, c'mon,' Joey chided me. 'Ya know whatcha did, why don't you just admit it?'

"'Admit what?'

"'Admit that you fucked her!' Joey demanded.

"I insisted nothing happened, since it didn't. When I started getting angry, and hurt by the accusation, Joey dropped it—for the night. Cindy was
someone I'd probably been in the same room with three times in my life.
And after asking what happened between Cindy and me a few more times,
when he was really drunk, I began to see that this was not rational thinking.
Joey was beginning to view the world in absolutes: black and white, good
and bad, pro-Ramones and anti-Ramones, pro-Joey or pro-Johnny."

Though Joey Ramone was still a great guy, funny, and a blast to hang
out with, there were definite changes happening within my brother, Jeff
Hyman. The most obvious was an increased display of insecurity. He also
seemed to be trying too hard to transform himself totally into Joey Ramone,
Rock Star.

I understood that in the early days he had to do this to some degree in
order to keep his chin up and to keep himself strong emotionally. But now
his Joey Ramone character was becoming a bit callous. Maybe this was his
way of fending off Johnny's belittling.

It seemed that my brother now realized that Joey Ramone could wield
a lot of power. But periodically he seemed to enjoy his status just a little
too much. There were many occasions when his wish was everyone's command. Joey came to expect star treatment not only from fans, but also from
the rest of our family and from me.

It was beginning to worry me. The guy I'd grown up with was starting
to make less frequent appearances. It seemed as if Joey wanted to take back
a little of that thoroughly kind, gentle, and generous person and now take
a little advantage of a world that had taken advantage of him for so many
years.

If you were a loyal, awestruck, dedicated fan, you were totally in his
graces. But I was bonded to Jeff Hyman, my brother; I would only go so far
to appease Joey Ramone, Rock Star.

My family didn't seem to care about drawing lines: My mother began
referring to herself as "Mommy Ramone" in an interview in *Rolling Stone*.
It seemed harmless enough, and maybe even cute to some people, but it
gave me a weird feeling. The most confusing thing was that when Joey was
twenty-two years old, our mother had forced him out to sink or swim on
his own. But now that he was successful, she was becoming subservient far
beyond normal parental parameters—and Joey didn't discourage it. Our
mother now preferred to oversee and handle his finances and fulfill as many

of his needs as possible rather than pass the responsibility on to his live-in girlfriends/fiancées like Angela, or Linda before her.

"Charlotte was always there," Angela confessed. "That was part of the problem: It was me, Charlotte, and Joey. And of course Charlotte had control of everything. If Joey was going to buy me something, he had to tell her first. She thought Joey really couldn't take care of his own finances, and that was not untrue.

"Joey couldn't even take care of the money in his pockets because of his OCD. He had so much crap in there that the bills would just drop out. I'd be walking down the hall behind him picking up dollar bills, tens, twenties. People would trail behind him and pick up money. I could see Charlotte's point of view. But when somebody with a half a brain came along Joey didn't need her to do that anymore. She was hesitant to trust me, and that made Joey hesitant, too, like he didn't want to hurt his mother's feelings. That made things between us a little strained."

My mother was basically being . . . a mother. Instinctively, mothers need to be needed. But Joey was unusually needy and always had been. This created a very strange dynamic between the two of them. It was strange and beautiful at the same time. Obviously Joey knew this wasn't normal.

While Joey appreciated it, he also resented it. The special treatment he received from our mom comforted him tremendously but also reminded him of his inadequacies. I believe that this internal conflict was a huge source of frustration, because he would periodically lash out at her. But in Mom's mind, she had no choice.

"I got to the point where I was going to leave him," Angela continued. "I told him if he didn't trust me enough and we couldn't take charge of our own lives, I was leaving.

"So he did let me handle our affairs. Joey gave me the responsibility of the bookkeeping. I wrote all the checks for the bills. Charlotte no longer had control over everything, and I'm not sure if she was happy about it. Finally we were a real couple, living together."

IN THE FALL of '85 Joey called and asked if I could come to his house and help him out with a new Christmas song. I brought over my little Fostex four-track recorder and we laid down the first recording of "Merry Christmas (I Don't Wanna Fight Tonight)," the way the Ramones would do it. Then we came up with another slower, steamier, more romantic version.

Joey loved it, so we recorded that as well. He crooned a beautiful, soulful vocal that was part Nat King Cole and part Elvis, but ultimately pure Joey Ramone. Angela was there and getting a real kick out of it, as she knew it was about her. We all knew it was Joey's musical apology for practically strangling her a few weeks prior.

"Joey and I had a major blowout a few weeks before they recorded that song," Angela recalled. "We walked into Joey's mother's house on Thanksgiving, and I had welts all over my neck and head. I don't think Mickey, or *anyone*, realized how bad Joey's temper had become.

"Charlotte looked at me and said, 'Angela! What's that on your neck? What happened?'

"I said, 'We had a little fight. Joey's temper got outta control.'

"Charlotte said, 'Well, are you sure you didn't provoke him?'

"Charlotte got me thinking," Angela recalled. "But I don't really know if I provoked him. Joey used to get turned on by our fights."

Either way it was an odd thing for my mom to say, considering the treatment she'd once been subjected to by her first husband and that she'd always told us, "No matter what, you never raise your hands to a woman."

But things were different now. Apparently the rules were changing. Joey's life and his relationship with his family, fans, and some of his friends would occasionally take on a reality that mirrored an episode of *The Twilight Zone*, specifically the episode where little Billy Mumy possesses a mystical power and sends people into the cornfield—*permanently*—when he doesn't like the way they treat him. Everyone in town, including his own mother and father, is deathly afraid of his wrath and would respond by telling him what he did is a good thing, lest they be sent to the cornfield, too.

Our father, the tough-love advocate who'd smashed Jeff Hyman's rose-colored glasses and shaved off his long hair, would now do just about anything to avoid upsetting Joey Ramone.

Did all this make me resentful, bitter, and disturbed? I'll be honest: It could get really annoying.

On July 15, 1986, Dad was taking Arlene, Joey, Angela, me, and his longtime girlfriend Nancy out to celebrate my thirty-second birthday. He made a reservation at a seafood restaurant on Hudson Street in the West Village. Dad and Nancy would be coming in from her condo in East Hampton, so I told him that Arlene and I would meet them all at the restaurant.

Then he told me it would be inconvenient for them to pick Jeff up on their way and that I better go get him.

The truth is, it was just as convenient for him as me. The unspoken truth was that *nobody* preferred to pick up Joey, as opposed to meeting him somewhere. A million times my father had expressed how he couldn't understand Joey's OCD. Most of all, he couldn't stand sitting around waiting for him.

So Arlene and I wound up picking up Joey and Ange and sitting almost an hour waiting. When we got to the restaurant, Nancy and my father were standing on the curb, and the old man had smoke coming out of his ears.

"WHERE THE HELL WERE YOU?" he yelled at me. "GODDAMN IT!! THEY JUST CANCELED OUR RESERVATION!"

The old boy was fuming, so we all hushed up and let him blow his stack. Apparently I was supposed to get to Joey's house an *hour* before, so that I could wait for him to come down and still arrive on time. Since it was my birthday, I got distracted and only got to Joey's place forty-five minutes before it was necessary. But we still wound up being twenty minutes late for dinner. Given that my family was now walking on eggshells around Joey, the old man directed his anger at me.

"*Now we have to wait!*" Dad barked. "*For cryin' out loud!*"

"Well, at least it's nice out," Arlene said, trying to break, or at least lessen, the thick tension.

"*I DON'T CARE! I'M HUNGRY!*" Dad snapped at Arlene.

I was beginning to feel like the abused stepchild when I went in to talk to the hostess to ask how much longer it might be. There was a line of people waiting to do the same. After five minutes, the old man and Joey walked in.

"We're waiting for you out there!" he started. "Why didn't you tell us what the story is?"

"Well, there is a line here, isn't there?" I answered, getting a little tired of this treatment.

When I got to the hostess, she said, "It'll be about fifteen more minutes—maybe less."

"You want to go back outside?" I asked.

"No! It's hot out there!" Dad said.

Joey and I looked at each other and shrugged.

"Well, can I buy you a drink?" I offered, really needing one myself.

"I don't want a drink!" Dad answered gruffly. "I want to eat! I told you what time the reservation was—we would have had a table already!"

I looked at Joey again, hoping he would accept at least a little of the heat. Instead he just let out a muffled laugh. It appeared there was a possibility Joey was enjoying this.

Or maybe it was just his nervous reaction.

"Why didn't you leave earlier?" my father went on. "We didn't have to be standing here like jackasses."

Enough of this bullshit: My brother had problems, and we all knew it. I was not going to let my self-respect get stripped away from me any more than it already had been.

What was our father afraid of—that "Hot Poppa" might not get invited to the show and be brought backstage next time? This big, tough man was afraid to confront his rock star son.

"You know what?" I finally blurted. "This is bullshit, man! You know damn well why we were late. You know damn well whose fault it is. You need to blame someone? Blame the person whose fault it is!"

My father gave me a look that said I had just betrayed him. I had exposed him; the jig was up. I'd basically told him I was no longer going to play his game, or get played, while he scored his points. I'd spoken the unspeakable.

Everything I'd said was true, and he knew it. I'd finally stood up for myself. I stomped back outside and left the two standing there.

It was obvious I wasn't happy.

"What happened?" Nancy asked, grinning sheepishly. "Noel's upset, isn't he?"

"*He's* upset?" I responded.

Finally we got a table and sat down to "celebrate" my birthday. Though my father adopted a more relaxed manner, he was still acting like I'd insulted him. He was ignoring Arlene and me, giving us the silent treatment.

We ordered a round of drinks, and when someone called for a toast to wish me a happy birthday, the old man said it without even glancing my way. Angela looked at me, shaking her head.

Arlene was ready to start crying. Joey was either oblivious, or didn't know what to do, or was savoring the moment.

The old man acted like I wasn't there.

"So," Dad said, turning his back to Arlene and me and facing Joey with a big smile, "tell me what's happening, Jeffy? How was the tour?"

I did a slow burn and bit my tongue.

Motherfucker!

I motioned to Arlene in the direction of the door, took out a $100 bill, and threw it on the table. I looked at my father and deadpanned, "Thanks for a great dinner . . ."

Dad's jaw dropped open—and I walked out.

I swore I wouldn't talk to him without at least getting an apology. Of course, everyone has his or her own idea of an apology. As far as I was concerned, I never got one.

"After Mickey and Arlene left," Angela said, "I started yelling at Noel, 'You know damn well it wasn't his fault!'"

"It started getting ugly because the more famous Joey got," Arlene explained, "the more the roles switched in the family. Joey became the boss— and Joey's parents became the disciples. It was weird to see, because basically my brother-in-law went from selling plastic flowers on the street to becoming a big rock star."

ON CHRISTMAS EVE in 1986, a bunch of us were hanging out at my mother's apartment in Queens. She had moved back to the neighborhood. Her third marriage, to Phil, had broken up amicably. After exchanging presents, Joey suddenly came up with the idea of finding a nearby studio to record a song he'd been working on called "I'm in Love with the Elevator Operator."

Outside a snowstorm was gathering, but we were all feeling jolly and ready to go. Joey, Richie Ramone, Rattlers bassist Dave U. Hall, and I grabbed a guitar and bass and all headed to a studio in Long Island City. When the engineer decided he wanted to go home for Christmas, Joey insisted we find another studio, even though it was two a.m. and the snowstorm had now turned into a raging blizzard. We found a studio in Flushing, Queens, where the engineer said he would let us finish the song as long as we shared our blow with him.

That night Joey seemed particularly obsessed. Ultimately, recording the song was a fun adventure. We all contributed little parts. Though it turned out well, it wasn't worth getting snowbound in Flushing.

It was becoming apparent that Joey was in a rut and digging for material.

One day we drove out to a little studio in Long Island to record another new song he'd written, one of Joey's sentimental, early-sixties-inspired romantic rocker ballads called "Rememberin'." I played guitar. The legendary sixties Brooklyn doo-wop band the Mystics backed us up.

We also recorded a song I know Joey had been dreaming about since we were little kids, Gene Chandler's "Duke of Earl." My brother's love for the song, as well as the music of that era, poured out in his vocal. I love his version and listen to it often. But these were things that would not be appearing on a Ramones album anytime soon—if ever. As Joey would tell me, he was "all blocked up upstairs," and he didn't mean his sinuses.

He wasn't the only one who was floundering. The whole band was frustrated, confused, and bewildered.

This was where the leadership and organizational abilities of original manager/spokesman/drummer Tommy "Ramone" Erdelyi would have been helpful. At this point in their career, the Ramones were confounded as to what to do next.

Legs McNeil had started writing for *Spin* magazine. Joey would call and ask, "Hey, Legs, when's *Spin* gonna do an article on us?"

Legs said he kept pitching the band but was turned down repeatedly by the publisher.

"In 1986, the band was in professional limbo," Legs recalled. "By then they'd been around for twelve years. They were accused of playing catch-up to the more youthful hardcore scene and becoming less and less newsworthy as time dragged on. They had already launched the punk rock movement. They'd done a movie and a big album with Phil Spector. By the mid-1980s, there was nothing to write about from a rock & roll publisher's point of view."

Joey would tell Legs, "Push, push even harder, they've had the Talking Heads and Sting and Simply Red on the cover—everybody but us!"

"Joey was right," Legs admitted. "*Spin* was selling itself as the king of 'alternative' music magazines, as well as an alternative to *Rolling Stone*. The Ramones were arguably the band most responsible for launching alternative music, yet no one at *Spin* really paid them any attention. It was very unfair, but that was the reality of the times. Thank God Bob Guccione Jr. was big on celebrating holidays, like punk's tenth anniversary issue, or the Ramones would've probably been waiting another ten years.

"John Holmstrom and I used to joke about how ungrateful the Ramones were," Legs commented. "We had art-directed the Ramones' first album cover. Holmstrom had put Joey on the cover of *Punk* number three, and he did the back cover and inner sleeve drawings for *Rocket to Russia* as well as the cover art for *Road to Ruin*. I had written a bunch of articles about them—yet they always found something to complain about. John and I both loved Joey, but the four Ramones together were like a giant pit of resentment."

John Holmstrom and Legs McNeil decided to tell the story of the world's greatest punk group from the beginning and to show how difficult it had been for the Ramones to remain together for ten years, and how they rallied to put out *Too Tough to Die*, reenergizing the hardcore punk generation.

After Legs and John handed in the article, the editors at *Spin* sat on it for three or four months. Since punk started in 1976, they could have published the article anytime during 1986 to make their "tenth anniversary of punk rock" issue.

In the interim, the magazine started running celebrity interviews such as "Ozzy Osborne Interviews Dr. Ruth Westheimer," the sex therapist. They garnered so much publicity that Bob Guccione Jr. quickly wanted more. They set up an interview with Pia Zadora. Legs was asked to get Joey Ramone to pose the questions. A cover line that screamed JOEY RAMONE INTERVIEWS PIA ZADORA would highlight it.

In order to prepare for the Pia interview, Joey asked if *Spin* could get Pia's movies and CDs over to him.

Legs was busy, so he sent another writer, Annette Stark, to deliver the material to Joey's apartment. Angela had moved to the studio apartment next door. When Annette arrived, Linda Danielle, Joey's ex-girlfriend, was sitting there.

"Apparently Linda and Johnny weren't getting along, because Johnny was still seeing Roxy on the side," was the way Charlotte Lesher remembered it. "I think Joey had hopes that they would get back together. I felt that Linda was just playing Joey against Johnny."

Personally, I doubt that Linda was playing Joey against Johnny or trying to make Johnny jealous by seeing Joey. I doubt even more emphatically that Johnny ever knew about Linda's visits, or there would have been an explosion we would *all* have heard. It *is* possible that Linda was confused and still had feelings for my brother. But only Linda knows for sure.

When Holmstrom and McNeil's article about the Ramones appeared, strangely enough, the Joey and Pia interview was in the same issue.

"I walked into Paul's Lounge on the day right after the story was published," John Holmstrom remembered, "and all of the Ramones were sitting at a table—Johnny, Dee Dee, Joey, girlfriends.

"So I said, 'Hey, guys, how ya doin'?' When I sat down with them, there was stone silence. Somebody said, 'Well, that article you did . . . '

"Dee Dee said, 'I oughta kick your ass for that!'

"*I* didn't think we said anything bad about the Ramones, but *they* did," Holmstrom recalled. "At the time, Joey was totally shocked, because this was the first time anybody ever said that the Ramones were not really this happy family.

"Joey resented the article until he died," Holmstrom confirmed. "He felt betrayed. That ended our friendship—a low point in my life. I didn't really talk to Joey again until a few years later."

Though Joey was trying to keep his sense of humor and character, the more coke he did, the more he drank. The only two songs he contributed for the next Ramones album, *Animal Boy*, were the aptly titled "Mental Hell" and "Hair of the Dog."

At heart my brother truly was a gentle person. *Nobody* knew the guy better than I did. Possibly no one loved him more than his mother, but nobody knew him better than me. And I can sincerely say he was one of the sweetest, most gentle, caring, loving people this planet was ever blessed with—at heart.

But at this point in his life, Joey was definitely getting more temperamental and was more apt to go into rages, which mostly were directed at people with whom he could comfortably act out—namely, Angela.

"Joey and I actually lived in the studio apartment 10-M for over four years," Angela recalled. "Then he bought the studio apartment next door, 10-N. We were gonna break down the wall so we could have a bigger place, but that never happened. While Joey was on the road, I decided I was gonna move from 10-M into 10-N. By then, I couldn't deal with him anymore.

"Joey was pretty angry. One night he came home and begged me to open the door. I knew he was drunk, so I kept saying, 'No, no, go away, I'll see you in the morning.'

"He said, 'Please . . . '

"Joey could be so sweet," Angela emphasized, "and I did love him. He was a sweetheart, but it was more apparent than ever that he had a drinking problem. So I said, 'No, no, no, go away!' After he finally convinced me to open the door, *bam!* He punched me right in the nose.

"After I finally got Joey out of my apartment, I looked in the mirror and said, 'Oh my God!' My nose felt three inches wide. The worst thing was that Joey didn't remember it.

"He probably *chose* not to remember it," Angela laughed. "When I went to the doctor the next day, he took X-rays and said it was broken in two places. He said it would heal if I just left it alone and that I probably would go through more pain and hassle to have it fixed—so I never did. My nose would be fine, but at that point, I'd had it with Joey. I still loved him, but he was too much to handle."

By then, Angela had met a guy named Mark Bosch, who played in a band called the Hot Heads. He convinced her to move in with him. They decided to move her things out of the apartment one night while Joey was asleep, but he heard them.

After Joey and Mark got into a fistfight in the hallway, someone called the cops. When the cops saw Joey, they started singing, "Rock, rock, rock, rock 'n' roll high school." They pulled Angela aside and asked her, "You don't want to arrest *Joey Ramone,* do you?"

The cops told Joey to go back inside. The rock star had skated.

"Joey was really pissed when I moved out," Angela confessed. "But after a while, he got my number from my sister and started calling me again. We didn't talk about getting back together or anything but kept in touch periodically, and somehow, we remained friends."

29.

WE'RE THE MONKEYS!

By this point, Joey was really down. "I'd had it with the Ramones," he said. "'Mental Hell' is about that. Part of it came from breaking up with Angela. The other part was that I had really had it with the band."

Since Joey was struggling, Richie Ramone stepped up as a songwriting talent and came through with one that remains among the Ramones' most popular songs.

"Joey was always encouraging me to write songs," Richie explained, "but I didn't really need encouragement. I wrote 'Somebody Put Something in My Drink' for the next album, *Animal Boy*. At one point I dated Frankie Valli's daughter, from the Four Seasons. We used to go to nightclubs, and when people would dance, we'd go to their table and drink their drinks. We'd drink shit all night long, and I got somebody's drink that had something in it. That's what the song is all about."

Producer Jean Beauvoir, whom we'd known since the seventies when he played bass for the Plasmatics, was also represented by Ramones manager Gary Kurfirst. Based on the success of his collaboration with the band on "Bonzo Goes to Bitburg," it was decided that Jean would produce *Animal Boy*.

"Jean Beauvoir wanted to mix the vocals in Sweden," Joey remembered. "I didn't really want to go there, because it was the middle of winter, but it worked out because I got away from the band. And I had a real good relationship with Beauvoir. The only problem was that in winter, Sweden has six months of darkness. It's dark all day, and then later, it just gets darker! You never know what time it is!"

"I was highly disappointed when I heard the vocals for 'Somebody Put Something in My Drink,'" Richie admitted. "Joey was just straining and making it sound too rough, you know? There was nothing I could do. I should have bought my own fucking ticket and gone to Sweden to oversee the vocals."

Richie wasn't the only one who experienced disappointment with the album.

"I wanted to shoot the cover for *Animal Boy* at the Bronx Zoo," photographer George DuBose recalled, "but that didn't work out. Plan B was hiring Zippy the Chimp, who later starred as the 'monkey-cam' chimp on *Late Night with David Letterman*. I built a monkey house out of wood and hung tires from a chain. We had Legs McNeil and one of the Ramones' roadies, Mitch Keller, dress up in gorilla suits and hang out in the background."

"Joey asked me if I wanted to pose as a gorilla for the cover of *Animal Boy*," Legs McNeil recalled with a laugh, "in exchange for a gorilla credit on the record cover. I had to change into my underwear because the gorilla costume was so hot, and then George turned on the photo lights! I was supposed to stand in the cage, grab the bars, and stare at the Ramones. The only problem was Zippy the TV chimp. I could tell right away that he didn't like me. Richie Ramone was holding Zippy, and every time Richie loosened his grip on the monkey, Zippy turned around and punched me in the head! It doesn't sound that bad, but it caused my gorilla head to rise up five inches—and slam down on my head. The gorilla head was made out of solid wood and it hurt every time. The Ramones just laughed, while Zippy turned around and kept punching me."

Within a few months, while the Ramones stayed in limbo, Zippy the chimp skyrocketed to national attention, appearing regularly on *Late Night with David Letterman* with a little television camera strapped to his head.

"The Ramones had been upstaged by a *chimp*," Legs stated. "How much worse could it get?"

When *Animal Boy* came out, Legs saw that he didn't get credited for being the gorilla. He called Joey, who laughed as he told him that Johnny didn't want to give anyone credit for being a gorilla, because he wanted everyone to think the gorillas were real!

"I was beginning to feel bad for Joey," Legs admitted. "After seeing the band together during that photo shoot, it seemed to me that being in the Ramones wasn't very much fun anymore."

Ten years after "Blitzkreig Bop," the band was still playing in clubs. The crowds were still enthusiastic but had peaked in number. The whole punk thing already seemed a bit retro—and the face of the Ramones' competition had changed vastly.

In 1986, after punk melded into new wave, which melded into something called new romantic, the only imprint of punk that remained was a bit of fashion—but now the motorcycle jackets weren't being worn by the Clash or the Sex Pistols or the Runaways, but by groups with names like A-Ha, Wang Chung, Scandal, and even Hall and Oates.

After the success of Blondie's disco-rock song "Heart of Glass," disco music evolved into "dance-rock." In clubs where the Ramones and the Rattlers were both playing, when the bands finished they would lower the disco ball and play Culture Club's "Karma Chameleon" while the girls did that eighties "We Got the Beat" white-girl dance.

When the Rattlers' album *Rattled* came out in the summer of 1986 on the indie label JEM, it was getting very impressive reviews.

From Lester Bangs's former place of employ, *Creem* magazine:

There must be something to the gene theory, 'cause Mickey Leigh's Rattlers inhabit the same kooky world as his brother Joey Ramone's. Same wry vocals, same goofy Alfred E. Neuman perspective ("I'm In Love with My Walls"!?), though these guys rarely feel the need to break the speed of sound. Anyway, this is boss wax from start to finish, with ten rockin' cuts of snazzy power pop. Among the pearls: "On the Beach," which finds our hero searching for his baby, kidnapped by a radioactive sea monster, "Bottom of the Barrel," a spunky Velvet Underground salute, and the title cut, wherein Leigh confronts the eternal dilemma of whether to be a good boy or a bad boy. It's records like *Rattled* that make the idiocy of the "real" world a little easier to bear. Gabba, gabba, hey!

In addition, I was finally seeing my work reviewed by one of the most revered critics, in one of the industry's most influential columns, Robert Christgau's "Consumer Guide." Thankfully, it was worth the wait:

> Led by Joey's little brother Mickey [Leigh], this is the terrific little pop band the Ramones never convinced anybody they wanted to be. The Ramones' conceptual smarts earned them an aura of significance even when they made like sellouts. The Rattlers are neater — sharper formally and technically, terse and tuff. The KKK didn't take their baby away, just some radioactive mutant, and they cover "I'm in Love with My Walls" as if Lester Bangs wrote it just for them, which he half did.
> Grade: A–.

Though the reviews were great and thoroughly flattering, the comparisons between my brother and me were incessant.

The first question I was asked in 95 percent of the interviews we did was "Does it help or hurt being Joey's brother?" The debate was never-ending. Changing my name and going incognito was not a practical option at this point. Eventually, I realized it was a battle that couldn't be won and stopped getting upset about it. I was damned either way, because if I protested, that didn't bode well, either.

So when a writer would ask if I minded talking about my brother and the Ramones, I would always answer, "No." Then I'd inform the writer, totally deadpan, "You know, Joey and I agreed we would never divulge this, but the *real* reason I started playing in bands was actually to help my brother and the Ramones get more publicity."

Finding the humor in these situations never failed in helping me deal with them.

HAPPILY, JOEY WAS encouraging about what was happening in my career now and was actively trying to be of as much help as he could.

The best radio station in the New York area, WLIR, had a call-in contest called "Screamer of the Week," where the DJs would nominate several songs and listeners would cast their votes to choose the winner. The Rattlers' "I Won't Be Your Victim" was nominated three weeks consecutively.

Each week we'd all gather in someone's apartment, usually Joey's, and everyone would call in to cast their vote for the Rattlers. Joey had his finger on the redial button constantly, probably due to his OCD. He called so much that by the third week, they finally recognized his voice.

"Joey? Is that *you*?" One of the receptionists had finally caught on.

"Yeah, it's me," he said, laughing. "Can ya put me on the air?"

"Hang on, Joey."

In a few seconds, they had Joey live on the air telling everyone to vote for the Rattlers.

It was for no reason, Joey said, other than he truly loved the album and enjoyed helping bands; but I think there was also a little pure, old-fashioned brotherly love in the mix.

Joey was also encouraging about the Birdland album.

When Dave Merrill and I finally recovered the Birdland tape we'd recorded with Lester Bangs back in 1979 and lost track of for eight years, Joey began seriously thinking about starting a record company. He couldn't get it together at the time, but he urged us to somehow make a record out of it, and he would help find a label to release it. Frank Gallagher and I began to mix down the ten bare-bones tracks, and then Ed Stasium offered to come and help salvage the sessions.

We all believed this deserved to be released as an album. Plus they were Lester Bangs's last unreleased recordings, and we felt obligated to ensure that his work got an opportunity to be heard. Ed Stasium tried but couldn't find a label willing to pick up the album. Joey couldn't, either. Even Lester's journalist buddies Billy Altman and John Morthland could not help us locate a record company willing to put out Lester's album.

One day I pulled out a record that Arlene and I had picked up in St. Thomas, the Virgin Islands. The album, made by a local solca (soul/calypso) band called the Imaginations, had ads for local stores, goat farms, and taxi services on the back cover. I thought, "Why not try it here?" To raise money for the Birdland album, I decided to sell ads to local artists, bands, designers, and businesses in the community, which would appear on the back cover of the album. Nobody had done that in New York City. Robin Rothman and I wrote up a proposal and took it door to door, pitching the idea all over lower Manhattan. We actually raised enough money to print up a thousand copies.

I started my own label, called Add On Records. ("Add-on" is also what they call a song added on to a radio playlist, so it was a two-sided joke.) As with the Rattlers' album, *Birdland with Lester Bangs* received incredible critical acclaim. *Creem* magazine wrote:

> Stop the presses, Bob, this one's THE best rock & roll album of 1986—it's got Springsteen and Thelonious Monster beat seven ways from Sunday! Soon after this album was recorded, Bangs and Birdland parted company, even as the brutally wordy Bangs clutched his beloved fantasies of betrayal (takes two) to his breast and trudged off to Texas.
>
> Down there Lester recorded "Jook Savages on the Brazos" with the Delinquents, but even that amazing set sounds a bit muddy compared to the naked clarity and raw fire of this new/old Birdland recording. Listen to both sets and note how much more terrifying Bangs's warbly drawl sounds framed by Birdland's angular rhythms, especially the fat abrasive guitar of Mickey Leigh. Bangs conquers all his demons on this one.

The album also received another high grade from Robert Christgau in *The Village Voice*. It was well worth the effort. The funny thing was, we got more press about the advertisements on the back cover than about the record itself.

In the spring of 1987, Joey asked me to accompany him on acoustic guitar for a "live on tape" performance on DJ Vin Scelsa's radio show on WNEW-FM. Vin's idea was to have artists perform their songs in a stripped-down acoustic format. It was rare for Joey to perform on a major New York radio station without his band, and I was honored that he'd asked me to do it with him.

I knew one of the songs we'd be doing, "Death of Me," from when we recorded it on cassette in his house. The second song was a new one called "Waitin' for That Railroad."

A few days before the radio show, Joey told me that he had asked Daniel Rey to join us. It was funny, because the way he told me about it was as if he didn't want me to be offended. I wasn't at all. I knew Joey and Daniel had been collaborating and was glad Joey had found someone, aside from me, to help him with his songwriting.

I was a big fan of Daniel's former band Shrapnel and had a lot of respect for his abilities as a guitar player and songwriter. The Rattlers and Shrapnel had done many shows together over the years, from Jersey to Toronto, and we'd all become foxhole buddies.

But when we got together to go over the songs, I got a weird vibe from Daniel, a strange coolness in his attitude. It gave me the impression he felt I was his competition and that somehow I was now intruding on *him.* Daniel was cordial and professional, but in a very superficial manner, as if he were tolerating me to placate Joey. Daniel had also been collaborating with Dee Dee, much more successfully than he had with Joey. Then again, writing songs with Dee Dee was easy in comparison, as he was so incredibly prolific. After struggling with his own bands, Daniel was now attempting to eke out a career for himself as a producer.

I felt no animosity toward Daniel, even wished him luck, but when I shook hands with him now, I felt like I was shaking hands with a politician on a campaign trail. To Daniel's credit, his talent as a producer was decent, and he was able to play the diplomatic role well enough to work his way into the Ramones' trust.

"Joey and I did a few songwriting sessions together," Richie Ramone recalled, "but Joey always brought Daniel Rey with him—and I'd butt heads with Daniel. I like writing with just one other person, but with two, it's just annoying. It's one head butting against the others. I guess that's kind of why I never cowrote anything with Joey, because Daniel always came with the package.

"What bothered me the most was that when we finally got to make the albums a little more radio-friendly," Richie explained, "nothing really came of it, because it costs money to promote something. Johnny Ramone and Gary Kurfirst didn't want to spend the money, probably because they thought it wouldn't make a difference. But I thought, why would you not want an album to be as successful as it could be?

"Gary Kurfirst seemed to want to keep the Ramones an underground band," Richie mused. "I guess his thinking was, he'd profit more."

On the other hand, Joey wanted major success. He wanted to go on tour and open for some other big band playing Madison Square Garden and be important. Johnny wouldn't go for it.

"It's hard because people want to see the main act, but you *can* grab a thousand fans at a time opening for someone big—and sell more records," Richie continued. "But Johnny would say, 'Fuck it. They're not going to buy the records anyway, so why bother?' Johnny's whole thing was to make the album as fast and cheap as possible, and that's how Daniel Rey came in the picture to produce *Halfway to Sanity*."

"Johnny heard some four-track thing that I did in my basement for a punk band called the Dirge," Daniel explained. "He thought it sounded better than the Ramones' last record. Plus I got along with all four of the guys in the band, which was extremely unusual. And they could get me cheap, because it was my first album. Hell, I would've done it for *free*."

But the group wasn't happy with the job Daniel did.

"The production on *Halfway to Sanity* was terrible," Richie claimed. "One night, at four a.m. Joey called me and said, '*Richie, Daniel fucked this whole thing up! We gotta fix this record!*'"

My brother's friendship with Daniel didn't hold him back from being concerned or critical about his production job; Joey knew Daniel was not as experienced as the producers the band had previously worked with.

"It was a tough record to make," Daniel admitted, "because it was the first album I ever produced. My goal was to make the best record with what we had at that time. Not to make the best *Ramones* record ever—because that just wasn't gonna happen. The Joey-and-Johnny problems were really bad then; they couldn't be in the same room together. I'd rehearse with the band, and then I'd record it and play it for Joey and work with him. We did a few odd rehearsals with everybody, but Joey would usually make excuses, like his throat wasn't doing well. He just didn't wanna have to deal with the rest of them.

"I had to walk a fine line," Daniel explained. "I couldn't crack on Johnny to Joey, because Johnny was Joey's guitar player. Even though they were enemies, they were still in the same band, and it could be misconstrued that I was making fun of the Ramones."

"Nobody would listen to Daniel," Johnny Ramone explained. "They weren't letting Daniel do what he wanted, and certain people were complaining. But Daniel always handled it well, as far as staying diplomatic."

In the end the Ramones hired producer Joe Blaney—who had recorded the Clash's *Combat Rock* album—to mix all the tracks.

"Johnny just said his usual thing," Richie continued. "'Okay, hurry up. Let's get it done. No one's gonna buy it anyway, so let's finish up.'

"Around that time, I started thinking about leaving the band," Richie recalled. "We had just signed to Radioactive Records, Gary Kurfirst's label.

It would have been stupid to continue to play to get the cash. I didn't make any money off the records or the T-shirts. It was just my salary. What was in it for me? It was just a job. There was no chance of us being any more successful than we were. It was just gonna go downhill from here. And as far as I was concerned, it did.

"On the the first tour," Richie recounted, "when we had a bus, Joey and I always rode in the back of the bus together. We listened to music together and we'd play our air guitars. When there was no money, we couldn't go spend $700 a week on a bus. Johnny said, 'Oh, we'll just go in a fucking van, you know, with a driver in the winter.' We'd drive to Vermont, play the show, and drive home right after—on the icy roads. I was putting my life in danger, every night. I just got completely disgusted."

"I never really knew why Richie left the band," Johnny Ramone stated. "What I heard was that one night, Joey was out and he's had too much to drink and he starts telling people, 'Johnny's gonna get rid of Richie!' Richie finds this out and then quits. I thought with Richie, we'd negotiate and reach some sort of compromise."

"There was never any negotiating," Richie insisted. "I knew I was leaving. Before the show in Islip, Long Island, on August 12, 1987, I called a car service. Right after the show, I just changed my clothes and left. I left the Ramones right before two gigs at the Ritz. I'd received a phone call from an anonymous person who said, 'After these two gigs, they're going to fire you anyway.' So I said, fuck it, I'm not going back. Johnny's plan was to have me play the gigs and then dump me.

"The next day, they started pounding on my door in New York City. Ira Lippy, the business manager, even said, 'We can lose Johnny before we can lose you!' But I knew that wasn't gonna happen. I never regretted leaving the Ramones. It wasn't going to get any better, because of Johnny's mind-set. Tour, tour and tour and tour, and play for five thousand or six thousand dollars a night."

"We weren't gonna throw Richie out," Johnny Ramone insisted. "After he left, I didn't want to go through the whole process of changing drummers and startin' to look for a new one—again. But somehow everything always works out for the best. People leave and it always worked out."

30.

> ## "THE BOTTLE IS EMPTY,
> ## BUT THE BELLY IS FULL"

Three and a half years after he'd been kicked out of the Ramones, Marc Bell got a phone call from Monte Melnick telling him Richie had left them flat. They were facing a lawsuit because of jobs that they might miss, ten or fifteen of them.

"Richie wanted to fuck them because he was only getting salary," Marky said. "He wasn't getting merchandise money, he wasn't gettin' nothin'!"

Monte told Marky they'd tried Clem Burke from Blondie for a few shows, but his style didn't fit with the Ramones.

"Then Johnny called me," Marky recalled. "He knew I'd been sober for a few years. They asked me back in the group. When I went back, the fucking tension in the band was so thick you could cut it with a knife. Things had got even worse. So I kept to myself and went to AA meetings. Joey was still doing coke. I could tell the drinkin' was affecting his personality. His moodiness was getting worse."

Marky tried to talk Joey into going to AA meetings with him, but Joey would say, "I don't want to know about that born-again crap!"

Marky wasn't the only one who was having problems with Joey's moodiness.

"Joey and I fell out," Legs McNeil coughed up, "when Richie left the band and Joey started talking shit about Richie. I told Joey, 'I don't think Richie's such a bad guy,' which was absolutely the wrong thing to say. Joey fumed and called me a 'traitor.' By now we'd been friends for twelve years or so, and I was getting tired of his thinking. He hated a person one day and loved them the next, according to what they had done for the Ramones. It was very high school–ish. I started to withdraw from the Ramones' scene.

"Joey was hurt by what I wrote about them; he felt betrayed. It didn't matter that I never wanted to hurt Joey, it didn't matter if it was real or not, just if Joey believed it—like that I slept with Cindy."

"Joey was mad at Legs McNeil and John Holmstrom because he felt those guys were part of the family," Daniel Rey asserted. "The Ramones were like the Mafia. If you are in the Mafia and you did anything to slight anyone else in the family, you'd be whacked!"

Another confrontation occurred when Legs went to see Blitzspeer, a band fronted by Shrapnel's former bass player, Phil Caivano.

"I went to the band's dressing room to get a beer," Legs recalled. "Joey came rushing in, grabbed my tape recorder out of my bag, and began smashing it on the floor. He never looked as pissed as he did at that moment. My initial feeling was that I was very embarrassed for Joey, because he was acting completely out of control. My second thought was, 'Damn, I'm gonna need a new tape recorder!'"

In the fall of '87 Joey and I went into a studio with Marky to record another song Joey and I wrote, called "We're Gettin' Out of Here." The song was okay, but I could see why the Ramones rejected it. I put a difficult guitar riff in it.

By the time *Halfway to Sanity* had run its uneventful course, the band was pretty much at its lowest depths.

Dee Dee was still ingesting his daily doses of psychostabilizers, some of which were actually prescribed, and Joey was still drinking far too much.

Johnny had thrown in the towel in his quest for the title of "superstar" and his attitude reflected it. He now viewed what he was doing as merely "a job," and he punched the clock like a champ.

Joey directed his enthusiasm toward other projects. He would do guest DJ stints at East Village clubs like the Cat Club, Lizmar Lounge, and Luna Lounge. Using the occasion of his birthday, he'd throw a big birthday bash at CBGB or the Ritz or Irving Plaza, where he'd showcase new or unsigned local bands. For a big finale, Joey would always put together a band composed of his friends to play a set of Ramones songs and other favorites.

My brother seemed to have far more fun putting these shows together than doing anything else. And he derived great pleasure from helping bands get to the next level. This was more like the guy who had put my band in the studio and produced a record when he was sixteen years old.

Dee Dee had begun to seek relief in his side projects as well. Apparently Dee Dee was serious about his desire to become a rapper and was not going to let Johnny stop him this time. Dee Dee began dressing like Run-DMC and Public Enemy and mimicking the jargon of black rap stars. But Johnny was extremely protective of the band's name, and one thing he remained adamant about was not allowing Dee Dee to use the name "Ramone" for his side project. Dee Dee King, the punk rapper, was born.

"It was my job as a collaborator to do what Dee Dee wanted to do," Daniel Rey said. "He'd write these raps and I'd put them to music. Then Dee Dee got someone to pay to make a record, and next thing I knew we're in the studio doing this thing for real—to my horror. One day at the end of the project, I stopped in my tracks, thinking, 'Oh my God, this thing is gonna come out!' Luckily it's a hard record to find."

AFTER TEN YEARS and several personnel changes in the Rattlers, I finally concluded that it was time to try another approach. We'd had ups and downs but had never gotten over the hump financially. There was a lot of admiration from peers and much praise critically, but while that feeds your heart, it doesn't feed your belly.

I kept hold of our multitalented and extremely pallid drummer, Neil "Whitey" Benezra. Whitey and I forged ahead to put together a new band, with a new name. In order to put an end to comparisons to Joey once and for all, I decided to get a lead singer.

In the meantime, we wrote and recorded some songs we could play for any interested candidates. We waded through every type of singer imaginable before finding one we thought was a gem in the rough.

He had a great, powerful midrange voice and looked like a cross between Bono and Robert Plant, with a big mane of curly, ginger-colored hair. He was very intelligent—a Harvard grad even—and had a good sense of humor. I was a little surprised when he said, "Well, I call myself Joshua

Lyon," as in "lion." I figured he would've thought of something better than that; then again, I'd certainly heard cornier names.

Within weeks, Josh, Whitey, and I had already written enough songs to start playing, but one piece was still missing. I filled in on bass for the time being and produced four of the new songs on an eight-track tape, at a cost of $250. It came out really well, and when Joey heard it, he got excited immediately. We did a show or two with Dave U. Hall filling in on bass temporarily.

Chris Moffett, the lead guitarist of the Cycle Sluts from Hell, introduced me to a tall, thin, slightly muscular guy named West Rocker. West wore horn-rimmed glasses and sported a Mohawk haircut. He possessed the presence, talent, personality, and attitude of a winner. West was a truly funny guy, and we hit it off instantly.

"I was a huge Ramones fan," bass player Westley "Rocker" Crawford recalled. " 'I Wanna Be Sedated' was one of the first songs I learned to play. When I finally met Joey, I asked him about my glasses. I was thinking I should get contacts. Joey said, 'No, no, no. You look cool. It's your personality. The glasses suit you.' From that point, I never felt uncomfortable about wearing glasses onstage."

The whole band clicked immediately. We even had a built-in joke. West, who is black, would kid around with our drummer and yell, "HEY, FUCK YOU, WHITEY!"

We called ourselves the Tribe, the name we would eventually change to Crown the Good. My biggest worry was Joshua, who had a big ego even for a lead singer, which tends to be troublesome in bands—that's an understatement.

We started drawing crowds pretty quickly. Joey thought West was fantastic, Whitey was great, Josh was great; we were all great together, and this was the best thing I'd put together yet. He vowed he wouldn't rest until we were signed to a major label.

Unfortunately Joey would have no choice but to rest, temporarily.

He had finally moved out of his studio apartment and into a one-bedroom unit down the hall from the two studios he owned. Since he wasn't living with anyone now, his place was once again a real mess—more like a minefield. Joey had stepped on something in his apartment and cut his foot. I picked him up and drove with my mother to a specialist she'd found in a hospital in Princeton, New Jersey. Sure enough, my brother was diagnosed with another foot infection. It was so bad that the doctor talked about possibly having to amputate part of his foot.

Joey was put on intravenous antibiotics and was out of commission for at least three weeks. Of course, during this time the rest of the Ramones were stewing because once again they were losing money as a result of shows being canceled.

As soon as he could, Joey started making phone calls about the Tribe to A&R guys at major labels. In July 1989, after returning from California, Joey got us on a bill during the New Music Seminar in New York, where record companies actively check out new bands. The show happened to fall on my birthday.

Dave Frey, who later went on to work for legendary promoters such as Bill Graham and Ron Delsener, was working for the New Music Seminar when he got the call from Joey.

"I worked booking bands at the New Music Seminar in the late eighties," recalls Dave. "Joey would showcase these New York bands on what he called 'Joey Ramone's New Music Nights!' at a place called Bond Street. But the club got red-tagged for all kinds of violations and closed about ten days before the seminar came to town.

"I found him a new venue called the Rapp Art Center, an old church on Fourth Street between Avenue A and Avenue B. He was supposed to have only three or four bands, but he'd overbooked the bill. He asked me to come over to his house to talk about it, which was an experience in itself.

"You open the door, and there's money all over the floor: change, wadded-up bills and stuff," Dave mused. "The kitchen was piled high with dishes. It wasn't very tidy.

"The rest of the apartment was very precarious, with every flat surface stacked as high as could be," Dave recalled. "It looked like a physics problem: 'How many objects can you place on a flat surface, and stack as high as possible, without them falling over?'"

Dave discovered Joey had promised everyone, from Dee Dee Ramone to the Cycle Sluts to Blitzspeer, that they could have half the door.

Dave laughed. "Fortunately, I knew a lot of these people and was able to call and say, 'Listen, you are playing from eight fifteen to eight forty-five, and you are going to make one hundred dollars.'

"They all said, 'Oh, hey, it's Joey, that's fine. No problem.'

"At the last minute," Dave recalled, "Joey called and said that there is this awesome band called the Tribe, and there's a lot of interest in them. We had to put them on the bill somehow. So we figured it out and we put the Tribe on, too. I had no clue it was Joey's brother's band. Joey never said a word about it."

"Mickey tried so hard, at every turn of the way, to divert the fact that he was Joey Ramone's brother," West Crawford laughed. "I mean, I would say to myself, 'Well, damn, we could use a little help! Just tell them who your brother is!' But he was so dogged and determined."

"Joey was *so* into these shows," West remembered, "and *so* into turning people on to new bands. Once I was standing by the stage with him as a new band was getting ready to go on. Two young girls came up to Joey, in awe: *'Oh, Joey Ramone, I can't believe it! I'm your biggest fan! Can I get your autograph?!'*

"Joey was so cordial and polite and sweet," West recalled. "The thing that really struck me is that the girls just kept on talking as the band was getting ready to play. The minute they started, Joey turned to the girls, put his index finger to his lips, and said, 'Shhh,' and pointed to the stage. This band was a bunch of nobodies. It was probably their second or third gig. Not only did Joey stop and focus on the bands, he stood there and listened and watched them very intently. The girls stopped and turned to the stage and listened, too. Joey was such a lover of rock & roll!"

Because of the energy and thought Joey had put into the Rapp Art Center show, the whole night felt like one big party—especially with the surprise birthday party Joey threw me in the basement. The best part of the night, though, was that after I blew out the candles on the cake, Joey told us that Michael Kaplan from Epic Records had come to see the band. We all got very excited and everyone thanked Joey profusely for putting the whole thing together. It got even better the next day, when Joey told me that Kaplan said he liked the band and was very interested.

About a week later we were doing another show at CBGB, basically for Kaplan again, though Joey had invited as many record companies as he could. I was backstage at CB's, just about to go on, when Joey and Monte walked into the dressing room. I was concerned because Joey had a strange look on his face, like something was very wrong. So did Monte; then again, Monte *always* looked like that.

"What's the matter?" I asked them.

"Dee Dee quit," Joey muttered.

"*What!?*"

"Yeah," Joey continued, "he wants to be a rapper or some shit. So, ya know of any bass players? Someone a little younger than us?"

"Yeah, I *do*, actually," I told him. "West was just talking about some bass player he knows in Long Island. I'll ask him."

"Thanks," Joey said.

I hadn't been talking to Dee Dee much, probably because I hadn't been to many Ramones shows lately—and I had pretty much stopped selling pot. When I did talk to Dee Dee, he didn't hold back from venting his frustration with the Ramones, especially Johnny's "Gestapo-like" control over everything from their music to their haircuts.

"When I left the Ramones in July 1989," Dee Dee recalled, "I made a lotta changes in my life. I left my wife, I left my girlfriend, and I left the band. It was hard, but I had to do it because I had to become myself. I'm not a puppet. I don't write music according to a certain style. I write how I feel at the moment. I write current. I don't try to re-create the past. And that was becoming the Ramones' thing—recycling the past—which was hard to deal with.

"Johnny wouldn't grow," Dee Dee continued. "He acted like Adolf Hitler. His nickname was 'the Führer.' And I was also sick and tired of the little-boy look, with the bowl haircuts and motorcycle jackets. It was just four middle-aged men trying to be teenage juvenile delinquents. You should wanna strive to become a man. I think it's better to be an adult, to be secure enough not to hang on to what may have worked at one time. I was getting sick of playing in a revival act, which would be fine if the Ramones wouldn't have put out any more albums.

"When I was in the Ramones," Dee Dee sighed, "I just wanted the songs to be sung with a sense of wisdom—and that was really hard to do because no one in the group was really growing up but me. Which is pretty weird, 'cause there was no one in that band more self-destructive. For the last fifteen years, basically we played the first three albums. No matter how much you like those songs, playing them every night is gonna make it crap. There's not one kid I met on the street who didn't say that if the Ramones had any dignity they would've broken up after *Too Tough to Die*. That was when *I* wanted to leave."

"In 1989, when Dee Dee decided he didn't want to be in the Ramones anymore," Vera Colvin recalled, "I thought it was another phase that was gonna pass.

"He didn't wanna be on the medicine or see doctors anymore. He had been doing it for about ten years—AA meetings, NA, CA, you name it. He went every night, every day—now he was throwing it all away. Dee Dee told me he wanted to change and that I had to change with him. But the direction he was taking was completely unacceptable. I told him, 'As long as you're not on your medication, you can't come back to me. You're putting your life in your own hands.'"

"I think if Vera helped me, we could have still been together," Dee Dee mused. "She threw me out. She was throwing me out every month, so I was running to the Gramercy Park Hotel for a couple of days, and then I'd get a call from Vera saying, 'Okay, you can come home now.'"

There were things bothering Dee Dee—Joey was one of them.

"Joey's alcoholism was getting too ugly," said Dee Dee. "There was a double standard in the group. Even when I was totally straight, I was being constantly watched and criticized and not given any money. Joey could do whatever he wanted. He was starting to give bad shows and pass out on the plane. One time Joey had to be carried onto the plane on the last tour. I had to be carried to the plane too a few times, but we were younger then! Joey was like thirty-nine now—there's no dignity in that!"

Dee Dee's remarks about Joey's drinking, and why he quit the band, got around. Eventually they got back to Joey, who then ranted about Dee Dee's drug use to anyone who'd listen, including "shock jock" Howard Stern. A month later, turnabout became fair play when Stern aired a recorded message of an audibly plastered Joey canceling just hours before his scheduled appearance on the early morning radio show. He'd been out drinking 'til dawn and was so fucked up he could hardly talk.

My phone started ringing early that day, with people laughing hysterically about the message Stern had played. It *was* pretty entertaining, unless of course you were Joey, or in his band, or a member of his family.

I felt really bad for my brother. Though Howard Stern was a big fan and supposed friend of Joey's, he played the tape repeatedly, mercilessly, for weeks. But, of course, that *is* Howard's job. Joey was furious, but he wouldn't say anything to Howard Stern. Joey knew very well who would take his shit and who wouldn't.

Dee Dee, for one, could no longer deal with Joey's condescending bullshit. In fact, he'd had it with all of them.

"When I found out Dee Dee was leaving, I was shocked," Johnny remembered. "I always figured Dee Dee and me would stay until the end.

"They all called me up and said, 'Come on down here for a meeting!' I said, 'If he quits, let him quit!' I go to the meeting and Dee Dee doesn't even show up.

"I said, 'Fine, we're having tryouts tomorrow.' I'm gonna let this defeat me? I'll find a young replacement. I already envisioned that when this calmed down, I would get Dee Dee to continue writing songs for the Ramones."

While Johnny was busy convincing Dee Dee to keep writing songs for the band, Joey was busy finding a replacement. He called West Rocker and asked him about the bass player he knew.

"I got off the phone with Joey and called this kid I'd grown up with on Long Island, Chris Ward. I said, 'You got a bass?' He goes, 'Yeah.' I go, 'Listen, I got you an audition with the Ramones, if you want it.'

"Chris said, 'Yeah, I want it! Definitely!'"

"We thought Chris Ward was good," Johnny Ramone recalled. "I knew that once he was in the band, he'd be playing with a pick and get a bowl haircut. I had the vision."

"Chris shows up at my house," said West. "He goes, 'It looks like I got it! It's just a matter of picking out a name. It's either gonna be Izzy, Dizzy, or CJ.'

"I said, 'CJ. All the others sound crazy,'" West laughed. "The rest is history."

CJ Ramone was now the newest member of the band.

By the end of the summer, Joey had just about found us a record deal, and West and I had found the Ramones their next bass player.

But even though Dee Dee was out of the band, his presence was still felt.

"After Dee Dee left the group," Daniel Rey recalled, "he needed to spew some venom, so he wrote an unflattering piece about the Ramones for *Spin* and was quoted saying some bad things about the guys. Joey was pissed off."

With many of Joey's old friends abandoning ship, he was feeling lonely. Joey would never come right out and admit he missed people, but I could tell. So Joey was very lucky to run into Robin Rothman on the street and reconnect with her. Robin was working for our old friend James "Ratso" Rizzi, the artist who had sponsored the first Rattlers record. Jimmy was doing quite well now.

"I was walking down Lafayette Street to Rizzi's house," Robin Rothman laughed, "when I saw Joey with his new friend Susan Calamari on his arm.

"I hadn't seen or talked to him in almost seven years. I just looked at him and said, 'Oh, my God. Hi, Joey!'

"Joey says to me, 'Listen, I moved down the hall and gotta rent my studio apartment . . .'

"I said, 'Wow! That's great!' I was living in Brooklyn and had to get outta my apartment there.

"Joey gives me his mom's number and I call her up and tell her I'm interested in the apartment, and the first thing Charlotte says to me is, 'All right, but if you move in, you *cannot* interfere with his life!'

"I will never forget that as long as I live," Robin howled, "because from the day I moved into that fuckin' apartment, *Joey never left me alone!*"

JOEY SET UP a meeting for my band with Michael Kaplan at the offices of Epic Records. Since the band had only been together for about six months, Kaplan could only get the go-ahead to offer us something called a "development deal," which is a step closer than a "demo deal." But it ain't the *real* deal.

In a development deal, the band got $30,000 to take four months off from work, buy some equipment, rehearse the show, write a slew of hit songs, and make another demo tape. Then the label had one month to decide if they wanted to pick up the option on what would be a twelve-year, eight-album recording contract.

I recommended Steve Massarsky represent us, but Josh had a guy named Michael Guido in mind who had a far more impressive client roster. Guido represented a lot of the glitzy and suddenly popular heavy metal "hair" bands like Skid Row and had just engineered a huge bidding war for a band called Warrior Soul.

So Guido won out.

The first thing Michael told us about the development deal was, "Don't do it!"

"You guys really have a great buzz going right now," Michael said. "Let me shop a better deal for you. I'm pretty confident I can get you one."

"Well, what about my brother?" I asked. "We promised him ten percent."

"Right, but not from this development deal money," Michael explained.

"He *would* get ten percent *if* they pick up the option on the whole twelve-year record deal. There's also the possibility they won't. You should keep that in mind. Three out of four times the company goes through with the deal. But it's a gamble."

"And if we don't take this deal," I asked, "the band doesn't have to give Joey anything?"

"That's right; if he is not involved you certainly wouldn't have to give him anything from any other deal you might enter into. In fact, legally, at this point you don't have to give him anything anyway. He doesn't have a contract with you guys. I'm not saying that would be right or wrong, just business. It happens all the time.

"But Joey thinks that you *should* take this deal," Guido continued. "And I'm telling you I think you can do much better. But I'll be happy to negotiate this Epic contract for you, if that's what you want. You guys decide."

The smart thing would've been to take Michael Guido's advice and let him pursue a deal for us that would ensure we could make at least one album—and get a lot more money.

Some of the other guys were on the fence but leaning toward letting Guido go for it.

I thought it over and remembered how enthusiastic my brother had been, how happy he was that he had been able to get things this far, and how much work he had done for us already. There was no way I could allow him to get screwed. Call it faithfulness, loyalty, naïveté, guilt, pure stupidity, or a combination of any of the above; for better or worse, I just wasn't going to do that to my brother.

So I pushed hard to have everybody agree to go ahead with Epic. I urged them to consider the possibility that Guido might not be able to pull it off and that the Epic offer might not still be there in six months. More than likely, they would move on to other acts. I successfully convinced them to go with the deal Joey had gotten us, and negotiations began.

Then things got more complicated when Joey informed us that Andrea Starr from his manager's office had helped him make a lot of phone calls and sent out packages on our behalf. Joey was now pushing for Andrea to get 10 percent as well.

He also wanted us to give something like a 5 percent finder's fee to a writer friend of his, Joan Torshes, who had been his connection to Michael Kaplan at Epic. Kaplan and Guido both thought that was totally absurd. We didn't have a manager yet, and Kaplan said we would have to get one. That person would take at least 15 percent, too. Kaplan told all of us, including Joey and Andrea, that if the band had to give away 40 percent of its advance, it would drastically cut into our recording budget and our ability to tour, and there would be no sense in them giving us any record deal at all.

Kaplan made complete sense and thankfully got his message across to Joey. We kept negotiating.

I tried to make it as good as possible for Joey, so much so that some of the other guys speculated I was getting some kind of kickback, which was nonsense. I was merely trying to show my appreciation for what my brother had done and continued to do. Eventually we worked out something agreeable to all, and Epic began preparing the contract.

While Guido and Epic were working on the contract that would make one of my dreams reality, Joey had another fantasy of his fulfilled: He'd gotten his first radio show on WZRC Z-Rock, 1420 on your AM dial. He called it *Joey Ramone's Radio Revenge* and brought on Handsome Dick Manitoba as his sidekick/cohost. He had my band on the show to perform live several times, hoping to sway Epic to pick up the option. Joey's *Radio Revenge* was a mix of music from vinyl, CD, and live performances, spiced with humorous banter between Dick and Joe and interviews with guests such as Motörhead's Lemmy, Johnny Rotten, Cycle Sluts from Hell, and the Tribe.

While all this was going on, in a serious attempt to be more responsible and avoid blowing this opportunity, I drastically cut back on partying and drinking, and everything else, for that matter. Unfortunately, Joey had been delving deeper and deeper into the bottle.

One night he went out with photographer Bob Gruen to a hippie-ish club in the West Village called Wetlands. He wanted to catch the set of our friends in a band called Raging Slab. Joey decided to get up and do a song with them, and he wound up putting on quite a show, replete with a highly dramatic exit off the stage.

"I was with Joey the night he had his last drink," Bob Gruen remembered. "We were at the bar at Wetlands, and my girlfriend said, 'Let's have some tequila.'

"Since we were with Joey, the bartender came over and poured us all mega-sized shots of tequila. Joey picked up the glass and said, 'I know I'm gonna regret this.'"

The crowd was thrilled when Joey came onstage to join Raging Slab for their encore song but startled when, coming off the stage, Joey slipped on the steps and hit the ground, twisting his ankle.

A few hours later, stepping out of a cab at an after-hours joint, Joey told Bob, "I really hurt my ankle. I think it's starting to swell up."

At that point it was four a.m. Joey called Monte, who got out of bed to come and take him home. The Ramones' tour had to be postponed because Joey had broken his ankle.

"The next time I saw Joey," Bob recalled, "he was recovering from his broken ankle and said he decided not to drink anymore. As the years went on, I never saw Joey Ramone with another drink in his hand."

Neither did I, or anyone else.

31.

"GIMME SOME TRUTH"

In March 1990, the Tribe's development contract with Epic Records was finally signed, kicking off our four-month agreement to write, rehearse, and record. In July, we handed the finished recordings to Michael Kaplan, and the monthlong wait began. We were all on pins and needles as our fates were determined.

In the interim, West had the misfortune to be picked up in a drug raid.

The Kentucky Fried Chicken on Fourteenth Street and Third Avenue was not only a popular hangout for dead chickens; it was also a well-known hangout for coke dealers. The police were doing one of their randomly scheduled sweeps on the Lower East Side, and West happened to be in the Kentucky Fried Chicken and had bought something . . . to go.

Just about everybody in the music business had been in rehab around this time, phasing out of the cocaine heyday of the eighties. So Kaplan assured us this would not kill the deal, as Epic was very understanding.

A few weeks later, in August, Arlene's dad Charlie passed away from a heart condition he had been dealing with for many years. Charlie was a really good guy, and needless to say, Arlene was devastated. I was pretty distraught, as well. Her parents had moved to Florida, and we went down there for the funeral.

When I got back, I called our new manager, Mike Lembo, and told him I had just gotten back from my father-in-law's funeral.

"Well, Mickey, unfortunately, there was another death while you were away—your record deal died," he said, citing the usual causes. "Epic passed. They didn't hear a hit song on the tape, and the marketing people couldn't quite figure out what category you guys fit in. Also they think your singer, Josh, is a little too generic—not unique enough. I'm sorry."

He said he was willing to keep trying other labels and that we should keep writing and performing, but basically we were back to square one. We recorded another batch of songs live at CBGB, and Lembo began shopping another tape to the labels.

I'd written a few songs with West, and that didn't sit well with Josh. The tension among us continued to increase. One night after rehearsal we all decided to go downtown and have a drink. Josh and West were in the backseat of my car kidding around with each other. Then they started arguing, and it started getting physical.

So I turned onto Forty-second Street and pulled over to the curb.

Josh and West spilled out of the car and began to rumble, rolling around on the street. None of us were tough guys or fighters, so Whitey and I were laughing at first. But then it looked like they were really serious.

This was not good.

"C'mon, you guys. Cut it out!" we yelled at them.

All of a sudden a blinding light flashed down on us from the heavens. As Whitey and I looked up, a deafening boom followed. It was one of those thunderclaps that sound as if skyscrapers are tumbling down like dominoes. It started to pour, and Josh and West were still rolling around on the sidewalk.

Things were really starting to deteriorate.

I had written a song on the eve of the U.S. bombing of Kuwait called "With Our Blood," a slogan Iraqi Muslims had been chanting to show how much they were willing to give for their cause—which was supposedly all about their religion.

"With our hands we pray, with our blood we pay," the chorus to the song went, as now Americans would be paying with their blood, as well as Iraqis and Kuwaitis. Instead of Josh, I sang lead on the song, simply because it sounded better. Even Joey agreed with that.

Joey's friend Joan Torshes had written a review of one of our shows for *The Music Paper*, in which she said that the song was the highlight of our set. Josh accused Joey and me of coercing her. Things were getting progressively worse for the Tribe.

A meeting at Joey's apartment culminated in us parting ways with Josh. Joey supported our decision, agreeing that we would be better off with another singer. As we were auditioning singers, equipment began to mysteriously disappear from our rehearsal room, and not long after, so did West.

That's how quickly bands rise and fall in the music business, not that that was news to me, as Johnny had warned me years before. I knew the odds and that the ratio of those who actually find success to those who try is minuscule. I'd known that since I first picked up a guitar in 1965. I didn't get down on myself too hard; I'd seen and known so many great bands and incredibly talented people who also just couldn't get over the hump, many of whom had given up, either because they couldn't afford the expense involved in forging on, or because they just ran out of gas. But I still had the main ingredient necessary to pursue my dream, which is not so much talent, but *drive*—and if you have enough fuel, you keep driving.

We auditioned a singer named Stephen Siegel, a.k.a. Steven Sane, who also played guitar and bass, and decided to go ahead as a three-piece band with Steve singing and playing bass.

Joey was busy putting together a band called the Resistance as a politically oriented side project to coincide with the presidential primaries and MTV's "Rock the Vote" effort to get kids to come to the polls. He'd been working on a remake of John Lennon's "Gimme Some Truth" for their performance at a rally for Democratic hopeful Jerry Brown, which was coming up soon.

A few nights later he called me up about another song he was working on.

"Can ya help me with this song?" Joey said desperately. "I got the opening line but I can't seem to get any further. Ya gotta help me!"

I had made an agreement with myself that I would not, again, do something I would later regret—or get pissed at my brother for. It was pretty clear by this point that no matter what kind of contribution I made, I wasn't going to get acknowledged for it. After a while, as my brother surely knew, that takes a lot of the pleasure out of the whole process. I knew it was not going to be easy or pleasant, but I had to take a stand about it sometime, so I gave it a shot, opened my mouth, and expressed my feelings about it to my brother for the first time.

"I don't know, man," I said apprehensively. "I've helped you with a lot of songs already. You know, I wrote all that music on '9 to 5 World' and that riff and ending on 'Real Cool Time,' 'Chop Suey,' a lot of stuff—but I never get credit on anything. Why?"

"Well, it's really 'cause of John," he replied. "If I had put your name on any of those songs, John wouldn't have let them be on the album."

"So why is this gonna be any different?" I asked.

"Because this isn't for the Ramones," he said. "It's for the Resistance. It'll be all right. I promise you."

"Okay," I said, "whadda ya got?"

"It's this song called 'Censorshit,'" Joey told me. "It's about Tipper Gore and that PRC thing and how they want to put ratings and shit on records. The first line is, *Tipper, what's that sticker hanging on to my CD?*' And that's all I got."

I thought about it for a few seconds. "How about, *Is it some kind of warning that's supposed to protect me?*'" I offered.

"That's great!" Joey said excitedly.

"You want some more?" I asked.

"No, no, that's enough," he said, "I'll take it from here. Can ya come over and help me put it on a cassette?"

"Yeah, yeah," I said. Of course, I wound up adding some music, as well, but this was different, because it "wasn't for the Ramones."

I told Joey about the new lineup with Steven Sane and that we had our first show booked. He came down to see us at a crappy club on Houston Street that had no stage and a putrid PA with no monitors.

When I called him a few days later to see if we could pick up where we left off with the Tribe, Joey sounded a little strange. He said he had good news and bad news.

The bad news was that he didn't think Steven Sane was impressive as a front man. He had a great voice and was a talented guy, but my brother didn't think this was nearly as good a lineup as I had before. Joey even added that I had blown it. I'd had a great thing, but I blew it, along with all the hard work he'd done, as well. He was also upset that he never saw any money from the Epic deal. Though it would be unusual for most people to bring up something like that, it seemed on par with my brother's sometimes-paranoid behavior. I got the distinct impression he now thought he'd been taken advantage of in the ill-fated Epic deal. Our lawyer had told us Joey was only going to receive a percentage if the full deal went through, which would have brought him around $40,000. The development money was to be used strictly to get the real deal, which was not in the cards.

I argued that Joey knew what had happened with Epic; and as far as losing the singer, he'd agreed with what we'd done.

"Yeah, well it shouldn't have mattered what *I* thought," Joey said. "You should have tried to keep it together."

Though I was pissed, mostly I was disappointed that he didn't really want to pursue things.

"Well, you're entitled to your opinion," I responded.

His good news was that the Ramones had landed a song on a TV commercial. It would pay the band $100,000. This was a first for the Ramones, and Joey was thrilled about it. He told me that "Blitzkrieg Bop" would be used in a commercial for Bud Light that would start airing in the spring of 1991.

Though they were still the kings of punk, the Ramones were no longer at the top of the "alternative music" food chain and were on the brink of being swallowed up by a new phenomenon known as "grunge." A punk-inspired form of rock & roll made famous in the early nineties, grunge had been incubating in Seattle, where it was hatched. Now in its formative years, it was making its way toward the heartland, flattening everything in its path. To me, it appeared as if Neil Young and the Ramones had an offspring and named it Nirvana. The press and the media were eating it up.

Throughout the 1980s, the Ramones had been vilified, patronized, smeared by the mass media and the major marketing brain trusts. They were ignored by some and ravaged by others. Finally in 1991 a smart advertising executive realized what radio programmers never did—that the Ramones' music could sell beer to a thirsty nation. Contrary to what some people perceive as "punk ethics," which the Ramones never really espoused to begin with, the band had no ethical or political problem whatsoever with licensing their music for a beer commercial. While they always maintained their creative integrity, they were not exactly huge proponents of anticapitalist ideals, such as not taking money from corporate sponsors—depending on the sponsor, of course. To me it seemed more like the poor taking money from the rich—the band's record sales were still averaging only about seventy thousand units per album—and who's got more money than Budweiser?

The Ramones remained virtually unknown to the general American public until the Anheuser-Busch Brewing Company chose to showcase "Blitzkrieg Bop" in its summer 1991 Bud Light advertising campaign.

"Hey, ho, let's go drink a Bud!"

My initial reaction was excitement—for my brother and the Ramones. But I was also leery that something would get fucked up, as it usually did for the band.

Overall I was extremely happy for Joey when Bud Light finally put the Ramones on the national map. I was thrilled when I saw the commercial for the first time. I started bopping my head watching the thirty-second, race-car-themed spot. The director of the commercial used more of the song than I thought they would.

Then all of sudden I heard the little part I did on the song.

"Cool!" I thought. "That's great!" And it *was* cool—the first thirty or forty times.

Months went by, and the commercial kept running strong. I was hearing my voice on TV four or five times a day, and after a while I started thinking, "Hmmm, something is wrong with this picture."

I had done a little dabbling in the jingle business after my friend and former Ramones roadie "Big" Matt Nadler hooked me up with an agency. I did some demos for them and knew that background singers got paid very well. Of course, this was a different circumstance, as the original recording was already done and this was a licensing deal. But I thought that since I never got paid for the original sessions, maybe something could still be worked out.

I was as broke as could be except for the little bit of money I was making bagging weed. Yet I heard myself singing on a TV commercial for which the band had been paid $100,000. It seemed to me that this would be the perfect opportunity for the Ramones to offer a little gesture of appreciation for all that I'd contributed over the years. Even a union-scale, hourly-rate payment for singing on that record—maybe $500—would have been *huge* to me at the time. Way over a month's rent, right there!

My brother, and undoubtedly Johnny, knew how badly I was doing financially. I knew from the way I'd heard John talk about other people who hadn't made it—mockingly labeling them "losers"—that he was probably getting a kick out of my lack of success. These were not comforting thoughts. No, they were not making their life's fortune from the ad and would only wind up with $12,500 each after all was said and done with copublishers, etc.

But they knew I had gone into debt when I was working for them for $50 a week, when that was all they could afford. And given that I was the only one who wound up *losing* money while working for the Ramones, I didn't think I was out of line feeling I should have been considered for at least a taste of this Budweiser round — especially for singing on this song. Had I not been so desolately broke, selling pot to cover my bills, I probably wouldn't have cared. But the more I heard it, the more it irked me. That no one ever said anything about it irked me as well. I guess I shouldn't have been surprised. But as the commercial played on for months, I got more annoyed.

In August I called my brother to get the phone number of someone he knew who worked at a record company.

I was talking to Joey when the commercial came on TV, and I said, "Hey, Joey, here's the commercial . . ."

Joey said, "Oh yeah, ha ha!"

I said, "Oh, and there's my part . . ."

"Yeah . . . ," Joey said, sounding slightly embarrassed, suppressing a nervous laugh.

As pleasantly as possible, and with absolutely no malice, I asked, "Do you think I should have gotten something for that?"

Joey said, "Well, you know . . ."

That was it.

I said, "I guess, umm, you don't want to talk about it?"

Joey said, "Nahhhhhh . . ."

After I had that little "conversation" with Joey, I could tell he didn't want to deal with it. I had a feeling of foreboding in my gut. This could be either big trouble, or a happy ending and the rectification of many years of disregard.

Joey never disputed that I sang on the song, and he'd probably been expecting me to bring it up sooner or later, but he did not want to deal with it at all. I could tell Joey knew something was not right; this was *really* bothering me. I just didn't think it was fair.

I decided to call my friend, lawyer, and former manager Steve Massarsky to see what he made of the situation. Maybe there was nothing that could be done; maybe there was nothing that *should* be done. The next day, before I got around to calling Steve, I went up to my mother's house to show her how to use her VCR. Mom and her friend June, who was like our second mother, were having coffee, so I sat down and told them what was going on.

I said I was thinking of calling Steve to help me straighten out this potential mess with the Ramones.

"Didn't they pay you at the time for that?" Mom asked.

"Not for that," I explained. "They were paying me to be a full-time roadie—fifty dollars a week."

"Fifty dollars—a *week*?" June asked. "For working seven days a week, going on the tours? That's not even ten dollars a day!"

"Well, I got a little extra on tours," I added.

"Well, I think you *should* call a lawyer," June advised. "Maybe they'll finally respect you if you stand up for yourself."

My mother said, "I don't know if you should do that, though. What would you do, have Steve call Jeff?"

"No," I told her. "This isn't between me and Jeff. It's between me and the Ramones, or me and the record company; I'm not sure who it's between, to tell you the truth. Most likely Steve will call Gary Kurfirst, their manager, and maybe he can straighten things out."

My mom was very apprehensive, which was the first indication to me that if there *were* a conflict, I wouldn't be getting any support from her.

I'd hoped she would be supportive, as her friend June was. It was not like our mother to approve of or be complacent about people being taken advantage of, especially when it was one of her children. If it had been any other band, I'm sure she would have been saying, "Those cheap, lousy bastards!"

But now she seemed different, for reasons I was not quite sure of.

Steve Massarsky told me he had to have more information but that there was a good possibility I could stand to make a substantial amount from the little background vocal depending on whether it was still running nationally or regionally and with what frequency. He estimated anywhere from $500 to $5,000.

Not bad. I sure could have used it.

Steve called back a few days later and told me, "Kurfirst said the spot would be running another three months, but they don't want to give you anything. Let me know what you want to do."

In the interim, Mom asked what was happening. I think she sensed there was going to be trouble. I saw absolutely no big deal in what had been done so far: Steve had put in an inquiry call, and that was it. No threat, no lawsuit, not even a raised voice—just a business call. I was merely looking out for myself, exploring a possibility of being compensated for work I'd done.

About a week or so later, I got a call from my brother. He was out on the road, in Washington, DC. I could tell all was not well. He had an attitude from the word "hello."

"So," he started off, "I hear you had your lawyer call Gary?"

I said, "Yeah, so?"

"I hear you're looking for money," said Joey.

"Steve just put in a call to Gary about the commercial, Joey. That's all."

"Well, what's there to talk about?" Joey asked rhetorically. "Background singers don't get paid."

I said, "Yeah, they certainly do. How much depends on the situation."

He said, "Background singers and hand-clappers don't get paid."

Joey suddenly remembered that I also did the hand-clapping, as well as other things, on that first album, but his tone was extremely belittling.

I said, "That's not true. What are you gonna tell me, that you don't have hundreds of albums in your collection with background singers credited on them? And you're going to tell me that none of them got paid anything? Bands a lot smaller than yours have paid me for studio sessions. Come on, man!"

Joey said, "Well, you did it because you *wanted* to do it."

"First of all," I said, "*you* are not going to tell *me* why *I* did it. I know why I did it. And I did it for several reasons. I did it to help out your band—and because I was going to get my name on an album. And yeah, because it was fun and I wanted to.

"*You* wanted to sing on that record too," I told him. "I don't see you guys turning down the money you got because you wanted to make a record. You're not turning down your share and saying, 'Hey, Budweiser, it's okay. I just wanted to sing this song.'

"Yeah, I wanted to do it," I said, "but I also expected to be credited for it, and possibly even paid a little something if you guys ever did well, which you did.

"Come on, Joey, you know how much I got paid for working for you for two years. I had to borrow *hundreds* of dollars to get out of hock after

I worked for the Ramones. Do you know that after I quit working for your band, Talking Heads paid me for one night what you guys paid me for a week? Have fuckin' mercy!"

Then my brother said something that changed our relationship forever: *"WELL, YOU ONLY WANT MONEY NOW BECAUSE YOU'RE A FAILURE AND A LOSER, AND YOU NEVER MADE IT!"*

That was like a knife through my heart.

For a moment I was in total shock. Then my own defense mechanisms kicked in.

"Listen, man, maybe I never made it," I told him, "but I could have done worse, too. And I'm proud of what I've done."

"Yeah, well, you're bitter," Joey snarled, "'cause ya never got where you wanted to go!"

"Well, neither did you," I countered. "If you wanna play this game, if anyone is bitter, it's you guys. You're the one who's so resentful 'cause you never had a hit record and always complaining how all these bands that came up after you got so successful. You never played the Garden. You never got asked to do *Saturday Night Live*—and *I'm* bitter? I suppose those things don't bother you at all, right?"

"Yeah?" Joey said. "Well, I'm fine with where I'm at."

"Well, good for you!" I said. "So am I."

"Listen, man, if you try to do anything," Joey threatened, "I'll come at you with my lawyers, and we'll blow you out of the water! I'm gonna call Seymour Stein and tell him and everybody in the business not to work with you, because you're greedy and you're a troublemaker. I'm gonna blackball you in this business!"

Then he hung up the phone.

Another knife in the heart—not to mention a wave of fear. Was he serious?

Needless to say, I wasn't expecting that reaction from my brother. I didn't know if he was bluffing. I had no idea how far he would take this.

I didn't cry, but I was definitely devastated. I was pissed. If somebody tells you "You're a loser and you just want money 'cause you never made it!" those are *fighting words*. If you said that to a stranger, you'd be taking a good chance of getting punched in the face.

I was feeling all kinds of emotions . . .

I was mad.

I was sad.

But I was pissed off at Joey more than anything else. Though I hoped I was wrong, it appeared that the thing I feared most was now surfacing— some kind of need for revenge or retribution on my brother's part. I always worried that someday he would want to punish me for years of things not in my control, such as being more normal physically and faring better socially and academically in our youth, getting more accolades from our mom and Hank and even our father when we were children. He was now willing to make the big separation between him and me, and with whoever took my side in this dispute—be it a friend or family member.

And Joey was indignant, knowing he would prevail now as the more powerful figure. But I couldn't back down, just on principle. I never did buy into the old "might makes right" adage. The little guy has rights and has to stick up for himself at some point.

Steve Massarsky called a few days later with some options. If, as was promised at the time, I'd been credited for the background vocal, even if it was in tiny little print somewhere on the back cover, I would have been eligible to collect performance residuals through the Screen Actors Guild. The money would come via the ad agency and Anheuser-Busch, and the Ramones wouldn't have to part with a penny. Steve informed me that if Ramones Productions would simply agree to certify my performance in a document, that would be sufficient. I told him I was sure that was never going to happen, but I would never be sure why not.

"Well, we could do a voice analysis," he said, "but we'll have to get the master tapes."

They take a sample of a voice, isolate the track, and legitimately prove that it was me singing through voice recognition patterns.

Steve said, "We could pursue this thing, but since they're being so reticent, it might cause some friction. It could also cause some family problems for you."

"Well, it's too late for that, Steve." I told him what had happened and that I didn't want to take it any further. There was nothing to gain at that point except a lawyer bill that would probably negate anything I might have been awarded. Plus it would only exacerbate things. I was still worried about my brother's threats.

Steve knew my brother, and he was pretty shocked at Joey's reaction.

There was someone else, however, who seemed to have expected it from Joey.

"I thought that might happen," Mom said when I told her what Joey had said to me. She added, "*I told you it was not a good idea to call a lawyer.*"

"So you would have rather I just shut up, and just let myself be taken advantage of, without making a whimper?" I asked her.

"Well, like Joey says, a lot of people out there would just be honored to be on their record. Isn't that true?" she said.

I could see where this was going.

The real issue was that if Joey *did* think it was fair for his band to give up a fraction of what they got paid to compensate me, and Johnny didn't, he might have had to get into an argument with Johnny about it. But if Joey really did think it was the right thing to do, then maybe he *should* have gotten into an argument with Johnny, whether it was for me or anyone else. I'm not talking about a life-or-death duel but an objective argument.

Joey was no longer a shy, introverted kid just going with the flow. He was a bona fide rock star now and could speak up when he wanted to. He could certainly speak up to me, his mother, his girlfriends, and even his father.

I knew I might be playing with fire, but I truly never thought it would end up like this.

In hindsight, what I had done regarding the Bud Light fight probably wasn't the smartest thing considering Joey's ever-increasing paranoia, a symptom of his psychiatric/medical condition. But is that a good reason not to respect yourself or stand up for your rights? How many times did I say to myself, "Ahh, just let it go. Don't let the little things bother you"? I'd done it too many times, about too many little things.

I think that's why my mother was upset. She knew I was putting my brother in a position where he might have to stand up to Johnny, and she probably knew instinctively that Joey still wasn't able to do it. To be honest, I was hoping that Joey would come through for me—and for himself. After all, this wasn't a problem between Joey and me but between the Ramones and me—or, more likely, between Johnny Ramone and me.

Joey was my big brother, and I think I wanted him to stick up for me just once, the way I had always been forced to stick up for him when everyone in the neighborhood was picking on him. Instead, Joey called our mother. One day when I was dropping her off in front of her building, she said to me, "Joey said that you called him up and said, 'You owe me fucking money, man!'"

That's the way Joey defended himself—he had to defame me. Instead of telling Mom that he was mad I had put him in an awkward situation, he had to demonize me.

"Ma," I said, "honestly. Does that sound like me?"

"Well, that's what Joey says," my mother said firmly, as if it had to be true—*because Joey says.*

If anyone should have known how my brother reacted when being confronted about doing the wrong thing, it's the woman he'd threatened at knifepoint back in Birchwood Towers. This was the first time Mom had believed his side of the story over mine in many, many years. It was the first time in all these years a situation like this had come up; that threw me, too.

"Well, you know what?" I said. "The next time he needs me to do something for him, I'm not going to be there. That's it."

"Well, I don't know what *you* could possibly do for him," she responded. "I already do everything for him. Whatever he needs done, *I* already do."

"Riiiight. Okay, Ma. Bye."

Holy mother of God.

Now it was a competition for the right to be the rock star's main custodian.

As justified as I believe I was to inadvertently put Joey in an awkward position, I'd known for some time that there was more to this than just Johnny Ramone. Though we both pretended it didn't happen, the truth had come out that very drunken night in Puerto Rico when I was still writing songs with Dee Dee, and Joey had confessed, "Well, if you ever make it, I don't know what I'll do . . ."

I'm sure I hurt Joey on several levels when we were kids—not intentionally, of course.

On the other hand, I had to stop my brother that day he held a knife to my mother's chest in the hallway. I had to live in his squalor and essentially share his compulsions: him switching lights on and off all night, opening and closing the door, and holding his glasses in and out of running water in the bathroom for hours on end, like some kind of Vietcong torture procedure. And of course that's the short list.

I never thought I'd really done anything that Joey wouldn't understand as we matured. But that was the problem: Joey never really matured—he *adapted.*

Maybe I had never really matured completely, either, but I was a lot closer. Then again, if I'm that much more mature, I wouldn't have to go around saying it.

As angry as I was about not receiving even the slightest consideration for the Bud commercial, the aftereffects were far more upsetting. The reality was that I was really angry—because it hurt so much.

A COUPLE OF months later when I came over to my mother's house for dinner, she said, "You know, the Ramones are playing at the Palladium next week. Joey told me he invited the *whole* family to the show. Are you going?"

My mom made the best turkey meatloaf *anywhere*—with tomato paste, rice, and raisins—but my appetite immediately began to fade.

I said, "Well, he didn't invite *me*."

She said, "Oh, really? That's odd, because he specifically told me he was inviting the whole family."

The story was unfolding. I got the message.

I said, "Do you see what he's doing here? We're not talking to each other, and he's inviting my whole family to this show, but he's not inviting Arlene or me. Don't you get it? It's a little power play. And he's doing it to punish me.

"And you're gonna go to this thing," I added, "when he's just trying to stick it to me here?"

"Well, I don't know if that's true," my mother argued.

"Mom, your son told me that he was going to blackball me in the music business—that he's gonna do his best to fuck up my career. And you're gonna go to this show, and, what, congratulate him? Pat him on the back and tell him how wonderful he is?"

"Well," she countered, "what do *you* want me to do? Shoot him in the head? Cut his legs off?"

"*Shoot him in the head?*" I responded in disbelief. "What are you talking about? I'm just asking you to show just a *little* disapproval of this ploy. I think it would have a good effect. Maybe he'll go back to being more humble, maybe come back down to earth. You do realize he's using you all to prove a point, right?"

I don't think she hated being in that position.

Of course she didn't like it, but she also hadn't said, "Leave me out of this, okay?"

Normally our mother would try to patch things up if there were family problems. She'd always ask, "Well, did you guys talk?"

I said to her, "You've been to over a hundred shows."

"Well," Mom said, "he always invites me. He *always* wants me there."

"That's very sweet," I countered. "But considering the circumstances, I'm asking you not to go to this *one* show, this one time, to maybe show a little support for me in this, because I'm the one left out here."

"Well, I'm not going to cut off my relationship with my son," Mom said. "That's what you're asking me to do!"

"*Cut off your relationship?*" I asked. "Are you really afraid that he's going to cut you off? His own mother—just because you didn't go to one Ramones show?"

"It means a lot to him that I come to this show," she said defensively. "He even told me that."

"Yeah, why do you think it means so much to him?"

I'm sure I could have gone if I'd called my brother, or even Monte, but did I really want to do that? It was a horrible position to be in; I hadn't mentioned any of this to the rest of my family. Either way I lost: By not going, I was hurting myself, and if I did go, I was either looking for—or asking for—trouble. Bottom line was, I certainly did not feel wanted.

The day after the show, my mother called me up and started gushing: "It was great—and they treated me like royalty! Monte came over and made sure we were okay, and someone showed us to our seats.

"Everybody fussed over us—I signed autographs. It was a wonderful show. *Everybody* was there . . ."

What was I gonna say?

"I think he does feel a little something," Mom continued, in a warm glow, "because he said to me, 'You know, Ma, it was really great to have my whole family there.' He sounded wistful, like a little boy."

"Mom!" I exclaimed, snapping her out of her moment. "Who are you telling this to? You're telling me how happy he was to have his whole family there, but remember me? *I wasn't there!*"

"Oh, right," she said, displaying the closest thing to contempt I'd ever heard from her. "I forgot who I was talking to."

She almost didn't seem like herself. I knew she was smarter, more sensible, and more sensitive than this.

I think she was confused, a bit lost in a cloud of celebrity euphoria—and she just wanted me to get off of her cloud.

———

BY THE NEXT summer, about a year after the Bud Light fight, the band I had with Whitey and Steven Sane had totally fallen apart. I started a new band with Handsome Dick Manitoba, the former lead singer of the Dictators and Manitoba's Wild Kingdom. We called it the Plug Uglies. Manitoba was one of my favorite performers of all time. He was an incredibly gifted front man, even though he wasn't what you would consider a musically adept singer. Working with Handsome Dick was kind of like working with a funnier, less complicated version of Lester Bangs.

Over at Manitoba's house, we were trying to write some songs together. Handsome Dick pulled out a copy of the Ramones' *Mondo Bizarro* album, which had just come out.

"Did you see this yet?"

When he passed it over to me, I saw "Censorshit" on it.

I didn't know it was going to appear there. Joey had told me that it was for the Resistance, not the Ramones.

I looked at the album and said, "That motherfucker!" It read "By Joey Ramone"—no Mickey Leigh, and no Robin Rothman, who I knew contributed lyrics as well. That he also excluded Robin made me feel a little better, knowing that at least I wasn't alone and would have someone to commiserate with.

I couldn't imagine that Robin would be okay with it. She had helped him with a lot of material for his Resistance project while she was renting his apartment, including, ironically, a rewrite of John Lennon's "Gimme Some Truth."

"I was really pissed," Robin Rothman recalled. "In fact, I was *furious*. Just like he'd told Mickey, he said we were all doing this one together. That's what really killed me. After we wrote the words, I published it as a poem, and I put my name on, Mickey's name on, Joey's name—and Charlotte's name on it, because she had actually come up with several lines, too.

"I'd been helping Joey with all kinds of things for his various projects—lyrics, whatever—and sometimes I wasn't thrilled with the way he treated me. But this time, *Joey really hurt me*," Robin said sadly.

"I confronted Joey and said, 'You didn't even give your *own brother* credit?' That's when he threw a pillow at my head. I used to love him, but I couldn't trust him anymore. Now I felt like he was . . . a thief. So I moved out."

There wasn't even a thank-you, to me *or* to Robin. The only ones Joey thanked on the album were Robin's cats, Precious and Spatz.

Andrea Starr, from his management's office, also said she wrote some words in the song. I found out later that Marky had originally come up with the title. That didn't leave a hell of a lot left that Joey could've written.

Aside from being pissed, I was really disappointed in Joey. This time I thought he'd really crossed the line.

When I got home from Manitoba's, I thought about calling my brother. I hadn't seen or spoken to him since Christmas at Mom's house, when she and June convinced me to go shake his hand and wish him a merry Christmas. "Be the bigger man," they told me.

Maybe I was the bigger man then, but now I was fuming. I called my brother up and said, "I *saw* the album . . ."

"Yeah?" Joey said.

"Well, don't you think you at least owe me a phone call?" I asked him.

"No," Joey said angrily.

"You told me there was not going to be a problem with that song, right?" I asked.

"So?" he challenged me.

"Don't you even think you owe me an explanation?"

"No," he hissed.

Now *I* was pissed.

"Well"—I took a deep stab—"tell me, how does it feel to rip off your own brother? And your friend? And even your own mo—"

Bang!

As expected, he hung up on me. We didn't talk after that for a long while.

Before the Bud Light fight, never in our entire lives did we go months, or a week, or even a couple of days, without talking.

After my mother heard about it, she called me and said, "Well, *of course* he didn't put your name on the song. You two weren't talking. He was mad at you."

"That's a reason for him not to put my name on it? Because he was mad at me because I had the audacity to make a peep about the Bud commercial? You're saying because I thought I got kinda screwed once—and he got mad—that's why he screwed me again? Does that sound rational to you?"

She didn't have an answer for that but finally replied, "Well, what did you expect? *You called a lawyer!*"

This was becoming more and more confounding.

32.

CLOWNS FOR PROGRESS

SCENE I

Pushin' Too Hard

I SUPPOSE I could have been doing worse—if I were sick or dead. The little money I'd been able to squeeze out of the Tribe's development deal was long gone, the jingle work opportunities were few and far between, and my wife was complaining about the lack of a regular paycheck. Things were looking grim.

So like so many other struggling musicians and entertainers, I resorted once again to what I had previously done to make ends meet when all other profitable avenues were closed: selling pot. I had gotten out of the weed business when my band had actually generated enough money for us to live on, but now I was drawn back in.

I had written some songs over the course of the year and I wanted to record them and come back strong with a new band. I wasn't going to let myself be intimidated or overcome by anybody's power trip; nobody should, no matter what his or her famous brother, sister, mother, or father thinks.

If you want it, you have every right to go for it. For me, though, this would take some money—and I wasn't going to my family, who told me I would do much better in life if only I'd kiss the Ramones' ass a little more.

They didn't say it in those words, but my mother did tell me that if I apologized to Joey for talking to a lawyer regarding the Budweiser commercial, then maybe Joey would be nice to me again and help me out. *Fuck that.*

Guided by pride, I opted to take my chances, as perilous as they might have been. After all, we're only talking about a little bit of marijuana here. I had no moral problem at all with selling pot. In fact, one of my customers was a cop at the 112th Precinct. Another was a middle-aged neighborhood truck driver, who would split what he got from me with his son, who also was a cop at the 112th Precinct.

So I knew they knew about me and didn't give a shit. I figured I had to be below the radar of any higher authorities—or drug rip-off bandits, many of whom pretended to be cops, complete with police badges.

My normal procedure was to take a pound or two—which was fronted to me—and sell it in ounces, or quarter pounds, over the course of a month. I wasn't your lowest-level pot dealer, but it was relatively small and safe. I didn't deal with hardened criminals, mostly friends.

On one occasion, I took a few pounds from a connection named Sam and brought them to my old friend and former Rattlers drummer Matty Quick. Being the middleman in something like this didn't make you much money. They'd actually set the price with each other and just pay me a delivery fee. It was a quick $100, but I *had* introduced Matty and Sam—at least over the phone.

In the summer of 1992, there was a "drought"—a severe reduction in marijuana crops. During those times, it wasn't uncommon for my pot connections to call me to see if I had a line on any product.

In September, Sam called me to see if I had anything for him. He came over to my house and bought a half ounce of hash, a relatively small amount. As Sam was counting out $120, which he did several times—loudly—he began to tell me about a trunkload of Thai weed that his "buddy" was going to be driving in from San Francisco.

"Do you think Matty would be interested in it?" he asked.

"I don't know," I said. "Maybe, considering how dry it is out there. I don't know about a trunkload, though."

"Come on," Sam cajoled, "Matty does huge amounts, doesn't he?"

"Well, you know what he does, Sam. He does what *you* do."

"Why don't you give him a call?" Sam suggested. "Ask him if he'll take the whole load. Or would you rather I call him? Matty remembers me, right?"

"No, I'll call him if you want," I said, "but I doubt he'll do anything. He doesn't like to go outside the people he deals with, but I'll tell him what you got going on and see what he says."

With that one phrase, I opened a can of worms that are still squirming around to this day.

In the following weeks, Sam called several times and came back over once to talk.

"If not Matty," Sam wondered, "do you know anyone else we could do this with?"

I told Sam I really had no prospects for moving that kind of weight, except for Matty Quick, and maybe Donny Denuccio, another guy I dealt with. Sam gave me a beeper number and in a day or so I got a call back from a guy named Mark. I got a strange feeling from Mark, and I didn't like getting involved with large amounts and new people. I guess I was getting apathetic, as well as desperate and reckless, thinking, "Fuck it, I'm just gonna make as much money as I can!"

I mean, it was just *pot*. I actually believed I was doing people a service until it eventually became legalized. I still do.

Sam's friend Mark called, so he could bring me a sample to bring to Matty.

"We'll give him fifty pounds," Mark bargained. "We'll give him a *hundred* pounds, but he'll have to pay cash. How much can Matty afford?"

I told Mark that Matty *might* take five or ten pounds from him, at the most. Mark urged me to convince Matty to take more.

"How about you?" Mark asked. "How many are you taking? You gotta pay for it up front, though."

"Me?" I asked him. "I don't have a lot of money. I could buy maybe one pound. That's really all I would want, anyway."

I took the sample to Matty, but he decided he didn't want to do business with these guys. After all the talk, nothing happened, so I went back to my small weed business.

Later that fall, on November 2, 1992, to be exact, my buzzer started ringing at about eleven a.m. As usual, I turned over and went back to sleep, assuming it was someone ringing the wrong buzzer. Suddenly there was someone knocking on my door, and as it got louder, I realized they were not going to go away. I got out of bed and headed for the door, wearing only my underpants. Before I got there, the door blew open and in charged men with guns and badges.

They pushed me up against the wall in my hallway, yelling, "DEA!" and, "FBI!"

"We've got a warrant for your arrest for the sale of narcotics," one of them said as they handcuffed me, "to your friend Sam!"

Holy Shit! Sam?

I started to replay it all in my mind—that day Sam came to my house and counted the money out loud, and asked me all those questions about different people.

It all made sense now. Sam had been fucking wired!

Motherfucker!

"Okay, okay," I told them, "you got me, so I sold a little piece of hash to Sam. You got your man, but tell me two things: First, can I put on some pants? And second, what the fuck are *ten* of you guys doing in my house? And where do you get *narcotics*? It was just hash!"

"Well, pally," one of the agents answered cajolingly, sounding very much like Bullwinkle the Moose, "under federal law hashish *is* a narcotic, and it comes with a *very stiff* penalty."

"But you haven't heard the good part yet!" Agent Bozowitz gleefully informed me. "We got you on conspiracy charges, too! Remember your friend Mark? Well, guess what? He works for the FBI!"

They told me they could smell pot in the apartment and went to the closet where I had a triple-beam scale and about three-quarters of a pound of marijuana.

"Well, well, well!" Agent Emmett Kelly gloated, proudly posing by the scale and the sneaker box containing the marijuana. "Look what we have here! Where's the rest?"

"Uh, that's about it," I told him. "You guys scored big today; back up the tractor-trailers . . ."

I was nervous but figured the charge *had* to be just a small step up from a misdemeanor, at the very worst.

Still dressed in just the handcuffs and underpants, they sat me on the couch in the living room.

"We want to search the house," one of them asked.

"Do you have a warrant for that?" I answered him.

"No, but like I said, buddy," Agent Chuckles quipped, "we got you on a conspiracy charge, ha ha! That could land you in jail for *fifteen years*. It will look a lot better for you if you let us search the house."

"Go ahead." I shrugged. "You already found everything there is."

"Listen," Agent Keystone said in a very serious tone, "we *know* what you do. We know you sell *hundreds and hundreds* of pounds of marijuana!"

"Oh, really?" I responded, getting pissed, even though I was now scared shitless. "And how do you know that—because Sam told you?

"I'm sure you caught Sam with a big bundle, maybe he was crossing state borders, maybe he was selling coke, too. I'm sure Sam is really screwed. And I'm sure he told you he's giving you a big dealer so he can get himself off.

"Don't you get it? What Sam told you is bullshit," I argued truthfully. "Sam went down the ladder instead of up, because he was scared. Sam told you I was a big guy, but I'm not. Don't you guys do any kind of research or anything before you do this?

"This is where I live," I tried to rationalize with them. "It costs $350 a month. I drive a ten-year-old Nissan my father-in-law bought us as a wedding present. This apartment isn't a front. I don't have a mansion on Long Island or a yacht in some marina somewhere. That big box of phone cords in the closet? I sell them at flea markets to try and make extra money. I mean, *are you guys for real?*"

"Yeah, sure, you sell all kinds of things. Nice try," Agent Skelton answered me. "We *know*, Mitch. *We know all about you.*"

"Great," I said. "You know all about me. So, yeah, I was selling some pot, but what I just can't believe is that *this* is what you guys *really do*? You bring ten DEA and FBI agents into the house of a little Jewish pot dealer? I mean, do you see any guns here?"

"Yeah, yeah." Agent Clarabelle smiled. "We know *everything*, okay? And you are going down!"

Then they spotted bowls of cat food.

"Oh, you have cats here, huh?" Agent Coco asked suspiciously. "How come I don't see them?"

"Well," I confessed, "it's lunch hour now, so they go out to sell crack to children in the schoolyards."

One of them pointed to a poster of the Ramones on my wall.

"You know these guys?" Agent Crusty asked.

"I thought you knew everything," I snapped.

Then one of them walked in from my bedroom with a stack of cash. I had $10,000 in my drawer. About half of it was owed to Donny Denuccio for pot he had fronted me the week before. The rest was everything I had saved up over the past couple of years.

"All right," they told me, "we're going for a ride."

They put a jacket over the handcuffs when they took me out of my apartment house, because they didn't want anyone to know I had been busted. They drove me into Manhattan, entered the FBI/DEA headquarters through a secret entrance on Tenth Avenue, and put me in a cell. I knew they wanted me to start freaking out in there, begging to be let out and telling them whatever they wanted to know. So I did my best to meditate and stay as still and calm as possible. And I actually did; but inside I was very much freaking out. About five hours later they brought me into the office, and the grilling began.

"You better tell us everything," one of them barked. "Who you get it from, who you sell it to—we want names, addresses, everything!"

"Can I talk to a lawyer?" I asked. "Can I make a phone call?"

"Yeah, when we're finished," Agent Smiley said. "Now tell us *everything.*"

"I don't think so," I shot back.

They let me call Arlene, but I didn't tell her everything on the phone—just that she couldn't tell anybody I got arrested and that she should try to be as calm as possible.

Then in walked a familiar face. *"Hey, buddy! Remember me?"*

Oh, Jesus. It was Mark, Sam's "friend."

Mark even had his hand out to me—like I would ever shake it.

I just glared at him.

He was giddy and highly animated, telling me, "Well, it looks like you're gonna be talking to us, buddy! We're gonna be your new best friends! Or you could be going away for a *long, long time!*"

Mark was acting like such a clown that even the DEA guys were looking at him funny. Then he got even more dramatic.

"This is the real thing, Mitch," Mark said, spreading his arms out before resting his hands on his hips. "This ain't no movie now, friend. *This is not a television show!*"

He leaned over and looked me in the eyes.

"This is no act," he said, shaking his head side to side as he slowly came in closer for the kill. "I'm not an actor."

He backed off, still staring at me.

"Well, maybe not," I told him, "but you sure are a ham."

Even the DEA guys had to laugh at that one.

After that brief moment of relief, things turned very dark.

"Look," one of them said sternly, "we have you on a charge of conspiracy to sell over one hundred pounds of marijuana."

"*What?*" I gulped hard.

This was looking bad.

"That's right." Mark grinned. "And it's all on tape. We know *everything* you do, we know *everything* about you—so you may as well talk to us!"

"Or you can *not* tell us anything," the stern one continued as they began forming a circle around my chair, "and we can take you out of here and put you in a special cell in Rikers. And believe me, you will not last ten minutes there!"

Rikers Island is the huge city jail facility in Queens, located in the middle of Flushing Bay. It's where the city's most violent criminals are interned.

"What do you mean by that?" I asked. "Do you *know* that someone is going to do something to me there?"

"We didn't say that." Mark began backpedaling, since it is improper to threaten a suspect. "That's just what happens. *You* know. You've heard about what happens at Rikers Island—you'll be torn to pieces. So give us some names!"

"It's called survival, Mitch," one behind me whispered.

"You want to see your wife again?" asked a voice from the right side.

"Or your family?"

Then they peppered me with threats from every direction.

"You better talk to us or . . ."

"You won't last ten minutes . . ."

"They call it *survival* . . ."

"*Okay!* Okay," I blurted out.

I invented a bunch of names, Benny from the Bronx, Jackie in Manhattan, Cisco from Newark . . .

"What about a guy named Matty?" the stern one asked. "Come on, Mitch, you *do* know a guy named Matty?"

"Um"—I hesitated—"I was in a band with a guy named Matty, but that's all."

That did not go over well.

"*Bullshit, man!*" one of them yelled, and they started assaulting me from every direction again.

"This guy doesn't get it, man. Let me have him . . ."

"*We don't believe you, Mitch!*"

"Talk to us *now* or we take you to Rikers!"

I took a long breath, slumped over in the chair, and said, "Well, then, okay, take me to Rikers. I'm not telling you anything else. You haven't even let me talk to a lawyer, so just take me to Rikers Island."

Rikers Island was just a scare tactic. If they took me to Rikers, the charges would go from federal jurisdiction to state, which has more lenient drug laws. Also, the case would then be out of their hands.

They all huddled in the corner for a few minutes, staring me down the whole time.

"Okay, you know what?" Agent Crusty said. "We're going to let you go. You go home, you call a lawyer, and you will find out that you are still going to talk to us, okay? Either that, or go away for about ten years. And we'll be checking into your story about what you do, and we'll be watching everyone else, too."

"Now while we're investigating you," Chuckles picked up, "you won't tell *anyone* that you've been arrested. Understand? If you do, we will consider it interfering with the investigation, and you'll really be screwed. I mean instantly. You won't see the light of day until who knows when. Got it? Now get outta here!"

I heaved a giant sigh of relief and started to get to my feet, but my body felt like it weighed a ton. I was still in shock. I still couldn't fathom how, with all the horrible shit going on in this city, in this country—in the *world*—the FBI had decided to use their resources to take *me* out.

This is how they are going to make the world a better place?

"Anybody got a subway token?" I asked these clowns for progress.

As I walked out, it all started to sink in. This nightmare was real; I could be going to jail, *for years*. I started shaking on Fourteenth Street, looking around constantly to see if someone was following me. I just wanted to see Arlene, cuddle with my cat, and never leave the house again. I just wanted to get on the train, get home, and stay there.

I thought everyone on the F train knew what had happened to me. The little girl sitting across from me, staring . . . she knows I'm in trouble, big time. The nebbishy Jewish guy next to her is making sure *not* to make eye contact with me, just as he was taught to do around dangerous types.

The gray-haired Puerto Rican lady at the end of the car . . . she's *definitely* FBI or CIA—and so is that kid with her, the one in the stroller. The muscular black guy with the prison tats, he's just lickin' his chops, waiting to get me alone in that cell.

I started shaking again.

I don't think Arlene realized the severity of the mess I was in until she saw my face—and then she panicked. I explained to her that they had me on the sale to Sam and they also had me for conspiracy, for some ridiculous amount—and it was all on tape.

I told Arlene, "When Sam asked me, 'Will Matty take a trunkload?' and I said, 'I don't know,' they had me on a conspiracy charge right there, because I didn't plainly say no. I said, 'I *don't* know. Maybe.'"

The half ounce of hash, under federal law, is practically in the same class of drugs as heroin. They were talking about three years in prison just for that one sale.

I broke down. I started banging my head against the wall and crying, just like you see in those prison movies, or like Robert De Niro did in *Raging Bull.* But as Mark had said, this was real.

All of a sudden the phone rang. It was Agent Chuckles: "Hey, buddy! Just wanted to let you know we're thinking of ya, ha ha. Sweet dreams. We'll be seeing you real soon!"

My stomach was churning. I knew what they wanted—my good friend Matty Quick. They had wanted him all along, and I was just a stepping stone to get to him. They were going to have me do to Matty what Sam did to me—set him up, so they could bring him down.

Then I had a thought: What if I appeared to be cooperating with them but really wasn't? Would that be good enough to get out of this?

Immediately I left the apartment and walked a few blocks to the Seventy-fifth Avenue subway station, where the only entrances are at the far ends of the station. I knew there was a pay phone right in the middle, by the token booth, where I could see anyone watching me from every direction. I waited there for a long minute, and then I called Matty Quick.

"Stickman?" he asked. "What's wrong?"

Matty could tell right away something was up, just by the sound of my voice. "Listen to me," I told him, "if I ever call you and ask you for some-thing—just say *no* to me. Just say that you don't know *what* I'm talking about."

"Did something happen to you?" Matty asked.

"I can't say any more than that," I told him, still watching every corner of the subway station for the feds. "If I call you, just *don't* ever sell me any-thing. Don't even *talk* to me about anything!"

"Stick, you wouldn't hurt me, would you?" Matty pleaded.

"I gotta go now," I told him. "Just be careful."

Then I hung up and got the hell out of there.

"You know, Mickey took a big risk calling me," Matty Quick confessed. "I wouldn't have done that—warn anybody. I *know* what Mickey did, and he took a big chance—because they would have killed him if they fucking knew that he had warned me."

When I got home I called my mom and told her what happened. I felt horrible, but I really had no one else to turn to. She didn't get down on me. She was certainly not happy, but she was supportive. She was just worried about me going to jail.

Mom called later that night and said she'd found me a lawyer, a woman named Isabelle, who used to work for the DEA and for the prosecutor. She'd switched over to being a defense lawyer because she didn't like the way the DEA operated. I called Isabelle, made an appointment, and went to see her the next day.

"A half ounce of hash and three-quarters of a pound of pot?" Isabelle asked. "This is a joke! Do you realize that this is the smallest federal pot bust in twenty-five years?

"They came to *you*, right?" Isabelle asked me. "Sam, and this guy Mark—who, I got news for you, is not named Mark. *You* were the 'mark,' the target. Sam approached you about this. *That* is entrapment, so that should take care of the conspiracy charge."

I felt a lot better after talking to her.

Isabelle was confident that she could get the prosecutor to dismiss the charges. She called it a "deferred prosecution." She advised me to continue not to say anything to anybody until she set up a meeting with the prosecu-tor, Bette Wilson—whom Isabelle had worked under.

The next week Isabelle told me, "It looks like they really want this other guy, Matty, and they want to use you to get to him. They're being very firm about it. They might want to indict you. I'm sorry, Mitch, but I think you have to talk to them."

I looked at Isabelle and thought, "Fuck, is she one of them? Maybe she's still on their side. Maybe this is all a setup. Maybe she is giving me up to get someone else off."

"What the hell happened, Isabelle? You said this was going to get dropped, and now . . ."

"I know, I know," Isabelle responded, "but they are making this into something else. They were trying to scare the shit out of you with the going-away-for-ten-years stuff, but I do think you might have to at least give them *some* information.

"Or you could not," Isabelle said, describing the second scenario, "and if they decide to indict you, we can go to trial, but that will be very expensive, and there is no guarantee you will win."

"Well, what if I didn't win?" I asked. "What's the worst-case scenario? How much time would I be looking at?"

"Well, they got you on the sale and the possession," Isabelle thought out loud, "which could be six months to a year, but if they get you on the conspiracy charge also, it could be as much as six years, *possibly* more."

"Oh my God," I groaned, almost collapsing on the floor.

"Listen," Isabelle said, trying to calm me, "go home, stay cool, and we'll talk tomorrow."

I was freaking out. I may have been wrong, but I *didn't trust her.* I considered the possibility of giving up Matty but was immediately overcome with nausea and had to run to the bathroom and puke. There was no way; I could never do it and live with myself. I'd rather take my chances in jail, the prospect of which also made me nauseous, but at least I wouldn't hate myself the rest of my life. I had to find another lawyer. I remembered my father telling me he knew the assistant district attorney of Queens, and as much as I didn't want to, I called him.

"Well, when you play with fire, this is what happens," he said.

I told him what had happened with the lawyer my mom had found me.

"Your mother didn't get you a good lawyer," Noel declared. "Sounds like that one was just dancing you down the aisle, telling you what you wanted to hear."

It became a competitive thing for my father—to prove who knew the better lawyer and who had the better connections. Mom agreed that maybe the former assistant DA, Paul Pickelle, might be more effective and that it was worth a shot. The next morning, I called Paul and hired him.

It was New Year's Eve 1992. My father and I were talking again and he seemed to be trying to help.

"You know," my father told me, "there *are* ways of getting around these things. Sometimes, with a little money . . ."

"You mean a bribe or something?" I asked him.

"Well," he said, "*maybe* something can be arranged. But first, I want you to call Jeff and wish him a happy New Year."

Dad made it sound like if I called my brother, then he and his lawyer friend would somehow help me get off the hook.

At that point, I'd have done just about anything.

Arlene and I had made plans with some friends to go see our friend Rob Falcone, who was beginning his career as a comedian and had his first New Year's Eve show that night. There we were at a comedy club, and I was pale as a ghost, trying to look like I was laughing, when actually I was shaking. It was all quite surreal, given how scared I was. I went out of the comedy club around ten p.m. to a phone on the street. It had started snowing, and I had no idea if my brother would even be home. Fortunately, he was. Joey sounded surprised to hear from me, especially when I wished him a happy New Year. He had no idea what was going on at my end.

"Oh, well, thanks," he said. "Same to you."

It felt good to talk to my brother—almost too comfortable. I so much wanted to be able to talk freely to him, like I used to, to tell him everything, confide in him—but I felt I couldn't really count on him. I was very scared. Our conversation was short and sweet, and then it was over. My mission had been completed, and I'd kept up my end of the agreement with my father.

I thought my father was going to take care of this, but he told me that *I* should ask Paul Pickelle if there were any other ways we could get this thing taken care of. So I very discreetly put it to Paul, who did not sound very enthusiastic. In fact, he responded by asking me if I knew that he had been head of the anticorruption department at the Queens district attorney's office.

"Uh, no." I cringed. "My father didn't tell me that. I hope I haven't insulted you."

"Don't worry about it," Paul told me.

He also told me that things were not looking good. Pickelle had heard the tapes, and even though I said on them that all I personally wanted was one pound—which was a good thing for me—I had also attempted to broker a deal with Matty and Mark. Paul explained that a trial could be a crapshoot. He recommended that we play along—not unlike what Isabelle had told me.

I was on my own—again. I was scared shitless.

SCENE II

Without a Net

THE FEDS WOULD call frequently and arrange clandestine meetings with me in dingy diners on the West Side near their offices. They would read off lists of names and ask if I knew any of the people. I would say no, and I wasn't lying. They also had the names of people I had talked to Sam about on tape—fortunately mostly nicknames, like Harry O, Nickles, Root Man, and Donny D—and they would tell me that I was going to have to call this one and set up that one.

I told them that this was pointless, because I wasn't going to do it.

"Oh, you will, you'll see," they would tell me.

"No one is going to do anything with me, anyway," I told them. "Everyone already thinks something is strange. I'm walking around white as a ghost, and I told everyone I stopped dealing . . ."

"Well, that wasn't very smart, Mitch," they said.

"Oh," I protested, "I should keep dealing just for you guys? Like you wouldn't bust me again, I suppose?"

"Well," they laughed, "we didn't really say that."

"Yeah," I said, "exactly."

IN JANUARY, I took my father out for lunch and he brought up the Bud Light, fight night debacle. He wanted me to know that I was wrong about the *whole* thing.

"Joey never paid you anything because you didn't have a contract," he informed me.

"Dad, that's bullshit," I said. "First of all, I never asked *Joey* to pay me.

And second, if the Ramones wanted to pay me something for the work, they could have paid me. Simple as that!"

"No, no, no," he argued, "Joey says you have to have a contract. You *always* have to have a contract."

"Listen," I told him, "lots of things are done in this business on good faith, with no contracts being drawn up. It depends on the people."

"You're wrong," he insisted. "Joey says that in this business, if you work on something and expect to get paid for it, ya gotta go to a lawyer first, and ya gotta have a contract. Joey says they couldn't have paid you even if they wanted to, because there was no contract."

"You're kidding me, right?" I asked him. "Dad, do you remember the thing we recorded, your 'Cold Turkey for a Hot Poppa' song? I did a lot of work on that, right? Do you mean to tell me that if somehow that ever came out as a record and you guys made a bunch of money off that, you wouldn't give me anything for what I did because I don't have a contract with you?"

"That's right," the old man said, shaking his head.

"I can't believe this," I said. "You are gonna go that far just to back up what he says? You're my own father, and you're telling me that we need a contract with each other for something like that? I can't fucking believe this."

"Well, what can I say?" my father said, shrugging. "That's business. That's what Joey says—and he knows. He's been successful in this business. I believe him. And I *would* pay you. Go to a lawyer and get a contract for 'Cold Turkey' and of course we will pay you."

"Please." I shook my head. "I wouldn't want anything from that, anyway!"

"Ya see? You're too stubborn for your own good," he informed me. "That's why you are where you are. Ya don't wanna learn."

My old man asked me if he should give me some money for the food.

"I don't know. Talk to my lawyer," I snapped, "I don't have a contract."

"Okay," he said angrily. "That's it for us. I don't need this from you."

Then he got up and left.

Once again, we didn't talk for years. Of course, my dad went right back and told my brother I got busted, even though it could have seriously jeopardized my case if Joey went and spilled it. My mother told me Joey was mainly pissed off that nobody had told him about it. Maybe he was more insulted than concerned. Or maybe he was actually upset because he was left out of a family crisis.

A few weeks later, the Clowns for Progress set up another meeting with me at a greasy coffee shop on the West Side Highway.

"We want you to call Matty," they said. "We want you to go see him, and we will prepare you."

"What do you mean . . . prepare me?" I asked. "You mean you want me to wear a wire? I have to talk to my lawyer."

"Okay, Mitch," they told me on my way out. "You talk to your lawyer, but we gotta tell you, this isn't nearly over, you know. We still have big plans for you."

The next day, February 26, 1993, something happened that would put this whole bit of stupidity into perspective, at least for me. A well-planned terrorist attack on the World Trade Center was carried out successfully. Bombs were detonated in the basement, and though the explosion failed to bring the towers down, six people were killed and close to a thousand more injured. Fortunately—for the rest of the city—the FBI and DEA had their priorities structured so that the agents had been assigned to keeping a close eye on *me* for the six months leading up to the terrorist attack, ensuring that the pound of marijuana in my closet did not explode.

In March they scheduled another meeting.

"Listen. We think you've been protecting Matty. Get him to do something, and we will consider letting you out of this. Otherwise, it's up to the prosecutor—and she wants you screwed. You'll be saying good-bye to everyone for a very long time."

"You know, I don't get you guys," I told them. "Back in September, Matty didn't even want to do anything, right? He always suspected something was odd about the whole thing. What makes you think he would do something now?"

"This could be it for you, Mitch," they went on. "What about one of your other connections? On the tape, you mentioned there might be other possibilities."

"But these are people I got things *from*, not the other way around. I don't go around offering people a hundred pounds of pot! It's not going to look right. *Nobody is going to do it.* Don't you get it? I'm too small to do what you want me to do. You guys are trying to catch a shark with a minnow!"

SCENE III

Under the Big Top

IN MARCH, PAUL Pickelle called and said they'd requested one more thing before they would decide if they were going to take me to trial. They wanted me to call Donny Denuccio, and they would record it.

"Paul," I explained, "everyone says this guy's family is 'connected.' And not only that, his brother is on the police force. He's a *lieutenant*, for Christ's sake. That would be a death sentence. You may as well just hang me."

"I see what you mean," Paul said.

"I'm not wearing a wire," I continued. "I'm not setting anyone up, that's it. For what I did, this is insane already, Paul. You told me you got a guy off that got caught with *forty handguns*—but they want to put *me* away? Tell them I'm done."

I sweated it out for a week, waiting to hear what the prosecutor decided. Finally Paul Pickelle said that they would drop the conspiracy charge if I would plead guilty to a lesser charge of "possession with intent to distribute small amounts."

I took the deal.

I was convicted of a class D felony—the lowest-level felony charge. It was over, almost. Sentencing was still an issue. Outside the court, I saw a couple of the agents, who actually told me they were glad it was over—that they knew all along I was not a bad guy, just a small pot dealer. They were just doing their job, which was basically to scare the shit out of me and try to get me to cooperate with them. It was a quota thing.

I told them that I appreciated their honesty, and that while I admired their bravery in dealing with dangerous criminals, it didn't take a hell of a lot of balls to bust into my house. They laughed and agreed.

Finally, I could tell everybody what had happened. I met with Matty and told him everything. He didn't really listen like he should have, though— he kept dealing.

Unfortunately, my May sentencing had been put off until September. I was still freaking out, as they could still send me away for anywhere from six months to a year, possibly more. I had to go through a process called a PSI, "pre-sentencing investigation," in which you meet with a probation officer to tell your life story and he or she recommends a sentence to the judge. I got character reference letters from Chris Frantz and Tina Weymouth of the Talking Heads, lawyers, managers, and other people in the music business. They were all very supportive. Even though the feds said I should just get probation, especially as it was my first offense, the PSI woman assigned to my case did not agree and very much wanted me to get jail time. I had to sweat it out until September.

I wanted to do something for my mom for Mother's Day. She had been so cool with me and I wanted to show my appreciation. What would make her happiest would be if we *all* got together, including Joey. So I called him up. The last time we had talked was on New Year's Eve.

"Hey," I said.

"Hey," he said back. "So I heard what happened," Joey said with a bit of an attitude.

"Yeah, I know," I said, adding, "I guess you were never even gonna call me, huh?"

"Well, yeah," Joey answered. "I was, ya know?"

I swallowed my pride and said, "How 'bout we get together and do something for Mom on Mother's Day?"

"Yeah, okay, that sounds good," Joey agreed. "So what's the story with you and the cops?"

"Well, I still don't know what's gonna happen," I told him. "I didn't get my sentencing. The feds and the prosecutor don't want to see me do any time, but this woman at the probation department is a real ballbuster, and she wants me to do at least six months!"

I told him I was still pretty scared about going to jail.

"Well," Joey laughed, "if you do, don't get a sore ass!"

It was a joke meant to break the tension, but I certainly wasn't laughing. However, we *were* talking again, and we took our mom out for Mother's Day. Joey was being very cool. He seemed to be sincerely concerned and even got infuriated about my arrest. He suggested we go to the press to expose the archaic pot laws and what the federal government had done with taxpayer money. He was ready to take up the cause.

I was afraid of running to the press. I didn't want to push my luck. Joey took me out to dinner with a friend of ours, a club owner who had gone away on a tax fraud charge. He wanted to help me relax about the fear of jail. Our friend told me not to worry too much, that there was certainly nothing to be scared about. If it did go bad for me, at least I'd go to a federal prison, like he did, to a minimum-security facility—a "Club Fed."

Our friend told my brother, "We just gotta make sure he stays cool now, out of trouble."

Joey nodded in agreement, and I really appreciated the gesture he'd made.

Finally the day of judgment was upon me. The prosecutor was in the courthouse. The FBI and DEA agents were there, as well as the probation officer. The agents reiterated that they didn't want to see me go away and said the probation woman had a stick up her ass. The prosecutor concurred with them and practically admitted that the conspiracy charge wouldn't have held up.

"We came to *you*, didn't we?" Bette Wilson asked me.

They conferred with the judge, and a few minutes later I was sentenced. No jail time, just two years' probation. Justice was finally served.

And now—as I had been doing the morning of November 2, 1992—the children of America could sleep safely in their beds.

But look out for those clowns!

33.

SIBLING REVELRY

Having escaped the slammer, I was answering phones, cleaning up after bands at Coyote Studios in Williamsburg, driving a cab, doing production sketches for my mom—anything I could to show my probation officer I was an honest tax-paying citizen and an upstanding contributor to society. I was also financially devastated.

Handsome Dick Manitoba and I did our first show with the Plug Uglies at Harry Slash's Space on Third Ave. and Thirteenth Street and afterward had a falling-out. Manitoba complained that I had been putting more effort into my songs than his; the thing was, he hadn't written any songs. So, in actuality, Mr. Manitoba was right. This was typical rock band bullshit. We decided it wasn't working and that it was better to remain friends, so we unplugged the Uglies.

With money borrowed from my mom and some friends, I started recording some new songs at Coyote Studios, playing everything myself, except the drums. I still had the drummer from the Plug Uglies, Frank Siatta, and we were hoping to start a new band. A few weeks later, by odd coincidence Frank said the Ramones had called and offered him a roadie gig. He was gone.

Then, out of the blue, Joey called and said that Seymour Stein had offered him the opportunity to start his *own* record label, as he had done with Madonna. He wanted my band to be the first release. I explained to him that I currently didn't have a band together, as his road crew had scooped up my drummer. Joey didn't know anything about the Ramones hiring Frank, but he felt bad about it.

I thanked Joey profusely, wished him luck with his record label, and told him if he had any job openings to let me know. Joey told me to let him know what was happening and said he would keep an eye out for drummers for me. About two months later, Joey called saying that it wasn't going to work out for him to do the record company thing, but he had another idea.

"We should make a record together," he said. "You and me, ya know, like a side project."

"That sounds like fun," I said enthusiastically. "What would you want me to do, play guitar or something?"

"No, no," Joey said firmly, "I don't mean like a solo record with you playin' on it—I mean an actual Joey Ramone/Mickey Leigh record. We'll come up with a name for it and everything, ya know?" Though I was apprehensive about, well, just about everything at this point, I was comfortable with the way Joey outlined the project. I needed something positive to latch on to.

"Sounds great, Joey," I told him. "I just wanna thank my probation officer in the credits, okay? Maybe then she'll chill out a little on the urine tests."

Joey laughed and said, "I want us to have fun with this, ya know. No pressure, just a fun project."

I was really happy when I hung up the phone. Joey sounded totally sincere. This would be a project born out of mutual respect and done for all the right reasons. It was something we'd talked about doing for years, but now we were finally getting it together.

Joey suggested we record a song I'd done with the Tribe called "See My Way," originally done by a band called Blodwyn Pig. We'd switch off on the lead vocal, like we did when we were kids. We got Whitey Benezra and Steven Sane in on it and had a great time recording the song. Joey arranged a deal with Jello Biafra, founder of the punk band Dead Kennedys, to release the record on his Alternative Tentacles label, and he decided on two other songs that would fill out the three-song EP.

When it came to a name for the project, Joey insisted on titling it *Sibling Rivalry*, which I wasn't crazy about. I felt that name defeated the purpose of the project, which was to bring us together, not invoke tension or some sort of a battle for supremecy. But it seemed to make Joey really happy, so I agreed.

We had a blast making the cover with our old friend George DuBose. The shot was of Joey and me sitting at the dinner table, while our "mom"—a professional actress who looked convincingly scary—stood poised, ready to bop the first one who got out of line with a rolling pin. We were thinking of using our real mom, but she didn't look nearly scary enough, even when she tried.

There was a lot of talk in Joey's "circle" about the record.

"The Sibling Rivalry record was initiated by Charlotte," Daniel Rey claimed, "because when Mickey got busted, he really embarrassed Joey. It also put Joey's mom in a really bad place, and Joey didn't want to see her rattled in any way.

"Charlotte really wanted the boys to get along," Daniel continued, "and she wanted Joey to do something to help Mickey out. Joey agreed and did Sibling Rivalry just to appease Charlotte."

I knew it was not my mom's idea.

"I don't know what Daniel is talking about," Charlotte said when interviewed on the subject. "I never had anything to say about the boys' music unless they asked me, and they never asked me anything about Sibling Rivalry. I thought it was great that they were working together, but I never suggested to Joey that he do a record, or *anything*, with Mickey.

"I also don't believe that Joey was embarrassed about Mickey getting busted for pot," she added. "Joey wasn't exactly a proponent for strict drug laws, especially marijuana. Joey had sold pot before he was in the Ramones and had gotten into trouble once himself when he was a teenager. If anything, Joey thought it was a travesty."

There was a definite void created when Joey and I stopped talking to each other—and Daniel appeared eager to fill it. When interviewed about the band, Daniel gave only "the company line" about how great the new album was going.

When the Sibling Rivalry record came out, Joey and I did a few cable TV shows and some press. Though we were getting along really well again, I always feared that potential for trouble bubbling underneath.

Shortly after we did Sibling Rivalry, Joey called to tell me that the Red Hot Chili Peppers were auditioning guitar players; he could hook me up with an audition. Normally I wouldn't have considered being a hired guy in *any* band, but, under the circumstances, I appreciated the opportunity.

He told me that Joan Torshes, his friend who had written those great reviews of the Tribe, knew the Chili Peppers' manager. Joey and Joan also had a close but occasionally volatile friendship.

Joey told me to call Joan about the Chili Peppers audition. But when I did, I hit a wall—a *flaming* wall.

"I know what happened between Joey and you," Joan growled. "Joey told me all about what a greedy troublemaker you are. He said I should never talk to you or write about your bands ever again. The Chili Peppers are *wonderful* people who are clean and sober now. You are a convicted felon and you smoke pot, and I would never introduce *you* to those guys in a million years!

"You should find a rock and crawl back under it!"

"Umm . . . so . . . Does that mean I *don't* have the audition?" I joked before she smashed the phone down.

Joan later explained her actions: "I was newly sober then. I wasn't *me* yet. Fifteen sober years later, I can admit that I did something really shitty. I didn't submit Mickey's stuff to their manager because of my loyalty to Joey. *Now* I can question my thinking. It could have been I was just making myself feel more important than I was."

I called Joey back and told him what Joan had said.

"Oh, man!" he said. "She's fucked up; she doesn't get it!"

"Get what?" I asked.

"Oh, never mind," was his response. "Just forget about it."

"All right," I replied, anxious not to inflame the situation. "Well, thanks for thinking of me."

I realized that Joan thought she was simply doing what Joey wanted. She was being a good soldier. But Joey didn't realize that once he let his attack dogs loose, he couldn't call them back.

She didn't consider that Joey had said a lot of those things in anger—or possibly one of his paranoid, steroid-bolstered rages. That's most likely what Joey meant when he said "she doesn't get it." However, Joan is a very smart woman, and I think she really did get it; but at that moment, she didn't care. Proving her loyalty was more important.

I let it slide. I'd been through too much to let Joan bother me, though it did make me worry about perceptions other people might have of me.

It certainly made me more than a bit paranoid and inhibited, but it was nothing compared to staring down a roomful of FBI agents. The only thing worse is hearing you have a life-threatening disease. And that's exactly what happened in the spring of 1994, when my mother called and said she had some bad news—about Joey.

34.

MURPHY'S ROAR

Joey had gone to see a general practitioner for a checkup," Charlotte remembered. "Then he went back out on the road for a short tour with the Ramones. The doctor called and told me, 'You've got to get him home!'"

When Mom asked what was wrong, the doctor said that they'd found too much abnormal protein in Joey's blood. My brother needed to come back for more tests. She told the doctor that Joey was almost ready to come home anyway. Was there any point in upsetting the band's whole tour schedule?

"We think it's something called myeloma, a form of cancer," the doctor said. "It's not nearly at a serious stage and possibly won't even require any treatment at this juncture. But we need to do more tests as soon as possible."

When my mother called and told me what the doctor had said, she wasn't freaking out, because at this point the illness didn't even require treatment. It was treatable—and still asymptomatic. But hearing my brother had cancer, mild or not, scared me enough to bring me to tears and made me pound on the table.

"Joey came back from the tour, but he really didn't like this doctor; he was very arrogant and had a dictatorial attitude. I started asking around,"

Charlotte added. "Joey and Mickey's aunt was a doctor at NYU. She suggested one of her colleagues, Dr. Morton Coleman."

Our dad's brother, Uncle Sy, had married a sweet, energetic, highly intelligent woman named Sandra. Sy's mother would have been very proud that he married a doctor—a Jewish mother's dream. Joey liked Dr. Coleman right away. He was very good and very tactful. After additional tests, it was determined that Joey had lymphoma in his bone marrow.

Dr. Coleman told Joey not to worry because it had been caught early. Though nowhere near a life-threatening stage, the disease had to be watched very carefully. My brother had to be tested every month or so.

I knew how fragile Joey's health was and feared that something like this could be devastating. Then again he'd faced so many health problems already and had persevered; there was good reason to believe he'd prevail with this one, too. When my brother got home from the tour, I called him to tell him I'd heard what was going on and tried to ease any fears he was having.

"Don't worry, Joe. They say it's just something that needs to be watched. You're gonna be all right!"

"Yeah, I know," he said. "It just sucks, it's like, it's always something, ya know?"

My brother seemed to be handling it—like he'd handled all his other health problems—with the bravery of a boxer. This time, however, Joey was in the ring with an unknown opponent who, while seemingly not a threat, could at any time unleash a knockout punch that could take him down—permanently.

Before Joey was diagnosed with lymphoma, he'd *already* been suffering from something called spina bifida, a result of the surgery he'd undergone when he was six weeks old to remove the teratoma. It caused a gap in the bones in the spine. Now his spine didn't connect properly.

"From birth, pain was a big part of his life, and Joey had learned how to live with it," Charlotte noted.

Joey usually kept his health issues close to home, due to potential problems in the band.

"Joey didn't tell me that he had been diagnosed with lymphoma," his former girlfriend Angela Galetto remembered. "Not right away. He didn't tell me for a couple months, actually. Then when he did tell me, we were just crying. I kept telling him, 'You'll be okay, don't worry, I'll be there. You'll be fine!'

"But Joey kept saying, 'I could die, I could die!'

"I kept telling him, 'No, you won't die. They've got lots of cures for cancer now, you know?'" Angela recalled.

"Joey was never healthy. Between the foot infections, the neurological problems, and the spina bifida, I always knew there was the possibility Joey was going to be a cripple," Angela confessed. "We made jokes about it. I used to tell him, 'Well, you know, we'll get you a wheelchair—we'll put ramps around the house and I'll wheel you around!' We dealt with that. Now we had something else to deal with."

After Joey underwent further tests confirming that the lymphoma was not at a stage that required any treatment, we all relaxed—but only a bit.

A FEW MONTHS later, on July 15, 1994, Joey and my mom threw me a big surprise party for my fortieth birthday. It was at my favorite restaurant, Sugar Reef on Sixth Street, which was owned by Joey's friend and collaborator Al Maddy and his wife Judy. They invited around forty of my new friends, former bandmates, *compadres* from the music business, and old friends from my neighborhood. I was very grateful, and Joey's participation was very significant to me.

Sadly, Joey's core of old friends seemed to be more depleted than ever.

He was still in touch with Angela, but there was no major reconciliation in the works. Plus he had been seeing a new girl for a while. This one was subservient to the point of being neurotic, as she poured a constant stream of praise over her "gigantic rock star boyfriend." She came with us on some of the interviews Joey and I did for the Sibling Rivalry record, and it was exasperating.

"Joey is the handsomest man in the world," she would say, stroking his head, "and the most talented ever. He is the greatest songwriter. The biggest rock star . . ." She had a foreign accent, which, for some reason, made it even more annoying.

On and on she would go, relentlessly, until my brother would finally say, *"AWRIGHT! SHUT THE FUCK UP ALREADY!"*

This was around the time he met another fan who would become a close friend. This one, at least, had far too much self-respect to slobber. Chris Snipes lived in South Carolina and was the lead singer of a band called the Independents.

"Before I met Joey, I met Johnny Ramone in 1994," remembered Chris,

Joey's friend to the end. "It was my first Ramones concert. After the show I went out with CJ Ramone, and we became friends. About six months later, CJ got us on a Ramones tour, opening for them for five shows. Joey came over and started talking to me and I gave him an Independents demo. He'd always watch us from the side of the stage. We just hit it off."

At this point, I was still working as a custodian at Coyote Studios in Williamsburg. The owners, Mike and Al, told me they were renovating the place and had attempted to contact my brother several times. They wanted him to pick up a box containing a master tape he'd left, but Joey never responded. They said they had to toss any boxes that hadn't been picked up. So I took it home.

I had a hunch about what might be in the box, as I remembered Joey calling before all the fights to tell me he was at Coyote Studios trying to re-record a song we'd recorded years earlier called "Out of Here." He asked if I would want to come down there and show some guitarist how to play the part I'd done, because they were having trouble figuring it out. But I'd turned down that flattering offer.

When I got home and opened the box, I was surprised to see the title on the track sheet, which read, "Cold Turkey for a Hot Poppa."

Joey had apparently done something with the tape and forgotten about it.

I could only laugh, thinking about all the grief that stupid recording had caused. And after all that, I wound up with the tape. I wasn't about to bring it to my brother's attention and start the whole argument all over again. I was glad he'd just left it there at Coyote and didn't seem to care about that song, or whatever else was on the tape, if anything.

I shook my head, put it on the shelf with a few dozen other tapes, and forgot about it as well.

IN THE RAMONES' world, it was business as usual. They would tour, make a record, have the video rejected by MTV, not get a hit, and tour some more. Joey still wasn't talking to Johnny, nor was Johnny talking to Joey. The only thing that changed was which one of them the other guys in the band sided with at any given time. It was a game they played constantly, and a very stressful one. And it added to the same damaging, unhealthy environment that had been festering for thirteen years. After all this time, it had become the norm.

Thankfully the Ramones were beginning to be acknowledged by the crop of grunge bands that had become increasingly popular in the mid-1990s. It was a strange sort of compliment, as these bands had far surpassed the success of the Ramones, selling records by the millions and playing sold-out arenas.

While the Ramones were still playing small clubs, these guys were enjoying the kinds of careers the Ramones had dreamed of. Joey went back and forth between resentment and approval of bands like Soundgarden and Pearl Jam. He'd gone on record in several interviews to say that Nirvana had ripped off their act and owed their entire success to the Ramones. For me, they at least proved there was still some hope for new bands.

Steven Sane and I decided to form a band with me singing lead this time. I called it STOP. I liked the name because it's such a powerful word, as well as one you see on just about every street corner in suburban America. I figured it was an economical marketing gimmick. Better than that though, I was quite amused by the prospect of a huge crowd of people yelling "STOP" at a band onstage and meaning they wanted *more*.

We'd put an ad in *The Village Voice* for a drummer, but no luck. Around Christmas of 1994, Joey called me to say that his friend and Ramones' video director George Seminara knew a drummer who might be interested. This was one of the best Christmas presents Joey ever gave me: Pat Carpenter turned out to be not only an amazing drummer, but also one of my best friends.

"I wasn't looking to get into a band with Joey Ramone's brother," Pat states. "I just wanted to find a band that had really good music. So I gave Mick a call and he sent me a tape. I thought the stuff was great. From day one I loved it."

Joey came to a few STOP shows and was very impressed. He thought Steve was much more effective as a bass player, with me as the lead singer/front man.

In March of 1995 he told me that the Ramones were going to be playing in London in June and he wanted STOP to be the opening act.

In twenty years of being in original bands I'd opened up for the Ramones only a half-dozen times. It was always fun but not necessarily a ticket to success. More meaningful was that this was a huge breakthrough in the wall that had formed between Joey and me. And even more meaningful was that Joey told Johnny Ramone, who was adamantly opposed to our being on the bill, that if we weren't allowed to open for them, he would not do the show.

"I'm really proud of him," I told Mom. "It's about time he stood up to John—about *something*."

"Well, don't say that to him," my mom warned me. She knew that if I said something like that, he would most likely take it as an insult, even though it was meant to be a positive remark indicating a big breakthrough for him in his relationship with Johnny. It was sad that I couldn't be honest or blunt with him anymore. Sometimes I really wanted to say to him, "Hey, come on, man. That guy is just steppin' all over you. Put him in his place. Do your solo record. Show him up. You can do it!" But I couldn't. Even sadder, neither could his own mother, or just about anyone else, for that matter.

I was still on probation for another five months, so I had to present my probation officer with all kinds of information to get permission to leave the country. He soon informed me I'd received definite clearance to travel. As we were about to purchase our plane tickets, the officer called to tell me that even though I had their permission, I couldn't go because British customs does not grant anyone on probation permission to enter the United Kingdom. The probation officer had neglected to inform me of this little detail.

I dreaded calling Joey to break the news to him—and understandably he was pissed. There was nothing I could do but apologize.

"Joey once said to me," Daniel Rey recalled, "'Whenever I try to help Mickey, it always comes back and blows up in my face.'"

"It sucked," said Pat as he shook his head. "But I thought it wasn't the end of the world, just one show. We had a really good band. George Tabb had even written an article in the *New York Press* proclaiming STOP 'the best band in town,' and I thought if that show didn't happen, there would be something else."

Joey cooled down after a while. He said he wanted to introduce me to his friend Veronica Koffman, the president of the UK Ramones Fan Club, and said maybe she would help us get a tour together. Veronica was coming to the U.S. to attend a show Joey was putting on at the Continental during the New Music Seminar, which as usual fell right on my birthday, July 15. MTV was coming at ten p.m. to film a segment for their news program. Unfortunately for STOP, Joey had put us on at eight thirty p.m. Veronica wondered why Joey had put us on so early, but we had no answer for her.

Later that night, Steven Sane fell and cracked his head in the bathroom of the Continental. I waited with him at the Beth Israel emergency room while they stitched him up. When we finally got back to the club, everybody was gone. I called Joey from the bar and told him what happened, and thanked him for putting us on the bill.

The next day, my mother told me that Joey called her and said he was pissed that I didn't thank him. I told her Veronica was standing right there when I called him. It was getting weird again.

A few days later, Joey went to L.A. to meet the owner of Epitaph Records, Brett Gurewitz. Packages I'd sent to the label inevitably wound up in a box under someone's desk. I was never able to get a response. When Joey got back I asked him if he happened to drop a STOP package off with Brett. He gave me a terse, snappy reply.

"I didn't go there for you!" he said, bristling. "I went there for me."

Joey said he had gone there to talk about a solo album, but Veronica later informed me and Steven Sane that he had dropped off a kit at Epitaph for the Independents, who he was now managing. Veronica thought it was odd considering Joey was supposedly trying to help us get a deal.

"I don't understand," she told Steve and me during lunch at Dojo on St. Marks Place. "Why wouldn't he just hand Brett a package while he was right there?"

"You know, Veronica," I confided, still baffled myself, "just between us, I'm never really sure if he really wants me to make it or not."

She said she couldn't figure it out.

The next day I got a call from Joey. He was madder than I'd ever heard him.

"*I hear you're badmouthing me again,*" Joey yelled. "*Well from now on I don't ever want to have anything to do with any of your bands ever again, okay?*"

Then he hung up on me. Again.

Joey would offer to help—it seemed that he really wanted to. But when it started to look like something might happen for one of my bands, he got strange.

Pat, Steve, and I recorded a few more songs, including a version of the Ramones' "Outsider," and continued looking for a label. Another former friend of Joey's, Aime Elkins, was now married to Lee Josephs, who owned a small indie label called Dionysus in L.A. Lee and I couldn't agree on terms for a STOP album, but he and Aime hooked me up with a tiny little label out of Chico, California, called Smut Peddlerz, who would press up the CDs. And I worked out an arrangement with my old friends at Bomp records to distribute them. The album would be called *STOP . . . Never.*

In November 1995, I got a call from someone at BBC's Radio One saying they had received a copy of our tape from Veronica Koffman. They wanted to know if a CD and tour was forthcoming, and if so, they would like us to come and do a live performance on *The Mark Radcliffe Show.* This was amazing news! *Jimi Hendrix had played on Radio One!*

"That's when things got a little twisted, and I got my own glimpse of the picture," Pat Carpenter explained. "I really can't say why Joey was running so hot and cold, but all of a sudden, Joey was again interested in helping STOP. Joey and Mickey weren't talking to each other, but Veronica called Mickey and told him that Joey wanted to *manage* the band now, and shop us around while we were over in England."

I could further and more accurately explain this oscillating behavior, but I would need several years studying psychiatry to do it properly.

"Joey's people handed me a management contract," Pat continued, "requesting fifty percent of any record deal we got anywhere in the world—as well as publishing, merchandise, and firstborn children, etc."

Here we go again—contracts, lawyers costing thousands of dollars . . .

We had no money for lawyers. This led to more insanity and turmoil. Of course, my mom felt the urge to step in and try to help the situation. After all, she really wanted to see it happen for me—always had.

"Let me lend you guys a thousand dollars for the lawyer, so you can work this contract thing out," she offered. Given that Joey and I weren't really speaking at that point, Mom was acting as go-between.

"But what if it's more?" I reasoned with her. "Why don't you just tell Jeff to chill? If we say we'll give him ten percent of any record deal he gets us, then *we will.*"

"Oh, he'll just tell me that I'm taking your side again," she replied.

Joey and Veronica kept threatening to cancel our tour if we didn't sign something before we left. The closer it got, the more heated it became. Veronica would call from England and tell me that I had to learn to treat Joey more like his other fans did—that I needed to learn how to kiss my brother's ass a little better.

I would have to remind her that she was the fan club president, not me.

"They came back with a slightly better offer," Pat Carpenter recalled, "but the possibility of ever making any money was very limited.

"It was a pretty cold deal," Pat added. "George Seminara said to me, 'You guys are crazy! *Whatever* the deal is, Joey Ramone wants to manage your band, and you're going to turn that down?' It just seemed to always come back to that: Joey is a rock star and Mickey should just accept it. A lot of people expected Mick to just step in line.

"Mickey and Joey were going at each other again. I don't think Mickey was fighting with Joey Ramone as much as he was fighting with his brother. I saw two brothers who got along beautifully, and then they didn't. When my brother and I didn't get along it was like, 'Screw you! Okay. I'll call you later.' With them, it could get pretty bad."

35.

LOWLIGHTS IN THE HIGHLANDS

At this point they couldn't cancel our tour just because we wouldn't sign some crazy contract. They would look bad to the promoters, and Joey still wanted to get the Independents over there. Veronica had been convinced that we weren't to be trusted and was told she should come with us on the road to collect all the money, ensuring she'd get paid back.

"Five of us were squeezed into a little car," Pat recalled, "including Veronica, who kept insisting she had to come."

We appreciated everything Veronica had done, but this was just not practical. After two weeks of pickle and sauce sandwiches and sleeping on the cold dirty floors of the clubs we'd just played—which comprised the guaranteed "food and lodging"—our patience was being tested.

"We were in Edinburgh, Scotland, a grueling twelve-hour ride to the next place we were playing. So we asked Veronica to please take the train back to Brighton, where she lived and was putting us up. She got angry, crying, 'Why are you doing this to me?'"

Veronica started yelling and threatening to throw all our stuff onto the street once she got home. When she walked away, I went after her. "Mickey ran back and told me to call Joey from the phone booth," Pat continued. "I told Joey, 'Veronica is freaking out!' He said, 'Why can't you guys just deal with this?'

"I said, 'Joey, she's walking away with all our money, and said she was going to throw our stuff out on the street, including our passports. She's heading for a train! Can't ya just talk to her?' He started laughing."

My brother finally agreed to talk to her, so I ran down the street after her screaming, "Joey's on the phone!"

"Looking back, it *was* pretty comical," said Pat.

All in all it was a memorable trip. The BBC show alone was worth all the discomfort and grief. And the CDs sold out in every store that took them—close to two thousand in total. Smut Peddlerz only pressed two thousand before going out of business, but we got some great reviews. As flattering as the comparisons were, they were still as much about the Ramones as STOP.

Like this one in *Guitar World:* "Joey Ramone's brother, Mickey Leigh, has never been able to unload his weighty family baggage, but now that the Ramones are fading into history, Mickey may finally have his shot at the slime light . . . His new band, STOP, has all the snarl and swagger of the Ramones in the days before they got comfortable and complacent . . . If the Ramones had developed some chops and enlarged their repertoire, they'd sound a lot like STOP."

From *Stereo Review:* "Fronted by Mickey Leigh (Joey Ramone's kid brother), this is as devastating a piece of neo-punk as I've heard in years. Imagine the drive and intensity of his sibling's outfit but with real guitar playing and a far more expressive lead singer, and you've got the idea."

I suspected these reviews may have caused even more friction between my brother and me, but I hoped not.

Either way, I was *still* getting him press.

STOP came back from the tour a lot poorer than when we left, and a few months later, Steven Sane quit. Pat and I stuck together but couldn't afford to put ads in *The Village Voice* or pay for rehearsal studios to audition new bass players. I was bartending and working the door at rock clubs—and had to give up any idea of having a band. Pat and I joined forces with our friend Tim Heap's eponymously named band Heap.

I was at a real low but still grateful for whatever I had. Any time I got too down, I thought how lucky I was that I wasn't in prison. Any day aboveground and out of jail was a good day.

My friend Jesse Malin, a onetime Rattlers roadie and now lead singer of the very popular band D Generation, gave me a bartending shift at his rock club Coney Island High on St. Marks Place. Jesse was also a friend of my brother's, but to his credit he didn't let it be a factor in hiring me.

I began hanging out at after-hours joints after my bartending shifts, feeling sorry for myself—getting fucked up and carousing until the sun came up. One night/morning I ran into an old friend, a girl named Lucky Lawler, who published a little downtown paper called the *New York Waste*.

She offered me a shot at writing a column. I took her up on it. I called it "My Guitar Is Pregnant." It was a mishmash of whatever I felt like writing about: news, fiction, fantasy; I had a sports section called "Balls!" Basically it was for my own entertainment, so I liked to try to make myself laugh as much as possible. A favorite was about the first male to undergo a successful womb transplant surgery, who subsequently cloned himself, enabling him to give birth *to himself*. The *Waste* was later voted "Best Underground Newspaper" in the *New York Press*'s annual "Best of New York" issue, and my column was mentioned as one of the reasons.

After I came back from the English tour, Joey and I were talking guardedly, but speaking to each other nonetheless. He told me the Ramones were pissed at him because they had an offer to go to South America for a lot of money. The Ramones had become like the Beatles in South America, but he didn't want to do this tour.

"I haven't been feeling just right, ya know?" Joey told me. "I just don't feel like I have the strength to do another tour like that, not right now, anyway. But the Ramones are really pressuring me. I don't know what to do."

"Fuck 'em," I advised him. "Your health is more important—and if you don't think it's gonna be good for you, then don't do it. You can always go down there and play another time! You gotta think of yourself."

"Yeah," Joey said, "but it could make us, like, a million dollars. Everybody wants to do it. They all say I'm taking money out of their pockets!"

"Of course they want you to do it," I said. "But apparently they don't care if you drop dead in the process."

The offer to go to South America had come while the band was on the Lollapalooza tour.

"Joey wanted to do Lollapalooza," Johnny explained. "I just wanted to do our final Ramones tour. But Joey wanted to do that—like that was gonna make us something?

"Lollapalooza was ridiculous. Metallica was the headliner, Soundgarden was second. We went on between the two bands. I mean, half of the crowd was there to see Metallica, and the other half was there for Soundgarden. We played every other day for forty-five minutes, and I didn't feel like I was even working.

"At least if we played South America," Johnny complained, "we would've made a lot more money than we had on the six-week-long Lollapalooza tour. Joey felt well after doin' Lollapalooza, and he booked Lollapalooza while he was supposedly sick. So what's the difference if we go play four more shows in South America?"

"I even told Johnny," Joey told me over the phone, "that I would do it if they just gave me two or three months after that last show in L.A., ya know?"

"Joey said, 'I'll do it in a coupla months,'" Johnny recalled. "Come on, he was playing games! I said to him, 'Well, ya know, I don't need the money, but we got two other guys in the band that *do* need the money. They don't make what we're making. What about them?'

"Joey said, 'I gotta think of myself.'

"Everyone in the band," Johnny claimed, "was pissed off at Joey at that point—both Marky and CJ."

"Whether it was because Joey found out he was sick with lymphoma," Marky explained, "or because he just wanted to spite Johnny, I don't know.

"Joey didn't tell me he was sick with lymphoma," Marky admitted, "but I sensed, by looking at Joey's skin, that something was going on.

"Sometimes Joey would look a little green," Marky added, "and on his neck were these little pockmarks. I thought Joey was on all kinds of medication because of his neurological problems, so I never suspected it was something serious. But Joey shoulda told me he had lymphoma, because if anybody in the fuckin' group shoulda known, it shoulda been me!"

At this point there were two factions in the band, with Marky and Joey comprising the liberal, Democratic camp, and Johnny and CJ the Republican, conservative camp. Joey even performed with his side project, the Resistance, at presidential candidate Jerry Brown's campaign rally. He had Marky play drums and recruited a bunch of his friends for the band. He didn't ask me to join him, but I really was not surprised. He'd stopped including me in his side projects over the past several years. Of course, I felt left out; but I suppose that was the idea.

"Then Joey went on Prozac, for his OCD, I guess," Marky recalled, "and he was talking more."

Joey was finally communicating again.

"I was sitting in the van one day and Joey started talking to Johnny as if he was his good friend. Joey actually tried to talk to Johnny—who wouldn't have any part of it. I couldn't believe it. So I said to Joey, 'What happened there?'

"Joey said, 'Well, I tried, so now I don't care.'

"Joey didn't give a shit that Johnny wouldn't talk to him, which I thought was pretty cool, because that was probably what stopped Joey from confronting Johnny all those years. Maybe if Joey had been on the Prozac earlier," Marky mused, "he could have overcome the Linda thing better and moved on.

"Meanwhile," Marky continued, "Joey never explained why he didn't want to go to South America—and he would have made a pretty penny on that offer."

Johnny's perspective on the South American tour was that there was no point in doing it later.

"When Joey said that maybe he would go to South America in a couple of months," Johnny Ramone said, "I said, 'I'm not gonna go home, and stop rehearsing, and then go back! Let's just do it now, let's just get it over with!'"

"Johnny was an asshole," Joey told me. "Johnny was like, 'Once we do that last show, once I put that guitar down, that's it! If they can't book it now, then forget it!'"

"The way I grew up," Johnny explained, "you didn't miss nothin'! Same with Dee Dee—he played no matter what was wrong. He went on tour with hepatitis. I got my skull fractured in 1983, and Joey went to the hospital at the same time for his foot. I have a craniotomy done on part of my brain, but I'm back and ready to play shows—and Joey's still in the hospital for his toe? I was like, 'How long is he gonna milk this for?'

"Okay, Joey was sick. But everybody kept saying that it's very treatable with medication. I still hear that people don't die from lymphoma. But Joey just said to me, 'Nah, I gotta think of myself.'"

Joey turned down the tour, but they didn't let him forget about it too quickly. Nobody in that band forgot about anything too quickly.

IN THE SUMMER of 1995, Legs McNeil and Gillian McCain had interviewed me for a book they'd been working on for several years called *Please Kill Me: The Uncensored Oral History of Punk*. I took the title literally and spoke bluntly. How else can you speak in a book about punk rock? Though

I was assured that everything I said would be cleared with the people I talked about, sometimes shit *doesn't* happen.

"I thought *Please Kill Me* would be like everything else I'd ever done," Legs confessed, "that it would be interesting, no one would notice it, and it would quickly fail. But that's not what happened.

"I knew Joey would hate the book," Legs added, "because he hated everything else I'd ever written about the Ramones, so why would this be different? I didn't know what exactly would piss Joey off, but I knew it would be the last thing in the book I'd think Joey would object to—and of course it was. Joey Ramone hated *Please Kill Me* because Mickey said Joey had been a hippie in the 1960s and that when he became a singer in a glitter band he called himself 'Jeff Starship.' I think that is one of the most moving scenes in the book. Mickey is so impressed seeing his brother singing onstage for the first time. But the truth is, Joey never read books; he only read something if it was about him.

"I had planned on reinterviewing Joey for the book," Legs said, "but when I read my old interviews with him, they were so good. I knew that Joey had changed so much that he probably couldn't be that honest anymore. So Gillian and I just went with the old interviews. What we were trying to capture was how you can take chances and reinvent yourself."

Shortly after the book came out, Legs and Joey ran into each other on St. Marks Place. Legs was carrying a hard cover of *Please Kill Me*. He stopped and wrote in it, "Joey, you really did save rock & roll! I love you, Legs."

"Joey took the book," Legs recalled, "read my inscription, and then stared at me, almost in disbelief. I think Joey really thought I delighted in making fun of him—he was that paranoid. I told him, 'I know you'll hate the book, but I really believe what I wrote to you. Take care.'"

He thanked Legs and they parted ways. It was the last time Joey spoke to Legs McNeil. I have a strong feeling that another reason Joey was pissed at Legs was because Legs and Gillian had hired me to play guitar, making some ambient background sounds while they would do readings from their book at bars and bookstores.

They did readings for almost a year, and then the paperback came out. At the end of that promotional tour, Gillian and Legs were in Los Angeles staying at the Chateau Marmont. Legs was sitting by the pool, eating eggs Benedict, when he got a phone call from Dee Dee Ramone alerting Legs to the fact that the last Ramones show *ever* was that evening.

The fans had been anticipating a final tour from the Ramones, but since the band had already done several "final" tours, they were never really sure which was *really* the Ramones' last show until a show on August 6, 1996, in L.A. was promoted as the actual, definite farewell performance by the band. There would be special guest star performers joining in, and it would all be filmed.

The band had invited Dee Dee to perform with them.

"Dee Dee said he was nervous and unsure what to do," Legs continued. "So I invited him over to the hotel for lunch. When he asked me if I was going to go to the last Ramones show that night, I said no. I wanted to keep my memories of the old Ramones, and ignore all this new bullshit."

36.

"WEIRD, RIGHT?"

At the last show, Dee Dee sang 'Love Kills' all wrong," Johnny Ramone laughed. "Totally lost, in the middle of the song he stops and goes, 'This is how I am.'

"The show was fine. It was just hard for me to get the people on and off the stage. We had Lemmy from Motörhead do his 'R.A.M.O.N.E.S.' song. Then we had Rancid come out and do '53rd and 3rd,' and we had Eddie Vedder come on and sing the last song, 'Any Way You Want It.' Eddie and Joey sang it together because my thinking was, 'The more solo people we can get on this film, the better.' I was looking at the big picture, not worrying about egos—whatever was gonna sell the video. But the video was badly filmed. They shot the *entire* show with a wide-angle lens! It didn't sell very well," Johnny confessed.

The show itself, while undoubtedly interesting and historically significant, was unusually messy and completely uncharacteristic of the Ramones, with the band stopping to introduce the guest performers, some of whom took long guitar solos.

John had bought a house in L.A., where he was now living and buddying up with Hollywood celebrities—which was historically uncharacteristic for John, though Linda had to be thrilled. He insisted on having the band's final show there, which seemed like an odd choice—quite incongruous for a band so iconic to New York City.

The atmosphere at the last performance was typically strained. The band displayed their usual dourness. They didn't appear to be celebrating their remarkably groundbreaking and illustrious career. It seemed more like they just wanted to get it over with. The big event was hugely uneventful and highly anticlimactic, especially for the band members.

"I never said good-bye to any of the Ramones individually," Johnny confessed. "But I did say a general good-bye, like, 'See you guys.'

"I don't know if anyone responded." Johnny paused. "It didn't matter. Twenty-two years . . . weird, right?"

So weird that even Johnny noticed.

"The way the Ramones ended," CJ Ramone recalled, "with everyone walking away at the end of the night, it was kind of fitting. I didn't even say good-bye to anybody."

"I wanted out of there," Marky Ramone remembered. "I didn't say good-bye. I left, got some ice cream, went back to the hotel, and watched TV."

"I was more worried about Eddie Vedder," Johnny Ramone explained, "because me, Vincent Gallo, and Eddie were running out for dinner with Tim Burton. And this guy there was worried about getting Eddie in the car safely, because all the kids were swarming us. I didn't ask any Ramones to go to dinner with us. I mean, I saw them every day. We had a retirement party here at my house, and we didn't have any of the Ramones here, either. The only person I would've invited would have been CJ. I'm surprised I didn't invite CJ, 'cause he was friends with Soundgarden. No one from the band got invited. I don't know if they were all pissed off; and if they were, I didn't care. I mean, I never talked to Joey, so why would I have him at my house?"

The only sentiment Joey expressed to me about the last Ramones show was that he was glad when it was finally over. But what happened between Johnny and Joey during their last few seconds onstage together was more telling. In the most mutually passive-aggressive act of their career, Johnny and Joey practically rammed into each other as they crisscrossed the stage, exiting in separate directions.

Each one stared straight ahead as he walked and went on his way.

What a way to go.

WHILE I WAS out of favor with my brother, Joey told some people straight off that if they were friends with me, they couldn't be friends with him. It was still so confounding how Joey could be the kindest, most generous guy in the world but was also capable of a vengefulness the likes of which were hard to fathom.

And the harshest treatment was saved for people whose relationships with him went beyond friendship or fandom—that's what family was for!

When Joey would yell and curse abusively at my mother, I reacted protectively: "Hey! You don't fucking talk to her like that!"

"Oh, yeah?" Joey taunted. "What are you gonna do about it? Tell everyone? You're gonna badmouth me some more? Nobody cares what you say," he jibed. "Nobody wants to deal with you. You'll just be screwing yourself again."

And he was right. No one cared if it was because I was defending my mother that Joey might be mad at me—just that he *was*.

Once again, the fireworks would explode between Joey and me.

Once again I would appear to be the troublemaking sad sack—out of favor with Saint Joseph of Obsessive-Compulsive Disorder.

"You're just alienating yourself more and more," Joey would tell me, sounding more like Our Lady of Perpetual Damage.

Typical brother shit—maybe.

I went to talk to my uncle Sy, the brains of the Hyman family, the one Joey and I always thought was the coolest. I recounted the whole sordid story to Sy. Uncle Sy didn't quite see how anything Joey would do could really affect my career but did agree that it was odd that he had been so unwilling to share credit with his own brother and was puzzled by his extreme reactions. He also felt bad that Arlene and I had been excluded from Hyman family events, such as the recent Thanksgiving dinner they'd all shared and Nancy's son Jonathan's wedding, at which Joey sang.

He realized that, basically, we'd been passively exiled from the family, and he wasn't happy about it. Uncle Sy set up a summit. Appropriately, he arranged it to take place in the dining room at the United Nations Building, where he had some kind of affiliation. Participating would be my father, Joey, Uncle Henry, Sy, Sy's first son Andrew, and me. We all met at Sy's apartment on Fifty-ninth Street and rode in his car to the UN.

We parked across the street from the UN and I watched as the men of the Hyman family crossed First Avenue in single file.

Uncle Sy, bless his soul, had a very bad hearing problem, and his hearing aid was on the blink. Uncle Henry, bless his heart, was one of the sweetest people in the world and practically incapable of a harsh thought about anyone. My father, bless his reproductive organs, hadn't talked to me in years. Cousin Andrew, bless the child, had some emotional problems of his own and didn't have the slightest clue what was going on. Brother Joey, bless the stars, followed.

"I don't know where this is gonna take us," I thought, "but we're on our way!"

After we ate, my father, my brother and I finally confronted each other. First we tackled the "ya gotta have a contract" issue, and then we got to the singing and songwriting credit/acknowledgment thing.

Uncle Sy had to temporarily excuse himself from participation due to an equipment failure.

Basically, Joey and I bashed it out. Uncle Henry said he didn't need any contracts. He said that he trusted both me and Jeff and he would put both our names on his record if he ever made one. Surprisingly, my old man agreed with his big brother.

Joey started getting pissed and started to belittle anything and everything I'd ever done with him.

"Oh, so what, man!" he said dismissively. "So you come up with one line of a song and some guitar parts? That means you gotta have your name on the song? Who do you think you are?"

"What about that song 'We're Getting Out of Here?' " I asked, referring to the song we'd recorded on the demo tape I was unknowingly holding in my closet. It was on the same reel with the "Hot Poppa" track, but I didn't know it at the time. "What about the chords in the beginning? You even put words to the guitar line I came up with for the middle. I mean, come on!"

"Yeah," he snapped, "so you came up with a guitar line—that doesn't mean you wrote the song!"

"I didn't say I wrote the song!" I snapped back.

"Yeah, that's right. Because you didn't! You just said it yourself!" he laughed.

I looked around the table.

Uncle Sy apologized for not being able to hear the question. Our old man shrugged, threw his hands up, and headed back to the buffet table.

"See what I mean?" I said to Andrew jokingly.

Uncle Henry, still smiling, shook his head sadly.

I had brought my guitar with me. I'd told Uncle Sy earlier that day that I had a recording session to do and I might need to leave early. I lied. Sorry, Sy.

I said I had to go, and we got up to leave. Joey and I avoided talking to each other on the way down to the lobby.

The good part was that my father and I were talking again. He'd actually come through for me this time. It felt really good, and before we broke up the summit I told my father I was glad he and I had cleared the air.

Joey was pissed off, now probably more so. He reverted back to his punishment routine: not putting me on bills, not inviting me to parties he'd invite everyone else to, etc., etc.

If I did go to some show Joey was putting on, I'd have to hear, "Hey, how come you're not playing? How come you're not on the guest list? How come Joey didn't ask you to play with him?"

The snubbing was effective, at least, in making me *feel* like I was being perceived as someone who should be avoided. In essence, I was being subjected to sanctions by a superpower—an outcome typical of most UN summits.

Getting people on your side to help you punish someone else had become a recreational activity for the Ramones. It continued to be a favorite pastime even after the members of the group retired.

Joey and Marky got into a major brawl on *The Howard Stern Show*. It was insipid, embarrassing, and, of course, hilarious. Howard treated the situation like "Okay! Let the games begin!"

THE HOWARD STERN SPECIAL OLYMPICS PROGRAM

Howard: Marky wants you to know he's not a drunk, even though you called him one.

Joey: He's a dry drunk.

Marky: So are you. You got a big mouth and you're a liar.

Joey: What am I a liar about? That you drink? I didn't say you drank.

Marky: Yes, you did! You said that I'm drunk now, which everyone knows is a bunch of baloney!

Joey: You're a drunk.

Marky: Howard, he's pissed off because the last time we were on the show the OCD thing was brought up, and he's upset about that.

Joey: I ain't upset about anything.

Marky: C'mon, Joey, stop it, what, the Prozac's kicking in now?

Joey: Why don't you just go back to sleep?

Marky: You got up pretty early to put me down last week, didn't ya?

Joey: I didn't say a word.

And the winner is . . . ?

37.

"TOO TOUGH TO DIE"?

That winter I was working the door at the Continental, right across the street from Joey's building and right around the corner from Coney Island High, where Joey was playing that particular night. As I was frigidly finishing out my shift, Joey was finishing up one of his famous Joey Ramone Christmas parties, to which—violin music, please—I hadn't been invited.

"Five more minutes, Mickey," Trigger, the owner of the club, said to me. "Then you can come in."

Just as I was about to do so, my mom, her ex-husband Phil Sapienza, and my former bandmate Dave U. Hall came around the corner, all laughing and joking. They were coming from Joey's party. As they got closer, they spotted me.

"Hey!" they shouted, surprised to see me.

It was awkward for all of us.

We talked for a minute, and Trigger invited them in for a drink. We had a quick, awkward drink together and they left. Then the Continental started closing up.

I decided to go over to Coney, figuring a lot of my friends would still be there. When I got there, the main room was cleared out. So I went to the downstairs bar, where the dressing room was located. At the bottom of the stairs, standing guard outside the dressing room, was Jerry Adams, Joey's bodyguard. Jerry was like a guardian angel to Joey and to me. He was attentive to emotional danger as well as physical.

"Mickey!" Jerry said, greeting me with a hug so hard I could feel his bulletproof vest. "Go in and say hello to your brother," Jerry urged me.

"Come on, Jerry, you know we're not talking," I said, spotting a friend holding a beer for me.

I started walking over.

"Mickey!" Jerry said, pulling me back. "I'm serious, go in and talk to him. He needs you."

Jerry seemed very concerned, so I poked my head into the narrow dressing room. There was no one there but my brother, sitting on the couch by himself, his head down, twirling his hair.

"Hey," I said to him quietly.

"Oh, hey," he said, looking up.

"How you doin'?" I asked him. "You all right?"

"I dunno," Joey replied, sounding tired, dazed, and confused. "I'm feelin' a little weird. I don't know what it is, ya know?"

"Yeah, I know the feeling," I said. "Maybe it's the holidays?"

"Yeah, how are you?" he asked, still twirling his hair. He was at an angle where I could see his eyes as he looked at me. I saw a familiar look in those doelike brown eyes. A look of vulnerability and fear—almost controlled panic. Jerry was right; something was bothering him.

"Well, you know. I'm surviving."

"Yeah," he said. "Well, nice to see ya."

"You, too," I said. "Happy holidays."

"Thanks."

"What's the matter with him?" Jerry asked me. "He's not doing too good, is he?"

"I don't know," I answered, shaking my head. "Something doesn't seem right."

In the following days, I couldn't get out of my head just how sad and troubled Joey looked in the dressing room. But I wasn't gonna go looking for more punishment, either.

Let it be.

"ONE MORNING IN the winter of 1997," said Jamie Forster, Joey's chiropractor, "I came into the lobby of Joey's building on Ninth Street and the doorman buzzed and there was no answer. My routine was to go to Joey's lobby, be announced by the doorman, and have Joey say, 'Could you tell him to come up in ten minutes?' I'd just take a seat and wait. But that morning I knew that something was fucked up, because Joey always answered the buzzer, even if he was on the crapper."

Jamie waited awhile, but there was still no response. Since the doorman knew him well, he encouraged Jamie to go upstairs and knock.

"I took the elevator to the tenth floor and knocked on the door, calling out, 'JOEY? JOEY?'"

When there was still no answer, Jamie called our mom. "Something's going on," he told her. "Joey's never done this. He's not answering the door or the phone—and either nobody's home or something's wrong."

Joey had a combination lock on his door because he had lost his keys so many times it was easier for him to remember a combination than to lose more keys. Mom immediately gave Jamie the combination.

"After I hit the numbers and opened the door," Jamie said, about to burst into tears, "I saw Joey lying on the floor unconscious, with blood spilling out of his mouth. Immediately I thought he was dead. I ran over to him, turned him over on his back, and checked him out. I did feel a pulse, so I knew Joey was still with us."

Holding Joey in his arms, Jamie called 911 and told them he had just found an unconscious Joey Ramone in his apartment. They sent an ambulance in about two minutes flat. Then he called our mom and told her what happened.

"Charlotte said she'd meet us at the hospital. Even though I was panic-stricken, I kept my head together until the EMS and the fire department and the police all arrived at once," Jamie recalled.

The EMS crew determined that Joey had been lying there for at least twenty-four hours, possibly as long as two days. They injected him with epinephrine and adrenaline and gave him oxygen. He regained consciousness, barely, but was extremely disoriented. It took five EMS techs to get him on the stretcher. They got him down the elevator and over to Mother Cabrini Memorial Hospital in just minutes.

"They rolled Joey into the emergency room," Jamie remembered, "and that's when I really started to panic, because he was losing color and wasn't getting attention fast enough. He went from white to green within minutes. No one was doing anything. They didn't have a room for him. We were in the hallway.

"I flagged down the doctors," Jamie explained, "and called for immediate attention when I saw Joey turning purple. They stabilized him and then went to the other bleeding people with gunshots and knife wounds. It took between one and two hours for them to get Joey into his own room, and by that time Charlotte and her friend June had arrived."

Jamie tried to keep Joey talking and to act like he wasn't worried. In truth, he was panicked, thinking my brother was at death's door. After Joey was stable, he told Jamie that the last thing he remembered was getting off the phone with Mom on Saturday around lunchtime.

Dr. Coleman, who was treating his lymphoma, called my mom afterward and said that if Jamie had found Joey even fifteen minutes later, he just might not have made it.

MY MOTHER CALLED me shortly after she and June got to the hospital. Of course, when she told me what was going on I panicked, got right in my car, and sped into the city. I suppose my fraternal instincts kicked in, because the *last* thing on my mind, if I even thought of it at all, was our senseless bickering. When I got to the hospital, Joey was conscious and alert but extremely drained. He was too weak even to get up to go to the bathroom, so he asked me to hold a paper cup so he could pee in it.

Of course, I obliged. Joey said there weren't too many people he would have felt comfortable enough with to ask that favor—if any.

Needless to say, in more ways than one he was very relieved I had come, and I was *more* than relieved he was going to be okay.

We spent several hours with Joey, and then me, June, Phil Sapienza, and my mom went down to get something to eat.

"You know," June started, "Joey told me how glad he was that you came and that things are going to be different with you two now."

"Well, that is truly nice to hear," I said both sincerely and sadly. "I just hope he still feels that way when he gets better. But you know how it is with him, June. Even if there's nothing to fight about, he seems to find something."

Phil snapped, "Ah, see how cynical Mickey is!"

That really hurt. I threw up my hands and put my head down. I had held some hope for our future, but now once again I felt hopeless.

I didn't go back to the hospital for a while, until my mom told me that Joey had had a bad reaction to some medication and had broken out in a nasty rash. She said Joey didn't really want any visitors other than family, as he was embarrassed about how he looked, and was kind of lonely. I went to see him several times, until he got better and was released from the hospital.

Joey soon began to have days where he was feeling pretty good. He was able to begin working on his solo album. He had a band lined up that included Daniel Rey on guitar and Andy Shernoff on bass.

"Joey had started talking about a solo album a long time ago," Andy Shernoff recalled. "I remember hearing about it in the 1980s. Seymour Stein was talking about doing something with Joey alone. But I didn't think Joey had the guts to go out on his own. He was in this bubble that was the Ramones. And I think there would've been problems with Johnny Ramone and with his manager Gary Kurfirst."

"Joey was constantly talking about his solo record," Johnny Ramone griped. "From 1979 on, it was 'Joey's solo record! Joey's solo record!' It had become a joke already. If the Ramones were selling seventy-five thousand, a hundred thousand records, what is Joey gonna sell? It's hard enough to write twelve songs for a Ramones record and hopefully get three or four really good ones. How are you gonna do a solo record? You need checks and balances, a system. Someone has an idea, and other people say if it's a good idea or not. If you let one person run wild and do everything they want, you run into problems."

"The Ramones were Joey's security," Andy admitted. "Maybe they weren't superstars, but they were a working, touring band. Joey couldn't fall on his face in the Ramones."

Joey was still on the fence about who would play drums on his record. In a weird parallel to our relationship, his feud with Marky continued to be on and off again.

"Joey didn't want to work with Marky," Andy Shernoff stated matter-of-factly. "He hated Marky because of that big fight on Howard Stern. But Joey loved Marky's drumming. Marky has that Keith Moon element to him, which Joey loved."

Initially Joey had wanted to use former Dictators drummer Frank Funaro, who was currently drumming for a relatively successful band called Cracker.

"We did a session with Frank at Chelsea Studios on Fourteenth Street," said Andy Shernoff. "It was a good session, and Joey wound up using Frank on some of the songs. But it wasn't the sound he really wanted, so Joey called up Marky and asked him to do the rest. Joey swallowed his pride. He knew Marky's drumming was gonna make it a better record. In the studio, they were fine together. It was very cordial."

" 'What a Wonderful World' was Joey's idea," Daniel Rey remembered. "I don't know where he got the idea from, but he always liked that song."

Sometime in the early 1980s, Joey told me that the Ramones had been considering covering the Sinatra song "Young at Heart," and we started tossing around some ideas about what other standards would be cool to cover.

I told him that there were a few I'd been thinking about for years. One was a metal-bebop version of Benny Goodman's "Sing, Sing, Sing," another was a psychedelic punk version of the Irving Berlin classic "Blue Skies," and another was the Louis Armstrong hit "What a Wonderful World."

I pretty much forgot about it after that, but thankfully, Joey didn't. I never would have done "What a Wonderful World" the way he did, anyway. His version is classic—to me, second only to Louis's—though it seemed to take him forever to finish it.

"Some artists," Daniel Rey said, "have a fear of completion, and I think Joey absolutely did. It was hard to get him out of the studio.

"I'd say, 'Okay, we're done.'

"Joey would say, 'Can I just do this one thing?'

"I'd say, 'No, we're done, somebody else is coming in.' It was hard to say no, because on a Ramones album Joey would only have ten days to finish everything. Either Johnny or someone from the studio was always telling him what to do. With his own effort, he wanted to take his time.

"The tracking for the music took only two days. We did two big recording sessions and over the next couple of years probably two hundred vocal sessions. Joey would come over to my house, where we recorded most of his vocals. He would sing when he was feeling well enough. Some days he would come over and sound fucking great. It would all depend on his mood and how he was feeling."

I never begrudged my brother for wanting to use the musicians of his choice for *any* of his side projects, but, of course, I would have loved to be part of his solo album. Any little bit would've been nice, but at this point he was keeping me at a distance, I suppose to prove some kind of point. By now that was something I completely expected and accepted.

38.

"BE MY BABY"

As much as Joey had been hurt by Linda's betraying him with John, his disappointment at losing Linda paled in comparison to his disappointment at losing Angela. His relationship with Angela was far more meaningful—and the one worth keeping.

Joey had always stayed in touch with Angela, who moved upstate in the early 1990s to a town called Saugerties, near Woodstock and close to her sister Mary. Mary and Angela had a relationship that more or less paralleled mine with Joey. Mary had married a lawyer who had done very well. While Mary and her husband lived in a tremendous house on a huge spread of land replete with barns, horses, stables, and a corral, Angela lived in a scanty little trailer on their property a few hundred yards from the luxurious house.

Naturally, Angela had been seeing other men since leaving Joey. In 1994 she had gotten pregnant. She wanted to have the baby but opted not to marry the father. She gave birth to a beautiful girl she named Raven.

"Joey wanted to be with me in the delivery room when I had Raven, but Raven's father had a fit!" Angela giggled. "I wasn't really in love with Raven's father, and her father knew that."

Joey loved the little girl so much he actually offered to adopt her. But

Raven's father loved his daughter. Joey visited Angela and Raven frequently in the trailer on her sister's property. Eventually he helped her out with just enough money to put a down payment on her own house and buy some furniture and a TV—the bare necessities.

Angela took whatever work she could find to support herself and Raven. Joey didn't want Angela to be dependent on him, but he did want them to be safe and comfortable.

"Sometimes when Joey came up to Woodstock," Angela explained, "he'd be feeling sick, but soon he would feel better. It seemed like he'd get energy from being around Raven in the fresh air.

"Joey, Raven, and me used to stand around in a circle," Angela laughed. "We'd hold hands and chant, 'Ooooooooooom,' and see who could hold it the longest.

"I'd take Joey to see the animals at the petting zoo," she continued. "He loved them. There was this one goat that always followed him around until Joey put his arm around him. He got the biggest kick out of it.

"Everybody in Saugerties and Woodstock thought Joey was Raven's father. They looked so much alike. I was in a store shopping," Angela recalled fondly. "Joey and Raven had gone across the street to sit on the green in Woodstock. When I came back, Raven was sitting in Joey's lap, hugging him. She just loved Joey."

Sometimes after Angela went to work, Joey took Raven to a sandy area along the Esopus Creek for the day, carrying a chair, an umbrella, and the lunch he'd packed for them himself.

"Joey never wanted to leave Woodstock," Angela continued, "but he'd always have to go home to New York and *do something*. His OCD would start kicking in, and he would have to go.

"Of course, there was still always something strange going on with him—like the time we went to a carnival with Raven and some of her friends. Joey got all out of whack because he laid out around a hundred dollars for some of Raven's friends to go on the rides, and he wanted their parents to pay him back. When we got home we had a big fight. It was just weird. He thought he was being taken advantage of. To get *that* crazy about a hundred dollars seemed more like paranoia than cheapness, but who could tell with him?

"The next time he'd come up, he'd be fine again." Angela laughed. "Well, let's say he'd be his usual self.

"Once my sister Mary said to me, 'What the fuck are you doing with him? What do you see in him? He's crazy!'

"I said, 'You don't know him.'

"Nobody knew what the real Joey was like, except for people that got really close to him. There was a side to Joey that was wonderful. People thought he was such a sweet guy. To a certain extent, he was. Then there was the other Joey, the one who said, 'You're an asshole! Get me my fucking coffee! Don't you know how to make a fucking egg?'"

(Note: If you'd like to meet that Joey, play the Ramones song "We're a Happy Family" and turn it up loud on the fade-out at the end.)

"When I was with Joey," Andy Shernoff remembered, "a lot of times he was still Joey Ramone instead of Jeff Hyman.

"When we'd sit in his apartment talking about food or movies, he was more like just Jeff. It wasn't like he was being pretentious otherwise—he was just easier to deal with without all that Ramones craziness going on.

"Then every time he walked out of his apartment, firemen in their trucks would throw on their sirens and yell, 'Hey, Joey!' Everywhere he went, it was, 'Joey, Joey, Joey!' You couldn't miss him. As soon as he left his apartment, he was Joey Ramone, whether he wanted to be or not. Girls wanted to talk to him, people wanted to give him drugs—for Joey, not Jeff."

"There were all these girls," Angela explained, "that he treated like dirt. They'd become obsessed with him, and then Joey would say, 'Get away from me!' He wanted to kill them. It was wrong, of course, but that's what fame does to you."

It was around this time that Joey and I had yet another clash.

He called one day to say that he couldn't find the "Cold Turkey for a Hot Poppa" tape. He wanted to do something with the song. I told him the story of how I got it and that it was safe in my house. I told him I would be happy to give it to him, but there were two things I wanted in return: an apology for the insults and threats he made to me over the Bud Light thing, and to straighten out the old man, and the rest of our family, about how the stuff about needing contracts between us was bullshit.

"Well," he replied, "I don't know about getting any apology. I'll have to think about that."

I told him that I'd just noticed there was also another song on the tape that we'd recorded in the 1980s, "We're Getting Out of Here," one of the songs we'd argued about at the UN summit. He seemed really pissed that I'd found out about the other song being on there. Apparently that was really what the hubbub was about.

"I want that tape," he demanded.

"You can have the Hot Poppa track, no problem," I assured him. "But if you want the other song on the reel, I want a guarantee you'll give me a writing credit for my contributions on it. Then it's all yours."

"Bullshit, man!" he blurted. "That's mine."

"Yeah, well, part of it is mine, too, Joey. I'm just trying to protect myself, and you too, indirectly. You might want to screw me, but I'm not going to let it happen, not again. It's for *both* of our sakes. But I don't know if you can understand that.

"Hey, if you wrote the whole song, then you don't need this version," I went on. "Why don't you just go and rerecord it?"

"Fine, asshole! Be a baby. Keep the tape. You just keep screwing yourself, man."

And he hung up.

Once again, the roller coaster took a dive.

The off-again on-again aspect of our relationship was confusing for our friends as well. One month Joey and I could be hanging out talking, hugging, laughing like old times—and the next we would be standing in a club, possibly even back to back, and refuse to turn around to acknowledge each other, except for maybe a nod and a grunt.

"The fighting between Joey and Mickey was ridiculous," Legs McNeil claimed. "Even though Joey and I were no longer on speaking terms, I knew how close these two brothers were.

"One night," Legs recalled, "I went to Coney Island High, the night-club on St. Marks Place, and Mickey was upstairs, bartending to an empty bar, because everyone was downstairs, enthralled with his rock star brother onstage. Joey was having another of his shows and hadn't asked Mickey to play. It was heartbreaking because it was so petty. It was curious that they always had to be in the same room while they were fighting and act it out in front of everybody. It was very public sibling rivalry—and everybody was supposed to take sides. Joey always won because he was more famous. This was grammar school stuff—getting the other kids in the playground not to talk to someone because you're fighting.

"If you really hate somebody," Legs laughed, "you don't *always* end up in the same room together. There were a lot of rock clubs in New York City at that time, so Joey and Mickey could have avoided each other very easily. I think they had to stay very close to each other, because *they were* so close, even when they were fighting. They were both so close with their mother."

As Phil Sapienza observed, "Once Jeff had a real home base, he held on to it."

I'm sure the same held true for me, as well as for my mother, though maybe not to the same degree. The three of us kept struggling, striving to get back what we had had before things went bad with the Bud Light fight—and before other issues were brought to the surface.

My brother, my mother, and I had been through a lot together. As far back as I can remember we'd experienced tragedies that we had gotten through only by holding on more tightly to each other. After our parents' divorce, after Hank's death, after David and Reba were taken away, all Joey and Mom and I had were each other. There was a void we all felt when we were fighting. As mad as we'd be at one another, no matter what Joey would say to his friends—or what I said to mine—we always kept looking to come together again.

But something always seemed to get in the way.

There were periods where Joey and I would become like fire and gunpowder. All we needed for an explosion was a fuse, and there seemed to be plenty of those around.

Joey barely hung out with anyone anymore who'd known him from the early days of the Ramones—not Legs or Holmstrom or Stotts or Robin Rothman. Except for Andy Shernoff and Daniel Rey, barely anyone from the old crowd was around anymore, and I think he missed us. I believe Joey missed his old best friend, his brother.

I know I missed mine.

Even if we weren't talking, I could feel in my bones he wasn't as happy as he could, or should, have been. I know I wasn't. But I honestly don't know what more I could have done about it.

My mother would always say, "You know, Joey always asks, 'So what's up with Mickey Leigh?' He asks what you're doing and if you're making any records."

"Yeah?" I shrugged. "Well, he knows my number. If he really wants to know how I'm doing, he should call me. I'll talk to him."

"Well," she'd say, "that's exactly what *he* says—'I wanna talk, but I'm not gonna call him. He can call me.'"

Truth was, I was about as down and desperate as I'd been since I got busted, with a multitude of health and financial problems of my own. Though I worked constantly, the money only came in dribbles. Bartenders didn't make much at Coney, and even with income from some occasional background acting and singing on jingles for things like Pillsbury Toaster Strudel and promos for the *Hey Arnold!* and *Angry Beavers* cartoon shows on Nickelodeon, I was still sinking. Fortunately, I had some very good friends who wouldn't turn their backs on me to please Joey Ramone. They generously bailed me out, spiritually and financially, when I needed them, as did my mom. But it was kind of pathetic. I didn't cave in. I maintained my spirit and wit and stayed driven and creative, but I certainly felt beaten.

A friend hooked me up with some work at Irving Plaza, loading heavy equipment in and out of shows. It was risky. I had a ruptured disk in my back, a hernia, and no health insurance. But the money was good, and they gave you pizza.

Of course, I did not compare my problems to Joey's health issues—and I truly did feel bad for him. But I had a hard time acknowledging it to him. When you're lugging a two-hundred-pound amplifier down a flight of stairs and there's a golf ball popping out of your groin, believe me, you ain't thinkin' about *no one*.

My brother was also taking the stance of rightful indignation—possibly over the tape I wouldn't give him, or what I'd said in Legs and Gillian's book, or what I'd said to Veronica Koffman, or even what some stranger on the street had told him that I'd said about him. I had no idea, really, and didn't care anymore.

I suppose the bottom line is that we were both being stubborn fools.

As fall 1998 approached, Joey's lymphoma worsened slightly, and Dr. Coleman determined that my brother needed to undergo chemotherapy.

"Joey was feeling fine," Daniel Rey recalled, "until he got chemotherapy. The first treatment kicked his ass and scared the hell out of him. He said it was the worst thing he'd ever had to go through. I think it fucked with his head. It makes you feel crazy. They did it in the doctor's office, so he wasn't expecting it to be nearly as bad as it was. Joey wasn't ready for it."

The chemo treatments went on for several weeks and knocked the shit out of Joey. I don't know where all his friends were while he was in this weakened state, but apparently they were not around. According to my mother, he was lonely.

That loneliness, as well as his physical pain, was expressed in an e-mail exchange between Joey and Ramones publicist Ida Langsam:

ISLPR (Ida): how r u feeling today?

HeyYoJoe (Joey): talk about having too much time on ones hand. . . .

ISLPR: *yeah*

HeyYoJoe: my last appointment, which was Monday, i got a IV of steroids to raise my blood counts and though it gave me an energy boost, i haven't really slept in 2 nights, especially last night, i been up most the night

ISLPR: that's not too good—what did the dr say about getting sleep?

HeyYoJoe: he stopped givin me steroids, cause of these side affects . . . so i'm feelin a bit shitty . . . but my white count is low, and i've had this infection in my system for 3 weeks, he's trying to raise my immune system to fight it off . . . steroids boost the white count, but make me very speedy

ISLPR: i'm sorry you're going through such a difficult time

HeyYoJoe: good in the day, bad at night, stays with me for a few days . . . this has been a very tough time for me and i'm having another infusion next Thursday. Last time it knocked me on my ass.

ISLPR: anything you can do in advance to prepare for it?

HeyYoJoe: nothing . . . take my antibiotics and hopefully get this infection out, which is what i'm doin . . . so this record thing is real, but who knows when i'll get around to doin it . . . it's more of a morale booster . . .

ISLPR: it must be really tough on you. Are you going out at all or basically staying in the apt?

HeyYoJoe: basically in . . . i try and go out though, especially during the day . . . in the meantime, i keep getting all sorts of offers . . . for dinner

ISLPR: do you have enough people keeping you company?

HeyYoJoe: not really, i tend to stay by myself, which sucks, but then, if i don't feel well, i can just crash . . . it is nice getting together with people, though, i miss it . . . sometimes i don't have the energy to make a phone call

ISLPR: well, if you're feeling up to it next week, we can go for dinner if you'd like. You can let me know how you're feeling then.

HeyYoJoe: okay, sounds good. have a good day out there in the wilds of Manhattan

ISLPR: you try to get some sleep!

My mom called about a month later to tell me that Joey was actually doing better.

"What is Dr. Coleman saying?" I asked. "Is he going to be all right?"

"Yes, he is," my mom told me. "They say his blood count is improving, but slowly. He's on steroids and a few other things."

"Well," I told her, "as long as he is doing better, that's the important thing."

"Yes, he's doing better, but he's still a bit weak and achy," she said, hoping to elicit a proactive reaction from me, like, "Okay, Ma, I'll call him right up and go right over. Anything he wants."

She kept pouring it on: "He's kind of miserable . . ."

"I'm sorry to hear that, Ma. I really am," was all I could muster.

But Joey was definitely improving, and Dr. Coleman was confident that he would continue to do so. Hearing that made me relax. In hindsight, I wish I had acted differently. Though I wanted nothing more than for my brother to be okay, I felt I had to go about my life and not raise hopes or expectations about my relationship with him.

What would be, would be.

It's all right, Ma, we're only brothers.

Of course Mom meant well, but this approach was doing damage to a relationship that had been so loving and trusting all my life. Finally she was beginning to realize it.

"I'm not a hypocrite," Charlotte Lesher explained. "And I'm not a hero. The trouble started in the early 1990s when Mickey wanted the Ramones to include him in on the money from the 'Blitzkrieg Bop' beer commercial. I hoped it would get settled and blow over, and everybody could forget it and be friendly again. But it didn't happen. I don't think Joey had enough confidence in himself at that time to say anything to John.

"Except for that one time about STOP opening up for him in England, Joey didn't stand up for his brother. That was pretty obvious—because Joey even told me a few times he would have wanted the Rattlers to open for them at various shows. But Johnny said, 'No, I don't want that.' So it just never happened.

"Mickey felt that Joey took him for granted. He would play for Joey, practice with Joey, and help Joey write songs. So eventually Mickey resented it and felt that he should be recognized—that if Joey didn't pay him for things, Mickey should at least get credit for his contributions, which could have legitimately helped him along in his career. Joey felt that Mickey, like the rest of his adoring followers, would do anything for him. Joey took the attitude, 'Well, other people do it for me, so why shouldn't he?'

"And he'd say, 'I'm always plugging his bands in interviews. I just mentioned him on MTV!' But he plugged lots of bands he liked. They didn't all help him write his songs. Mickey would have preferred acknowledgment for his abilities rather than be included in a list of Joey's current favorite bands. Joey was not properly appreciative—and I told him that. I said, 'He's your brother. Why can't you feel that he deserves something?'

"And Joey resented that Mickey felt that he deserved some kind of thanks or recognition. He felt Mickey was trying to use him to get ahead, the easy way.

"At that point I said to Joey, 'That's Noel Hyman talking. When you do things like that, I can only feel you're a chip off the old block. Those were his tactics.' That used to get Joey very upset.

"He would get angry at me and say, 'You're always taking his side!' And Mickey said exactly the same thing! They're both stubborn, another Noel Hyman characteristic they shared. I never could get anywhere with them. I got more criticism from Mickey than I did from Joey—because I think Joey knew he was being vindictive.

"Joey would say things about Mickey to other people. And Mickey would say things as well. Of course, Joey knew people were more concerned about their relationships with him than Mickey, including even their own father—and he rubbed that in pretty well. So, each resentment just compounded the whole thing."

Charlotte sighed. "I was between a rock and a hard place, and I could never come out right with either one of them."

It was getting so bad that Mom and I decided to go to a therapist together to work it out. We cared too much to let it get any worse. Dr. Cynthia Luft determined that my mom had been justifying my brother's behavior as a way to protect him, which is not uncommon but may have been a bit unnatural at this stage of his life.

Of course, the shrink did not know my brother or the uniqueness of the situation. We did our best to enlighten her on past conflicts and to convey our feelings. I explained that my mom rode around in a car with three big Ramones stickers on the back and called herself "Mommy Ramone," and that I didn't think that was exactly helping to keep my brother grounded— more likely the opposite.

"Well, I'd be happy to wear STOP or Rattlers T-shirts and put *your* stickers on my car, too!" she said. "But you don't want me to. You don't even want me to come to your shows half the time . . ."

"No, Mom," I informed her, "I don't *need* you to do that. What you don't seem to get is that I want you to act like a *mother*, not a fan. You are not exactly in the demographic we're going after."

The shrink concluded that my mother and I were *both* acting a bit immature, especially in our squabbling over who was wrong or right regarding the issues with my brother. She said we should just concentrate on our relationship with each other. She told me that I could not get mad at my brother for my continually offering to help him and repeatedly not getting treated the way I would have treated him, basically imposing my values on Joey.

Dr. Luft went on to say that just because I behaved a certain way did not give me the right to demand or expect the same from other people. She advised me to stay away from my brother if he needed to play power games with me to resolve issues from our youth, which is what she believed Joey had been doing.

Our former stepfather Phil Sapienza, also a therapist, had a similar take.

"Surprisingly enough," Phil recalled, "Mickey was always a threat to Joey, because he represented normalcy, something Joey couldn't achieve on any level.

"What Mickey never realized," Phil explained, "was that Joey *wanted to be a normal guy*. You have to remember that there was a kind of generalized anger in Joey at that point in the early 1970s when I came into their lives— because he was not recognized. While Mickey had friends around him, including guys like John Cummings, Joey was a guy who sat in the corner of the bedroom by himself. Two guys in one room—and he's the phantom presence. Joey wanted to be on the other side of the bedroom. He thought that becoming a big star could win some normalcy for him. He didn't get it, of course. Mickey was comparatively normal. Joey resented it. It's as simple as that.

"On the other hand," Phil Sapienza explained, "it may very well be that the Ramones saved Joey's sanity. Otherwise he could've spent his life in the hospital. Remember, Joey pulled a knife on his mother, and on his brother, too. When he started doing that, I got really scared. What's the gap between brandishing a weapon and doing something with it? With a mind that unbalanced, if it weren't for the Ramones, I don't know if Joey would have survived."

Though Phil and our mom had long been divorced, they'd continued to be friends, and Joey continued to call Phil for advice and counsel.

"As a professional, I am not supposed to see someone I have a relationship with, or a family member, but I knew he wasn't going to go to anybody else. Most of Joey's sessions were devoted to his OCD. Joey would ask, 'What is this shit? Why do I keep doing this? Where did it come from? Why me? What does it mean? How do I get rid of it?'

"Joey would say to me, 'I have visions sometimes, and I don't know what they mean. I hear voices sometimes and they're always negative voices.' So I'd ask him, 'Who's talking to you?' Sometimes Joey knew, and sometimes he didn't know he knew. It was very revealing, to me, that many of these voices were his father."

39.

THE OLD MAN AND THE SEAFOOD

One day I got a call from my father's girlfriend Nancy. Dad had given up his apartment in Chelsea and moved into her town house in Eastchester, an upscale suburb north of the city. She was in a panic, as my father had fallen down in the living room and seemed a bit disoriented, and she couldn't lift him up by herself. My father had diabetes. He had been hospitalized once, when lack of circulation required several of his toes to be amputated.

Arlene and I jumped in the car and immediately rushed up to her house.

My father was still a bit dazed when we got there, but we got him up. Nancy called the doctor, who told her to call an ambulance and get him to the hospital right away. It was strange that Nancy had called me instead of my brother, as they had become so much closer, and I'd been so estranged for so many years. But I was glad she called.

Over the next month I visited my father in the hospital several times. Joey never made it. I could sympathize; he'd seen one too many hospitals.

I think my brother appreciated my caring for the old man, because out of the blue he called and asked me to help out with a benefit he was staging at Don Hill's for his friend Chris Snipes's band, the Independents, who'd had their truck and all their equipment stolen. Joey wanted me to do the old Rattlers song "On the Beach," with the two of us singing the choruses, as we'd done on the original record.

With my brother and I onstage together for the first time in quite a while, it felt like the old days. For those few moments, at least, it was as if nothing bad had ever happened between us. A videotape of the event shows us hugging warmly at the end of the song. Then it was over; but it did open up a channel of communication. Once again we were talking, sort of. More specifically, we weren't *not* talking.

In the winter of '99, Mom's best friend June passed away after losing her battle with lung cancer. Though Joey and I didn't talk to each other much at her funeral service, when we all went back to Mom's house afterward, we did.

He told me that the steroids he had been on for much of the past decade had really messed him up. That they made him say a lot of things he didn't want to say.

Not exactly an apology, but getting closer.

In April the Hyman family gathered for a Passover Seder at Uncle Henry's favorite fish restaurant on Brooklyn's Sheepshead Bay, near his Brighton Beach apartment. It was Arlene and I, my father and Nancy, Uncle Sy, Uncle Henry, and Joey. The restaurant was right across the street from the pier we used to fish off of when we were kids. We reminisced about the day forty years prior when Joey and I had been sharing a fishing pole that almost broke in half as we hauled up a monstrously heavy catch, which turned out to be a sea-filled rubber boot.

It was a pleasant dinner and quite funny when Uncle Henry kept asking the waiters and busboys if they knew who the Ramones were, proudly telling them, "This is Joey Ramone!"

They were Russian immigrants and had no clue what he was talking about.

It was the first time we'd all gotten together since the UN summit, and it felt strange to be talking to my father more than to my brother. But it was good. The old man was not doing very well. His diabetes was getting worse, and he was not walking easily.

When we were finished with dinner I walked my father out of the restaurant, holding his arm. Going down the steps, he couldn't keep himself balanced, and though I tried to keep him up, his weight was too much for me. I can still feel him slipping out of my grasp—but there was nothing I could do as he stumbled forward off the staircase and hit the pavement face-first.

I panicked and ran back into the restaurant to get my brother and Sy to help me pick up my father. He was okay, though he'd hurt his hand and head slightly. I could see the concern on my brother's face and sensed he felt as bad as I did about letting Dad fall.

IN THE SUMMER of '99, Coney Island High closed down, a victim of Rudy Giuliani's sanitizing mission to improve the "quality of life" in New York City. At this point, Joey's condition was coming along very well. He'd been on a regimen of cancer-fighting drugs, a "cocktail," as they called it, and it was proving to be effective.

In March of 2000, Dr. Coleman sent Joey a copy of his blood test results along with an encouraging note exclaiming, "Jeff: We're getting there! Hang in there."

He was feeling stronger and getting very active again, working on his solo album, and even contemplating entering into other businesses. Believe it or not, Joey and I, along with our father and Uncle Sy, had been e-mailing each other about investing in a new rock club with Jesse Malin. The potential spot was on the Bowery, just a block away from CBGB. We were all going to invest $10,000 each. I would be borrowing my share from them and would pay them back as it came in. But it was all contingent on my giving Joey the tape he'd been after.

It was the principle of it, he said. Of course, I felt the same way. Then he notified me that even if I borrowed the money elsewhere, without handing him the tape, I would not be welcome, or necessary, in this venture.

"We could easily do it without you," my brother informed me. "They really just want *me* involved. It's your choice, if you wanna be stubborn about it."

Once again I stated my terms; and once again he refused to even consider giving me acknowledgment on the song. I didn't give him the tape, we stopped talking, and the sanctions began again.

I had no steady work, no steady band, and no resources. Pat Carpenter and I were still playing together in Tim Heap's band. Pat offered to help me get into the video editing field, in which he was doing extremely well. He suggested I take a course on Avid, a digital editing computer format, and then he could hook me up with at least an entry-level job at his company. The Avid course was $4,500 dollars but would be worth it in the long run.

I called my father and asked him if he would lend me the money for the course. I was shocked when he turned me down. I'd heard him and my brother talking about all the money they'd made in the stock market lately. Joey had actually become a big player. He had done so well he'd developed a crush on CNBC financial reporter Maria Bartiromo. He'd even written and recorded a song about Maria for his solo album. Of course, picking stocks in the late 1990s was like shooting fish in a barrel.

Even though my father had bragged about having $100,000 in his stock portfolio, he turned me down.

"Well," he told me, "you gotta make it on your own. Nobody helped me, nobody handed me the money. I had to work my ass off to get everything I got!"

"I know what you're saying, and I have no problem working hard. But that's not what I heard," I told him. "I know you worked very, very hard too, but Mom told me that even you had to borrow some money from her parents to start your trucking business. Sometimes people just need a little help and they flourish, ya know?"

"Ah, ya know, you gotta make it on your own, kid."

"I can't believe it, man," I told him. "Except when we were little kids I never asked you for a thing my whole life. I worked when I was going to college. My mother paid for that. You never had to spend a penny for either of our educations. I'm asking you to help me one time, for something that will help me survive on my own, and you won't do it? Well, can you help me with any of it?"

"Sorry, but no. Like I said, you gotta make it on your own."

I couldn't hold myself back. I unloaded on him.

"Ya know, I don't know why you even had children if you wouldn't help them when they needed it. Why the hell would you even want to be a father if you weren't willing to do that?"

Then I hung up. Though quite harsh, it might have been a fair enough response to him, but it's one I'm not proud of.

My mother told my brother about it and relayed to me that he offered no help either. And, after hearing that, I certainly wasn't going to ask him myself. Of course, she wound up lending me the money for the class.

In the beginning of October, I got a call from Uncle Henry telling me my father was in the hospital up in Westchester. It was very serious.

I got up there as soon as I could. The old man was in bad shape. He grabbed my hand when I came to him. Of course I put all our shit aside. He was still my father.

Nancy seemed to be panicking again and didn't seem to know how to handle it. So I talked to the doctors and got all the information I could and tried to make sure he got the best attention possible. I went there just about every day. Uncle Henry was usually there, as well. Eventually, as my father got worse, I had to drop the editing course. He was slipping in and out of consciousness.

"I love you, Dad," I got to tell him one day before he slipped too far away.

My father held my hand and mouthed the words back to me.

Joey hadn't been coming to the hospital but it certainly wasn't due to lack of concern for the old man. For whatever reason he just couldn't make it up to Eastchester. Actually Joey and the old man had become quite close, especially during the past ten years. I'm sure it had a lot to do with the turn-around in the old man's behavior.

But ultimately their relationship became solid. Joey frequently visited him at Nancy's house in East Hampton. The old man would pick Joey up in the Caddy and take him out there. They would play checkers, go out to eat, to the movies — all the things we all used to do.

The affection that had developed between the two longtime antagonists was a beautiful thing to see, even if I could not celebrate it with them.

Joey still needed Dad's approval desperately, as well as his love, no doubt. And the old man, as prickly as he could get sometimes, certainly did have a lot of love in him. Like most of us, he just didn't always know how to show it.

Before June passed away, Joey seemed very nervous. He didn't visit her in the hospital, almost preferring to avoid the reality that we were going to lose her.

He couldn't seem to face the situation at hand here, either. My father's condition was now at the point where we would have to make a decision about keeping him alive on life-support machines. We all went to the hospital, and this was the first time I'd seen my brother there. Two days later, I learned that my dad was virtually gone. We were not in agreement about taking him off the machines and decided to gather one more time to make a decision.

Joey had organized a big show at CBGB where he was debuting some of the material from his upcoming solo album. The meeting was to take place the morning after Joey's show. This was one night I was almost glad he hadn't included me, as we would be meeting at the hospital at nine a.m. I couldn't think about anything else. I don't know how my brother did it: I give him credit for having the strength to go on with the show that night.

We met at the hospital, and I said my good-byes to my father, but Henry and Joey still could not give their approval to end his life. They were undecided.

Fortunately they were spared that decision—my father passed away later that night.

Joey and I went to the funeral separately. He went with Henry, while I went with Arlene, Mom, and her boyfriend Larry. Larry and my Mom had been together for about fifteen years, and he was like yet another father to Joey and me. Though Joey and I went up together to speak, at the last moment he asked me to speak for both of us.

I told a story about our father being responsible for teaching us about having a sense of humor.

"When we were really little," I told the congregation, "and we were out in the city or in a department store, our dad used to play this little trick on us where he would hide around a corner from us, or behind a pole, and watch us as we'd begin to panic, thinking we were lost.

"Then just as we were about to burst into tears," I explained, "he would pop out, laughing, and grab us.

"We thought, 'Oh, this is a *funny* thing. Let's try it, too!' So me and Joey would walk a few steps behind dad and then hide from him, until we saw him looking around for us, panicking, and then we'd jump out laughing."

When I finished telling the story, I turned to my brother, who had a big smile on his face. He told me he had forgotten all about that stuff until I reminded him, and it was really nice to hear. As we looked into each other's eyes, all kinds of memories came flooding back—only the good ones, though. The ones that made us remember how much the guy loved us: how hard he used to hug us when we were kids; how he took us to the dude ranches—even when he was so tired from working and getting up early, he'd shake his head in the car to keep from falling asleep at the wheel.

And how he took us to the rock shows we wanted to see. My brother and I did have a lot to be thankful for, even if the old man was not a perfect father. Who is?

Who is a perfect son? Or brother?

Afterward, though, Joey and I again went our separate ways.

A few days after the funeral, my mother called and asked, once again, if Joey and I had been talking. She told me Joey's cancer had notably improved and that the doctors were now very hopeful he was going to pull through. She asked if I was going to his annual Joey Ramone Christmas show at the Continental in a few weeks and if I would be playing. I told her I didn't know, since he hadn't asked me.

We both thought it was pretty sad. My brother was still trying to punish me or hurt me by excluding me from his party. We had Thanksgiving dinner together at Mom's, but things were still tense between us, and I left early.

40.

A NEW BEGINNING FOR OLD BEGINNERS

Joey Ramone's Christmas parties held a very special place in the heart of the East Village rock & roll community. And that community, which Joey nurtured for so many years, owned a sweet spot in his heart as well. An everlasting love affair had developed between Joey Ramone and downtown New York City. All of the locals came out in force to be part of it. Jimmy Gestapo from Murphy's Law was there. Jerry Only from the Misfits came to play with Marky Ramone and Dez Cadena from Black Flag; Ronnie Spector would sing Christmas songs; Steve Bonge and some of his Hell's Angels pals even enjoyed the festivities.

At the last minute, I got a call from the owner of the Continental, Trigger, who told me that Joey now wanted me to do a song at the party.

"Well, that's nice, Trigger, but it would be nice if *he* asked me himself, don't ya think?" I asked him.

It was out of the realm of Trigger's comprehension why I was a bit disappointed that my brother hadn't called me himself—and called a little sooner as well. Trigger lambasted me for having the audacity to raise the question.

"You always have to be negative, Mickey," Trigger answered, with the response and logic typical of those who'd come to be protective of their relationship with Joey Ramone. "Why don't you just be grateful Joey is willing to have you play? I see what Joey means; even when he tries to do something nice for you, you always have to make a problem. I've called a lot of people for Joey, and nobody has a problem with it but you."

"Well, Trigger, nobody else is his brother, are they?" I argued pointlessly.

At this point—two nights before the show—Joey asking Trigger to ask me to play seemed a halfhearted gesture, but a gesture nonetheless. I decided not to be stubborn and accepted the invitation. I wound up doing a solo act, a bizarre version of the Bee Gees song "Holiday" with just my guitar and drummer Joe Rizzo bashing along for the hyped-up bridge.

Ultimately, it turned out to be a great night for Joey and me.

Joey and I hadn't really talked to each other for over a month, since our dad died. This night was a small icebreaker, melting a thin layer of the ugly wall we'd spent the last decade manufacturing. But we certainly weren't the only ones who enjoyed the evening: Joey's good pal George Seminara did his customary Santa Claus S&M act, spanking the fishnets off his scantily clad Elvettes, and a dozen local bands each did half a dozen songs.

"Maybe it was because it was Christmastime," Legs mused, "but everyone was in a great mood. John Holmstrom and I were in the back, saying, 'This is amazing!'"

Joey did a set of his favorite songs with a band comprised of his friends Daniel Rey, Andy Shernoff, Marky, Al Maddy, Chris Snipes, and other guests. Joey would crack jokes, make a toast, and thank everybody for coming. Everyone knew it was going to be a night filled with familiar faces, familiar freaks, good loud music, free-drink tickets—and even freer inhibitions. Somebody would be giving someone head in the bathroom stall; somebody would be puking all over someone's sneakers on the stairway.

That intoxicating holiday revelry was not really being sold at the bar, but there was plenty available, and you could grab it as easy as a longneck bottle if you were thirsty for it.

It was the kind of night Joey had become notorious for in the "neighborhood," the "neighborhood" being Manhattan, the capital of the world. But on these nights it felt like a small town. And on this particular night, it seemed especially small.

There was something strange in the room that night—like the tinsel hanging off the ceiling, which seemed to glisten like shreds of sterling silver, and the lights glowing more like small torches. It felt warmer and seemed cheerier than usual. Maybe it was the effect of the double Bacardis I'd been drinking. Maybe it was because it was the first Christmas Joey and I had been together for quite a while.

Maybe it was the great news about Joey's health: If things kept going the way they were for a few more months, the doctors were actually going to consider his lymphoma in a state of remission.

Something about the night also seemed a little sad. Maybe it was just the typical holiday blues. Maybe it was that Joey and I still didn't *really* talk before we left the club. Maybe it was because our dad had died only a month earlier, and this was our first Christmas without him.

Whatever it was, it led to Joey coming back over to the Continental the very next night when I was playing with my friend Tim Heap's band. It was a surprise visit.

I was about to slam my pick into my guitar strings to kick off the first song of our set when I picked my head up to take a quick gander into the crowd. With a mere glance from the stage I could instantly identify the hulking silhouette entering through the door at the opposite end of the club. I could even identify the winter coat he had on, because my mom had given me the same one.

Every person who'd come to see Heap that night knew who'd just walked in without having to see his face. Joey Ramone was that recognizable.

My big brother had come to see me. And I was really happy to see him.

When we got off the stage, Joey came over to say hello, and we sat in a booth and talked. Joey and Chris Snipes invited Heap and me to come over to Manitoba's, the bar where the Independents were playing at ten p.m. Well, it was actually Chris who asked us to come over, since Joey seemed a bit apprehensive about extending the invite.

When we eagerly accepted, Joey warmed up quite a bit.

A few minutes later, my brother leaned over and whispered in my ear, "Ya know, it's Chris's birthday today; I'm gonna sing 'Happy Birthday' to him with his band. We're gonna do it the way the Ramones did it for Mr. Burns on *The Simpsons*, ya know?"

Then Joey asked, "Ya wanna sing it with me?"

"Sure, that'd be fun," I answered.

Manitoba's was shimmering with decorations. The craving for celebration seemed unusually prevalent in the city that holiday season, maybe because people were nervous about the future and really needed to party; 2000 had been a really bad year. The stock market, which had climbed to miraculous heights, had suddenly tumbled in record proportion. We were all hopeful for 2001: hopeful the economy would rebound, hopeful people's health would rebound, hopeful the New York City music scene would get better and that Mayor Rudy Giuliani would leave us the hell alone.

There was something else altogether happening between us two brothers—and "hopeful" was the key word here, as well.

We quickly went over the arrangement of the song, and with the Independents thrashing out the music behind us Joey and I sang "Happy Birthday" to a beaming Chris Snipes. When we finished, Joey suggested we do another one.

So we did.

"That was fun!" Joey said. "C'mon, let's do some more!"

We wound up singing all kinds of songs together, trading lead vocals on verses and harmonizing on choruses. Neither one of us wanted it to end, so we kept going until two a.m.

"That was great, right?" Joey said when we finally stopped.

"Man," I said, "that was a fuckin' blast, Joe!"

We gave each other a big hug. Joey and I had shared many an embrace over the many years, but none with that kind of significance.

"Look," Joey said, "let's just forget about everything, okay?"

"Hey," I said, "fine with me. It's about time, don't ya think?"

With that out of the way, we went back to talking about how much fun it had been to sing together and how we used to do it a lot, going back to a time when we were little more than infants—not musicians or rock stars, just kids.

We hung out for a while and talked about those days, about the two of us singing together, standing on top of the piano, down in the basement.

It was a new beginning for us old beginners. It was another new morning in our brave old world.

41.

"IN A LITTLE WHILE"

There had been some debate about whether 2000 or 2001 was actually the start of the new millennium, so we'd been celebrating both.

At about six a.m. on Sunday, December 31, 2000, me, some bartending coworkers, Jesse Malin, and a few other unhinged consumers slid out of Jesse's new bar, Niagara, and into a white wonderland on Tompkins Square. The gates covering the windows had been down since "closing time" at four thirty, and nobody noticed that the snow had begun to pile up.

If this snowfall had begun at four thirty in the afternoon on a weekday, the rush hour activity would have rendered these inches of white stuff into black slush on the street corners. But now the city was beautiful, muffled, quiet and still, except for an occasional cab passing by and the big foamy flakes swirling down. This looked like it could be a big one.

Joey was probably waking up on Ninth Street around the time I got home. He'd spent Christmas upstate with Angela and Raven and had come back to the city. I had hoped we'd all have a Christmas party at Mom's house, the way we used to every year, but was actually happier to see that he and Angela were getting along so well again. I had a gut feeling that Joey was gearing up for reconciliations across the board—maybe even Johnny would be next!

Something about Joey did seem different now, and anything's possible around holiday time.

We were planning on getting together for a little New Year's celebration sometime in the next day or two, and since we were all about putting our problems behind us and finally getting on with the reparations and reformation of being brothers, it seemed like a perfect way to start the year.

However, there was something else terribly important that Joey needed to do before the end of the year, or so the imperious voices in his head had convinced him.

Despite the freezing temperatures and the snow coming down on top of already icy streets and sidewalks, he couldn't ward off these demons on this morning—or he just didn't have the energy. As he had thousands of times before, he submitted and obeyed the silent orders to make completely sure that something got done that he may not have done "correctly." He headed uptown to Jamie Forster's office to repeat a movement, to push a button or turn a doorknob—and do it right this time—so he could silence the voices and move on into the next year without them challenging him.

He made it there and back, presumably doing what needed to be done, and wisely opted to get out of the storm and return to his apartment—mission accomplished.

Or was it? It was. Wasn't it?

Wasn't it?

No, it wasn't. Off he went. The demons had won again—and finally more than just the battle.

He never made it back to Jamie's.

He slipped on the ice and fell hard onto the cold street, feeling something pop on his side. He lay still for a moment, unsure if he'd done any damage, before attempting to gather himself together and get back on his feet. But the sudden shooting pain in his side prevented him from straightening up. He lay there in the snowy street, alone, writhing in pain. He called out to a few passersby, who looked at him, assumed he was drunk, and kept walking.

Finally a female cop came upon him. She radioed for an EMS team, who came and took him to New York–Presbyterian Hospital. Tests taken that morning would later confirm that he'd broken his hip in the fall. The cumulative effect of all the medications he'd been taking for the cancer, and for his vast assortment of maladies, had softened his bones, making them more susceptible to fracture. He would need hip replacement surgery.

When my mother called me from the hospital in the afternoon, Joey was already in surgery. She said there was no sense in me coming in as he was under heavy anesthesia and most likely would not be awake until the following morning. She would be leaving soon herself, once they assured her the surgery had been successful.

I didn't feel like going out that New Year's Eve, especially knowing I'd be going to the hospital in the morning and seeing someone who would undoubtedly be in extreme pain, physically and emotionally. Joey was back in the hospital—again.

I was really feeling for him. How many weeks, months, had this guy spent in hospital beds—and now this?

He'd been on a good health streak the past few years, too.

He was not in horrible spirits but was certainly frustrated and obviously in pain. He was happy to see Mom and me, though, and happy to hear that he should be able to recover and be back in action within a few months if all went well. He'd be in Cornell for one week and then spend the next three weeks in the Rusk Institute for Rehabilitation. While he was there, they would teach him how to do everything that affected his new hip, like how to get in and out of the wheelchair, get out of bed, bend over to tie your shoes—even how to walk, initially.

He seemed to be recovering right on schedule.

I went to visit him as much as possible, but turning down any work was inconceivable. I was writing bar and restaurant reviews for *Time Out New York*, moving equipment at Irving Plaza, night-managing a rock club called Under Acme, and interning at Pat's editing facility. But I was still broke and horribly in debt to Pat and several friends who'd kept me going while I was looking after my father in the hospital and taking the digital editing courses.

Of course, my mother was at the hospital every day. She told me there were so many things that she needed to do for Joey but still had to worry about her other job. I had offered to get him things from his apartment such as sweat pants, toiletries, and such, but she somehow concluded that I wouldn't know where to find these items. As usual, she insisted she had to do it all herself.

I'd almost forgotten about my mother's protectiveness and unusual need to be the sole provider of anything Joey required. After what I'd been through with them, and what I'd learned in our therapy sessions, I wasn't going to argue with her. In my observation, I still didn't think it was healthy for either of them; and sure enough, Joey started to become resentful.

On one of my last visits to Joey at Rusk, he and Mom and I walked around the visiting area, where they had a little botanical garden and bird zoo. Joey was progressing well physically, but he was also getting crankier and a bit ornery again.

As my mother became increasingly concerned and attentive—"Where did you put your dirty laundry, Jeff?" and "Do you have enough clean?" and "Do you have this?" and "What about that?"—he began to lash out at her. He mimicked, cursed, and prodded her nastily. It was like old times.

She looked to me for confirmation that the treatment she was receiving was undeserved. But this was the *abusive* Joey Ramone again, the one his "friends" and family did not talk about, lest they fall from his good graces and get "buried in the cornfield." Or as Daniel Rey feared, "You'd get whacked."

"Is it me?" she said to me.

I threw up my hands. "Don't look at me. I'm not gonna get into this with you two again," I responded, visibly frustrated and disappointed.

I'd hoped he was beyond this now. But at that moment, her son, my brother, was once again taking us for granted. For me, there was no more "taking" to grant. Though they both seemed to get my message, it was worrisome.

When we left, my mother asked again why he was acting that way with her when she was just trying to help him. She explained that she had fixed up his apartment to accommodate all his post-surgery requirements, putting railings on the bathtub, a higher mattress on his bed, etc. She said she would have to stay there with him for an indefinite amount of time, because it was possible his body might reject the new hip.

"Mom, there *are* people you can hire to come and help him, ya know?" I offered, envisioning a monthlong run of the production I'd just witnessed, only much worse.

"How could I think of having a stranger come in?" she said, aghast. "Maybe that's what *you* would do! What kind of person do you think I am?" she sneered, supposing I'd feel like a pretty small one. "I wouldn't trust anyone but myself, anyway," she continued. "And he wouldn't want someone else taking care of him."

"Mom, I understand. But he may *need* professional help," I reasoned. "Maybe you should see how *he* feels about it, anyway. Did you ever think he might be getting irritated and embarrassed with you constantly fussing over him? Maybe he'd show a little more respect and appreciation for you. He's a grown man, don't you know that?" I was becoming exasperated all over again, thinking I would not be able to deal with another go-round of this scenario. I never could just stand by passively when my brother treated my mother so harshly. "Don't expect me to be pushing him around in that wheelchair if he's gonna keep cursing you out like that."

Joey called me the next day and thanked me for coming to see him all those times in the past month, which was a big surprise—and an even bigger relief. It was enormously encouraging, and I was thrilled. It seemed that some progress was actually being made. As usual with him, you had to take a stand or he'd take advantage.

My mom was right, though. He was going to need a lot of help when he got out of there—the very personal kind. The kind of help he didn't like to get from his friends and that you really only get from your family, if you're fortunate enough to have one. With June and my father gone, maybe he was seeing the value of his immediate family. Maybe he was finally acknowledging the value of his brother. I got the feeling he didn't want to lose me again.

After we spoke for about ten minutes, Joey said he was kind of tired and had just found out he was running a slight fever. Then Mom called and told me that his doctors at Rusk wanted to let him go home as scheduled, but Dr. Coleman thought he should get a blood transfusion. He saw something in Joey's blood work that he didn't like, possibly a change caused by the various adjustments in the medications they'd been giving him.

When Joey had hip replacement surgery, it necessitated the administering of the drug Coumadin, a blood thinner routinely used to prevent clotting. However, for the Coumadin to be effective, they had to temporarily hold off on the medications he had been previously taking for lymphoma. His blood test results were nothing to get alarmed about, Dr. Coleman said, adding that he was just a bit concerned. The transfusion would be a good precaution. He also thought it was time Joey got back to his former drug regimen.

The transfusion was administered the day before Joey would be released from Rusk. But the transfusion did not produce the desired results, and

Joey's fever had not gone down. In fact, it had gone up for the third day in a row.

Dr. Coleman instructed that he not be taken home but readmitted to Cornell until they could determine the cause of the fever, which was rapidly approaching dangerous levels. At least there had been no mention of anything related to the lymphoma.

When I got to Cornell later that day, Joey's fever was close to 104 degrees and still rising. He was having trouble talking and couldn't swallow the aspirin tablets or stomach the sweetness of the liquid aspirin concoction they were trying to get him to take.

Dr. Coleman hadn't arrived yet, and none of the nurses seemed to have a solution, so I decided to crush the aspirin tablets into powder and mix them with some applesauce so he could get them down. It worked. A few hours later the fever came down slightly, and Joey was able to drift off for some sleep.

Needless to say, my mother and I were somewhat relieved but still extremely worried; we wanted some explanation as to what was causing the fever.

Given that he'd just been admitted that day, no one on the floor was familiar with his case yet, and they couldn't give us any answers. They had to wait for Dr. Coleman to see him first.

One doctor came by to examine him and *did* seem to have some information. We cornered him in the hallway, and he spoke to us matter-of-factly, as if we were aware of the situation. He informed us that the fever was *possibly* being caused by an internal infection but that that was probably not the case. More likely, he said, it was the beginnings of the cancer advancing.

That was when it hit me; I realized why Joey was on this particular floor of the hospital. It was the floor for cancer patients.

When we asked if it could be controlled and curtailed, he said that only Dr. Coleman could answer those questions for us thoroughly, but that in *his* opinion . . . it did not look good.

Anyone who's been on the receiving end of news like that knows what happens next. You feel like the outer layer of your entity has been peeled away, like on an onion. Peeled and peeled, layer after layer, until you are just a raw nerve, totally exposed.

When he said those words, my mom and I stopped breathing temporarily. We had to force ourselves to inhale and then exhale. It's hard to inhale when you feel like you've been knocked flat on your back and someone is standing over you pushing his foot on your chest. It would be a long time before we breathed easily again.

We walked into a lounge area, looked at each other, and broke down crying in each other's arms. Nothing else mattered anymore, only our own flesh and blood. All the problems that had loomed so dauntingly did not even appear as specks now. The whole world, all its complications, everything but the floor we stood upon, quickly melted away. Nothing mattered at that moment except my brother's survival.

This couldn't be happening. That guy couldn't be right; he wasn't Joey's main doctor. We prayed to the powers that be that Dr. Coleman would have a more hopeful outlook on the situation. We wouldn't accept anything less.

Walking back into Joey's room was the hardest thing I'd ever done in my life. Thankfully, Joey was dozing off and unaware we had been speaking to the doctor in the hallway, or he certainly would've asked us what the doctor had said.

Though Joey wasn't visibly alert, he was still totally observant. He wanted to know everything that was going on within him, good, bad, or otherwise. He was always brave when it came to ominous encounters with bad health, but this time he appeared more uneasy than usual. I could see it in his eyes. Or maybe it was that he could see it in ours. It wasn't only the persistent fever that had him, and us, extremely worried; he barely had the strength to move.

After several doses of aspirin applesauce, the fever had come down a few degrees. Joey seemed to be more comfortable now. He jokingly called me Doctor Leigh and congratulated me on my aspirin administration technique.

It was hard for us to leave that night. Joey didn't want us to go, but he was tired, and we told him we'd definitely be back in the morning. We left him around ten p.m. with an assurance from the floor staff that Dr. Coleman would call as soon as he arrived.

I was in shock, and Mom was completely shaken.

When Dr. Coleman called her around eleven thirty that night, he did, at least, dispute what we had been told by the other doctor. He assured her that there could be several reasons why the fever was not going down, and that even if it *was* due to the cancer advancing to a heightened level, there were still definite options available that could help turn this thing around. He wanted us to come in and see him in his office the next day.

Joey's friend George Seminara got there early in the morning. George was one of the few people Joey wanted to have as a visitor at this point. He was still very weak and tired. George would come every morning after he dropped his son off at school and would call Joey in the evenings.

I was by Joey's bedside when he got a phone call from George.

"I saw Joey quite a bit when he was in the hospital," George Seminara recalled. "I'd come in the mornings, and Joey would want me to read him Harry Potter books. He loved 'em!

"At this point I didn't really know what was happening, just that he was going to be there for a while. His third night there, I called to see how he was feeling and Joey told me, 'Well, I always feel better when my brother's here.'"

When my brother said that, I smiled and rubbed his hand. I had to put on the good face, 'cause I got choked up inside again. This moment was huge for us. It obliterated every bad thing that had happened between us over the past ten years. Those words meant everything to me, and that he had said them to his friend George made it that much more meaningful.

At the same time, his words intensified this feeling of urgency—that we *had to* make up for all that misspent time as soon as Jeff got better. He just *had to* get better. And, yes, I was starting to think of him as Jeff again. Maybe because that's the name we now consistently used to refer to him, as did the doctors and nurses. Maybe it was because he was acting like my brother again.

But what really got me nervous when he said that to George was that I sensed something else happening—something *I* didn't want to even think about but that Joey may have been thinking. The possibility . . .

Mom's boyfriend Larry would come by after work. Joey didn't want a lot of visitors. Until he was feeling a little better, he didn't even want anyone to have the room or phone number. We wanted him to have as much rest and as little stress as possible for the time being, as per the doctor's recommendations. Having visitors was totally his call. Fortunately, the first week or so, nobody even knew where he was, except for the few people he wanted to see. We contacted Angela, who came down from upstate.

Mom and I met at the hospital and checked in on Joey before our second appointment with Dr. Coleman. He was doing better. They'd started some treatment after Dr. Coleman examined him, and it seemed to be having a good effect. We were so relieved. Joey was in much better spirits but still very weak and nervous.

When we got to Coleman's office we told him how much better Joey seemed to be doing. It's so easy to get overly enthusiastic when you see improvement. You want so badly to believe that it was all just a big scare and that everything is going to be fine. No one wanted to hear good news more than Joey, who was anxiously awaiting our return.

There *was* good news. There was bad news, as well.

The roller coaster ride had begun, and so had the fight of Joey's life. These were the kind of fights he'd been facing since the day he entered the arena forty-nine years ago, and he was intent on winning this one, as well. Joey was looking forward to his fiftieth birthday, and to continuing work on his first solo album. He knew there was an issue of *Spin* magazine coming out in April celebrating the twenty-fifth anniversary of punk rock, and that *his face* would be gracing the entire cover.

He was confident that the Ramones were going to get inducted into the Rock and Roll Hall of Fame when they became eligible in 2002. But he wasn't nearly so concerned with any of those things at this juncture.

He only wanted one thing—life.

And to watch the new season of *The Sopranos*.

AFTER A WEEK or so, the fever went down, but other problems arose.

His friends were concerned, and he started to take some phone calls and have some visitors. His problem was that half the people on the Lower East Side were his "friends."

One Sunday afternoon I came into a room filled with people. At least they were from his inner circle of friends. I don't think they understood what was really happening or the severity of the situation. In fact, I'm sure they didn't.

For whatever reasons, Joey didn't want them to know anything more than they already did. As much as I wanted to talk about it to some of our mutual friends, I respected his wishes. So the room started to buzz with everybody socializing. There were about a dozen of us: Bob Gruen, Jesse Malin, Chris Snipes, Kevin Patrick, George Seminara, Larry, my mom, and I. Some of the guys had brought their wives and girlfriends, too.

Everybody had brought something—food, cookies, and beverages. We needed plates and glasses. It seemed more like a party. All the action was just making me worried about my brother. I was too nervous to enjoy socializing. Though they all meant well and thought that the visit would be a good distraction for Joey, I didn't think he was ready for this.

I took a glance over at him, and he was looking at me with a pleading expression. I worked my way through the crowd to ask him what was up and see how he was doing, if he was tired and wanted to rest. With one look from him, I knew he'd had enough. He still couldn't speak very loudly, but he indicated to me that all the talk and activity had been a bit dizzying. He didn't want his friends to be insulted if he closed his eyes and didn't talk to them, but he needed some quiet.

I asked the nurse to help me out. She understood completely and was surprised that so many people had stayed in the room so long, considering that the patient couldn't even walk to the bathroom without help. It was a strange situation: All of us had spent so many days visiting Joey in hospitals that this scene was not out of the ordinary. But those occasions were not nearly as distressing. This was not just another one of his foot infections.

The nurse announced that she had to do some tests on Joey and needed to clear out the room. Joey was happy that his friends had come but relieved when they left. We could now go back to biting the nails off our fingertips without having to explain anything to anyone.

Another week or so went by, with Joey improving slightly day to day. When my mother and I went to Dr. Coleman's office to get his latest diagnosis, he said he was very concerned. The doctor in the hospital had been partially correct. The cancer was advancing. But Dr. Coleman wasn't nearly giving up, and there was still a list of options he would explore. Dr. Coleman still hoped he could turn this thing around. The main goal was to get Joey strong enough so that he could withstand the chemotherapy again.

One day I came in to see Joey, and of all people, Victoria Gotti, daughter of mob boss John Gotti, was in the hallway. Her friend Andy Capasso was in the room down the hall. She looked drained. Her friend wasn't doing very well. Guess it doesn't matter how well connected you are when you're up against this enemy.

Joey was actually strong enough to start walking around a bit. The nurses told us that he had been spotted walking in the hallway late at night in a bit of a dreamlike state. He was on all kinds of medications, and one night he either tripped or just fell. So, to keep a better eye on him, they moved him to a room closer to the nurses' station.

A few days later, Chris Snipes left to do some shows with his band. Chris had been tremendously supportive and helpful.

When Chris left, Daniel Rey showed up. Daniel had been in England, working on a record. Joey was glad to see him. My mother and I were too, at first, but then we both began to sense an odd possessiveness about him. We needed all the support we could get, but Daniel had this air about him—as if to let us know that since he was now there, we could leave, and *he* would take care of Joey. He hovered around Joey's bed constantly, often preventing my mother from getting near her son if he needed something. It was strange.

Daniel seemed to be dismayed by the closeness he was seeing between my brother and me. Whereas Chris Snipes, George Seminara, Kevin Patrick, and the rest of Joey's friends were thrilled that we'd gotten over the hump, Daniel did not seem to trust this supposed reconciliation that had transpired between us—or did not want to.

Both my mom and I got the distinct impression from Daniel that he did not think I deserved to be this close to Joey again, because he was acting extremely aloof and cool with me, even considering the emotional upheaval we were going through. It seemed to distress Daniel that when a nurse or doctor came in and needed a signature in order to administer a different medicine, they discussed it with me, not him. It seemed like he was dying to tell them, "Don't trust Joey's brother. He'll fuck everything up. Ask Joey. Joey hates his guts."

Joey was getting stir-crazy. He had spent two solid months now in hospitals, and there was no foreseeable release date. He wanted desperately to go home, to see his own walls and sleep in his own bed—even if just for a short time.

Although Joey had shown some slight improvement, Dr. Coleman was very apprehensive about allowing Joey to leave the hospital. However, at this point, the doctors were not discarding the possibility that there might be a way to stabilize Joey's condition that could buy him several more years of life. In that time they might find a way to improve his condition even further. But we were told this was unlikely. Also unlikely was that a cure would be discovered anytime soon.

Even the possibility that Joey would still be with us for a few years, in any way, shape, or form, was miraculous. We were overjoyed at the prospect but probably shouldn't have allowed ourselves to be.

His quality of life had to be considered, as well. We began to discuss how it could be worked out so he would be able to reside in his own home. Dr. Coleman said it was not likely that Joey would ever regain his strength or abilities. If he did survive, he would need constant care and the presence of someone strong enough to manage a six-foot-five man.

"*You* should take care of me," Joey suggested to me.

"I don't think I'm qualified, Joey. I'd really rather see someone who knows what they're doing in that capacity. And I still have these other jobs."

"I'll stay with him," my mother assured Dr. Coleman, "I'll stay in his apartment 'round the clock."

I thought this was a bad idea—a recipe for possible disaster, even. I didn't think he should go home in this condition unless a pro could at least check in on him every day.

But this was what my mother wanted to do—maybe even *needed* to do. So I didn't force the issue any further for the time being. The doctor allowed Joey to go home for one week, and then he would have to come back.

"If there is *any* change whatsoever, call me immediately," Dr. Coleman warned my mother.

Joey was brought home in a wheelchair by an ambulette that Friday and was thrilled to see his apartment again. Unfortunately I came down with a slight cold, and my mother insisted I stay away until I was better.

I understood. The last thing in the world I wanted was to take any chances with his fragile health. I also understood her despair and was doing everything I could to keep everyone, including myself, calm.

Two days later I was feeling better, so Arlene and I went to Joey's house. He was in decent spirits but had hardly gotten out of bed. He did not look good to me at all. My mother was insisting he needed to walk a bit, to get his circulation going. But she couldn't handle his weight should he need to lean on someone.

Her boyfriend Larry was there. Larry was *always* there for us, and though he was a big guy, he had health problems of his own. So I helped Joey get up out of the bed, and we walked with him up and down the hallway one time and then got him back into bed.

Mom and Larry had ordered some Chinese food and were dishing it out at the dining room table. Arlene and I were by Joey's bedside making meaningless, light conversation and just trying to get him to laugh and joke around a little. He was still in bad pain. His leg hurt and his foot was swollen; in fact his whole body seemed bloated. A dozen other things were paining him. But somehow we still managed to have some laughs.

Out of the blue, my brother suddenly said to all of us, "You know, I really love you guys. And I just want you to know that nobody is more important to me than you guys, and I mean *nobody*."

With that, Arlene started tearing up.

I held back as best I could.

Larry smiled.

Mom brought in the egg drop soup.

After a little food we got Joey out of the bedroom, and he sat down in a chair for a while. But then he couldn't get up.

I tried to put my arms around his chest to lift him up, but the higher I lifted him, the more it hurt him, and I had to stop halfway. I just couldn't get him up all the way. Either I didn't have the strength, or I couldn't stop panicking when he would cry out in pain. So I called Arturo Vega, who came over in ten minutes. Somehow, Arturo was able to deal with lifting him up and out of the chair, and we got him back in bed.

I thanked Arturo profusely for coming over and helping us.

"This is what I've always done," he said bluntly. "I've always taken care of Joey."

"Well, thanks anyway," I told him. "I really appreciate it."

Arturo stayed and visited with Joey for a few minutes, and then left.

"This is not good," I said to my mother. "He needs to be looked at. He is swelling up all over the place. This is crazy."

"Well, I'll put in a call to Dr. Coleman and see what he recommends," she said.

Later that night my mother called and said that Dr. Coleman insisted Jeff be brought into his office first thing in the morning. She had arranged for the ambulette to come at nine thirty a.m.

"I'll be there," I told her.

When I got to Joey's the next morning, he looked even worse.

He was extremely weak and kept falling asleep with his head leaning to one side. The ambulance worker got Joey into the wheelchair and dropped us uptown at Dr. Coleman's office.

Coleman took one look at him and said to leave him in the wheelchair, get him back to Cornell immediately, and get him readmitted. Once again, my mother and I were thoroughly distraught. Mom rushed back to Joey's apartment to collect his things and would meet us at the hospital. I put a blanket over him and pushed him to the elevator and down to the street.

The hospital's admissions office was only about four blocks from Dr. Coleman's, but the journey was totally surreal.

Here I was, pushing my barely conscious brother in a wheelchair down York Avenue on a cold but sunny March morning, with all kinds of hustle and bustle going on all around us.

Normally walking down just about any street in Manhattan with my brother, he would have been stopped at least ten times by fans. But nobody noticed who the man in the wheelchair was, or the tears dripping from the face of the guy pushing it.

While we waited in the admitting office, Joey slipped in and out of sleep. He'd pick his head up and show a relieved but weak smile when he'd see Mom and me sitting on the bench next to him. There we were once again, just the three of us, supporting each other, as we'd done back in the house all those years ago.

"It's gonna be all right, Jeff. We're gonna be all right."

When Arlene and I came in to see him the next day, he was on a different floor. I thought that was a good sign, but all the nurse at the desk would tell me was that Joey had been given a platelet transfusion and was certainly doing better than when he was admitted. Mom, Larry, and Joey's dear friend Rachel Felder were already in the room when we arrived.

When I walked in, Joey opened up his arms and said, "Come here, I want to hug my brother."

"Wow," I laughed, "you really are feeling better."

I bent over his bed, and he wrapped his long arms around me, really tight. That was fine with me.

He pulled me down to him, and he just didn't let go.

I can *still* feel that hug.

Maybe that was his hope.

When he finally did let go, I looked over at Larry, my mom, and Rachel, who seemed to be crying.

"Whoa, I couldn't breathe there!" I joked to conceal my feelings and keep his spirits up. "Well, you still have plenty of strength in those arms!"

My brother just had this big smile on his face.

"It was one of the most beautiful, emotional things I'd ever seen," Rachel said. "I knew what had been going on with these two guys. And those moments, that hug—it was like Joey was making up for the past ten years.

"It brought tears to my eyes—and Charlotte's. We were all pretty broken up. It's one of those things I'll never forget."

My mom thought that since Joey was feeling a little stronger, it would be good for him to walk a little bit. The nurse on duty warned against it, but Mom convinced her that Dr. Coleman recommended it.

He made it up the hall and back, with me on one side and Mom and Rachel on the other. He seemed to be doing all right and was even joking around again.

When we got back to his room, I asked him if he wanted to keep going down the hall. He said he felt okay and wanted to give it a try. When we got a few feet down the hall, he stopped for a second. Suddenly Joey's legs just gave out, and though I tried to hold him up, I couldn't. I got behind him to try to cushion his fall as best as possible, but he was two hundred pounds of dead weight. His legs got tangled underneath him as he fell, and he crumpled right on top of them. I was trying to hold him upright in my lap, on the floor, and at the same time trying to untangle his legs. We got his legs out from underneath him, and I sat there holding him up while he screamed in excruciating pain.

It seemed like an eternity until enough help came to lift him up, get him in a wheelchair, and put him back onto his bed. The doctor on the floor did not believe that any damage had been done. But I wasn't sure because Joey's leg was already swollen when he entered the hospital. After a while, and several doses of pain medication, the pain subsided and Joey was able to sleep. Hopefully no damage had been done.

The next day Joey seemed to be feeling better again, but we were told he'd been admitted to the wrong floor. He was supposed to be back on the floor he was on before he went home. We gathered his things and he was taken back to his original room, which was very gloomy, with no windows and damaged walls.

There had been a young teenage girl in the room next door, a fan of Joey's. But she was not there anymore. We didn't see Victoria Gotti around, either. Andy Capasso, her boyfriend, didn't make it. But Joey had seen his room and of course it was much nicer, with a big window overlooking the East River. And it was available so he moved in. Joey wanted to move to a room where he would feel more comfortable, especially with *The Sopra-nos*'s season starting in a few days. There was only a tiny little "personal" speaker unit by his bed coming out from the TV, which had a pretty limited selection—certainly no HBO.

So I got him a VHS player, jerry-rigged the wire from the back of the set, and hooked up a little speaker on each side of the bed. This way, I could tape the show and bring it to him the next day, for us to watch together. And people could bring him movies and concert videos. It was the only distraction he got. He would begin to feel a little better, and we would feel hopeful; but his condition continued to fall into a "one step forward, two steps backward" pattern.

Amidst all this, Joey had Rachel Felder use her contacts to get me tickets to see Jeff Beck at Roseland, which was sold out. He knew I was a big Beck and Yardbirds fan, and he wanted to surprise me with the tickets. I went with my friend Tim Heap, and though I really appreciated Joey's gesture, I couldn't enjoy the show at all. I was just emotionally void. Tim and I left halfway through.

Joey had been in and out of the hospital so many times that until now, the general public and media thought nothing of it. But now after he'd been in for over two months, the rumor mills started to spin out of control. My phone started ringing more frequently, with calls coming not only from my friends in the media but also from strangers who wanted to know what was going on. Joey still did not want anyone knowing his status.

Arturo Vega felt compelled to talk to the *Daily News*. He gave them a statement but with a vague message. This only fueled the fires.

Then I got a call from Kurt Loder of *MTV News*. Kurt had called to inquire about Joey. Though I never really knew Kurt personally, I remembered he had written something about the Rattlers in *Rolling Stone* in his pre-MTV days. We *sort of* knew each other, and of course he and Joey knew each other very well. Kurt told me everyone in the industry knew that there was something going on, that there was something very wrong with Joey.

I explained to Kurt that Joey did not want to talk about it to the press, but that I had been getting a lot of calls and didn't know what to tell them anymore. It's pretty hard to keep convincing people that there is nothing going on when someone is in the hospital going on three months without even a tentative release date.

Kurt had been around, and had known Joey for so long, I figured I could confide in him. The first thing he asked was if there was anything he could do. Then he said he understood and would not betray my confidence and let anyone know how bad it was—and to his credit, he didn't.

The calls still came relentlessly from press people. There was speculation of all kinds: Did Joey have another bad infection? Was he going to lose a foot this time? Was it cancer? Did he have AIDS?

Then one day Gideon Yago from MTV called. I had met Gideon when he worked in Forest Hills as a stock boy at a record store called the Wall. He was a really nice kid, very knowledgeable about music, and he'd actually tried to help me get the STOP and Sibling Rivalry CDs on the racks but was thwarted by the manager. Now he was working for *MTV News*, and doing his job, looking for info about Joey.

"Tell me honestly, Gideon," I asked him. "Are they going to eventually give up and move on to someone else?"

"Honestly?" he answered. "No. They are going to keep calling you. And if you don't talk to them, they will start bombarding your mom, and then your uncles, aunts, whoever they can find."

"But Arturo Vega said something already in the *Daily News*," I told him.

"Yeah" he said. "Well, they'll take that for starters. But what they are really after is a statement from the family, and they are not going to let up until they get one.

"I feel bad for you," he said, "and I'm not going to push you, but you might want to talk to Joey and consider that. I'm just being honest with you."

Toward the middle of March it was becoming harder and harder to fend them off. It was overwhelmingly difficult and draining, and I had to discuss it with Joey.

Joey was still adamant about it.

"What're ya, lookin' to get yourself some press?" he said.

"Don't be ridiculous, man," I told him.

I explained to him how it had been and what Kurt Loder and Gideon had told me—that it was really bad, and that these people were ruthless. Any day now they would be pouncing on Mom. If we just put out some kind of official statement, whatever he was okay with, then at least they would leave us alone. He didn't want to, but he finally understood and agreed.

We wrote up a rough draft that I would fix up when I got home and call

him to approve. I asked Joey's friend Jan Uhelski, a journalist, to help me fi-
nalize it. Basically it acknowledged that he was being treated for lymphoma
in the hospital and had responded positively to the treatments. That he was
now doing well and should be going home sometime soon.

When I called Joey that night to read it to him, Daniel Rey answered
the phone.

Daniel told me that he didn't think Joey should talk at that moment, because this press release thing was upsetting him. He went on to express that
he didn't think it was a good idea for *me* to make a statement for the family
because of the way things had been between Joey and me.

"Just put him on the phone, Daniel," I told him.

Joey approved the statement Jan and I had written up and said to give it
to Kurt Loder first.

I had been confiding in Kurt, who knew that our press release totally
understated what was really happening. He said he had spoken *privately*
to Bono and that if things got worse, U2 were willing to do a show to raise
money to help Joey pay for his medical expenses if necessary. I told him
how incredibly nice that was and that I would tell Joey about it. In the
meantime, Kurt continued to keep Joey's condition confidential. I had only
spoken about it to a few people outside the family.

After the news came out that Joey was doing well with his treatments,
hundreds of get-well cards started pouring in from all over the world. People
began calling him like crazy and wanting to visit. I hooked up an answering
machine to his phone so that he could screen his calls. But the phone rang
nonstop.

For the most part, everybody meant well. Everybody was trying to have
Joey see how much people cared about him. People in bands called from
the road and passed the phone around in their dressing rooms—because *everyone* wanted to talk to Joey and wish him well. But it took energy to listen
to and talk to so many people. It sapped him badly.

One day he yelled at Jesse Malin for giving his number out to the guys
in Green Day and a bunch of other high-profile people.

"What are you trying to do, impress people that you have my number
here?" he chided Jesse, as he'd chided me about the press release. It was
kind of a good sign. At least we knew he was getting some strength back and
being a little of his old self.

He chewed out Handsome Dick Manitoba when he called joking that he'd heard Joey was having wild parties in his room and asked why he hadn't invited him. Understandably Joey was irritable. Who wouldn't be?

No offense to them, but he really didn't give a shit about talking to Billie Joe from Green Day or Lars from Rancid. He wanted to get a call from Dr. Coleman saying there was good news, and that was about it.

Then he yelled at me when someone read him the rough draft of the *Spin* article, where Johnny says that he didn't hang out with Joey before they had the Ramones because Joey was a hippie.

"Oh, that fuckin' hippie thing again. See? You and that fuckin' Legs book, with the hippie thing—that's what started it. Thanks a lot."

That really hurt.

"Oh, man, don't tell me you're gonna start that again," I pleaded.

"Well, you had to go and open your fuckin' mouth, huh?" he went on.

I didn't say anything, but I was really disappointed. I didn't know what to do because I didn't want to start fighting with him. I got frustrated and just couldn't deal with it.

He had Daniel and Chris Snipes there, our mother, and Angela. I left. He could tell I was upset about what he said. He was getting chemotherapy the next day. I was working so I didn't go.

"Mickey brought Joey a VCR," Angela remembered. "Mickey was bringing all this stuff to Joey's room, taking care of him. I got there one day and everybody had left. When we were sitting alone, Joey says to me, 'Maybe I've been wrong about my brother all these years. Look what he's doing for me! He's here for me!'

"I said, 'What have I been fucking telling you for how many years?'

"Joey said, 'You were right.'

"I said, 'Yeah, I know I was right!'

"The next day," Angela continued, "when he was going to get the chemotherapy, he was asking Charlotte and me, 'Hey, where's my brother? When is he coming?' But I didn't know what to tell him."

I called his room, and my mom was there. She had been there every day. She said he had a pretty hard time with the chemo, and he was sleeping. It was one of the few days I hadn't visited.

I'm sure he thought that I hadn't come because I was mad at him for yelling at me, because the next day the phone rang. It was Joey, which surprised me because he hadn't been making many phone calls. He called very early in the morning, and I didn't even hear the phone ring. When

I got up, I heard his message on the answering machine. He sounded so weak.

"Hey, Mickey, it's me. Just callin' to see how you're doing, and I hope I'll be seeing you later today."

Yeah, he felt bad about what he'd said. I could tell. And I felt like the world's largest turd. I called him up to say I'd be right over.

The chemo drugs had really done a number on him. He'd had these treatments before, but it never affected him as drastically as it had in this weakened state.

He had the *Spin* article on his bed, and I looked down at it.

"Uh-oh," I said.

"Don't worry," he told me, "I don't want to argue with you about that ever again. It's really stupid."

"I couldn't agree more," I said, letting out a huge sigh of relief.

My brother was seeing life with more clarity now than I'd ever known him to. I suppose it's the nature of our species to recognize what's most important mainly when we're in peril, when the things we've fabricated and the things that are real need to be separated. My guess is that it probably has something to do with our instinct for survival.

Amidst all this distress, he had conjured up such bravery and wisdom; I felt like I was learning so much from him now.

Bob Gruen, a world-renowned photographer, brought in a poster-size blowup of a photo of Joey performing. It was a great action shot.

"Put it up on the wall here, Joey, so the nurses here know who you are," Bob suggested.

It was a nice gesture on Bob's part, but he didn't really understand. Joey wasn't so impressed with himself as a rock star at the moment and didn't seem interested in impressing anyone as Joey Ramone. That wasn't what he was concerned about when the doctors and nurses came into his room. He didn't even want to keep the picture on the wall so that people could point to it and say, "See? This is Joey Ramone lying here."

Not that he wanted to relinquish his career or his alias; he just wasn't concerned about it then. As his situation worsened, he became even more lucid—through the pain, the fear, and all the uncertainty.

The pattern of "one step forward, two steps back" became "one step forward, four steps back." When Dr. Coleman called my mom and said we should come to his office, we knew what was happening before we got there. But he told us that he still wasn't giving up. There were still options on his list, but the list was getting shorter, and he was getting more and more concerned about the outcome.

My brother's system was slowly breaking down, the doctor told us. Not that we didn't know that already from talking to the multitude of doctors that had been coming in to see him.

One of us—my mom, Angela, Joey's friend Chris, or me—would accompany him while he got his dialysis treatments. We'd bring a little boom box down to the treatment room.

The first things Joey asked for when he came into the hospital were the Beatles new release *One* and the new U2 CD *All That You Can't Leave Behind.* He still loved to start his morning listening to music.

We'd open the curtains so he could see the East River and put on "It's a Beautiful Day." He said the song gave him energy.

Sorry, fans, but it's the truth.

Life became more and more surreal as his condition spiraled downward. Get-well cards started coming in by the boxload, all festive-looking and cheery. From all over the country, everyone from rock stars to junior high school kids sent their good wishes. Bono sent him a plant we called the Bono Bush.

His favorite thing was the poster Little Steven Van Zandt sent him, of him posing in his *Sopranos* "Silvio" guise.

Then it got to be like a circus. People just started showing up in his room, with things for him to sign and cameras. A multitude of his casual friends from downtown wanted to see him. There were people who were really just fans of his who seemed intent on making sure they saw him, regardless of his condition or the fact that he was not really in any kind of shape to host a greeting line. There were people who, for whatever reason, he explicitly did not want to see.

If there were certain people he wanted as visitors, we would arrange it so they came at a time when he wasn't being treated or tested for something, which he was most of the time. Some people were understandably hurt, and some even got a little testy, even when it was explained that the man just did not have the energy to receive so many visitors. They didn't understand why *this* one or *that* one could see Joey, but *they* couldn't.

As if things weren't bad enough, now we had to become like social directors for cretin hoppers. What was also really strange was that except for Tommy, none of his bandmates called during this period.

Marc "Marky Ramone" Bell had visited Joey just once after he broke his hip, when he was in Rusk rehabilitating. Dee Dee was in Europe, on tour or something. Richie Ramone was in L.A. and possibly not even aware of what was happening. CJ lived in Long Island, an hour away, was always in touch with Arturo and must have known.

All the time Joey was in the hospital dying from cancer, not one of them came to see him. None of them ever called me to see how he was doing or how my mother was feeling during this devastating time. But for those guys, it was not that surprising.

While Joey's body was deteriorating, our relationship continued to heal, and the bond between us had never been more solid. As eating and breathing became increasingly difficult for him, it became that way for our mother and me. We had no appetite for food or pleasure. Our only goal was to make Joey as comfortable as possible.

I got him a little silver wind chime, and while he was sleeping I went to hang it from the bar above his bed. But he caught me when the jingle it made woke him. I smiled to him as I stood above his bed holding the chimes.

I still had to work when I could. I got a call to do some background acting work—playing a waiter, a photographer, and a businessman—in a movie about the life of Howard Cosell starring John Turturro.

When I phoned Joey from the set, he asked when I would be coming to the hospital. I had to tell him I couldn't come until they were finished shooting. He sounded so sad that it broke my heart.

I almost got thrown off the set, as it was getting so late I realized I wasn't going to be able to make it to the hospital. I actually made a comment to the director about a way he could have saved time shooting that last scene. Turturro gave me a look that said, "Are you nuts or something?"

After that I didn't even try to work. There was no point. It was impossible to focus on anything else. We needed to spend every moment humanly possible with Jeff, and he needed that, too. He appreciated it greatly, which was evident in his gestures.

As he seemed to be more perceptive than ever about certain things, he could tell his mother was suffering as well. One day he asked me to ask Mom to get him some peppermint tea. She wasn't in the room then.

"I can get it for you, Joey," I offered. "I know how to make tea."

Apparently one thing that never changed between us was the ability to know what the other was thinking, because he gave me a look and a little smile, and his expression conveyed to me exactly what he really wanted—and what he was doing. He knew it made her feel good and kept her busy, so he wanted *her* to do it. It was really a beautiful thing, and it made a lot of other things much clearer for me as well.

Joey was all about making us feel appreciated now. He told my mother and me that he wasn't finished with his solo album and that he wanted me to do some work on it when he got out of there. After all we'd been through, our mother was thrilled to hear him say it.

We were both so happy that he was still thinking so positively despite everything, keeping his will strong and his spirits up—even as he became weaker and the doctors started to give us signals that there was little more they could do. As his pain became more agonizing, he still talked about returning to the stage—though it finally became harder and harder for him to talk, or just to watch *The Sopranos*.

I was downtown visiting my bartender friend Tom Clark when I went outside to call my mom to see if she had heard from Dr. Coleman. When I came back in, Tom looked at me, and without saying anything he poured me a shot. Dr. Coleman had ordered Joey be taken to the intensive care unit the next day. He said that this didn't necessarily signal the end, that there was still something he thought might buy Joey some time. Though I knew in my bones that my brother was slipping away, I still couldn't believe it. I prayed for a miracle, from anywhere or anyone, even God.

I even thought the luck of the Irish might help when Bono called to talk to Joey in the ICU. Bono had called me a few times at home to offer his support and give me a pep talk, and I arranged the call to Joey with him. The guy really went out of his way.

Joey was too weak to hold the phone, so I held it up to his ear as he talked to Bono, or, more accurately, as Bono spoke to him.

That night was the anniversary of the closing of the rock club Coney Island High, and they were having a Coney Island High reunion at Don Hill's. Everybody from the old staff and their bands would be doing a song or two. I'd been planning to do Joey's song "I Remember You" for the occasion. It seemed like the perfect song for a high school–themed reunion.

Earlier that day I had asked Daniel if he would come up that night and do it with me, but he declined, saying it would be disrespectful. He said that because people knew that Joey and I had been fighting I'd get flak about doing one of his songs, especially that one.

"People are going to talk," Daniel warned me as he left the hospital.

Bono had performed the song at Irving Plaza, so after he spoke to Joey, I asked him if he thought it was a good idea or not. He said, "Of course it is. It's a great song Joey wrote. Go represent."

Joey agreed, whispering to me, "Yeah, you should do it. Definitely. It's perfect. I want you to."

Those were about the last words he spoke to me.

The next day, when I drove into the city, I saw huge posters on the streets advertising the new issue of *Spin*, the "twenty-fifth anniversary of punk" issue. There was Joey, larger than life, his face covering a good two feet of wall space, plastered in multiples on every available site in the city.

When I got to the hospital I told him about it.

He was barely conscious but still reacting, so I knew he could hear me.

"I'm so proud of you, bro," I told him.

He squeezed my hand, looked over, and smiled.

"Thanks," he whispered.

That night was sleepless.

My mom called me around eleven thirty, just as I was thinking about calling her. We were as distraught as could be.

In the morning, the phone rang.

"The hospital called," Mom told me. "They said we'd better come in."

Chris Snipes had left to do a tour with his band, so I called Arturo Vega and Andy Shernoff and told them to come to the hospital if they wanted to say good-bye.

The ride into the city was dreamlike. I couldn't even drive. My mother took the wheel. After all this, she was still holding up, even stronger than me. It was really amazing how this woman found the strength she did. She'd been through so much in her life but was still intrepid. Jeff and I were so fortunate to have her.

On the ride in, a song kept going through my head. It was a song that my friend James Llorandi played several times on the jukebox at the 5 Burro Café in my neighborhood, where he bartended and I'd been drowning my sorrows. It was another U2 song, called "In a Little While," a slow, soulful, 1960s Otis Redding–style tune. I thought it would be nice for my brother to have some soothing music to help him pass on to the next realm.

I hadn't even thought of the irony of the title or the words, not consciously—it was just a beautiful song. But when I put it on, I, Arlene, my mom, Larry, Andy, and Arturo just broke down, crying uncontrollably. The guy had been in such pain for so long, we just wanted his suffering to be over.

While the song played, we just rubbed him and held his hands, and told him, "We love you, Joey. You'll be okay soon. No more pain, no more suffering. It's okay to leave us now. We love you."

A few seconds after the song ended, the nurse said, "He's gone now."

He was gone. He went with the song, I thought, to that place where songs go after they're played—wherever that is.

But when we left the hospital, I saw my brother all over the city. Not only on those posters on the walls, but all over the place. I saw him in the thousands of kids on the streets who wore holes in the knees of their jeans and oval-shaped sunglasses. I felt him in the songs he'd written and sung.

He was still everywhere. But mainly, he was in my heart and my soul, in my flesh and blood, and in my mind. To his kid brother, he was a towering hero—not just because he was Joey Ramone but because he was so much more. He was the ultimate underdog who soared to a place far beyond mere overachievement. As low as he'd been, he never let it prevent him from setting his sights on astronomical heights. His brave plight was inspiring, as I intend his story to be.

"Come along with me because we're gonna have a real cool time," he sang.

We sure did. Thanks for including me, bro.

Even if you can't stand by my side, you'll always be my best man.

ACKNOWLEDGMENTS

In loving memory of Charlotte Lesher (1926–2007).

Legs and I would like to thank the staff at Simon & Schuster for their enthusiasm and patience, especially Mark Gompertz and editors Amanda Patton and Zachary Schisgal.

My heartfelt appreciation to Susan Lee Cohen, the agent whose encouragement and support of this "first-time author" pushed me past the doubters, enabling me to actually write my story myself, and ensuring it didn't turn into an oral history.

And thanks to freelance editor Pat Mulcahy, who spent the past year and change helping me transform this book into its current shape.

I would also like to thank: Arlene Leigh, my wife (who has lived with me for the past thirty-two years. Need I say more?); Legs McNeil, for sharing with me his experience and experiences and for making me prove, as well as improve, my abilities as a writer. Much gratitude to Jen "You're as good as any of 'em" Osborne, Sy and Sandy Hyman, Renee and the Mandells, Robbie and the Rymans, the Fontanas, Mel Berger (William Morris Agency), Tom Clark, Lynn and Lilly Probst, Dave Frey and Wes Kidd of Silent Partner Management, Rory Rosegarten, Brad Rose, Jon O'Keefe, Kurt Loder,

Dr. Morton Coleman, Dr. William K. Main, Dr. Gary Goldberg, Michael Friedman (both of you), Tyler Lenane, George Tabb, Mitch "Bubbles" Keller, Bob and Shirley (how many pages you write today?) Boyd, Diane Barton, Carole Cassidy, Larry Marks, Kenny and Robert Klein, Stella "Ramone" Cummings, "Crazy" Glenn Wernig and Lucky Lawler of the New York Waste, Michael Beiber and Tom Gogola (wherever you are), Lori Eastside, Trigger, and all my family and friends still on earth.

Also in loving memory since 2001: Rose Kohn, Henry Hyman, Larry Finkel, Doug Colvin, John Cummings, Robin Rothman, Steve Massarsky, Andrea Starr, Linda Stein.

Legs McNeil would like to thank: Sean and Moira McNeil, my niece and nephew, for being such great kids. And also to Matt Mulhall and Ryan Adie for finding the lost Richard Freed tape the week I moved into my new house.

Also hats off to my agent, Susan Lee Cohen, and to my generous friends who indulged me during the several years it took to get this book into shape; Kristina Berg, Gillian McCain, Jim Marshall, Danny Fields, Stacey Asip, Tom Hearn, Carol Overby, Bob and Elizabeth Gruen, Ellen McNeil (my mom), Craig and Amy McNeil, Mrs. Diane Brown, Matt and Ryan and Amie and Keion, Fred and Regina Geller, Mary Greening, Tom Greening, Noel Ford, Jeff Goldberg, Mr. O'Neil, Jonathan Marder, and Jimmy from Trash & Vaudeville.

Legs McNeil and I would like to thank all the people we interviewed: Jerry Adams, Allan Arkush, Joe Blaney, Roberta Bayley, Jean Beauvoir, Neil "Whitey" Benezra, Tony Bongiovi, Bono, Pam Brown, Clem Burke (Elvis Ramone), Ellen Callahan, Pat Carpenter, West Rocker Crawford, Ira Cohen, Rosanna Cummings, the late Laurie Doll from Neon TV, Rachel Felder, Danny Fields, Jamie Forster, Chris Frantz and Tina Weymouth, Dave Frey, Richard Freed, Dr. Donna Gaines, Angela Galetto, Frank Gallagher, Michael Goodrich, Bob Gruen, Debbie Harry and Chris Stein, Dave U. Hall, Tim Heap, Tom Hearn, John Holmstrom, the late Noel Hyman, Aime Elkins McCrory, the late Hilly Kristal, the late Gary Kurfirst, Scott Kempner, Reba (Lesher) Kushetsky, Ida Langsam, Matt Loyla, Arlene Leigh, Craig Leon, Charlotte Lesher, Al Maddy, Jesse Malin, Terry Malloy, Handsome Dick Manitoba, Steven Massarsky, Monte Melnick, David Merrill, Matt Nadler, Ira Nagel, Kevin Patrick, Matty Quick, the late Dee Dee Ramone, the late Joey Ramone, the late Johnny Ramone, Marky Ramone,

Richie Ramone, Tommy Ramone, Vera Ramone King, Genya Raven, Marty Rev, Daniel Rey, Andy Ritter, the late Robin Rothman, Bob Roland, Phil Sapienza, Janice Schacht, Doug Scott, George Seminara, Andy Shernoff, PJ Soles, Phil Spector, Chris Snipes, Annette Stark, Ed Stasium, Hilly Kristal, the late Linda Stein, Seymour Stein, David (Lesher) Stein, Howard Stern, Richie Stotts, Joan Torshes, Marty Thau, Little Steven Van Zant, Holly Vincent, Alan Vega, Arturo Vega, and last, but not least by any means, Cynthia "Roxy Ramone" Whitney.

And much gratitude to our editorial assistants: Jennifer Osborne, Kristina Berg, Ryan Adie, Keion Nostadt, Aime Mulhall, Sabrina Hawkins, Alex Woodhouse, Debbie Belfie, Melissa Kurtis, Emily Schlesinger, Deb Sokolowski, and Mary and Eugenia Borkowski; as well as our transcribers Ed Web, Jeff Guziak, Adam Rehmeier.

Special thanks to John Holmstrom for his editorial scrutiny and contributions.

Extra special thanks to Gillian McCain for all her editing suggestions.

PERMISSIONS

PERMISSIONS

ROBERTA PRYOR

24 WEST 55th STREET • NEW YORK, NEW YORK 10019

Imaginary Men

The

John

Simmons

Short

Fiction

Award

University

of Iowa Press

Iowa City

Enid
Shomer

Imaginary
Men

The   University of Iowa Press, Iowa City 52242

publication   Copyright © 1993 by Enid Shomer

of this book   All rights reserved

is supported   Printed in the United States of America

by a grant   Design by Richard Hendel

from the   No part of this book may be reproduced or utilized in any

National   form or by any means, electronic or mechanical, including

Endowment   photocopying and recording, without permission in writing

for the Arts in   from the publisher. This is a work of fiction; any resemblance

Washington, D.C.,   to actual events or persons is entirely coincidental.

a federal agency.   Printed on acid-free paper

Library of Congress Cataloging-in-Publication Data

Shomer, Enid.

Imaginary men/Enid Shomer.

p.   cm.—(John Simmons short fiction award)

ISBN 0-87745-399-3

I. Title.   II. Series.

PS3569.H5783I4   1993

813'.54—dc20   92-34204

                                                     CIP

97 96 95 94 93 C 5 4 3 2 1

For Nirah and for Oren

ACKNOWLEDGMENTS

I am grateful to the National Endowment for the Arts and to the Florida Arts Council for fellowships which helped to support me during the writing of these stories.

Acknowledgment is made to the editors of the following publications in which these stories have appeared:

Florida Review: "Taking Names"
Midstream: "Tropical Aunts" and "Street Signs"
New Letters: "Goldring among the Cicadas"
New Yorker: "Disappeared"
Orlando Sentinel (in the Sunday supplement, *Florida Magazine*): "Companion Planting"
Plainswoman: "Stony Limits"
Woman's World/Woman's Weekly: "Imaginary Men"
Zelo: "The Problem with Yosi" (under the title "A Solution for Yosi")

"On the Boil" won the H. E. Francis Fiction Award offered by the Ruth Hindman Foundation as well as the *Iowa Woman* Fiction Prize. It appeared in *Hometown Press* and *Iowa Woman* and has also been reprinted in the anthology *Lovers* (Crossing Press, 1992).

"Street Signs" is included in *New Directions in Prose & Poetry 55* (New York: New Directions Press, 1991).

"Tropical Aunts" has been reprinted in *NEW VISIONS: Fiction by Florida Writers* (Tampa: Arbiter Press, 1989).

Contents

In the
Family

Street Signs

My brother, Beryl, was eleven when he decided to change his name. The kids at school had taunted him about it for years, insisting it sounded like a girl's name or a kind of fruit. Raspberyl, blueberyl, blackberyl. My parents were reluctant to agree: he was the only namesake for my mother's Great Uncle Beryl, a man famous for overturning with his bare arms a wagonful of Cossacks who had called him a Jew-dog and ordered him off the road. The story went that when the Cossacks came looking for him in the village the next day, even the gentiles lied to protect him. This all happened in the Ukraine, in the dim ages before we spoke English.

"Pick a name that begins with 'B,' all right?" my mother said. "Maybe Bruce?"

My brother said he liked the name Brad.

"Brad is that little brass thing on envelopes. Like a paper clip."

He must have given it quite a bit of advance thought. "Then Bart," he said. "I want to be called Bart."

"Rhymes with fart," my father said.

He was not discouraged. "Bob? Just plain old Bob?"

Finally they settled on Barry. It didn't sound too ordinary, my mother said, or too gentile. It sounded a little French, a little continental.

They went downtown to the courthouse the next day after school. My brother told me if I ever called him Beryl again he would pour calamine lotion in my eyes while I was asleep.

After that, only my brother's best friend, Asher Levandowski, was allowed to call him Beryl, and only in private. Beryl and Asher were both born in August, which accounted, Mother claimed, for their sticky temperaments, her way of saying they were pests. I hated them most of the time. They were boys. They were vulgar. They picked their noses and ate it. They said bad words when no adults were listening, then denied it on their lives. At the movies on Saturday afternoons they waited until there was kissing on the screen, then exploded their popcorn boxes. Worst of all, they played the pinball machines on Georgia Avenue, a known hangout for hoodlums.

Asher would have liked to change his name, too, but his parents were religious—recent refugees from Europe. Because the Levandowskis had paid dearly for their heritage, Mother said, they were determined to keep it intact. The Levandowskis made no concessions to the *meshugos*, the crazinesses of "Amerikeh." The result was that Asher behaved as if he were two different people. At home he was obedient, dutiful, and careful. He took piano lessons and was not allowed to read trash like comic books. Asher's house on Friday nights and Saturdays was a dreadfully quiet place even my brother avoided.

The other Asher was hell-bent on adventure, despite the oversized galoshes, the leather cap with earflaps, the heavy wool mittens, and, of course, the umbrella. Mrs. Levandowski believed that the umbrella was the first bulwark against catching colds. She fastened it to Asher's coat sleeve with a giant safety pin. Later, he carried the large black umbrella hooked over his forearm. It gave him a formal appearance, as if he were about to bow. Like Beryl, Asher wore thick eyeglasses which he broke about once a month. That may have added to their camaraderie. Also, Asher understood Yiddish. He had always known that the name Beryl meant a great, ferocious bear.

Now they are widening the road that leads to my brother's house. Alongside the hilly, winding blacktop, giant backhoes churn and shovels drool uprooted sod. These are the first road improvements since Barry and his wife moved out there twenty-five years ago. He wanted his kids to grow up with plenty of trees, birds, and fresh air, the occasional wild rabbit and raccoon. He didn't want them subject to the push and tumble of city life, by which he meant our old house on Garfield Place. I thought we had enough of the countryside in the old neighborhood. We had stinkbomb trees and mimosas and acorn oaks. We had room in the backyard for Mother to raise a few tomatoes. We had the workmanlike sound of the garbage trucks in the morning and the dreamy whir of the street-cleaning machine at night.

He moved farther out than he had to, but then that was always his way.

From the sidewalk outside Rudy's Pinball Palace you could hear the machines—they sounded like a hundred cash registers going at once—and see their lights flashing. It was a hot day in late September when I bribed Barry and Asher with a dollar apiece to take me there. I had saved up three weeks' allowance and scoured the house for *gefineneh gelt*—the loose change that disappeared into sofas, chairs, and the washing machine.

The double entrance doors were open, and three ceiling fans chopped away at the heat. I followed Barry and Asher into the deepening gloom, past boys of all ages intently pushing buttons and flipping levers.

They chose a game called Frisco Goldrush. Barry said he'd kill me or Asher if we touched the machine. He released the first ball, then began pushing and leaning on the machine with all his weight. That was just like him: he was always making rules for other people and breaking them himself. Asher didn't seem to mind. Mother said Barry was a born ringleader and that he had Asher going in circles.

Around us, buzzers and bells rang as less skillful players made their machines go tilt. His score climbed rapidly: 500, 900, 1,200.

"His best is 42,000," Asher said.

"Shut up!" Barry hissed. "I can't concentrate."

But he was concentrating. The lights of the machine reflected off his glasses, giving him a powerful look, as if the colors were zooming out from his head, like Superman's X-ray vision.

"Shit!" he cried, as the silver ball dropped into an alley.

"Double shit," Asher said. "Piss."

There was almost nothing as satisfying as hearing them curse. I had no desire to do it myself. My mother's speech was filled with euphemisms like heck, darn, and shoot. Naturally, she disapproved of indelicate language, which for her also included speaking Yiddish in the presence of non-Jews, something she considered rude and old-fashioned. On the other hand, nothing pleased her more than to hear a gentile use the word "goy" or Sammy Davis, Jr., say "*schvartza*."

Some older boys draped themselves around our machine and lit cigarettes. They had thin, sharp noses and stiff, oiled pompadours. They were what we called "rocks."

"Who's the slit?" one of them asked.

"His sister," Asher said.

They glared at me. "This is no place for girls," the same boy said. I moved to the next machine and dropped my dime in.

"Give me a drag," Barry said.

"Yeah," Asher said. "I want to hotbox it."

The older boys passed their cigarettes to them. Barry and Asher inhaled deeply and made the tips of the cigarettes glow bright red. The idea was to see how long an ember you could make.

Afterward, they bought peppermint candies to sweeten their breath. I had been scared to go to Rudy's alone. When I returned home, it struck me that Barry and Asher might have been afraid, too. But together they acted like they could take over the whole world.

Do you think the teachers at school were diplomatic about my brother's name change? They kept remarking on it, or forgetting it momentarily, so that the two names were strung together into a horrible long new one—Berylbarry. This marked the beginning of my brother's difficulties at school.

In those days bad behavior wasn't called hyperactivity or social skills deficits. It was called simply "discipline" and occupied an intimidating square outlined in bold black on our report cards. That fall, his grades changed from SP for Satisfactory Progress to UP, Unsatisfactory Progress, with remarks in the discipline box like "talks too much," "constantly disrupts the classroom," and "challenges the teacher."

Things went from bad to worse. Finally, during Passover that year, he crumbled some matzohs he had brought to school as snacks and dumped them inside Sheila Green's jumper. Sheila had to be sent home. Her mother told my mother her skin was red and irritated. Mother said yes, she was sure that it was, because no cracker in this world had edges as sharp as a broken matzoh. Barry was suspended from school for two days. I remember how agitated my parents were about this incident. Could it be the teachers had said something derogatory about the matzoh in the first place? Did they know it was a ritual food? And most important of all, what was Barry thinking, desecrating the matzoh like that? On the eighth day of Passover, Mother threw out the leftover matzohs, something she had never done before.

The next afternoon, Barry came home from Asher's house and went up to his small attic bedroom and cried. Mother and I both heard him. He didn't cry the way I did—silently into a pillow until it was soggy and cold. His tears were always accompanied by temper tantrums. He beat on the wall with his fists and wailed.

"Barry!" Mother shouted up the stairs. "What's wrong?"

"None of your business." His voice was muffled by the closed door.

If Dad had been home, he wouldn't have dared to answer her like that. She looked crushed and then, gradually, angry.

"Come down here this instant!" she yelled.

No sound from his room. She mounted the stairs and pushed the door open. Then she dragged him by his shirt collar down the steps into the kitchen and poured him a glass of cold milk to calm him down.

"What is it, Beryleh?" she asked quietly.

"Barry."

"Barry, then."

"Mrs. Levandowski heard about the matzohs." He choked up a little.

"And?"

"She kicked me out of the house."

Mother was silent for a moment. She glared at me so that I wouldn't say anything. "She'll get over it," she said.

"No, she won't. She said I can't come back." Barry sipped at the milk.

Though there was always a lot of yelling and screaming in our family, there was very little of the kind of quiet terror I imagined Mrs. Levandowski to be capable of. In our house, no matter what anyone said, we all knew that the person didn't really mean it. The glue that held us together could not be dissolved by a flare-up in temper, no matter how severe. It was a special kind of permissiveness—perhaps a Jewish permissiveness. We were made to feel guilty, but we never doubted that we could redeem ourselves. There were no absolutes, only a kind of ongoing tug-of-war run by parents who almost never stuck by anything they said if we pressed them hard enough. I could not imagine my mother ordering a child from her house. It was far too rude and arbitrary. But Mrs. Levandowski was another case. She reminded me of my Russian Grandma Bella—a stubborn and strict woman who stuck to a gallstone diet long after her gall bladder was removed and whose favorite food was laxatives.

"Just like that?" my mother asked. "What else did Mrs. Levandowski say?"

My brother looked up from his glass of milk. "I already told you."

"I mean, I want to know her exact words." Mother was always asking for people's exact words, as if she could insert herself into another person's head if she had enough information.

Barry gazed out the window toward the alley that separated Asher's street from ours. I looked out expecting to see one of the neighborhood kids there, but it was empty. "She said she was ashamed for me. About the matzoh and all."

"Oh." Now mother was getting indignant. "Who is she to call names?"

"She didn't call me any names. She just said I couldn't come to the house."

"We'll see about that," Mother said.

"I don't want you talking to her for me." Barry stood up. "I'm not a baby, you know. And it's none of your business."

From there on, the argument grew familiar. I knew Mother would win but that it would take a long time to bring him around. She explained that when he beat his head against the wall it was her business, that the whole neighborhood was her business if she said it was, even Mrs. Levandowski. But she promised to be tactful. She promised not to get angry at Mrs. Levandowski. Barry made her swear that she wouldn't say anything to make the situation worse.

Once I saw a film of a house-raising in an Amish community. The sides of the house were laid out and nailed together on the ground. Ruddy men wearing overalls, straw hats, and carpenters' aprons swarmed over the wood frame like bees over a hive. Nails poked cheerfully out of their mouths instead of words. In the distance, other farmhouses they had built squatted like salt cellars on a great laid table. A field of summer corn swayed behind them, its deep treads and waves repeating the grain of the wood, the hanks of their hair. You could hear a communal hum of pleasure when the sides went up. This happened near one of those towns in eastern Pennsylvania like Paradise or Intercourse where tourists are always stealing the road signs.

Barry moved into Wildwood Estates right before his first child was born. All the streets bear the names of trees and woodland flowers. At the corner of Azalea and Bluet lived a profoundly deaf child whose parents arranged to have a special yellow sign like the ones used for dangerous curves and deer-crossings installed at the entrance to the subdivision. It said Deaf CAUTION Child. At least that is the way I always read it, because the word "caution" was sandwiched between the other two. I remember thinking that like all signs, it would become invisible after a while. But I liked the idea of a public notice for a single child. It seemed both extravagant and absolutely essential. I could imagine a neighborhood full of such signs: Blind Caution Child, Lame Caution Child, Shy or Fat Caution Child, Doesn't Understand Where Road Leads Caution Child.

Whenever Barry gave directions to his house, he'd always say turn right one block after deaf child. Then he'd take pleasure in explaining what that was.

Mother telephoned Mrs. Levandowski the next day. Barry stood right next to her, listening. I was arranging my dolls under the kitchen table in their own little fallout shelter.

"Sadie?" Mother said. "Sadie Levandowski?"

I had been to Asher's house many times to play the piano. I knew Mrs. Levandowski would be standing in the kitchen like Mother, most likely stirring or kneading something. She kept a kosher kitchen, which meant, basically, that nobody else could touch anything in it, not even Mr. Levandowski. There was no neutral zone for the uninitiated among all those cabinets, shelves, and drawers. I felt like a barbarian, stranded between the *milchadik* and the *fleshadik*. When I drank a glass of milk, I was afraid to set it down anywhere, even in the double sink. I always handed it back to her.

"Danken Gott, the whole family is fine," Mother said. "Yours?"

Of course when Mother said the whole family was fine, she was referring to about forty people—all our aunts and uncles and cousins and grandparents. Mrs. Levandowski had one cousin in Detroit, her husband, and son. The rest of the family had been killed in the War.

"Sadie, how would you like to come over for a cup of coffee?" Mother's voice was warm and sincere. "Sure, I have tea."

They decided on Saturday afternoon. Mrs. Levandowski preferred Saturday after shul because she'd already be dressed.

Barry was three years older than I. Three years in the life of a child is a crucial, heartbreaking span. It is the difference between counting on your fingers and long division, between being confined to a few streets and wandering freely through the neighborhood. People were always assuring me that three years would be nothing once we were grown. But at the time, it seemed that Barry would always be smarter, taller, and faster, that I would never catch up. Even when I tried to imagine the two of us in our dotage, Barry was a white-haired gentleman walking ten steps ahead, talking a mile a minute to the blank air in front of him, and I was an old lady scrambling to keep pace like our Grandma Bella, who couldn't get out of the way of her own great fallen bosoms.

I often sneaked into his room to see the Lionel train setup which occupied most of it. He always left little scraps of paper jammed into the tracks and wheels so that he could tell if I played with it while he was out. But I didn't need to turn it on. I'd stare at the miniature cows and sheep fastened to their painted green pasture until I felt myself settled peacefully in that tiny, immobile landscape. Then I'd comfort myself with the thought that along with more privileges, Barry also ran into more trouble. As a toddler, he had been kept on a leash. He had set the house on fire accidentally the year before during a paper drive. He was sicklier than I was. His eyes itched and watered, and he suffered sneezing fits. The doctor said Barry was allergic to himself but that he would outgrow it.

Several times in going through his desk I'd encountered his Hebrew books. That was one advantage I had over him. Because I was a girl, I didn't have to go to Hebrew school. Barry, like Asher, spent three afternoons a week at Agudas Achim synagogue to prepare for his bar mitzvah. The synagogue was walking distance from our house, but it was orthodox. Did the other members know that we ate hardshell crabs by the bushel in summer and ordered Lobster Cantonese at the Shanghai restaurant?

The thick black Hebrew letters reminded me of the symbols in cartoons when the character is exasperated and runs out of words. Though I had heard Barry read Hebrew out loud, I was still amazed that such foreign sounds could come from his mouth. Even my parents could not understand most of it.

The next Saturday morning was spent in preparation for Mrs. Levandowski's visit. My mother insisted that we make our beds and clean our closets just in case Mrs. Levandowski wanted to take the ten-cent tour. I always hated it when we had company, for then she would stalk the house anxiously grumbling as she checked for dust, fingerprints, smears, and stray hairs.

It has always struck me as odd that children become intimate with their neighbors while their parents often never set foot in their houses. I had seen Mr. and Mrs. Levandowski in their pajamas on Sunday morning. I knew that Mrs. Levandowski wore a thick layer of Noxzema cream on her face at home, even if Asher brought company. I had seen her watch TV in the living room in the evening, white-faced, smelling like a Vick's cough drop, dead to shame about her appearance. I had even heard her burp once at the kitchen table. She had excused herself, but she wasn't embarrassed.

Mrs. Levandowski arrived at 2 P.M. She was dressed in a navy print dress with a large white collar that spread out from her cleavage like wings and flapped into her face when she leaned forward. Her accent was Polish, her speech, even in English, filled with the gentle clicking and mewing of that tongue. The blood red lipstick she wore made her face look extremely pale. Barry and I said hello, then sat down on the loveseat opposite the sofa where the two women sat, each turned slightly on one haunch toward the other. Mrs. Levandowski withdrew a huge deadly hatpin from her hat, removed the hat, and patted her hair. "In Europe we had cafés where to talk," she said.

"Oh? You mean sidewalk cafés?"

"Sidewalk, yes. On the street. In Warsaw we had many. We walked there."

"I see," Mother said.

"We didn't drive. Who needed a car in Warsaw?"

"I hate to drive," Mother said. This wasn't exactly true. We used to have a blue stick-shift Ford that Mother was unable to master. But once we got the Chrysler with the automatic transmission, she was jumping into it every chance she got.

"My husband, Zaichik, he drives."

"Yes," Mother said.

The kettle was whistling. Mother got up to fix the tea and told us to keep Asher's mother company. The three of us sat silently until she returned. Mrs. Levandowski looked around at everything in the room, not furtively, but as if she were searching for something familiar. She picked up the plate of cookies my mother had set out, chose two, and put them in her lap. Her hands were meaty and slow-moving. They were as big as a man's.

Mother returned with the tea service on a tray. "I have sugar cubes, if you like," she said, offering her the good crystal sugar bowl.

My grandparents from Russia drank tea with sugar cubes in their mouths. Mrs. Levandowski took her tea unsweetened.

Suddenly, the two of them were speaking the secret language, Yiddish. Mrs. Levandowski spoke much faster than she had in English. Mother stumbled a bit, groping for words. They talked for a long time, until their voices were a drone in the room. I looked at Barry fidgeting and was happy to see he couldn't understand them either. Then, all of a sudden, dead silence. Mother lit a cigarette and blew a plume of smoke to one side.

"The world," Mrs. Levandowski said, addressing me and Barry, "is not a happy place. Once maybe, but never again . . ." Her voice trailed off.

"Dos iz nisht Warsaw, Sadie. Dos iz America," Mother said.

Mrs. Levandowski glowered at her and spoke some more in Yiddish. I could pick out the words "matzoh" and "Pesach." She pointed to Barry and counted off four fingers on one hand, each accompanied by a name.

Mother continued to smoke, but with her free hand she was pressing her thumbnail along her jaw, a nervous habit I'd seen before. Then, her voice quaking and high-pitched, she said something long and pleading in Yiddish to Mrs. Levandowski.

"Nein." Mrs. Levandowski shook her head. Her teacup rattled in the saucer as she set it down. She pushed up her left sleeve until small blue numbers appeared on her forearm. "Don't be fooled," she said. She reached across the sofa, took Mother's arm and gently turned it over to expose the wrist, with its tracery of veins and smooth, finely textured skin. "Your arm is the accident," she said, "not mine."

Mrs. Levandowski stood up to leave. "Asher understands," she said. She picked up her hat and walked to the door. Mother thanked her for coming. They shook hands, something I had never seen two women do before. They looked like heads of state. "Goodbye to you," Mrs. Levandowski said.

Mother watched through the living room window as Mrs. Levandowski trudged down the pavement. Then she burst into tears and went upstairs to her bedroom. "I knew you wouldn't be able to change her mind," Barry shouted up at her, a note of righteousness in his voice, as if Mrs. Levandowski had not disappointed him.

For some time after that, Barry and Asher continued to be friends, though only on the street. Barry was not allowed in Asher's house, and Asher avoided our house, not because his mother had forbidden him to enter it, but because, I think, it held too much for him to reconcile. Eventually, of course, he had to choose. Perhaps if he had been a few years older, he'd have chosen Barry. But he was young then. So young that the choice must have felt to him simply like a gradual turning in the direction of his mother's pale insistent face and dark lips, a slight inclination of his head so that her lament came clearer to his ears and became, finally, his lament.

When Barry saw that new neighborhoods and shopping centers were sprouting near his subdivision on land formerly given to tobacco and horse pasture, he thought about moving farther out. But of his three children, only one lives at home now, and she'll be going away to college in the fall. Instead, he and his wife bought a large cabin-cruiser where they spend every weekend in good weather. He says the sea is the last open road.

I was surprised to see the old Deaf CAUTION Child sign relocated to the side of the newly widened road to his house. I like to imagine that the road workers preserved it out of reverence, for surely they could have guessed from its battered condition that the deaf child was long since gone. But perhaps they were simply daunted by the prospect of discovering whether, in all those houses, there was still someone who lived in a markedly different world, one which could not be changed and needed protecting.

Barry says he barely remembers Asher, and he does not know what became of him or his parents. This is nothing unusual or sad for a human being. The memories of children do not so much record the past as bury it.

The full story about Mother's Great Uncle Beryl is this: when he overturned the Cossack wagon into the ditch he wasn't just showing off. He was in quite desperate circumstances. He was a drayman and made his living hauling things—barrels of salt herring, household goods, sacks of flour and barley. His buckboard was full that day. He couldn't have moved it out of the way if he had wanted to. The road was narrow and steep, with deep culverts on either side. Mother said he must have reached the breaking point, sitting up high on his rig, looking into that dark ditch where the Cossacks expected him to tumble without a fight. It was perhaps the tenth or the hundredth time he had been called a Jew-dog. That was a common insult in his world of shtetls and pogroms. What matters—what aroused such ferocity—is what he saw from his rig: the dark ditch waiting for him.

After he overturned the Cossacks, it was said that their horses were so frightened by the sight of a wheel that they had to be sold for meat and glue. In the countryside, word of his bravery spread, exciting admiration among gentiles and Jews alike. The family celebrated and toasted him that night with wine, even his aged mother, for whom I am named, and who, I am told, tossed off her shoes and danced.

Tropical Aunts

Aunt Debs and Aunt Ava. They were my father's sisters. Dramatic, glamorous women who, my mother said, had "been around." I saw them every July when we traded the humidity of Washington, D.C., for the even more oppressive heat of Miami, where my father's people lived amid piña coladas, guava jelly, and floral print clothing. I still have a picture of them mounted in one of those plastic telescopes that were popular key chain trinkets in the 1950s. They look tan and healthy and non-Jewish standing arm-in-arm in front of the cardboard palm trees.

Debs was the older, a stormy, rich blond who had been widowed. She lived a reclusive life in a houseboat on the Miami River. Without a phone, she could only be contacted through her attorney, like a movie star. Ava was a redhead with a reputation for borrowing money. Everyone knew she'd had to get married to her first husband. This was the biggest scandal so far in our family. After she had the baby, she got divorced, lost custody, and married an osteopath who worked nights as a stand-up comic in the hotels of Miami Beach.

My Florida aunts came north to visit us only twice. The first time was for my sister Fran's wedding. They drove up together in a big white Chrysler sedan. "My teeth started to chatter as soon as we hit North Carolina," Aunt Debs said, hugging herself as she closed the car door. She regarded our snow-covered lawn as if it were the surface of the moon. Then she picked her way slowly up the front walk. Ava followed, relatively surefooted in doeskin loafers and thick white socks. She leaned down to touch the snow shoveled into a heap along-side the front stoop and put a drop of it on her tongue. "Sometimes we put Hershey's syrup on it and make snowcones," I told her. I knew they'd be exclaiming and complaining about the weather but that the cold fascinated them. Also, when I saw my aunt Ava eating snow, just like that, I understood how she could have gotten pregnant.

As soon as they had hung up their clothes, they unveiled the presents: chocolate-covered coconut patties (my favorite candy), sea-grape jelly, and fresh papayas. For my mother, a white lace bathing suit cover-up, for my father, a book called *Fish of the Southern Waters*. My gift was a pearly pink comb-and-brush set with tiny shells and seahorses embedded in the handles. For Fran they'd chosen salmon-colored lingerie that made my father blush as my sister eagerly held it up for us to admire. "Baby-dolls," Aunt Ava explained to Fran. "I hope your Herb will like them."

The night before the Florida aunts arrived my mother had given my sister and me a briefing. "Don't mention Uncle Teddy," she cautioned. Teddy was Aunt Debs's dead husband.

My father, within earshot in his lounger, pitched in. "Did you put away the liquor?" Fran and I looked at each other. The only time my parents drank was at Passover, when they sipped reluctantly at four glasses of Manischewitz Concord wine. Beer had never crossed our threshold. Once at a restaurant I had seen my mother drink a Brandy

Alexander, but afterward someone told her mixed drinks were fattening and she never had another one.

"All I have is the bottle of schnapps," my mother said. I knew exactly which bottle she was talking about. It belonged to my grandfather, Velvel. My mother kept it on hand for him the way you'd keep medicine for an emergency asthma attack.

"Are we supposed to pretend Uncle Teddy never existed or what?" Fran asked.

"She took his death so hard," my mother said. "Just avoid the subject if you can."

I remembered when Great Uncle Benny had died. The whole family mourned for a week at my aunt Florence's house where the gilt mirrors were covered with black cloth and the satin loveseats crowded out by low, uncomfortable, wooden folding chairs.

"Aunt Debs must have really been in love," I said, looking at my sister and remembering an old movie about a girl whose fiancé was killed on the way to the wedding. Would Fran turn to drink if Herb were tragically killed after the final head count had been given to the caterer?

"Teddy was a real charmer," my mother said. "Could charm the birds out of the trees."

My father lit a Lucky Strike. "That girl really suffered when he went. I even had to hide the scissors. No hospital could have handled it."

This explained, at last, my father's prolonged visit to Florida the autumn before. My parents had flown down for the funeral, but my father had stayed an extra three weeks. At the time he had said he was helping Aunt Debs settle Uncle Teddy's estate. Now my imagination ran wild with passionate scenes in which my aunt Debs, her large blue eyes reddened by grief and alcohol, was saved from self-destruction by *my father*, who in my experience had not been up to dealing with bloody knees or temper tantrums.

Later that evening I persuaded Fran to let me into her room. She was setting her hair. I eyed the birch bedroom set and pink clock-radio, the wallpaper with its soothing dusky primroses being visited by small yellow birds. As soon as Fran was married I'd be moving in. I smeared some of her Dippity-Do on my hair.

"Your bangs will look like sheet metal if you use that much," she said through a mouthful of bobby pins.

"Who do you like best, Aunt Ava, Aunt Debs, or Aunt Florence?"

"You must be joking. Ava and Debs treat us like their own kids."

"Mom says they spoil us rotten."

"That's because they don't get to see us very often," Fran said.

"I wish Aunt Florence would move to Alaska," I said. Aunt Florence was our mother's brother's wife. She was a stout woman, later diagnosed as diabetic, whose bleached-blond hair was done up in a zillion curls like a telephone cord on top of her head. She referred to her kids as "my Maury" and "my Melissa," even if they were standing right next to her. I was jealous of and hated both these cousins. "I'm glad you're getting married before Melissa," I said.

"Melissa's a bit young to be thinking of marriage," Fran said, from her great tower of eighteen years. Melissa was sixteen.

"Aunt Ava eloped when she was sixteen." "Eloped" was the word everybody in our family used for her shotgun wedding.

"Aunt Ava's different," Fran said as she opened the door and gestured me through it. "You can't talk about her and Melissa in the same breath."

Fran was right. The Florida aunts were different. Aunt Ava was a model, but not the kind who strolls down runways or appears on the cover of *Vogue*. Her portfolio was full of magazine ads for shoes, gloves, detergent, and jewelry. She had supplied the hands and feet for the photos. "A perfect size 7B," she'd say, pointing her toe. "And feet don't show age like a face does."

Aunt Debs had kept her husband's accounts. "They weren't ordinary books," my father had told my mother last fall after Uncle Teddy died. "Well, when he had the dry-goods stores, all right, pretty regular. But after the deal in Las Vegas?" His voice had trailed off to a low, knowing snicker.

At the wedding the two sides of our family would have a chance to get to know one another better, my mother said at breakfast the next day. The Florida aunts were still upstairs asleep.

The northern half of my family—my mother's side—had always acted superior to the Florida half. It had nothing to do with pedigrees—they were all immigrant Jews from Russia, Poland, Hungary, and Romania. I think now it was envy, for the northern relatives vacationed in Florida for two weeks each winter and talked of retiring there to a life of golf, sunshine, and shrimp cocktails. For them, Florida meant relaxation. Anyone who lived there year-round had chosen good weather over hard work. My father had told me at least a thousand times that I wasn't a Yankee like them. This was confusing coming on the heels of my mother's pleas that I attend Hebrew school and join the Young Judea group at my junior high. Would they need to know if I was a northern or southern Jew?

My father's family—fifteen of them—had left Baltimore's harbor district in the early 20s, part of the Florida land boom. My father spoke of this period with such reverence that as a very young child I pictured them in covered wagons, carrying rifles and beef jerky. My grandmother Minerva opened a beauty shop in Lemon City, claimed to have invented the permanent wave before Nestlé, and dropped dead of heart failure at the pari-mutuel window when I was four. She and her children took to the tropical landscape without a hitch. They ate hearts of palm, gambled on dogs, horses, and jai alai, and carried fishing tackle at all times in the trunks of their cars. Though my father claimed that the aunts spoke Yiddish just like my mother's side of the family, I'd never heard a word of it pass their lips in eleven summers in Miami. They had picked up *un poquito español*, which, Ava said, came in handy on weekends in Havana.

"I want to sit with the aunts at the wedding," I told my mother, handing her my empty cereal bowl.

"Out of the question. We've already discussed it."

"It's *my* sister getting married," I argued. No good. I looked at the wall calendar where the large red circle that represented Fran's wedding loomed at me like an angry eye. The entire month of December was full of arrows and asterisks and my mother's notes to herself. If I ever got married, I'd run away to Elkton, Maryland, just for spite.

On the day of the wedding, Debs and Ava included me in all their beauty rituals: eyebrow tweezing, oatmeal facials, shampooing, hair setting, leg waxing, manicuring, and eyelash curling. Much of this was new to me because my mother, a size 20 most of her life, spent her cosmetic energy experimenting with the silhouettes various corsets and girdles provided. She paid little attention to her face. I'd watched her countless times after her morning bath. She used no foundation but blotted her shiny freckled face with a puff dipped in light rachel powder. The lipstick was applied the way you'd put a dash in a sentence.

Finally, after six hours of primping, we got dressed. Debs wore a green satin sheath that showed off how slim she was—without dieting, my mother said. Ava was startling in a silver sequined dress that fell from her body like enchanted water. I stepped out the door in my red french-heel pumps as if I were wearing someone else's body, one that was fragile, required stiff posture, and allowed no contact with anything that might smudge my makeup.

The wedding went exactly as rehearsed. I had to eat with Maury and Melissa, but after dessert Debs and Ava made room for me at their table. Debs was a little drunk. She leaned on her elbow, her chin in her hand, and spoke slowly, drawling and cooing like a pigeon. Ava spent much of the night on the dance floor, sometimes dancing alone. The light bounced off her silver dress as she twirled and dipped. At eleven o'clock Fran tossed her bouquet—right through Aunt Debs's arms and onto the floor. Debs stumbled trying to pick it up but managed not to fall.

After the wedding my mother relaxed, went off her diet, and spent a week with her feet up playing card games with the aunts while a record snowstorm buried the capital city. She set aside the donor luncheon she was organizing for the synagogue where she was president of the sisterhood and where the rest of us set foot only for the high holidays.

Looking back now, I think she didn't quite approve of the Florida aunts. If they had been men, she'd have had no trouble appreciating their guts and eccentricities. But as women they must have frightened her. They had survived hurricanes. They had moved alone through nightclubs, funeral parlors, divorce courts, and casinos.

Under their influence my mother recollected her girlhood. "When I was fourteen I had a blue silk matching coat and dress that cost $200," she told Aunt Debs. She turned to me to explain. "That was when you could buy a dress for $6.95."

"Hen," Aunt Debs said, taking the pack in a canasta game, "you wouldn't believe some of the getups I've seen in Vegas."

"Not in your wildest dreams," Ava added. She had visited Debs and Teddy while the casino was being built. "It's hard to tell the hookers from the rest of the crowd."

"Hookers?" I asked.

"Whores," Debs explained.

"Please watch what you say," my mother whispered, glancing at me.

"I'm old enough to hear," I protested.

"I'll decide that," my mother said.

"Teddy knew everybody," Debs said, without a hint of wistfulness in her voice. This remark was met with silence by my mother and Ava.

"Even Frank Sinatra?" I asked.

"Sure," Debs said. "You want to know something about Frank Sinatra?" I nodded. "He still calls his mother every day. Just to check in."

They talked, too, about people who were long dead, people out of the family mythology. They ran through a slew of names and infamies, recalled favorite foods, recited the names of my grandmother Minerva's eight brothers and sisters, listed every set of twins on both sides of the family, and praised the spirit which had brought all our relatives out of the hopeless bondage of eastern Europe and onto the shores of America.

"You know you're part Gypsy, don't you?" Aunt Ava asked me at the end of one of these recitations.

We were playing rummy in teams. My mother and I against the aunts. "Gypsies?" my mother and I repeated.

"Our grandfather's father was a Gypsy who became a stable boy for a branch of the royal Romanian family," Ava explained.

"Really?" I asked, my mind already full of campfires, gold hoop earrings, and wide, colorful skirts.

"Absolutely," Debs said, stubbing out a cigarette and lighting another.

"I never heard that one," my mother said.

Aunt Debs cupped my chin in her free hand. "That's why you're so dark. Like your great-great-grandfather."

"Come on," my mother said. "There are no Jewish Gypsies." Her laughter was met with silence.

"Hen, we wouldn't kid about a family thing," Debs said. "He worked in the stables, taking care of the horses. And the riding boots."

"Riding boots?" My mother's voice sounded for a second just like Eleanor Roosevelt's, it was so shaky and high-pitched.

Ava elbowed me and smiled. "If you ever get the urge to roam, you'll know where it comes from."

I knew it had to be true. I could already feel the Gypsy blood in my veins. It had always been there. It was the reason I didn't want to join Young Judea. I couldn't belong to any group.

"He must have converted," my mother said, still puzzling out loud.

After the aunts left, I moved into Fran's room. The wallpaper with its profusion of birds and flowers reminded me of the house we had rented the year before in Miami with its hibiscus bushes and iridescent hummingbirds. But we didn't go to Florida the following summer. My parents sent me, instead, to a Jewish camp in the Poconos, where I stumbled through transliterations of blessings and songs and sneaked out at night to smoke with the boys. I didn't see the aunts again for eleven years. They stayed in touch, though—chatty letters on pastel stationery arrived several times a year.

Debs continued to live in seclusion on her houseboat. She became involved with the Humane Society, gave up meat, and adopted a variety of dogs and cats. Ava gave up Judaism, a faith she claimed only barely to have embraced, for the teachings of an Indian avatar named Meher Baba. When I was about fifteen she sent us a photograph of him with his finger to his lips. Her letter said he'd taken a vow of silence more than twenty years before and that she was going to India to live in an ashram with his followers.

I wasn't too surprised to learn in the mid-60s that Ava and her husband were living in a religious commune near Orlando and that Debs, who'd been hitting the bottle again, had been persuaded to join them.

I like to tell my friends that I was the poster child for my family—the one with something wrong that no one could fix. After

Fran married, she moved into a split-level home ten minutes away from my parents and had four children in quick succession. I tried not to hold it against her that my parents never complained about her, that she was my mother's idea of a model daughter. My own interactions with my father and mother over the following years went something like this.

"Have you met any nice boys lately? What about that boy Maury introduced you to? What does his father do? Is he going to college?"

"*What* boy?"

"Maury's friend."

"Maury *who*?"

"Your Aunt Florence thinks you should go to college here in town. What's wrong with George Washington University?"

"It's here in town."

"She hates me. My own daughter hates me."

My brilliant report cards failed to impress them. In my mother's eyes, I was valuable cargo waiting to be unloaded. Then her marriage mode would set in: invitations, napkins, and matchbook covers with a red embossed heart and my name intertwined with the name of someone nice, someone they approved of, someone Jewish. Caterer. Photographer. Bridesmaids' gowns. Ushers' handkerchiefs. Dyed silk pumps. And me, dressed up in white, an offering to the same God my mother served at her donor luncheons.

At last I graduated from high school and won a scholarship to a college in New England, a Yankee after all, my father complained. I didn't come home for the summers. After college, I went to Europe for a year. I threaded my way across the continent on a Eurail pass, picked grapes in Italy, and worked as a secretary in London. I pictured my relatives speaking of me the way they used to speak of the Florida branch—with the slightly disapproving nonchalance reserved for the inexplicable. My parents sent me a couple of hundred dollars every month, an emotional blackmail I gladly extorted knowing they felt helpless—except financially—to influence my life.

It was a beautiful fall day when I picked up my mother's letter from general delivery in Edinburgh, where I was visiting friends from college. General delivery was the only address I used that whole year;

it gave me the illusion that I never had to settle down, that I was beyond the reach of family. The letter was marked URGENT and explained that Fran was very sick. It ended with a plea for me to telephone as soon as possible.

"She had a tumor on her spine," my mother said when I finally reached her. "We think it came from a bad fall when she took the kids roller skating. They removed it," she whispered. "It was malignant."

The word "cancer" filled my mind, hordes of fiddler crabs with their pincers upraised like the ones I'd chased every summer as a child along Biscayne Bay. I tried to imagine Fran with a life-threatening disease but could only produce the image of her with baby after baby in the maternity ward of the hospital. "Will she be all right?" I asked.

"I waited to write you, hoping to have good news."

"When—?"

"Two months ago. She's had radiation and all her hair fell out. She weighs eighty-six pounds."

I remember looking through the window of my friends' house at the heather that purpled the September fields and wondering if heather grew anywhere else in the world. Everybody was pitching in, my mother said. Herb, though, was falling apart. Could I come home and take care of the kids? I could sleep in the guest room in the basement. I agreed and made arrangements for the next plane back to the States. In my mother's voice there had been a music, a music that caught me up in its melody, its refrain. We can save her, it said, if the sacrifice is big enough.

———— ————

But we couldn't save Fran, and my mother, who lived all her life conservatively as a kind of white magic against such a tragedy, was beyond consolation. My father called in the Florida aunts toward the end of Fran's illness. They flew to Washington and stayed at Fran's house with me, sleeping on cots in the rec room. They took on cooking and cleaning and babysitting with a fervor I wouldn't have expected of them. But even they, with their perpetual Florida tans and tropical radiance, were lost in the larger crowd of family, in that swaying throng of mourners dressed in black.

The funeral was held in the poshly appointed Zimmerman's Star of David, the largest Jewish establishment in town. I had never experienced grief before, and now I used it as an excuse to avoid Melissa, Maury, and the rest of the Washington clan. Everyone overlooked my aloofness, impressed, I knew, with my devotion to Fran, with my selflessness. I held onto my sacrifice like a shield and refused to cry through the rabbi's long eulogy. All the time I kept waiting for the grief to hit me like a tidal wave, for it to grab me like a claw.

At the cemetery, a beautiful snow-covered hillside in Virginia, both my parents fainted and were helped back to their feet by the Florida aunts. Those two were everywhere, consoling the family, lending a hand when the awning threatened to blow down at the graveside, helping mourners into and out of cars. They wept unashamedly, not so much for themselves, as Debs confided to me in the limousine, but on my parents' behalf. Ava was more silent than I had remembered her. She had a silver streak through her hair—whether natural or peroxided—like Indira Gandhi. It gave her an otherworldly look, as if it were the badge of some wisdom obtained at great expense. All she said to me that afternoon was, "There are no rewards for us here." Her green eyes swept the horizon and arced into the clouds and back.

After the burial, there was the *shiva*, the period of ritual mourning. Zimmerman's had delivered to Fran's house a dozen wooden chairs small enough to be elementary school furniture. When we returned from the grave, my aunts dutifully unfolded them and set about serving the platters that friends of the family had sent. Only the immediate family had to sit in the little chairs, terribly uncomfortable on purpose to keep the mourners' attention on pain and grief. The aunts brought us food and encouraged us to eat. During all of this service they were as humble and quiet as geishas.

The eating and crying continued all evening until the last guest left and my sister's husband, Herb, collapsed into sleep. Finally, only my parents, the aunts, and I remained. Ava suggested my mother switch from her mourner's chair to the sofa. My mother, mute as she had been all day, obeyed, moving in a daze. She took off her shoes and stretched out the length of the couch. "God," she suddenly said. "I helped Frannie pick out this fabric." She felt the nubby tweed of it and sobbed. "What's the point?" she asked us all.

"Oh, Hen, I'm so sorry," Ava said.

"I know," my mother said.

"But Hen," Ava went on, "there's something I want to tell you. Something you have to know."

All of us looked at her.

"She isn't really dead," Ava announced. I could hear the sound of genuine jubilation in her voice, of conviction. "No one really dies. We all come back. I knew it when I was in India. You mustn't think of her as lost forever."

My mother looked to Aunt Debs.

"Yes," Debs agreed. "It's a comfort. Somewhere your Fran and my Teddy go on. Transformed." She exhaled, and we watched her cigarette smoke hang in the air for a moment like a magician's rope trick.

Then my mother bolted upright on the couch. "You're crazy!" she shouted. "Both of you."

"No, Hen, you don't understand—"

"You've always been crazy. Only now you call it religion. We're leaving. Get our coats," she ordered my father.

"Please," Aunt Debs begged, tears streaming from her eyes.

"Wait, Ma," I called to her as she punched her fists through her coat sleeves.

"Wait for what?" my mother said, turning on me the same venom she felt for the aunts. "My Frannie's dead. Who cares if she comes back as something else? She isn't coming back to those four children. Or," she socked her chest, "to me."

That was the last time she ever saw the aunts, though she and my father eventually retired to Florida. The aunts tried to contact her repeatedly, but she dismissed all apologies and offers of reconciliation and returned their letters unopened. And I think, mild as she was, that she took pride in having taken so absolute a stand against them. Years afterward she refused to speak their names. She tended her anger like a rock garden, nourishing it once a year on the anniversary of Fran's death. Fifteen years later, when I came home for a visit, I saw her light the *yahrzeit* candle and heard her say bitterly, "Back as a flame? Only a little flame?"

The aunts left the day after the funeral, hugging thin coats around their print dresses at the airport as we waited for their call to board the plane. I knew I'd want to defend them if their names ever came up, if I ever found myself sorting through the family mythology. And

I knew I'd never change my parents' minds about the incident. They needed that anger too much. I could imagine myself far into the future, living perhaps in Taos or San Francisco, some place I'd never been, talking to a child with a face I couldn't picture clearly, a dark face like mine. I'd tell her about the wedding—not my own, but Fran's.

When their plane taxied down the runway I wished I were on it with them, our faces leaning together in a threesome toward the small window, the city spreading out below us like a game board. The trip south would have felt like walking under a very large shade tree, a tree so large that the coolness under its branches went on and on into nightfall.

Goldring
among
the
Cicadas

Harry Goldring was fifty-nine years old and still worried about upsetting his mother, Bella. On alternate Wednesdays, he ate lunch in her apartment. Today, he was going to talk to her about moving to a retirement village. He really was. She would pitch a fit. He would feel disloyal.

Despite his age, Harry still felt like a young man with his whole future stretching out before him. When he dealt with Bella, though, he felt old. He thought this was unusual. Most people he knew complained of feeling like little kids around their parents.

While Bella stuffed peaches with cottage cheese, Harry studied a photo of his younger brother. Mel was pushing fifty, but in the picture on Bella's mahogany sideboard he was a perpetual nineteen, tan and muscular from months of holding action against the Japanese.

Bella noticed Harry staring at the picture. "Such a handsome boy," she said. "We almost lost him."

Harry asked if she wanted a glass of tea, but it was too late.

"Quinine, quinine, quinine," she chanted, cutting her peach into bite-sized bits. "I never saw a human being take so much medicine. We supported the drugstore."

Next she would be calling Mel her Yiddishah Marine. Harry resisted the urge to remind her that he had tried to enlist, too, but had been declared 4F—volatile blood pressure even then. In Bella's mind Mel held the title of family hero while Harry was the family mensch. That meant Harry bought ambulances for Israel while Mel invested in the Redskins and socialized with goyim, knocking back martinis and who knows what other poison. Mel was shrewd, Bella always said, while Harry—*Harry had a heart as big as his body.* He'd always been fat. He loved food. He was married to a fat woman and his son, Maury, was even fatter. Harry couldn't recall a single movie or book that showed what fat people were really like. They never got to rescue anything but leftovers.

Harry always pretended to be on a diet when he visited his mother. Now he arranged his cottage cheese in a neat mound and rehearsed what he and Mel had agreed on. *Ma, it's time to give up the apartment. Even with the maid you work too hard. You need people around you.* But Bella didn't just live in her apartment like other people, Harry realized, looking at the mirrors from Czechoslovakia, the Persian rugs. She was a curator, for Christ's sake, and the apartment was a museum of Velvel's success and her own good taste. You couldn't fit a museum into the one-bedroom units of the Potomac Retirement Village. Still, Bella was eighty-two years old. She'd fallen twice in the two years since Velvel died. Once she'd fractured an ankle and the other time suffered a mild concussion. Both times she'd been waxing the floor. When Velvel was alive, if he caught her climbing a stepladder to vacuum drapes, he'd yell something in Russian, and she'd giggle and stop. Now there was no one to make her giggle or stop.

Bella put their plates in the sink, then walked slowly to the bedroom and returned with an ornate hat in a plastic bag. "I want Florence to have this. I wore it for your thirtieth anniversary."

Harry thanked her, though he knew that Florence would give it to the maid. The day he'd won the low-income housing contract—his biggest deal ever—he'd been relaxing in the den, feeling kingly in his household, the master of a notable destiny, when Jolie Mae walked by, dragging the Hoover and wearing Bella's mink-collared sweater over her uniform. Now he frowned as he imagined the old black woman in the fancy beanie.

Bella moved carefully toward the TV and flipped on an afternoon soap. "Mama," Harry began, "I've been thinking—"

"Not now," Bella said. "I want to see if that stupid Ann keeps her baby. You'll think later." She angled her cheek toward his face, prompting him to lean down and kiss her goodbye. He felt the blood rush to his head. Then something sputtered right under his breast bone, like a failing car starter. Something scurried there, threatening to run away.

Harry sat staring through the french doors at the patio where a small wind-devil of autumn leaves sucked at the flagstones. Soon it would be his busy season. The nation's capital would be limping through another winter. Pipes would be freezing and bursting all over town.

He let a Hershey's Kiss dissolve in his mouth and thought with pride of his fleet of four white panel vans. *Goldring's Plumbing*—the "o" a gold ring set with a huge diamond solitaire. Under it, his slogan: *Service is an engagement we take seriously.* There were worse ways to make a living. He didn't expect his customers to remember him when they were taking a nice steamy shower. But when the tap ran cold, when the toilet backed up or the garbage disposal choked on steak bones, then, *then* they were calling his name.

The phone rang. His son, Maury, was having a problem. His wife needed breast reduction surgery, and their insurance company wouldn't pay. The plastic surgeon had sent two letters explaining that her heavy breasts were straining the thoracic vertebrae. "'Purely cosmetic,'" Maury read to Harry from the insurance company's letter. "These guys have no compassion. Can you imagine? All her life, she thinks she's lucky to have big boobs, and it turns out they're making her hunchback."

"How much will it cost?"

"Five thousand, give or take."

"That's a lot of money," Harry said. The exact amount he'd put aside for a down payment on that condo in West Palm Beach.

"I'm not asking for myself." Maury's voice dropped. "Damn it, the doctor told us it would be covered. She's scheduled for next Friday afternoon."

"What about a bank loan?"

"I'm willing to pay you interest, Dad," Maury said. "Why should the bank know Elaine's bust size?"

Elaine was such a nice girl. From Georgia, where they knew what good manners were. Hunchback. Harry remembered Charles Laughton's twisted face as he lurched around like a wild animal in the bell tower.

They agreed on 5 percent a year. *"Rachmones,"* Harry mumbled as he hung up. Compassion.

Maury just couldn't seem to break in as a lawyer. Harry had thrown him customers over the years, but they drifted away. It wasn't personal, they assured Harry. Maury was such a nice guy, maybe even too nice. At least Elaine substitute-taught a couple days a week. They had two adorable sons. The kids were on diets, but when they visited Harry, they stuffed their pockets with bounty from his candy drawer—Snickers bars, Milky Ways, caramels.

When the doctor suggested he get psychotherapy for his hypertension, Harry had laughed, but now he regarded his Wednesday afternoon session as a small oasis in his week.

Dr. Toland's offices were dimly lit, like a bedroom. The layout reminded Harry of a series of check-valves. There were two waiting rooms and a separate entrance and exit so patients never saw each other. Even though he detested waiting, he always arrived early for appointments. Why was that?

It had taken Harry a while to relax with Dr. Toland. Bella and Velvel had ingrained in him the idea that he mustn't trust anyone who wasn't family. A few times Harry had gone home angry at not knowing anything about the doctor except what schools he had graduated from, information Harry had gathered from the diplomas on the wall. Also, he had asked if the doctor happened to be Jewish. The doctor happened not to be.

During the first session, Dr. Toland had explained that high blood pressure was one of the ways Harry had developed to cope with the world, but there were other ways, and he could learn them. The doctor said it was a little like switching from being right- to left-handed.

"Ready to go to work?" Toland asked as Harry entered the office. Harry heard him click on the tape recorder.

It felt good to have his legs up, to stare at the dimpled ceiling while the doctor lavished attention on him in the form of simple questions. When Toland asked, How are you? he really meant it. Sometimes, though, Harry thought Dr. Toland was trying to trip him up, trying to get him to admit to something awful once his defenses were down. Harry was sure he wasn't hiding anything. He'd long ago decided that he wasn't a very deep person. He was conscientious, but his politics and philosophy were only about an inch thick. Under that lay strange questions and ideas not fit for conversation, such as: How many people worldwide still named their sons Adolf? Had there always been Jewish prostitutes, or were they a result of the establishment of Israel?

"You were saying you get along well with people."

"Sure, people like me," Harry said. "They can see I haven't got a mean bone in my body." Those were Mel's words, the family's words. His official description. Possibly, his epitaph.

"Why else do people like you?"

"I'm generous—not to brag, but I am. And I'm easy to please. You know," Harry lifted his head, "there's only one food I don't like. Beets. I hate beets."

"What exactly pleases you?"

"People please me," Harry said firmly.

"All the time?"

Harry scanned a portrait gallery of his family in his mind. Only Florence had ever really been angry with him. But that was natural. "Yes."

"You always get your way?"

"Who's talking about getting my way?"

"What animal are you this instant? Say it now."

"I'm . . . a Budweiser Clydesdale. I've got big white shaggy feet."

"Where are you?"

Harry let the images flood his brain. "I'm pulling a wagon full of beer through a cobblestone street. Part of a team."

"Now you're going up a steep hill."

"My feet make a lot of noise. My big chest is pulling the wagon up."

"Feel your body," Dr. Toland ordered.

Harry became aware of his tight stomach muscles, his hands curled into fists, his forehead furrowed with effort.

"Hold that tension for a moment," Toland said. "Now the day's work is done. You're in a pasture, lying down with the other horses. Night is falling."

Harry felt his body begin to go limp. He sank deeper into the leather couch. His legs relaxed until his feet formed a V.

"Now you see your mother and brother, wife and children. All the members of your family are slowly walking into the pasture."

Harry could see them clearly. First was Bella, and holding her arm, Mel. They were dressed up like royalty, but they looked sad. "They're all crying," Harry told the doctor. He felt tension return to his body as his relatives filled the pasture, which had sand traps and rolling hills like a golf course. He watched the horde of people arrive until the pasture was tweeded with color like a football stadium on TV. And then his time was up.

Harry and Mel were having lunch at Duke Zeibert's, a restaurant where people went to be seen and where the owner, Duke, circulated among the tables. Normally, Harry brought in deli and ate it one-handed as he presided over the office hustle-bustle. He liked to eat fast. He looked at the menu. What could he order that would take a long time? Something leafy. Maybe something with bones, tiny bones.

The waiter appeared. Mel ordered a soufflé. Harry ordered smoked whitefish with cucumbers and sour cream.

"I've been thinking we ought to talk to Mama together," Harry said.

"Hmmm," Mel said.

Unlike the rest of the family, Mel talked little. Harry figured this was the result of being in the War, of having seen things that words could not change. *The Goldring Boys*, that's how they were known. But the two of them were so different. Mel vacationed at a hacienda in Mexico; Harry went to Miami where his overeating was practically deemed a mitzvah. Mel had a future as an alcoholic. Harry imagined himself keeling over on the golf course. Heart. The big heart would just stop.

"You'd think an eighty-two-year-old woman would be starved for company," Mel finally said.

Harry tried to picture Bella in the retirement home, but her figure kept looming out of focus, an expression of terror on her face. "The only people she ever wanted around was the family."

Mel set his fork down. "Suppose I call her? Make it real casual?" He signaled the waiter to bring a phone.

"You're going to tell her on the phone?"

"Mama, how are you feeling?" Mel began. A long silence followed during which, Harry knew, Bella was reporting on the condition of her bowels. "Listen," Mel said. "I want to tell you a secret." Harry perked up. "Your apartment building is going for condominiums. So Harry and I have found you a new place." Long silence. "It's big, sure. Roomy. Harry will take you to see it"—he looked over at Harry for a date—"next Thursday morning."

Harry couldn't believe it. Snap. Just like that. He had more trouble tying his shoes.

Mel was purring into the phone again. "Oh, Mama, I love you, too." He hung up. "At least she's agreed to look at the place."

"What if she doesn't like it?"

"I'm not a magician."

"Think about it," Harry countered. They both reached for the check.

Moments later, Harry handed his ticket to the valet and watched him sprint into the parking lot. When was the last time Bella had told him she loved him? His car squealed to a halt in front of him. The day of the Japanese surrender. They were listening to the radio—he and Velvel and Bella and Florence. "My Mel is coming home!" Bella shouted. She wrapped herself around Harry. "I love you," she said. "Today I love the whole world."

"Mrs. Liberman has agreed to let us look in on her." The director of the Potomac Retirement Village punched the elevator button for the eighth floor. Bella gripped the railing and stared at the numbers. They had toured the card room, the pool deck, and the arts and crafts center. Bella hadn't said a word.

Harry tried to imagine his own old age. He'd be bald as a cue ball, like Velvel. Still fat. Maybe a cane. He'd live in a condo in Florida and eat snapper almondine. Once a year he'd go north to pay his respects to family, dead and alive. The rest of the year he'd play golf and lie in the sun.

The door of 804 opened before the bell stopped chiming. "Come in!" Mrs. Liberman sang, ushering them into the foyer as the director made the introductions. Harry noticed the doorway made extrawide for wheelchairs, the red emergency buzzer, and speaker on the wall. He steered Bella to the window. "What do you think of this?" he asked. He pointed to the gardens below. "Some nice view, huh?"

"View?" Bella said. "Who sits and looks out a window all day? You have children?" she asked, turning to Mrs. Liberman.

"Of course. Over here by the sofa." Harry and Bella followed the woman to the coffee table where she picked up two framed photographs. "My son, Alan, and his wife, Marian. He's in ski equipment. Three children. All smart as a whip."

They could have been Harry's niece and nephew. His own kids, even. He'd read somewhere that the entire human race consisted of fiftieth cousins. How many pictures of children, grandchildren, and great-grandchildren were there at the Village? The faces ran together in his mind, interchangeable. Weddings, bar mitzvahs, kids in braces. Pieces of paper. Pieces of paper.

"Your children visit you?" Bella pressed.

"They moved to Colorado." Mrs. Liberman gently returned the faces to their shrine. "They used to visit. Every Saturday. Now they drop me beautiful postcards."

"Terrible," Bella whispered.

Bella the nosy. Bella with her talent for going straight to the heartache.

Mrs. Liberman scooped a handful of glossy cards from the end-table drawer. "See? The Grand Canyon. Coulee Dam. A prairie dog. A coyote."

Bella took the woman aside by the elbow. "You like it here?"

"Mrs. Liberman has been a Villager for more than three years," the director said. "She's practically a founding member, aren't you?" Mrs. Liberman nodded uncertainly.

"You have good shopping nearby?" Bella continued her interrogation. "A&P? Shoe store? Dress shop?"

"They take us on a bus." Mrs. Liberman smiled. "Sometimes we sing on the way. You'll see."

"Me? A bus?" Bella laughed. "I haven't been on a bus since Roosevelt." Harry's heart sank. His temples began to throb. Bella continued. "But I wish you long life and *nachas* from your children." She started for the door. "I hope they move back from Colorado." She exited into the hallway and stood puzzling over which way to go.

During the car ride home, Bella called the retirement village a highpriced, high-rise shtetl. Harry pointed out that she'd have maid service, a doctor on call night and day, and planned social activities. Bella said Harry had taste in his mouth. In his rear end. She wasn't going to be buried on the eighth floor like poor Mrs. Liberman. Why couldn't she buy her apartment when the building went for condos?

"You can't afford it," Harry said.

Bella glared at him. "You'll have to drag me," she announced. "I'll lie down on the floor like a hippie before I'll move."

It'll be her last move, Harry thought to himself. He was sorry he hadn't allowed the director to show them the nursing home wing. Bella could use a little humility. She'd never once referred to her own death, unlike Velvel who planned for it the way other people plan for a vacation. Oh no, mustn't aggravate Bella. That was the first commandment at home. *I'm the complaint department*, Velvel would say, smiling.

"So I'll get old like everybody else," Bella said, back in her apartment. "But not in front of strangers."

———

Harry and Florence agreed to watch their two grandsons the weekend after Elaine's breast surgery. Bella would join them for Friday dinner. Late that afternoon, Harry went around the den salting the overstuffed sofas with loose change so the boys would have something to hunt for. Weren't those kids lucky to have a grandfather like him? Still in good health, able to help out with a summer camp tuition here, a basketball hoop there. A grandfather who *spent time* with his grandsons. So what if Maury wasn't on his feet yet? Florence always said generosity and love never hurt anybody.

Maury phoned at 5:30 to report on Elaine. He told Harry the doctor had removed enough tissue to make another pair of breasts. Now they had Elaine packed in ice to prevent swelling. While Maury talked, Harry's gaze wandered to the den wallpaper, a pattern of grape leaves wound around fuzzy black vines. The room looked like a god-damn fruit farm. Why didn't he have a room like the ones in Chivas Regal ads? A leather-topped desk with gold flourishes all around the edges like a stock certificate. Wallpaper with a fox being chased by spotted dogs. The hunt. That's what he should have insisted on when Florence redecorated.

"Elaine's hot to take tennis lessons again," Maury was saying. "Nothing to get in the way of her forehand now."

"She should live and be well," Harry said. "Kiss her for me." He hung up.

He lay back in his Barcalounger, waiting and fidgeting. Florence had taken Bella with her to the beauty parlor and then to pick up the kids. Jolie Mae was in the kitchen fixing a feast. He could smell the caramel cake in the oven. His mouth watered. He remembered Bella's cooking—stuffed derma, eggplant salad. Chicken soup with kreplach on Fridays. And the cooking odors that hung in the hallways of the apartment building where he grew up. Something happened to food smells trapped there. When they all came together, the result was awful, like inhaling someone else's belch. It made him sick to remember it.

He readjusted his chair, closed his eyes, and tried to summon the Clydesdale he'd invented at Dr. Toland's. He wanted to lie down in the pasture again, but it eluded him. Instead, the evening to come played like a home movie. Florence would arrive with Bella and the boys. Bella would have that damn blue hair, and Florence's hair would feel like wire lath.

When he opened his eyes, the grapevines of the wallpaper began to twist and slither like snakes. Stress, he told himself. He shut his eyes and opened them quickly. The room was glowing, as if it had heated up. The vines were so thick and active now they threatened to pull down the walls. The bookcase leaned and swayed, ready to crash to the floor. Harry jumped up and threw his back against it. Overhead, the chandelier glinted, its long crystal drops a hundred sharpened blades. He pushed until the bookcase knocked against the wall. Suddenly he felt his heart. Not the beat of it, but its weight and shape. Big and slippery and fragile. Like one of his top-of-the-line porcelain bathtubs being delivered through a window. His whole body was slick with sweat, little pools of it in the bags under his eyes, in the folds of his neck and chin. "I'm cracking up," he said. "The end. Finito." The sound of his own voice gave him courage. He began to feel cool. He let go of the bookcase and willed the walls plumb again, the furniture upright. Then he staggered to the bathroom and took a blood pressure pill.

He returned to the den, eyeing the room from the doorway until he was certain everything in it was normal. He stretched out in the lounge chair. I'm all right. I'm in my own house. So then what was all this tumult, this brooding? he asked himself. And in the same instant he had the answer. Dr. Toland had told him to pay attention to his fantasies, to the weirdest ideas that crossed his mind. He did. And what they meant was clear: he was dying.

It wasn't as if he had pains in his chest or down his arm. He knew the signs of heart attack. This was more subtle, not symptoms but a premonition. On Saturday morning he made an appointment with the family doctor for Monday.

In the meantime, he enjoyed the easy courage of the condemned. He felt a sense of wisdom descend and wait nearby along with his own death. He was starry-eyed, like someone who had fallen in love. It irritated everyone around him. He was slow to answer questions, indecisive in the car on Sunday when they took the boys and Bella for a drive in the country. In exasperation, Florence took the wheel and drove them to Martin's Dairy. He didn't eat ice cream with the others but stood at the farm fence and watched the clouds float by, forming and re-forming like ideas in his head. A certain elegance inhabited his body.

He took the wheel for the ride home. As he pulled onto the main highway, he looked into the rearview mirror and saw Bella there, stiff as a little doll, a great-grandchild on each side of her like a set of bookends. Bella had never driven a car. How many times had she sat in the backseat, obstructing his view? A hundred? A thousand? "Mama, you're not made of glass," he said.

Bella didn't move.

"Switch places with one of the boys," he told her. "Sit by a door."

Bella was making faces, unaware he could see her in the mirror. She squirmed over and sat directly behind him.

Harry looked at the countryside flowing by. It was so beautiful, even in November with the fields died back. And the foothills, curved like a woman. Like hips and thighs and ass. God, the world was gorgeous. And he'd be leaving it soon. He'd seen his share though. He'd been to Puerto Rico and Las Vegas and everywhere plumbing conventions were held. He'd been to Israel. He and Florence had been pampered at the Duke University fat farm. He'd lived it up in Manhattan—Broadway shows, Mama Leone's, the works.

"I'm not going," Bella suddenly whispered in his ear. "I even told Mel."

Harry swerved onto the dirt shoulder of the road and stopped. A cloud of reddish dust engulfed them.

"Where are we?" one of the kids asked.

"Nowhere," Harry said. "I'm resting."

"Resting my eye," Bella snapped.

"Mama!" Harry twisted around to face her.

"Grandpa's getting *mad*," the younger boy said.

"We're going for a walk, Mama." Harry opened the door of the Buick and helped her from the car. She was biting down on her lower lip. She was always biting down on her lower lip. He did all her banking, the hiring and firing of her maids. Schlepp, schlepp. He brought her to the house once a month for dinner. What did he get for it? Bella, biting down on her lower lip.

They started walking down the white sideline of the road. Harry turned briefly back to the car, sending a signal that nailed Florence and the boys to the spot. Don't move, his eyes said. Don't you dare move or speak. His chest was pounding. His lungs felt like two pockets turned inside out. Dust went up his nose, in his mouth.

"Crazy," Bella said. "*Meshugge.*"

Harry held her by the elbow as they walked along, taking small steps.

"I'm ruining these shoes."

"Shoes are meant to be walked in, Mama." A bird flew by. "Look at that," Harry said, pointing.

"A bird," Bella said. "So what?"

"So nothing. The whole world could be without birds. Would it bother you?"

"You dragged me out here to talk about birds?"

"I want to tell you something, Mama."

Bella stopped and pulled her coat around her.

"The story of the happiest day of my life," he said, not knowing what he would say next. What was the happiest day? His wedding? The day Maury was born? The day he moved into his big new office? No. Something farther back, simpler. "Remember when I graduated high school? June 1929. The seventeen-year cicadas were out."

"Birds," Bella said. "Now bugs. So?"

"So I was eighteen, and I had a white robe and a mortarboard with a gold tassel." He hadn't looked fat in the graduation robe. He'd looked massive, imposing, a walking Greek column. The day came back to him clearly. He could see the old-model cars on the street, big and shiny and black. "It was so hot," Harry said. The day had been all green and gold and white. On the bandstand were two hundred white scrolled diplomas tied with gold ribbons. Nearby, a green-and-white striped pavilion shaded long picnic tables full of iced lemonade, the glasses already sweating in the heat. The principal read the long list of names. It was hard to hear over the racket of the cicadas, the fuzzy gold insects that lived underground for seventeen years at a stretch, then emerged for a month to mate. *Harry Goldring*, the principal said. "Remember how slowly I walked across the platform?" he asked Bella. "I kept thinking, I'm the first person to graduate high school in the whole entire family. Me. Number one."

"Number one," Bella repeated.

"I remember that Polish girl who was the valedictorian," Harry continued. "She wrote the class motto. 'Each of us will go our separate ways, holding high the banner of excellence.'" *Separate* ways. He had believed it that afternoon. He had pictured himself living in his own small apartment, riding on trains, going to the movies on his own. He stared at Bella. "Everything was gold—the drinks, the sun, the cicadas sitting in the trees. Singing. That's a love song, that noise they make—"

"I'm getting cold," Bella said. "It's nice you graduated. I'm getting cold just thinking how hot it was that day. A person could have passed out—"

"Oh God," Harry cried at the sky. "Why are You letting her interrupt me?" He grabbed Bella by the shoulders. "Don't you understand? That day," he said more quietly, tears springing to his eyes. "That day. I'm telling you everything."

She looked at him blankly. "What?" she raised her voice. "What do you want from me?"

She didn't know. None of them knew. There was a fire in him now. The fat man starving, the shoemaker who goes barefoot. I can't get enough, he thought. Why can't I ever get enough?

"Take me home," Bella said. She looked frightened. He let go of her.

They walked back to the car and got in. Florence and the boys seemed to have stopped breathing.

"I'm begging you, Harry," Bella said, pulling out a handkerchief. "Don't make me go to that place."

"I'm not making you go," Harry answered. "Just promise me you'll try it for six months. Just that long."

The idea of a compromise had obviously not occurred to Bella until now. She took a long time to answer. "No," she said.

On Monday, Harry went for a checkup. His EKG looked good, blood count completely normal. His pressure was a little high, but nothing alarming. Harry described in detail what had happened on Friday afternoon: the vines turning to snakes, the furniture about to topple, the certain knowledge that he would soon be dead. The doctor said it sounded like a panic attack.

"Do these panic attacks cause heart attacks?" Harry asked.

The doctor said they didn't. Judging from Harry's EKG, he wasn't going to have a heart attack any time soon. Harry was not relieved. The doctor suggested he talk to Toland.

On Tuesday afternoon Harry didn't lie on the couch right away. He sat across the desk from Toland. Toland nodded the whole time Harry talked, writing notes occasionally. "I still feel like I'm dying," Harry said as he finished the story.

"Yes," Toland said. "I can see that."

"You can?"

"It's just an expression."

"Oh."

"Let's try some imaging on the couch," Toland said.

Even as he stretched out, Harry saw himself blanched white as an almond, lying dead on a rug somewhere, looking much heavier than he actually was because in that position the fat spread out. He banished the image from his mind, but it hovered at the edge like a page number.

"First, tell me what's been happening. At work. With the family."

Harry told him about visiting the Village with Bella. "Bella's eighty-two, and she's not worried about dying."

"Everybody's dying," Toland said.

"It's like a job," Harry said.

"What is?"

"Dying. You're born, and then you spend the rest of your life dying. Breathing in and out. Looking at trees."

"Close your eyes," Toland said. "Let your mind drift. You're very relaxed."

But Harry couldn't relax. What about Bella? What about the Village? No, *not* the Village. Screw the Village. Good God, why had he ever considered the place? Mel's stupid idea. What did Mel know? *Gornisht.* Bella would be miserable with a social life. Better to hire a companion, someone bossy with a sense of humor. An older Jewish woman, maybe, a pensioned widow—

"You're not relaxing." Toland got up and put on a tape recording of masted ships in the wind. "Try again."

"All right," Harry said. Behind his eyes he saw nothing but a deep orange color. He listened to the peaceful creaking of canvas and rigging. The ocean yawned gently. The ships rocked in the white-toothed waves.

"Go wherever you like," Toland said.

Harry drove to Florida in a dove gray Cadillac. The car had a sail, like a boat, and sped down U.S. 1 and then I-95 on gusts of wind. The trees changed from hardwoods to pine and then cabbage palms and magnolias. Farther south, swaying royal palms bowed down before him. He could smell the cold steam of the ocean. When he reached Coconut Grove, he parked his car on the beach, aimed at Africa, where the surf would be crashing over it by morning. He got out and walked toward a dense thicket of mangroves. Weeks passed, months. "I've gone into the tropics. Into the wilderness," he told Toland dreamily. He was going to live off his own fat, ha ha, instead of the fat of the land. Much much later, he surfaced on Collins Avenue in Miami Beach, a thin figure in a white suit that caught the neon glow of the hotel signs. "No one recognizes me," Harry said. He opened his eyes and grinned.

"Give them a little time," Toland said.

Her Michelangelo

Riva Stern was going to save Paul Auerbach. She was going to save him for college and law school and a house in the suburbs and three or four children. She would save him for the world, like bolstering Albert Schweitzer at a crucial point early in his career.

Paul was the poorest person Riva knew. He was poorer than the maid who had taken care of the Sterns for more than fifteen years. He was poorer, even, than Tante and Uncle, her old Russian relatives who still had a party line and lived in a black neighborhood. They spoke hatchet English, and their dingy little apartment always smelled of candle wax and boiled beef with carrots. Riva had never seen Tante in anything but a housecoat. Because of their age and piety, no one in the family took note of their poverty in a critical way. No one pointed to it as a sign of failure. They did not drive a car. They couldn't afford to go anywhere but the synagogue, and they received the hand-me-downs and charity of at least twenty-five family members with utter dignity. And Paul Auerbach was poorer even than that, though his poverty had the same sort of grace, a kind of storybook quality.

Paul had been working for his uncle at the wholesale produce market in downtown Washington since he was nine years old. He hawked fruits and vegetables from 4 A.M. to noon on Saturdays and on Wednesday mornings until it was time to go to school. Once, right after she got her license, Riva had driven there and from her car had watched the customers surge along the narrow streets and alleys lined with pushcarts and trucks. Haggard men in knit caps and shabby coats weighed and bagged tomatoes, celery, endive, calling out their bargains to passersby. Torn vegetables slicked the pavements, and the gutters ran with the juices of the discards, the overripe, the accidentally dropped. Paul, wearing big leather gloves and a dirty white apron over several layers of old clothes, was carrying bushels of something heavy, his body moving with the fierce rhythms of concentration, his face red with effort and the cold. He hadn't seen her.

You couldn't tell Paul was poor. Until she began to date him, Riva thought he was shy or antisocial. He had a beat-up car, which, she found out later, he owned with his older brother who had already left home. Paul, in fact, spent most of his energy trying to look and act as middle class as anyone else, even though his home life was a nightmare. Riva didn't mind having to buck him up. He was worth it. Because poverty was abstract to Riva, she had a bottomless faith in his ability to overcome it, and her faith was contagious. Also, she was good at talking people into things.

Now she sat in her mother's Buick in a downpour in front of the public library waiting for Paul. She had told her parents she'd be out until ten, studying for a Latin exam. On the phone, Paul had said something was wrong. He needed to see her. Riva loved being needed. She thought she would make a wonderful wife for some brilliant, successful man, like a physicist or a writer.

Through the sheeting rain, she made out his finned, grass green Oldsmobile. She pulled up the hood of her raincoat and when Paul drove up alongside, darted from her car to his. Then she slid across the seat and kissed him on the cheek. "I don't know why I came," he said. "Talking about it isn't going to change a thing."

"Let's go someplace."

He headed in the direction of Tacoma Park, to a back road that dead-ended under a train trestle. They often went there to neck. They had discovered it one Sunday in the fall when they took a hamper lunch to the park.

It had taken Riva months to get Paul to confide in her. He was deeply ashamed of his family. But now he trusted her completely in a way that he would probably never trust anyone again in his life. His need was that great.

The sky was a dull red above the glistening street lights as he maneuvered through traffic along Georgia Avenue. The rain made liquid jewels of the neon signs for Little Tavern hamburgers and Midas mufflers and Ramco Auto Upholstery. Riva had become more aware of her surroundings lately. She would be leaving for college in the fall, and she would probably never live here again, except for the summers. She and Paul planned to write to each other and spend vacations together. She liked thinking about that arrangement—Paul tucked away in her life, like a lucky coin you could keep in your pocket and never spend. Riva was a "brain," and Paul was the only boy at Hoover High School she had ever dated. Unlike most boys, he wasn't afraid to date a girl who made better grades than he did. Or maybe he figured that his grades would have matched hers if he had more time to spend on schoolwork.

Paul parked under the trestle, and they cracked their windows. It was the end of March, and they could smell the change of seasons in the sharp, damp air. Outside the car, the first green shoots worked their way up through a thick brown carpet of dead grass.

"I won't be going to San Antonio," he said. He linked his hands together and cracked his knuckles. Paul had won the school debating contest. The prize was $300 and the honor of representing the school at the National Polemics Competition.

"Oh no," Riva said. The story would be terrible; it would make her cry for Paul. The story would be about his disreputable father and his pathetic mother. She put her arms around him and lay her head on his shoulder and waited.

"He heard about the money. He said he had to pay these bills. He showed me a bill for three months' rent for the apartment."

"How did he find out?"

"What difference does it make?"

"Maybe he heard your mother telling somebody about the prize." As soon as Riva said it, she could see Mrs. Auerbach herself telling her husband about the money—being proud of Paul, not realizing what would happen next. "You have to go. You could win the $2,500 grand prize."

"I know."

"You've still got three weeks. Maybe your brother can help you out. Maybe you'll let me help you out—"

"No!" His eyes flashed. He punched the dashboard with his fist.

"Don't do that to yourself." Riva stroked his hand.

He forced a smile and combed through his hair with his fingers. "Right. New topic. You've got your big test tomorrow. Come on, let's conjugate a couple of verbs." He whispered it into her ear. "You're so luscious."

"God, you're sweet." She kissed his hand. "You could take the money out of your college savings."

Paul had a savings account at the bank that only Riva—not even his mother or brother—knew about. In three years he had managed to save $1,500 toward tuition at George Washington University.

"I can't do that. I'm already short for the first semester unless I can get a loan. I'm counting on getting a loan."

She stroked his sand-colored, slightly greasy hair that felt like silk in her fingers, like silk embroidery floss. She comforted him, and together they tried to figure a way for him to accumulate the money before the end of April. Then they necked, just a little, just to cheer him up. She unzipped his pants and drew circles around his cock with her fingers until he was hard, and then they kissed a little more, and then he drove her back to the library.

The next morning was a Friday, and Riva lay in bed before the alarm clock rang pondering Paul's problems. Paul had a secret that no one at school except Riva knew: he supported himself. Sometimes he had to help support his mother and father. This had been going on since he was fourteen. In the past, in addition to working at the farmers' market, Paul had held various part-time jobs, most of them in sales. He had sold Kirby vacuum cleaners and the Encyclopedia Judaica and men's monogrammed golfing shirts. He had demonstrated the Kirby for Riva and her mother one Sunday evening. Mrs. Stern had taken quite an interest in it until she realized that she didn't care what kind of vacuum she owned since the maid was the only one who used it. But she admired its engineering, she told Paul. In two months' time, he sold only one Kirby.

Riva had tried to lend him money, but he refused it. The most she could offer was a gift now and then—a sweater for his birthday, a shirt at Hanukkah. Paul loved clothes. He took fastidious care of his few things, ironing the shirts himself, keeping them folded in Saran Wrap in his drawer. He was the only boy she knew who polished his shoes. He couldn't achieve the flashy look of the wealthier boys, but he bought quality. He watched the papers for sales. He chose conservative colors and styles that blended together. Almost nobody noticed him one way or the other. When Riva first talked about dating him, her friends had difficulty calling up the matching face: "Paul Auerbach? Who does he hang out with?" And Riva would patiently explain where he sat in Chemistry or World Lit and that he didn't have time for a real social life like other kids.

She could remember the exact moment she had noticed him. It was the third week of school, in Civics. She was in her assigned seat in the first row and he was standing right in front of her giving an oral report and the edge of her desk cut into his thighs. He was nervous and stuttered a little. His intense hazel eyes stared fixedly at the back of the room where Dr. Voski sat, grading him on completeness, accuracy, and presentation. For a moment, it looked like he was getting a hard-on from his nerves. That happened to some boys, Riva knew, but then he shifted his weight and the bulge disappeared. He dropped a note card on her desk toward the end, and when she handed it back to him, he had looked startled, as if he hadn't noticed her before. That night she had dreamed about him. It was one of those dreams that makes you fall in love, whether you want to or not. This had happened to Riva before. When she was twelve, she had dreamed about Tab Hunter after she saw him in a movie. She had a terrible crush on him after that. And in eighth grade she'd had a love dream about Eliot Finkelstein that rendered her mute for weeks in his presence. After her dream about Paul, she had talked to him in school the next day. What had been the pretext? She had sold him a ticket for the

Latin Club's raffle, and then he had walked her to the cafeteria and asked her for a date.

"Riva! Riva diva!" Barry called out. "I'm leaving here in exactly five minutes." Barry was her twenty-one-year-old brother. He dropped her off at school every morning on the way to work.

Riva lunged from between the covers and reached for the day's clothes draped across a chair, a cerise wool skirt and matching sweater. "Be right down," she called back.

Paul was absent that day from school. During lunch she called his house. She had to be careful about phoning there. His father did not like Paul to receive calls from girls. His mother was more understanding. His mother, Riva thought with a start, would not know how to push a rat away that was gnawing on her face.

"Why aren't you here?" Riva asked.

"He's left again. She's very upset."

"He left even though you gave him the money?"

"Yeah. Look," Paul whispered, "I can't talk now."

"Call me tonight. I love you."

"Tonight."

That night, after she and Paul talked, Riva wrote in her diary. She made a list of ways she could help him raise the money for San Antonio. She wrote down everything she could think of, as fast as she could write:

1. *Get the money somehow and make him let me lend it to him.*
2. *Give the money to the school (after I get it) and have them give it to him, compliments of "anonymous."*
3. *Give the money to his mother to give him. Swear her to secrecy.*
4. *TALK TO POP GOLDRING!!!*

She had been keeping a diary for nearly three years. When she entered high school, her mother had bought her a "Chums" desk set—a matching blotter, pencil holder, scrapbook, and five-year diary in pink leather. Carefree teenagers resembling the "Archie" cartoon characters strolled along each piece, their books slung casually across their hips. The diary had lasted a little more than a year. Then Riva spilled over into a serious-looking lined notebook with a black-and-white marbleized cardboard cover. She kept the diary and the notebook hidden in her closet at the bottom of a tall Kotex box, along with the novel she had written in eighth grade. "Once Only" was the story of a fifteen-year-old girl who fell in love with an alien from another galaxy. It was based loosely on her crush for Eliot Finkelstein.

Riva had devised a code for her diaries. She stashed the code-key in the pages of an old Honey Bunch mystery. *The blood the first two days this month was the color of crushed rubies. . . . I like the sickening feeling I get before my period comes—like when you eat too much chocolate and the stomachache reminds you of all that pleasure. Only this reminds me that I can bring a new human being into the world any time I want!* She would have died if anybody else read these passages. Especially Barry. Even though he was grown-up, she still remembered the days when he unscrewed the heads of her dolls, put raw oysters in her bed, and shot food at her across restaurant tables. Barry had grown into his lanky body and turned out to be handsome, much to Riva's surprise. Now he was engaged to Olivia Wykowski, a beautiful redhead two years older than he. Riva's family believed in early marriage. Her sister, Fran, had married at eighteen and so had her cousin Melissa. Whenever Riva saw distant relatives, they talked about living to dance at her wedding.

Olivia had the look of an airline stewardess—a permanent smile and perfect makeup, her hair sprayed into a stiff beehive. Riva couldn't stand her. Her diary was full of invective for PV (Olivia's code name, short for Professional Virgin) who, five years Riva's senior, treated her like a little mouse. Now that they were officially engaged, Barry and Olivia were planning to go to Atlantic City the last weekend in April. They talked about it all the time in front of her parents as if to forestall suspicion that they would Do Anything. Riva was sure Olivia hadn't done it. You could tell by looking in her eyes, Riva believed. She got up from her desk and studied her reflection. Anybody could see she was still untouched, even though Paul had been pressing his case hard since January. Riva hadn't worked out a philosophy to justify why she hadn't done it yet. It was just safer to say "no." She felt the same urges Paul did. Sometimes she nearly went crazy when they were fingerfucking. She had to remind herself that it wasn't just a technicality, the difference between a finger and the real thing.

―――――――――――

Riva had a four o'clock appointment with Pop Goldring on Tuesday. As soon as school let out at three, she took the streetcar and bus to Du Pont Circle, stopping for a cherry Coke at the drugstore on the ground floor of his building so that she wouldn't be early.

Pop Goldring was prosperous. He had a construction company with his son, Mel, and had built many office and apartment buildings around the city. Mrs. Stern kept a scrapbook of clippings about her father and brother, who were periodically honored for their philanthropy. Pop Goldring had planted a lot of trees in Israel. He probably had a whole forest by now. But he wasn't generous just for the publicity or the tax deductions. Once, many years before, he had supported an American artist in Italy. Alongside the plaques and certificates in his office hung a huge painting by the man, the portrait of a family of jesters. They wore velvety red clothing and stocking caps with bells. They were traveling to their next court performance, the artist had explained. The father jester walked along, playing the flute. The mother and one child perched astride an ox. A mysterious winged infant balanced on the ox's rump, his back to the viewer. Behind them, fields, sky, and mountains flattened into shapeless daubs of bright blue, yellow, and orange. No one in the family knew what had happened to the artist—whether he kept on painting or was butchering meat somewhere for a living. Pop called the painting "my Michelangelo," and he thought it just as artistic as the bust of Moses by the other Michelangelo that sat on his desk.

The receptionist buzzed his office, and he promptly appeared in the reception area. He was a squat, heavyset man with light blue eyes and wisps of white hair around a large bald spot. His face was wide and Slavic-looking, with high cheekbones and a broad forehead. "Sweetheart," he said, giving her a big hug. He had a heavy Russian-Yiddish accent. Years later, Riva would melt whenever she heard that accent, even from the mouths of second-rate stand-up comics.

His office was uncluttered, outfitted with modern furniture that was sleek and low-slung like cats relaxing all around the room. Even the desk top was clear except for a few letters and an ashtray with a half-smoked cigar in it. His home was the opposite—it glittered with gilt tables, Victorian whatnots, and crystal decanters. Grandma Bella was constantly rearranging it like a gigantic still life. Only the den was livable. As a child, it was the only room Riva had been allowed in.

"How's my Einstein?" he asked.

"Everything's great. I came to ask you a favor."

His gaze intensified. Riva had never asked him for anything before.

"I have a good friend who needs money, and I want you to give it to him. I want you to buy him an airline ticket to San Antonio, Texas."

"You're asking for a complete stranger?"

"Actually, you met him during Christmas when he picked me up at your apartment. His name is Paul Auerbach."

Pop Goldring narrowed his eyes, trying to recall the boy. He shook his head. "I don't remember any Paul. What does his father do? He's a Jewish boy?"

"Yes. His father drives a cab."

"A taxi driver?"

"They're very poor. His mother can't work. She's an invalid. She got polio right after Paul was born. She has an awful limp and a bad lung."

"A shame," Pop said. "He's smart?"

Riva told him about the debate contest and how hard Paul had worked all his life. He listened attentively. "You love him? You're going to marry him?"

"I'm too young to marry anybody," Riva said. It was the one area where she and her grandfather would never see eye to eye. While he celebrated her triumphs at school, he would never really be relaxed about her future until she married.

"All right. I'll do it. Call Nancy with the details."

Riva jumped up and kissed him. "Thank you, thank you, thank you."

"He'll take charity, your Paul?"

"He doesn't know about it yet. I hope I can make him accept it. He'll probably want to repay you someday. He has a lot of pride."

"I hope so, if only for your sake."

"Pop? Can we keep this a secret? I don't want anybody else in the family to know. It might be embarrassing later."

Riva's family had memories like elephants, especially for foibles and mistakes. The only way you could live something down with them was to be reincarnated. If she did end up marrying Paul, it would be bad enough when her family learned how disreputable the Auerbachs were. That would be soon enough for them to begin doubting Paul. Riva was certain that Paul's noble character had survived and maybe even been honed by his terrible family, but she knew how adults saw these things. They wouldn't praise him for overcoming so many handicaps; they would wait for the day when the offspring reverted to type, when the ugly head of the parent reared up in the child.

Paul lived in a small apartment building in a neighborhood tucked between a Trailways bus terminal and a complex of warehouses. Tonight, when she arrived, Riva was relieved that Mr. Auerbach's cab wasn't anywhere in sight. The parking lot was brightly lit, but the stairs to the entrance were dark, and the hallway smelled rank. The Auerbachs lived on the ground floor. Their living room was full of black vinyl furniture and cheap pole lamps. Everything in it was ugly except for the afghans that Mrs. Auerbach crocheted and draped over the furniture.

If she had called first tonight, Paul would have wanted to meet her someplace. She wanted him to know she didn't care where he lived or who his father was. She wanted to tell him about Pop Goldring. She would tell his mother, too, if she felt like it. There would be nothing any of them could do to ruin it. The airline ticket was in Paul's name. Nancy, Pop's secretary, had reserved a room at the Gunter Hotel, and when Paul tried to settle the bill, he would find that it was already paid.

Paul was embarrassed at first to hear her news. Then he was very grateful. Afterward, he followed her home in his car. They told Mrs. Stern they were going to the Hot Shoppe for a snack. She and Paul went to the park.

"How can I ever pay you back? It worries me, Riva. Money between friends can lead to problems." He was carefully unbuttoning her blouse.

"What kind of problems?"

"I don't know exactly. I know my father hasn't got a friend left in the world, and they've all helped him."

"You're not your father."

He buried his head between her breasts, then rolled from one to the other, kissing. He had the softest lips of any human being alive and a tongue like a sweet little animal. "Oh God," he moaned, "I love you so much. You'll never know how much it means to have your love."

Before he went to San Antonio, Paul spent every spare minute beefing up his debate skills on the assigned topic: Should the U.S. Recognize Castro's Cuba? Three-by-five index cards accumulated in drifts on his desk in study hall. Paul would be called upon to argue both sides. That was the thing about being a good debater—you had to be able to fake the passion of your argument, and you had to know what the opposition was going to say. Paul would make a fine lawyer. His poverty gave him an appetite for justice in the world.

Things at home improved. His father had returned after a spree in Florida and was driving his cab every day. A couple of mornings he had slipped Paul a five spot at breakfast.

Paul left for Texas on a Thursday evening at the end of April. He called Riva twice. On Saturday, he sounded ecstatic. He praised Tex-Mex foods she had never heard of—sauces concocted of chocolate and hot peppers, cactus fruit and *cabrito* and tequila. He had gone to a nightclub where a Mexican mariachi band with huge guitars played until dawn. He cursed the afternoon tour-bus driver and called one of his debate opponents a "pubic hair" in Spanish. He had made dozens of friends, he said, despite the pressures of the competition. Everyone was so friendly. He loved the Lone Star State. It was southern and western at the same time—the best of both worlds. The weather was perfect. He'd even been swimming at the hotel pool. He didn't worry about the chlorine ruining his new madras shorts. He was having too good a time to worry about anything. His joy confirmed what Riva had long believed about Paul—that given half a chance in life he would be a raving success. He would know how to work hard and play hard. He would achieve what Pop Goldring had—the happiness of the self-made man.

"What about your debates?"

"I'm doing great. I'm here, I'm having fun. For the first time in my life, I'm really having fun. You know," he grew wistful, "now I see what I've missed all my life."

"You mean a vacation?"

"Some people's lives are vacations," Paul said. "I've got to go. I'm on early tomorrow morning again."

A huge storm front lashed the mid-Atlantic states that weekend. It rained in Washington and Virginia and Maryland and Delaware and even in Atlantic City, New Jersey, where Barry and Olivia huddled, no doubt, against the dampness in their hotel suite. Riva missed Paul. She watched her parents moving past each other all weekend and thought what a waste it was that they were in the same house yet kept their bodies completely separate. She walked from room to room, staring out at the rain. She imagined herself inside a paperweight, a raining paperweight. Beyond her windows, it wasn't raining. The sun was beating down everywhere else on shining streets, giving off that summery odor of heat and growth, especially in San Antonio, Texas.

Olivia and Barry brought back saltwater taffy twisted in waxed paper like party favors for everyone in the family. Paul brought Riva a silver pin from Mexico—the figure of a peasant in a serape drowsing under a huge sombrero, kind of like the Frito Bandito, he said, describing it over the phone to her late Sunday night when he returned from the airport. Paul finished seventh out of two hundred in the competition—not in the money but close enough for a special certificate of Honorable Mention. "'Know Ye by These Presents,'" he read to her. "Well, you can imagine the rest."

"I'm dying to see you. I really missed you. I love you so much."

"I know. I want to see you, too. Tomorrow," he promised.

Would she ever say these words to any other boy or man? She had nothing to go on but movies and the books she'd read. If her parents traded endearments, they did it when they were alone, never in front of the children.

She and Paul kissed outside of school the next morning, before the first bell rang, but he was busy after that. He was a celebrity, with tall tales to tell. She let him shine in his glory. This is what it would be like when they were older—Riva behind the scenes, modest, sure of his unswerving love. Maybe a couple of trusted servants to buffer them from the clamoring world. Deep, knowing looks—a raised eyebrow, the slightest inclination of the head. They would hardly need words at all. And Riva would take pride in believing in him when no one else did, like Van Gogh's brother, Theo. They would be completely devoted to each other. Forever. It would take that long for her to finish loving him.

This blood, Riva wrote that night. *This is the lifeblood. This blood belongs to Paul Auerbach. My wonderful, hardworking Paul who will never take me for granted.*

"I won't be going to college after all," Paul said. He gripped the steering wheel with one hand, turning it rapidly from left to right.

"What?"

He repeated himself. His voice was shaking.

"But it's all worked out, you'll get a loan, you might get a scholarship."

"Forget the scholarship. I never counted on the scholarship. That's just a fairy tale you believed in."

"I thought you had a chance."

"Maybe if I do well the first year. But they'd rather give it to an out-of-state student than to me."

"And the loan by itself isn't enough?"

"It might be if it were big enough."

"Well then what's the problem?" Riva asked, her voice rising against her will.

"My savings are gone as of tonight."

"Oh my God. You gave him the money?"

"I had to." He started to cry. "I had to," he said again. "That bastard. I hate him. I wish he'd die."

"I'm so sorry."

"He doesn't care about my life. I'm his son, and he doesn't care shit for me."

"You have to go to college. You have to. Even if it's part-time at first. Even if you have to go at night."

"I'm so tired of fighting for every little thing."

Riva looked around. In the distance, past the train trestle, a few houselights glowed, smears of yellow and white beyond the windshield, blurred in the thick, low-hanging mist. The trees were fringed with little flaglets of leaves that shook in the evening air. They made a rustling sound, like something breathing out there. "You can't give up," she said.

"Yes I can. I can get that job at Hahn's. There's nothing wrong with selling shoes."

She took his head in her hands and kissed his forehead. "You deserve better. You're going to be a great lawyer. I believe in you." Riva's mind was already racing: how would he raise $1,500 in five months when it had taken him three years to save it up the first time? Maybe it was cruel to keep on encouraging him. After all, she had never been poor. Her closet was jammed full of clothes. She'd never ironed a shirt in her life. She didn't even pick up her dirty underpants off the floor if she didn't feel like it. "You'll get the money somehow."

"I don't care anymore," he said dully. He looked askance and nodded to himself. "I'm going to take you home now."

"No! I don't want to go home yet."

"I'm really tired," he said.

"This could be the most important night in your life."

"Just the worst," he said.

"This is the night you have to be very strong. I love you," she told him, pulling him toward her. She was going to make him believe in himself as much as she did. Couldn't he tell how much she loved him? "It would be like a betrayal if you gave up. What about our life together?"

"You should find somebody else."

"Come here," she said. She opened the door and got out of the car. "Let's take a walk." Within a few paces, she had disappeared into the ground fog.

"Riva?"

"I'm over here. Come on. Bring the blanket."

He got out of the car and walked toward her voice.

She kissed him all over after they lay down on the blanket. She traced his face with her fingertips and wrote "I adore you" on his brow. She could make him forget how bad he felt. She had that power over him.

"God, Riva," he said. "You're driving me crazy I love you so much."

"Do you have . . . protection?" she asked.

"I won't finish inside you."

Paul had met lots of subtle people in San Antonio. That was his word—"subtle." Cool, neat, hip. Sophisticated, though they were only kids. They came from New York City, Santa Barbara and Grosse Pointe, Lake Forest and New Canaan. They went to prep schools like Miss Porter's in Farmington and the Friends School in Shaker Heights and Groton and Andover. It wasn't just that they were rich. Money hadn't spoiled them, Paul said, it had refined them. They could afford to be nice to everybody, because jealousy was practically beyond them. They all had jolly nicknames—Puffer and Ships and Ironlegs for the boys, Beanstalk, Barnum, and Smash for the girls. Naturally, he'd also met kids from public schools; they were bright and well-off, too. The weekend had been a revelation to him. Riva tried her best to keep track of all the people in the anecdotes Paul told—a succession of minor pranks and triumphs over authority, at least half of which hadn't happened in San Antonio at all but had merely been retold there. "They made me feel like one of them," Paul kept saying. "They treated me like one of them."

"You *were* one of them, silly," Riva said. "You won the right to be there just like they did."

"I have to laugh now at the kids here at school, like Duke Weinstein acting so stuck-up because his father is the Pabst Blue Ribbon distributor. Ships Stewart's father owns a steel mill, and Donald, from Chicago, is *the* heir to the Quaker Oats fortune."

Now that Paul had had a taste of real money, his own poverty in relation to the wealth of the kids at Hoover High seemed less extreme. This despite the fact that his financial problems were never greater. He'd been accepted to GW, gotten a small loan, been turned down for the scholarship, and had no way of paying for the first semester. Somehow, though, when he talked about San Antonio, it soothed him. He had seen the effects of great wealth and they were so pleasant, so ordinary, that he was able to dismiss the present as a temporary state of affairs. He had, in short, learned that he was worthy, that poverty was indeed not a punishment but a caprice of fate. His pride softened and two weeks later, when Riva suggested that he meet Pop Goldring about borrowing the money for college, he agreed.

"What kind of lawyer? Corporate? Tax? Malpractice?" Pop Goldring's voice was calm, like an animal grazing over a vast field. He spoke slowly, one question after another. The Spanish Inquisition, Riva thought. She had tried to prepare Paul for the interview. Now she had to sit quietly, without interfering or interrupting. She didn't want to make Paul look weak. He could answer any question himself, anyway. The worst would be about his family. His face would get red and blotchy and circles would spread under his armpits beneath his gray tweed sport coat. Inside the white collar of his shirt and the thin black suede tie she'd given him, his neck looked as delicate and vulnerable as an antelope's. The skin there was soft and smooth. His Adam's apple reminded her of his cock.

Riva studied the huge painting by her grandfather's Michelangelo. The watercolors were so soft and muted that the harlequins' bodies could have been clouds as easily as flesh. The jesters walked toward her as if borne in a wash of their own music and the sweet heavy breath of the ox.

"You plan to live at home?"

"I have to. If I could afford it, I'd join a fraternity and live at the frat house," Paul was saying.

"Your parents are a bad influence on you," Pop Goldring said. He flicked a gold Ronson lighter, and the end of his cigar glowed briefly while he sucked on it.

Paul said nothing.

"Your father drinks?"

"No, sir."

"Where does all the money go?"

"He gambles, sir."

"You're not a good risk." Pop turned away and pulled open a desk drawer.

Riva stopped breathing. Paul's face flushed with rage or shame or both. He looked down at the floor.

"I couldn't give you the money directly. I'll pay the school. Like I'm going to do for Riva. For the first year. Then, we'll talk again. You'll pay me back when you're established."

"I'll put it in writing, sir." Paul's voice cracked with emotion as he stood and offered her grandfather his hand. "I don't know how to thank you enough, sir."

"I don't need it in writing. I build apartments with five hundred units on a handshake." He pumped Paul's hand, then inhaled on his cigar again. "You'll send me a letter, with the amount and the address."

"Yes, sir."

Riva kissed her grandfather and hugged him and kissed him again. As she turned to go, she eyed the harlequins, watching to see if their gaze followed her across the room. It didn't. She supposed that meant it wasn't a very good painting.

"You've saved my life!" Paul said in the elevator.

"I'm so happy for you. And proud. You made a very good impression."

"You've saved my fucking life." He slipped his hand under her yellow cashmere sweater and inside her bra in one swift move. "My life," he said again.

In Chemistry class, Riva stared out the window at the green curtain of mulberry trees that lined the athletic field and imagined the two of them lying on a soft blanket beneath them. Paul was on top, launching himself into her. Love was a presence, as real and invisible as the elements that expanded and contracted that late spring according to the beautiful, orderly laws of gases. Exotic substances evaporated and then collected again, distilling in the beakers, dripping from the retorts. It looked like magic, and Riva could only fathom it a little at a time, like love or God. She and Paul sat miles apart in the old-fashioned classroom with the floor that sloped like a movie theater. She could see the back of his head, his shoulders attentive through an oxford-cloth shirt. She knew his body intimately now—how the knobs of his spine disappeared between his shoulder blades like an underground spring and rose up again where the neck connected to the torso; the lobes of his ears, delicate as the rolled edges of silk scarves; the tawny odor of his sweat and semen. They owned each other now. The radio was a boxful of love songs. The days grew warmer, and Paul already looked collegiate in his chino pants, V-neck pullover, and plaid shirt. They never went anywhere on dates anymore. They lived in the car.

On the first Saturday in June, Paul called Riva. He had just returned from the produce market, showered, and changed clothes. He sounded excited. His brother had a friend who had an apartment in downtown D.C., and Paul had arranged for them to use it that night.

"Use it?" Riva repeated.

"Yeah."

"Oh." Riva hesitated. Another technicality, wasn't it, whether they made love in the car or in some stranger's apartment? "Okay, great," she said.

"Do you want to go to the movies first?"

"Sure."

The movie flickered across the screen like the shifting patterns in a kaleidoscope. It felt like a long delay and only made Riva nervous. She remembered stories she'd heard of priests and rabbis being found in the arms of prostitutes after hotel fires. Whatever happened in the car, no one questioned their right to be in it. But an apartment was premeditated. It scared her.

"Here we are," Paul said. He turned the key in the second-story walk-up. They were somewhere on the unfashionable edge of Georgetown. The building was ugly red brick in a fake castle style with turrets and bulging bay windows. "This place gives me the creeps," Riva said.

"You'll feel better once we're inside."

"I hope so."

The furnishings were ordinary, but you could tell a single man lived there from the dark, suit colors and the piles of sports magazines. Paul turned on a table lamp and held out his arms. She went obediently to his embrace. "Come on. I'm going to make you a famous Tequila Sunrise," he said. He walked her to the kitchen where a bottle of tequila was waiting on the counter. It was the first time they had ever had a drink together.

"You had this in Texas?"

"Right."

"Make mine real sweet," Riva said. "I hate the taste of liquor."

He added an extra measure of grenadine, and she watched the fuchsia color swirl and dissipate into the orange juice. Her legs started to feel numb after a couple of swallows. "It's strong, isn't it?"

"Pretty strong. It's a shot and a half of liquor."

He took their glasses into the living room, turned off the lights, and undressed down to his Jockey shorts. "No steering wheel and no seat back," he said. "What luxury." He came over and kissed her on the neck. But when she began to remove her skirt, he grabbed her wrist. "Leave it on," he said. "Please." He reached up under it and pulled her underpants down and unhooked her bra under her blouse. Then he dragged a bar stool into the middle of the room and sat down on it. "Come over here and sit on my lap," he said.

She sat on his lap sidesaddle, as if he were going to tell her a story. His soft lips nuzzled her ear and jawline. Everywhere his warm breath touched, she ached with longing. "Turn around and face me," he said, and then he was inside her, thrusting, his hands gripping her breasts under her blouse. A wave of nausea washed over her. "Wait," she protested.

"I'm really hot," he said.

"It hurts!" she lied.

He pulled out of her abruptly, still rocking back and forth slightly. She got up and sat on the sofa, her skirt wound tightly around her legs.

"I don't feel very good," she said.

"Maybe it's the booze."

"I don't know." But it wasn't the booze. "It makes me feel bad being here," she blurted.

"I thought you'd like it. It's like being married, in a way."

"It makes me feel cheap."

"I'm sorry."

"I want to go home."

"Come on," he argued. "We just got here. Come on." He sat down next to her and began kissing her neck again, and her eyelids. "Come on. It'll be all right."

But it wasn't all right. "Something's different," she said.

He sighed and sat back against the sofa cushions. "Yes," he said. "For the first time in my life I'm not worried about money. God, I'm so happy not to have to worry about money for five minutes."

He got up and went into the kitchen to fix another drink. When he came back, he stood at the window and stared out. "I just can't lie to you," he said. "You mean too much to me."

He was going to say something she didn't want to hear and she couldn't stop him.

"I met this person in Texas," he began. "Her name is Merle. She's from New York."

Riva pulled on her underpants and fastened her bra while he spoke. If she kept busy, if she could just keep busy, she could hear the words but they wouldn't penetrate, like knives clattering along the surface, not sinking in. Later, when she was alone, she could call up the words and turn them over slowly.

Merle this and that. Merle who looks like you, the same dark hair and friendly eyes. Merle whose father invented contact lenses. Something came over me. Merle who didn't know I was poor. She's written every day. We've been talking on the phone. I feel better now that I've told you. Oh Riva, I'm sorry. I didn't want to hurt you. Do you have to be hurt? I still love you, Riva. It's confusing. I didn't have to tell you.

"Yes you did," Riva said. "Oh yes you did. But you didn't. You made me make you confess. I don't want to hear your shitty confession."

He took her home, holding her hand as he drove, trying to comfort her, apologizing over and over. Making her swear she forgave him. By the time he dropped her off, he'd stopped talking about loving her and had made her promise they'd stay friends.

Mrs. Stern was insistent: she wanted the specific reason that Riva and Paul had broken up. Riva was too humiliated to say she'd been jilted and too loyal to use the loan from Pop Goldring as an excuse. She considered telling her mother the exquisite lie that they had broken up over whether to have sex or not, but a sense of dread and superstition stopped her. Finally, she said that she and Paul had incompatible values. When Mrs. Stern asked what that meant, Riva said he laughed at all the wrong parts in the movies and probably wouldn't make a good father.

So this is how the broken heart beats. The same way as the whole heart, only you feel every contraction like a refusal. That was very nice. It was really very nice. *Someday, years from now, I will see Paul, maybe with this Merle, maybe with someone else. And we will greet each other and act very polite and civilized. But I will know the minute I see him, even if it's thirty years from now, I will know from looking in his eyes if he ever forgot me. And that,* she wrote, *is the only time, those are the only circumstances when I would ever consider making love with him again.*

On
the
Land

Taking Names

I'd never served on a jury before. In fact, I hadn't
been downtown for years—ever since they built the Falling Waters
Mall. Stan assured me I'd have no trouble spotting the new courthouse. "It'll be the only building with portholes over the entrance,"
he said, "like a big ship in dry dock." He drove me to the kiss-and-
ride, and from there I took a bus.

The woman in the information booth pointed me to an elevator
before I got close enough for her to hear my question. Everyone got
off at four and streamed into the jury pool room.

I sat down and picked up an old copy of *Life*. "Nine o'clock. Let's
get going," a man at the microphone announced. "Anybody here
who can't serve this week?" I leaned forward, thinking of Stan alone

at the farm with all the grafted trees that needed repotting. About fifty people stood up, waving their jury duty notices and talking. "Form a line," he ordered over the hubbub. I read about John Hinckley wanting to go home for Christmas until I heard the man's voice again. "Listen for your name," he said. A long scroll of computer printout spilled from his podium. "It's a punishable offense to be absent, so make sure I get you." As he went down the list, one by one people slumped back in their chairs, as if released from a magnet.

"Now you wait. When we need you, we'll call you. No leaving the room. You've got two TVs, books, cards, magazines, checkerboards, puzzles, restrooms, and a coffeepot."

The woman next to me had brought knitting—blue yarn with a silver fleck running through it that matched her tinted hair. Across from us, a group was forming to work a thousand-piece puzzle. "I'm good at finding the borders," I said, diving into the confetti-like mess. The box lid pictured an iceberg drifting at sundown, the colors of sky and sea nearly indistinguishable. Hard on the eyes but a good test of concentration.

A bell rang. "Williams, DeBaro, Feldman, Sanchez—that's Rosario—Gold, Eaugalle, Chesterton, Whelan, Eisenblatt, Samuels, Lattore, Jabotinsky, Wood, and Helms." He read the list rapidly, as if they were all one name. We congregated near the double doors. Then he led us like schoolkids across the marble hall.

The courtroom was beautiful, with dark walnut paneling and molding. I half-expected carved faces where the walls joined the high ceiling. The light was dim, and voices were muffled by thickly upholstered blue chairs.

The judge explained the procedures with great patience. He sounded like Johnny Cash and had a long, sallow face. "The victim was a young child, and some of the evidence is graphic." He looked at his hands forming a steeple on the bench in front of him. "It won't be pleasant," he cautioned, "but it's your duty." Two women behind me spoke up at the same instant. "I'm a grandmother," they said. "I couldn't stand it."

"We need grandmothers," he said. "Are you sure?"

They were both sure.

After we gave our addresses and occupations, two lawyers fired questions at us. Had we read about the case in the papers? Had we been abused as children? Did we know an abused child or abusive parent? More people were excused. Then we were removed to the jury room while they haggled over us.

"Helms," the bailiff read, then five more names and two alternates. So that was it. I had a case, a duty to perform, then home to Stan and the nursery where five hundred citrus trees were waiting to be re-potted. Valencias and Parson Browns. Mineola tangelos and Satsumas. The grafts had taken well and were ready for two-gallon containers and new homes. It always pleased me to think of my trees taking root all over the country in climate zone 10.

Elvis Thornberry, the defendant, entered the room, accompanied by a guard and a washed-out-looking pregnant woman who sat behind him. The D.A. aligned his pad and pencil.

Elvis didn't look like the famous Elvis. He had sandy hair thin as seedlings and stooped shoulders. His chest caved in under a limp white shirt and brown polyester jacket. He was a man you'd never notice unless he held a gun to your head or saved your life.

The D.A. promised to present circumstantial evidence convincing enough to take us beyond a reasonable doubt. The public defender assured us that a crime without a witness was difficult to prove.

At lunch, I asked the knitter what was happening in the jury pool room. "Same as when you left," she told me. "The young ones are plugged into Walkmen. They might as well be on the moon." I turned to dump my sandwich wrapper. "Oh, a big bunch was called for a cocaine case, but most of them got excused. They're afraid to serve," she whispered. "I hear you can get a person's legs broke for under a hundred dollars these days."

"Hmm," I said. I was glad that Elvis Thornberry didn't look like he had those kinds of connections.

"And," she went on, "I played solitaire for nearly an hour without a five of hearts." She spun the counting spool on her knitting needle and stuffed the yarn into her bag.

Elvis, his wife, and their toddler, Elvis, Jr., lived in a truck on the beach for two months before they found a cheap rental in the Palm Breeze Trailer Court. Elvis told the authorities that the refrigerator had fallen on his little boy. But when the police checked, they found no dents in the floor where he said it landed. We studied pictures of the floor. The refrigerator was banked so deeply in the gummy linoleum that I was pretty sure Elvis had lied.

Next were the photos of Elvis, Jr., not as terrible as I had dreaded because he didn't look dead and there were no outward signs of violence. This, the coroner explained, was because he had been killed with a single blow, a blow named the knee-slam by child abuse experts. The killer had lifted three-year-old Elvis over his head like kindling and smashed the child's abdomen across his upraised knee. All the damage done in one stroke, irrevocable and irreparable. I remembered the citrus counties ravaged by the '84 freeze: 160,000 acres destroyed in Marion, Lake, Orange, Polk, Hillsborough, Osceola, Sumter, Pasco, and Hernando. Only the coastal groves like ours spared.

The prosecution rested. Then, without rising from his chair, the defense rested. Not one witness. During his closing argument, Elvis's lawyer leaned over the jury box banister, pleading that no man should be put behind bars for a lifetime on the basis of his kitchen floor. We retired to reach a verdict.

The first ballot was five guilty, one abstention from a young TV cameraman who didn't understand the difference between Murder Two and Manslaughter. The foreman read the definitions from a sheet the judge had provided.

The next vote was four guilty, two abstentions. The cameraman still didn't get it, he said, and now the woman next to him was confused by the legal jargon, too. We didn't know each other's names so the conversation was blunt. Comments were offered around the table without apology or explanation, like chips in a poker game. "Murder is more brutal, then?" the cameraman asked. "Yes," we said.

The next vote was unanimous for Murder Two. The foreman rang the buzzer, and we returned to the beautiful room. No one was in the gallery, now a place of doom for Elvis Thornberry. The silence was cold and penetrating, like the nights in the nursery before we light the smudge pots when a freeze threatens. Soon there would be fire and the falling and rising of voices and heartbeats.

The judge read the verdict and polled each of us individually, tying our names to the word "guilty" forever. We passed into the grandeur of public record.

Back in the jury pool room, smoke rings hung in the stale air like complicated nooses. The boss man crossed our names off his list and said we'd get our checks in ten days. "What about the sentencing?" I asked. "The judge takes care of that. You're finished," he said.

At home, I told Stan about the case. He said I should get it off my mind. "The trees," he said. "Think about the trees."

But I kept thinking of Elvis Thornberry and Elvis, Jr. Two weeks later I phoned the judge's chambers. "He got life," his secretary told me. "He was a convicted felon in Kentucky and Tennessee, but they couldn't tell you that."

"So he'll be there for as long as he lives?" I felt relieved.

"Oh no," she said, after putting me on hold. "Legally, he's eligible for parole in seven years, but His Honor recommended no hearings for at least fifteen."

Good, I thought. Maybe by then I'll have forgotten his name and his face. I turned to the latest citrus grower's bulletin which reviews the major threats to citrus: hard freeze, Medfly, canker, *Phytophthora* foot and root rot, orange dog, and tristeza, the only incurable virus. It attacks the bud union, the graft, the scion.

Imaginary Men

Momma is trying on a pair of Sears 440 running shoes. The catalog clerk took her driver's license as collateral, and now she sits in the anteroom to the Sears portrait studio, studying her feet.

"I'd hardly call this powder blue," she says to Diane, her daughter who is in the process of getting a divorce. "More like aquamarine." Momma gets up and walks around in the orthopedically designed sneakers. She stands on one foot, then the other, like a marsh bird. "They're still too narrow," she says, out of breath. "I'll have to re-order the double E's."

A couple wheeling a stroller comes through the heavy brown drape at the studio entrance. "What a darling baby," Momma coos. Behind the couple is the photographer, a young woman heavily made-up and perfumed, wearing what Diane calls the "working woman's uniform"—a dress, panty hose, and heels. Diane prefers pants, even though she has nice legs.

"I'm sure we got at least one good one," the photographer says, handing the couple a receipt.

"Did you get one with Timmy looking straight ahead?" the young mother asks.

"Well, I think so." The photographer fidgets with her appointment book.

"He's going to have his eyes operated on next month," the father announces. "Didn't you notice he was cross-eyed?"

"I wondered what that was," the photographer admits. "His eyes did move around a lot. He seems so young for surgery."

"The doctor says it's common to operate at nine months," the mother recites. "He won't even have to spend the night."

"It's not a serious operation," the father adds, slipping his arm around his wife. "They do about three a month."

The photographer smiles. "Your pictures will be ready in two weeks."

Momma stuffs the shoes into their box with the accompanying brochure, *Relaxing Adductor Muscles*. "It's as complicated as buying a washing machine," she mutters. The couple, bracketed together at the waist, makes a slow right-hand turn at the cash register and heads toward the exit.

In the parking lot, Momma hooks her arm in Diane's. "I still think Joe ought to have a second chance."

Diane's stomach tightens at the sound of his name. The night four months earlier when Joe confessed is etched into her mind like a TV commercial. Now it plays again.

"I have to talk to you," Joe had said, stroking her arm. She remembers putting her arms around his neck. "Here or in the bedroom?" She nibbled his ear.

"It's not that." He unwrapped her arms. "I'm leaving."

"Do you need something from the store?" Diane glanced at the wipe-clean memo board they used for grocery lists. *Lunch bags. Oranges.*

"No. I mean you. I'm leaving you. I'm in love with Maryanne Snyder."

The warm sensation of anger radiates again through Diane's body as she walks across the parking lot. She thinks about the men she refused over the last nine years. Some were tempting, like the one she met in Norfolk when she went to her cousin's wedding without Joe. If Diane had gone to his hotel room that night she might not be so furious now with Joe. She regrets all—she counts four—of the lost opportunities for romance. And she would never have picked someone Joe knew!

Diane retrieves the car keys from her large pocketbook, but Momma has strayed to a nearby pickup truck—the couple with the baby. Diane hurries over just in time to hear her saying, "Isn't this the baby who's going to have surgery?"

Diane has watched her mother strike up conversations with many strangers over the years. "Here you are," she says. Momma ignores her. Diane is anxious to get home to Gerald, her eight-year-old, who otherwise will stay up to watch "The A-Team."

The couple is happy to show off the baby despite his wandering eyes. "See?" the woman shows Momma, "how they move in and out? Sometimes they're perfectly straight, but other times both eyes turn right in to his nose."

"It's a very common defect." Momma chucks the baby under the chin. "My younger brother had it, and that was fifty-two years ago."

Diane nearly drops her keys. Momma doesn't have a brother.

"He was as cross-eyed as a chicken," Momma says. The couple huddles closer as if they're getting a second medical opinion.

"Did the operation work?" the woman asks. "The doctor said the surgery will make it possible for him to see straight, but it won't automatically fix his eyes."

"My brother never had another problem after his surgery," Momma assures them.

"I'm so relieved to hear that." The mother smooths the baby's rompers over his bottom.

Momma is just hitting her stride. "I remember them saying it was just a weakness in the muscle."

"Actually," the father corrects her, "the doctor said the muscles are too tight."

"Yes, well. My brother *has* worn glasses all of his life. But I'm not sure it's related to the crossed eyes."

"You know," the woman confides, "they say it's safe and all, but it really helps to meet someone who's been through it."

"Don't you waste another minute worrying." Momma turns to go. "My brother had it fifty years ago and it worked and he's just fine."

"Thanks a million," the woman calls out. Diane watches the couple load the stroller into the truck. They're smiling. She waits until she and Momma are out of earshot.

"How could you lie like that?" Diane asks.

"They looked so troubled," Momma says. Diane doesn't say anything. She is thinking how simple life would be if you could just lie. Sometimes she wishes Joe had lied and never told her about Maryanne Snyder.

"Besides, I read all about it in *Redbook*. Everything I said was true to the best of my recollection." She pauses to blow her nose. "Except the part about the brother."

Diane puts Gerald to bed halfway through "The A-Team." Momma answers the telephone. "Alice is coming over," she tells Diane. "She just had a phone call from Joe."

Diane plugs in the coffeemaker because Alice always likes a cup. She loads the day's accumulation into the dishwasher, giving each dish a halfhearted scrub before placing it in the rack. She and Alice have discussed men and life in general since high school. They spend hours on the telephone analyzing the people they know and working on their female consciousness. Momma is what they call "another wasted woman." Diane and Alice define this as anyone born before 1958 or anyone whose female consciousness hasn't been raised. Most of the women they know have had their consciousnesses raised for them by unfaithful husbands, divorce, single-parenting, and humdrum jobs. Alice has been divorced for three years. "It isn't all negative," Alice told her. "I don't have to worry about what to make for dinner anymore. Plus I lost a ton."

Momma answers the door. Alice throws her purse onto a chair and hurries to the kitchen. "Guess who I just had a heart-to-heart with?"

"I give up," Diane says, setting spoons around the table.

"He wants you to take him back."

"I knew it!" Momma says. "What did I tell you, Diane?"

Diane had heard that Maryanne dumped Joe after two months and that he's living alone in a trailer on the edge of town. She had driven by a few times during her lunch hour. She'd felt twinges of sadness at the sight of his laundry stiffening on the line and the dented mailbox with the broken flap hanging down like the tongue of a thirsty dog. But she isn't willing to be anybody's second choice. And she doesn't like the idea of him slinking back with his tail between his legs. That wasn't the Joe she had married.

"I'm not taking sides." Alice lights a cigarette. "Just reporting the news."

"This isn't a natural disaster," Diane says. "I don't need Peter Jennings. He could call me himself."

"There's a lot to be said for hanging on to old problems instead of trading them for new ones." Momma stands behind Diane and strokes her hair. "You still love Joe, don't you?"

Diane thinks about it. "Love's easy. It's the living together that's hard."

"He wants to move back and go for counseling. Can you believe it?" Alice asks Momma.

"Couldn't you just talk to him?" Momma rests both hands lightly on Diane's shoulders.

"Sure," Diane whispers. She and Joe have been perfectly civilized every time they've been together since he left. The problem is that afterward something strange, beyond her control, happens, usually when she's getting ready for bed. She imagines he's watching her as she moves through the quiet upstairs rooms. She pretends he's small enough to squeeze under the bed or thin enough to hide behind the door. In the hallway she invents a hidden camera like the one at the Sun Bank. Sometimes she finds herself pointing her toe in an alluring way as she peels off her hose or stroking her neck too long as she applies moondrop lotion, almost as if her hands had become Joe's.

"He's basically a good man, you know." Momma pours more coffee.

"He sounds genuinely miserable," Alice adds, "not that I'm defending him."

"I'm sure the experience has changed him," Momma says.

Alice speaks into her upraised cup. "He said to tell you he'll be by tomorrow at 5:30."

"Have you ever thought of joining the diplomatic corps?" Diane asks Alice.

Momma calls Diane at work the next day to check on her. Diane promises she'll listen to Joe. She remembers all the comfort and advice Momma gave her when she was growing up—what to wear on dates, how to handle her first job interview—and wonders now if Momma got all that from ladies' magazines, too.

Joe, always punctual, rings the doorbell at 5:30. Considerate, Diane thinks. She knows he still has a house key, and he knows she never bothered to change the locks, even though the legal clinic recommended it. Joe brings a grocery bag full of goodies for her and Gerald—an econo-pak of Juicy Fruit gum, three cantaloupes for her perpetual diet, and a couple of frozen pizzas.

"Gerald here?" he asks, neatly folding the bag.

"No, he's sleeping at Billy's tonight." Diane grips the countertop as she leans against it.

"Mind if I make myself a cup of coffee?"

Diane stares at the refrigerator as he putters at the sink. A butterfly magnet holds a picture of suffragettes marching down Park Avenue. Above it is a photo of a mule standing in a kitchen full of overturned garbage with the caption, Some Days Nothing Goes Right. A gift from Momma.

Joe sits down at the table and stirs powdered creamer into his coffee. "I'd like to come back," he says. "Do you want a cup? I should have asked . . ." His spoon clinks against the saucer.

"How do I know there won't be another Maryanne?"

He thinks about it for a long time, rotating the cup in its saucer with one beefy finger. This unsettles Diane, who is used to the old Joe who had a quick answer for every question. Finally, he says, "I can only tell you that I'm not looking for another Maryanne. Before," he adds, "I was looking."

Diane slumps into the opposite chair, her hair falling forward onto her face. "Jesus," she says.

"I'm only telling the truth."

"Well, it isn't a very nice truth, is it? You lied to me before, but now you say you don't intend to lie again. How can I believe anything you say?" Suddenly she's crying, but her voice is angry. He hands her a tissue.

"I can't answer that. I've had the shit knocked out of me, too, you know."

She nods.

"How about a couple of hands of gin? It might make you feel better."

"I'm confused," Diane says, retrieving the cards from a drawer. "You deal."

Diane knows that Joe hates cards. She can count the number of times they've played. The first was on their honeymoon cruise to Jamaica. It rained for two days straight. She remembers Joe saying he wasn't good at any game where he had to sit still. Then, when her father died three years ago, Joe played cards with the relatives from Baltimore who hung around after the funeral to fulfill the seven-day requirement on their Super Saver flights. She remembers best their gin tournament in the hospital after Gerald was born, slightly jaundiced and premature. They'd play to five hundred, then walk down the hall to peer at Gerald, whose treatment was to lie in a special cubicle under ultraviolet light, wearing only a blindfold and a diaper. "Look at that one," a tactless visitor said one day. "Must be a blue baby." And Joe had answered loudly, "No, no. He's just getting a head start on his tan."

Now Joe shuffles the cards solemnly, then counts off "she loves me, she loves me not" as he deals. Diane knows that the knock card will be "she loves me," but she doesn't comment. They play for more than an hour, Diane winning nearly every hand.

"I'm going home for a week to my folks," he tells her.

"Everybody okay there?"

"Yeah. I just want to talk to them. My counselor agreed it was a good idea."

"Your counselor?"

"Yeah. I'm seeing a counselor twice a week. I think she's helping me. I'd like you to come with me sometime."

"I'll think about it." Diane knocks with three points. Joe's hand is loaded again with face cards.

At seven o'clock Joe tucks the end flaps over the cards and puts on his jacket. "Will you tell Gerald goodbye for me?" He pauses at the doorway like he used to when they were dating. Diane feels the old ache she felt then. "I'm sorry that I hurt you," he says. "I wish I could undo it." Tears magnify his eyes.

Diane would like to comfort him. But she was the one who cried at the movies while Joe put his arm around her. Suddenly she feels awful about the way she's treating him, yet, at the same time, put off by his tears. She can't forgive the old Joe or warm up to the new one. But just to be on the safe side, she undresses that night in the dark.

Momma takes Gerald on Sunday because Diane has finally agreed to go with Alice to the Trinity Singles meeting and picnic.

"You look great, Alice," Diane says as she gets into the Toyota.

"Didn't we decide not to comment on each other's looks?" Alice reminds her. "Unless one of us has spinach on her teeth or something."

"Oh yeah, I forgot." Diane finds it hard to remember all their resolutions. The primary one is to talk about their work, just the way men do, even if it means being a bore. Diane practices on the way to the Trinity church. She tells Alice about the new software program for inventorying paper goods. "It's supposed to save the city about $5,000 a year in overstock assets alone," she concludes.

Diane knows she's supposed to care about her career, but despite her new title as executive assistant, Purchasing, and her new computer terminal, she can't generate much enthusiasm. Between her job and Gerald and her dissolving marriage she feels like a juggler frozen in midstroke, forever waiting to catch the third ball. Alice, on the other hand, has mapped out a strategy to net herself an elementary school principalship within ten years.

The Trinity Singles meeting is boring. The men busily scan the women. Diane senses many eyes roaming her body. She recrosses her legs and tucks strands of hair into her French knot. Alice is giving her the scoop on the members she's dated. "Why do you keep coming back if they're all such creeps?" Diane asks.

"Uh oh," Alice whispers. "Clam up."

A man of about forty-five wearing a silver dollar belt buckle and yellow jeans sits down next to Diane. "Name's Harding," he says, extending his hand to her.

"You look familiar." Diane cocks her head. "Do you work at city hall, too?"

"Everybody says I look familiar. I'm the guy that does the waterbed commercial on TV. You know, the one for the Waterbed Ranch."

Diane remembers instantly. In it, Harding is sitting on the edge of a waterbed surrounded by three women in nightgowns. "Want something new in your bedroom?" he leers at the camera.

"You new in town?" he asks. "Or just newly divorced?"

"Separated."

"So," he says, leaning back, "you've seen me on TV?"

"I guess you're famous."

"So what did you think of it? The commercial?"

"Oh, it's fine," Diane lies, "but I'd like to see one with men in their pj's."

"Hey, I volunteer," Harding says seductively.

The meeting adjourns to nearby Morning Glory Park. The men light barbecue pits, and the women spread blankets under the trees. A volleyball game begins. Harding sits beside Diane, telling the story of his life. His voice is southern and soothing. The sky is so blue she can hardly look at it. It reminds her of the sky painted on the background of a cereal box—the one with the bowl of granola set on a checkered cloth in a field of wildflowers.

"The Boogie-Woogie Bugle Boy of Company B," Harding suddenly sings. "That's my real love," he explains, "music of the '40s."

"Do you want to take a walk?" Diane longs for the cool shade of the forest at the edge of the picnic area.

They follow the hiking path, a mile-and-a-half loop through the park grounds. The terrain changes from sandy pines to overarching hardwood trees. Harding walks briskly, talking most of the time. "Resurrection ferns!" she interrupts, running over to a low limb of live oak where the supple, shiny fronds have uncurled from the rain.

"I bet you have a real green thumb." Harding doesn't move from the path. "Even though my daddy was a farmer, I never could grow anything." He scuffs at the loose soil. "But ask me anything about the Andrews Sisters."

"What?"

"Go ahead. Ask me anything."

"I don't know anything about them. Besides," she feels the moss along a branch, "I don't care."

"Oh."

Diane, surprised by her own honesty, notices that Harding is finally silent. "Look!" She points to the electric fence that demarcates the county prison from the park. Beyond it, the windowless white concrete building generates a glare in the full sun. As they get closer, Diane makes out men in gray prison suits walking and smoking in the compound. "Let's go back," she urges Harding.

"They can't hurt you from over there." He goes right up to the fence and stares at the prisoners.

"Yeah, but I bet they hurt a lot of people on their way in." Diane imagines Joe there for a second, convicted of mental cruelty or infidelity or whatever it is that used to be against the law between two married people. Irreconcilable differences is like a traffic ticket, she thinks.

"Hey little lady." Harding's voice is conspiratorial. "Want to smoke a joint?"

Over the next three days Harding calls twice to chat, most of the time reviewing why his two marriages failed. Momma calls every day, and Joe phones every evening from Georgia. By Thursday, Diane is actually waiting by the phone for his call. She knows this is regressive—she's read enough articles confirming that it's a waste of time for women to wait for men.

"I found my high school yearbook," Joe tells Diane on Friday. "I used to wear my hair greased. It looked wacky. I was sure a different person then," he muses. "Diane?"

"Yeah?"

"I really love you."

"I'll talk to you tomorrow," Diane forces herself to say.

The next night he tells her three times that he loves her, but now there is a happier ring to his voice. "I've figured it out," he says. "I think I've figured it out."

To this Diane says nothing, even though she's pretty sure she loves him, too. Still, there's something in the way, though Diane can't quite identify what it is. She agrees to meet him on Sunday evening on the neutral ground of Harrison's Cafeteria in the mall.

Sunday is Family Night at Harrison's, and the place is packed. The big, intact families with grandparents, parents, and children cluster in noisy groups. A few of the unescorted women have their hair in rollers under bright bandannas, as if they are already preparing for next Saturday night.

The line snakes around in front of a mirrored wall where Diane and Joe hesitantly study their reflections as they wait. Diane thinks Joe looks thinner and older. She thinks, too, that they still look as if they belong together. It's partly the way the top of her head comes right up to his ears, the stair-step silhouette they make standing together. But now they stand apart, as if they don't know each other very well. Diane has the same eerie feeling she gets at night—that Joe is secretly watching her and that she wants him to. He stares into the eyes of her mirror image. "Diane," he says to her reflection, "do you miss me at all?"

"Of course I miss you." She touches his sleeve.

"I've learned a lot about myself," he says, handing her a brown plastic tray.

"I'm glad."

"No, you don't understand. Now I want to learn about you. I want to know everything about you. I don't even know what size shoe you wear," he says incredulously.

"It's all right," she says. Her heart thumps a little at the prospect of Joe wanting to know her so intimately, so individually.

"Salad, ma'am?" the server asks in a bored voice. Diane becomes aware of the long buffet of food. She surveys the assortment of desserts—bright red deep-dish cherry cobbler, tall chocolate layer cake, key lime pie heaped with whipped topping.

"It's too bad I know what this stuff tastes like," she tells Joe. He squints back a question mark at her. "The desserts. All the food here," she explains. "It looks delicious, but it's a . . . lie. It tastes like . . . nothing." Her voice rises in anger. "It fools your eyes."

"Yeah," Joe drawls. "There are people like that, too."

Diane passes over the entrées and heaps her plate with corn bread, butter, and fried okra. They take a corner booth in the brightly lit lime-colored room.

A moment later, Harding's bejeweled hand is on Diane's shoulder, and his silver dollar belt buckle gleams at the corner of her eye. "I've been trying to reach you," Harding says, ignoring Joe. "I got a great new Benny Goodman recording I wanted you to hear—"

"Harding," Diane interrupts, "this is Joe."

"Nice to meet you. You can come along, too, Joe. I'm talking about a smooooth sound. How about after dinner?"

"I don't know." Diane holds her buttered corn bread in midair.

"And," Harding continues, "I'm making another commercial this week. I told them your idea about the pajamas, and they want to meet you. You might even get to sit on the bed."

"We're trying to have a conversation here. Do you mind?" Joe points a fried drumstick at Harding, who gets the message, tips his cowboy hat, and retreats, promising to call Diane at a more convenient time.

"Do you like that guy?" Joe asks.

"He's all right."

"Since when do you like Benny Goodman?" Joe pauses. "Is that how I've acted for the last nine years? I mean, he just assumed you wanted to hear all about him and his record."

Diane puts her hand over Joe's. "I think you *were* like that for nine years, but I didn't notice it most of the time. Now I'd notice it though, you know?"

"Yeah. I guess I owe you nine years of listening. No—not owe. I want to hear you out."

"About the pajamas—"

"You don't have to explain anything."

"I know." Diane drains the last of her ice water from the glass and watches Joe pick at his food. She remembers the countless times Joe heard her moaning in and out of sleep with menstrual cramps. He would take her in his arms and stroke her face until she fell asleep.

At least he had always understood pain. Now, she thinks, he might be trying to understand friendship, even joy. "Let's get out of here," she blurts. "We have to pick up Gerald from Momma's."

Diane makes popcorn while Joe plays the short version of Monopoly with Gerald. Then they all watch TV, sitting on the floor eating popcorn out of a big wooden bowl. After a while Gerald goes to bed. Joe shuts off the TV, sits down, and takes Diane's hand.

"Will you come with me tomorrow for my counseling?"

"Okay."

Joe removes Gerald's baby book from its shelf under the coffee table and starts looking at the pictures. "How can I expect you to take me back?" He points to Gerald at two in a bedraggled diaper.

"What do you mean?"

"I look at Gerald now and I look at this snapshot of him, and all I can think is, how did I treat Diane then? I mean, I don't think it was just Maryanne."

"Please don't mention her name anymore."

"I'm sorry. I just don't seem to know how to do it." Joe leans back and studies the ceiling.

"What?"

"Love someone the right way."

Diane watches Joe flip the album pages backward. Gerald gets smaller and smaller until finally he's a bulge at Diane's middle in the photo taken a week before he was born. Joe touches the picture lightly with his forefinger. For the first time Diane notices deep lines in Joe's face.

Diane leans back against the couch and closes her eyes. Joe begins stroking her forearm. Her body goes slack. She drifts into the half-sleep she often experienced between night feedings when Gerald was an infant. Words begin to form unexpectedly in her head, pulling her back to consciousness like the instinct that brought her sharply awake when the baby fretted even slightly. "There's something I want to tell you, Joe." Her voice is grave but relaxed. Joe's expression is identical to Gerald's when she interrupts him playing with crayons or airplane kits.

"Remember when I went to my cousin's wedding in Norfolk two years ago? You stayed home with Gerald?"

"Mm hmm."

Diane's head is a jumble of thoughts—the New Woman, equality, divorce, sex—but she speaks easily, as if reciting a familiar bedtime story. Images of Momma flit through her mind: Momma dancing at the wedding reception; Momma talking about her cross-eyed brother in the mall parking lot; Momma hip-deep in glossy magazines, each one rolled up like a diploma.

Diane describes the man she met at the wedding—a friend of the groom—and how lonely she felt watching the bridal pair all evening. Joe doesn't move a muscle. Swallowing hard, she tells how the man invited her to his hotel room. "I knew why I was going there," she admits. Joe looks stricken, though he still doesn't move. Diane sees the man fold back the orange floral bedspread, then pull the thickly lined drapes closed with a long plastic wand. He hangs the Do Not Disturb sign on the door. "What I noticed about him first," she says, convinced herself, "was his hands."

Stony Limits

When I wheeled through the door of Room 12A at the Heloise Gumm High School for Exceptional Children, the first thing I saw was a shiny red football helmet looming over a blond wooden desk. Well, I thought, at least the dress code is lenient. The last school I attended was pretty strict: no denims or T-shirts, no high heels, no more makeup than Jackie Kennedy wore.

Mrs. Page motioned me toward the front of the room. "Class," she began officially, "this is our new student, Maggie Freer. I'm sure that you'll all make her feel at home." I hate being reduced to third person, so I stared at my little toe which was wiggling. It's the only part of me from the waist down that moves. When I'm nervous it gets going on its own.

Mrs. Page asked all the kids to state their name and handicap. "It saves a lot of time and questions later," she explained.

"I had polio when I was ten," I said when my turn came. "Six months before the vaccine came out." There was a little awed hush in the room. This was familiar to me—I call it the Prestige of Polio. When it comes to wheelchair disabilities, it's the top of the heap. Maybe because a U.S. president had it. I don't know. But for six years now people have always been impressed when I mention my disease.

The football helmet was called Julio, and there was a kid with real bad cerebral palsy named Carl. And I was wrong about the dress code: Julio had hydrocephalus and wore the helmet day and night for protection. What would it take to get him to remove it for me?

Mrs. Page was teaching Geography. She pulled a glossy map of the world down in front of the chalkboard. Lots of pink, yellow, green, and blue blotches. I noticed that Thailand was still called Siam. The bell rang, but no one left. They wheeled their chairs back from the desks and huddled, chatting, in small groups. Only Julio stood, tall and lean, without a chair. Then, in about ten minutes, the bell rang again and Mrs. Page began English. I had gone to regular schools all my life, and I missed being carried along with the crush of students changing classes at a regular school—the commotion, the sly remarks and quick digs.

"*Romeo and Juliet* is a tragedy," Mrs. Page started, "of doomed love, of a love which tries to go against tradition and the weight of social custom." I detected a faint snicker behind me. "But there are many other important messages in this play, as in all of Shakespeare." She quoted: "'He that is strucken blind cannot forget the precious treasure of his eyesight lost,'" then paused respectfully. "But mainly," she went on, "we could sum it up with these words: 'Alas that love, so gentle in his view, should be so tyrannous and rough in proof . . . violent delights have violent ends.'" Having read the play aloud with my dad many times after my spinal fusion, I quoted to myself the apt, "She speaks, yet she says nothing," while I doodled a cartoon of Julio on the inside of my notebook.

At lunch the kids were real friendly. First everybody in chairs went through the line, then Julio, then the born-deaf kids from the second floor who talked rapidly with their hands in miniature karate chops. The only sign language I knew was the international screw-you finger, so I smiled a lot at them but didn't try to join in. I showed Julio my sketch of him, thinking he'd be flattered.

"Someday I won't need this," he said, adjusting his chin strap. "Otherwise, I'm completely normal."

"That's good."

"What about you?" he asked, looking at my small legs.

"This is it," I answered.

"Yeah, well, at least you're not in a potty chair like some of them."

"I'll remember that next time I say my prayers."

"You wanna take a walk?" He didn't hurry to rephrase his question, which was a good sign. I was tired of people adjusting their vocabularies to accommodate my wheels.

We headed out the door onto the playground—a dismal paved area surrounded by very tall fences. Across the alley was a body shop and an envelope warehouse. I remembered the photograph on the school brochure. It showed the front with its wide, spanking-white double doors and closely cropped shrubs. Julio twined his fingers in the chain link and was silent. I felt like a parked car with all the glare and concrete. My wheels were hot to the touch, and my foot pedals were starting to burn. Then we saw Carl motioning us and returned to the lunchroom.

"She's going to announce it after lunch," Carl said, fighting for each word.

"You sure?" Julio asked. I watched Carl struggle to maintain control of his movements. He nodded, then rested against his chairback.

"What?" I asked.

"Another field trip," Julio said. He tore open a pack of Tom's Peanut Butter Crackers, dropped the wrapper, and crushed it under his foot. The cellophane unfolded spastically, just like Carl.

"I saw a cow in person once," Carl managed to say.

"Oh yeah," Julio said, "we've had some stellar field trips."

"Now I'm going to get to see God," Carl continued.

"Like one time they loaded all of us into a bus," Julio crunched down on the whole bundle of crackers at once. "You know how *long* that takes? And then they drove us over to the rich end of town to—get this—see the azaleas in bloom." At that moment his front teeth were blooming with orange flecks of cracker and peanut butter.

"And music," Carl said, touching my hand.

"Yeah," Julio explained for him. "We go to the symphony four times a year. They have to take out the whole first row of seats for us."

"I like music," I said. "It makes me feel like I'm flying."

"Me too," Julio conceded. "The music part is great. It's the way they talk to us that gets me. You know, like we're retarded, too."

"*Bolero* was good," Carl said. "Have you heard *Bolero*?"

The deaf kids were returning their trays through the cafeteria pass-through. They were a rough-and-tumble group—punching each other on the arm, banging the trays around. It never occurred to me that deaf people would be so noisy. "What about them?" I asked. "Do they go to the concerts?"

"Course not," Julio answered.

The deaf kids lined up at the bottom of the stairs. It was a steep metal staircase with one landing and rivetlike pockmarks all over it, like something salvaged from a battleship. The noise was tremendous as they stampeded up. Julio pointed out their teacher, Miss Simons, who brought up the end of the line—a powerful-looking woman with meaty arms and legs and a long chestnut-colored ponytail. She looked about forty but bounded up the steps energetically, her arms extended to catch all of them if the tide turned.

After lunch we had a rest period in the physical therapy room. Everyone got out of their chairs and lay down on thick leatherette mats. Mrs. Page brought me an upholstered cube and placed it at the end of my mat. I got into Fowler's antigravity position—my knees crooked as if I were seated in a chair that had been tilted back onto the floor. Mrs. Page put on a recording of *Swan Lake*, and my mind began to drift.

The next thing I knew a little dog was licking my face, a toy poodle with pink skin and eyes streaked like marbles.

"Oh my poor, darling, sweet thing," a voice behind me said. I twisted my head around to see two heavy brown walking shoes and thick support hose. Then a hand brushed my face. "Lamar! How rude of you." She scooped the dog up, then touched my face again. "You precious little thing," she crooned. I realized, then, that she was talking not to the dog but to me.

"Who are you?" I asked, raising up on both elbows and reaching for my chair parked alongside.

"Let me help you, dear," she said, going for my armpits.

"No!"

Mrs. Page lunged between us. "Maggie, this is Mrs. *Gumm*." Suddenly I made the connection—she was Heloise Gumm, the benefactor and founder of the school.

"Pleased to meet you." I hoisted myself into my chair.

We arranged ourselves in rows for Mrs. Gumm. Then the deaf kids torpedoed through the doorway, laughing and poking each other.

Mrs. Gumm beamed. "My dear silent angels," she said. They ignored her. Miss Simons settled them in and joined her at the front to translate into sign language.

"My dear children," said Mrs. Gumm. "It's all been arranged for two weeks from Friday. A big field trip." She looked to Miss Simons for help, then mimicked the sign for "big." "Pilgrims and tourists from all over the country come to Withlahatchee Springs, Florida. The radioactive waters are said to be healing."

Carl, seated next to me, raised his hand jerkily.

"Yes?" Mrs. Gumm noticed.

"Are we spending the night?"

"No, dear. But we'll have lunch and dinner on the road, and the park has refreshment stands. Won't that be fun?"

I quickly scrawled a note to Carl: OH GOD, JUNK FOOD AT LAST. He smiled.

"Where was I?" Mrs. Gumm asked Lamar, whose head peeked out from her arm. "Yes. Christ of the Orange Grove. A magnificent statue. A holy shrine without the great expense and danger of traveling to the Holy Land. A modern wonder of the world."

I looked over at Miss Simons, trying to verify what I'd heard. She jabbed the palm of her left hand with her right index finger, then punched a similar "hole" in the right hand. Then she tapped her way up one arm, like someone playing "this little piggy." She kept repeating these gestures. A fat tear slid down Carl's cheek. Taking my pen hand in his own, he made me circle the word "GOD" on my notepad.

Mrs. Gumm visited our classroom every morning to give an inspirational message. "I was without shoes," she began on Wednesday in an ominous tone, "and wanting the pity of the world until I saw a man without feet." I knew it was supposed to make me feel better, but all I could see the rest of that day were stumps.

After her pep talk, she went upstairs to her silent angels. Rumor had it that the deaf room was a scientific wonder, with state-of-the-art earphones and oscilloscopes. Kids said it was brightly painted and wallpapered and had shag carpeting. Amanda Frank's mother had told her there were all kinds of posters—polar bears with "real" fur and photographs of castles that Mrs. Gumm had visited on her yearly European vacations. I itched to see it. Could it really be so much nicer than our shabby room with its green chalkboard overhung with the cursive alphabet? Mrs. Page often brought flowers from home for her desk, but otherwise the room was a dull beige designed to hide dirt for years.

Thursday at lunch I convinced Julio to eat with the deaf kids. Carl tagged along. We waved hello as we pulled up to the table where they were bent over their macaroni casseroles and milk. A few returned the wave, then ignored us.

"I told you," Julio said, grabbing hold of Carl's chair handles to return him to our side of the lunchroom.

"Wait," I said, throwing on the brake lever of Carl's chair. He lurched slightly forward.

"They don't want us," Julio said, his foot tapping in annoyance.

I looked at the ten or so faces at the table. Most of them seemed relaxed as sleepers but with open eyes. They sat much closer together than hearing people and leaned and rubbed against each other. I decided to go for it and put my arm against the thin arm of a girl with reddish hair. She turned to acknowledge me and kept on drinking her milk. I felt a slight pressure back from her warm, smooth flesh. Then, as if someone had lowered a curtain, she turned away and began gesturing to the boy on her right.

"They don't like us," Carl said.

"No. They just like each other better," I said. Julio's face brightened. He moved his hands from Carl's chair to my shoulders.

"I like you," he said, and began to massage my neck. Out of the corner of my eye, I saw Carl blush furiously, then move his wavering hand to touch Julio's leg. We froze for a moment. Then Julio released his gentle grip and pushed Carl to the wheelchair side of the cafeteria.

"The Christ is seven stories tall," Carl said, his face returned to its usual pale color.

"All I want to know is do they sell cotton candy," I told him.

"I heard the Christ is so white. When you touch him your hands come away all silvery. And beautiful. Like moonlight."

"Or chalk," Julio said.

"They have a big Bible," Carl continued. "I heard the pages are made of steel."

"I heard they have lots of natural springs, and Mrs. Gumm wants us all to get baptized." Julio fiddled with the straw in his milk.

"Oh no!" I lamented. In the two years I spent at Warm Springs, clergymen of every faith had visited me, not to mention the evangelists I attracted on weekend family outings who tried to talk me into attending tent revivals.

"On the other hand, maybe they have rides," Julio offered.

"Oh sure," I said, "like the Tunnel of Sodom and Gomorrah."

Julio cracked up.

"I could get cured," Carl said, staring out the window at the body shop where blue fire flared from an acetylene torch.

Back in the PT room, Mrs. Page arranged us on our mats, put on Beethoven at low level, and left the room to join Miss Simons and the rest of the staff in the faculty lounge. Beethoven always reminds me of someone having a temper tantrum, so for the first time I stayed awake. I looked at the other kids lying on the floor, some with knees bent and legs elevated like mine, others on their sides, and some curled up like unborn babies. Julio's red helmet stood out like a Christmas ornament three mats away. He was reading *Battle Cry*. It looked like a steamy sex novel from the cover, which showed a couple kissing, the man's uniformed body pressed hard against the woman.

"Hey, Julio," I whispered. "Are you getting ready for *Romeo and Juliet*?" We were going to read parts of it aloud in class for the next few days. Julio shushed me and kept reading. A moment later he said, "I'll turn down the pages with good parts for you."

"Thanks." Just then I heard thumping from the ceiling. Nothing so loud as to startle and not that creepy groaning that makes you think the roof will collapse. This sounded like people batting tom-toms.

"What is that?"

Julio came over and sat down beside me. "I don't know. Maybe it's some kind of vibration therapy. Or dancing."

"Have you ever been upstairs?"

"No. But they do it just about every day." He suspended the book in front of my eyes. "Read this," he instructed.

"So what?" I said, after speeding through it.

"I thought only babies sucked women's tits," he admitted.

"Well that just shows how much you know," I said, trying to sound cool.

Mrs. Page had turned off the classroom lights and lowered the window shades to simulate night. She was posted by the switch to bring the dreaded dawn on cue to Romeo and Juliet. Amanda was reading the part of Juliet, and Julio was Romeo. "It was the nightingale," Amanda insisted, trying to get Romeo to stick around even though he'd been banished.

"It was the lark," Julio argued. I waited for my lines, but it took forever. Besides, Juliet's nurse didn't have a lot to say in this scene. "Yon light is not daylight . . . It is some meteor that the sun exhales," Amanda said. She sounded like someone reading the ingredients on a cereal box. But Julio was really getting into his role. "Let me be put to death," he screamed, clutching his chest. "Come death and welcome! Juliet wills it so." This startled Amanda, but she continued to read flatly. "Now be gone," she told him with equal emphasis on each word. Mrs. Page flipped the light switch. Julio looked at the ceiling as if he were seeing it for the first time. "More light and light. More dark and dark our woes!" he wailed. I quickly wheeled over to the couple. "Madame!" I reprimanded Juliet. "The day is broke, be wary, look about." Julio planted a wet one on Amanda's hand and retreated to the back of the room. By then Amanda was very interested in her part, and her "Oh think'st thou we shall ever meet again?" was passionate.

From the doorway Julio's voice boomed in an astounding stage whisper that gave me goose bumps. "I doubt it not," he reassured Amanda, "and all these woes shall serve for sweet discourses in our time to come." Amanda just sat there, a lovesick expression on her face.

"Cut!" Mrs. Page ordered, returning to her desk. "That was good. Would anyone like to talk about the meaning of this scene? I mean, how we might apply it in our own lives?"

"Can we rehearse it again?" Amanda blurted.

"We won't have time today, I'm afraid," Mrs. Page said.

Carl was thoughtful. "You just know they aren't going to live happily ever after," he said. "I don't know how, but you do."

"That's true," Mrs. Page agreed.

"But you want them to so bad, like wanting to believe in miracles."

Four days before our trip Mrs. Gumm delivered an orientation lecture to the whole school. I took plenty of notes, figuring that a studious, attentive attitude might come in handy if I had to bargain for taffy apples and chili dogs.

"Gethsemane Sinkhole," she intoned. "Even the name is magical." She paused while Miss Simons signed for the deaf kids. Julio passed me *Battle Cry* with a juicy passage set off by blue-ink brackets. I read it as I continued to take notes about our destination. It was a strange combination of facts and word pictures: Harold J. Wilson whose money had built the Christ and whose features it supposedly bore. . . . *A dressing gown, sheer, white—it flowed like a billow to the floor.* . . . From a distance the outstretched arms (sixty-five feet across) give the appearance of a mammoth cross surrounded by 20,000 orange trees. . . . *Across the room each heard the other's deep breath.* . . . *He could see the nipples of her breasts through the film of silk net.* . . . Three automobiles can be suspended from either wrist without affecting the statue. Free juice samples. . . . *Their bodies seemed to melt together; she sank her fingernails into his flesh.* "Oh God, God, God," she said. Seventy feet tall. White cement.

"Bring your cameras," Mrs. Gumm suggested, "and some mad money. The Christ Only Art Gallery has lovely crucifixes." She pulled a large crocheted handkerchief from her purse and stretched it taut against her black dress. The familiar gossipy groupings of *The Last Supper* emerged in incredible detail. "Handmade," she crowed, pivoting so that everyone could see the sacred scene displayed on her chest.

On my notepad I wrote Julio a message: I NEED TO TALK TO YOU.

Rest hour was the obvious time to get a look at the deaf room. Julio and I sneaked out of PT together. The other kids were asleep as usual and the teachers safely out of earshot in their lounge.

"This is perfect timing," I reassured Julio, as we contemplated the steep staircase to the second floor.

"I'm not worried about getting caught." He shoved his shirttails into his trousers with abrupt pecking motions. "Maybe I should bring you up in your chair?"

"The chair would make an awful racket against the metal."

He kicked the bottom tread, and a slight ringing filled the stairwell. "You're right," he said.

"I'm strong," I told him. "I can pull myself up by my arms. Come on, Julio, I'm dying to see that room."

"Me too. Mrs. Gumm's 'heaven on earth' for her little angels! And we can see what the noise is, too."

"Yeah." Actually, I hadn't thought about the thumping since that first day I heard it, but now I noticed again random thuds right over my head. I slid onto the second step. "Only seventeen more to go," I said cheerfully.

"I can help you," Julio offered, as I began my slow ascent. "Tell me what to do."

I have been called "fiercely independent" so many times that I practically answer to it as my name. I looked at Julio's pale cheeks against the red of his helmet and his hands outstretched vaguely in my direction. "Stand on each stair as I climb. That way I won't get scared looking at the spaces between the steps."

He stood above me, backward, on the stairway, his arms extended straight from the shoulder to grip the iron railings on either side. It was comforting to see his legs firmly planted in front of me instead of the floor receding below as I hoisted myself along. His black trousers were neatly cuffed and his sweatsocks nice and clean. Soon I began to use his ankles to grab onto as I climbed.

I stopped at the landing to catch my breath. "Let me pull you the rest of the way," he whispered. "We can practice here first. I'll drag you along a little bit and you can see how you like it."

In my mind a big neon sign began flashing BREASTS BREASTS HANDS HANDS. I knew that for him to get a good grip he'd have to touch me there, but I told myself it would be like a doctor doing it. "Okay," I muttered. Very gently he put his arms around me and, locking his hands together, slowly pulled me six inches closer to the steps. "Try to relax and just let it happen," he urged. I recognized this as the line that the soldier in *Battle Cry* used to seduce his girlfriend but said nothing.

I couldn't completely relax as he pulled me or my bottom would have been bruised blue as a berry. His helmet frequently grazed my cheek, and more than ever I wished he'd take it off. I knew the bones of his skull hadn't joined together, but I was sure I wouldn't be shocked by the sight of his head.

Finally we reached the top of the stairs, outside Room 22. Julio straightened up, turned the doorknob slowly, opened the door a crack, and peeked in with one eye. "Oh!" he gasped, and closed the door.

"What is it?"

"Oh boy," he said, his face a deep pink, the color your hand turns when you shine a flashlight through it.

"I can't reach the doorknob, Julio. Open the door," I pleaded.

Wordlessly he turned the knob, pulled the door ajar, then flattened himself against the wall. I squirmed to the door and Julio goosenecked around me. We looked in. My throat closed and my eyes popped open like umbrellas. There they were, the silent angels, partly undressed, some of them doing it. Julio slumped down beside me. I eased the door shut. We sat there for what seemed like an eternity. Finally he said, "I don't feel sorry for them anymore."

"Right," I said.

Julio took my hand in slow motion and placed it inside his helmet against his cheek, kissing it as it passed his mouth. I felt all my blood flow into that hand, as if the rest of me had gone to sleep. My fingertips tingled. "Oh Julio," I said, moved beyond the point of trying to sound original, "that feels so nice."

We snuggled closer. I squinted my eyes shut and kissed him on the mouth. The air around me felt thick as cotton batting, and for the first time in my life all I could do was feel pleasure, a sensation of floating. After a while, he unbuttoned my blouse and very gently placed his hand over my heart. I felt the blood throbbing in his neck with my fingers. Then suddenly, I felt his body stiffen. He yanked his hand from my blouse, squeezed my shoulder, and cried out, "Maggie!" From the corner of my eye I saw the bronze legs of Mrs. Gumm.

"What is going on here?"

I buttoned my blouse.

"How dare you! How dare you do this in MY school." Julio kept holding my hand on his thigh. Mrs. Gumm leaned into my face. "Maybe they allowed such goings-on where you came from, but not here. I won't have it," she hissed. "I won't have any tramps in my school."

"Open the door," I said.

"Girls like you have no—what door?" Mrs. Gumm was confused.

"Open the door," Julio said quietly. "Please, just open the door."

As if moving through someone else's nightmare, Mrs. Gumm complied. Though we couldn't see the kids from where we sat, we had a clear view of Mrs. Gumm's face as she beheld her angels caught in the act. Her mouth opened slowly, forming the shape a mouth makes before it howls in pain. "MISS SIMONS!" she yelled over her shoulder. "Come here immediately!" Then she froze. The deaf kids must have noticed her in the doorway, because I heard a scurrying inside like kitchen mice at night. Miss Simons came clanging up the steps. Mrs. Gumm turned to me again. "However you got up here, you get back down," she ordered. Then the two women strode into the room and slammed the door shut.

A special assembly was called that afternoon right before school let out. By then, of course, everybody knew what had happened. I regretted having left my wheelchair in such plain view. If I had asked Julio to fold it up and hide it behind the stairs, Mrs. Gumm might never have discovered us or the deaf kids. Other than that, I felt no regret whatsoever. Julio had already told Carl he was madly in love with me, and Carl had already told me that Julio had told him.

The buses waited in the parking lot like big yellow slickers waiting for rain. Mrs. Gumm and Miss Simons joined forces at the front of the room. "I have always thought of the deaf," Mrs. Gumm began, "as children who are seen but not heard by anyone . . . except God." Was she going to cry? I looked at the deaf kids. They were as relaxed as usual. "His real sheep," she went on. "And I am shocked and appalled." She sniffed. "I don't know how these perversities began, but they will not be tolerated." The deaf girl with reddish hair nudged my shoulder and smiled. Carl, sitting on my left, was as expressionless as a juror.

"If I cannot trust my children here in school, I cannot take responsibility for them out there," her arm swept up, "in the real world." Carl looked at his wristwatch. Julio circled something in his English book and passed it to me: *Rom: For stony limits cannot hold love out.*

"Therefore I have canceled our field trip," Mrs. Gumm announced. There was a low groan from the room. "You are not deserving of it, particularly considering the nature of your—" she searched for a word, "waywardness." Miss Simons's rendition seemed much more to the point: she jammed her finger in and out of a fisted hand.

Carl's voice cracked. "Not all of us were bad," he said, holding back tears.

"I cannot single anyone out for favors," Mrs. Gumm answered, making me hate her at last. I'M SORRY I wrote to Carl. Julio underlined it in blue and passed it to him, giving my hand a quick squeeze. Carl read it and pushed the notepad to the floor. I wanted to tell him it wasn't the end of the world, that maybe it was better in some mysterious way that he wasn't going to see Christ of the Orange Grove. But when I turned to tell him, the bell rang and he rolled past me through the door.

The
Problem
with
Yosi

Naomi's eyes swept the crowd in the kibbutz meet-
ing hall to make sure everyone was listening. Her head moved delib-
erately, like a gun turret searching out a moving target.

"Then, he reached over and touched my breast," she said.

A unanimous "oy" rose from the members.

"What does Zalman say?" a woman asked.

The kibbutz doctor, seated beside Naomi at the table on the dais,
leaned forward on his arms. "Other than his weight, he's in excellent
health for a man of thirty-two. He's got some appetite."

The crowd mumbled. Naomi stood to get their attention, her
silvery hair and freckled face shining in a beam from the overhead
lamp. "What about a psychiatrist?" she asked. "Maybe we should

send him down to Haifa to see Dr. Morganstern. She helped little Dafna that time. Remember?" she prodded them. "When Dafna pulled her eyebrows out?"

"Yes," the doctor said, "but that was what we call a neurotic compulsion. Yosi isn't sick. He's just lonely."

"No one ever wanted to marry him," a man called out. "I remember when he tried. Seemed like he asked nearly everyone."

"Last night on the path he touched my breast," Naomi repeated. "This is not a good omen. Something must be done."

Heads nodded agreement. The members—the *chaverim*—began to brainstorm, leaning forward and back in their folding chairs. "Order!" the leader, Lev, cried. "Let's take a break and have our tea." The *chaverim* aligned themselves at the back of the room near the samovar, their voices swelling and quickening. The name "Yosi" moved up and down the line like a password.

━━━━

In the cow shed, Yosi was settling the milk cows for the night and cleaning the stalls. Sharon was helping him.

"You are liking the smell of the hay?" he asked, handing down a bale from the loft.

"Yes," she answered in her careful, American-accented Hebrew. "I like the smell of the hay." They had agreed to have bilingual conversations so that each could practice the other one's language. "You like the cows, don't you?" Sharon led the oldest dairy cow, Tsiporet, into her stall.

"Oh, yes. I'm liking them very much."

"Better than Ton-and-a-Half?"

"No, not better," he said. "Just different. Like two different animals, like a cat and a dog."

"But they're all the same, cows—"

"No," Yosi interrupted. "No, the girls are cows. The boy cow is . . . is . . . I don't know the word in English, is *shor*."

"A bull. *Shor* is the Hebrew?"

"*Shor*, yes. He is a bull. He is different."

"Is he mean?" she asked, leading the last cow in from the outdoor pen.

"Oh no. He's a good bull. He always does his job."

"I know." Sharon lined up the water pails to be disinfected. She had seen Ton-and-a-Half do his job. He was a prize bull from America whose sperm was used all over Israel to improve the breeding stock. Yosi was the one who collected the specimen each week. Two months before, she had seen the bull pumping into the warm receptacle built into the "breeding wall." It was her second day on the kibbutz. Yosi had run back and forth, leading the "teaser" away just in time to turn the bull's attention to the surrogate opening. This had been Yosi's job for years, in addition to caring for the ten dairy cows the members kept for their own supply of sweet milk and cream.

"Ton-and-a-Half is very happy. So he's not mean. I think he knows what I'm doing. He doesn't mind. He never gets the heifer. Once in a while I bring him a real cow like Tsiporet to make fresh her milk."

Sharon scrubbed and hosed out the buckets. "How did you get your job?"

"I've always been a *bakar*," he laughed. "Like Roy Rogers, like Hopalong."

"A cowboy?" Sharon studied the face set on the thick neck. A fringe of wispy blond hair glowed halolike around his bald head, giving him an expression of perpetual amazement. "You don't look like any cowboy I've ever seen," she said.

Yosi lowered his gaze to the floor as if he'd dropped something of value.

"Oh, but I think all that's missing, really, is the hat," Sharon added.

The meeting resumed. "Order!" Lev shouted, pounding the table with his hand. "Eli?"

A burly redhead rose. "Let's try to arrange a *shiduch* for him. My mother knows a matchmaker in Tel Aviv—"

"Yosi doesn't want to live in the city," Naomi objected. "A match with a city girl? They don't like the kibbutz life. They like their fancy clothes and their typewriters and their lipstick." Though Naomi had brought the complaint against Yosi, she had only his best interests at heart, she explained.

"How serious is it, Naomi?" Miriam asked.

"He put his hand on my breast."

"Yes, but you're old enough to be his mother. Do you think it could go farther than that? Do you think," she hesitated, "he might force himself on someone? Become violent?"

"Violent?" Naomi swatted the word away with her hand. "We're talking about Yosi. He's not a criminal. But it's so unpleasant having to push him away, treating him like a child. Yosi? I don't think he has violence in him. Still, we must do something. We can't have him hiding in the bushes waiting to touch women in the darkness."

"I think he was staring at me when I came out of the shower house the other day," another woman offered.

"So what's the harm in looking?" Lev joked. The women in the room groaned in unison.

"You want him looking at your wife, maybe?" It was Miriam.

"Pardon me," Lev said earnestly. "All right. Let's be practical. Who has an idea? Don't be shy, *chevrai*."

The room seemed to inflate like a balloon as they sighed deeply and pondered the question. Finally, Shimon spoke. "I was just re-membering what my father did when I was seventeen. I mean, what he did to educate me about women."

The members waited as he groped for words, their eyes bright with anticipation. "He arranged for me a meeting in Tel Aviv."

"What does this have to do with Yosi?" Lev asked.

"A moment," Shimon continued. "He found a prostitute there, not an ordinary prostitute—"

"Tell me," Naomi chuckled, "what Israeli prostitute is an ordinary prostitute?"

"Order," Lev said calmly.

"She was very high-class. Superior in every way—gentle, kind—"

"And how did your father manage to find such a righteous whore?" Miriam asked.

The *chaverim* laughed. "A good qvestun!" shouted the old Rus-sian, Samuel, from the last row.

"I don't know," Shimon confessed, his face red. "Anyway, it's not important—"

"To *you*, mebbe," Samuel countered. "But to your mother?"

"Order!" Lev repeated. "I think Shimon has an idea here."

"Thank you," Shimon said. "If Yosi is lonely and awkward with women, why not get him a prostitute—a very nice one, of course. A prostitute of his own, so to speak."

"Tel Aviv is too far away. I never noticed any in Haifa," Miriam worried. "I don't think there are any."

"You, mebbe, didn't notice," Samuel said. "You mebbe didn't notice World War I, but I assure you it happened."

Dr. Zalman took the floor, twisting the band of his wristwatch into a pretzel. "This idea sounds practical to me. And if it doesn't work, we'll know the problem goes deeper."

Again the *chaverim* buzzed and turned in their chairs, discussing the pros and cons. "Do I hear a motion?" Lev asked.

Shimon stood quickly to claim his idea. "I so move: that the kibbutz send Yosi to an appropriate prostitute—"

"How often?" someone asked. More buzzing. Shimon looked out over the faces in the room, watching their lips move, catching the emphatic phrase. "Once a week," he concluded.

"Everyone in agreement?" Lev polled them. Every hand went up. "Done! And who will tell him?"

"Let the doctor tell him," Naomi advised. "Say . . . that his hormones are building up and that it's healthy for a man to have sex on a regular basis. True?"

"True," the doctor agreed.

"And you, Samuel, you know-it-all. You find the prostitute."

"Mit pleasure."

Yosi studied the woman's calling card.

> Leah Star (Strovosky)
> 18 Michael
> Haifa, Israel

A bright purple star exploded in the upper right-hand corner. The magenta letters were raised and seemed to flow like liquid under his calloused thumb as he touched them over and over.

Number 18 was the upstairs rear of a small apartment building overhung with bougainvillea, the orange blossoms bright against the white concrete. A small sign above the mailbox bore the same star as the calling card. In small script next to it were the words *Specialist in deep muscle massage.*

He had hardly pressed the buzzer when the door opened and a dark young woman took his hand, saying, "I'm so glad you could come."

"Thank you," he mumbled. His legs felt as if they were dissolving at the knees.

"Over here. Let's sit. I have made a small salad and we'll drink dry hock wine. You like hock, don't you?"

"Yes." He picked up a pillow decorated with metallic Yemenite embroidery and clutched it to his stomach.

"That was made by little deaf girls," she told him.

He looked around the room. "What was?"

"The pillow. The one in your lap. Would you like to eat now?"

"Yes." He was suddenly very hungry.

As he picked up his fork a large gray cat leapt onto the table. The utensil clattered to the floor.

"Oh Melech!" she chastised the cat. She removed him and set him gently on the floor, then came and stood behind Yosi as he leaned to retrieve the fork.

"Wait," she said, placing her hands on his shoulders. He froze. "You are very tense." Her fingers began to play his neck tendons like a keyboard. He let his head droop forward onto his chest.

"That feels good," he whispered.

She picked up the fork, letting her breasts graze his back as she leaned down. Then, with her arms around his neck, she wiped the fork with a napkin and pierced a tomato wedge.

"Open, please. Make big the tunnel for the choo-choo train." The fingers of her left hand stroked his lips. His mouth opened as if by reflex. She fed him the salad one piece at a time.

"That was delicious," he said, after she had wiped his mouth with the palm of her hand.

"Now it is my turn," she said, pretending to lift him from the chair.

"Your turn?" His eyes darted around the room.

"You feed me salad now," she explained. They traded places, and he imitated her perfectly. When he got to the last slice of cucumber he let the fork fall on purpose. She smiled, as if she knew what would happen next. The hard surface of his pants pressed against her arm as he straightened up and fed her the last morsel.

"And then what happened?" Sharon asked. She was standing in the barn doorway, a pail in one hand, the other hand on her waist.

"I'm embarrassed," Yosi admitted. "I know I promised, but . . ."

"What?"

"She is wonderful, my little Star. I am learning from her so much."

"Learning? Tell me."

He began to whistle and pull on Tsiporet's udder rhythmically. The cow's eyes looked waywardly at both of them as the fresh milk streamed into the bucket.

In the following weeks Yosi received letters every Sunday addressed in purple ink from Star. "Next time you come, bring me pictures from your childhood," the first letter requested. Another time she sent him green tea from Japan—a thin tissue-paper sack placed inside a note: "Steep this four minutes in boiling water," it instructed. "Next week kelp."

Yosi took a steamy shower every Thursday morning, shaved and readied himself like a bridegroom for his weekly visit with Leah. He had lost a few pounds, and his hair was slicked down now, leaving only a saucer-sized bald spot. Her insistence on touching his face convinced him that he was not as ugly as he had thought, that there was something exotic about his small gray eyes and fleshy ears.

Only Sharon knew what went on during his visits, and even she did not know everything. Nevertheless, she learned a great deal: the fourth week, Yosi had shaved Leah's legs for her; the sixth week he had licked honey from her breasts. She had given him a manicure and explained how the muscles in his arms worked. One Thursday morning, as Yosi left the dining hall in a cloud of hair tonic and cologne, Samuel had joked, "Look at him! A regular Mr. Hollyvood!"

As Yosi pried the cow's mouth open, Sharon forced a large pill down her gullet. "You are not bored," he asked, "working with the cows?"

"No. Do you get bored with them?"

"They are like sisters," he said simply, replacing the lid on the bottle of capsules. "We must watch the next few days for the worms," he reminded her.

"Yosi, do you ever get bored with Star?"

He grabbed a shovel from its hook on the barn wall. "I am like Ton-and-a-Half, you know? Besides," he said, stabbing the shovel under a fresh pile of manure, "I love her."

Sharon carried a chair under each arm from the storage room to the main hall. "Where is everyone?" she asked Naomi, setting them down with a thud and a sigh.

"Outside, kibitzing."

"Looks like they're having their own meeting out there," Sharon observed.

"Yes." Naomi sat down at the end of an incomplete row. "It's about Yosi."

"But Yosi is in town. It's Thursday—"

"I know."

"Oh, I see." Sharon frowned.

"They're just jealous, of course. But they want to quit sending him to the prostitute. They say maybe he's rehabilitated by now, ready for a real girl."

The rising inflection of Naomi's voice made Sharon suddenly realize that this was a question.

"A real girl?"

"You know him well. He talks to you."

"You're not thinking of me with Yosi?"

Naomi patted Sharon's arm. "No, I don't mean you and Yosi. I meant he confides in you. Maybe he's told you something? Has he got his eye on someone here at the kibbutz?"

"I don't think so."

"I've known Yosi since he was a baby." Naomi wiped her neck

with a handkerchief. "I only want what's best for him." She stared into Sharon's eyes, her forehead grooved with concern. "I don't want you to betray any confidences, exactly. Just tell me," she whispered loudly, "what's going on with him? What goes through his mind?"

"How good Leah is to him."

"The whore?"

"I don't think you ought to call her that."

"Aha!" Naomi exclaimed. "You've met her then?"

"Of course not. But Yosi's told me—"

"What?"

Sharon scrutinized Naomi. The freckles on her forehead, run together from the summer sun, suggested the shape of a land mass on a map. Asia, perhaps. "He loves her."

"I'm so glad for him." Naomi threw her arms around Sharon. Then her teeth bit into her lower lip, and she shook her head doubtfully. "We have a problem."

"We do?" Sharon followed Naomi's eyes to the doorway where a crowd of men had assembled. She could see their knobby legs as they shifted from one foot to the other and scuffed at the ground.

"The best defense is attack." Naomi held Sharon by the shoulders. "Are you willing to help?"

"Yes."

"Then here is what we will do." Naomi's eyebrows arched as she pulled Sharon closer. She unfolded a chair. The sound of its legs scraping the floor smothered her words as the hall began to fill.

Lev took up the usual business: first, a report on the grapefruit crop, a discussion of the new picking schedule. The allocation of money for a phonograph for the children's house was next. The poultry committee complained again about the unreliability of the itinerant chicken sexer and recommended employing one from nearby Kibbutz Shemesh in exchange for violin lessons with Samuel.

"Anything further?" Lev asked.

Shimon stood. "I wish to say I think it's enough, this sending Yosi to the prostitute. It's time for him to find someone on his own." The room remained quiet, so he continued. "I know practice makes perfect, but it isn't like he's going to make a career of it. We're not paying for him to become a concert violinist." The crowd fractured with laughter. Naomi's finger drummed on her ample thigh.

"Now?" Sharon asked her.

"Not yet."

"We never intended it as a permanent solution," Shimon went on.

"You can't cut a man's water off just like that!" Samuel objected, snapping his fingers for emphasis.

"We could wean him gradually . . . say, three more weeks," Shimon replied.

"That sounds reasonable," Doctor Zalman agreed. The *chaverim* buzzed briefly, an intermittent and unenthusiastic buzz, like the sound of a fly dying.

"Do I have a motion?" Lev asked.

"Now!" squeaked Naomi.

"*Rak rega echad!*" Sharon bellowed. "One minute please!" The *chaverim* were stunned first by the voice, then by the translation.

"Our newest member has the floor." Lev's voice was solemn.

"Thank you," Sharon said. Silence descended on the members like a sheet thrown over a bird cage. "The other night, when I was coming from the barn, he put his hand on my breast." Now the silence filled the room in heaps and drifts, engulfing her words. "And my leg," she added, "high up."

"Oh no," Miriam sighed.

"This sheds a different light," Doctor Zalman said, rubbing the side of his face as incredulity gave way to thought. Sharon glanced at Naomi, who was intently tracing the lines on her palm with a thumbnail.

"We could be the first kibbutz with a maniac on our hands," someone yelled.

"He could be working up to something bigger," the doctor said. "What did you do?"

"I told him," she cleared her throat with a low rumble, "that he must not do these things, because I don't feel romantic about him. I told him it was a serious matter. He was very ashamed." Naomi's plan was brilliant, but Sharon didn't quite know how much to embellish the story. She kept talking. "Actually, I felt he was trying to tell me something—"

"Exactly!" Naomi was on her feet. "Doctor, wouldn't you agree there is a pattern to his lapses?"

"A pattern?" the doctor echoed.

"First it was me," Naomi continued. "And who am I? Almost his mother, may she rest in peace. That's who I am. And now Sharon. And who is she?"

They looked at her blankly. Then, as if one candle after another were being lit, the room perceptibly brightened.

"Like a sister, perhaps?" Shimon ventured.

"Right. You see, he only does it to people he loves and trusts, people who would forgive him."

"Still—" Miriam objected.

"No. Listen, what does it mean?" Naomi raised her arms toward the ceiling. "He's sending us a message, *chevrai*—"

"Of course!" Samuel interrupted. "It's like the handwriting on the wall. But this time," his index finger wagged at them, "the handwriting is on, if you'll forgive me, the breast!"

"I know what the handwriting says." Naomi folded her arms and smiled broadly. An unspoken challenge radiated from her stout figure.

The buzz in the room was deafening, the sound of an airplane engine warming up.

"Would one of you prophets be so kind as to translate it then?" Lev asked, clapping his hands for order.

Naomi turned to stare at Shimon seated several rows behind her. He stood up slowly. "I, too, read the writing." He took a deep breath. "It says—" he watched Naomi as she wiggled two fingers alongside her ear, "it says that we should send him twice a week."

"And?" Lev prompted.

"I so move," Shimon said hurriedly, "that the kibbutz send Yosi to his appropriate prostitute twice a week—"

"Indefinitely," Naomi added.

A biblical "for eternity" from Sharon was muted by the enthusiastic clucking which filled the room.

The vote was again unanimous. At tea afterward, they congratulated themselves on the wisdom of their solution. Solomon himself could not have done better. In the barn, Tsiporet pulled hay from her rack and chewed it slowly as she waited for Yosi's hands.

Companion Planting

At Christmas, while I visited my new grandson in North Carolina, I wrote to Alice every day on the prettiest postcards I could find—Bat Cave, Blowing Rock covered with bluish snow. I stopped twice on the road home, once to buy her shelled pecans and once for a poinsettia plant. When I crossed the Florida line I called her. "You'll be a sight for sore eyes," she groaned. "Can you come over right away, Cleland?"

In spite of all that had happened in the last few months, when I heard her voice I missed that blond hair blazing in the sunshine and that nice smile of hers. A good-looking woman, even at fifty-five. "Anything wrong?" I asked.

"Just a surprise," she said. Then she blew me some kisses over the phone and hung up.

Surprise. That could mean trouble. It was the same word Alice had used when she stopped by the feedstore last April to tell me her niece Jackie was moving to Florida. "I figure she can fit her little single-wide right between your trailer and my A-frame, temporarily," Alice had said excitedly. "I've got it all worked out in my mind."

I didn't doubt it. When Alice had something worked out in her mind, it might as well be standing and breathing and talking in front of you. She explained that Jackie was a certified PE instructor in California and that she'd lost her job and her fiancé the same week. "She calls it 'bad karma,'" Alice had said.

I told her any kin of hers was kin of mine. It was almost true—two weeks before I'd bought her a diamond solitaire at Thurgood's. We hadn't set a date yet, but Alice, being a Roman Catholic, put a lot of stock in engagements. It was the third ring I'd given to a woman. You might say I'm an old hand at it.

Now the rows of pines fanned out as I sped down the dirt road to Alice's place. I passed the beef steer in his small pasture—a cleared area with a bathtub and a bale of hay. His ears stood up and followed me like radar dishes. He was nearly big enough to slaughter.

The setter, her whole body wagging, met me at the path. I heard music throbbing from Jackie's trailer. The words of the song were garbled, like people screaming into the wind. I knocked on the door of Alice's A-frame. No answer. I walked back to the barnyard. One of the milk goats baaed at me over the fence rail, her udders hard and full. The place had the feel of something gone wrong—a stillness, like when you find the cattle loose in the sugarcane, bloated and woozy from overeating.

I heard banging from the barn, then Alice's voice. "Damn you!" she hollered. The new foal bolted through the dutch doors and galloped off toward the mares. Alice appeared, wrapping a blue halter around her arm like a bullwhip. "Glory be," she said, and waved to me. From Jackie's trailer the pitch changed, and a woman belted out the song "What's Love Got to Do with It?"

"Listen to that racket, will you?" Alice took both my hands. "I really missed you."

"Me too. What's going on around here?" I nodded toward the trailer.

"Jackie's driving me crazy."

"She's taken up rock and roll music?"

"Worse than that." Alice opened the door to her A-frame. "She's taken up with a man."

"I don't believe it."

She opened the refrigerator and took out two beers. We sipped, then kissed, our mouths cold and wet.

We had to knock hard on Jackie's trailer door. Finally she appeared, wearing a housedress covered with parrots and flowers.

"Welcome back," she said, clapping me hard on the shoulder. "Come on in and join the party." I looked into the dark living room. A man was sitting on the sofa, his boots up on the coffee table.

"Who's this?" I asked. The man stood and walked toward me, moving a big chaw of tobacco from one cheek to the other.

"Name's Hudson," he said.

"Cleland, meet my new fiancé," Jackie said.

"How do," he said. We shook hands. He was real thin, this Hudson, with long, slicked-back hair. He was wearing spurs, a tight denim jacket, and jeans. His voice was quiet and polite.

"Flip the tape over, will you, honey?" Jackie hooked a finger in one of his belt loops and pulled. I took a slug of my Bud and coughed as I whispered to Alice, "How long?"

"She's been catting around with him since the day before Christmas," she whispered back.

"Hudson's got a booth at the Waldo flea market," Jackie said.

"I sell collectibles." Hudson inserted the cassette. "And smoked turkeys and hams for the holidays."

"That's how they met," said Alice. "We had smoked turkey for Christmas supper."

"A real good meal," Hudson told Alice. "I appreciate the way you all been treating me." He looked me in the eyes as if to ask, Are you gonna make trouble for me? "Alice showed me the beautiful ring you give her. Hope I can buy Jackie one like it someday." He reached his skinny arm up and around Jackie's shoulders.

Alice set her beer down on the table. "Jackie, I told you this morning we need to talk."

Willie Nelson began singing "Always on My Mind." Jackie joined in.

"Jackie," Alice began again. "I've got to talk to you about the chores."

"That's our song," Jackie said, closing her eyes. Hudson pushed her chin sideways with his fist in a mock punch.

"Why don't you sing it, then, while you milk the goats or clean the hog pens?" Alice was getting riled, but Jackie just slouched down into the sofa cushions. Alice stamped her foot. "Jackie! You're not listening. Did you hear what I said? Even the cabbage is going to seed. It doesn't make sense after all the work we put in."

"I guess I'm just a fool in love," Jackie said, lighting a cigarette Hudson had rolled for her.

"I guess I'm the fool!" Alice snapped.

Jackie had arrived in late April, bringing her trailer and an old cat named Harmony. She was a tall, broad-built woman, flat as a board front and back, with short, frizzy red hair. The first thing she said when she got out of her car was, "Looks a little bit like California." Then she threw herself on Alice and cried about her ruined romance and her unemployment. "I'm swearing off men," she said. "No matter how good a shape you're in, your heart can still be broken."

At first things picked up for her. She got a job right off teaching PE part-time at Archway High. She hooked up her trailer between Alice and me and minded her own business. But only two weeks after starting, she lost her job in an argument over coed football. "Florida sure is behind the times," Jackie told us, waving her pink slip like a flag on the Fourth of July.

That night Alice and I were lying in bed jay-naked. Alice said, "What am I going to do with her? She's so damn independent. I told her this wasn't California, that people don't change their ways so quick here."

"I have a cousin who moved to California to raise cantaloupes," I said. "He's not so independent."

"It's not the same thing," Alice explained. "See, Jackie never lived anywhere but California."

I kissed Alice, but she couldn't keep her mind off Jackie.

"She's thirty-nine years old and got nothing going for herself." Alice smoothed back the hair from my forehead. I poked at the little dimple she has below her waist. "I told Jackie she could stay here permanently, Cleland, if she wants to."

I felt myself being wrapped around her little finger. But it was Alice's property, and the bed was warm and she smelled so good that I didn't care. Then Alice rose up on one elbow and commenced to pull the hair on my chest with gentle tugs. All my women have done that, even my first wife, who died in childbirth at the age of twenty. Alice told me Jackie had a plan for them to become totally self-sufficient, to live off the land. It wouldn't affect her pension, either. They'd buy livestock and farm the place, not just a few laying hens like she had now.

"How're you gonna do that with most of your twenty acres already planted in pines?" I asked.

"Jackie got a bunch of books from the library. Young women today are resourceful," Alice said. I buried my head between her breasts and rooted around a little. "It'll work out, you'll see," she said. "You can get us a discount at the feedstore. That'll help some."

For the next few weeks when I came home from work, I found Alice and Jackie digging up the backyard and nailing wood slats together. Jackie showed me diagrams of their garden, explained that she'd take the chicken lime and toss it right into the compost heap. Everything was going to be organized and energy efficient. Intensive gardening, she said. Nothing wasted. The garden would be grouped into what Jackie called happy combinations of crops by companion planting.

"*What* planting?" I asked.

"Companion planting—putting crops together so they strengthen each other. Beneficial pairing," she said. "Marigolds smell bad to most bugs. Garlic repels them, too. Sunflowers make nice shade for bush beans." She went on down the list. According to Jackie, every pest from tomato hornworms to aphids could be avoided if the right companions were planted.

Alice lapped up every word of it. I'm a Georgia boy. I've worked in cane fields and cornfields and soybean fields, but I'd never heard of "plant partners" or seen crops laid out in circles. Still, I wanted to show the women I was behind them one hundred percent. So I bought them a young steer.

"How cute!" Jackie said when I coaxed him out of the truck. She ran into her trailer and returned with a bottle of Coca-Cola. Then, sprinkling a few drops of it on the steer, she said, "I christen thee Sir Loin." The animal licked the soda off his muzzle and blew out through his nose.

"He ought to fill your freezer without too much waste," I said.

Jackie stood there, running her finger around the rim of the bottle. She looked at Alice and scraped her feet in the sand. "You'll have to feed him," she told me. "If he's going to be butchered, I'm sure neither of us could bear to get to know him personally."

"That's right," Alice said. "I draw the line at chickens."

The first time Jackie saw Alice and me leaving for square dancing I thought her eyes would fall out. "Petticoats!" she screamed. Then she positioned Alice in the middle of the living room and asked her to twirl—first slow, like a figure on a music box, then so fast that Alice's skirt blew up to a bell shape. "That's really quaint," Jackie said, clapping her hands. Alice pointed the toe of her shiny black shoe.

I hooked my fingers in her green satin cummerbund that matched my shirt. "You look like a prize at the county fair and good enough to eat." I pulled her to me as we stepped into the cool night air.

"She looks like an antique," Jackie said, closing the door behind us.

By the end of May the women had moved the chickens to their new coops and built all the animal pens. They bought two milk goats and five shoats. They took in a stray for a watchdog—a twitchy red setter who wagged her tail at everybody—and gave each animal a name.

Jackie got a part-time job at Mrs. Yancy's thoroughbred farm. She was on duty nights with the pregnant mares. All her salary went for calf manna, hay, growing mash, laying mash, goat chow, and minerals to balance the soil. The backyard looked like moles had been set loose in it. Piles of black muck, dolomite, and perlite were added to the sandy soil, a shovelful at a time. All my life I thought loving a woman meant taking care of her. Now it seemed to mean sitting back and watching her tote a bucket of manure. I did enjoy watching Alice work. No matter how serious she was, when she carried a hoe her hips swung back and forth in the same old way that made my heart flop around in my chest.

"Liberace owned a piano-shaped diamond," Jackie told me. I was helping her set collars made from tuna cans around the spinach seedlings to keep off cutworms.

"I never cared for all that glitter myself."

"John Travolta's got a weight problem," she went on.

When Jackie wasn't talking about gardening, she talked about Hollywood stars. Her favorite TV show was "Entertainment Tonight."

"My daddy used to sprinkle vinegar down the spinach rows," I said.

"Not good for the soil pH." She adjusted another tuna can.

Just then, Alice came out of the A-frame carrying the Heavy Hands that Jackie had loaned her to build up her biceps and pecs. She reminded me of a cheerleader with red dumbbells instead of pompoms. "Don't you get enough of a workout tending your farm?" I asked her.

"That's not the same as a regular program of exercise." She wiped her forehead on her sleeve.

It was another one of Jackie's ideas. Every morning when I left for the feedstore, Jackie was outside her trailer, doing chin-ups from a bar over the door. No amount of working out, though, changed the shape of her behind, which was flat as the bottom of a skillet. The seat of her jeans was always a couple of shades lighter than the legs.

It was at Mrs. Yancy's that Jackie heard about a half-blind quarterhorse that was going to be sold for dog food. "I've got to save the poor thing," Jackie told us. We were having supper in the A-frame: bean sprouts grown under the kitchen sink, meatless meatloaf, and acorn squash. Jackie's cooking. "I can get her for nothing," she said.

"This place already looks like the petting zoo at Busch Gardens," I said, buttering a stony biscuit left over from breakfast.

"It would be nice for Amanda to have company," Alice mused.

Amanda was her Appaloosa, in foal to the palomino down the road. "Jackie and I could ride together every afternoon."

So they paid $25 to trailer the mare over and another $150 to the vet. "Isn't this putting a pinch in your pension?" I asked Alice the next week. "It's not practical to spend so much time and money on livestock."

"Maybe Catholics feel different than Baptists about animals," Alice said. She was milking one of the goats. I watched her hands pulling on the udders and wished Jackie would go back to California.

"I'm a believer," I said. "That's what counts."

"God intended us to care for His dumb creatures. Roman Catholics take these things more seriously."

Maybe she was right. I'd been going to church since I was six years old but couldn't remember a single Baptist sermon that mentioned a horse, cow, pig, or goat.

"It's in the Bible," she said, scratching the nanny's face.

"Everything's in the Bible if you look hard enough."

When Labor Day rolled around, I couldn't get Alice to go to the Baptist Singles beach party. She said she had to pickle cukes and to-matoes over the long weekend and she couldn't leave home anyhow, because Amanda was due to foal. "We're gonna have a whole pantry full of homegrown crops." She was washing green tomatoes.

Through the kitchen window I could see Jackie pushing a wheel-barrow full of mulch along one of the spokelike paths through the circular garden. The big African marigolds on the outer rim made the whole thing look like it had caught fire.

"It's worth all the work," Alice said, inspecting another tomato as she rolled it across the drainboard into the sink. "No insecticides. Everything natural."

"Seems like you got time for everything natural but me." As soon as I said the words I wanted to take them back, but there they were, lined up like another crop waiting to be picked over by Alice.

"I'm not sure I catch your drift." She pulled the sink stopper and wiped her hands on a towel.

The last time I'd heard those words was right before my second wife, Leota, threw her V-neck sweater in my face. "I don't catch your drift," she'd said. I'd asked her to stay home more with our son, Ellis. If she had, maybe Ellis wouldn't have turned out so rotten and ended up serving time. Leota's last words on the subject, right before the divorce, were, "Children grow up in spite of their parents, not because of them. It's all in the genes, nothing to be done about it." I always wondered how come if Ellis was half mine and half hers, it didn't break her heart when he went bad.

"Look at that," Alice said suddenly, pointing out the window. The wheelbarrow was stuck on a hose. Jackie spit into her palms, bent her knees like a weightlifter, and cleaned and jerked the wheelbarrow over the hump. "She sure has upper body strength," Alice said. Then she turned back to me. "Just be patient, Cleland, things will be back to normal soon." She kissed me juicily. It was hard to stay mad at Alice. If there's one thing I've learned from my years with women, it's that where patience leaves off, your hormones take up the slack.

Amanda's foal came two days later. Sturdy, all right, but real pale. The first week, half of Archway paraded through the paddock. Against my advice, Alice turned down a quick $500 for him. Then those china blue eyes got lighter and lighter. "Oh boy," the stud owner said, "you've got yourself an albino."

That didn't sour the women on him. They rubbed sunscreen on his muzzle and said it didn't matter that they couldn't register him. Jackie wanted to sell him to a circus that ran an ad in *Saddle Bred* calling for blue-eyed white horses. But, as I pointed out, he was dun-colored. The $500 beauty was a $50 misfit.

"You can't keep him," I told Alice. He had gained forty pounds in the first three weeks of life. "I love you, Alice, but I can't feature us working to pay for animals that don't bring a return."

"We just don't see eye to eye like we used to," she told me, slipping a bright blue halter over the foal. The diamond ring sparkled in a bar of sunlight coming through the barn door. "I think we ought to re-consider our engagement."

"Because of a horse?" I swatted at my knees with my feed cap.

She took hold of my arm. "I think we need some time apart."

I could hardly believe my ears. Being apart from people I love has never made me feel anything but sad.

"You think all this farming and husbandry is a waste of time, don't you?" She put her hand on her hip.

"Not exactly. I think it'd be a waste of my time. Problem is I want to spend my time with you, like we used to."

"Well I want to be more independent." She leaned her whole body against the foal to budge him toward the stall.

"You are independent. You were independent when I met you."

"I was doing woman's work though."

"I'm gonna move my trailer back to my property for a while," I told her.

"We can keep on courting," she said, "like before—square dancing, the movies. All right?"

It always surprises me that when I'm feeling the worst I act the nicest. "I'm gonna miss making love to you." I could feel my neck turn red.

Her eyes flashed. "No you aren't. I don't plan to let you off that easy."

What's a man to do? My first wife, Ina, died before she grew up enough to talk so free. When I think of her I remember a thin young girl who sat for hours on end with her hands folded flat as road maps in her lap.

I moved my trailer three miles the other side of Archway and kept busy at the feedstore. It was deer season and rainy. We sold out of everything—ammo, camouflage duds, rifles.

Alice let her hair go gray and quit polishing her fingernails. She said she didn't have to be stylish around her animals, that she was getting in touch with her real self. It might as well have been Jackie speaking to me from under the pink-striped sheets.

We went square dancing every Tuesday. And every Sunday after church there was dinner with Jackie. I don't hold with being rude to women, but Jackie pushed pretty hard.

"We're doing fine without a man around the house," she said one cold November afternoon, serving up her vegetarian chili.

"If I'd never tasted chili with meat, I guess I wouldn't miss it," I said, spooning the red gunk over my rice.

"I've been in love," she said. "I know just what I'm missing."

Alice didn't say anything—just drank her goat's milk and stared at us.

When I left for North Carolina to see my new grandson two weeks later, Alice didn't even notice I hadn't invited her to come along.

——— ═══

Now, standing in Jackie's dim little trailer, I felt bad for Alice. I looked at her blue jeans with straw stuck to them. Her hair was a two-tone mess, gray around her face where it had grown out and blond at the ends. It was like seeing both my wives at once—the one no more than a child, the other a gadabout who kept closing doors in my face.

Alice was shaking her head and sighing. "Yep. I let you change my whole life. I've been blind as a bat."

Hudson smiled and nodded. "You know, Jackie changed my whole life, too. This woman's charm runs deeper than the Chattahoochee River."

"Boy, oh boy!" Alice let out a breath.

"Well, honey," I reminded Alice, "you wanted to be more independent."

"That's not the same as never having a minute to myself because Miss Physical Fitness here won't keep her half of the bargain. I didn't set out to change my way of living and my looks." She plucked at her torn western shirt and fought back tears.

Jackie snuggled into Hudson's shoulder and sniffed. "I'm sorry, Alice. I thought you wanted a new life as much as I did. I never twisted your arm." Hudson handed her a big plaid handkerchief. "I've got better things to do right now than rake hog pens."

"Oh, I get it." Alice was shouting. "You don't give a damn about intensive gardening, do you? It was just something to do till this cowboy came along."

Hudson opened his mouth to speak, but nothing came out.

"I'm living in harmony with nature, all right, all by myself!"

"Listen," Jackie said, "I'm real grateful for everything you did for me."

"That's the truth." Hudson leaned forward. "She's told me how grateful—"

"Oh shut up!" Alice said. "I don't care what she told you or what you think."

"But you have to," Jackie said. "We're partners now, Hudson and me. And you've still got Cleland."

"You jilted me," Alice said to Jackie. "I've been jilted."

"Me too," I said. Alice turned to me, moving as slow as a housefly on a cold day. We both looked at Jackie.

"It's your karma," Jackie said.

Alice smacked her own thigh hard enough to sting. "Is that what you call slopping pigs and mucking out stalls? Karma? I call it work. Work you wanted to do. Those animals and crops out there were your idea."

Jackie blew her nose; Hudson patted her like he was burping a big baby. Alice's chest was heaving up and down, but she looked spunkier than ever. "I could wring your neck," she said.

"She's right about one thing," I told her. "You've still got me."

Alice stared at me like she was trying to remember something real hard. Then she took my face in her two hands. "I'm a real lucky woman."

I put my arms around her.

"Don't you go thinking I'm beaten because of her. I still plan to live off the land, partly. And keep the animals tip-top."

"I know it," I told her. "We're adults. I guess we can work it out."

She said she was sure we could now that she realized how much work was involved. We looked over at Jackie and Hudson entangled on the couch, his blue denim and her bright print housedress heaped together like a pile of laundry.

"Isn't puppy love sickening?" Alice said.

Hudson and I sat across from each other, smoking and staring at the ceiling, while the women divided up the farm animals and equipment. Jackie halfheartedly agreed to help get in the cold weather crops before she and Hudson moved on. "We can sell the new coops at the flea market," she told Alice. "You can have my subscription to *Organic Gardening*."

"What am I going to do with three horses?" Alice asked.

"Mrs. Yancy can help us find buyers for them."

"Just for your half-blind mare," Alice said. "I'll keep Amanda like before." She turned around and stared at me as I swallowed some beer. "And the foal?"

"Oh, all right," I said. "He'll make a good pleasure horse, at least in the winter." I knew I was agreeing to more than a blue-eyed white horse that needed sunglasses, just like when the truck salesman asked, "Would you like it in red or green?" and I spent $7,000 on a color. In my head I started figuring an asking price for my lot and trailer and pictured my old rocker in the A-frame.

"The garden was a success," Alice told us. "But it's too big for one person. I'll have to make a smaller circle next planting season." She tried to catch my eye, but I looked away. "Maybe half a circle." She tapped a pencil on the table. "I'm gonna try nasturtiums next to the blueberries. And black salsify for the carrots."

"There's a companion for every plant," Jackie said.

The two women talked a while longer. Then Alice came and knelt by me, talking under her breath. "She wants us to hold on to Sir Loin till she and Hudson get settled. They're going to keep him. As a pet."

"That's fine."

I pulled Alice onto my lap. I couldn't rightly imagine Jackie and Hudson settled anywhere but in each other's memory, but I smiled at the thought of that big steer eating his way through our life, getting fatter, sleeker, safe as a sacred cow.

Disappeared

"Look at my life," Fontane said. She clutched her robe together below her neck. Fontane was a thin, lithe woman with springy black curls that lay close to her scalp. Even in grief she was beautiful, like a piece of sculpture in the rain. "It's as if I'm being punished for killing people in another life."

"I know, I know." Leila Pinkerton sprinkled sweetener into a glass of iced tea. "There's no explaining it."

"Why would the Lord give me two children if He was going to take them away?"

"I'm sure Hiram is all right," Leila said, hoping Fontane wouldn't get angry at the ease with which hope poured from her mouth. Leila had never had children herself and was well past the age for it. "I just know it in here." She pointed to her heart. "It's only been three days. He could have amnesia, he could have gotten lost." She stopped before saying that he could have run away. What would he be running away from?

Leila Pinkerton and Fontane Whitley were as close to friendship as they could get, given that Leila was white, Fontane was black, and they lived in a world full of people who claimed to know what that meant. They came together in crisis, like an emergency room team. At other times, a formality neither of them had created restrained them, driving them back into their separate shells. They trusted each other hesitantly, the way you trust a relative you've heard bad things about since childhood but who has always treated you with the utmost kindness.

Fontane began weeping again. Leila put an arm around her and squeezed her shoulder. "Did you search his room?"

Fontane's eyes caught fire. "Do you think I'm an idiot? We tore the house apart, hoping for a note."

"I'm sorry. I know you did. I thought you did."

"If this is some prank of his, I'm going to kill him when he gets home." She laughed at herself; then she began to cry again.

"There was nothing missing from his room?"

"Not that I noticed." Fontane stirred and sat upright.

"Like a favorite book or toy, his sneakers?"

"I don't think so." But as she said it, Fontane stood and began walking up the stairs, and Leila followed.

Leila had never seen Hiram's room, and it wasn't at all the way she would have pictured it. It was futuristic, like the inside of a spaceship. "Handsome," she said, looking around. One wall, covered with black corkboard, had posters from the video store thumbtacked all over it, and four intricate circuit boards hanging from hooks. Shelves spray-painted silver held books and magazines jammed in at all angles, including a few titles Leila had given Hiram. She believed reading kept the mind sharp, and she liked to turn a phrase herself. She'd rearrange a thought or observation in her head until she got it just right, as if she intended to write it down, though she never did. Her favorite author was Mark Twain.

"I fought the beer sign." Fontane pointed over Hiram's desk to a Miller High Life neon sign with a whale spouting a bright-blue plume of water. "That was a birthday gift from Dayton." Dayton was Hiram's father. He had refused to marry Fontane when she got pregnant at seventeen and had left town two months after Hiram was born.

Leila felt Hiram's absence more here than she had downstairs. Stuffed animals, model planes, an afghan draped across the foot of the bed: without their owner, the objects seemed forlorn. She remembered sorting through her husband's clothes after he died. She had felt sad and then had fallen into a rage. Colonel Pinkerton's ties and shirts were uncooperative messengers, not the measure of the man but a pile of anonymous hand-me-downs. It reminded her of what happened when Claude Rains removed his suit and unwound the bandages from his hands and face. There was nothing left but his cigarette and the desperation in his voice.

"Is it O.K. if I look in here?" Leila's hand hovered at the pull of the center desk drawer.

Fontane began to rummage through the bureau. "Yes, oh yes," she said. "You can look anywhere at all."

Hiram Whitley, aged twelve, had been missing officially since Monday. On the noon news that day, Hiram had been described as a slender black boy, five feet two inches tall, last seen at home on Sunday morning wearing a T-shirt and pajama bottoms. Leila, who lived next door to the Whitleys, was no alarmist. Having no children herself, she had nothing to relate Hiram's disappearance to but her own childhood, so long ago. In those days, instead of sassing, children often ran away from home or vanished into the woods for a day. She'd never known of one who hadn't come back. She imagined that Hiram was off hunting squirrels with the BB gun his father, Dayton, had given him, or exploring the bat caves formed by the interstate crossing Bellamy Creek.

But Fontane and Evan Whitley, Hiram's stepfather, were more modern, and, Leila supposed, more realistic. They were half out of their minds with worry. No doubt they were thinking of the little girl who was kidnapped last year from a department store in Palm Beach and then murdered. The killer was never found. That had happened three hundred and fifty miles to the south, in the glittery, crime-ridden part of Florida, which seemed a crazed foreign country compared to Bellamy County. Bellamy County had hummed along for more than a hundred years on lumber mills, tobacco, cattle, and truck farms. The town of Waccasassa was a transparent place, like a piece of old glass with impurities in it. Its inhabitants had long ago accommodated themselves to its flaws. They had their troubles, like people everywhere. There were bar fights and convenience-store robberies, but Leila had never heard of a child being snatched and murdered in Bellamy County.

"Have you got any notion at all where Hiram might be?" Fontane had asked her on Sunday afternoon, when she first discovered Hiram was missing. Hiram had made himself scarce right after breakfast, Fontane said, probably to avoid his stepfather's weekly attempt to persuade him to go to church.

"The last I saw him was yesterday, when he did the yard for me," Leila said. It had been overcast and windy on Saturday, and the whole time Hiram was cutting her grass, she had worried about lightning, staring through the window as the mower slowly peeled narrow swaths of lawn from dark to pale green. "I'm sure he'll turn up by supper."

"I tried to call Dayton, but wouldn't you know it, his phone's been disconnected," Fontane said. According to Fontane, she and Dayton had been on good terms only for the amount of time it took to conceive Hiram.

After Fontane left, Leila got in her old white Valiant and drove over to Vern's Kwik Stop, where kids often hung out to play video games and read comic books. Then she tried the middle-school playground. She stopped for a glass of iced decaf at Sinrod Drugs, swiveling slowly on her counter stool as she tried to put herself—a plump, sixty-eight-year-old white woman—in Hiram's place, tried to divine his whereabouts.

Leila had run away once, but she was nearly an adult at the time. It was during the war, and the Colonel was being sent to an island in the Pacific that was so small it wasn't on the big globe at her teachers' college. They spent his last weekend pass in a motel room in Myrtle Beach. Her parents didn't approve of the Colonel. Too impulsive, they said. Reckless. White trash was what they meant. He had a thick north-Georgia drawl, and he was big and raw-boned and had crooked front teeth. She loved him, she remembered, she loved him so much that just seeing the golden hairs bristling on his arms made her feel safe. And then, after forty-three years, he had disappeared into the earth as if he had never existed.

By Monday, the Whitleys were frantic. Mr. Whitley stayed home from the lumber mill where he was a foreman to be with Fontane. It was especially trying for them, coming so soon after the death of their six-year-old, Beckah, who had succumbed the year before to leukemia. AN ANGEL CAME TO EARTH AND TOOK THE FLOWER AWAY, Beckah's headstone said. The cemetery was at the end of two miles of washboard road. Beckah's first-grade teacher and Leila were the only white people at the funeral. Leila remembered the smell of freshly turned clay, and Mr. and Mrs. Whitley standing in front of the small coffin. Hiram had patted his mother's arm and tried to act like a grownup man, but Mr. Whitley dropped to his knees and began rocking back and forth, sobbing, "Lord, O Lord, you took her away." Fontane knelt down and wrapped herself around her husband. Hiram had stood behind them, suddenly tall and alone.

Leila believed that Fontane had married Evan Whitley out of spite, to get even with Dayton for leaving her. Evan was upstanding and proper. Once, at a Fourth of July street party, Leila had asked him to call her by her first name instead of Mrs. Pinkerton. He had raised his index finger to his eye and rubbed it and blinked repeatedly, as if a gnat were trapped in his lashes.

Dayton, on the other hand, was the kind of colorful, lying, energetic man whom adults saw right through and children adored. Hiram adored him. When Dayton visited, he was extravagantly attentive. Then no one heard a word from him for six months. He drove a hot rod with airbrushed flames licking the fenders and the rear end hiked up like a scorpion's tail. He never had money, though he always had some kind of recent good time he could tell you about. For Dayton, charm was a means of locomotion, like a swift pair of legs.

When Hiram was five or six, Dayton started bringing his women around. Leila had overheard some nasty arguments. Last Easter, Mr. Whitley had ejected Dayton from the house and stood screaming at him until he drove away, and Leila could understand why. She didn't care for Dayton's values or his women, with their black leather shorts and tube tops and tall boots. "They're all nurses, according to him,"

Fontane had told her. Leila responded with a questioning look. "That's how he introduces every one of those trashy women. He says, 'Have you met Sharanda, my scrub nurse friend?'" Fontane had burst out laughing. "He must think I have the brains of a bowling ball." But, for all his flaws, Leila could see that Dayton had a little fire in his soul and that the same light flickered in Hiram.

The Atlanta police had gone to Dayton's last known address on Monday. He wasn't there. His employer said he hadn't given notice, just quit showing up. The Bellamy County police stopped by to question Fontane that afternoon. Was it possible that Dayton had kidnapped Hiram? Fontane was sure he hadn't. "He's never even invited Hiram to come home with him for a weekend," she reported to Leila later. "Hiram is just a toy he plays with when he wants to show off for one of his girlfriends."

The neighborhood where Leila and the Whitleys lived had been built at the turn of the century for the new middle class—for meek, polite women like Leila's mother and grandmother, women who held the line between public and private life and feared shame. All the houses backed onto service alleys, as if the household functions—garbage pickup, stove-wood delivery—had to be handled as discreetly and invisibly as bodily functions. When Leila was growing up, everything about family life was thought to be proper and just, and you weren't allowed to talk about anything personal. Nowadays, nothing was right anywhere in society. Just tune in "Donahue" or "Oprah": people confessed everything, absolutely everything, in public. The sound of the daytime talk shows was one gigantic lamentation. Were there shameful secrets in Hiram's family? Late Monday, the police had questioned Leila privately, asking whether she'd noted any tension between family members, any bruises on anybody. She told them she was certain there was no violent behavior among the Whitleys. When Hiram misbehaved, he got a "time-out," not a slap.

Fontane was not trained to be meek, but to be scrappy and vigilant. She was born to adversity, while Leila was born to the smugness typical of Southern white people of a certain class. She and Fontane had never discussed it, would never discuss it. Fontane, the solitary dancer on the music box, with long legs like exclamation points. What must it be like for Fontane to climb into her bed tonight, Leila wondered. Mr. Whitley would pat her, turn over, and fall asleep. The house would be utterly quiet. All Fontane would hear would be the sound of her own breathing, the goddam regularity of it, and a prayer repeating in her head: Please, God, let Hiram be breathing, too. Eventually her eyes would grow accustomed to the dark. Visual purple— Leila remembered that phrase from somewhere. The room would take shape, the empty hallway beyond it like a bend in a river that leads nowhere.

Leila had worked or lived next door to Fontane for seven years— two when the building was only a store and five more since Leila had moved into it. Colonel Pinkerton's Treasure Trove was a cracker cottage with Victorian touches—gingerbread trim on the eaves and porch gallery, a fancy iron fence. Inside, it was set up like a model house, the used furniture and collectibles for sale displayed in rooms organized around color themes. Leila had a knack for arrangement and for color. The attic playroom was a cartoonish blue and yellow. The kitchen bustled with green glass Depression-era mixing bowls, red-handled eggbeaters, and gingham.

At first, Fontane Whitley kept her distance. But when the Colonel died, six years ago, it was Fontane who noticed that something was wrong with Leila. Fontane liked old things; she regularly checked the new arrivals after a truck had been unloaded. She collected hand-embroidered pillowcases and anything made of copper. One day, Fontane parked Beckah, who was sleeping in her stroller, next to Leila's desk. The adding machine was plugged in and she was paying bills. Leila remembered staring at the small red "on" light. The baby dozed; the red light burned steadily. It was like a tiny traffic signal that made her want to stop doing everything. Time passed—she did not know how much time—and the baby's eyes were open. She was grabbing at a string of plastic keys suspended above her, drool running from the corner of her mouth. Her feet kicked and her eyes watered as she reached for the toy with her whole body. Once in a while she touched one of the keys, and it clicked against its neighbor. Otherwise, the store was quiet as a folded quilt.

"Leila, honey, you're not talking today. Something's wrong with you, you're not saying a word." The voice was Fontane's. "Can't you say something?" The silence had brought Fontane hurrying down from the third floor to the front room. Usually she could hear Leila's voice, uncurling tentatively at first, then climbing, as she chattered at Beckah. "You're not even talking to the baby?"

Leila looked at Beckah and then at Fontane and burst into tears, but still she couldn't talk. The red light burned. The baby slept, then played. The Colonel had been dead for six months.

The doctor said Leila's depression was "profound"—as if, she thought, he were describing a symphony or a speech. He prescribed an antidepressant drug that gave her a great deal of energy after just a few weeks. She felt happiest in the store, each room of it like a bright nest she had woven for herself. The colors and textures suddenly brought shivers of delight, almost as if she could taste them, as if they satisfied some physical appetite. The doctor said not to worry about this odd joy; it was just her aptitude for pleasure coming back. But it was the reason she had decided to sell the house outside of town where she had lived with the Colonel and move into the store.

The police visited the Whitleys three times on Tuesday. They brought a specialist from the Missing Children's Registry, who asked detailed questions about Hiram's playmates and habits and interviewed children in the neighborhood. The church auxiliary sent covered dishes. The Whitleys' phone rang continuously with calls from well-wishers, friends, psychics, and the parents of other children who had disappeared. Two camera vans stayed parked on the street.

By Tuesday afternoon, Fontane was under a doctor's care for her nerves. She took small yellow pills every four hours and received visitors from the striped sofa in her front room. Mr. Whitley had gone back to work, but not before posting pictures of Hiram all over the county: "Missing Reward," the fluorescent-green paper said above Hiram's seventh-grade picture. Newspapers in Valdosta, Tallahassee, and Jacksonville carried the story on the front page.

Leila brought lunch for Fontane that afternoon—a platter of chicken salad with sliced cucumbers and a pitcher of Crystal Light lemonade. The Reverend Dozier Jones was there, holding Fontane's limp arm as they prayed together in front of a silent TV screen where well-dressed white people moved through spacious rooms. Fontane had taken to watching a lot of TV since Beckah got sick. She still hadn't gone back to work. Mr. Whitley said she would never have to if she didn't want to.

"Ma'am," the Reverend said, rising to his feet, as Leila leaned down to place the food on the coffee table.

"You remember my neighbor, Leila Summer Pinkerton," Fontane said.

"What a pity we keep meeting under such trying circumstances," the Reverend said. For a second, Leila imagined his voice emanating from the afternoon soap unfolding in miniature behind him.

"Lemonade?" she asked.

Leila hardly watched television anymore. Her favorite programs in thirty-five years were the Milton Berle Show and the Bicentennial Minutes. She wished they would re-run Uncle Miltie—there was nothing funnier than a man dressed as a woman, pitched forward in high heels like a gawky bird.

After Beckah died, Hiram developed an interest in movies like *Frankenstein* and *The Shining* and *Alien*. His weekends were filled with gelatinous creatures, mummies trailing gauze, and body snatchers shaped like giant snow peas. Leila was happy to let Hiram use the Colonel's VCR. He talked a mile a minute while he watched movies. Leila had difficulty keeping up with him; her attention would settle on the film or be sidetracked by a bird at the feeder in the yard. Hiram talked mostly about school. Fontane bragged to anyone who would listen that Hiram was in the gifted program, and sometimes, in front of company, she had him recite the names of all the presidents.

After lunch, the Reverend followed Leila into the kitchen and stood running his finger along the Formica counter while she washed the dishes. "I'm certain we all appreciate your thoughtfulness to Mr. and Mrs. Whitley in this time of trouble," he said. His "t"'s were little firecrackers going off in the middle of words. It was probably the way he preached, drawing the words out, making them sizzle and hiss.

"Don't you remember me from the shop?" Leila turned to face him. Sometimes she couldn't bear the way her black neighbors deferred to her, exchanging nothing more than pleasantries and homilies. She wanted to grab them and shake them and scream *It's me.* She often imagined the awkwardness dissolving: a door suddenly coming unstuck in a room full of people, every face furrowed at first with alarm, then softening as though a baby with wings had fluttered through the open doorway.

"The Colonel was a fine man, a fine man." The Reverend stayed behind his mask.

Mabidda thirty, I got thirty, mabidda thirty, who'll say thirty-five, bidda thirty-five where? The Colonel used to stand at his auctioneer's podium, the walnut gavel in his hand, a cowboy hat on his head. His voice was a bullwhip, gathering the crowd in, circling, snapping in the air. Whenever Leila thought of him now, she had to remind herself of his bad traits as well as the good ones. That way she missed him less. He was too stuck on himself to adopt a child. Afraid he'd get a defective one. Being from north Georgia, he wasn't open-minded, and, if the truth be told, in the beginning he did business with his black neighbors only because there was money to be made off them.

"He was just a human being, " Leila said. "You don't have to sweet-talk me."

The Reverend looked shocked. "I know he's with Jesus," he said, "the Colonel. And I hope you've taken Jesus. I've taken Him into my heart, and I am ready to go to Him whenever I'm called."

Leila picked up a knife in the sink and imagined brandishing it in his direction. *How about right now? Are you ready to go this minute?* Instead, she scrubbed the blade with a sponge until clear water danced off it. The Reverend waited as if for an "amen" from Leila, still unwilling to acknowledge her candor. "I'm in no big hurry myself," she finally said. She knew he'd find the remark too playful, but wouldn't take issue with it. A moment later, he left, promising to return the next day, urging Fontane to call him any time.

The sheriff organized a search party. At dawn on Wednesday, deputies and citizens began combing Waccasassa and its environs. It made Leila sick to her stomach when she saw volunteer fire fighters going through the dumpster behind Video World. Soon Hiram's face would appear like a reverse cameo on milk cartons, and children throughout the state would compare his birth date to their own over bowls of breakfast cereal.

Leila would have liked to join the search, but her legs and back were not what they once were. She knew the local terrain well—from the sand-hill pines near the northern county line to the swampy sweet-gum woods that fringed the Waccasassa River at the western border. Bellamy County was full of creeks, dry creek beds, quarries, and dense forests, all of which now seemed threatening. It was still possible that Hiram had run off and gotten lost; Leila believed that. When he was in elementary school, he had gone camping with Mr. Whitley and his Boy Scout troop. He knew, presumably, the basics of survival: how to light a fire, find fresh water, and sleep in safety from the snakes, bobcats, and wild hogs that Leila knew roamed Bellamy County. Still, as the days passed, the vision of him that occupied her mind changed. On Sunday, he tromped in slow motion through a field like someone in a shampoo commercial, the wild phlox and rye grass waving him on. That night, he slept in the crotch of one of the huge live oaks that lined the old Bellamy plantation road to the black cemetery. By Tuesday, his clothes were ragged and his hair was starting to mat. She saw him smeared with mud to the elbows and knees, bent over a brook, catching crawdads. By Wednesday, every imaginary glimpse of him was terrifying; he was becoming wild, a feral child. He had taken on an existence in which ferocity alone could save him. Finally, it was impossible to picture him at all—he had regressed too far from the boy she knew. Hiram had become a complete mystery. And another mystery had been revealed: Leila loved him. She felt the love deep in her body and all the way out to its edges—in her teeth and nails, skin and bones she wanted him back.

The search teams quit at sundown, having netted two garbage bags full of what looked like shreds of clothes, newsprint, and beer cans, all of it described as potential evidence.

Now, with Fontane's approval, Leila pawed through crayons and rulers and Magic Markers and gum wrappers and balled-up homework assignments. The disorder of Hiram's desk felt vital as it touched her hands, like the boy himself. "Nothing," she said when she was done. She walked to the closet and opened the two louvered bifold doors. Fontane nodded her agreement. "Help me," Leila said. "You know where things belong."

The two of them bent into the dark of the closet. Fontane was a good housekeeper. At home, when Leila opened a closet or looked under a bed, dust bunnies drifted in the small updrafts. Leila recognized a lavender-and-black plaid shirt and remembered a wisp of conversation, Hiram's head framed by hickory leaves. The shirt seemed ghostlike.

"Oh, my God," Fontane said. She had been squatting. Now she sat back on the floor. "My God, my God."

"What is it?"

Fontane pointed to the flamingo-colored high-tops lined up neatly at the back of the closet. "I put his sneakers there myself. They were alongside the bed on Sunday. But where are his dress shoes? Do you see his dress shoes? Black leather wing tips?"

The two of them pulled out everything on the closet floor. While Fontane pushed through the clothes on hangers Leila dumped the contents of a toy box on the bedroom rug. Legos, blocks, a small, deflated football, an old T-shirt. "I don't see them anywhere," she said.

"His good black pants," Fontane said. Her voice was shrill with excitement. "His dress clothes are gone. They're gone!" Fontane grabbed Leila around the waist and jumped up and down, holding on to her. Then she raced down the steps and into the yard, to the toolshed. Leila watched from the window as Fontane removed the padlock, ducked inside, and returned weeping and thanking God. "The BB gun's gone!" she shouted. By the time Leila made her way downstairs, Fontane was on the phone with her husband, her voice wobbly with excitement, then rushing out in a torrent. Leila hugged Fontane and sat next to her as she made one call after another.

That night Leila lay in bed thinking about the last time Dayton had visited. He had brought Hiram the BB gun against Fontane and Evan's wishes. Worse, he had taken the boy out to the Bellamy plantation road for target practice. It was a Sunday morning, and Fontane was furious and humiliated when she discovered that the gunfire that punctuated the Reverend's sermon was from Dayton's shotgun. He and Hiram were shooting mistletoe out of the live oaks. Several parishioners had seen the two of them resting in the culvert, their guns propped against a tree.

On Friday afternoon, Leila donned her tattered straw hat and pink cotton gardening gloves. She knelt on the soft rubber mat she had bought to save her kneecaps and began weeding the herbs. Fontane was arguing with her husband. Leila could hear their voices rising and falling through the open kitchen window.

The sun beat down through the torn weave of Leila's hat, dappling her hands and the ground. Then Fontane was standing beside her. "Any news?" Leila asked.

"The police keep telling me it's easier to find two fugitives than one. They don't know Dayton."

Los Angeles, Detroit, Leila thought, that's where Dayton would take Hiram, some crowded place where people disappeared into each other.

"Evan's idea of finding Dayton is to pray." Fontane reached beside the parsley and pulled out a big tuft of wood sorrel and another of spurge. "If I could kill Dayton, I would," she said.

"I bet Hiram will come back on his own. At the end of the summer, when the novelty wears off." But Leila knew that a runaway could be running *toward* something as well as away from something. She had wondered about that: which would be lonelier for Hiram—to settle into the quiet that Evan Whitley cast around his family like a heavy net or to listen to the laughter of Dayton and his women behind locked doors? And what if Dayton settled down? What if he suddenly learned about Crockpots and oral thermometers and encyclopedias? Fontane would become bitter, and then, for all her cynicism, pious. Leila could picture her in lace-collared dresses, offering up her love for her two lost children on the unyielding altar of the Zion church. In any case, even if he came home, Hiram would be changed. There would be a different light in his eyes—a satisfied shine, or, more likely, a sullen glint.

Leila took Fontane's hand and squeezed it hard and pressed it against her forehead, the way a magician touches and presses and smells the article of a stranger to surmise the past or the future.

On the Boil

From an airplane, the Suwannee River resembles a tree more than a body of water, a gigantic tree with all its roots exposed, intricate as the tunnels and chambers of an ant farm. When the sun hits it a certain way, the river water glistens like sap, and the tree seems to be growing right before your eyes, branching out until it empties into the Gulf where whitecaps flurry like blossoms.

Everyone has heard of the Suwannee, though almost nobody has seen it, including Stephen Foster, who wrote the famous song. He picked the name out of an atlas after his brother complained that "Way down upon da Pedee River" didn't sound musical enough. I'm an expert on the Suwannee. I've drunk the water, eaten the fish, picked my way through the poison ivy and stinging nettles, and danced away from its snakes. I love it the same way a person comes to love her own body or a close relative—not with a sense of choice but with a sense of destiny.

That's the way it is with Dory, too. Something grand, like destiny, between us, despite our differences. I've grown sick of explanations: more than anything else, love feels to me like a kind of being lost. Maybe that's why at first Dory and I spent so much of our time together camping in remote areas. In the wilderness, you expect to feel a little lost; you can tell yourself that the second thoughts you have at night in your tent come from the vastness of the place, not from a hollowness in yourself.

After we knew each other well, we started going to state parks. The public land was tamer, and we noticed each other more there. We spent the first warm Saturday in May at Manatee Springs. The park was crowded. We snorkeled around the boil and watched spelunkers diving into the craggy grottoes. I lay in a patch of sun while Dory worked his foxhound, BJ, letting her out on a twenty-five-foot lead, then hauling her in and rewarding her with dog snacks. Afterward, he tied BJ to a tree and went to buy lunch at the concession stand. He walked in a determined way, but slightly hunched over. If I hadn't known him, I'd have said he looked shifty from the back, as if he was trying to disappear, like a pickpocket in a crowd.

Dory bit into his hot dog and pointed toward a stand of big trees on the opposite bank. "See those cypresses over there? They're as old as the Bible."

"They remind me of an old sci-fi movie where the stones in a certain valley had recorded the past like video cameras. A scientist played back a hunk of rock and saw dinosaurs and all." What I didn't say was that I'd seen the movie before Dory was even born.

He slipped his hand down the back of my bathing suit. "You and me could live right here in a houseboat. Cook with Sterno, fish for our dinner," he whispered. "I'd love you all night long."

"Quit it." Sometimes I get so sick of the word "love" that I wish Baptists had convents. But, of course, if you spend all your energy denying a thing, it's nearly the same as believing in it.

"That attitude is going to make you miserable someday." He gazed straight at me. "I mean it, Lavell." He threw the stump of his hot dog to BJ and spilled the dregs of his soft drink at my feet.

He stopped formally proposing in March when I promised I'd give him an answer in a month. But when April came, warm and rainy, I still hadn't decided. That's when he got the tattoo on his shoulder: "Marry me, Lavell," on a placard like one of those gas station signs that sticks up over the interstate, except Cupid was holding the pole.

"Don't get into one of your moods," I told him.

Once in a while he fell into a deep quiet and refused to talk for hours. He called it "down time." He usually went home because I told him it agitated me to sit in a room with another human being and still feel alone.

"BJ's having a miserable day," he said. The dog had tangled herself around the tree and stood softly whining, one foot lifted as if it were broken. "Marry me," he said, forcing a smile, "shut me up forever."

Dory worked construction, but he was studying welding at the county trade school at night. He said welders could pick their jobs, work half a year, cruise the Caribbean the other half. "The world is made of metal," he kept telling me, "and it's forever coming apart at the welds."

His mother died when he was six, the same age I was when my father left home for good. My mother never bothered to get a divorce—she knew she was finished with men. She took up gardening. When I think of my childhood, the memories are set against her bent-over back framed by shiny green vine tomatoes, bushy orange and pink cosmos. Mama and I worked quietly together in the yard, stringing up pole beans, cradling the glossy eggplants like newborns as we cultivated around the plants. I like growing things, even if they don't always turn out. When I look at garden rows, I see pure goodwill, the weeds cleared, each little plant set out like a promise. Mama and I gardened even in fall and winter—pruning, mulching with cypress chips, putting the stamp of patience and expectation on the ground, telling ourselves we would be there three months, six months, down the road.

Dory's father was a postal worker in Lake City, so it was natural for Dory to take up stamp collecting. But his real passion was fox hunting. It's against the law to kill a fox, so the men just let the dogs roam in the preserve while they sat on the tailgate drinking beer, picking out their dogs' voices. They talked pedigree and cold nose trailing and told tall tales all night. I don't believe you could interest people in this sport once they're grown. They have to be bred to it, like the dogs.

Dory had ten hounds, with numbers dyed in their fur: Preacher, Luther, Belle, Digger, Highball, Tad, Willie, Frypan, Minute, and the new bitch, BJ, the high-spirited one nobody could catch. He took on training BJ when her owner, Uncle Jones, the bigwig at the Dixie County Hunt Club, threatened to shoot her. She had stayed in the swamp alone for three weeks, chasing deer from dew to sunset, living off the carcass of a buck Uncle Jones had shot but couldn't get to. For three weeks he came calling for her in his pickup. Once he spotted her running alongside the highway, her white hide flickering through the dark green of the scrub. Dory was determined to break her of running. She lived in a tall pen at my place (with Frypan for company) so he could spend more time working with her.

I flipped on the television while I waited for Dory to get home from school. I practiced different ways of crossing my legs so the cellulite in my thighs would be less noticeable.

"Entertainment Tonight" was celebrating Barbie doll's thirtieth anniversary as if she were a real person. They held her so close to the camera she looked life-sized. They showed her getting a spiral perm, dirt-biking with Ken at Big Sur. Barbie relaxed in a tiny hot tub while Ken barbecued at a matchbook-sized hibachi. She had changed a lot since 1960—not just her clothes and hairdos but her life-style. She used to be formally engaged to Ken, but now, even though the announcer didn't say so, it was clear they were living together.

Dory came up the path to my trailer, singing "Bridge over Troubled Water," which he called "Our Song." He could get romantic over nearly anything. I have a big blood mole right between my shoulder blades. My mother said when I was born she was afraid to bathe me, that the red bubble looked as if it would burst at the touch of a washcloth. Dory said it was my heart showing through to the other side, that I was a bighearted woman. According to him, everything about me was perfect. I wasn't fooled. No woman is perfect. Even Loni Anderson didn't make the big time till she bleached her hair blond.

"Mail for you." He handed me an envelope as big as a grocery bag. "It wouldn't fit in the box."

The front was plastered with "Love" stamps, but there was no postmark. On the greeting card inside, a bee all covered with fuzz, like a stuffed animal, said, "For you I'd go a million miles. . . . Just because you're my honey." It was signed, "Name the day, Love, Dorrance Shore." He always signed his full name on notes to me, as if they were legal papers.

"That's adorable." I kissed him so hard I felt his teeth through his lips. Then, all of a sudden, I started to get mad. Wherever I turned there was this boy begging me to marry him. I fully expected to see our names spray-painted on the overpass some day, a big question mark instead of a heart wound around them. "You know, you're just too nice all the time," I said. "It's not natural. It's weird."

His Adam's apple jumped up and down like a cat in a sack. "Nobody in high school thought I was so nice."

"You had a girlfriend."

"Didn't I ask you not to bring her up, Lavell? Sue Ellen's got nothing to do with us."

About two months after we started going together, Dory had disappeared for a week. By the time he phoned, I'd worked myself up into a lather, worrying over his safety, convincing myself I didn't love him. He told me he'd gone to visit his old girlfriend, Sue Ellen, but wouldn't explain except to say she was having a "confidential, personal crisis."

"Do you realize I've never seen you lose your temper?" I pressed. "I keep hearing about romances that go sour after the honeymoon."

"Quit trying to pick a fight with me, Lavell. You're going to have to marry me to see if I turn into Frankenstein."

"Why can't we leave things just as they are? We've got the best of both worlds." It was true. At thirty-eight, I was set in my ways. If I felt like being alone, he stayed at his place for the night. I had the sexual revolution, plus I knew that in the morning my panty hose would be hanging on the shower rod where I put them and not thrown to the floor in a damp heap.

I went to the Springs the next week to think. I walked the trail from the point to the deep turquoise lagoon of the boil and imagined women lifting their hooped dresses along the muddy path. When I saw the tiny gowns they wore, it made me feel like the Jolly Green Giant. No diet or exercise program in the world is going to make me shorter, which, in a way, is a relief. If you've got to have a flaw, it's best if it's something you can't correct.

Dory had found the invitation to my high school reunion on the kitchen counter the day before. His mouth was wide open, like a two-year-old's, as he read it. "We're going, right?"

"Give me that." I put the invitation back in its envelope.

"Why'd you do that?"

"I don't want it to be the topic of conversation."

"Okay, but I'll tell you right now, if I could go to my twentieth reunion, I wouldn't miss it for the world."

When the number "twentieth" came out of his nineteen-year-old mouth, it had burned into my heart like a hot spark.

Now, on my way back to the parking lot from the boil, I saw the park ranger putting up a display of Indian pottery. Pencil renderings showed how a whole piece of pottery must have looked and matched clay fragments that hung alongside on leather straps. Some were checkered, and some had fine lines like bird footprints. The ranger said gophers had dug up the shards not twenty feet from the display. "Are we standing on sacred ground?" I asked.

"We're standing over the kitchen." He locked the glass case.

I looked out through the trees and tried to imagine them growing over my trailer, rooted around the microwave and sink a thousand years from now.

Dory began bringing BJ into the house. He claimed that if he could tame her spirit just enough, she'd be the best dog in Dixie County. Then he'd breed her. You had to have one running fool somewhere in the pedigree to make a good hound. He'd play around with her in the living room before taking her for extended romps on longer and longer leashes. Sometimes he had to reel her in ear-over-ass because she'd lift her head, open her mouth to scent, and then take off, running to the end of her rope, refusing his commands, whistles, and shouts to return. In May, he began working her tied to the back bumper of the truck.

"Isn't that dangerous?" I asked. I'd heard stories of hunters running over their own dogs. It was a common accident, especially at the end of the day when the men were tired and the dogs were eager to be put up in their boxes on the trucks.

"The last place BJ wants to be is with me." He scratched behind her red-and-white ears. She turned her head away, closed her eyes, and panted. "She's like one of those convicts at Raiford or Cross City, just waiting for an opportunity."

Dory and I spent that whole evening in bed. We made love, took a shower, had a snack, and made love again. He knew the names for all the parts of my body and liked to talk about them while we were making love. It was like receiving one Academy Award after another. Best nipples: Lavell Beacham. Labia majora: Lavell Beacham. Areolas, and so on. Even when we were just lying there, he kept on touching me, drawing pictures and diagrams on my belly and back. If I felt talkative, he'd listen all night long.

A few days later Dory saw my new purple dress and knew something was up. "I guess you've decided to go?"

I was rummaging in the freezer for ground beef. That winter, Dory had shot a buck, dressed it, and wedged the long hind legs into my side-by-side. Every time I opened the door, a pair of lean silver legs leapt across packages of green beans and blackberries. "I'm thinking about it. You want to chop some onions for the burgers?"

"No. They always make me cry." He walked to the bedroom. I followed and sat down next to him on the bed.

I didn't want to be cruel. I was afraid that if I asked Dory to go I'd have such a terrible time explaining who he was that I'd never want to see him again. I'd always felt self-conscious in high school and had never really found a niche for myself. Too tall to be a cheerleader or a prom queen. Not smart enough to be a brain. I finished on the Business Ed track. I was a crack typist before word processors swept the country. Almost nothing I studied prepared me for the survey work I do now. The best thing that happened to me in high school was going steady with Fred Packett for two years. We broke up when he left to study business administration at college. The last I heard he took a job with a plywood manufacturer in Mobile.

"All right. I do want you to go with me."

He threw his arms around me. "You can say we're engaged."

"I don't have to say anything!"

After dinner, he produced a gift and a card that read "For Your Graduation," to which he'd added the word "reunion." I unfolded the tissue paper and pulled out a white shawl with rhinestones knitted into the pattern.

"I thought it was beautiful," he said, watching my face.

"Yes." I held it outstretched in front of me, a tacky triangle that threw off light like a disco globe.

"I was going to give it to you whether you invited me or not."

From age eighteen to thirty I felt proud and sassy when I printed the word "single" on applications for Visa, homestead exemption, Avon. Then the years began to zip past. It's true that as you get older, time speeds up: when you're ten, a year is equal to one-tenth of your life. By the time you're fifty, it's one-fiftieth, so naturally it goes by five times faster. Suddenly, I was pressing forty. Christmas came round so often I felt like I was constantly buying gifts or packing up decorations.

As for dog years, I couldn't say. BJ was three. She had two hunting seasons to shape up or Uncle Jones would put a bullet in her head instead of retiring her. BJ was making progress. She finally understood that she was attached to Dory by a rope, now almost one hundred feet long. He never took her off it. The idea was to trick her into thinking the rope would always be there, that his voice was the rope, that the horn of his truck was the rope. One night, at the beginning of June, she began howling, piteously at first, then with the full belling of a hound on the scent of an animal. It was three o'clock in the morning. Dory went out and beat her with rolled-up newspapers. "She must have whiffed something real big. BJ wouldn't waste herself like that," he said.

I'd never seen anything in our trailer park but rabbits, muskrats, and possums. Roadkill casserole, not fit for a hound to fiddle with. Besides, Frypan, her kennel mate, had remained silent. "Maybe she's howling to come inside the house," I said, though BJ never seemed to notice our company much. She wouldn't even look you in the eye. She wouldn't even let you that far into her dogsoul.

I had thought a lot about what to call Dory at the reunion—my roommate? boyfriend? fiancé? Finally, I settled on "friend." It left room for interpretation and gave me a fresh perspective on him. Perspective—that's what I love about going up in the one-engine mapping plane. I feel insignificant and important at the same time. I'm responsible for sighting landmarks while the aerial photographer lines up the shots and clicks away. Between us, we piece together the landscape like blocks in a quilt. From 6,000 feet the woods seem as stiff and artificial as those toilet-brush Christmas trees.

Fred Packett, my old beau, was glad-handing people at the door when Dory and I arrived at the reunion. His eyes were the dark green of magnolia leaves. I did a double take. They had been gray behind horn-rimmed glasses all through school. His hair was combed forward, but a small spot like an egg in a nest showed through on top. "It's real good to see you, Lavell." His arms felt meaty and familiar through his sport jacket. A gardenia leaked sweetness from his lapel.

I introduced him to Dory. "I'm divorced," Fred said, by way of a reply. "From a real nice woman in Mobile. No kids. She didn't want any."

"That's too bad," I said. Dory nodded in agreement.

Fred guided us toward the punch bowl. A big banner saying "Welcome Back Wildcats 1970" hung above the refreshment table.

Fred was as friendly as a long-lost relative, and before I knew it we were talking and laughing. Dory stood silently next to me, holding my elbow. "You're a lucky fellow," Fred told him, squeezing me into his shoulder.

While Fred and I danced, he told me about his divorce. He'd been married for twelve years. He and his wife went to Mexico at the end to try to patch things up. "Vacations are a true test of marriage," he said. "When you're in a foreign country you end up liking the person you're with a lot more or a lot less. We ended up practically hating each other."

"I've never been to a foreign country."

"You're not missing much." He grimaced. "All Lola wanted to do was visit ruins." He gulped down a cup of wine cooler. I told him how I'd worked my way up from clerk to assistant director of Maps and Surveys at the Farm Bureau.

I'd never seen Dory drink anything but beer, but he downed six glasses of champagne during dinner. He sat in a stupor, staring at the back of my neck, while the class president read our statistics. Three class members unaccounted for. Sixty-four college diplomas and eighty-two children. Three grandchildren. We bowed our heads as he read the names of the deceased—one girl dead of cancer and two more in car wrecks; three boys killed in Vietnam. We stumbled through the school fight song, and even though I never cared much for sports, I got teary-eyed thinking of all of us back then, so young and stupid and hopeful.

A bunch of us hit the ladies' room after the presentations. When I returned to the ballroom, I didn't see Dory anywhere. Fred, looking morose, was leaning against a column wrapped with orange and black crepe paper. He caught my eye and motioned me over. "What do you think about this business with Sue Ellen?" he asked.

"Where's Dory?"

"He went outside to get a little air. Actually, I think he felt like throwing up."

I found Dory on the balcony, leaning on the railing. He smelled sour and looked disheveled. He put a limp arm around my waist.

"Tell me about the week you went away."

"Sue Ellen and I—" Tears collected in his voice, but he swallowed them down. "She had a baby. My baby."

Sometimes people talk and nothing gets said, and other times, using the same two-cent words, they say something so big it feels like an avalanche. When my daddy left us, all he said, according to Mama, was "I'm not coming back, Norma."

"She wouldn't get an abortion. I don't love her, Lavell. I was sure I did at the beginning. At first, I was as happy with her as I am with you. Then one day the feeling just vanished. It was horrible."

"Oh God." I pulled away.

"You don't understand." He reached for me, but I hurried back inside.

I don't believe in astrology, crystals, or liquid diets. My mother, though she went to church, was not a religious woman. She spent her free time bowling and canning. She was a kind of Benjamin Franklin of the kitchen, always entering recipe contests. I suspect she didn't win because she used quantities of fresh sage, lemon balm, basil—herbs and spices that people can't buy except dried-up like mummies in those little bottles in the supermarket. Mama would cringe to see what Dory and I eat: frozen pizzas and quiches, canned corn, instant mashed potatoes—the food Dory grew up on. Broken-home food. Loneliness food.

Fred opened the sunroof of his car, and warm air fragrant with night-blooming jasmine blew through my hair. We passed Six-Pack Creek, named for all the beer the boys drank and peed into the water those hot summer afternoons we tubed down it. I didn't want Dory finding me. I'd grabbed Fred by the arm and asked him to drive me anywhere but home. He'd looked confused but eagerly agreed.

After we parked the car, we squeezed under the gate to the recreation area. We sat on the seawall and watched the moonlight reflecting across the current. Mosquitoes whined around my ears.

"I'll always remember this place," Fred whispered, as if testing to see if I wanted to talk. "We had some good times here."

"Yeah." In high school Fred and I went to the river to make out. It had taken months before I let him touch me below the neck. I'd never slept with him.

"Everything's so different now, except the river," Fred said. "The river's the same."

"Oh no it's not."

"Polluted, huh?" He lit a cigarillo.

"I don't know about pollution. I just know it's always changing a little. You know, Indians used to cook their food right here."

"That so?"

"Who knows what people a thousand years from now will find of us."

"You've grown real philosophical, Lavell." He took the rhinestone-studded shawl off my shoulders, walked to a live oak tree, and draped it over a low limb. Then he spread his coat jacket on the ground. "Let's study the stars a while."

Cobwebs floated across my face as I knelt down. We lay back on the jacket and breathed deeply. "I'm up for plant manager," Fred said.

Suppose Dory couldn't tell the difference between teenage love and mature love? He might be falling in or out of love all his life. Or worse yet, suppose there was no difference between the two kinds of love? Mama always said that women were after love and men were after sex and they spent their whole lives angry at each other for an unavoidable confusion. I glanced from the star-studded sky to the shawl nearby, the rhinestones blinking in the tree. "What would they make of that shawl a thousand years from now?"

"They'd put it in a museum, I guess."

"That's the thing about time. Junk, I mean even real garbage can become valuable. Something you never thought about could be important."

"I know you're real upset, Lavell." He pulled me down by the neck and kissed me hard on the mouth.

I felt my face redden and the veins in my neck stand up. "That's really crude, Fred, especially if you know I'm upset."

Fred twisted away from me and flung his arms over his head. "You gotta overlook it if I'm awkward. Divorce really messes you up."

"I wonder if the Indians had it."

"What?"

"Divorce."

"Marriage is an unnatural institution," Fred sniffed.

"It must be terrible to fall out of love," I said. I wasn't thinking about Fred but about Dory. I'd never fallen out of love. I'd had a broken heart a few times. I'd fallen into love so hard that even the sight of shoes like my boyfriend's in a store window or a car like his in traffic made me giddy, as if they had eyes to watch me. But usually I lost interest by degrees so that the end was never a shock and I could hardly remember that crazy feeling. Now I tried to imagine worshipping a person one week, and the next week finding him ordinary, completely unmagical, his possessions ordinary—sagging topsiders, a beat-up Ford Escort.

"I don't regret marrying Lola," Fred said. "That's the funny part. I don't think I've learned a single thing from twelve years of marriage."

I caught sight of a blue heron lifting off from a cypress tree. The river was warming up, getting ready for another day. I picked up the shawl and bunched it in my arms. We started back to the car. Cypress knees stuck up on either side of the boardwalk in their usual ragged fashion, competing for space. Like seedlings, with no one to thin them. Though it wasn't yet dawn, I could feel the light just below the horizon like a humming in my bones.

Fred dropped me off at 5 A.M. I was relieved that Dory's truck wasn't in the driveway, but he had left a note on the kitchen table: "I'm SORRY. Love you so much. Taking BJ to the trials. See you tonight. XXXX" I drew a hot bubble bath and soaked. Gray light turning to pale pink filtered into the room through the rippled glass of the small east window. I added more hot water, and the room filled with steam. Dory's face floated in the mist, along with a squalling infant and a sad-faced woman holding a phone to her ear. It was bad enough trying to decide whether to marry Dory when I was just worried about the age difference. If I could have ten good years, just ten, I had thought, it would be worth it. I'd keep on working, keep parts of my life to myself, like a cash reserve in the bank, something to fall back on when he finally left.

I decided not to go to bed at all. It was a Saturday morning, a fine Saturday morning in June. The oak tree overhanging the dog pen was tipped with tender, waxy new leaves. I dragged a webbed lounge chair from the carport into the backyard to nap instead. Dory had left the gates of the dog runs ajar and hadn't picked up the food pans from the night before. The kennel looked peculiarly sad and mysterious without BJ or Frypan in it, like the scene of a kidnapping.

I remembered that Dory hadn't planned to take BJ out until Sunday, the second day of the hunt being held east of Horseshoe Beach, in the Waccasassa swamp. Maybe he was just afraid to face me. I was glad he wasn't around now. I got enraged just thinking about the begging tone he'd have in his voice when he asked me to forgive him.

My neighbor's daughter came into her yard and waved hello. Emmy was fifteen and dressed crazily. She wore iridescent exercise tights, a long T-shirt, and a black leather belt cinched around her hips to school. Other times she dressed in clashing plaid pants and blouses, with men's white shoelaces braided through her hair. I didn't know what clothes meant anymore. All the fashions seemed designed to confuse you about a person's values and financial status. When I was growing up, I was taught that clothes told the world what you thought of yourself.

"Your dogs was crying all night long," Emmy called out to me. "My dad was fit to be tied."

"I was out all night."

"That's what Daddy said."

On Saturday, the judges spotted BJ first behind the fox three times. But at the end of the day, when the pack gathered, their tongues hanging out like sodden rags, she was missing. Dory had remained until after dark, calling, honking the horn, playing the radio full blast.

We spent Sunday searching for her. We set aside our differences like parents do when a child is in danger. Dory wore his Wellingtons, and I drove the truck from point to point. People don't realize this end of the Suwannee, being so close to the Gulf, has tides. The water was high in the swamps and in the river basin. By nightfall, we were both hoarse from calling. Uncle Jones was waiting by my trailer when we got back. "It's in her blood," he said, without getting out of his truck. "She's more wild than domestic."

Dory said he didn't think it was wildness, because the feral dogs he'd seen always looked scared, as if they'd trade their terrain in a minute for a feed bowl and a warm place to sleep. BJ was another story. BJ had a job to do—chase all the foxes and deer in the world, though she would likely never have been able to bring one down on her own. "I guess you were right about her. It was real bad that she got along so fine that time she was gone for three weeks," Dory said.

"Yeah," Uncle adjusted his cap. "She'd have been better off if she'd broken her leg or got cut up real bad, instead of finding that carcass to eat."

We went looking for her every day that week after work. Once Dory thought he saw a spotted red-and-white dog slip through a patch of shadow not far from the road, but he was never sure.

A week later, Uncle phoned to say BJ had shown up in his backyard but that she was doing poorly. He suggested Dory come over to see her. It was hours before Dory returned to the trailer. His face looked hard. "She ran herself to death. Busted her heart. She came back to die, was all."

Sometimes, when I'm lying here alone at night and can't sleep, I think of what it must have been like for her out there, among the trees and stars and all the animals of the kingdom. I imagine that on nights when the deer and foxes stayed hidden, she chased ripples on the water, birds, finally, maybe, even the moon. I know what it would feel like to run that hard, the pulse in your head so loud that it drowns out any name you might once have answered to.

Other Iowa Short Fiction Award and John Simmons Short Fiction Award Winners

1991
The Ant Generator,
Elizabeth Harris
Judge: Marilynne Robinson

1991
Traps, Sondra Spatt Olsen
Judge: Marilynne Robinson

1990
A Hole in the Language,
Marly Swick
Judge: Jayne Anne Phillips

1989
Lent: The Slow Fast,
Starkey Flythe, Jr.
Judge: Gail Godwin

1989
Line of Fall, Miles Wilson
Judge: Gail Godwin

1988
The Long White,
Sharon Dilworth
Judge: Robert Stone

1988
The Venus Tree,
Michael Pritchett
Judge: Robert Stone

1987
Fruit of the Month, Abby Frucht
Judge: Alison Lurie

1987
Star Game, Lucia Nevai
Judge: Alison Lurie

1986
Eminent Domain, Dan O'Brien
Judge: Iowa Writers' Workshop

1986
Resurrectionists, Russell Working
Judge: Tobias Wolff

1985
Dancing in the Movies,
Robert Boswell
Judge: Tim O'Brien

1984
Old Wives' Tales,
Susan M. Dodd
Judge: Frederick Busch

1983
Heart Failure, Ivy Goodman
Judge: Alice Adams

1982
Shiny Objects, Dianne Benedict
Judge: Raymond Carver

1981
The Phototropic Woman,
Annabel Thomas
Judge: Doris Grumbach

1980
Impossible Appetites, James Fetler
Judge: Francine du Plessix Gray

1979
Fly Away Home, Mary Hedin
Judge: John Gardner

1978
A Nest of Hooks, Lon Otto
Judge: Stanley Elkin

1977
The Women in the Mirror,
Pat Carr
Judge: Leonard Michaels

1976
The Black Velvet Girl,
C. E. Poverman
Judge: Donald Barthelme

1975
Harry Belten and the
Mendelssohn Violin Concerto,
Barry Targan
Judge: George P. Garrett

1974
After the First Death There Is No
Other, Natalie L. M. Petesch
Judge: William H. Gass

1973
The Itinerary of Beggars,
H. E. Francis
Judge: John Hawkes

1972
The Burning and Other Stories,
Jack Cady
Judge: Joyce Carol Oates

1971
Old Morals, Small Continents,
Darker Times,
Philip F. O'Connor
Judge: George P. Elliott

1970
The Beach Umbrella,
Cyrus Colter
Judges: Vance Bourjaily
and Kurt Vonnegut, Jr.